SPEED HEALING

More Than 2,000 Quick Cures and Fast Fixes to Ease Everything From Arthritis to Wrinkles

Bill Gottlieb, CHC

BottomLineBooks

BottomLineInc.com

Bottom Line's Speed Healing

ISBN 0-88723-762-2

10 9 8 7 6 5 4 3 2 1

This book is based on the research and observations of the author. The information contained in this book should by no means by considered a substitute for the advice of the reader's personal physician or other medical professional, who should always be consulted before beginning any health program.

The information in this book has been carefully researched, and all efforts have been made to ensure accuracy as of the date published. Readers, particularly those with existing health problems and those who take prescription medications, are cautioned to consult with a health professional about specific recommendations for supplements and the appropriate dosages. The author and the publisher expressly disclaim responsibility for any adverse effects arising from the use or application of the information contained in this book.

Bottom Line Books® is a registered trademark of Bottom Line Inc.
3 Landmark Square, Suite 201, Stamford, CT 06901
www.BottomLineInc.com

Bottom Line Books® publishes the opinions of expert authorities in many fields. The use of this book is not a substitute for health or other professional services. Please consult a competent professional for answers to your specific questions.

Offers, prices, addresses, telephone numbers and website listed in this book are accurate at the time of publication, but they are subject to frequent change.

Bottom Line Books is an imprint of Bottom Line Inc., publisher of print periodicals, e-letters and books. We are dedicated to bringing you the best information from the most knowledgeable sources in the world. Our goal is to help you gain greater wealth, better health, more wisdom, extra time and increased happiness.

Printed in the United States of America

Contents

Feel Better Faster

When you don't feel well, what you want is to feel better—*fast*. And your desire for quick and effective remedies and cures is the reason behind the writing and publication of the book you're holding in your hands—*Speed Healing*.

I'm Bill Gottlieb, a health educator and book author. I've worked with the editors of *Bottom Line Books* to create this unique resource for health and healing, after readers like you said it was the type of book you wanted most.

I reviewed thousands of recent clinical studies to find the hidden gems of scientifically proven speed healing that so often stay buried in medical journals (where they're certainly not doing you any good).

I located and interviewed hundreds of top-notch doctors and other canny clinicians (such as nutritionists, herbalists and massage therapists) who specialize in speed healing—and asked them for their best secrets in helping their patients and clients achieve quick relief. And believe me, they were *delighted* to share those secrets, in the hope of helping more people than the grateful folks who end up in their offices, entering with misery and departing with relief.

Then I sat down to write—and compiled more than 2,000 of the *fastest* remedies I'd found for 101 different health conditions. The result—a book that I think you'll find is like no other, a book that offers you quick and effective relief for health problems that may have defied the slower, ineffective solutions you've already tried.

These unique and surprising remedies include…

For adult acne: Stop eating this seemingly harmless food and your blemishes will vanish. Plus, an easy way to instantly rid yourself of any pimples you already have.

For arthritis: The two all-natural supplements that work the fastest to relieve pain.

For asthma: The fastest, safest way to short-circuit an asthma attack.

For back pain: The most comfortable position for an aching back (it relieves the pain in seconds). Plus, a 30-second self-massage that stops a back attack from turning into a chronic problem.

For colds and flu: The nutrient that can clear up a respiratory infection in a day or two (surprise: it's not vitamin C), and the exact amount you need.

For diabetes: How to balance your blood sugar by exercising *four minutes a week*. (No, that's not a typo! *Four minutes* is all it takes, says a new study.)

For drug side effects: Seven simple secrets for avoiding the drug-caused disasters that kill more than 100,000 people every year.

For fatigue: Easy ways to protect yourself from "energy vampires," the family members, friends and coworkers who routinely drain you of energy.

For headaches: The fastest way to use medications to treat mild, moderate and severe headaches—the right drug, at the right dose.

For heart disease: A revolutionary diet that reverses heart disease in just three weeks, making you virtually "heart-attack proof."

For heartburn: Just one teaspoon of vinegar can solve the problem!

For high blood pressure: A cardiologist's simple-to-follow program for lowering pressure without blood pressure meds (and their likely baggage of fatigue and impotence).

For insomnia: How to cure a case of sleeplessness by turning *on* the lights.

For memory loss: Five easy-to-follow rules for *never* forgetting a name again. "I've taught millions of people this fast and simple method—and it works," says a memory expert.

For menopause: The newest, scientifically proven natural remedy for hot flashes. Amazingly, it can also help menopausal women overcome insomnia, fatigue, headache, vaginal dryness and low libido!

For osteoporosis: A surprising new finding—the strange, bone-saving power of *prunes*.

For PMS: The number-one strategy for relieving symptoms is a multivitamin-mineral supplement—but you have to take it at *exactly* the right time.

For psoriasis: This registered dietician cleared up a 25-year case of hand psoriasis in six months *without* medications. She reveals her secret method.

For stomachache: The "best-studied and safest" remedy for stomach pain, abdominal cramps and nausea is an herbal formula from Germany. But almost no one knows about it!

For stroke: The breakthrough advice that can save your life. (It's not what you think. Calling your doctor or the hospital when you think you're having a stroke can kill you!)

For yeast infections: 98% of women who used this simple remedy cleared up their recurrent problem—even after anti-fungal medications had failed.

For wrinkles: The hype is over, because here are the five dermatologist-tested ingredients that can *really* smooth skin.

And that's only a small sampling of the more than two thousand remedies in this remarkable book.

But that's enough introduction. It's time for you to turn the page and discover the fastest remedies for your health problems—so you can start feeling better *now*.

For speedier healing,
Bill Gottlieb

How to Use Speed Healing

Needless to say, *Speed Healing* is speedy (and easy) to use.

The health conditions are arranged alphabetically—from problems such as Arthritis, Back Pain and Constipation…to Stroke, Urinary Tract Infections and Wrinkles. You can find your problem—and its solution—in a flash.

Each condition also includes several informative features…

See Your Doctor If… tells you when self-care isn't sufficient and professional treatment is a must. Symptoms may indicate a medical emergency.

Speed Healing Success are stories of people just like you who discovered speedy solutions to long-term health problems. For example, you'll read about a man who cleared up a 20-year case of heartburn in three days with a low-carbohydrate diet, and a woman in her seventies who uses a 30-second exercise to help her feel thirty years younger.

Super-Quick Fix indicates *really* speedy remedies. All the remedies in *Speed Healing* work fast—but in most sections there are one or two that are so rapid, we wanted to make sure you didn't miss them.

This symbol means "proceed with caution" when using the following product or medical remedy.

Rapid Resource supplies a phone number, website, e-mail and/or mailing address for all name-brand products recommended in the book so you can obtain the remedy that was discussed. We've even provided websites and other contact information for many of the hundreds of top health professionals interviewed for the book.

Conditions A–Z

ADULT ACNE

There are plenty of headlines about modern-day epidemics, such as the rapidly rising rates of obesity and type 2 diabetes. Well, you can add *adult acne* to that list.

"In the last fifty years, there has been a significant increase in the rates of acne for all age groups, and many adults are now experiencing acne for the first time," says Alan C. Logan, ND, a naturopathic physician and coauthor of *The Clear Skin Diet* (Cumberland House).

New finding: A survey of more than 1,000 adults conducted by Julie C. Harper, MD, associate professor of dermatology at the University of Alabama School of Medicine, found high rates of acne among women and men in their 20s, 30s, 40s, 50s and older. During their 40s, for example, 26% of women and 12% of men reported experiencing acne.

"Acne is one of the most common skin diseases—and there is a general misconception that it only affects teenagers," says Dr. Harper. "It is a persistent problem for people of all ages. And it can significantly impact a person's quality of life,

leading to anxiety and depression, regardless of when it occurs."

New thinking: But getting acne isn't the result of a genetic lottery, as was once believed. Like the modern-day epidemics of obesity and diabetes, the skyrocketing rates of adult acne reflect *lifestyle* factors, says Dr. Logan—specifically, a diet with too many processed foods, and a day filled with too much stress.

Which means you don't have to schedule a dermatologist's appointment (and you know how long *that* can take) to clear up adult acne. *You can start getting rid of those embarrassing blemishes today...*

➤ **Dump the dairy.** "The fastest, most effective action you can take to clear up acne blemishes is to stop eating dairy products," says Dr. Logan. Why does milk get a bad rap? There are two theories.

All dairy products—organic or conventional—contain growth hormones that can spark acne.

Eating dairy products boosts levels of *insulin*, a hormone that ushers blood sugar (glucose) into cells. Insulin also triggers the manufacture of excess pore-blocking sebum.

Better: Unlike other dairy products, plain or unsweetened yogurt doesn't cause an increase in insulin.

The Anatomy of a Pimple

Under each pore of your skin is a tiny canal that contains a hair and an oil-producing gland. Normally, the oil, or *sebum*, migrates to the skin's surface via the hair shaft. But...if there is too much sebum...or the canal clogs with dead cells...or a bacteria called *P. acnes* runs amok, triggering inflammation...or if one or more of those problems causes the canal to rupture and leak...you can end up with pimples—blackheads, whiteheads, papules (red bumps) or pustules (yellow bumps).

➤ **Watch out for watermelon and mashed potatoes.** Like dairy, they can drive up insulin levels.

• Enjoy all other types of fruits and vegetables.

Better: Eat potatoes with their high-fiber skin intact, which helps keep blood sugar levels steady and insulin in check.

➤ **Eat low-glycemic foods.** A diet emphasizing vegetables, fruits, whole grains, legumes, lean meat, poultry and fish—a so-called *low-glycemic diet* that keeps blood sugar levels stable—can reduce acne.

New finding: Australian researchers divided 43 people with acne into two groups—one ate a low-glycemic diet and the other didn't. After three months, the group not eating the low-glycemic diet had developed twice the number of blemishes. "Nutrition-related lifestyle factors may play a role in the development of acne," wrote the researchers, in the *Journal of the American Academy of Dermatology*.

What to do: Eating a low-glycemic diet is easy, says Jennie Brand-Miller, PhD, a professor of Human Nutrition at the University of Sydney in Australia and coauthor of *The New Glucose Revolution* (Marlowe).

• Favor breakfast cereals based on oats, barley and bran.

• Use breads with whole grains.

• Use basmati, long-grain or brown rice.

• Enjoy pasta and noodles. (Firm, briefly cooked, "al dente" style is best, says Johanna Burani, MS, RD.)

🕐 Super-Quick Fix

➤ **Get rid of that pimple—right now!** You have a new and embarrassing blemish—and a big presentation in a couple of days for your firm's top clients. If you could get an appointment tomorrow with a dermatologist, he would probably inject the trouble spot with cortisone, a powerful anti-inflammatory drug that can deflate pimples. But his waiting list is six weeks. What to do?

New approach: Try Ain't Misbehavin' Medicated Acne Control Serum, from DERMAdoctor. It contains a combination of natural ingredients that simulate the pimple-pulverizing effect of a cortisone shot. And it isn't drying, a big drawback of other "spot" acne treatments, says dermatologist Audrey Kunin, MD.

Rapid Resource: To order the product, visit *www.dermadoctor.com* or call 877-DERMADR.

➤ **Take a fish oil supplement daily.** Acute inflammation is the redness, swelling and heat in the area of a recent cut or injury. It's caused by well-meaning immune cells that rush to the spot to control infection, but trigger "collateral damage."

Surprising: New research shows that acne is caused or complicated by those same inflammation-causing immune cells. However, they're in first rather than fifth gear, a condition scientists call *low-grade chronic inflammation*.

One of the fastest and safest ways to douse chronic inflammation is to take a daily fish oil supplement rich in two anti-inflammatory omega-3 fatty acids—EPA (*eicosapentaenoic acid*) and DHA (*docosahexaenoic acid*). Dr. Logan recommends a supplement supplying one to two grams of omega-3 fatty acids, with an emphasis on EPA, which blocks the inflammatory factors that are typically elevated in people with acne.

Try this: The supplement Perfect Skin delivers not only the right amount of EPA, but also zinc, selenium and chromium, three trace minerals shown to fight acne.

Rapid Resource: To order Perfect Skin, visit *www.genuinehealth.com*, call 877-500-7888 or e-mail *customerhelp@genuinehealth.com*.

SPEED LIMIT OTC Acne Products Not Overly Impressive

Channel surf for a while and you'll probably encounter a Hollywood celebrity hawking an over-the-counter acne product that (so the smiling spokesperson claims) can "miraculously" clear up your blemishes better than anything else on the market. Americans spend $100 million a year on these and other over-the-counter (OTC) acne products. Blemished buyers beware.

Red flag: There are no new OTC acne products with astounding and unexpected results, says Dr. Logan. In fact, the active ingredients in all OTC acne products, such as benzoyl peroxide and glycolic acid, have been available for years. Their results are well known—50% of users will see a 50% improvement. For OTC acne products, that's as miraculous as it gets.

➤ **Green stops the red.** Drinking green tea lowers levels of DHT (*dihydrotestosterone*), a hormone that pumps up sebum production. Drink six, four- to six-ounce cups daily, says Dr. Logan.

⚠ *Warning:* Stay away from sugary green tea beverages, which can spike blood sugar levels and worsen acne.

➤ **The best way to wash your face.** Once a day or twice a day? Mild cleanser or strong? Dermatologists (and their patients) have been debating these points for years. *Well, the cleansing controversy has finally been cleared up...*

New finding: You get the best acne-reducing results from washing twice daily with a mild facial cleanser, such as Neutrogena Fresh Foaming Cleanser, says a new study from researchers at Harvard Medical School.

Trap: Washing once a day worsened acne. Washing more than twice a day didn't produce better results.

Try this: Another scientific study shows that washing twice a day with Cetaphil Daily Facial Cleanser for Normal to Oily Skin helps clear up clogged pores.

➤ **The best makeup to hide a pimple.** Green-based concealers (such as Smashbox Photo Finish Color Correcting Foundation Primer) do the best job of masking redness, says Dr. Kunin.

Trap: Don't make the mistake of applying the concealer on top of the foundation, which creates a smudge on the skin that draws the eye just like the pimple you're trying to conceal. Apply it to the blemish *before* you put on your foundation makeup.

➤ **Decrease stress.** "For years, many dermatologists have noted that stress promotes acne flare-ups," says Dr. Logan. That's because stress bullies the adrenal glands into pumping out more cortisol, a hormone linked to acne. The simplest way to counter that stress, he says, is to "Practice the Relaxation Response." *Here's how...*

1. **Pick a focus word,** short phrase or prayer that is either neutral like the word "one" or firmly rooted in your belief system.

2. **Sit quietly in a comfortable position.**

3

Speed Healing Success

The Three-Day Acne Cure

Chris Gibson claims he cured his acne—in three days! How did he do it? Although he's not a doctor, like many innovative dermatologists Gibson concluded *diet* was the cause of acne. Specifically, he indicted a sugary, fatty diet that loads the intestines with toxins—which then try to find their way out of the body through the skin.

To correct the problem, Gibson went on a high-fiber, colon-cleansing, three-day fast. "By not eating the offending foods, my body completely shut down the digestive process and expelled all toxins," he says. *His approach…*

He ate nothing but 10 or more Red Delicious apples a day for three days, peeling them before eating (to avoid pesticides).

He drank only water, downing six to eight, 16-ounce glasses a day.

On the third day of the fast, he also drank three ounces of grape juice and took two tablespoons of olive oil. "This ensured that the apples were moved through and out my system," says Gibson.

At the end of each day, he self-administered a Fleet enema, to wash out the lower bowel. "The enema guaranteed that I didn't reabsorb the very toxins that I was working to remove."

Another nighttime ritual—massaging castor oil into his affected skin before retiring, to keep his pores open.

By the second day, he noticed "the acne really calming down and much of the sores and bumps quickly receding."

By the third day, his acne had cleared up—and hasn't returned for the last 18 years.

Rapid Resource: You can find out more about Gibson's approach in his book *Acne Free in 3 Days* (Universal Marketing Media).

3. **Close your eyes.**

4. **Relax your muscles,** progressing from your feet to your thighs, abdomen, shoulders, head and neck.

5. **Breathe slowly and naturally.** As you do, say your focus word, sound, phrase or prayer silently to yourself as you exhale.

6. **Don't worry about how well you're doing.** When other thoughts come to mind, simply say to yourself, "Oh well," and gently return to your focus word.

7. **Continue for 10 to 20 minutes.**

8. **After you're done, don't stand up immediately.** Continue sitting quietly for a minute or so, allowing other thoughts to return. Then open your eyes and sit for another minute before rising.

9. **Practice the technique once or twice daily.** Try before breakfast and before dinner.

Also try: Inadequate sleep also disturbs your adrenal function, increasing levels of cortisol. ("Patients frequently report that lack of proper sleep aggravates acne," says Dr. Logan.) If you're having trouble falling asleep—at bedtime, or after waking up in the middle of the night or early in the morning—practice the Relaxation Response to help you fall asleep.

See Your Doctor If…

The following symptoms characterize severe acne and may require medical care with prescription treatments such as oral antibiotics, or *isotretinoin*, says Dr. Logan.

- *More than 10 red bumps or pustules (red bumps with pus) on the face, chest or back.*
- *Acne nodules (red bumps bigger than about 1/3 inch, or the size of a cranberry).*
- *Pitted or bumpy scars from acne.*

AGE SPOTS

Lighten Your Load

If the word "sunspot" hadn't already been claimed by astronomers, it would have been the perfect name for those blotchy dots of skin that can pepper faces and the back of hands—because they're caused by decades of sun exposure.

What happens: Too much sun puts the color-producing cells (melanocytes) of the skin in overdrive.

The good news is that the spots are rarely precancerous. (However, if you notice an age spot that is growing rapidly, see your doctor.)

The better news is it's never too late to lighten your load of age spots. *And you can do it quickly...*

➤ **Use sunscreen.** The sun caused those spots. The sun darkens them even more. Block that sun with sunscreen, says Audrey Kunin, MD, a dermatologist in Kansas City, Missouri and author of *The DERMAdoctor Skinstruction Manual* (Simon & Schuster).

Look for a sunscreen with "broad spectrum protection," a term on the label indicating the product blocks both ultraviolet A and ultraviolet B rays. The sunscreen should have an SPF (sun protection factor) of 15 or higher.

Trap: "Don't be fooled by a product's claim to be 'waterproof,' " says Dr. Kunin. "I find this term both confusing and misleading. Many consumers simply apply a waterproof sunscreen early in the day and neglect to reapply it. You *must* reapply sunscreen—whether it's labeled waterproof or not—after water exposure, or every two hours while outdoors."

🕐 *Super-Quick Fix*

➤ **Try a multi-ingredient lightener.** "I like the idea of using a multi-ingredient lightener, as compared to monotherapy," says Dr. Kunin. A multi-ingredient product typically works three ways, she explains. It bleaches the skin. It increases the turnover of skin cells, reducing darkened areas. And it cuts melanin production, stopping the formation of new discoloration.

Recommended: Solage, a prescription product containing 2% mequinol (a bleach) and 0.01% tretinoin (a topical form of vitamin A that speeds cell turnover and blocks melanin production).

Newest research: In a four-month study, 200 people with age spots used either Solage or 3% hydroquinone (a bleach). Solage produced better results, with the researchers calling it a "highly effective and well-tolerated treatment" for age spots, "superior to three percent hydroquinone."

➤ **Skip the freezing and burning.** Some dermatologists freeze off age spots with cryotherapy (liquid nitrogen) or burn them off with a laser. The results are, well, spotty.

"I've seen more spots worsened than helped by freezing," says Dr. Kunin. "The freezing inflames the skin and further darkens the problematic area. Lasers can do the same thing."

SPEED LIMIT
Is Hydroquinone Safe?

The bleaching ingredient hydroquinone is found in many OTC and prescription products for lightening age spots. But it might not be safe, says the FDA, which wants to remove the ingredient from the market. The agency says hydroquinone might cause *ochronosis* (a disease in which pigment is deposited in cartilage and other connective tissue) de-pigmentation (the loss of skin color) and skin cancer.

Hold your regulatory horses, FDA, says James J. Nordlund, MD, a clinical professor in the Department of Dermatology at Wright State University Boonshoft School of Medicine, in Dayton, Ohio.

"Ochronosis is rare. There are no cases of hyperpigmentation from hydroquinone. And skin cancer has never been reported following its use. The history of hydroquinone is a history of safety. It isn't necessary to remove the ingredient from the market. Consumers should continue to have access to hydroquinone."

Recommended: Volunteers, testers and a supervising dermatologist at the Good House-keeping Research Institute spent four weeks investigating several hydroquinone-containing OTC products for age spots. They determined the most effective product to be Murad Age Spot and Pigment Lightening Gel.

AGING

Feel Younger Faster

"Aging is not inevitable. It is a treatable condition. The clock can be reversed." Those bold and hopeful assertions were made by Philip Miller, MD, founder and medical director of the California Age Management Institute (*www.antiaging.com*) in California, and author of *The Life Extension Revolution: The New Science of Growing Older Without Aging* (Bantam). And he's not the only one making them.

"Your body wants to live to be a hundred," says Dr. Maoshing Ni, a practitioner of Traditional Chinese Medicine (TCM) and author of *Secrets of Longevity: Hundreds of Ways to Live to Be 100* (Chronicle Books). "All you have to do is give your body the factors it needs to thrive. In fact, it's never too late to get healthier, stronger

and younger—whether you're fifty, sixty-five, or eighty years old."

And it doesn't have to take a decade to slow, stop or reverse the aging process. Or even a day.

"There are quick and easy steps to avert the seemingly inevitable insults of aging," says Mark Liponis, MD, medical director of Canyon Ranch Health Resorts and author of *Ultra-Longevity* (Little, Brown).

Here are the fastest ways to feel younger, from these and other antiaging experts…

➤ **Four "must-have" antiaging supplements.** "If I had to list the must-have daily supplements for slowing the aging process and living longer, I would pick resveratrol, fish oil, vitamin D and curcumin," says Joseph Maroon, MD, professor and Heindl Scholar in Neuroscience at the University of Pittsburgh Medical School and author of *The Longevity Factor* (Atria Books).

Let's look at those supplements one by one…

1. **Resveratrol.** In the 1930s, researchers at Cornell University discovered they could extend the lives of rodents by 40% to 50%— by severely restricting calories. This scientific finding has been repeated hundreds of times, in rodents and other laboratory animals, including flies, worms and fish. For decades, however, no one could figure out why calorie restriction increased lifespan.

Then, in the 1990s, researchers at Harvard Medical School discovered the *genetic basis* for the effect, says Dr. Maroon.

Their experiments showed that the stress of calorie restriction activates "survival genes" (sirtuins) that energize an enzyme (Sir2) that stabilizes DNA, slowing cellular aging.

In 2003, the same Harvard researchers discovered that stressed plants (such as red grapes fighting fungus) generate survival molecules that strengthen and repair their cells—and that those molecules, when ingested, activate survival genes!

One of the most potent of these molecules—because its small size and specialized shape allows it to switch on the genes—is resveratrol.

Scientific research on resveratrol shows that the compound can…

- **Lengthen life**
- **Stop metabolic harm from a high-fat, high-calorie diet**
- **Balance blood sugar, protecting against diabetes**
- **Strengthen heart cells and block heart disease and stroke**
- **Prevent and treat cancer**
- **Clear away amyloid-beta,** the toxic protein that has been linked to Alzheimer's disease
- **Boost the burning of body fat**
- **Improve memory**
- **Transform muscle fibers** into the "slow" type seen in well-trained athletes
- **Increase endurance**
- **Enhance muscle strength**
- **Reduce fatigue**
- **Improve coordination**

Suggested intake: 250 to 500 milligrams (mg) daily.

Product: There are more than 300 resveratrol-containing products available. *The best have the following characteristics, says Dr. Maroon…*

- Made with *trans-resveratrol* (the active form), not *cis-resveratrol*
- Shown by professional testing to activate the sirtuin "survival genes"
- Produced by manufacturers who comply with Good Manufacturing Practices (GMP)

- Produced in an oxygen-free environment
- Sealed in airtight bottles and vials
- Free from fillers or additives such as sugar, starch, gluten and artificial colors or flavors

Resveratrol products from the following three manufacturers contain most of those characteristics…

Longevinex, at *www.longevinex.com.* Order online or call 866-405-4000 or e-mail *info@longevinex.com.*

Biotivia, at *www.biotivia.com.* Order online or call 866-459-2773 or e-mail *care@ biotivia.com.*

RevGenetics, at *www.revgenetics.com.* To order online or call 888-738-4363 or e-mail *orders@revgenetics.com.*

2. **Fish oil.** "Hidden inflammation can invisibly drive age-related disease processes, from heart disease and cancer to Alzheimer's and arthritis," says Dr. Miller. A fish oil supplement provides omega-3 fatty acids, which convert to certain *prostaglandins,* that fight inflammation. "Most of us are extremely deficient in these essential fatty acids, and adding fish oil supplements to the diet can bring about astonishing improvements. Simply stated, fish oils are magic."

Suggested dosage: Choose a supplement containing at least 1 to 2 grams of EPA/DHA (the omega-3 fatty acids in fish oil), says Dr. Maroon.

Product: Fish oil supplements are widely available.

3. **Vitamin D.** Scientists used to think that vitamin D had only one important job to do—help with the absorption of calcium, to build and maintain strong bones. Now they know that every cell in the body uses vitamin D—and that the nutrient is crucial in keeping you young and healthy.

New finding: In a study of more than 13,000 people, researchers from Johns Hopkins University found that those with the lowest blood levels of vitamin D had a 26% higher risk of dying than those with the most D. "Our results make it clear that all men and women concerned about their health should make sure they have a sufficient intake of vitamin D," say study researchers

Suggested dosage: Taking a daily supplement that provides 1,000 IU of vitamin D is quickest and most reliable way to maintain healthy blood levels of vitamin D, says Michael F. Holick, MD, PhD, director of the Vitamin D, Skin and Bone Research Laboratory at Boston University Medical Center.

Product: Vitamin D supplements are widely available.

Important: Please see page 253 in the chapter "Osteoporosis" for more information on the healthiest blood levels of vitamin D (50 to 80 ng/ml) and bi-yearly testing to ensure your levels are in that range.

4. **Turmeric.** This spice—from a gingerlike perennial plant native to South Asia—is a staple in India. Its active ingredient is *curcumin*. And thousands of animal and human studies have shown that curcumin can combat 66 serious illnesses, including Alzheimer's disease, diabetes, heart disease and various types of cancer. That's because curcumin, like fish oil, reduces chronic, low-grade inflammation.

"Curcumin appears to possess all the desirable features of a synthetically created multipurpose drug," says Gregory Cole, PhD, a neurologist at the University of California. "The data obtained thus far in scientific studies have surpassed the expectations of most researchers. It is probably only a matter of time before we appreciate the true potential of curcumin in the management and eradication of various chronic diseases."

Healthy Aging Secrets From 100 Centenarians

One hundred Americans who turned 100 were asked for their secrets of healthy aging. Here are their top ten—none of which take a whole lot of time!

1. **Stay close to friends and family.**
2. **Laugh and have a sense of humor.**
3. **Keep your mind active.**
4. **Continue to look forward to each day.**
5. **Maintain a sense of independence.**
6. **Keep moving and exercising.**
7. **Stay in touch with your spirituality.**
8. **Eat right.**
9. **Continue to follow current events.**
10. **Continue to make new friends.**

"This survey shows that the keys to living longer are about the things that are *under our control*," says John Mach, MD, a geriatrician and chairman of Evercare, the health organization that commissioned the survey.

Suggested dosage: 500 mg curcumin supplement (not turmeric). Look for a supplement with *bioperine*, an extract of black pepper than aids absorption. And down that supplement with a glass of milk or cup of yogurt, which also increase the absorption of curcumin, says Bharat Aggarwal, PhD, Professor of Cancer Research, in the Department of Experimental Therapeutics at the University of Texas M.D. Anderson Cancer Center.

Product: Curcumin supplements are widely available.

➤ **Smile—and live longer.** A Dutch researcher recently analyzed 30 studies on happiness and longevity. Among people who weren't ill, happiness boosted longevity by 10% to 40%. "The effect of happiness on longevity in healthy populations is remarkably strong," he concluded, in the *Journal of Happiness Studies*.

That's great news—unless, of course, you're unhappy. Well, you can *learn* how to increase happiness, says Robert Biswas-Diener, PhD, a life-coach, instructor at Portland State University in Oregon and coauthor of *Happiness* (Blackwell). *Here are his fast-action (and science-tested) secrets for achieving and savoring happiness…*

1. **Ask yourself, "Am I happy now?"** Many people get happiness backward, says Dr. Biswas-Diener. "They think it's an end result, a kind of emotional finish line. But many of us are *already* happy. So sit back, ask yourself if you're happy *now*—and if you are, *appreciate* your happiness, rather than trying to achieve a mythical ideal."

2. **Hyper-happiness isn't better.** People who rate themselves as 7 or 8 on a happiness scale of 1 to 10 outperform people who rate themselves as 9 or 10. (The happier people aren't as conscientious.) "People who hear this are often quite relieved," says Dr. Biswas-Diener. "It takes the perfectionist edge off the pursuit of happiness."

Pray to Stay Alive

Researchers at Albert Einstein College of Medicine analyzed data from more than 90,000 postmenopausal women and found that weekly attendance at religious services reduced the risk of death by 20%, compared with people who never attended.

"The protection against dying provided by religion cannot be entirely explained by expected factors of religious affiliation, such as enhanced social support of friends or family, lifestyle choices or reduced smoking and alcohol consumption," says Eliezer Schnall, PhD, a study researcher. "There is something here that we don't quite understand."

3. **Accept the fact that happiness isn't constant.** You're not *always* going to be happy. You're bound to experience anger, sadness, regret, embarrassment and other negative emotions. That's normal.

4. **Savor your happy memories.** A researcher at the University of Chicago found that intensively visualizing a "happiness moment" for 10 minutes a day produced more day-to-day happiness. "Take that positive moment—whatever it was—and stretch it out mentally," says Dr. Biswas-Diener. "Who was there? Was it night or day? Is there memorabilia to help you visualize, such as a wedding picture or a trophy? Really savor and feel good about that moment."

   Trap: Studies show that *analyzing* the past actually makes you *unhappier*. "It sucks the soul out of a happy moment," says Dr. Biswas-Diener. You want to *replay* the positive moment, not figure it out so you can do it again."

5. **Imagine a happy future—and write about it.** Imagine yourself in a future where you achieved everything you wanted, whether it's financial well-being, a good relationship or a beautiful place to live. Now *write* about that future, flooding the page with your thoughts, without concern for punctuation or grammar. Do this for a few minutes, once or twice a month.

6. **Count your blessings.** Every day, write down three things you're grateful for. "Research shows this exercise is very effective in increasing happiness," says Dr. Biswas-Diener.

   Also try: At the end of the day, write down ways in which you were kind, e.g., holding a door open for someone or helping your niece with her homework.

7. **Identify your strengths.** People who acknowledge their personal strengths (such as curiosity, courage or creativity) are happier. "When you know and employ your strengths, you feel good," says Dr. Biswas-Diener.

Try this: To discover your top five "signature strengths," take the VIA Survey of Character at *www.viastrengths.org*.

Super-Quick Fix

➤ **Turn aging upside down.** Gravity is a drag. A lifetime of earth's constant downward pull can wizen your spine, robbing you of an inch or more of height. But you can turn the tables on gravity, effortlessly lengthening your spine and reversing aging—by using an inversion table or chair, says Dr. Liponis.

"I recommend daily use of an inversion table or chair—a device that safely and comfortably tilts the body, placing your head slightly lower than your feet and decompressing your spine. A gentle incline of forty-five degrees is enough to do the trick. Start with one minute or so a day, and gradually increase the time to ten minutes a day."

Best: Use the device mid-afternoon or later, to unload the day's burden of gravity.

Rapid Resource: For a wide selection of inversion devices, visit the website *www.inversion tables.com* or call 888-880-4884. Address: Hayneedle, Inc., 9394 W. Dodge Rd., Suite 300, Omaha, NE 68114.

➤ **Foods for more future.** Dr. Ni examined the diets of nearly 100 centenarians. "What they consumed, for the most part, was a variety of legumes, whole grains, vegetables, fruits, nuts and seeds," he says. "These sound nutritional practices have been confirmed by Western science to contribute to health and longevity."

Recent study: Scientists at the Harvard School of Public Health analyzed 18 years of dietary data from more than 72,000 women. They found that women who ate a "Western" diet (lots of red and processed meat, refined grains, French fries, sugary foods and desserts) had a 21% higher risk of dying from any cause compared with women who ate a "prudent" diet (lots of vegetables, fruit, legumes, whole grains, fish and poultry).

New research has identified three of the best antiaging foods...

● **Broccoli for a younger immune system.** Researchers at UCLA found that a chemical in broccoli (and other cruciferous vegetables, which include cauliflower, Brussels sprouts, kale, collard greens, arugula, cabbage, bok choy, watercress, radish and horseradish) perks up an aging immune system by blocking *free radicals*, a supercharged form of oxygen that damages cells.

"As we age, the ability of the immune system to fight disease and infections and protect against cancer wears down, because of the impact of oxygen radicals on the immune system," says Andre Nel, PhD, of the David Geffen School of Medicine. "Our study shows that a chemical present in broccoli is capable of stimulating a wide range of antioxidant defense pathways, and could interfere with the age-related decline in immune function."

● **Nuts keep you nimble.** Scientists in the Division of Nutritional Sciences at Cornell University spent three years studying 700 men and women aged 65 and older, publishing their results in the *Journal of the American Medical Association*. They found that those with the lowest blood levels of vitamin E had the fastest decline of physical function, as measured by walking speed, the ability to repeatedly stand up and sit down with the arms folded across the chest, and balance while standing. Foods richest in vitamin E include nuts and whole grains.

● **Longer life is a bowl of cherries.** Researchers in Spain and the US found that a diet rich in *melatonin*—a compound produced in the body and found in many foods—slows the aging process. Foods rich in melatonin include cherries, corn, oats and red wine.

Speed Healing Success

Think Yourself Young

Ellen Wood is 72 years old and growing younger every day.

"I have more energy and vitality than I had even thirty years ago," she says. "If I chose to, I can work as many hours as I did when I was thirty-five, without feeling fatigued. My mind is clearer and sharper than it was. And I'm flexible enough to handle any changes in life that come my way."

What's her secret? *The Law of Attraction.*

"This law is a fundamental cosmic force, like the 'law of gravity,'" explains Wood. It states that your inner thoughts attract similar outer situations and circumstances. If you constantly worry about aging—if you constantly think about and imagine a dismal future of memory loss, frailty and dependence—you create those very realities. But if, on the other hand, you constantly affirm youthfulness—you become more youthful!

"The root cause of the deterioration and infirmities of growing old is *expecting to be old*," says Wood. "To grow truly younger, you must reprogram your mind to replace previously received notions of aging with thoughts of the vibrant, joyful, active person you wish to become. You need to become aware of your negative thoughts about aging *each time they occur*, and replace them with positive thoughts." *Here's how she does it—and how you can, too...*

⏰ Super-Quick Fix

The 30-Second Grow Younger Method

1. *Catch yourself.* Notice a thought that you look old, feel old or have a memory lapse—or that you will in the future.

2. *Center your awareness in the middle of your forehead.* Let go of the negative thought—without judgment—and allow your consciousness to drift to your forehead, which helps center you in the present moment.

3. *Say: "With every breath I take, the cells in my body grow younger."* Say it out loud or silently.

4. *Feel the emotion of a younger you.* Straighten your posture. Relive a positive feeling you had when you were in your prime.

"Practicing this method will interrupt your negative programming and consciously change your thoughts so you can attract youthfulness," says Wood.

Rapid Resource: You can learn more about Wood's techniques for growing younger in her book, *The Secret Method for Growing Younger: A Step-by-Step Anti-Aging Process Using the Law of Attraction to Help You Stop Aging, Grow Younger and Enjoy Life* (StarHouse Creations). Her website is *www.howtogrowyounger.com.*

"Melatonin can provide many potential health benefits that are important to people as they age, including protecting the cardiovascular system and improving sleep," says Russel J. Reiter, PhD, a nutrition researcher at the University of Texas Health Science Center, and an author of the study, published in the journal *Free Radical Research*. "As people look for natural ways to promote longevity, including cherries in their daily diet may be helpful."

"What's especially great about cherries is that they're available year-round as dried, frozen and juice," says Cheryl Forberg, RD, author of *Positively Ageless* (Rodale). "They're an easy, convenient and colorful addition to the daily diet, from whipping into a smoothie to

Dr. Maoshing Ni's Six Best Antiaging Foods

1. *Asparagus.* "It supplies glutathione, a master antioxidan that aids DNA synthesis and repair," says Dr. Ni. "A deficiency can be a factor in premature aging." Other good sources include avocado, walnuts and fish.

2. *Ginger.* "It's anti-inflammatory—and inflammation is one of the main mechanisms underlying aging." Use it as a condiment in cooking, especially in soups.

3. *Pine nuts.* "Evergreens are a traditional symbol for longevity. Pine nuts contain pycnogenol, a potent antioxidant." Include them in trail mixes or add a handful to stir-fried vegetables.

4. *Seaweed.* "Vegetables from the sea have long been considered to possess powers to prolong life." Common types include nori (sushi wrap), kombu, kelp, dulce and Irish moss. Use nori in place of a tortilla, wrapping turkey or chicken. Try seasonings made from sea vegetables. Soak sea vegetables in water for a couple hours, chop them and stir-fry like any other vegetable.

5. *Sorghum.* "This grain was the first cultivated food in the world. As a wild grain, it is rich in chi, or life force." Cook it like rice.

6. *Sweet potatoes and yams.* "They deliver the hormone DHEA, which turns into estrogen, progesterone or testosterone, all essential for your body's antiaging defenses to work."

mixing into a rice pilaf or folding into a sweet dessert such as gingerbread."

Rapid Resource: For cherry recipes, visit *www.choosecherries.com.*

➤ **Whatever you eat, eat less of it.** "It's well known that calorie restriction is the most effective way to increase longevity in animals,"

says Dr. Ni. "Most centenarians surveyed around the world follow the 'three-quarters' rule: they stop eating when they are three-quarters full."

"One of the ways to live a long, healthy life is by reducing the *quantity* of the food we eat," agrees Dr. Liponis. "The ideal pattern of eating is to eat frequently, but take in fewer calories." Eat smaller portions, five times a day.

➤ **Strong-arm aging—with quick-and-easy at-home strength-training.** Australian scientists recently studied 67 people aged 65 to 84 for six months and found that just a *little* strength-training (working out with weights) improved their muscle strength, power and everyday functioning, compared to a group that didn't work out.

"The benefits of strength-training for the older person are irrefutable," says Tim Henwood, PhD, a study researcher. "Not only does it increase muscle strength and power, protecting the independent lifestyle of aging adults, but it also builds bones, improves balance, boosts energy, speeds reaction time and deepens sleep."

The best way to strength-train is to go to a gym or other exercise facility, learn a strength-training routine from a qualified professional and practice it twice a week.

But if you can't or won't do that, Dr. Henwood says to do these four quick-and-easy strength-building exercises, which he designed for you to perform at home. Do the exercises 10 to 15 times, two or three times a week.

⚠ *Caution:* If you experience pain in a joint or back pain while doing any of these exercises, stop—and talk to a qualified health professional before proceeding.

1. **Chair stand.** Use any hard-backed chair where you can sit and have your feet touching the ground. Start the exercise standing, keeping your hands on your hips or across your chest. (Don't use them to help you.) Sit down

and then stand again. Keep your eyes looking forward, your back straight and your head up. Repeat 10 to 15 times. If you have trouble with the exercise, swing your arms forward as you stand up.

2. **Standing lunge.** In an open space, place a chair on either side of you. Take a large step forward with your left leg, leaving the other foot on the ground. Lower yourself straight down until the knee touches the ground, using the chairs to maintain your balance. Rise up to the starting position. Repeat 10 to 15 times. Switch legs and repeat the exercise.

Longer Life, for Free

Researchers at the University of California in San Francisco studied 24 people for three months, asking them to eat a healthy diet (rich in fruits, vegetables, whole grains and legumes), exercise regularly (walking half an hour a day) and increase their happiness levels (by practicing stress-management methods including yoga and meditation).

After three months, the participants had an average increase of 29% in *telomerase*—an enzyme that repairs genetic factors known to control longevity.

"If a new drug had been shown to do this, it would be a billion-dollar drug," said Dean Ornish, MD, the lead researcher of the study and founder and president of the nonprofit Preventive Medicine Research Institute in Sausalito, California. "But this is something people can do for free."

Find out more: For more information about the telomerase-increasing program used in the study, see *The Spectrum: A Scientifically Proven Program to Feel Better, Live Longer, Lose Weight, and Gain Health* (Random House), by Dean Ornish, MD.

As with the previous exercise, keep your head up, your eyes looking straight ahead and back straight.

3. **Towel rows.** For this exercise, you need a bath towel and a solidly anchored towel rack. Place the towel around the rack and take each end in each hand. Place your feet together. Slightly bend your knees. Lean backward. Only moving your arms, draw the towel toward you until your elbows are behind your body and your shoulder blades are pinched together. At the end of the exercise, you should be upright. Return to the starting position and repeat.

4. **Wall push-ups.** Standing up, place your hands on a wall at shoulder height, with your arms fully extended. Keep your body straight from your ankles through your hips. Bend your elbows to lower yourself toward the wall. Return to the starting position.

➤ **New shoe, new you.** At some time in our lives, many of us develop a vision problem such as nearsightedness that requires correction. Similarly, many of us also end up with a foot problem such as fallen arches or a narrow forefoot—but it never gets corrected! The possible results of a 60- or 70-year stroll on flawed feet? Chronic foot or knee pain, a harrowing hip replacement or even a life-ending fall. Fortunately, these all-too-common problems of aging have a quick and sole-satisfying solution.

"Purchase a new shoe or shoe insert that provides enough padding and corrects natural imbalances," advises Dr. Liponis.

He recommends investing in a high-quality walking shoe.

Try this: New Balance 755, Nike Air Pegasus, Mizuno Wave Rider and Asics Gel Cumulus are enthusiastically endorsed by satisfied walkers.

You can also add an insert, such as a Dr. Scholl's Custom Fit Orthotic Insert.

Rapid Resource: Go to *www.footmapping. com* to locate a store near you that sells these products.

Smart idea: Once you've got the right walking shoes and inserts—go for a walk! Researchers at the University of Georgia found that when people 60 and over walked regularly (40 minutes, three times a week, for four months) they decreased their risk of disability and dependence by 41%. "This study shows that walking on a regular basis can make a huge impact on quality of life for older people," says M. Elaine Cress, PhD, of the Institute of Gerontology.

ALZHEIMER'S DISEASE

Prevention Can Start Today

Thirty-three percent of 75-year-olds have *dementia*—loss of memory, personality changes and a descent into dependence. By age 85, it's 50%. And even if you're under 75, the statistics are scary. In recent decades, the rate of Alzheimer's disease—the most common type of dementia, accounting for 60% to 80% of cases—has increased 10-fold among those over 65 and 24-fold among those under 65.

That's the bad news about our brains. Now for the good—no, the *remarkable*—news.

"Seventy percent of people can prevent Alzheimer's and dementia," says Vincent Fortanasce, MD, a clinical professor of neurology at the University of Southern California, director of the Fortanasce-Purino Neurology Center, in Arcadia, California, and author of *The Anti-Alzheimer's Prescription* (Gotham). The other 30%—those with genetic risk, such as having a parent with the disease—can delay its development by 15 to 20 years. How is such powerful prevention possible?

Dementia Isn't One Disease

"Saying a person has 'dementia' is like saying a person has cancer," explains Marwan Sabbagh, MD, director of the Cleo Roberts Center for Clinical Research at the Sun Health Research Institute in Sun City, Arizona, and author of *The Alzheimer's Answer* (Wiley). "There are many types of cancer, such as leukemia, lymphoma and sarcoma. Likewise, there are many forms of dementia." *The three most common are...*

- *Alzheimer's.* "This progressive brain disease causes gradual memory loss, a decline in the ability to perform routine tasks, disorientation, difficulty in learning, loss of language skills, impairment of judgment and personality changes," says Dr. Sabbagh.
- *Dementia with Lewy bodies.* The second most common type of dementia, its symptoms include slow movement, stiffness, walking problems and hallucinations. ("Lewy bodies" are changes in brain cells.)
- *Vascular dementia.* This type of dementia, in which blood vessels in the brain are damaged, is often caused by multiple small strokes.

Alzheimer's is caused by a type of brain aging—the buildup of *amyloid*, protein plaques that destroy *neurons* (brain cells). "It is fully within your power to control the factors that cause brain aging—starting today," says Dr. Fortanasce.

➤ **Sleep more, stress less.** Doctors are typically intelligent and motivated, but they are also common victims of Alzheimer's. Why? Because they are chronically sleep-deprived and stressed, says Dr. Fortanasce.

"These two factors lead to lower levels of dopamine and serotonin, *neurotransmitters* that regulate many brain functions," he explains. When these two neurotransmitters are low, you have less discipline and willpower to establish and maintain brain-protecting healthy habits such as regular exercise. And you always feel anxious, and sedate yourself with brain-harming foods, such as refined carbohydrates.

"The damage from too little sleep and too much stress may be the greatest risk factor for developing Alzheimer's," says Dr. Fortanasce. In fact, studies show that stress can *quadruple* your chance of getting the disease.

To lower your stress levels and get more sleep…

• **Just say no.** Rather than automatically saying yes to yet another responsibility or task, say "Let me think about it" or "Let me get back to you"—and then take your time deciding whether or not you can do it without additional stress. *Also try…*

• **Once a week, evaluate all your commitments.** Do only those that are the most important to you—and say no to the rest. "Don't feel guilty about prioritizing," says Dr. Fortanasce. And put "Keep my brain young" at the top of your to-do list!

From 1926 to 1954, the average American got 9.4 hours of sleep per night. Now, it's less than 6.5 hours nightly. This drop in daily zzz's parallels an increase in new cases of Alzheimer's.

Starting tonight…

• **Meditate at bedtime.** As you're falling asleep—or trying to—focus on the sensation of each breath as it moves in and out of your body. Every time you notice that your attention has wandered, gently redirect it to the breath, without judging yourself. This will produce the "relaxation response"—calming your heart and draining tension from your muscles—and help you fall asleep.

• **Use the same technique to help you get back to sleep** if you wake up in the middle of the night or the early hours of the morning.

• **You can also practice this meditation during the day,** while sitting up, any time you feel stressed.

Other ways to improve your sleep life include…

• **Take a 10- to 30-minute nap—** especially between 2:00 and 4:00 P.M., when sleep hormones peak.

• **Go to sleep and wake up at the same time every day,** weekday or weekend. Establishing a regular sleep pattern is a must for satisfying sleep.

• **Use earplugs if you are bothered by noise.**

• **Reduce the light in your bedroom,** particularly light that flickers or pulses, from an alarm clock or TV screen.

➤ **Build up your brain.** Your brain has a fixed number of neurons. Every year, you lose millions. Eventually, there are so few left that you develop Alzheimer's.

Surprise—that's *not* true!

"Contrary to popular belief, your brain doesn't have a 'fixed bank account' of neurons," says Dr. Fortanasce. "Your brain has an 'interest-bearing account'—if you make regular deposits with brain-building mental exercises."

The secret of building the neuron-to-neuron "bridges" that strengthen the brain is *novelty*— doing things you've never done before. *Starting today…*

• **Eat a meal with your other hand.** If you're right-handed, eat with your left hand, and visa versa.

• **Other ways to stimulate your brain at mealtime** include eating dessert first, using chopsticks instead of silverware and eating in a different room.

• **Play the name game.** Each day, pick a new word from a foreign language for an object that you see frequently, such as a car. (That's *coche* in Spanish…*voiture* in French…*auto* in German.) Throughout the day, when you see the object, say that word aloud.

Rapid Resource: To translate an English word into any one of 10 different languages, use the free translator at *www.freetranslation.com.*

- **Take your brain on vacation.** The new sights and sounds of travel stimulate your brain. *To stimulate it even more...*

While traveling by car, train or bus, select an image from the road and remember a pleasant memory associated with that image. For example, a tractor plowing a field might remind you of spending time at your uncle's farm. Challenge yourself with a new memory every few minutes.

- **Checkmate a computer.** Chess is a super brain exercise—and you don't even need a partner. Play against a computer at *www.chess maniac.com.*

➤ **Strong Body = Strong Mind.** There are two types of hormones—youthful and aging, says Dr. Fortanasce. The youthful hormones include estrogen, thyroid hormone, growth hormone and testosterone—and from age 20 to 70 they plummet by about 90%. The aging hormones are cortisol and adrenaline—and from age 50 to 70 they increase by up to 70%.

"A youthful brain requires a 'hormonal symphony'—a balance between youthful hormones (which are like the violins and piano) and aging hormones (which are like the brass and drums)," he says.

One of the best ways to balance your hormonal symphony is with *physical exercise.* Regular exercise also increases brain size, improves the connections between neurons and improves blood flow to the brain. *You can start today...*

- **Take 8,000 steps.** In a six-year study of nearly 2,000 people aged 65 and older, researchers at the University of Washington found that those who walked for as little as 10 minutes a day reduced their risk of Alzheimer's by 38%, compared to non-walkers.

One of the best ways to motivate yourself to walk every day is by wearing a pedometer—a small device that clips to your belt or waistband and displays the number of *steps* you take each day. In one study, women who wore a pedometer walked a mile more a day than women told to take a daily 30-minute walk.

A pedometer helps you do what behavioral scientists say you must do to make any positive change—set a goal, monitor it yourself and feel the satisfaction of success once you've reached it, says Caroline Richardson, MD, an assistant professor in the Department of Family Medicine at the University of Michigan.

A brain-protecting daily goal—8,000 to 10,000 steps.

To reach that goal...

- When shopping by car, choose a parking space as far away from the entrance as possible.

- When using public transportation, get off two stops before your destination and walk the rest of the way.

- In buildings, use the stairs, not the elevator or escalator.

- At home or work, take a step break every hour—walk briskly in place, until you accumulate a few hundred steps.

If you don't like stepping, any moderate exercise will do, including biking, jogging, calisthenics, tennis, golf (without a cart) and even normal daily activities such as house cleaning, mowing the lawn, gardening and washing windows.

➤ **The top 12 anti-Alzheimer's foods.** "I call these twelve foods the 'Golden Dozen,'" says Dr. Fortanasce. "Every one of them can help protect you against Alzheimer's."

- **Berries.** "Berries are rich in *anthocyanins*, which reduce inflammation, a primary 'brain killer' that destroys from within," says Dr. Fortanasce. *Quick uses:* Toss berries in dinner salads, sprinkle on yogurt as a topping or eat for snacks.

- **Apples.** Apples also douse inflammation. *Quick uses:* Bake, slice in garden salads or eat anytime for a snack.

- **Fish.** Fatty fish such as salmon, mackerel and tuna are rich in omega-3 fatty acids, which reduce inflammation. *Quick uses:* Broil salmon, serve tuna for lunch, snack on sardines and crackers.

- **Cruciferous vegetables.** Cruciferous vegetables, such as cabbage, broccoli, cauliflower and Brussels sprouts, are a major dietary source of *isothiocyanates*, special compounds in food that may protect against Alzheimer's. *Quick uses:* Steam, sauté, mix in casseroles or shred for coleslaw.

- **Nuts.** They contain monounsaturated fat, which helps to reduce 'bad' LDL cholesterol and keep the brain healthy. *Quick uses:* Add to rice dishes, toss in cold salads or eat a few nuts at snack time.

- **Low-fat dairy.** A diet rich in low-fat diary significantly lowers blood pressure—a risk factor for Alzheimer's. *Quick uses:* Drink fat-free or low-fat milk with meals, pour on cereal, use in cooking, eat yogurt or eat low-fat cheese for snacks.

- **Dark leafy greens.** They are loaded with the antioxidants that nourish and defend brain cells. *Quick uses:* Steam, sauté or chop for salads.

- **Dried beans or legumes.** They are high in folate, a B-vitamin linked to lower risk of developing Alzheimer's. *Quick uses:* Serve hot at mealtime, mix in casseroles or toss in cold salads.

- **Soy.** Like nuts, they help lower LDL. *Quick uses:* Use soy milk on cereal or in baking. Use soy-substitute crumbles instead of meat in

---

Don't Forget to Drink Coffee!

In a 26-year study, Scandinavian researchers found that people who drank 3 to 5 cups of coffee a day from middle (39 to 53 years) to old age (65 to 79 years) had a 65% lower risk of developing Alzheimer's and other forms of dementia, compared with their low- or no-coffee drinking compatriots.

How does coffee brew better brains? Caffeine, antioxidants and blood sugar balancing may be the keys, say the researchers.

---

recipes. Use dried soy beans in recipes such as chili and baked beans.

- **Sweet potatoes.** With a high-fiber content, they help control blood sugar levels and prevent diabetes, a risk factor for Alzheimer's. *Quick uses:* Use in place of white potatoes.

- **Tomatoes.** They are rich in lycopene, an antioxidant more powerful than beta-carotene and vitamin E. *Quick uses:* Stew them, add to soups and sauces, eat sliced on sandwiches or in salads.

- **Whole grains.** They also help control blood sugar. *Quick uses:* Use whole grain bread for sandwiches. Have oatmeal for breakfast. Add barley to casseroles.

Rapid Resource: You can find out more about Dr. Fortanasce's approach to preventing Alzheimer's disease—with diet, exercise, attitude and rest (D.E.A.R.)—at *www.healthybrainMD.com* and *www.anti-alzheimers.com*. Or contact the Fortanasce-Purino Neurology Center, 665 W. Naomi Ave., Arcadia, CA 91007; call 626-445-8481.

➤ **Toast to your brain.** A neuroscientist at Loyola University in Chicago reviewed 44 scientific studies on drinking and Alzheimer's disease

Be a Red Head

Researchers at UCLA and the Mount Sinai School of Medicine in New York have found that compounds in red wine called *polyphenols* are uniquely effective in blocking the formation of *amyloid beta*, a clump or "plaque" of toxic protein that destroys brain cells and may cause Alzheimer's.

Why it works: Polyphenols can stop the clumping. They can also stop existing plaques from harming cells.

Try this: A "Brain Healthy" Sangria, created by Marwan Sabbagh, MD. "Combine five ounces of red wine with four ounces of polyphenol-rich pomegranate juice. Garnish with berries. Don't consume more than one of these a day—and don't chase it with anything."

Also try: Red wine is one way to get your polyphenols. Taking a daily polyphenol-rich nutritional supplement is another, and might be a good strategy to help prevent Alzheimer's (and even improve the condition of Alzheimer's patients), said David Teplow, PhD, a professor of neurology at UCLA.

A polyphenol extract from red grape seeds, called MegaNatural-AZ, from Polyphenolics, stopped the development of amyloid plaques in mice genetically programmed to develop Alzheimer's disease, says Giulio Pasinetti, MD, PhD, of Mount Sinai School of Medicine, in a study in the *Journal of Neuroscience*.

"The ability of the compounds found in MegaNatural-AZ to inhibit the formation of amyloid structures suggests that MegaNatural-AZ might even help prevent memory loss in people who have not yet developed Alzheimer's disease," said Dr. Pasinetti.

Recommended: MegaNatural-AZ is not yet on the market. But Polyphenolics' red grape seed extract is an ingredient in several brands, including Vitamin Shoppe Grape Seed Extract, Nature's Way Grape Seed Extract, and Enzymatic Therapy PCO Grape Seed.

and other types of dementia and found that moderate drinking lowers the risk of dementia.

"Too much alcohol is bad for the brain," says Michael Collins, PhD. "But a little might actually be helpful."

What helps: Moderate drinking is defined as 1 to 2 drinks or less a day for men and 1 drink a day or less for women. One drink is 4 ounces of wine, 12 ounces of beer or 1½ ounces of 80% distilled spirits or liquor, such as whiskey or vodka.

Surprising: Dr. Collins theorizes that alcohol may work to prevent dementia by actually stressing brain cells, toughening them up so they're able to cope with aging.

➤ **Don't get a divorce.** "The results were astounding," said Krister Håkansson, a researcher in the Department of Neurobiology at the Karolinska Institute in Sweden. She was talking about the findings from a study by Finnish researchers, recently reported at the Alzheimer's Association International Conference on Alzheimer's Disease.

The researchers studied 2,000 people for 21 years, starting around the age of 50. They found that those who lived with a spouse or partner had a 50% lower risk of developing Alzheimer's than those living alone. Those who divorced in midlife (around the age of 50) and never remarried had *three times* the risk. People who became widowers and widows in midlife and never remarried had *six times* the risk.

"If cognitive or mental challenges can protect against dementia, so should living as a couple in a relationship—because it is one of the most intense forms of intellectual and social stimulation," says Håkansson.

However: "If you are single and have a rich 'social network,' there is no reason to drag anyone to city hall to get married," says Håkansson.

New study: A four-year study of more than 2,000 women age 78 and older showed that those with large "social networks"—family or friends they could visit with, ask for help, phone or e-mail—had a 26% lower risk of developing dementia. Such networks have a "protective influence" on mental ability, say the researchers, in the *American Journal of Public Health*.

ANEMIA

Revive Your Weary Blood

One out of every five women has anemia, a shortage of red blood cells, or of the protein *hemoglobin*, the oxygen-carrying molecule in red blood cells. The condition chokes the body from the inside out, causing symptoms such as fatigue, brain fog, dizziness, shortness of breath, pale skin and cold hands and feet (though in mild cases it may be asymptomatic).

Anemia has dozens of possible causes, from intestinal ills to cancer. But the most common is iron deficiency. That's because iron is a crucial ingredient in the manufacture of hemoglobin. Imagine a red blood cell as a bicycle, hemoglobin as the seat and oxygen as the rider—without hemoglobin, there's no way for the cell to transport oxygen.

What you may not know: You probably know that iron-deficiency anemia is mainly a woman's problem, because both menstruation and pregnancy drain the body of iron. But pre- and postmenopausal women are at risk.

"A lot of women go through their entire lives iron-deficient and never replenish their stores," says John Neustadt, ND, a naturopathic doctor, and medical director of Montana Integrative Medicine. "Iron deficiency anemia is common in younger and older women."

Fortunately, you can start solving iron-deficiency anemia in a second, by taking an iron supplement. *But make sure it contains the best source of iron…*

Anemia Is Tough on Older Bodies

Studies have found that anemia is particularly tough on those over 60…

- **Weaker body.** In a four-year study, researchers found that older people with anemia had the greatest decline in standard tests of "physical function"—the ability to walk, maintain balance and get out of a chair. "Even mild anemia can reduce the ability of older people to function at their fullest potential," said the researchers, in the *American Journal of Medicine*.

- **Weaker mind.** Researchers at Johns Hopkins University found that older women with anemia had poorer "executive function"—the ability to problem-solve, plan and follow-up on important activities, such as taking medications and paying bills.

- **Hospitalization.** Older people with anemia have a 40% higher risk of hospitalization—and double the risk of death, say researchers at Wake Forest University Baptist Medical Center, in North Carolina.

Bottom line: If you're over 60 and feeling fatigued, don't assume it's an "inevitable" part of aging, says Dr. Neustadt. Ask your doctor to test you for anemia.

➤ **Rust Rx?** If you're diagnosed with iron-deficiency anemia, your doctor is likely to prescribe a form of supplemental iron called *iron oxide*. You might as well go lick a car at the junkyard.

"Iron oxide is essentially rust," says Dr. Neustadt. That's why so many women literally can't stomach it. The supplements often cause indigestion and constipation—and only 2% of the iron is actually absorbed.

Better: The best type of iron supplement is *chelated*—the iron is combined with an amino acid, increasing absorption to 65%–75%.

Recommended: Dr. Neustadt recommends the product FerroSolve, which delivers 45 milligrams (mg) of chelated iron. Take one capsule per day, with your doctor's approval and supervision.

Or you could try Supreme Fem MVM (with iron), a multivitamin/mineral supplement that delivers the same type of highly absorbable, non-constipating chelated iron *and* 1,000 mg of vitamin C—a nutrient that further boosts absorption.

Rapid Resource: You can order FerroSolve and Supreme Fem MVM (with iron) at *www.nbi health.com*, call 800-624-1416 or e-mail *info@nbi health.com*; Nutritional Biochemistry Inc., 1184 North 15th Ave., Suite 1, Bozeman, MT 59715.

➤ **Teatime isn't the right time for iron.** Tea (both black and green) contains tannins, which block iron absorption. So does red wine. Don't take your iron supplement at teatime or at dinner with a glass of cabernet.

⚠ **Caution:** Iron-deficiency anemia in men and older women often signals internal bleeding, which could be caused by an ulcer or even a cancer, and should be evaluated by a doctor.

➤ **The best way to take B-12—under your tongue.** Without enough vitamin B-12, your body can't build sturdy red blood cells. But as you age, there is a decrease in *intrinsic factor,* a molecule in the digestive tract that aids the absorption of B-12. Also, proton pump inhibitors such as *esomeprazole* (Nexium) can deplete the body of B-12. The result: 10% to 15% of people over 60 have a B-12 deficiency, which can cause megaloblastic anemia—large, sluggish red blood cells.

New approach: If you complain of fatigue, your doctor may order a test to detect low blood levels of B-12. But if he discovers you're low in the nutrient, he probably *won't* prescribe a supplement to treat the problem—because you probably couldn't absorb its B-12. Instead, he's likely to give you an injection of B-12.

Well, there's an easier (and pain-free) way to boost B-12 levels, says Dr. Neustadt. Take a *sublingual* form of the vitamin—a quickly dissolving lozenge that is placed under the tongue, delivering B-12 directly into the bloodstream.

Recommended: Sublingual Vitamin B-12 from Physiologics. It is widely available. Dr. Neustadt typically prescribes 2,000 mcg a day (two lozenges), for the fastest relief from B-12 deficiency and megaloblastic anemia.

See Your Doctor If...

If you have fatigue that won't quit, ask your doctor to test you for anemia. If an initial blood test (CBC, or complete blood count) shows low levels of hemoglobin, your doctor will then test you for ferritin, a stored form of iron.

Trap: The "normal" range for ferritin—with a low of 10 and a high of 350—is so broad as to be meaningless, says Dr. Neustadt.

What to do: If you have fatigue or other symptoms of anemia and your ferritin is below 70, talk to your doctor about taking an iron supplement, even though your iron levels may be considered "normal." *However:* Chronic ingestion of iron supplements can lead to iron overload, causing liver damage and other problems. And people with the disease hemochromatosis should never take iron.

ANGER

Quick Ways to Defuse

Are you so angry your blood is boiling? Well, so are your heart, lungs, skin and immune system. *Several new studies show how habitual anger can fry your body, part by part...*

➤ **Heart.** Researchers at the Medical University of South Carolina studied more than 2,300 people age 45 to 64—those who were the angriest day-to-day had a 70% higher risk of developing high blood pressure, and a 90% higher risk of blood pressure turning into heart disease.

➤ **Weight.** French researchers examined health data from more than 6,000 people and found that "higher levels of hostility" were matched by higher body mass index (BMI), a measure of weight and body fat.

➤ **Skin.** Researchers at Ohio State University asked 98 people to participate in an unusual experiment—each received a tiny, blistering burn on one forearm. Over the next eight days, the researchers tracked the speed at which the wounds healed. Those participants with the poorest control over their anger—the quickest to get angry and show it—were the slowest healers.

➤ **Lungs.** Researchers at Harvard Medical School and several other institutions analyzed data from nearly 5,000 seemingly healthy young people, age 18 to 30. They found that those with the shortest tempers had the weakest lungs—in fact, every notch upward on a hostility scale accounted for a 0.7% decrease in lung function! (Among the young, even smoking doesn't have the same measurable effect, noted the researchers.) Their conclusion: "Harboring hostility hurts."

Why is anger so harmful to health? *A brief anatomy lesson helps clarify the connection...*

Your autonomic nervous system (which controls heart rate, digestion and the functioning of internal organs) has two branches—*sympathetic* and *parasympathetic*, explains Deborah Rozman, PhD, a psychologist in Boulder Creek, California, and coauthor of *Transforming Anger:*

The HeartMath Solution for Letting Go of Rage, Frustration, and Irritation (New Harbinger). The sympathetic branch speeds up your heart rate and the parasympathetic branch slows it down. "Feeling irritated, frustrated and angry much of the time puts your sympathetic nervous system into overdrive," she says.

"An overactive sympathetic nervous system increases the risk of heart problems, exhausts the nervous system, causes hormonal imbalances, triggers excessive fat buildup, impairs immune function, decreases bone and muscle mass, impairs memory and learning, and destroys brain cells." Whew!

Fortunately, adds Dr. Rozman, there are quick and easy ways to defuse that anger, calm your nervous system and increase your odds of living a healthier, longer life...

➤ **Follow your heart—away from anger, to love, care and appreciation.** Dr. Rozman is a proponent and teacher of the HeartMath System, a series of techniques for anger and stress management based on the discovery that the heart (not the brain) is the master controller of emotions. *Here's why and how it works...*

Your heart has a slight *beat-to-beat rhythmic variation*, she explains. Scientists call this "heart rate variability" or HRV. When you experience anger, your HRV has a disordered, chaotic, *incoherent* rhythm, producing rough and jagged waves. When you experience positive emotions such as love, care or appreciation, the pattern of your heart rhythm becomes *coherent*, producing smooth, orderly waves.

"Because the heart is a primary generator of rhythm in the body—influencing brain processes that control your nervous system, your emotions and your thinking—the heart provides an access point from which these system-wide dynamics can be quickly and profoundly affected," says Dr. Rozman. "By learning to shift your heart rhythms *right when you feel frustration*

What Is Anger?

Anger is a survival mechanism, explains Dr. Rozman. "It is an emotion that is intended to help you get up and get going—to battle or escape threat and danger. But it is not meant to linger, to become a habit or way of life."

And anger never improves life in the long run, she points out. "Yes, it may feel good for a moment, as your body experiences a short burst of energy from adrenaline and other hormones," she says. "But afterward, you feel drained and distressed—in fact, even five minutes of recalling a situation that made you angry can depress your immune system for up to six hours afterward."

or anger, you harness the physiological power of anger and change the information going from your heart to your brain." *Here's how to shift your heart rhythms in one minute...*

🕐 *Super-Quick Fix*

➤ **The One-Minute Quick Coherence Technique.** "Quick Coherence is a simple yet powerful technique to release anger and bring more coherence to your heart rhythms," says Dr. Rozman. "Once you've learned the three-step technique, it only takes a minute to do. It's important to practice this technique as soon as you feel angry."

Step 1. **Heart Focus.** Focus your attention in the area of your heart. If this sounds confusing, try this...Focus on your right big toe and wiggle it. Now focus on your right elbow. Now gently focus in the center of your chest, the area of your heart. (Most people think the heart is on the left side of the chest, but it's really closer to the center, behind the breastbone.) You may want to put your hand over your heart to help you keep your focus there. If your mind wanders, just keep shifting your attention back to the area of your heart while you do steps 2 and 3.

Step 2. **Heart Breathing.** As you focus on the area of your heart, imagine your breath is flowing in and out through that area. This helps your mind and energy to stay focused in the heart area and your breathing and heart rhythms to synchronize. Breathe slowly and gently in through your heart (to a count of 5 or 6) and slowly and easily out through your heart (to a count of 5 or 6). Do this until your breathing feels smooth and balanced, not forced. You may discover that it's easier to find a slow, easy rhythm by counting "one thousand, two thousand," rather than "one, two." Continue to breathe with ease until you find a natural inner rhythm that feels good to you.

Step 3. **Heart Feeling.** Continue to breathe through the area of your heart. As you do so, recall a positive feeling, a time when you felt good inside, and try to re-experience it. This could be...a feeling of appreciation or care toward a special person or a pet...a place you enjoyed...or an activity that was fun. Allow yourself to feel this good feeling of appreciation or care. If you can't feel anything, it's okay; just try to find the attitude of appreciation or care. Once you've found it, try to sustain the attitude by continuing your Heart Focus, Heart Breathing and Heart Feeling.

"Practice Quick Coherence first thing in the morning," says Dr. Rozman. "Then use it whenever you feel angry, during the day or night. Practice it again, as the last thing you do before sleep."

➤ **Put the brake on anger—Go to Neutral.** When do you get the angriest? If you're like most people, says Dr. Rozman, it's when you're

Speed Healing Success

Quick and Easy Anger Control

Reynir Johnson is a construction manager in Idaho, with a wife of 23 years, an 18-year-old son and a 15-year-old daughter.

Reynir used to be angry. Really angry. All the time.

"My son was born, my wife stopped working, I started my own business, so that I wasn't collecting a steady paycheck with benefits. My stress levels went through the roof—and so did my anger. The smallest thing would set me off. I would vent and my wife would get mad at me and we would have shouting matches—every day. We went to see three different therapists and a marriage counselor, but I didn't really get any help for what was bothering me and my wife the most—my instant anger."

Then a psychologist recommended Heart-Math—and Johnson says it was life changing.

"In just a few minutes of practicing techniques like Quick Coherence and Go to Neutral (see pages 22–23), both my wife and I felt more comfortable than we ever had. Finally, we had simple tools that made it quick and easy for us to control anger on a daily basis.

"Now, if there are things that I can't control—an obnoxious driver on the road, or an angry worker at a construction site, I don't get angry. I disengage, shift my focus to the energy around my heart and in a split second I'm doing something *other* than anger.

"And I don't care who you are or where you're at in your life—*anybody* can do this."

going to happen. All the people, places, events and issues that push your buttons—triggering the feelings, images and thoughts ("She's always stupid and thoughtless"..."People always demand and expect too much of me"..."I'm a terrible mother.") that Dr. Rozman calls the *anger cascade*.

"To stop the anger cascade, you need to pay attention to the feeling or memory that triggers judgmental or angry thoughts," says Dr. Rozman. *The three-step Go to Neutral Tool is a way to do that...*

Step 1. **Take a mental time-out** so that you can temporarily disengage from your thoughts and feelings, especially stressful ones. When emotional triggers come up, recognize that you are triggering. As soon as you feel the trigger, tell yourself "time-out!" and step back from the reaction.

Step 2. **Shift your focus to the area around your heart.** Now feel your breath coming in through your heart and going out through your solar plexus. Practice breathing this way a few times to ease into a time-out in your heart.

Step 3. **Tell yourself, "Go to Neutral"—** then don't go one way or the other in your thoughts or feelings about the issue. Hold on to a place of being neutral in your heart until your emotions ease up and your perception relaxes.

"If you start to slide back into the anger cascade—use the steps of Go to Neutral again," says Dr. Rozman. "At first, you may have to practice Go to Neutral a dozen times before you have enough heart power to hang in neutral. That's fine. It's like building a muscle—it takes exercise." You might also find it useful to practice the Quick Coherence Technique after you use Go to Neutral.

Rapid Resource: To learn more about HeartMath, visit *www.heartmath.com* or call 800-450-9111.

dealing with a person or situation *you can't control*. A driver who cuts you off. The computer crashing. Pain that won't quit. Waiting on the phone. The thought that something you really want isn't

ANGINA

Rapid Help for Hurting Hearts

The chest pain of angina is a sign of *serious* disease, a warning from your heart that it's *suffocating*—because your arteries have become too narrow to provide your heart with a ready supply of oxygen-rich blood.

If you're one of nine million Americans with angina and you have yet to see a doctor, you should—and fast.

"Angina can be either unstable—life-threatening—or stable—something you can live with day-to-day," says Seth Baum, MD, a cardiologist in private practice in Boca Raton, Florida, and author of *The Total Guide to a Healthy Heart* (Kensington). "You must have an evaluation by a cardiologist to determine your level of risk and the appropriate treatments to control your condition."

But once that's done, you can also talk to your cardiologist about the following ways to help prevent angina attacks—and even short-circuit one that's in progress…

⏰ Super-Quick Fix

➤ **Take nitroglycerin right before exercise.** Regular exercise (along with losing weight and eating a healthful diet) is a must for the long-term management of angina, says Dr. Baum.

Problem: One of the most common kinds of angina is *exertional*—you get it *when* you exercise. Discouraging!

Solution: "If you have stable angina, talk to your doctor about taking one, artery-expanding nitroglycerin tablet under the tongue right before exercise," says Dr. Baum. This will help you exercise without angina.

"Most nitroglycerin is now prescribed in sustained-release preparations," he says. "Few cardiologists are recommending this helpful, single-table therapy for exertional angina."

➤ **Take these nutrients with nitroglycerin.** Sustained-release nitroglycerin—whether delivered by pill or patch—has another downside, says Stephen Sinatra, MD, an integrative cardiologist and author with James Roberts, MD, of *Reverse Heart Disease Now* (Wiley).

The preparations trigger an increase of *superoxide*, an oxidant that damages the endothelium, the thin layer of cells that line the arteries. "This is drug-induced endothelial dysfunction, and it actually increases the risk for heart attacks," says Dr. Sinatra.

Recommended: If you take nitroglycerin, he recommends also taking three antioxidants every day—1,000 milligrams (mg) of vitamin C; 200 to 400 IU of vitamin E; and 500 mg of N-acetyl-cysteine.

Speed Healing Success

Remarkable Improvement in a Few Days

"Louis had stubborn angina," says Dr. Sinatra. "He experienced chest pain with normal activity, such as walking across a room, or from just mild emotional stress. He had visited several cardiologists and had taken a number of standard heart drugs but his angina persisted.

"Louis was already taking low doses of L-carnitine and CoQ10, which I increased. I also added D-ribose. In just a few days, Louis showed such remarkable improvement that his son-in-law called and reported, 'You fixed Louis!'"

🕐 *Super-Quick Fix*

➤ **The 30-second way to ease an angina attack—rub your neck.** There's an old-fashioned technique that can quickly slow the heart rate and may help ease an episode of angina, says Dr. Baum.

1. Find the "carotid pulse"—the pulse on the side of the neck—by placing your index and middle finger along one (not both) side of the windpipe (trachea), which is located toward the front of the neck.

2. Rub that spot gently for about 10 seconds.

3. Now find the pulse on the other side of the neck and rub that spot gently for 10 seconds.

⚠ *Caution:* Only use this technique if you do not have blockages in the carotid arteries of the neck, which your doctor can confirm with a carotid ultrasound.

And only perform this technique while sitting down, since it slows the heart, lowering blood pressure, which could make you feel light-headed.

➤ **L-carnitine to the rescue.** L-carnitine is a combination of the amino acids lysine and methionine.

"It increases blood flow to the heart," says Allan Magaziner, DO, the medical director of the Magaziner Center for Wellness and Anti-Aging Medicine in Cherry Hill, New Jersey, and author of *The All-Natural Cardio Cure* (Avery). "People with angina taking L-carnitine experience improved exercise tolerance and decreased symptoms."

Study: For six months, 200 people age 45 to 66 with exercise-induced angina took either their standard drug regimen or that regimen *and* two grams of L-carnitine a day. After six months, those taking the nutrient had the greater increase in exercise tolerance.

Drugs Are as Effective as Surgery for Angina

Every year, nearly one million Americans with angina and heart disease undergo a two-pronged surgical procedure—an angioplasty (the insertion of a small balloon into a clogged artery, where it's inflated, popping the artery open) and a simultaneous insertion of a stent (a wire-mesh tube designed to keep the artery expanded).

Surgery not your style? Taking medications—a much faster procedure—might work just as well.

Landmark study: Doctors in the US and Canada studied more than 2,000 men, with an average age of 62, who had stable angina (several times a week, caused by exercise or stress). They divided them into two groups. One group was treated with several medications for heart disease (to lower blood pressure, lower cholesterol and thin blood). The other group was treated with an angioplasty and a stent. Both groups were asked to make lifestyle changes (exercise regularly, eat a low-fat diet and stop smoking).

Five years later, 70% of men in *both* groups were free of angina pain.

"If a patient with heart disease has stable angina, the latest available medications are very effective and there is no need for a stent," said Peter Liu, MD, scientific director of the Canadian Institutes of Health Research and a study researcher.

The study appeared in the *New England Journal of Medicine*.

Recommendation: For patients with heart disease, Dr. Sinatra recommends 1 to 2 grams, once or twice a day, taken on an empty stomach. (If you get a stomachache—which sometimes happens—take it with food.)

Helpful: Choose *L-carnitine fumarate* over *L-carnitine tartrate*. "We have found it to be

Women and Angina

For women, the narrowing arteries of heart disease may not produce the "classic" sign of an angina attack, such as pain in the center of the chest.

A woman may have "angina equivalents," such as a sudden shortness of breath or abdominal discomfort, says Dr. Baum.

Signs of heart disease in women include…

- *Unusual fatigue*
- *New, unusual shortness of breath, during everyday activities (or at rest)*
- *Nausea*
- *Dizziness*
- *Lower chest discomfort*
- *Back pain*
- *Upper abdominal pressure or discomfort*

What to do: A study shows that many women with heart attacks had milder versions of their symptoms *six weeks* before the attack, says Nieca Goldberg, MD, a cardiologist in New York City and author of *The Women's Healthy Heart Program* (Ballantine Books). If you experience these symptoms, make an appointment with your doctor now, and get evaluated for heart disease. You could avoid a trip to the emergency room.

If you think you're having the symptoms of a heart attack—call 911. Too many women think about how they're going to feel silly if they go to the hospital and their "heart attack" turns out to be nothing, says Dr. Goldberg. "Please, get over that concern! What is truly important is staying alive."

more efficient, especially among patients with oxygen-starved hearts," says Dr. Sinatra.

L-carnitine is widely available.

➤ **Count on CoQ10.** CoQ10 is a nutritional compound that helps cells make energy—including heart cells. "Many studies show widespread CoQ10 deficiency among patients with heart disease," says Dr. Sinatra.

"And research involving thousands of patients with heart disease—including patients with angina—also shows significant improvements in qualify of life and longer survival with CoQ10 supplements.

"CoQ10 enables the heart to function better with whatever limited blood flow it receives," he explains. "As a result, a person will have less chest pain—in fact, quite a bit less—not because the arteries are opened, but because of better energy production in the muscle."

Recommendation: For the treatment of angina, Dr. Sinatra recommends 90 to 180 mg a day of CoQ10 in the "Q-Gel" form, which is the most absorbable. (Look for the word Q-Gel on the label.)

➤ **Depend on D-ribose.** Diseased hearts are deprived of blood and oxygen—and their cells slowly but surely lose energy. D-ribose is a building block of ATP, the primary fuel for every cell in the body.

"If you have angina, an adequate dose of D-ribose usually results in symptom improvement very quickly—sometimes within a few days," says Dr. Sinatra.

Recommendation: He recommends 10 to 15 grams daily for treatment of stable angina. Take it with meals, or mixed into juice, milk or fruit. D-ribose supplements are widely available.

⚠ *Caution:* D-ribose can lower blood glucose levels, says Dr. Sinatra. "Insulin-dependent diabetes should check with their physicians before starting on the supplement."

ANXIETY AND WORRY

It's Easy to Feel More at Ease

You're irritable, impatient and restless, and find it hard to concentrate. You're tired all the time but can't fall asleep at night.

Sometimes you feel so nervous and on edge that your palms sweat, your heart races and you have a lump in your throat.

But most of all, you *worry*—nearly all the time, about nearly everything. Your bills. Your house. Your job. Your spouse. Your health. You figure that worry helps you prepare for the worst. And you *know* the worst is going to happen. Soon.

Psychologists call this condition *generalized anxiety disorder* (GAD). It's not just occasional worrying about the inevitable problems and setbacks of everyday life. It's *excessive* worrying that often doesn't match the situation you're worried about.

Example: Your husband is late getting home from work. You worry he's been in a car accident.

Not surprising, GAD is bad for you—too much worry causes problems such as headaches, digestive upset and insomnia, and tightens muscles all over the body. Unending hours of worry can also poison your practical life—clouding your mind so that you can't get much done, and eroding relationships, as loved ones, friends and coworkers feel barraged by your fretful concerns.

And older isn't always wiser about worry—GAD is the most common psychological problem among people 65 and over.

"People tend to worry more as they age," says Martin Antony, PhD, a professor in the Department of Psychology at Ryerson University in Toronto, Canada, and coauthor of *The Anti-Anxiety Workbook: Proven Strategies to Overcome Worry, Phobias, Panic, and Obsessions* (Guilford Press).

Psychologists aren't sure why seniors are prone to GAD. (It may be that as you age you have more to worry about, such as poorer health, a fixed income and increasing isolation as family and friends pass away.)

But psychologists do have plenty of recommendations to help you control excessive worrying, no matter how old you are. *And don't worry, they're easy to do...*

➤ **Think differently, feel differently.** "Anxious thoughts keep anxiety and fear alive," says Dr. Antony. "When you learn to change your anxious thinking, you'll reduce your level of anxiety and fear." *Here are quick ways to make that change...*

First, identify your worry-triggers: Anxious thinking is almost always triggered by something, either external (a situation or activity) or internal (thought or imagery). For a person with GAD, typical worry-triggers include...

- **Money** (*Example,* opening bills; *Thought:* I will run out of money and won't be able to care for myself.)
- **Work** (*Example,* a deadline; *Thought:* I won't be able to cope with the stress of work.)
- **Family** (*Example,* a spouse arriving home late; *Thought:* My husband is probably late because he's been in a car accident.)
- **Health** (*Example,* going to the doctor; *Thought:* This symptom could be the sign of a disease.)
- **Sleep** (*Example,* lying in bed awake; *Thought:* If I don't get enough sleep, I won't be able to function tomorrow.)
- **Worry itself** (*Example,* a worried thought; *Thought:* Worrying will drive me crazy.)

Next, ask yourself, "Is my worry realistic or not?" Once you identify your worry-triggers and anxious thinking, figure out if those thoughts are realistic or unrealistic, says Dr. Antony.

"For example, you might worry a lot about walking in your neighborhood at night. Well, if the neighborhood is perfectly safe and people walk around there all the time—your worry is unrealistic. But if there are muggings in your neighborhood, your worry is realistic."

- **If your anxious thoughts are realistic, brainstorm solutions.** If you're worrying about a real problem, generate real solutions, says Dr. Antony. "For example, Can you avoid walking at night? If you have to walk at night, can you walk with other people? Can you move out of that neighborhood?"

• **If your anxious thoughts are unrealistic, challenge them.** "Unrealistic thoughts are usually exaggerated predictions that something bad will occur," says Dr. Antony.

This is called *catastrophizing*. To challenge it, you have to *de-catastrophize*.

"Often, when you anticipate a negative event, you assume that it will be awful and that you'll be unable to cope. But you stop short of imagining what it will actually be like, and just how you'll react if it occurs," says Dr. Antony. "De-catastrophizing involves taking your catastrophic thoughts to this next, realistic stage, thereby taking away their power."

Do that by asking yourself two simple questions...

1) Realistically, what is the worst that could happen?

2) How would I cope with that?

• *Catastrophic thought*: "It would be awful if my car isn't fixed by the time the mechanic said it would be ready."

• *De-catastrophizing*: "What would happen if my car isn't ready? Why would that be such a problem? Could I cope with it? Well, if it's not ready, it would be inconvenient. I would have to get a ride with someone else or take public transportation to work. I could live with that for a few more days if I had to."

Bottom line: "Whenever you experience feelings of anxiety or fear, ask yourself what you're thinking in that moment," says Dr. Antony. "As you become aware of your anxious thoughts and challenge them, you will experience a significant drop in anxiety."

➤ **Antidepressants—a safer drug for anxiety.** Medications are an excellent way to treat anxiety, says Dr. Antony. "Anti-anxiety medications work relatively quickly—typically, within minutes or hours. And taking medication does not require much effort—all you have to do is remember to take a pill."

However, a commonly prescribed class of anti-anxiety medications—the *benzodiazepines*, or so-called "minor tranquilizers," such as *diazepam* (Valium) and *alprazolam* (Xanax)—can cause light-headedness, confusion and dizziness, and has been shown to increase the likelihood of falling in older adults. Also, stopping these drugs suddenly can *trigger* intense anxiety and panic attacks. There's a safer medicine for anxiety—antidepressants.

New study: Researchers at the Washington University School of Medicine in St. Louis studied 177 adults age 60 and older with GAD, dividing them into two groups—one took the antidepressant medication *escitalopram* (Lexapro); the other took a placebo. After 3 months, those taking the medication had an 18% greater reduction in anxiety, with better daily functioning. They also had a significant drop in blood pressure, a sign of less tension.

In older people, antidepressants may be a safer alternative to anti-anxiety medications such as Valium and Xanax, says Eric J. Lenze, MD, an associate professor of psychiatry, who led the study.

Recommended: The suggested starting dose of escitalopram for GAD is 5 to 10 milligrams (mg); the suggested maximum dose is 20 mg.

➤ **Mellower muscles.** If you have GAD, you probably have tense muscles—and releasing that tension can reduce anxiety. An effective way to release the tension is Progressive Muscle Relaxation (PMR). To practice PMR, read the script below into a digital or cassette recorder and then play it back while following the instructions, says Dr. Antony. For best results, relax with PMR for a minimum of 10 minutes a day.

Instructions: Settle back into a chair. Take a couple of deep breaths and look forward to taking some time to relax. Start to allow the chair to support your entire body.

Now go back and tense every muscle in your body at once. Curl your toes and at the same time try to point your toes at your knees. Press your knees together and tense your stomach and chest muscles, make a fist and pull your hands up toward your shoulders. Shrug your shoulders, tense your neck and clench your teeth. Close your eyes and wrinkle your forehead. Hold the tension for a few seconds, then release. Notice the difference between tension and relaxation. Pay attention as the tension flows out of your body and relaxation fills every muscle. Enjoy the feeling of being more and more relaxed. As you start to feel completely relaxed, focus all your attention on your breathing. Breathe slowly and deeply, in and out. Pay attention to the sensation of air filling your lungs and then flowing gently outward. As you breathe in, say to yourself, "In, two, three." As you breathe out, say to yourself, "Relax, two, three." *Keep repeating that to yourself:* "In…two…three…Relax…two…three…"

➤ **Mindfulness: Acceptance over anxiety and worry.** "There is a capacity inside each of us to be calm and stable—to effectively deal with even the most intense anxiety, worry and fear," says Jeffrey Brantley, MD, founder and director of the Mindfulness Based Stress Reduction Program at Duke University's Center for Integrative Medicine, and author of *Calming Your Anxious Mind* (New Harbinger). "Discovering your own capacity for a calm, steady awareness requires turning inward and using your natural ability to *pay attention.*"

This type of attention—"purposeful, non-judgmental and with a welcoming and allowing attitude"—is called *mindfulness*, he says. How does mindfulness work to counter worry?

Chinese Medicine for Anxiety

"A very high percentage of chronic anxiety conditions are rooted in the heart, which the Chinese see as the vessel that contains the spirit," says Angelo Druda, a practitioner of Chinese medicine in northern California and author of *The Tao of Rejuvenation* (North Atlantic).

To treat anxiety, Druda uses a traditional Chinese herbal formula. "It contains several herbs that are calming to the heart—and with a few doses, the whole pattern of chronic anxiety is typically resolved, and the person calms down and becomes grounded."

Rapid Resource: The formula is called *Heart Protector*. To order it, visit the product section of Druda's website, *www.traditionalbotanicalmedicine.com*, or call 707-291-9164.

However: Kava, an herb from the South Pacific often recommended for anxiety, is not effective. "Most studies on kava have been in people who don't have GAD," says Dr. Antony. "Studies in those with GAD generally find that kava is no more effective than a placebo."

"The habits of worry, anxiety and fear are like computer programs wired into your body and brain," explains Dr. Brantley. "Mindfulness—the practice of paying attention to thoughts and physical sensations without judgment, and with curious, open-hearted receptivity—disentangles you from these programs, so that you are no longer swept up in them."

🕐 *Super-Quick Fix*

➤ **What to do:** If you find yourself keyed up and anxious—whether because of a boss's deadline or a news report about a terrorist attack—try getting up and walking mindfully for a minute or two, suggests Dr. Brantley. "Pay attention to each step, to the sensations of the body and to your breath, as you inhale and exhale."

Another mindfulness technique is to name what's happening to you ("I'm feeling anxiety") and activate the intention to be loving and kind to yourself with a mental affirmation ("May I be free from fear, anxiety and worry").

"By using these types of mindfulness techniques to disentangle yourself from the reactive program, you may find that you feel better—even after just a minute or two," says Dr. Brantley. "When anxiety and fear pop back up—in ten minutes or in an hour—use the techniques again. These quick interventions don't immunize you against worry and anxiety. They are more like a surfboard—they allow you to surf the big waves of anxiety, to catch the energy and move on."

▶ **Count your breaths.** "Mindful breathing can help you establish mindfulness in different situations," says Dr. Brantley. "One key to staying present with mindful breathing is the strength of your attention, or concentration. You can use this meditation to improve concentration."

1. **Sit comfortably in a place where you won't be interrupted.**

2. **Give yourself at least 15 to 20 minutes for this practice at first,** and then vary the length, practicing for briefer periods and longer ones in future sessions.

3. **Begin breathing mindfully.**

4. **With your focused attention,** notice each in breath and out breath and the space between them.

5. **As you watch and feel your breath mindfully,** notice the point where the out breath ends.

6. **Quietly count each breath at the point it ends,** beginning with 1 and going up to

8. For example, "In, out 1…in, out, 2…in, out, 3," and so on, up to 8.

If you get to 8, count down in the same way until you get back to 1.

If you get lost or interrupted, go back to 1.

Remember to keep your count totally synchronized with the end of the out breath.

Rapid Resource: You can find more anxiety-reducing mindfulness meditations in *Daily Meditations for Calming Your Anxious Mind* (New Harbinger), coauthored by Dr. Brantley.

ARRHYTHMIAS

Say Whoa to Your Racing Heart

It races. It flutters. It skips a beat. That's what your heart does when its electrical system has a temporary or sustained short-circuit.

Doctors call it an *arrhythmia*—an irregular heartbeat.

Sometimes it's a *benign arrhythmia*, and produces a moment's discomfort, or symptoms that are slightly more bothersome, such as light-headedness.

But sometimes—particularly for people age 60 and older—an arrhythmia is the exact opposite of benign. The irregularity is so extreme and sustained that it increases your risk of a heart attack or stroke.

If you notice any type of arrhythmia beyond a skipped beat, such as a racing heart, a flutter in your chest, see a doctor ASAP. And talk to your physician about the following fast ways to harmonize your heart…

▶ **If your heart rhythm is fishy—take fish oil.** Doctors call the condition *sudden cardiac death*—a fatal disruption of the heart's normal rhythm. It kills 325,000 Americans every year. The heartbeat can become too rapid (*ventricular tachycardia*) or chaotic (*ventricular fibrillation*). *Fish oil can help smooth those choppy waves…*

"Any patient with risk factors for sudden cardiac death, such as ventricular arrhythmias, should consider fish oil supplementation," says Rishi Anand, MD, in the Department of Cardiology at the Ochsner Medical Center in New Orleans. Fish oil, he explains, improves overall "autonomic tone"—the steadiness of the part of the nervous system that controls automatic functions such as heartbeat and breathing—reducing the risk of arrhythmias.

Study: Researchers at Harvard Medical School conducted a one-year study on 402 people with cardioverter/defibrillators, a medical device implanted in the chest of a person at risk for a fatal arrhythmia. They divided them into two groups—one group took fish oil supplements; the other took olive oil.

At the end of the year, those taking fish oil were 38% less likely to have had a life-threatening arrhythmia and 28% less likely to die of any cause.

"Regular daily ingestion of fish oil may significantly reduce potentially fatal arrhythmias," say the researchers, in the journal *Circulation*.

And in another study of people who had recently suffered a heart attack—a particularly risky period for fatal arrhythmias—researchers found that fish oil reduced the risk of sudden cardiac death by nearly 50%.

"This study is important because there is really no effective therapy for arrhythmias," says Alexander Leaf, MD, professor of clinical medicine at Harvard Medical School.

Recommended: The American Heart Association recommends you eat four 3-ounce servings of oily fish weekly (salmon, mackerel, herring, sardines, anchovies) or take a fish oil supplement supplying a combined total of 800 to 1,000 milligrams (mg) of the omega-3 fatty acids EPA (*eicosapentaenoic acid*) and DHA (*docosahexaenoic acid*).

▶ **Block AF—with a walk around the block.** Atrial fibrillation (AF)—a rapid, irregular heartbeat—is a common type of arrhythmia. And it's especially common after age 65—by age 75, one in five people have developed it.

Good news: A walk around the block can help prevent it. A walk around two blocks is even better.

New study: Researchers at Harvard Medical School and Harvard School of Public Health studied more than 5,000 adults, with an average age of 73. Those who had participated regularly in one or more "light to moderate" leisure-time activities—walking, gardening, outdoor chores, golfing or dancing—lowered their risk of developing AF by 36%, compared with people who were inactive.

When the researchers focused their analysis on walking, they found that—compared to people who walked five or fewer blocks a week—those who walked…

- **Five to 11 blocks** a week had a 22% lower risk

- **12 to 23 blocks** a week had a 24% lower risk

- **24 to 59 blocks** a week had a 33% lower risk

- **60 blocks or more** a week had a 44% lower risk

How does exercise help prevent AF?

It keeps the heart muscle and arteries flexible…lowers the amount of fat in the body…builds muscle mass…lowers resting heart rate…lowers blood pressure…stabilizes blood sugar…and reduces inflammation.

"Each of these is a risk factor for AF," says Dariush Mozaffarian, MD, a cardiologist at Harvard Medical School and the study's lead author.

Mellow with Magnesium

"Among my patients with chronic cardiovascular disease are individuals who experience uncomfortable arrhythmias—racing of the heart, or a condition of extra or skipped heartbeats called PVCs, or premature ventricular complex," says James Roberts, MD, coauthor with Stephen Sinatra, MD, of *Reverse Heart Disease Now* (Wiley).

"Every one of these patients has a magnesium deficiency. I give them all a magnesium supplement and their PVCs disappear. They all feel better."

Why it works: Magnesium widens and relaxes arteries, decreases blood pressure and helps boost energy in heart cells.

Recommended: 400 to 800 mg a day. The chewable form has superior absorbability, say Drs. Roberts and Sinatra.

⚠ **Caution:** Don't take extra magnesium if you've been diagnosed with chronic kidney disease or suffer from kidney failure.

"Older adults who aren't currently active should talk to their doctors before starting exercise," he continues. "But most older adults should walk regularly and enjoy other leisure-time activities, such as gardening, dancing, golfing or swimming. We aren't talking about running marathons—or even running. Just enjoy regular walks to the park or around the neighborhood."

⏱ Super-Quick Fix

➤ **Get those headphones off your chest.** Maybe you have a pacemaker or an implantable cardioverter defibrillators (ICD)—a device surgically inserted to control potentially fatal arrhythmias. If you do, be careful how you listen to music. The magnets in the *headphones* of an MP3 digital music player (such as an iPod) can interfere with the devices and jeopardize your health.

New study: "We became interested in knowing whether the headphones, which contain magnets—not the MP3 players themselves—would interact with implanted cardiac devices," says William H. Maisel, MD, director of the Medical Device Safety Institute at the Beth Israel Medical Center in Boston, Massachusetts. To find out, Dr. Maisel and his colleagues tested eight different models of MP3 player headphones (including both the clip-on and earbud variety) with iPods on 60 defibrillator and pacemaker patients.

"We placed the headphones on the patients' chests, directly over where their devices are located, monitoring them for evidence of an interaction," said Dr. Maisel.

The researchers detected an interference with the device by the headphones in 14 of the 60 patients…

- **Pacemakers.** "For patients with pacemakers, exposure to the headphones can force the device to deliver signals to the heart, causing it to beat without regard to the patients' underlying heart rhythm," he said.

- **Defibrillators.** "Exposure of a defibrillator to the headphones can temporarily deactivate the defibrillator.

What to do: "Patients should simply be instructed to keep their headphones at least 3 centimeters (1.2 inches) away from their implantable devices," said Dr. Maisel.

In other words, don't place your headphones in your shirt or blouse pocket or drape them over your chest.

"And family members or friends of patients with implantable defibrillators should avoid wearing headphones and resting their head right on top of someone's device," says Dr. Maisel.

ARTHRITIS

Speedy Help for Stiff, Aching Joints

A storm is on the way…and the forecast is for mostly pain.

"People with arthritis *can* predict rain by the level of their joint pain," says Javad Parvizi, MD, PhD, of Thomas Jefferson University Hospital in Philadelphia. That's because joints contain specialized nerves called *baroreceptors* that respond to changes in atmospheric pressure, such as the lower pressure before a rainstorm. People with osteoarthritis are particularly sensitive to those changes—and their joints can hurt even more than usual.

Well, there are a *lot* of Americans out there who know when a storm is on its way…

Fact: Twenty-seven million Americans have osteoarthritis—usually in the joints of the knees, hips, neck, low back, feet or hands. (For information on rheumatoid arthritis, see page 37.) And many of them are older—65% of Americans over age 65 suffer from the disease.

What's going on inside those aging, ailing joints?

"In a joint afflicted with osteoarthritis, the cartilage that covers and cushions the ends of the bones degenerates, allowing bones to rub together" explains Jason Theodosakis, MD, coauthor of *The Arthritis Cure* (St. Martin's Griffin) and associate clinical professor at the University of Arizona College of Medicine in Tucson. "Bone spurs and cysts may also develop. And the structures around the joint—tendons, ligaments and muscles—may become strained, inflamed and painful."

Yes, *pain* is a prominent—and unfortunate—symptom of osteoarthritis (referred to as "arthritis" in the rest of this section). In fact, the disease is the number-one cause of chronic pain in America. Stiffness—sometimes with pain, and sometimes without—is another typical symptom. As the disease worsens, inflammation can become more common, with redness, swelling and warmth around the joint. And all that pain, stiffness and inflammation can stop people in their tracks—literally.

Arthritis is the number-one cause of disability in the US. Maybe you can't walk as well…or get up and down the stairs as easily…or screw open a jar…or turn your head to the side as you back up your car, or…well, you get the difficult picture.

But you can lessen (or even stop) the pain and stiffness and restore daily function, says Dr. Theodosakis. You can even reverse the disease, rebuilding damaged cartilage. You can usually do all that without drugs or expensive surgery. And, in many cases, you can do it fast. *For example, simply by taking one or more of the best disease-beating nutritional supplements…*

➤ **Dr. Theo's Speedy Seven, for faster arthritis relief.**

"There are several reasons why you need supplements to beat arthritis," says Dr. Theodosakis.

For one thing, he says, few people actually eat healthy, nutrient-rich diets. And, as you get older, you don't digest and absorb nutrients as well. And *treating* disease often requires higher quantities of nutrients, along with specialized, disease-defeating factors. "Yes, rely on a good diet for most of the nutrition you need. But you should add supplements that specifically treat arthritis."

And there are seven supplements that are scientifically proven to do just that—some a little faster than others. "In terms of relieving symptoms—ASU and Pycnogenol tend to work the fastest, followed by hyaluronic acid and vitamin D, and then glucosamine and chondroitin and fish oil," Dr. Theodosakis explains.

Let's look at those supplements…

1. **ASU.** ASU is short for *avocado/soybean unsaponifiables*. It's an extract from the oils of those two plants—an extract that can definitely "oil" your stiff, aching joints.

    Newest research: Researchers from Denmark analyzed data from four studies involving 664 people with arthritis of the knee or hip who took either ASU or a placebo for three months to a year. Compared to the placebo, ASU was 86% better at reducing pain, and 61% better at improving function in the activities of daily living, such as carrying groceries, doing the laundry or just walking from room to room. The study was published in the journal *Osteoarthritis and Cartilage*.

    Other studies show ASU can slow the progression of arthritis, limiting the amount of lost cartilage. It can also reduce the need for painkillers by more than 50%.

    ASU works by reducing inflammation, blocking enzymes that destroy cartilage, and reducing the abnormal bone formation in arthritic joints.

    Useful: ASU might help prevent arthritis in an athlete who has injured a knee or other joint.

    Recommended intake: 300 milligrams (mg) daily.

    Product: Avosoy Complete, which contains ASU and chondroitin and glucosamine, two supplements discussed below.

    Rapid Resource: You can purchase Avosoy Complete online at *www.drtheos.com*, or call 800-311-6883 or e-mail *drtheo@spexpress.com*.

2. **Pycnogenol.** This is an antioxidant-rich extract from the bark of the Maritime Pine, which grows in the southwest of France—and with over 220 scientific studies, it's one of the best-researched supplements.

    Newest research: Scientists conducted three studies on Pycnogenol and arthritis, involving 293 people. Compared to a placebo, Pycnogenol reduced pain by up to 55%…reduced joint stiffness by up to 53%…improved physical function by up to 56%. The studies were published in *Nutrition Research and Phytotherapy Research*.

    Pycnogenol blocks *nuclear factor kappa-beta*, a so-called "signaling molecule" that enters the cell, binds with DNA and triggers the production of inflammatory-causing compounds. This is the cellular genesis of arthritis—and pycnogenol disrupts it.

    Recommended intake: 50 mg, two or three times daily (100 to 150 mg).

    Product: Pycnogenol supplements are widely available.

3. **Hyaluronic acid.** This is a substance in synovial fluid, the movement-smoothing fluid inside joints. Hyaluronic acid keeps the liquid viscous and lubricating—but people with arthritis tend to have low levels.

    Injections of hyaluronic acid are a widely accepted, effective treatment for arthritis. New evidence shows that *supplements* of hyaluronic acid can work too.

    Newest research: Doctors gave hyaluronic acid supplements or a placebo for eight weeks to 20 people with knee pain from arthritis. At the end of the study, those taking hyaluronic had 23% better physical function and 16% fewer symptoms overall. They also had less pain and were more active. The study was published in *Nutrition Journal*.

    Recommended dosage: 20 to 80 mg daily.

    Product: The study used the product Hyal-Joint, which is available in Hyaluronic Acid Complex, from Country Life, and Doctor's Best Hyaluronic Acid.

4. **and 5. Chondroitin Sulfate and Glucosamine.** "Chondroitin sulfate (CS) and glucosamine are important factors in the creation,

maintenance and repair of cartilage," says Dr. Theodosakis. "Like pycnogenol, they also alter genetic signaling in cartilage cells, decreasing the production of molecular factors that inflame and destroy cartilage.

"There have been more than thirty-five positive human studies on glucosamine and/or CS, and the supplements are approved as over-the-counter or prescription drugs in more than forty countries. They work."

Newest research: French researchers studied 622 people with knee arthritis for two years, dividing them into two groups—one group received CS; the other, a placebo. After two years, those getting CS had a minimal loss of width in the joint space—a sign that cartilage was not disappearing. Those getting the placebo had a 31% loss of width. The CS group also had quicker pain relief and used less anti-inflammatory drugs. "Long-term administration of chondroitin sulfate can prevent joint structure degradation," concluded the researchers. The study was published in *Arthritis and Rheumatism.*

Recommended dosage: 1,500 mg of glucosamine and 800 to 1,200 mg of chondroitin sulfate, taken once a day.

Product: Avosoy Complete. "When ASU is added to glucosamine and chondroitin, the effect on arthritis is even more powerful," says Dr. Theodosakis.

Important: If after three months you're not getting sufficient relief, consider increasing the dosage, says Dr. Theodosakis. *Example:* If you're using Avosoy Complete, start with three pills a day; after three months, switch to four pills; after four months, five pills, and after five months, six pills, thereby doubling the dosage.

6. **Vitamin D.** "Vitamin D isn't just for healthy bones," says Dr. Theodosakis. The newest research shows that every tissue has vitamin D receptors and that it plays a role in many different functions. Low levels are associated with muscular weakness, loss of balance and falling, and chronic pain. And a study shows that people with the lowest blood levels of vitamin D have triple the incidence of arthritis of the knee, compared to people with the highest levels.

Newest research: Doctors in Ireland measured vitamin D levels in 231 people with osteoarthritis, rheumatoid arthritis and other bone diseases. Seventy percent had low levels and 26% had a severe deficiency. The study was reported at the annual meeting of the European Union League Against Rheumatism.

Recommended dosage: 3,000 to 5,000 IU daily. "I personally take five thousand IU because that's what my blood test showed I needed," says Dr. Theodosakis. "There is tremendous variability from person to person in the biochemical manufacture and absorption of this nutrient. So a somewhat higher level of supplemental intake—one that is still way below any risk of toxicity—helps guarantee an adequate blood level."

Product: Dr. Theodosakis prefers the brand Thorne Research, which tests its products for potency after manufacture, helping to guarantee their effectiveness.

Important: Please see page 253 in the chapter "Osteoporosis" for more information on the healthiest blood levels of vitamin D (50 to 80 ng/ml) and bi-yearly testing to ensure your levels are in that range.

7. **Fish oil.** "Inflammation can cause a lot of pain and discomfort in an arthritis joint, particularly in the later stages of the disease," says Dr. Theodosakis. "*Eicosapentaenoic acid* (EPA)—an omega-3 fatty acid found in fish oil—can help reduce inflammation, both in osteoarthritis and in rheumatoid arthritis."

Newest Research: Researchers in England gave either omega-3 fatty acids or a placebo for nine months to 97 people with rheumatoid arthritis. Thirty-nine percent of those receiving omega-3 were able to reduce their pain medications by 30% or more, compared to 10% for the placebo. The study was published in *Rheumatology*.

Recommended: "EPA has been mostly studied on people with rheumatoid arthritis, and the level typically used to reduce inflammation is 2.4 to 3.6 grams, which is not available in most fish oil supplements. I had my own supplement formulated to supply that amount of EPA."

Product: Advanced Premium Omega-3 Fish Oil, from *www.drtheos.com*.

SPEED LIMIT Is Your Painkiller Killing You?

On average, 45 Americans die every day—more than 16,000 every year—from taking the painkillers called *non-steroidal anti-inflammatory drugs*, or NSAIDs (pronounced, *en-saids*). The drugs also hospitalize 103,000 people yearly.

What happens: NSAIDs irritate the lining of the esophagus, stomach and intestines, often causing stomach ulcers and gastrointestinal bleeding. Nearly one in three of the 13 million people taking NSAIDs suffer from GI problems—and the thousands of deaths from the drugs are usually caused by sudden, massive bleeding from an ulcer.

NSAIDs can also mess with your cardiovascular system—for example, they can boost blood pressure, increasing the risk of heart disease, stroke and kidney disease.

Other side effects (to name a few) can include nausea, cramps and diarrhea…nervousness, confusion and drowsiness…and asthma attacks.

What's more, NSAIDs can destroy cartilage, worsening arthritis in the long run.

Many doctors recommend people with arthritis take *acetaminophen* (Tylenol) for pain relief, because it's a somewhat safer drug. But most actually take a NSAID, because it's usually more effective, helping control both pain and inflammation.

There are more than 20 different types of NSAIDs and over 100 different products. *The most commonly used and prescribed include…*

- **aspirin**
- **celecoxib (Celebrex)**
- **diclofenac (Voltaren)**
- **diflunisal**
- **etodolac**
- **ibuprofen (Motrin, Advil)**
- **indomethacin (Indocin)**
- **ketoprofen**
- **ketorolac**
- **nabumetone**
- **naproxen (Aleve, Naprosyn)**
- **oxaprozin (Daypro)**
- **piroxicam (Feldene)**
- **sulindac**
- **tolmetin**

Should you take a NSAID?

"To be fair, NSAIDs provide faster pain relief than supplements such as ASU, glucosamine and chondroitin," says Dr. Theodosakis. "But the relief quickly plateaus and often diminishes with time."

Smart idea: "If your symptoms are severe, use a NSAID for one to two weeks *with* ASU and glucosamine/chondroitin," he says. "Taper off the medication as the nutritional supplements begin to kick in and reduce pain." (Check with your doctor before beginning or changing any drug regimen.)

Rheumatoid Arthritis— When Your Body Attacks Your Bones

Rheumatoid arthritis is a joint-destroying auto-immune disease—for unknown reasons, your immune system mistakes your bones for a foreign invader, and attacks them. The condition afflicts 2.5 million Americans, most of them women. It can cause severe pain and disability.

In their latest guidelines, issued in 2008, the American College of Rheumatology recommended that doctors treat most cases of the disease with two drugs—an immune-suppressing drug such as *methotrexate* (Trexall), and "biologic" medication that can stop the activity of an immune factor called TNF that causes inflammation. Anti-TNF drugs include *adalimumab* (Humira), *etanercept* (Enbrel) and *infliximab* (Remicade).

"If you have rheumatoid arthritis and you are not using pharmacological therapy to halt the progress of the disease, you're making a mistake," says Dr. Theodosakis. He also notes that treating the disease as soon as it is diagnosed makes a big difference in how quickly it advances. "Consider it an emergency and get on medications immediately," he says.

But if you feel you must take NSAIDs, here are some ways Dr. Theodosakis recommends to protect yourself from the GI bleeding that kills and hospitalizes tens of thousands of people every year...

- **Take them with food.** Eat, take the pill and eat again.

- **Drink at least eight ounces of water when taking capsules or tablets,** to keep the lining of the esophagus and stomach from becoming irritated.

- **Don't lie down for 30 minutes or so after taking your medicine.** This assures the pill will pass through the esophagus to your stomach.

- **Take the exact prescribed dose.** If you miss it, don't take a double dose.

- **Don't drink alcohol with NSAIDs—** it increases the risk of stomach problems.

- **Don't combine acetaminophen with aspirin or other NSAIDs,** which can increase stomach damage.

- **Talk to your doctor about using acid-blocking proton pump inhibitors** such as *omeprazole* (Prilosec) or *esomeprazole* (Nexium) with NSAIDs. They can reduce the risk of stomach ulcers from 20% to 5% or less.

🕐 *Super-Quick Fix*

➤ **The fastest pain relief—ice. (If you use it right.)** "Ice should be the first therapy for anyone with arthritis of the knee, the most common type of arthritis," says Dr. Theodosakis. "It relieves pain and decreases inflammation, with almost no risk of side effects. But most arthritis sufferers don't learn to use ice properly, so it's not effective."

What to do: Buy two or three freezable soft gel ice packs, available at most sporting goods stores. Also buy one or two compression bandages. Store the gel pack in the freezer. When your knee hurts, place the pack on your knee, over a pant leg or a thin towel (never put the pack directly on your skin) and secure it to your knee with the ACE bandage. The pack stays cold for about 15 minutes— exactly the right amount of time to provide an hour or two of pain relief.

"This treatment with ice is *the* fastest way to get pain relief—faster than taking a NSAID or a Tylenol," says Dr. Theodosakis.

Rapid Resource: You can buy ice packs on the Internet, including packs that come with a compression sleeve that fits around your knee. Brands include Universal Cold Pack from Thera-Med, ColPaC Universal Ice Pack from Chattanooga Group, Dura Kold Knee Sleeve from Don Joy, Universal Cold Pack from Polar Products, and many others. They are available online.

➤ **Don't make your arthritis worse—learn how to sit down and stand up!** As you read earlier, arthritis is a "wear and tear" disease—your cartilage is worn away until bone is rubbing on bone. Ouch! But it's not an accident or trauma that damages most joints, says Dr. Theodosakis. It's the *little* things you do, day after day—actions that don't distribute your weight evenly throughout your body's joints and muscles (misalignment), putting undue stress on a particular joint and wearing it out.

Like sitting down and standing up.

"We get in and out of chairs all day long without thinking about the potential damage that results from our being temporarily out of alignment," says Dr. Theodosakis. "To remain aligned—to avoid placing extra force on your spinal vertebrae or your hip joints—use the following simple procedure." (It's much easier to do than to explain, he jokes.)

Sitting down: Stand tall in front of the chair, feet shoulder-width apart. Place one foot so that the back of that leg is barely touching the chair, with the other foot very slightly forward. Tighten your abdominal muscles as you bend your knees, and push your hips back. Keeping your back straight, moving down and never bending forward, use your leg muscles to ease yourself down into the chair. If the chair has arms, you can hold on to them as you sit. But don't reach down too soon. You want your legs muscles to do most of the work of lowering your body onto the chair.

Arthroscopic Knee Surgery Doesn't Work

Every year, 650,000 people with arthritis of the knee have arthroscopic knee surgery to treat the problem. The surgeon makes a small incision and inserts a thin, flexible fiber-optic scope into the knee joint, along with other instruments. Pieces of cartilage are removed and the inner surfaces of the joint are smoothed. There's only one problem.

The surgery doesn't work.

Newest finding: Researchers in England studied 178 people with knee arthritis. All of the patients received physical therapy and medications (ibuprofen and acetaminophen). Eighty-six people also had arthroscopic surgery.

Two years later, those who had the surgery *didn't* have fewer symptoms or better function.

"This study provides definitive evidence that arthroscopic surgery provides no additional therapeutic value when added to physical therapy and medication for patients with moderate osteoarthritis of the knee," says Brian Feagan, MD, a study researcher. "I don't think this surgery should be used at all for knee osteoarthritis."

"This study offers hope and encouragement to persons with osteoarthritis who would like to avoid the pain and emotional toll of surgery," adds Scott Ward, PT, PhD, president of the American Physical Therapy Association. "Too often, the first line of defense is surgery when it need not always be. Physical therapy can be equally effective and should be considered not only by patients themselves, but also the primary care doctors and orthopedists who are treating them."

To find a physical therapist near you, visit the website *www.moveforwardpt.com*, sponsored by the American Physical Therapy Association, or call the association at 800-999-2782.

Standing up: This should be the exact opposite of sitting down, says Dr. Theodosakis. *Don't* throw your upper body forward, bending severely at the waist, and pushing down on your knees with your hand as you rise. Instead, wiggle or slide yourself to the front of the chair, with both feet on the floor near the front of the chair, one slightly forward of the other. Then, keeping your back straight, use your leg muscles to push yourself straight up from the chair. If the chair has arms, press down on the arms with your hands for assistance as you rise.

Important: The key is to keep your back comfortably straight, so that it can support and disperse your weight properly.

▶ **Strengthen your quadriceps.** For years, doctors have debated whether strengthening the quadriceps—the muscles on the front of your thigh—helps relieve the pain of knee arthritis.

Newest research: Doctors at the Mayo Clinic conducted a 30-month study of 265 people with arthritis. They found those with the strongest quadriceps had the least cartilage loss in the *patellofemoral joint*—the spot where the thigh bone and the kneecap meet, and a typically painful area for those with knee arthritis. Those with the greatest quadriceps strength also had less knee pain and better physical function. The study was published in *Arthritis & Rheumatism*.

"Our findings suggest that greater quadriceps strength has an overall beneficial effect on knee osteoarthritis," says Shreyasee Amin, MD, PhD, of the Mayo Clinic.

What to do: To strengthen the quadriceps, Dr. Theodosakis recommends several types of exercise including the "Modified Lunge." *Here are his instructions...*

• **Stand with your feet about a foot apart.** Then move your left foot one large step forward (12 to 24 inches, depending on how long your legs are). Keeping your back straight and head up, try to bend the left leg until your thigh

is parallel to the ground. Then push back with the left leg (push the heel into the floor) to return to the starting position. The predominant movement should be more up and down than forward and back. When you do the exercise, you should feel the thigh muscles in the left leg working. Do eight to 12 repetitions on the left side, then switch and do the same procedure on the right side.

▶ **The easiest exercise for people with knee or hip arthritis.** "If you have osteoarthritis and you want to get better, you must exercise," says Dr. Theodosakis.

When you don't exercise, you lose muscle tone, your muscles weaken and the range of motion in your joints decreases (joint contracture). "In effect, your muscles and joints shrink and stiffen up, making normal movement even harder," he says.

But many people with arthritis don't exercise—because it hurts.

Smart idea: Spinning on a stationary bicycle—pedaling with no resistance—is typically painless. And it stimulates cartilage growth and decreases pain, says Dr. Theodosakis.

What to do: Pedal 20 to 30 minutes, three or four days a week. Increase "resistance"—the amount of tension on the wheel as you cycle—as you can tolerate it.

Rapid Resource: You can find a wide selection of home exercise bikes, for as little as $120, at *www.exercisebikes.com*, or call 888-880-4884. Address: ExerciseBikes.com, Hayneedle, Inc., 9394 W. Dodge Rd., Suite 300, Omaha, NE 68114.

🕐 *Super-Quick Fix*

▶ **Press your pain away.** *Acupuncture* is an ancient healing technique used by practitioners of Traditional Chinese Medicine (TCM). In TCM, healing energy called *chi* is said to flow through the body along channels called *meridians*. During acupuncture, tiny, painless needles are inserted into acupoints on the meridians that stimulate and balance chi. Acupuncture also increases blood flow to the treated area, and may trigger the release of *endorphins*, pain-relieving brain chemicals.

"But acupoints can also be stimulated with fingertips or knuckles, using a self-help technique called *acupressure*," says Michael Reed Gach, PhD, founder of the Acupressure Institute in Berkeley, California, and author of *Arthritis Relief at Your Fingertips* (Warner) and other books and CDs on acupressure (*www.acupressure.com*). "And the most amazing acupoint for arthritis is *Joining the Valley*—because it can help relieve arthritis pain *anywhere* in the body."

The point is located in the webbing between the thumb and index finger, at the highest spot of the muscle when the thumb and index finger are brought close together.

What to do: Rhythmically squeeze the webbing. As you squeeze, place the side of your hand that is closest to the little finger on your thigh or a tabletop. Apply pressure and press downward. This allows you to angle more deeply into the point, increasing benefit. Press for three minutes, once or twice a day.

"Use an amount of pressure that causes a sensation between pleasure and pain—pressure that 'hurts good,' " says Dr. Gach.

Also good for: Headache, toothache, hangover, hay fever symptoms, constipation.

⚠ **Caution:** This point should not be used by pregnant women because its stimulation can cause premature contraction in the uterus.

➤ **Shed pounds, shed pain.** If you have arthritis, extra pounds and extra pain go hand in hand...

Newest research: Researchers at the University of North Carolina and the govern-

---

See Your Doctor If...

No ifs, ands and buts about it—if you think you have arthritis, see your doctor.

"Many conditions, from infections to diabetes to cancer, *mimic* the symptoms of arthritis—and many people who self-diagnose their problem do so incorrectly," says Dr. Theodosakis. "In fact, as many as four out of five people with chronic symptoms in a joint haven't ever actually visited a health care professional for an accurate diagnosis. That's a mistake."

For the most accurate diagnosis, Dr. Theodosakis urges you to see a specialist—a rheumatologist, or a doctor who specializes in sports medicine, physical medicine or rehabilitation. "They spend more time than other physicians studying arthritis and seeing arthritis patients," he says.

However: An orthopedic surgeon is probably *not* a good first choice. "Despite specializing in the musculoskeletal system, a surgeon may not be your best first choice for evaluating your arthritis and recommending the proper *nonsurgical* care," he says.

Dr. Theodosakis also advises you to consult with your doctor before taking any supplements or engaging in any exercises for arthritis.

---

ment's Centers for Disease Control analyzed six years of health data on more than 3,000 people, ages 61 and older. Compared to people with normal weight, people who were overweight had a 30% higher risk of developing knee arthritis, and those who were obese (approximately 30 or more pounds overweight) had a 60% higher risk. In another study, Australian researchers analyzed data from more than 32,000 people and found that those who were overweight were three to four times more likely to need a knee or hip replacement because of arthritis. The studies were published in *Arthritis & Rheumatism* and *Arthritis Research and Therapy*.

What happens: "There are probably two reasons why overweight causes and contributes to arthritis," says Dr. Theodosakis. One reason is that extra pounds put extra pressure on joints, such as the knee and hip joint. The other reason is metabolic—overweight people manufacture more biochemicals, such as the hormone leptin, which break down cartilage, even in joints that don't bear weight, such as the fingers.

What to do: Lose weight, of course.

⚠ *Caution:* People who lose weight fast tend to gain it back because they can't sustain whatever dietary deprivation allowed them to shed the pounds.

"For permanent, long-term weight-loss—and permanent reduction of arthritic pain from those extra pounds—lose weight as *slowly* as possible, using a combination of a healthy diet and regular exercise," says Dr. Theodosakis. You may start to notice relief after losing only a few pounds, he says. Studies show you'll probably notice a big difference after losing about 13 pounds.

For no-deprivation weight loss, Dr. Theodosakis favors a tasty Mediterranean diet, with plenty of fruits and vegetables, whole grains, beans, fish, nuts and olive oil, minimal amounts of red meat and dairy products, almost no quickly digested, fat-creating carbohydrates (such as sugar, white flour, white rice and potatoes) and almost no processed foods and snack foods. *For successful long-term weight-loss, he also recommends...*

- **Make changes for yourself,** not others.
- **Exercise regularly.**
- **Never skip meals.**
- **Watch your fat intake**—the easiest and most efficient way to lower caloric intake.
- **Use alcohol in small quantities, if at all.** (Calories from alcohol quickly add up.)
- **Never "count calories" or diet**—instead, adopt a flexible, easy-to-follow general food plan such as the Mediterranean diet.

- **Be content with your body and realistic about your goals.**
- **Get organized**—food planning ensures full, well-balanced meals.
- **Understand your reasons for overeating and past dietary failures.** Many people eat to ease pain, deal with stress or relieve boredom. Once you figure out why you overeat, substitute another activity, such as going for a walk or reading a book. (Dr. Theodosakis broke his habit of mindless eating at work by instead throwing darts at the dartboard in his office or visiting a friend in another office.)

ASTHMA

Stop an Attack—Now

Nearly 27 million Americans have been diagnosed with asthma—a lot of them lately...

Fact: In the last 25 years, the number of people with asthma has *quadrupled*—and the number of deaths from asthma attacks has *doubled*.

What's going on?

It might be more air pollutants, outdoors and in...more stress...expanding waistlines...or diets loaded with fat, sugar and artificial chemicals.

All these factors (and many more) can set the stage for the inflamed, constricted and mucus-clogged airways of an asthma attack, producing symptoms such as wheezing, shortness of breath, coughing, phlegm and chest tightness. Symptoms that, in their most severe form, can be fatal.

New study: In a survey of 1,812 people with asthma, researchers at Wake Forest University School of Medicine found that 46% had had an asthma attack in which they feared for their life—even though most of them were seeing a doctor regularly and taking asthma medications!

Here are the fastest ways to repel an asthma attack…

Important: Use these recommendations only with the approval and supervision of your physician.

➤ **Use a peak flow meter—and use it correctly.** "A peak flow meter measures the fastest rate at which you can blow air out of your lungs," explains Thomas F. Plaut, MD, author of *One Minute Asthma* (Pedipress).

By establishing your *best* peak flow, you can use the device to measure if you're experiencing a drop in lung capacity—and treat yourself accordingly. (See below.) But, says Dr. Plaut, you have to use the peak flow meter correctly—and many people with asthma don't. *His instructions…*

- **Remove gum or food from your mouth.**

- **Move the pointer to zero.**

- **Stand up.**

- **Hold the meter straight.**

- **Keep your fingers away from the marker and vent holes.**

- **Open your mouth wide and slowly breathe in as much air as you can.**

- **Put the mouthpiece *flat on your tongue*** (like a Popsicle) and close your lips snugly around it.

- **Blow out as fast as you can**—a short, sharp blast (less than half a second).

- **Note your score, then move the pointer to zero.**

- **Wait at least 15 seconds.**

- **Repeat the process two more times.** Mark down the best score of the three.

Rapid Resource: The 80-page booklet *One Minute Asthma* offers a complete action plan that you and your doctor can use to achieve asthma control. You can order the booklet at *www.pedipress.com*, or by phone at 800-611-6081. Address: Pedipress, Inc., 125 Red Gate Lane, Amherst, MA 01002.

➤ **Know exactly what to do in an asthma attack.** "If you have asthma, you need to know what to do in a breathing emergency—how to act quickly and stay alive," says Richard N. Firshein, DO, Medical Director of the Firshein Center for Comprehensive Medicine in New York City and author of *Reversing Asthma* (Warner) and *Your Asthma-Free Child* (Avery).

Asthma is a complex problem, with a multitude of triggers, he explains. "Those triggers start a cascade of reactions in the lungs, leading to constriction and inflammation, along with mucous plugging of critical airways. In an emergency, you must address *each* of these problems. But the first step should always be to address the *constriction*. It is the failure to counter *this* problem that causes thousands of people to die needlessly every year."

If you're having difficulty breathing, first use your peak flow meter. "This will help you gauge the seriousness of the problem," says Dr. Firshein. "Sometimes people *feel* worse than their numbers indicate—and seeing your numbers are relatively good can reduce anxiety. *If your numbers are good, then…*

1. **Use a bronchodilator.** This inhaled medication—used in a "handheld puffer" such as albuterol (Proventil, AccuNeb, Vospire, ProAir)—can quickly relax airways and restore breathing. Use your peak flow meter again. *If your lung capacity has diminished by 20% or more compared to the reading you took before using the drug…*

2. Use a nebulizer. This device provides airway-opening medication in aerosol form—delivering four to ten times the amount of medication as an inhaled bronchodilator. (It should be part of your home medical arsenal.) Wait 15 minutes. Take another peak flow meter reading. *If your lung capacity remains diminished by 20% or more...*

3. Take a corticosteroid. This powerful anti-inflammatory medication—in pill or liquid form—can restore breathing. A typical dose would be 30 to 60 milligrams (mg). (This will help reduce inflammation, but it won't have an immediate effect.) *If the problem continues to worsen...*

4. Go to the emergency room. "One of the biggest mistakes people make is not seeking emergency care soon enough," says Dr. Firshein.

"This type of flowchart for action—formulated with your doctor *ahead* of your next asthma attack—is critical," says Dr. Firshein. "It provides an orderly approach to a frighten-

Early Warning Signs of an Asthma Attack

Along with respiratory distress and shortness of breath, there are other signs of an impending asthma attack...

Have you been feeling more fatigued than usual? Are your allergies worse? Do you have more heartburn? More sinus pressure? "These are all possible early warning signs of an impending asthma attack," says Dr. Firshein.

Smart idea: "You may want to pretreat the attack by slightly increasing the dosage of your daily medication," he says. "And talk to your doctor about your symptoms."

ing situation, and allows you not to panic—which worsens breathing even more, and renders you incapable of taking systematic effective action to save your own life."

➤ **Learn a breathing exercise.** "One of the best things someone with asthma can do is to learn to breathe properly," says Dr. Firshein. "It strengthens the muscles of breathing, such as your diaphragm, and allows you to relax during an asthma attack and breathe through it—in essence, using breathing as a natural bronchodilator."

Dr. Firshein says the most effective technique for strengthening the lungs...

• establishes a rhythm of breathing, coordinating breath with heartbeat,

• exhales slightly longer than inhales,

• builds "back pressure" in the lungs, and

• uses abdominal breathing, activating the diaphragm, a muscle necessary for good respiratory control.

"There are a number of different breathing techniques, and I have created one—the Firshein Technique—that is an effective combination of the others. It is the one I use myself and teach to my patients."

His instructions...

Sit down. Put one hand on your stomach, with the palm open and flat against your stomach; use this hand to monitor that your abdomen is rising and falling as you breathe. Use the thumb of the other hand to feel for the pulse point of the hand on your stomach. Let yourself relax. Next, synchronize your breathing with your heart rate. Breathe in through the nose, with the pulse—inhale 2-3-4-5. Breathe out through the mouth, with the pulse—exhale 2-3-4-5-6-7. Blow out through pursed lips, which builds back pressure. Continue for 10 to 15 minutes, practicing twice a day—or anytime you have an asthma attack.

➤ **Dr. Firshein's Favorite Five—supplements to help you breathe.** "At the moment an attack occurs, take a complete dose of each of these supplements—and then another dose later in the day, to make sure that you have adequate blood levels of these key nutrients," says Dr. Firshein.

- **Magnesium.** This helps lungs stay supple and relaxed—500 mg.
- **Vitamin C.** A mild antihistamine. It also strengthens your immune system—1 to 3 grams.
- **CoQ10.** Strengthens and energizes cells—100 to 300 mg.
- **Fish oil.** A natural anti-inflammatory—1 to 4 grams.
- **NAC (N-Acetyl-L-Cysteine).** A potent antioxidant—1,000 mg.

Super-Quick Fix

➤ **Walk away from the trigger.** "Many times there's a precipitant event that triggers the attack—exposure to cold, animals, dusty basements, to pollutants such as diesel exhaust and paints, to pollen, to molds or to perfume," says Dr. Firshein. "If you can remove yourself from the inciting or offending agent—if you can move away from where the inflammation began to another area that's relatively safe—the attack may proceed at a slower pace and give you time to recover."

BACK AND NECK PAIN

Are you having your first bout of back or neck pain? Don't worry too much about it. Eighty percent of Americans will experience back or neck pain at some point in their lives. Four out of five times it goes away in a few weeks—whether you do anything about the pain or not.

But if you're dealing with your second or third (or fourth or fifth) bout of back or neck pain, or pain that almost never quits and limits your activities—then you're one of the unfortunate 35 million Americans with a *chronic* back or neck problem.

Surprising: Seeing a surgeon is probably not your best bet.

"Ninety-five percent of the back and neck pain that brings people to a doctor's office is muscle related," says Gerald Silverman, DC, a chiropractor in Hauppauge, New York, and author of *Your Miraculous Back* (New Harbinger).

"And surgery is never appropriate for muscle strain," adds Stephen Hochschuler, MD, chairman of the Texas Back Institute and coauthor of *Treat Your Back Without Surgery* (Hunter House). "In fact, half the back and neck surgeries that are performed in the United States may be *unnecessary*. Virtually any non-surgical treatment that will not make you worse is worth a try before you resort to surgery." What kind of treatments?

"The best *self-treatment* techniques can significantly reduce or fully eliminate back or neck pain," says Lisa Morrone, a physical therapist in New York and author of *Overcoming Back and Neck Pain* (Harvest House).

And in many cases, she says, that pain relief can be quick...

Spine 101

"The spine is a complex tower of bones, discs, joints, muscles and ligaments," says Dr. Hochschuler. "There are twenty-five bones, or vertebrae—from the cervical vertebrae in your neck area to the lumbar vertebrae in your lower back. The vertebrae are separated by shock-absorbing discs. The tower is held in place by surrounding muscles, ligaments and tendons.

"The neck and back share the same anatomical parts, and both neck and back problems can come from muscle strain, disc problems, traumatic injury, arthritis or from spinal narrowing, which is also called stenosis."

▶ **For a back attack—ice first, heat second.** You lifted a heavy box without bending your knees. Or you worked in front of a computer all day and your neck is stiff. In other words, you stressed the muscles of your back or neck—and now there's an injured area that's tight, achy and sore. *For instant relief...*

• **Ice.** The area is inflamed—and ice is the best way to reduce inflammation, says Dr. Hochschuler.

"For treatment of acute back and neck strains and sprains, nothing beats good, old-fashioned ice cubes or chips in a plastic bag, applied over the area of pain for fifteen to twenty minutes, two to three times a day, for one to three days," says Brian Hainline, MD, chief medical officer of the US Open Tennis Championships and author of *Back Pain Understood* (Medicus). "Applying ice relieves pain and reduces swelling. It also helps prevent a spasm that could lead to more pain."

• **Heat.** Two to three days after the injury, begin applying heat to the area, says Dr. Hochschuler.

Best: A study by researchers in the Department of Physical Medicine and Rehabilitation at

UMDNJ–New Jersey Medical School in Newark showed that a *continuous low-level heat wrap* was 25% more effective at relieving lower back pain than over-the-counter medications such as *ibuprofen* and *acetaminophen*. Those who wore the wrap also had more muscular flexibility and were better able to perform their daily activities.

"A heat wrap goes beyond the simple pain relief provided by over-the-counter pills," says Scott F. Nadler, DO, who led the study. "It increases blood flow to the painful muscles, improving flexibility and mobility."

Rapid Resource: Dr. Nadler recommends the ThermaCare Lower Back and Hip HeatWraps from Procter & Gamble, which was the wrap used in the study. To learn more about the ThermaCare HeatWraps, visit *www.thermacare. com,* where you can search for nearby stores carrying the product.

Super-Quick Fix

➤ **The most comfortable position for a painful back.** "This position takes the weight off your spine while supporting it, and relaxes the muscles in your back," says Art Brownstein, MD, director of the Princeville Medical Clinic in Hawaii and author of *Healing Back Pain Naturally* (Pocket Books). And it's ideal for a back pain "emergency"—when your back has gone out and you're in so much pain you can't sit. *His instructions…*

1. **Lie on your back with your knees bent and your feet up on a chair or over a bed.** A stack of pillows or blankets under your knees and lower legs can be used in place of a chair or bed.

2. **Lying in this position, practice deep relaxation** by closing your eyes and paying attention to the gentle movement of the breath as it flows in and out of your body. Feel the breath expanding into your

stomach and abdomen as it enters into your body, and gently contracting your stomach and abdomen as it leaves.

3. **Relax all the muscles in your body.**

4. **Continue to observe the flow of your breath as you focus your awareness on the movement of your stomach and abdomen.** Do not try to control the rate or depth of the movement of your stomach and abdomen, but rather try to allow them to move on their own. Relax your mind as well as your entire body.

5. **Remain in this position with your eyes closed for a minimum of 20 minutes.** If you find yourself falling asleep, don't worry, it probably means your body needs the rest. Repeat this deep relaxation several times a day until your pain ceases. Many people sleep in this position when their backs are painful.

SPEED LIMIT
Ix-nay on the X-ray

Low-back pain ranks number five among reasons people end up in a doctor's office. And a study shows that, once they get there, four out of five people with back pain would consent to an x-ray or MRI to help diagnose the cause of their back pain if the doctor thought it was a good idea. *Well, it's probably a bad idea…*

"Performing routine x-rays or MRIs for patients with low-back pain does not lead to less pain, better functioning or less anxiety—in fact, it may even worsen outcomes," says Roger Chou, MD, scientific director of the Oregon Evidence-Based Practice Center at Oregon Health & Science University, and lead author of a recent study on the best ways to treat back pain.

"Clinicians may think they are helping patients by doing routine x-rays or MRIs," he says. "But these diagnostic tests increase medical costs and can result in unnecessary surgeries or other invasive procedures. And they may cause patients to stop being active—probably the best thing for back health—because the patients worry about common findings such as degenerated discs or arthritis, not understanding that these findings are rarely the cause of their back pain.

"Clinicians should not order x-rays or other imaging tests for patients with nonspecific low-back pain," he concludes.

However: Clinicians *should* order diagnostic imaging tests for patients they know or think have spinal or neurological disorders, or if the back pain persists for longer than a month.

➤ **"Targeted massage"—30 seconds to stop acute pain from becoming chronic.** If you strained your back or neck, wait for five days and then start long-term repair—with this speedy technique that can help stop an acute bout of back or neck pain from becoming chronic back or neck pain.

The trick, says Dr. Silverman, is to identify and isolate the source of your pain—the bound-together muscle fibers called adhesions that result in painful muscle spasm—and massage them out. "I teach this to all the patients in my practice with back and neck pain—and I know the ones who don't do it. They're the ones I see again in six months or a year." *His instructions…*

• **Targeted massage for the neck.** Lie flat on your back and look up at the ceiling. Place your fingertips at the base of your skull and gently press into the muscles. Then slowly run your fingers down your neck, covering all the areas between the base of your skull and the top of your shoulders. When you reach the offending muscle fibers, the gentle soothing pressure will suddenly turn into a localized, sharp, ice pick–like sensation. That's the spasm. It will feel like a tiny steel wire or perhaps a small pea in the midst of softer, more pliable tissue.

Now it's time for the massage. Apply firm and steady circular pressure over an area about the size of your fingertip, for 30 to 45 seconds.

There's no benefit to massaging for longer periods of time, says Dr. Silverman. Brief periods of targeted massage—30 to 45 seconds at a time, two times a day, for two or three months—is the way to stop acute neck pain from becoming chronic.

• **Targeted massage for the back.** To locate a muscle spasm in your upper or lower back, lie on your stomach and have someone apply light to moderate finger pressure over those areas, moving their fingers around until you suddenly feel a localized sharp or stabbing sensation—that's the spasm.

However, it's unlikely that you'll find someone to massage that area regularly, every day, day after day. The best way to perform a self-administered massage to the upper or lower back is with a tennis ball.

To massage the spasm, get into a semi-seated or squatting position near a wall, and then place the ball between your back and the wall. With the ball firmly on the spasm, spend one or two minutes applying heavier pressure to the site, using a limited up-and-down or side-to-side motion. Do this twice daily.

Helpful: If you can't find someone to help you first locate the spasm, use this same technique, moving the ball around until you locate the painful area.

Some people feel more comfortable lying on their back and placing the ball between their back and the floor.

➤ **Perfect postures for pain relief.** "Poor posture is the culprit behind many painful back and neck conditions," says Morrone. "Over time, improper posture can lead to muscle shortening, muscle weakness, fatigue and muscle spasms. But with postural correction, you can

Fore! Ouch!

Does a round of golf turn your back into a sand trap for pain?

If so, here are a few pain-preventing tips from Dr. Jim Suttie, a PGA Golf Instructor of the Year and author of *Your Perfect Swing* (Human Kinetics)...

- *Clubs.* Use longer clubs.
- *Address.* Stand erect at the address—avoid bending forward too much.
- *Knees.* Bend your knees more than a conventional instructor would tell you to do. This takes pressure off your spine.
- *Backswing.* Avoid coiling on the backswing—turn your hips and shoulders together. Never restrict your hips on the backswing. And let your head turn a little to the right—this avoids putting pressure on your mid-back.

feel immediate relief." *Some of her suggestions for better posture...*

- **Sitting.** The way in which you sit can actually create pain, she says. *To help correct poor sitting posture...*

- **Keep your feet on the floor.** "Sitting with your feet unsupported increases the pressure inside your discs by ninety percent."

- **Sit on a slight slope.** "This elevates your hips slightly above your knees, tipping your pelvis forward and thus creating an effortless, natural arch in your low back."

Rapid Resource: A wedge-shaped cushion on your chair can help you maintain this posture. The cushion is available at Morrone's website, *www.lisamorrone.com.*

- **Keep your shoulders down and back.** This helps line up your shoulders over your hips. "Roll your shoulders up toward your ears, then back behind you, then down toward the floor.

Now hold them there. This 'down and back' position should feel relaxed."

- **Keep your ears over your shoulders and slightly tuck your chin.** "Draw your head backward so your ear opening lines up with the bony tip of your shoulder. Slightly tuck your chin. This is a big help for neck-pain sufferers."

- **Sleeping.** If you have pain when you wake up, take a look at your sleeping posture.

If you sleep on your back: "Place the pillow under your neck and head—but not under your shoulders and head, which causes your head to tip backward, tightening the muscles in your neck," says Morrone.

If you sleep on your side: "Place a pillow lengthwise between your knees. This helps keep your spine aligned."

- **Don't sleep on your stomach.** It stresses the joints and discs in your spine.

Super-Quick Fix

➤ **The best stretch for morning stiffness.** "Doing a simple stretch before getting out of bed will help you reduce morning tightness," says Dr. Silverman. *His instructions...*

Lie flat on your back with your head on a pillow. Bend your upper leg and grab the front of your knee with both hands. Slowly pull your knee to your chest. When you feel some moderate pulling in your lower back and upper buttock, hold the position for 10 to 15 seconds. Let go and straighten your leg. Repeat seven to 10 times, each time bringing your knee a little closer to your chest. Repeat the entire exercise with the other leg.

⚠ *Caution:* Never bring *both* knees toward your chest at the same time.

➤ **Cross your legs at the movies.** "Our muscles are meant to move," says Norman Marcus, MD, founder of the Norman Marcus

Pain Institute in New York City (*www.nmpi.com*) and director of Muscle Pain Research at the NYU School of Medicine. "In a theater—or any situation where you've been sitting for a long time, and it's awkward to stand up and move around—just cross a leg. A bit later, cross the other leg. Simply crossing your legs moves a lot of back and hip muscles, helping to prevent back pain."

➤ **Toss and turn at night.** "Tossing and turning at night is the body's way of keeping you mobile in your sleep, which helps prevent back pain," says Dr. Marcus. But if your mattress is a decade old or more and has become saggy, you tend to sink in, and your body doesn't move. Not only that—a saggy mattress takes the spine out of its straight and healthy alignment, straining back muscles. The result is back pain.

What to do: Replace your mattress. It should be firm enough to support your spine, but still comfortable, says Dr. Marcus.

Helpful: When shopping for a mattress, bring a spouse or friend along, advises Dr. Hochschuler. Lie on your side and ask your companion to observe the alignment of your spine—it shouldn't curve, and your hips and shoulder shouldn't sink too deeply into the mattress.

See a Doctor If...

Top experts agree—the cause of most back pain is *muscular*. But in some cases, you may have damaged spinal discs that need medical attention, says Dr. Hochschuler. *See your doctor if...*

- *Your back pain continues to worsen over a few days,* or doesn't go away on its own after about three or four weeks.
- *You have back pain with radiating leg pain.*
- *You have leg numbness or leg weakness.* See a doctor within the next few days.
- *You have bowel or bladder incontinence or leg muscle paralysis.* Go to the emergency room.

BAD BREATH

Sweet (and Lasting) Relief

Do you have bad breath? Blame it on brimstone—or what scientists call *sulfur*.

What happens: Bad breath is caused by sulfur-producing bacteria that live under the surface of plaque (the "biofilm" that can coat your teeth and gums) and on your tongue. These bacteria are normal—they help digest amino acids, components of protein. But when they accumulate—in the hundreds of millions—the bacteria release an extra-large, extra-smelly cloud of Volatile Sulfur Compounds, or VSC.

The key to stopping bad breath (also called halitosis) is to deodorize the sulfur and shackle the bacteria's ability to produce VSC in the first place.

And you can do that in a jiffy...

➤ **Twenty-four hours of fresh breath (no morning breath!)—***if* **you make sure to use this mouthwash every 12 hours.** Most mouthwashes contain an antibacterial agent of one kind or another to slay the odor-causing bacteria. And it works. For a little while.

The bacteria are back in business in about an hour. In fact, many gums, mints and sprays—whether they're antibacterial or use a flavoring such as mint to mask bad breath—banish halitosis for an average of only 10 or 15 minutes.

Try SmartMouth mouthwash instead.

"It contains zinc chloride, which blocks the ability of the bacteria to ingest the amino acids that trigger the production of sulfurous gas," says Susanne Cohen, DDS, a dentist in St. Louis, Missouri. "It also contains sodium chlorite, a purifier and deodorizer. Combined, these ingredients stop the activity of sulfur-producing bacteria for twelve hours, not one or two."

After 12 hours, enough sulfur-producing bacteria are back in action to generate a noticeable amount of gas, says Dr. Cohen. "But if you rinse with SmartMouth twice a day, you'll *never* have bad breath." (Of course, if you chow down on odor-producing foods such as garlic or onion, you have to rinse again after the meal to restore freshness.)

Study: Researchers in the Department of Oral Biology and Pathology at the State University of New York in Stony Brook studied the mouthwash in 48 people with bad breath, measuring levels of VSC. After 12 hours, those who had used SmartMouth still had low VSC levels "where the breath is usually non-odorous," say the researchers, in the *Journal of Clinical Dentistry*.

Good news: The claims for SmartMouth are strong—no other mouthwash has been clinically proven to prevent bad breath for longer than one hour; with SmartMouth, your fresh breath lasts 12 hours after each rinse; if you rinse at night you wake up without morning breath; and you will have 24/7 fresh breath when you use the product twice daily.

Well, the National Advertising Division of the Better Business Bureau thought something might smell fishy, and investigated SmartMouth.

They looked at the science…they had the product independently investigated…they measured the breath of users with an odor-detecting machine…and decided the claims were perfectly "reasonable."

Rapid Resource: You can order SmartMouth mouthwash (and also toothpaste, breath mints and chewing gum) at *www.smartmouth. com* or call 800-492-7040. It's also widely available in superstores, supermarkets and chain pharmacies.

⏱ Super-Quick Fix

➤ **Scrape your tongue.** "The VSC are created by bacteria, so it makes sense to remove the bacteria," says Dan Smith, DDS, a dentist in private practice in Agoura Hills, California. "And one of the places those bacteria congregate is on the tongue."

He recommends purchasing a tongue scraper and using it twice a day.

Recommended: Dr. Smith favors tongue scrapers (and other breath-freshening products) from Breath RX. You can order them at *www.breathrx.factoryoutletstore.com* or call 800-816-0810.

Best: For the best removal of odor-causing bacteria, floss first, scrape your tongue next and then brush your teeth, says Dr. Smith.

"First, you want to get rid of the plaque between your teeth, where some of the bacteria hang out," he says. "Then you want to get rid of the bacteria on your tongue. Then the toothbrush can more effectively remove the rest of the bacteria, because it doesn't have a coat of plaque all over it."

🕐 Super-Quick Fix

➤ **Freshen up fast after a meal.** "If I eat garlic or onions or other 'smelly' foods, I freshen up by eating an orange or drinking a glass of lemonade," says Dr. Marvin Cohen. "These acidy foods reduce the pH of the mouth, cutting down on odor."

Also try: "Order the fruit dessert," says Dr. Smith. "Fresh fruits help cleanse the mouth and flush away odor-producing bacteria."

For an after-dinner drink, Dr. Smith suggests ordering a Mojito (go light on the rum), which contains a lot of breath-freshening mint.

➤ **If you breathe through your mouth, drink more water.** A dry mouth can produce bad breath. So if you have allergies, sinus problems or a cold and you breathe through your mouth—drying it out—you need more than the recommended 8 eight-ounce glasses of water a day to keep your mouth well-hydrated and your breath fresh, says Steven Kendrick, DDS, a dentist in private practice at the Midwest Dental Center in Midwest City, Oklahoma.

Suggested Intake: 10 to 12 glasses.

BEDSORES

Smart Advice for Vulnerable Skin

A bedsore can happen to anyone...You break a hip. Or you're felled by the flu—and then pneumonia. Or you're recovering from surgery. And suddenly you're lying in bed for days or weeks—at risk for developing a bedsore, or what health professionals call a *pressure ulcer.*

Fact: It can take only *70 minutes* for a bedsore to start forming. It can take a *year*—a year of discomfort, pain and even life-threatening infection—for one to heal.

If you're a senior, you're particularly vulnerable. That's because older skin is thinner and weaker, as cell-binding collagen fibers have frayed with age. Older skin has also lost most of the protective fat padding between skin and muscle.

What happens: A bedsore starts to form when circulation to the skin is cut off. If you're stuck in bed, that's likely to be at a spot where bone presses on skin from the inside, such as the hips or heels.

Bedsores are also caused by *shearing.* Old skin is like tissue paper, explains Nanette Lavoie-Vaughan, MSN, APN, a wound care specialist in North Carolina, the director of Nurse Nan Consulting (*www.nanettelavoie-vaughan.com*) and author of *The Baby Boomers' Guide to Senior Care* (American Media). If you take tissue paper between your hands and slide your hands back and forth, the paper starts to wrinkle, crumble and tear. Similarly, if you're stuck in bed and continually moving a circulation-deprived area of skin across the sheets, skin can tear and slough off, starting a bedsore.

The fastest way to deal with a bedsore is to spend time preventing one from starting! *Here's what you need to know...*

➤ **Choose the right bed surface.** The best way to prevent a bedsore is to "change the bed"—to provide a softer surface that minimizes pressure. If you're not chronically bedridden—if you've hit a rough patch of personal health, such as an operation or fracture that has you temporarily confined to bed—then you *don't* need a super-fancy pressure-reducing mattress, which can cost tens of thousands of dollars to buy or hundreds to rent. What you need is a pressure-reducing *padding. And scientific studies show the best kinds of padding are...*

● *Specialized foam,* convoluted or cubed rather than flat; and

● *Specialized sheepskin,* denser and thicker than regular sheepskin.

The best way to find these products is to call your local medical supply store, says Madhuri Reddy, MD, an Instructor of Medicine at Harvard Medical School and Director of the Wound Healing Program at Hebrew SeniorLife in Boston.

Trap: "You can't just go out and buy a sheepskin like the type you'd use over your car seat and expect it to prevent pressure ulcers," says Dr. Reddy. "You need *medical sheepskin.*"

➤ **Turn frequently.** The standard recommendation is to turn or be turned at least once every two hours, says Dr. Reddy. However, that might not be possible—maybe there's nobody to turn you, or you can't turn yourself.

Smart idea: Use a body-length pillow or foam bolster and, as you lay on your back, place it under your right hip and shoulder, to elevate them slightly. Every couple of hours, move the pillow/bolster to your left hip and shoulder.

"This helps take the pressure off sensitive areas," says Dr. Reddy. "It may not be the best thing to do, but it's better than doing nothing."

Emergency in the ER— A Bedsore Is Forming!

You're in the ER and you've been placed on a small gurney or stretcher with a hard surface. Well, if you're older, with frailer skin, make sure you're put on a better surface as quickly as possible, says Rose Jeans, MD. A bedsore can start forming in one to two hours!

➤ **Use pillows, cushions or pads under and between bony areas.** For example, put padding underneath the calves and ankles to keep the heels completely off the bed's surface, says Rose Jeans, MD, former director of an outpatient clinic for non-healing wounds, and medical director of the Advanced Rejuvenation Medical Spa in Burlington, Ontario.

If you're lying on your side, put padding between your knees and your ankles.

The two areas that get the most bedsores are hips and heels. Other areas to watch out for include the back and sides of the head, the rims of the ears, the shoulders or shoulder blades, the tailbone, the backs and sides of your knees, ankles and toes.

Most of all, use common sense, says Dr. Jeans. Check for areas where there's pressure, and put padding *there*.

Best: Gel foam is the most pressure-relieving type of padding, says Lavoie-Vaughan. Popular product: Geo-Matt cushions by Span-America Medical Systems.

Rapid Resource: Visit online at *www.span america.com*, or call 800-888-6752.

➤ **Check your skin frequently.** Every couple of hours, check for a reddened area that doesn't go away—the first sign of a forming bedsore. If you see one, pay special attention not to have any pressure on that spot. And let your healthcare provider know what's happening.

➤ **Keep skin dry—but not *too* dry.** Skin that is too moist—from sweat or urine—is a setup for bedsores. However, very dry skin can also cause the problem.

Smart idea: Keep the area clean and dry, but also moisturize with a basic, fragrance-free product, such as Vaseline, says Dr. Reddy.

➤ **Get out of bed.** Try to get off ulcer-prone areas as often as possible, says Lavoie-Vaughan. If

Self-Care for Vascular Skin Ulcers

Diseases that reduce circulation to the legs and feet—such as diabetes or peripheral arterial disease (PAD)—can cause vascular ulcers on the skin. Here are some fast ways to avoid them, says Lavoie-Vaughan.

Don't miss your doctor's appointment. If you have a disease that puts you at risk for ulcers, you must keep the disease under control.

- *Moisturize.* Moisturizing helps skin stay strong and not break open. Use a moisturizing lotion at least twice a day, on your lower legs and feet.

    Smart idea: Thick calluses on the bottom of the feet and the heels can break open and turn into ulcers. Put a prescription-strength moisturizer or emollient on your feet at night (Crisco works too) and wear socks to bed. "After a couple of days, the calluses will peel right off," says Lavoie-Vaughan.

- *Wear comfortable shoes.* Loose shoes that slide around can form blisters that turn into vascular ulcers. If you're ulcer-prone, a flat or a dress shoe might be better than a sneaker, because they're harder and molded to the foot. Shoe inserts can also help.

- *Check your skin carefully.* After each bath or shower, look for little open areas or blisters—because *any* kind of skin break can get infected and break open further. If you find such an area, put on triple antibiotic ointment and a Band-Aid for a couple of days, until a scab has formed. Don't pick at the scab—let it fall off on its own.

- *Know when to see a health professional.* If an area is red around the edges...or has yellow or green drainage...or there's a blister that won't go away...or a dark purple bruise that doesn't fade—you may have the beginning of a vascular ulcer. See a health professional immediately.

See Your Doctor If...

Self-care is not smart care for a bedsore or vascular ulcer. The best wound healing requires skilled nursing to prevent infection. (Medicare will pay for a home health nurse if you have a bedsore or vascular ulcer.)

What helps: The key to healing a pressure ulcer is to keep the wound as moist as possible (to stimulate new tissue growth) and to remove dead tissue.

The top new treatments, says Lavoie-Vaughan, include silver-impregnated dressings (for superb bacterial control), enzymes that painlessly eat away dead tissue but leave healthy tissue behind and chlorophyll to deodorize the wound.

Red flags: The older method of "cleaning" a bedsore with betadine (the brownish orange-colored sterilizing compound often used before surgery) makes the bedsore worse, because it destroys healthy tissue. "This is still sometimes used in wound care centers," says Lavoie-Vaughan.

Also avoid this old method of removing dead tissue—soaking gauze dressings in sterile saline, packing the dressing into the wound, letting it dry (so that it adheres to the dead tissue) and then ripping it out. "It's much better to use enzymatic products," says Lavoie-Vaughan.

there's someone who can help you, try to get up and walk around every two hours.

➤ **Provide yourself with protein.** Protein is a must for maintaining healthy skin or helping a bedsore heal. Meat, eggs and cheese are good choices. But maybe you don't have much of an appetite. If that's the case, add a scoop of protein powder to a glass of milk, suggests Lavoie-Vaughan. Or drink several eight-ounce bottles a day of Ensure High Protein, a supplement drink from Abbott Nutrition.

However: For many years, nutritionists and geriatricians debated whether supplemental vitamin C and zinc—two nutrients that play a role in maintaining healthy skin—might help prevent bedsores or speed healing. The final verdict is they don't help. In fact, extra zinc might even interfere with healing, by blocking the body's use of other minerals such as magnesium, says Lavoie-Vaughan.

BINGE-EATING DISORDER

Restoring Order, One Meal at a Time

Thirty percent of people who attend weight-loss programs such as Weight Watchers have a secret.

They're binge-eaters.

They might pull into the drive-through of a fast food restaurant and order not one but two meals—two burgers, two colas, two fries—and eat them both. Or down a quart of ice cream in one sitting. Or a large pizza. Or a bag of cookies. Or a couple of bags of chips.

They usually eat "comfort foods" loaded with refined carbohydrates and fat...eat in secret...eat fast...eat until they're uncomfortably full—and afterward, they feel disgusted with themselves or guilty or depressed or angry.

Who binges, exactly? A lot of people. Studies estimate that between 20% to 50% of people who are obese—the one-third of Americans who are approximately 30 or more pounds overweight—are binge-eaters. Many feel hopeless about their hidden problem. *But there is a way out...*

"If you have binge-eating disorder (BED), you need help—and working with a therapist trained in eating disorders or an organization such as Overeaters Anonymous *can* help you overcome the problem," says Carolyn Coker

What Caused Your Binge?

"Binges are caused by a variety of factors," says Joyce Nash, PhD, a clinical psychologist in California specializing in the treatment of eating disorders, and author of *Binge No More: Your Guide to Overcoming Disordered Eating* (New Harbinger). They include...

- **The Hunger Binge.** It's triggered by physical deprivation from dieting, says Dr. Nash. *Suggested:* Eat regularly and adequately.

- **The Deprivation Binge.** It's caused not only by restrictive dieting, but also by a sense of needing something and not knowing what it is. *Suggested:* "Legalize" formerly forbidden foods, such as ice cream. But eat a scoop instead of a quart.

- **The Stress Binge.** Your resources for coping with disappointment and difficulty have been stretched thin or exceeded, says Dr. Nash, and you feel anxious, depressed, lonely or insecure. This type of binge is also called emotional eating. *Suggested:* Identify and challenge the inner voices that tell you you're inadequate and that disaster is close by.

- **The Opportunity Binge.** You have a chance to be alone and binge—and you do it. *Suggested:* Plan ahead—decide how to minimize "unstructured" time that affords the opportunity to binge, says Dr. Nash.

- **The Vengeful Binge.** This binge is fueled by anger, says Dr. Nash. You're trying to hurt yourself or someone else. *Suggested:* You need the guidance of a therapist to feel and acknowledge your anger and restore faith in yourself and others.

- **The Pleasure Binge.** You want stimulation and entertainment. *Suggested:* Develop pleasurable, nonfood alternatives, says Dr. Nash. (See page 57 for some ideas.)

- **The Grazing Binge.** You're on autopilot. Food is available, and you eat it nonstop without thinking—for hours at a time. *Suggested:* A weight-management program that provides group support and includes "self-monitoring"—keeping daily records of food eaten and the circumstances under which it was eaten.

Ross, MD, an eating disorder and integrative medicine specialist in Denver, Colorado, and author of *The Binge Eating and Compulsive Overeating Workbook* (New Harbinger).

But while you work with a health professional or supportive organization, studies show there are also simple things you can do to help yourself—starting today...

▶ **Eat three meals a day—no matter what.** "A binge often happens because a person is trying to lose weight, restricts calories and feels deprived and stressed," says Dr. Ross. "Eating regularly will send your body and mind the message that you're *not* deprived—that you'll be nourished on a regular basis."

New study: Researchers in the Department of Psychiatry at the Yale University School of Medicine surveyed the food habits of 173 obese women and men with BED. The 55 people in the study who ate three meals a day had fewer binges and weighed less on average than the 118 who didn't.

▶ **Adopt-a-vegetable.** "Most people who binge don't eat a lot of high-quality foods, such as fruits and vegetables," says Dr. Ross. "But if you do eat more fruits and vegetables, you're less likely to eat sugary, fatty binge foods."

Dr. Ross instructs her patients to "adopt-a-vegetable"—pick one vegetable a week, try different ways of preparing it, and find one they enjoy and are likely to use over and over again. "Patients who do this find it's *fun* to eat more vegetables," she says.

Speed Healing Success

"I Shed the Old Me and Celebrated the New"

If you're a binge-eater, Megan Bartlett understands. A graduate student in psychology in Philadelphia, Bartlett has overcome BED. "I don't spend hours each day counting calories, obsessing over the number I saw on my scale that morning, or agonizing over what I should and should not eat," she says. "I'm gentler on myself. I have more space in my head to think about my family and friends."

Bartlett wrote a book about her eating disorder and her recovery: *Getting Out of BED: Overcoming Binge-Eating Disorder One Day at a Time* (Infinity). Here's what worked for her...

- *Establish a regular pattern of eating.* I typically skipped breakfast, ate a tiny snack at lunch, forgot about dinner—and at 7:00 P.M. started reaching for everything in sight. Now I plan my meals so that I eat throughout the day and never get really hungry.

- *Keep a food journal.* Much of BED is not even realizing you're eating throughout the day. You need to monitor yourself, review your journal, find out what triggers a binge and make more self-nurturing choices.

- *Incorporate so-called "bad" foods into your diet.* By allowing yourself to eat a small amount of a "forbidden food"—whether it's a slice of cheese or spoonful of mayonnaise or a piece of chocolate—you're less likely to binge on it.

- *Counter negative thoughts.* I learned to counter the thought, "You're so fat" with "I'm not fat. I eat a well-balanced diet and I exercise regularly."

- *Contact a friend.* I e-mail my family and friends and make promises to them, such as "I'm promising myself I'm going to go home and eat a healthy dinner. See you tomorrow."

➤ **Take supplements to improve mood and repair digestion.** Nutritional supplements can help people reduce bingeing, says Dr. Ross. "Bingers are emotional eaters—they typically binge when they're depressed, anxious or otherwise upset. They also tend to have more digestive complaints, such as bloating, gas and chronic constipation. Omega-3 fatty acids, B-vitamins and zinc can help balance moods. Probiotics—gut-friendly bacteria—can help correct bowel disorders."

Helpful: Dr. Ross has included these and other nutrients and food factors in a supplement she developed for people with eating disorders: ED Recovery Support. "My patients with BED and other eating disorders who take this supplement report more stable moods, milder or no digestive complaints, increased energy, better sleep and fewer cravings," she says.

Rapid Resource: You can order the supplement online at *www.carolynrossmd.com*.

➤ **Pay attention to what you eat.** "Most people who binge are eating quickly and compulsively and don't even *taste* the food they're eating," says Dr. Ross. "In other words, they eat *mindlessly.*"

She says to mentally note the taste and texture of the food as you eat, paying attention to every bite. Then notice the effect the meal had on your body—are you energized or stupefied, pleasantly satisfied or uncomfortably stuffed?

"Along with eating three meals every day, mindful eating has a huge benefit for anyone with a history of bingeing," she says.

New study: Researchers at Kent State University taught mindfulness techniques to binge-eaters who had recently undergone weight-loss surgery. They had fewer binges, were less depressed and were more motivated to change their eating behavior.

➤ **Keep a BED journal.** "You can take mindfulness a step further and keep a journal that analyzes your binges," says Dr. Ross.

Be mindful of what triggered your last binge, she advises. Where did you eat? When did you eat? What foods did you eat? Were you feeling bored, lonely, depressed, anxious, tense or sad? Were you hungry or not? Did you crave sweets? What emotions were associated with the binge—shame, guilt, embarrassment?

"By becoming more aware of what triggers a binge, you can find other ways to deal with those triggers—and stop the binge before it starts."

What helps: Dr. Nash offers several examples of ways to deal with triggers, such as…

• If you're watching TV and an ad for an attractive food comes on, change the channel or leave the room. Drink a glass or two of water.

• As soon as the thought of a tempting food enters your head, think, "No. Stop thinking about that. Think about something else." Then immediately turn your attention to another topic, such as a project at work or a pleasant memory.

• Temporarily "ruin" your taste buds—brush your teeth, use mouthwash or chew a mint.

Bottom Line: Engage in any activity that interests you and can distract you from thoughts of food or eating.

🕐 *Super-Quick Fix*

➤ **Surf an urge.** "Cravings peak and subside like waves in an ocean," says Dr. Nash. "You can 'surf an urge' by telling yourself to wait ten minutes before you eat—and then decide. In the meantime, get busy doing something else."

➤ **Soothe yourself *without* food.** Binge-eaters have very low self-esteem and don't think they deserve much in the way of pleasure, says Dr. Ross. Yes, they use food for "pleasure"—but in a mindless, self-destructive way that leaves them feeling worse.

"If you're a binge-eater, you need to find pleasurable, self-soothing behaviors that actually make you feel better," she says.

Some suggestions from Dr. Nash…

• Get a massage.
• Visit a friend.
• Read a good book.
• Go for a pleasant walk.
• Take a bath.
• Spend time on a hobby or other pastime you enjoy, such as playing music.

BURNS, SCRAPES, BRUISES AND STINGS

Patch Up in a Flash

It's a jungle out there—from the wasps in the backyard to the poison-laden plants in the woods. And it's a jungle in there, too—from hot stovetops to sharp kitchen knives.

So whether you're outdoors or in, it's very likely accidents will happen—burns, cuts, scrapes, bites and stings.

If you think an injury is serious (such as bleeding that won't stop or a blistering burn) call 911 or go to the emergency room.

But if an injury is minor, here's how to start healing in a hurry…

➤ **Cool a first-degree burn.** A first-degree burn is the least serious type—your skin is red and probably painful, but there aren't any blisters.

🕐 Super-Quick Fix

If the burn was sudden—for example, you accidentally touched a stovetop—douse it continuously with very cold water for about ten minutes, says Paul Auerbach, MD, a clinical professor of surgery in the Division of Emergency Medicine at Stanford University, and author of *Medicine for the Outdoors* (The Lyons Press).

Next, take an over-the-counter painkiller, such as aspirin or ibuprofen.

Then, cover the burned area with a cool wet compress (a cloth moistened with cold water and wrung out) for 20 or 30 minutes.

For post-compress soothing, try a moisturizing cream, such as Vaseline Intensive Care, says Dr. Auerbach.

For the fastest long-term relief of a first-degree burn, use aloe vera gel or lotion.

➤ **Repair a scrape.** You were summery in shorts on the tennis court, but fell and scraped your knee—and now you have a painful patch of oozing skin. *Unfortunately, the first thing you need to do is endure a little more (self-inflicted) pain...*

"You should scrub a scrape until every last speck of dirt is removed," says Dr. Auerbach. "Although it hurts just to think about this, scrubbing is necessary for two reasons. First, there's a potential for infection when an area of injured skin is exposed to dirt and debris. Second, if small stones or pieces of dirt are left in the wound, they can become like ink in a tattoo, leaving you with permanent markings that require surgical removal."

Scrub with soap and water, he says. Then give the wound a final rinse. Put on an antiseptic ointment, such as *bacitracin* or *mupirocin*. After the ointment, apply a sterile "non-adherent" dressing, such as Spenco 2nd Skin.

Smart idea: You can lessen the pain of the post-scrape scrubbing by first applying pads soaked with lidocaine 2.5% ointment, for about 10 to 15 minutes.

➤ **Soothe a bruise.** A blow, twist or tear ruptured tiny blood vessels under your skin. They're leaking. And you have a bruise.

What to do: A supplement of vitamin C and bioflavonoids can help reduce the black-and-blue more quickly, says Amy Rothenberg, ND, a naturopathic physician in private practice in Amherst, Massachusetts, and codirector of the New England School of Homeopathy. *Product:* There are many vitamin C/bioflavonoid supplements on the market, such as Hy-C tablets from Solgar, with 600 milligrams (mg) of vitamin C and 100 mg of bioflavonoids. Follow the dosage recommendation on the label.

She also recommends taking the homeopathic remedy Arnica. "It's quite miraculous for clearing up bruises." Arnica products are widely available. Follow the dosage recommendation on the label.

➤ **Take the sting out of an insect sting.** First things first, says Dr. Auerbach, remove the stinger (or pieces of it) as quickly as possible.

What most people don't realize: "It used to be taught that pulling the stinger out with fingers or forceps squeezed more venom into the victim, but that's no longer believed to be true. It's better to flick or pull a stinger and venom sac out of the skin, using a tweezers or your fingers."

See Your Doctor If...

You're bruising easily and frequently—particularly if you notice bruises but can't remember how you got them, says Dr. Rothenberg. They may be a sign of a serious medical problem, such as type 2 diabetes or cancer.

Speed Healing Success

How a Plastic Surgeon Treats His Cuts and Bites

"When I have a paper cut or other minor laceration, I always use Krazy Glue," says Matthew Schulman, MD, a plastic surgeon in New York. "It's essentially the same material that is found in the medical-grade 'skin glue' used by emergency room doctors and plastic surgeons in place of stitches. I also recommend it to my patients.

"For itching bug bites, I prepare my own topical cream. It consists of one fifty-milligram benadryl tablet, crushed into a powder, and mixed into an over-the-counter one-percent hydrocortisone cream. This has an amazing anti-itch effect that is better than any prescription drug I've tried."

And don't waste time searching for a straight-edged object, such as a knife or a credit card, to scrape away the stinger, says Dr. Auerbach. "In fact, crude scraping runs the risk of breaking off the stinger and leaving it embedded in the skin."

After you remove the stinger, apply ice packs to the site of the sting, which will help with the pain. *Next, you want to neutralize the venom...*

"After ten or fifteen minutes of ice, apply a paste made from water and unseasoned papain-containing meat tenderizer, such as Adolph's unseasoned meat tenderizer," says Dr. Auerbach. "Put it directly on the wound for no more than fifteen minutes."

However: Baking soda is "of no value" in treating insect stings, says Dr. Auerbach.

To control itching and mild pain, he recommends StingEze Liquid, from Wisconsin Pharmacal, which is widely available.

Super-Quick Fix

The jellyfish population is exploding! They're closing beaches in Australia and France, in Hawaii and Virginia—because of too many jellyfish.

"Human-caused stresses, including global warming and overfishing, are encouraging jellyfish surpluses in many tourist destinations," says a report from the US National Science Foundation.

And those jellyfish can *hurt*—their long, threadlike tendrils are lined with poison-containing stingers. Untreated, the painful burning from a jellyfish sting can last three to five hours, with itchy, red welts lasting for days.

What helps: "Of the methods I have seen to treat jellyfish stings, Jellyfish Squish is absolutely the most effective by far," says Captain Kevin Carvalho, who has treated hundreds of jellyfish stings as Medical Division Officer of the Okaloosa Island Fire Department, in Florida. "When we used Jellyfish Squish we could see immediate relief in our patients from the painful burning and stinging associated with jellyfish-to-skin contact. This product has made our job easier."

Jellyfish Squish—which was developed with the assistance of two marine biologists, and has been endorsed by the American Lifeguard Association—is a topical anesthetic. It also neutralizes the toxins from nematocysts—the pointed, corkscrew-shaped cells released when skin comes into contact with the tentacles of a jellyfish.

Rapid Resource: To order Jellyfish Squish, visit *www.coastalsolutionsinc.com.*

➤ **The best way to remove a tick.** The mouthparts of a tick are a combination can opener, harpoon and cement mixer. The creature cuts a hole in your skin, inserts its barbed hypostome, anchors itself with a cementlike substance and starts sucking your blood. That's bad enough. But a tick can also transmit a serious infectious disease, such as Rocky Mountain Spotted Fever or Lyme disease.

You want to keep ticks off your body and remove an attached tick as quickly and efficiently as possible, says Roger Drummond, PhD, author of *Ticks and What You Can Do About Them* (Wilderness Press). *Here's how...*

• **Prevention.** Hungry ticks hang out in fields and woods, waiting for their normal "hosts"—mice, rabbits, birds, deer and other wild animals. *Dr. Drummond has this advice to keep them from hitching a ride on your body...*

• Wear light-colored clothing, so any ticks are visible.

• Wear a long-sleeved shirt that fits tightly at the wrists and neck, and tuck it into your pants.

• Wear long pants with the legs tucked into your boots or your socks.

• As soon as possible after coming indoors, check your clothing and your body. "If possible, have another person examine you to make sure you have not missed any ticks," he says.

• Apply a product that contains DEET, an anti-tick insecticide.

"It's most effective against ticks when applied to clothing from a spray can," says Dr. Drummond. "Hang up your shirts and pants or lay them on the ground, hold the can about a

See Your Doctor If...

You're having a severe allergic reaction to an insect (or jellyfish) sting, including symptoms such as difficulty breathing, wheezing, swelling of the lips, throat and tongue, itching and hives (red, raised skin welts).

The Best Insect Repellant

DEET (N,N-diethyl-3-methyl-benzamide, to you chemists out there) is one of the best insect repellants around, says Dr. Auerbach.

However: It can be toxic. *To use it safely, Dr. Auerbach recommends you...*

• *Don't use concentrated products*—a concentration between 30% and 50% is fine for most adults.

• *Don't use repeated applications* or concentrations greater than 15% in children under the age of 6.

• *Don't inhale or ingest.*

• *Wash it off the skin* when you're back indoors.

Recommended: Ultrathon Insect Repellant, Sawyer Gold Insect Repellant and Sawyer Controlled Release DEET Formula, all of which are widely available.

Less effective: "Citronella and Avon Skin-So-Soft bath oil or skin stick are far less effective—fifteen minutes of protection versus six hours with twenty-five percent DEET," says Dr. Auerbach.

Nor is vitamin B-1 effective at deterring biting insects, he says. (Though it may decrease the skin irritation after an insect bite.)

And while garlic is famous for repelling vampires, it doesn't do anything to stop biting insects.

foot or less from the clothes and spray each side of each piece for about fifteen seconds."

• **Removal.** Popular folk methods don't work to remove ticks, he says. Don't cover the tick with petroleum jelly, nail polish or alcohol. Don't touch it with the hot, smoking end of a match.

Best: "The most effective method is a steady, direct pull away from the skin," says Dr. Drummond. *His advice...*

• Use blunt, curved forceps, tweezers or a tick tweezers-type removal device, such as Uncle Bill's Sliver Gripper or the De-Ticker. (Both devices are widely available.)

• Place the tips of the tweezers around the tick's mouthparts where they enter the skin.

• Remove the tick with a steady pull away from the skin—do not jerk or twist the tick.

• Take care not to crush or puncture the body of the tick or get any fluids on you. (You might release infectious components.)

• Examine the attachment site carefully to make sure you have removed all the mouthparts. If any are left, gently scrape them off.

• Disinfect your skin with alcohol and wash your hands with soap and water.

➤ **Poison ivy protection.** The "poison" in poison ivy and poison oak is *urushiol*, an oil produced by these three-leaved plants. It binds with the skin and you have about 30 minutes to wash it off before it's likely to trigger that notorious rash—bumpy, blistered, red, itchy and swollen. *Dr. Auerbach's suggestions…*

• **Prevention.** If you know you're sensitive to poison ivy or oak, use Ivy Shield or Stokogard Outdoor Cream before a walk in the woods.

If you've been exposed, use Tecnu Poison Oak-N-Ivy Cleanser, a combo of liquid paraffin and alcohol. Apply it as soon as possible after exposure…rub it in for two minutes…rinse it off…and repeat.

• **Treatment.** Calamine lotion can soothe and dry itchy skin. For a topical anesthetic, use pramoxine hydrochloride 1% (Prax cream).

Smart idea: Caladryl contains calamine *and* pramoxine.

Orally, try an antihistamine such as diphenhydramine (Benadryl) to stop the itching.

You can also try this "excellent" soothing bath, says Dr. Auerbach—lukewarm (not hot) water, with 1 cup of Aveeno oatmeal.

⚠ **Warning:** If you have the rash on your face or genitals, or the itching is intolerable, you may need a course of corticosteroids (prednisone).

🕐 *Super-Quick Fix*

➤ **Blow Your Itch Away.** "One of the best ways to relieve the itching in a small area of poison ivy or oak is with a hair dryer," says Dr. Rothenberg.

Put it on warm, hold it a couple inches away from the area, keep it on for five minutes and move it up and down the area.

"There is a slight intensification of itchiness while the hair dryer is on," she says. "But it stimulates the mast cells of the immune system to release all their itch-causing histamine—and you get an hour's relief from the itching."

CANCER

ancer is the second leading cause of death among Americans, killing 560,000 people every year.

However: One-third of cancers could be prevented with healthier lifestyle choices, says a recent report from the American Institute for Cancer Research.

What kind of choices? *The kind that don't take much time...*

➤ **Have a bowl of All-Bran for breakfast.** Researchers at the National Cancer Institute analyzed seven years of health data from nearly 500,000 people. They found that those with the highest intake of fiber from whole grains—such as whole wheat, whole oats, whole barley, whole rye and brown rice—had 49% less risk for bowel cancer, compared to those with the lowest intake.

Fact: Just one-third cup of Kellogg's All-Bran cereal delivers 8.5 grams of fiber, more than 30% of the daily recommendation of 25 grams. A cup of buckwheat groats (kasha) or brown rice supplies 10 grams. A slice of whole wheat or whole-grain rye bread supply 3 grams.

➤ **Women—drink more tea, eat more soy foods.** They're both rich in *isoflavones*— and Italian researchers found that women who consume more isoflavones have a 37% lower risk of ovarian cancer.

How they work: Possibly by blocking the cancer-promoting effect of the hormone estrogen on breast and other cells.

➤ **Men—eat a side dish of broccoli.** Researchers in England found that eating broccoli "upregulates" genes in the prostate gland that can help protect against cancer.

What to do: Eat two or three servings of cruciferous vegetables a week, all of which may upregulate those genes, says Richard Mithen, MD, the study leader. That class of vegetables includes broccoli, cauliflower, kale, collard greens, arugula and Brussels sprouts.

➤ **Women over 65—take B vitamins.** A daily supplement that includes the B vitamins folic acid, vitamin B-6 and vitamin B-12 may lower the risk of breast cancer in women over 65 by nearly 40%, say researchers at Harvard Medical School, who studied 5,442 women (average age 63) for seven years.

What to do: Look for a multivitamin or B-vitamin supplement that supplies the level of nutrients used in the study—2.5 mcg of folic acid, 50 mg of B-6 and 1 mg of B-12.

➤ **Eat a handful of almonds.** Researchers at the M.D. Anderson Cancer Center in Houston studied 2,392 people with lung cancer and found that those with the highest intake of vitamin E had a 55% lower risk of lung cancer.

What to do: Include more E-rich foods in your diet, such as almonds, wheat germ and sunflower seeds.

➤ **Get (low-fat) milk.** Women with the highest intake of calcium have a lower risk for any type of cancer...and men and women with the highest intake have a lower risk for colon cancer and other cancers of the digestive system, say researchers at the National Institutes of Health, in the *Journal of the American Medical Association.*

What to do: Three to four servings of low-fat dairy foods a day supplies the protective amount of calcium.

➤ **Women—take vitamin D.** Canadian researchers found that women with the highest intake of vitamin D had a 20% lower risk of breast cancer.

Another team of researchers found that only 24% of women with breast cancer had normal blood levels of vitamin D—and those with the lowest levels had a higher risk of developing metastatic breast cancer (outside the breast) and of dying from the disease.

What to do: Taking a daily vitamin D supplement of 1,000 IU is the easiest and most reliable way to maintain healthy blood levels of vitamin D, says Michael Holick, MD, PhD, director of the Vitamin D, Skin and Bone Research Laboratory at Boston University Medical Center.

Important: Please see page 253 in the chapter "Osteoporosis" for more information on the healthiest blood levels of vitamin D (50 to 80 ng/ml) and bi-yearly testing to ensure your levels are in that range.

SPEED LIMIT HRT May Cause Breast Cancer

In 2002, the Women's Health Initiative (WHI)—a scientific study designed to demonstrate the many benefits of hormone replacement therapy (HRT) for postmenopausal women—found that those taking a combination of the drugs *estrogen* and *progestin* had a 26% increased risk of developing breast cancer (along with an increased risk for heart attack and stroke). This unexpected result changed the outlook of doctors and their patients about HRT. Over the next four years, prescriptions for the therapy declined from 60 to 20 million—and breast cancer rates also declined.

However: Some experts questioned the connection, saying the drop was too rapid to have been caused by women stopping HRT.

New study: Researchers at Stanford School of Medicine looked at data from more than 56,000 women—15,000 in the original WHI study and 41,449 others. *They found…*

• Women who stayed on HRT for five years doubled their risk of breast cancer.

• A 50% decrease in hormone use between 2002 and 2003 was correlated with a 43% reduction in breast cancer rates.

• Among women who stopped taking HRT, rates of breast cancer declined by 28%—within one year.

The results appeared in the *New England Journal of Medicine.*

In addition, a study published in the *Journal of the National Cancer Institute* showed that breast cancer survivors who took HRT more than doubled their risk of breast cancer, from 9% to 22%.

What to do: "These studies are definitive," says Shannon Puhalla, MD, a breast cancer specialist and an assistant professor of medicine at the Magee-Womens Hospital of the University of Pittsburgh School of Medicine. "HRT causes breast cancer. Stopping HRT decreases the risk of breast cancer. Women at low risk for breast cancer should use HRT to control menopausal symptoms only as a last resort—and for the shortest possible duration. Women at high risk and women who have been diagnosed with breast cancer should avoid HRT."

Helpful: To access your risk for breast cancer—which depends on many factors, such as your age and the number of your first-degree relatives (mother, sister, daughter) with breast cancer—use the National Cancer Institute's Breast Cancer Risk Assessment Tool, at *www.cancer.gov/bcrisktool/.* Discuss the results with your doctor.

🕐 *Super-Quick Fix*

➤ **Marinate your steak.** Marinating meat in spice and herb mixtures before grilling can decrease the formation of *heterocyclic amines* (HCAs), cancer-causing compounds generated by cooking meat at high temperatures, say researchers from Kansas State University.

Preventing 30% of Prostate Cancers

The drug *finasteride* (Proscar) is a 5-alpha-reductase inhibitor—it limits the production of an enzyme that converts testosterone to *dihydrotestosterone*, a male hormone that stimulates the growth of prostate cells.

Landmark study: In 2003, an article in the *New England Journal of Medicine* announced the results of the seven-year Prostate Cancer Prevention Trial (PCPT), involving nearly 19,000 men 55 or older—those taking five milligrams (mg) a day of finasteride were 25% less likely to develop prostate cancer than those taking a placebo.

However: Twenty-four percent of the placebo group and 18% of the finasteride group developed prostate cancer during the seven years of the trial. And biopsies showed that those taking finasteride were slightly more likely to have "high-grade" cancer, an aggressive form that can spread quickly. Because of this, the medical community did not endorse the drug.

Latest development: In a recent study published in the journal *Cancer Prevention Research*, scientists from Fred Hutchinson Cancer Research Center in Seattle revisited the PCPT, conducting three new and careful analyses of the data. *They found...*

- **Men taking finasteride did not have a significantly higher rate of aggressive prostate cancer.** In fact, one analysis showed that men on the drug had 27% less high-grade prostate cancer than men on the placebo.

- **The original finding that finasteride increased the risk of high-grade cancer was due to what scientists call a "sampling error."** Finasteride shrinks the size of the prostate by 20% to 30%, making it much more likely that a six-needle biopsy (the type used in the PCPT) will find a "nest" of high-grade cancer cells.

- **The new analysis revealed that finasteride has greater cancer-preventing power than previously estimated.** It reduces the risk of prostate cancer not by 25%, but by 30%. In other words, it could prevent three out of every 10 cases of prostate cancer—nearly 70,000 cases a year!

Bottom line: "Men undergoing regular prostate cancer screening or who express an interest in cancer prevention should be informed of the opportunity to take finasteride for preventing prostate cancer," concluded the researchers.

"This breakthrough is particularly important for men with a higher-than-normal risk for the disease," says Peter Scardino, MD, chairman of the Department of Urology at the Memorial Sloan-Kettering Cancer Center in New York and head of the Center's Prostate Cancer Program, and author of *Dr. Peter Scardino's Prostate Book* (Avery). *That includes...*

- **Men with a family history of prostate cancer**
- **African-American men**
- **Men with a level of prostate specific antigen (PSA) that is 2.5 ng/mL or higher.** (PSA is the primary biomarker for prostate cancer.)

Talk to your doctor about whether finasteride is right for you.

The study: The researchers immersed steaks for one hour in one of three varieties of pre-packaged marinade mixtures—Caribbean, Southwest or Herb. Another batch of steaks wasn't marinated. Then all the steaks were grilled at 400°F, for five minutes per side. When the steaks were compared, the researchers found the marinades dramatically reduced the level of HCAs.

In another study, Portuguese researchers found that beer or red wine marinades reduced levels of HCAs by 88% during the frying or grilling of fish.

"Encouraging Americans to grill with spice and herb marinades may be one more nutritious way we can help promote good health—in a way that's both easy and delicious," says Wendy Bazilian DrPh, RD, coauthor of *The SuperFoodsRX Diet* (Rodale).

What to do: Use pre-packaged spice and herb marinade mixes, such as Grill Mates, from McCormick, which include blends such as Super Spice, Southwest, Zesty Herb and Mesquite.

If you want to create your own marinades, use one or more of the spices richest in HCA-defeating antioxidants—cinnamon, oregano, red pepper, ginger, rosemary, thyme or yellow curry, mixing it with a delicious base. *Example:* One tablespoon spice blend, ¼ cup pomegranate juice, 2 tablespoons honey and 2 tablespoons lime juice…or 1 tablespoon spice blend, ¼ cup strong brewed green tea, 2 tablespoons peach preserves, 2 tablespoons white wine vinegar.

Rapid Resource: For recipes using Grill Mates, visit *www.grillmates.com*. For homemade marinade recipes, visit *www.spicesforhealth.com*.

➤ **Drink red wine.** America's fastest-growing cancer is *esophageal cancer*—with a 500% increase in the last 30 years. The precursor to that cancer is often *Barrett's esophagus*, a condition that afflicts one out of 20 Americans and is caused when regurgitated stomach acid from heartburn permanently damages the lining of the esophagus. There is no treatment for this symptomless condition, which is typically discovered during an endoscopy for heartburn, an ulcer or other GI problem.

Newest research: Researchers at the National Institutes of Health (NIH) and the Kaiser Permanente Division of Research analyzed four years of health data from nearly 1,000 men and women. They found that people who drank one or more glasses of red or white wine a

day had a 56% reduced risk of Barrett's esophagus. (There was no reduction among people who drank beer or hard liquor.)

The NIH researchers also found that eating eight servings of fruits and vegetables a day and maintaining normal body weight can reduce the risk for Barrett's esophagus.

Why it works: The antioxidants in wine, and in fruits and vegetables, may neutralize the oxidative (rustlike) damage caused by heartburn.

What to do: "My advice to people trying to prevent Barrett's esophagus is to keep a normal body weight, eat a diet rich in fruits and vegetables and consider drinking a single glass of red wine a day, which we know is good for the heart," says Douglas Corley, MD, the study leader.

➤ **Don't overdo the packaged sweets and snacks.** Researchers at the University of California at Chapel Hill studied 622 people and found that those who ate the most *trans fats*—the processed vegetable oils found in many baked goods, snacks and crackers—were 86% more likely to have precancerous polyps in the colon.

Recommended: "This finding backs up the current recommendations to limit trans fat intake," say the researchers, in the *American Journal of Epidemiology*.

➤ **Extra "physical activity" for extra protection.** Many recent studies show that extra physical activity—from housework to gardening to running—can help prevent cancer.

• **Breast cancer in postmenopausal women.** German researchers studied more than 10,000 postmenopausal women between the ages of 50 and 74 and found that those who engaged in the most physical activity were 30% less likely to develop breast cancer. "Our advice to all women is to stay or become physically active in the second half of life," says Karen Steindorf, MD, the study leader. "You will not only reduce your risk of breast cancer, but will also benefit your bones, heart and brain."

● **Colon cancer.** Researchers at Washington University School of Medicine in St. Louis and Harvard Medical School analyzed 52 studies on exercise and colon cancer and found that people who exercised the most had a 24% reduced risk, compared to people who exercised the least. The protective effect was for *all* types of vocational and recreational physical activity—such as walking, lifting or digging on the job, or walking, jogging, biking or swimming for fun. "Physical activity is at the top of the list of ways you can reduce your risk of colon cancer," says Kathleen Wolin, ScD, the study leader.

● **Colon, liver, stomach, pancreatic cancers.** Researchers at the National Cancer Center in Japan studied nearly 80,000 adults and found that total daily physical activity—at work or play—was linked to a 15% lower risk of developing colon, liver, pancreatic and stomach cancer.

Why exercise works: It stimulates the cancer-defeating immune system and controls levels of cancer-causing hormones and growth factors, say the Japanese researchers.

SPEED LIMIT ## Do Statins Cause Cancer?

Researchers at the Fred Hutchinson Cancer Research Center in Seattle studied nearly 2,000 men. They found that those with a body mass index (BMI) of 30 or over who were also taking a cholesterol-lowering statin drug had a 50% increase in the risk of prostate cancer, compared to non-statin users. Among those taking a statin for 5 years or longer, the risk increased to 80%.

"Given the epidemic of obesity in the US and the frequent use of statins, our results raise substantial concern about the safety of these widely prescribed medications," says Janet L. Stanford, MD, the study leader.

Get Your Skin Examined!

In a survey of approximately 25,000 American adults, researchers at the University of Miami found that only 15% had ever had a full-body skin examination to detect skin cancer, the most common form of cancer in the US, with more than 1 million cases diagnosed each year.

What to do: The American Cancer Society suggests a monthly skin self-exam and an exam for skin cancer during your yearly health exam.

To conduct a skin self-exam, the American Dermatological Association says to…

1. *Examine your body front and back in the mirror.* Then examine your right and left sides with arms raised.
2. *Bend your elbows and look carefully at your forearms, upper underarms and palms.*
3. *Look at the backs of your legs and feet, the spaces between your toes and on the sole.*
4. *Examine the back of your neck and scalp with a hand mirror.* Part your hair for a closer look.
5. *Finally, check your back and buttocks with a hand mirror.*

You're looking for a possible melanoma, the most deadly form of skin cancer, with moles or pigmented skin spots that show one or more of this ABCDE—*Asymmetry,* one half unlike the other half…*Border,* irregular, scalloped or poorly defined border…*Color,* varied from one area to another; shades of tan and brown, or black; sometimes white, red or blue…*Diameter,* melanomas are usually greater than 6 millimeters (the size of a pencil eraser) when they are diagnosed, but can be smaller…*Evolving,* a mole or skin lesion looks different from the others on your body or is changing in size, shape or color.

➤ **Quick ways to soften the side effects of cancer treatment.** "Undergoing treatment for cancer—not to mention having the disease itself—can cause a number of side effects, ranging from unpleasant to debilitating to dangerous," says Keith Block, MD, Medical Director of the Block Center for Integrative Cancer Treatment in Skokie, Illinois, and author of *Life Over Cancer* (Bantam). *Here are some of his best recommendations for combating those side effects...*

● **Loss of appetite.** Chemotherapy can kill not only your cancer cells but your appetite, says Dr. Block. *He suggests...*

● Consider when your appetite is at its best. For most cancer patients, it's breakfast time—so try to get most of your nutrients and calories for the day then.

● Exercise can also stimulate appetite, says Dr. Block. "If it does, exercise shortly before mealtime."

● Snack. Rather than regular-size meals, have a snack every two to four hours, even if you don't feel hungry, says Dr. Block.

● Drink herbal teas. Fennel or anise, mixed with verbena or mint, may stimulate appetite.

● **Nausea and vomiting.** "Nausea and vomiting are all too familiar to many chemotherapy and radiation patients," says Dr. Block. They can now be tamed by *antiemetic drugs*, such as *palonosetron* (Aloxi) and *aprepitant* (Emend).

Complementary therapies can also combat nausea, he says.

● Try ginger. "Many of my patients with nausea and vomiting have successfully used ginger, either as a tea or supplement (five hundred milligrams every four hours)." But ginger should not be taken when your platelet count is low due to chemotherapy, he cautions.

● Try aromatherapy. Peppermint oil may tame nausea. "Carry a small bottle throughout the day and sniff it occasionally," says Dr. Block.

● Try acupuncture. You can buy a wristband with a small button that presses on the P6 acupressure point, which can relieve nausea. It is sold under the name Sea-Band.

● Suck on ice chips. "Vomiting can lead to electrolyte imbalances and land you in the hospital with dehydration," he says. "Try sucking on ice chips, sprinkled with a little salt."

● **Diarrhea.** Many cancer treatments—among them, chemotherapy, radiation, antibiotics and anti-nausea medications—can cause diarrhea, says Dr. Block.

● Sip small amounts of clear liquid throughout the day. That includes water, broth, green tea and herbal tea. "Choose room-temperature liquids, since very hot or cold drinks may stimulate bowel movements," he says.

● Avoid large amounts of food at one time. Eat small, frequent meals and snacks.

● Avoid greasy, fried, very spicy or very sweet foods. "Also avoid fruit juices such as apple, cherry or prune juice," he says.

If You Must Smoke... Drink Red Wine

A recent study by the American Association for Cancer Research shows that male smokers who drink one or two glasses of red wine a day had a 60% lower risk of lung cancer. There was no protective effect from white wine, beer or liquor.

Important: The researchers said stopping smoking was the best way to reduce the risk of lung cancer, noting that even the men who drank red wine faced a higher lung cancer risk than non-smokers.

Helpful: A recent study found that people who used support groups to help them quit smoking were twice as likely to succeed.

• Choose foods that may alleviate diarrhea, such as white rice, cream of rice cereal and refined white flour products.

• **Constipation.** "For cancer patients, constipation can be a side effect of chemotherapy or narcotic pain medications," says Dr. Block.

• Drink plenty of fluids. Eight to 12 cups daily is best, he says.

• Gradually increase intake of high-fiber foods. That includes beans, whole grains, vegetables and fruits.

• Walk. Walking or any type of regular exercise can relieve constipation. Even 10 minutes a day is helpful.

• **Taste changes or lack of taste.** "About half of cancer patients report changes in their sense of taste during and after chemotherapy, becoming more sensitive to bitter tastes and less sensitive to sweet tastes," says Dr. Block. "Chemo can also produce a metallic taste."

• Serve food cold or at room temperature. "It may taste better than food served hot," says Dr. Block.

• Choose strong-flavored foods. Use sauces, herbs and spices, and condiments such as mustard.

• Add tart ingredients. They help cover any metallic taste, says Dr. Block. For example, add orange juice, lime juice, lemon juice or orange marmalade to sauces, salsa, stir-fried or cooked vegetables.

• Add a sweet food to protein foods. For example, applesauce or fruit preserves.

• Rinse. "Before eating, rinse your mouth with tea, club soda, salted water or fruit juice to clear your taste buds," says Dr. Block.

• **Sore mouth or throat.** "Mucositis is an inflammation of the mucous membranes that causes a painful or dry mouth, mouth sores, and burning, peeling or swelling of the tongue," says Dr. Block. About 40% of those getting standard chemotherapy will develop the problem.

• Eat soft, non-irritating foods. Examples include bananas, applesauce, melons and other soft or canned fruits, soups, oatmeal or other cooked cereals, and pureed or mashed foods.

• Cut food into small pieces. "Use a food processor or blender to puree them, if necessary," he says.

• Drink through a straw to bypass mouth sores.

• Rinse your mouth often with water. This removes food and bacteria and promotes healing, he says.

• Swish and swallow one ounce of aloe vera gel two to three times a day. (Make sure it's a gel specifically formulated for internal use.)

Rapid Resource: Dr. Block's book—*Life Over Cancer: The Block Center Program for Integrative Cancer Treatment*—provides a comprehensive program for making cancer treatment more effective while reducing toxicity and side effects. It also includes a "remission maintenance" program to help keep you cancer-free. You can find out more about Dr. Block's integrative approach to cancer (combining the best of conventional medicine with scientifically supported complementary therapies) and the Block Center at *www.lifeovercancer.com*, or call 877-412-5625. Address: Block Center for Integrative Cancer Treatment, 5230 Old Orchard Rd., Skokie, IL 60077.

CANKER AND COLD SORES

Prompter Pain Relief, Faster Healing

Cold sores are little fluid-filled blisters that show up on the edge of your lip or nose, scab over and hang around

Speed Healing Success

Stopping a Cold Sore in Its Tracks

"Before I started taking lysine—five hundred milligrams, twice a day—my cold sores would develop over a period of five to seven days, blossoming into a painful, scabby, bloody mess," says Evelyn Chadwick, CHC, a certified health counselor in Fort Lee, New Jersey.

"At times, I've gotten them as often as every two weeks, usually when I'm stressed or lacking sleep. When I had surgery, for instance, I got one the night before. And because my relationship with my in-laws is challenging, I notice that every time I visit them in Texas I feel one coming on. The last time I was visiting I felt the telltale tingling, immediately went to the drugstore to purchase lysine—which I had read about as an effective natural remedy—and two days later the cold sore was gone!

"Now I take lysine for prevention and increase the dosage at the first sign of a cold sore. It always stops the sore in its tracks—the sore never develops and the tingling subsides in a day or two."

• **Rx for cold sores.** If you have recurrent cold sores, talk to your doctor about the once-a-day anti-herpes medication *valcyclovir* (Valtrex), says Tanya Kormeili, MD, a dermatologist in private practice in Los Angeles (*www.kormei liderm.com*) and a clinical professor of dermatology at UCLA. Taken at the first sign of an outbreak—tingling, burning, itching, pain or reddening—it can shorten the outbreak and lessen the severity of symptoms.

⚠ **Caution:** This is a very safe medication, says Dr. Kormeili. But if you're dehydrated, it can trigger the formation of crystals in the urine that can damage kidneys. "When you take the medication, drink plenty of water—enough so that your urine is clear-colored."

for about 10 days. They're caused by the herpes simplex virus.

Canker sores are whitish ulcers with a red halo that pop up inside the mouth, usually inside the cheek or lips or on the gums. They have many causes, from injury (you burn the inside of your mouth with hot cheese from a pizza and a canker sore is quickly delivered) to inflammatory bowel disease.

Aside from the fact that they both inhabit your oral landscape, cold and canker sores have another thing in common—they're both annoyingly painful. You want relief now and healing ASAP. *Here's how to get it…*

➤ **Lysine for prevention and relief.** Take 500 milligrams (mg) of the amino acid lysine, three times a day, to speed the healing of a cold sore, says Flora Parsa Stay, DDS, associate clinical professor of dentistry at the University of Southern California, and author of *The Secret Gateway to Health* (Morgan James Publishing).

Why it works: It stops the herpes virus from replicating.

Taking 1,000 mg a day of lysine as a preventive can help keep cold sores at bay, she says.

Also helpful: A topical remedy containing lysine and other anti-herpes nutrients and herbs can help shorten cold sore outbreaks to just three days, say researchers from the UCLA Geffen School of Medicine who studied the remedy. *Product:* SuperLysine+, from Quantum Health, available as a stick applicator, a salve or a tincture. You can find it in most Whole Foods and health food stores. Order it online at *www. quantumhealth.com*, or call 800-448-1448.

➤ **Topicals for turbo-charged pain relief.** Try one or more of these topical treatments for fast relief from the pain of a cold or canker sore.

For cold sores…

Preventing Outbreaks

Here are a number of ways to prevent outbreaks of cold and canker sores...

- *Protect yourself from sunlight.* Sun exposure can trigger a cold sore. When you're out in the sun, use an SPF 15 sunscreen, an SPF-15 lip balm and wear a wide-brimmed hat, says Dr. Kormeili.

- *Avoid contact with somebody else's sore.* If you or anybody around you has one, stop sharing—drinking glasses, food utensils, towels and kisses—until it goes away.

- *Throw out your toothbrush.* To avoid reinfecting yourself, throw out the toothbrush you used during a cold sore outbreak, says Dr. Stay.

- *Stress.* Physical, mental or emotional—stress can trigger a cold or canker sore. For fast-action stress relief, please see the section "Stress and Tension" on page 300.

- *Avoid toothpaste with sodium lauryl sulfate.* This irritating ingredient—a "foaming agent" found in almost every commercial toothpaste—can trigger canker sores, says Dr. Stay. *Better:* Cleure Toothpaste, which contains no sodium lauryl sulfate. Order it at *www.cleure.com,* or call 888-883-4276.

🕐 Super-Quick Fix

- **Ice.** "During the initial stages, apply ice on the cold sore for three to five minutes every hour," says Dr. Stay. "This decreases pain, itching and burning and may actually stop the development of the sore."

- **Aloe vera gel.** "Dabbed on a cold sore blister, it will hasten healing," says Dr. Stay.

- **Zinc oxide ointment.** "It can help dry a cold sore," she says.

Speed Healing Success

Wash Away Canker Sores— With Mouthwash

"I was tortured by huge, painful canker sores for years," says Anthony Dallmann-Jones, PhD, of Marco Island, Florida. "One day, I was talking to my son—a dental technician in the Air Force—about the fact that I hoped I didn't have any canker sores before some scheduled dental work. He said, 'Dad, I wish you had told me about this problem sooner. Just rinse your mouth out with full-strength Listerine every night. That's what we told the guys in the service to do and it worked every time.' That was ten years ago. I've been doing it ever since. And I swear to you that I have not had a canker sore in all that time!"

- **Pepto-Bismol.** "Apply Pepto-Bismol the moment you feel the tingle, and your cold sore will never rear its ugly head," says Rona Berg, author of *Fast Beauty: 1,000 Quick Fixes* (Workman).

- **Australian Sandalwood Oil.** "This essential oil is the most effective remedy for cold sores that I know of," says Lesley Hobbs, a certified aromatherapist in Redmond, Washington. "And even if the sore does erupt, the essential oil can relieve the severity and pain." To apply, put one drop on your finger and hold it on the affected area for 5 seconds or so. Do this every two or three hours. Wash your hands after applying. *Product:* You can purchase Australian Sandalwood Oil at the website *www.mountain roseherbs.com,* or call 800-879-3337.

- **Mouthwash.** "A cotton swab saturated with an alcohol-based mouthwash, dabbed on the blister two to three times a day, will usually dry up a cold sore in three days," says Dr. Stay.

For canker sores...

• **OTC sealants.** The OTC products Orabase and Zilactin act as chemical bandages to protect the ulcers from further irritation, says Dr. Stay.

• **Hydrogen peroxide.** A rinse with this astringent can help cleanse the canker sore, decreasing pain, says Dr. Stay. *Her instructions:* Mix equal parts of 2% hydrogen peroxide with warm water and rinse at least three to four times a day.

• **Mouthwash.** "Rinsing with the denatured alcohol in a mouthwash such as Listerine is helpful," says Dr. Stay.

🕐 *Super-Quick Fix*

➤ **Citrus oil and magnesium salts.** An Israeli study on 48 people with canker sores shows that an adhering, topical remedy containing these ingredients—which lower the level of inflammatory factors in the ulcer—can heal a canker sore in 24 hours. *Product:* Canker Cover, available at most drugstores and national retail chains, at *www. cankercover.com*, or call 800-433-6835.

CATARACTS

Surgery Isn't the Only Answer

More than 50% of Americans over 65 and 70% over 75 have a vision-blurring (and sometimes vision-dimming, vision-clouding and vision-yellowing) cataract. That's why cataract surgery is the most frequently performed operation among seniors, with about 400,000 procedures a year.

And cataract surgery works very well, says Marc Grossman, OD, LAc, an optometrist in private practice in Rye and New Paltz, New York, and medical director of the website, *www.natural eyecare.com*.

In about 15 minutes, the surgeon removes the damaged lens and inserts a clear artificial replacement. You recover in about a day, with your eye adjusting to the new lens over the next few weeks. Piece of cake!

However: If you have a cataract, it's a myth that cataract surgery is always a *must*, says Dr. Grossman. You can *reverse* a cataract without surgery. *And it might not take any longer than squeezing an eye drop or two out of a bottle...*

➤ **NAC—the super-antioxidant that can prevent, stop or reverse cataracts.** Cataracts are caused by the same process that scientists now understand contributes to and causes a range of age-related diseases, such as heart disease and Alzheimer's—*oxidation*, a kind of biochemical rust. Oxidation is carried out by molecular bad guys called *free radicals*, hyperactive compounds that damage the delicate outer lining (membranes) of cells and the DNA inside them, leading to cell mutation and death. Free radicals are generated by many factors, including sunlight (think age spots, wrinkles and skin cancer), smoking (think lung cancer) and diets high in fat and sugar (think heart disease and diabetes).

Fortunately, there are antiaging *antioxidants* such as vitamin C and vitamin E that can neutralize free radicals. And a particularly powerful antioxidant is *carnosine*, a combination of two amino acids, the building blocks of protein.

Now, scientists have found that a form of carnosine—N-acetyl-carnosine—is uniquely effective at stopping the aging process in the eyes.

"Research shows that N-acetyl-carnosine eyedrops can help improve cataracts—and possibly

Run Away from Cataracts

Researchers at the US Department of Energy's Lawrence Berkeley Laboratory studied 29,000 male runners for seven years.

Men who ran an average of 5.7 miles a day had a 35% lower risk of developing cataracts than men who ran an average of 1.4 miles a day. And when the researchers analyzed the results of 10K races, they found that the men with the fastest times—a sign of fitness—had a 50% lower risk of developing cataract.

"This study shows that, in addition to obtaining regular eye exams, people can take a more active role in preserving their vision," says Paul Williams, PhD, the study leader.

But do you have to *run* to get the benefit? Maybe not.

"We know there are important health benefits to walking, including lowering heart disease risk," says Dr. Williams. "It's quite likely that smaller doses of more moderate exercise also decrease the risk of developing cataract, though probably to a lesser extent."

enable the patient to keep their natural lens, avoiding the need for cataract surgery," says Dr. Grossman.

Study: Researchers in Russia studied 49 people (average age 65) with "minimal to advanced" cataracts, dividing them into three groups. One received twice-daily eye drops with N-acetyl-carnosine, one group received placebo drops, and one group didn't receive any treatment.

After six months, 90% of the group receiving the drops had an improvement in glare sensitivity (a common symptom of cataracts), 42% had an improvement in the light transmission through the lens and 90% had an improvement in "visual acuity" (they could see better). Those not using the drops had negative changes in all those parameters.

"As shown by this study, the N-acetyl-carnosine drops can help the aging eye to recover from cataract, by improving its clarity, glare sensitivity, color perception and overall vision," says Dr. Grossman.

"I recommend a minimum six-month period of use to evaluate the benefits."

Product: Can-C Eyedrops, available at *www.naturaleyecare.com*, or call 845-255-8222. Address: Natural Eye Care, 3 Paradies Lane, New Paltz, NY 12561.

How to use: "You can also use the drops to *prevent* cataract," says Dr. Grossman.

For prevention, he suggests one to two drops in each eye, one to two times per day. For treatment, he suggests two drops in the affected eye, two times per day.

"To apply the drop, lean your head back and look up. Put one drop into your eye, blink a couple of times and then gently close the eye. Do not blink again or reopen for sixty seconds. If you use a second drop, repeat this procedure. This allows each drop to be absorbed into the eye tissue."

Rapid Resource: *The Cataract Cure: The Story of N-acetylcarnosine*, by Marios Kyriazis, MD (iUniverse).

As with all natural remedies, use these eyedrops only with the approval and supervision of a qualified health professional, such as an optometrist or ophthalmologist.

➤ **Eat "The Vision Diet."** "If you're thinking about cataract surgery, try following these dietary recommendations for several months first," says Dr. Grossman. "You may find that your vision has improved enough to skip the surgery."

• **Cut back or eliminate sugar.** "High levels of sugar in the blood contribute to cataract formation," says Dr. Grossman. "People with diabetes, for example, are at three to four times the risk of cataracts. That's because blood sugar interferes with the lens' ability to pump out excess sugar from the eye and maintain its clarity."

• **Drink lots of water.** Dr. Grossman recommends eight to ten, 8-ounce glasses a day. "This maintains the flow of nutrients to the lens and the release of waste and toxins from the tissues."

• **Eat foods high in beta-carotene,** vitamins C and E, and sulfur-bearing amino acids. "These are antioxidants that combat free radicals," says Dr. Grossman.

Foods rich in these factors include garlic, onions, beans, yellow and orange vegetables, spinach and other green, leafy vegetables, celery, seaweed, apples, carrots, tomatoes, turnips and oranges.

• **Watch out for "congesting" foods.** "For many people, dairy, wheat and soy foods create sinus congestion, which impairs lymph and blood drainage from the area around the eyes—speeding the development of cataracts," says Dr. Grossman. "Try avoiding these foods for a month to see whether you are less congested," he says. "Then reintroduce them one at a time to help you identify your specific problem foods."

➤ **Wear (the right) sunglasses.** Maybe you routinely wear sunscreen to protect yourself from skin-damaging UV radiation. But UV radiation can also damage your eyes.

Fact: Eighty percent of Americans know that UV exposure from the sun can cause skin cancer, but only 5% know it can harm the eyes, causing cataracts.

"Whenever you're outdoors, you should wear sunglasses with UV coating," says Larry Jebrock, OD, a behavioral optometrist in Novato, California.

What most people don't realize: The degree of UV protection has nothing to do with the darkness of the lens of the sunglasses, says Dr. Jebrock.

Look for a pair with at least UV 400, which you should find listed on the product label or a sticker on a lens.

SPEED LIMIT | Can Cataract Surgery Cause Macular Degeneration?

Age-related macular degeneration (AMD) afflicts more than 20% of older Americans and is the number-one cause of vision loss and blindness. It occurs when there is damage to the macula, a tiny collection of cells in the middle of the retina, the structure at the back of the eyeball that translates light into brain-bound electrical impulses.

If you've had cataract surgery, you may be at greater risk for AMD.

What happens: "A cataract is like the lens of a pair of sunglasses—it filters out macula-damaging light," says Dr. Grossman. "Once you take out the cataract, light enters the eye more intensely, increasing the risk of macular degeneration. Anyone who has undergone cataract surgery should be on a preventive program for age-related macular degeneration," he says.

For more info on how to prevent AMD, please see Macular Degeneration, on page 232.

CELIAC DISEASE

Feel Better in Just a Few Weeks

You're gassy, and your stomach is bloated and painful. You feel tired all the time, even weak. Your hands and feet swell. You get migraines and mouth ulcers. Your joints hurt. And you're depressed.

Those are only some of the possible symptoms of *celiac disease* (CD), an autoimmune disease that has been called the "great masquerader" because its many possible symptoms mirror those of scores of other health problems.

The cause of CD is *gluten*, the protein found in wheat, rye and barley.

If you have CD, gluten triggers your immune system to attack and ravage the lining of your intestinal tract—perhaps creating day-to-day health disasters and setting you up for chronic illnesses such as anemia, osteoporosis and even cancer.

And if you have CD, it's likely you don't know it. Only 5% of people with the disease—which afflicts approximately 3 million Americans—have been diagnosed. Many of the other 95% spend years wandering from doctor to doctor…being misdiagnosed with irritable bowel syndrome, fibromyalgia, lactose intolerance or diverticulosis…taking prescription drugs…trying alternative methods…and doing their best to cope with unrelieved misery.

Good news: You could be feeling better by next week—if you eat a gluten-free diet.

"A strict gluten-free diet—a healthy diet that emphasizes fruits, vegetables, lean meats, dairy foods, nuts, seeds, legumes and non-gluten grains such as corn and rice—can clear up most if not all of the symptoms of CD," says Shelley Case, RD, a consulting dietician in Saskatchewan, Canada, a member of the Medical Advisory Boards of the Celiac Disease Foundation and the Gluten Intolerance Group, and author of *Gluten-Free Diet: A Comprehensive Resource Guide* (Case Nutrition Consulting Inc., Revised-Expanded Edition). Many people with CD who go on a strict gluten-free diet—the *only* effective treatment for CD—will start to feel better in a few weeks, she says.

But first you have to find out if you have CD…

➤ **Get an accurate diagnosis.** "CD is the single most underdiagnosed disease," says

Case. In fact, a study by Case and her colleagues showed that it typically takes *12 years* for someone with CD to receive an accurate diagnosis.

Problem: Most doctors don't think to test for CD because they were taught in medical school that it is a rare condition, found mostly in children.

Solution: If you suspect you have CD—if you have a long history of GI upset and other symptoms that nobody has been able to figure out—talk to your doctor about the following tests…

1. **The EMA (IgA endomysial) and TTG (IgA tissue transglutaminase) blood tests,** which are 90% to 95% accurate in screening for CD.

2. **A small intestine biopsy,** which is the definitive test to confirm the diagnosis.

Better: Celiac disease can appear in patches in the small intestine, so a single biopsy sample may show you're CD-free, even though you're not. Make sure your doctor takes at least four to six samples.

Trap: Don't start a gluten-free diet before the blood test and biopsy. For these tests to detect CD, your body needs to be reacting to gluten *at the time of the test.*

➤ **To eat gluten-free, use the best books on gluten-free living.** "A strict gluten-free diet for life is the only treatment for celiac disease," says Case. But staying on such a diet can be a challenge. "Wheat and wheat-based products are major staples of the North American diet," she says. "Hectic lifestyles rely on more meals eaten away from home and reliance on packaged, convenience foods, which often contain wheat. Another major challenge is that gluten is a hidden ingredient in many foods."

And a lot of the information that purports to help you through the maze of gluten-containing foods is outdated, inaccurate or confusing.

A Day of Gluten-Free Eating

There are a wide variety of gluten-free products on the market, with the category expanding by 25% a year, says Case. "That means you have so many options ranging from cereals, muffins, cakes, cookies, pancakes and more!"

- *Breakfast.* "It's easy to find gluten-free cereals, muffins, pancake mixes and waffles," says Case. Or try eggs with hash browns. And add a fruit smoothie, with a little bit of sweetener to taste.

  Product sampling: Instant Hot Quinoa Cereal, from AltiPlano Gold…Seattle Brown Bread, from Ener G Foods… Baking and Pancake Mix, from Pamela's Products.

  ⚠ *Caution:* "Most regular corn and rice cereals are not gluten-free, as they usually contain barley malt extract or flavoring," says Case. "Also, breads and other products containing the grains spelt or kamut are not gluten-free."

- *Dinner.* Dinner meals are the easiest because most people don't have a gluten-based food at that meal, says Case. You can have meat, chicken or fish as your main course, along with a potato and a vegetable.

- *Lunch.* "When you think of lunch, think of what I call 'planned-overs' instead of leftovers," says Case. "Cook extra food at dinner—an extra steak or pork chop or hamburger patty or fish, and make extra rice or vegetables, so you have something for lunch to heat up."

But maybe you want a sandwich-based lunch.

Problem: Many people don't like gluten-free bread, which can become dry and crumbly, says Case.

Solution: Here are some ways Case suggests to improve the texture and taste…

- When you buy rice bread, slice and freeze immediately, placing waxed paper between the slices and wrap tightly in a plastic bag so you can remove one at a time.

- Toasting gluten-free bread improves its flavor and keeps it from crumbling. Lightly toast the bread and freeze it for lunch the next day to use when making sandwiches.

- Consider buying a bread machine—homemade gluten-free breads are much fresher and more economical than ready-made breads.

- Try open-faced sandwiches toasted under a broiler—such as tuna or pure crab meat with shredded cheese, or a cheese, tomato and bacon combo.

Red flag: A gluten-free diet is not a weight-loss diet. "Many gluten-free foods tend to be much higher in starch, sugar and fat than their gluten-containing counterparts," says Case. "I caution my clients to limit their intake of gluten-free goodies such as cookies, cakes and muffins."

How to guarantee you're eating gluten-free? You need the most accurate, complete and easily accessible information, says Case. *A few key recommended books can provide it…*

One is Case's own book (*Gluten-Free Diet: A Comprehensive Resource Guide*), which is recommended by the National Institutes of Health and the American Celiac Disease Alliance. "I advise all my celiac patients to use this book," says Peter Green, MD, Director of the Celiac Disease Center at Columbia University in New York.

It includes…

- a comprehensive listing of safe, gluten-free foods and ingredients, and those to avoid;
- a guide to maintaining a nutrient-rich diet while eating gluten-free;
- meal plans, recipes, cooking hints and substitutions;
- how to eat gluten-free in restaurants and while traveling;

• more than 3,100 gluten-free specialty foods, listed by company and product name—from cereals, breads and snacks, to soup, sauces and even beer;

• a directory of more than 270 gluten-free manufacturers, bakeries, stores and distributors; and

• a list of helpful resources, such as celiac treatment centers, books and websites.

Rapid Resource: You can order the book at *www.glutenfreediet.ca*. Address: Case Nutrition Consulting, Inc., 1940 Angley Court, Regina, Sk. S4V 2V2 Canada, Phone/Fax 306-751-1000 or e-mail *info@glutenfreediet.ca*.

Another indispensable book is the *Pocket Dictionary: Acceptability of Foods & Food Ingredients for the Gluten-Free Diet.*

"Most people who are newly diagnosed with celiac disease spend a lot of time reading food labels, struggling to figure out what's gluten-free and what's not. This handy booklet allows you to read the ingredient list of most products in the store and figure out if the product is gluten-free or not," says Case. You can also get a downloadable version of the book for a PDA device.

Rapid Resource: You can order the book at *www.celiac.ca* or call 800-363-7296. Address: Canadian Celiac Association, 5025 Orbitor Dr., Ste. 400, Mississauga, ON, L4W 4Y5, Canada or e-mail *info@celiac.ca*.

Some of Case's favorite gluten-free cookbooks are those by Carol Fenster, including *1000 Gluten-Free Recipes, Gluten-Free Quick & Easy* and *Gluten-Free 101.* Visit online at *www.savorypalate.com*, or call 800-741-5418. Address: Savory Palate, Inc., 8174 South Holly, #404, Centennial, CO 80122 or e-mail *info@SavoryPalate.com*.

For eating out and traveling, Case says an excellent resource is *Let's Eat Out! Your Passport to Living Gluten and Allergy Free and other GlutenFree Passport Guides* by Kim Koeller and Robert La France. Visit online at *www.gluten freepassport.com*, or call 312-244-3702. Address: GlutenFree Passport, 80 Burr Ridge Parkway, Suite 141, Burr Ridge, IL 60527, email *info@gluten freepassport.com*.

➤ **Join a local organization.** "Local celiac groups and organizations can tell you where to shop, which restaurants are celiac-friendly and offer ongoing support," says Case.

To find a local organization, go to these websites...

• Celiac Disease Foundation, at *www.celiac. org*, which has a list of organizations in every state. Address: Celiac Disease Foundation, 20350 Ventura Blvd. Suite 240, Woodland Hills, CA 91364 (818-716-1513); e-mail *cd@celiac.org*.

• Gluten Intolerance Group, at *www.gluten. net*. Address: 31214 124th Ave. SE., Auburn, WA 98092 (253-833-6655); e-mail *info@gluten.net*.

• Canadian Celiac Association, at *www. celiac.ca*. Address: 5025 Orbitor Dr., Ste. 400, Mississauga, ON, L4W 4Y5, Canada (800-363-7296); e-mail *info@celiac.ca*.

CELLULITE

No-Sweat Reduction, for Real

Your fat cells are bigger. Your collagen—the fibrous protein that binds skin cells together—is thinner and weaker. You have three layers of fat around your buttocks and thighs, while he has just one.

And that's why you have cellulite and your hubby (no matter how chubby) doesn't, says Lionel Bissoon, DO, the founder and director of the Mesotherapie & Estetik Clinics in New York, Florida and California, and author of *The Cellulite Cure* (Meso Press).

Cellulite happens when fat cells swell up (because of poor circulation, falling estrogen levels and other factors) and squeeze out through collagen fibers. It's not a medical problem—cellulite isn't a risk factor for disease (unlike excess fat on your abdomen, which generates inflammatory biochemicals that can hurt your heart). But for most women (80% to 90% of whom will develop cellulite after the age of 18), those lumps, bumps and dimples are a cosmetic disaster.

Disaster relief is on the way.

"You can do something incredibly quick, simple and inexpensive to help prevent and reduce cellulite," says Dr. Bissoon…

⏱ *Super-Quick Fix*

➤ **Don't wear tight underwear with elastic bands.** In the US, an estimated one out of two women wear underwear with tight elastic bands that stretch across the buttocks and upper thighs. The elastic works like a tourniquet, says Dr. Bissoon—it cuts off the flow of *lymph*, the internal fluid that drains cells of debris and toxins. The result is swollen fat cells and worsening cellulite.

"The longer you wear this type of underwear, the deeper and more severe your dimples will become," he says. To correct the problem, he offers these "Rules of Underwear"…

- No elastic over the buttocks.
- No elastic over the groin area.
- Elastic is okay at the waist.
- Wear underwear with lace across the buttocks, rather than elastic.
- Or wear thongs and G-strings.
- Wearing no underwear is an option.
- Don't sleep in your underwear—sleep in the nude or wear a pullover nighty.
- Don't wear underwear and pantyhose together.

"You don't have to spend thousands of dollars to help rid yourself of cellulite," he says. "Just buy yourself some new underwear!"

Rapid Resource: For more information about Dr. Bissoon's specialty, Mesotherapy (injections of small doses of conventional and homeopathic medications and nutrients to reduce cellulite), see the website *www.mesotherapy.com*, or call 212-579-9136 (New York, New York), 415-810-2430 (San Francisco, California), or 561-838-4991 (Palm Beach, Florida), or e-mail *info@ mesotherapy.com*.

➤ **Roll cellulite away.** A study from researchers at the Vanderbilt University School of Medicine in Tennessee showed that deep massage with a handheld device can help smooth out cellulite.

Try this: "Roll a rolling pin over your hips and thighs for about five minutes each day," suggests Rona Berg, former beauty editor for the *New York Times Magazine*, and author of *Fast Beauty* (Workman).

⚠ ***Caution:*** But don't apply pressure to the point of bruising, cautions dermatologist Audrey Kunin, MD, founder of *www.dermadoctor.com*, and author of *The DERMAdoctor's Skinstruction Manual* (Simon & Schuster). It's unlikely this technique will provide more than "limited improvement," she adds. "But if improvement happens, it's better than none at all."

➤ **Try topical vitamin C.** Aging is a cause of cellulite—because collagen weakens with age. Topical vitamin C can trigger the production of collagen and may help improve the appearance of cellulite, says Dr. Kunin.

Recommended: Cellex-C Body Smoothing Lotion, which is widely available.

CHAPPED LIPS

Move to the Smooth

When Mother Nature gives you a big kiss on the lips, you may not like the result—particularly in winter.

Cold, dry, windy weather can desiccate your lips, leaving them cracked, flaky and uncomfortable—in other words, *chapped.*

Or maybe your lips are dehydrated year-round, probably due to a cause that could stump the sleuthing powers of Sherlock Holmes (not to mention your doctor).

But whether you suffer seasonally or non-stop, tell your lips to start smiling again. *Because they're about to get better...*

Super-Quick Fix

➤ **Brush your...lips!** Many people *exfoliate* their skin, using a mildly abrasive cleanser (or just a wash cloth) to remove old, dried cells and make room for moist replacements. The same approach can work for your lips, says Rona Berg, former beauty editor of the *New York Times Magazine* and author of *Fast Beauty* (Workman). So right after you brush your teeth, brush your lips.

"Wash your hands, mix a little honey and sugar in your palm, dip in the toothbrush and gently use that mixture to scrub away the flaky bits of skin on your chapped lips," says Berg. A minute or two is all it takes.

Also helpful: You might also want to use some honey later, says Stephanie Tourles, a licensed holistic esthetician in Maine and author of *Naturally Healthy Skin* (Storey Books). "Dab honey on your lips to soothe and protect," she says. "It acts as a *humectant,* drawing moisture from the air to your skin and helping lips stay soft and plump."

➤ **Balms away.** After you brush your lips, apply a lip balm for protection, says Berg. Her favorite ingredient is beeswax, the stuff worker bees secrete to build honeycomb cells in hives. You can find it in many products, such as Beeswax Lip Balm, from Burt's Bees.

Better: "Use wax-based lip balms *before* you've got chapped lips," suggests dermatologist Audrey Kunin, MD, founder and director of *www. dermadoctor.com,* and author of *The DERMA-doctor Skinstruction Manual* (Simon & Schuster).

"Think about it," she says. "How much moisture does a tube of wax give your lips? Wax is a protective barrier, not a healing agent. If you *start* the winter with healthy lips, a wax-based balm can keep them that way."

Red flags: Some lip balms contain irritating ingredients that can actually worsen chapped lips, says Berg. She advises staying away from Blistex and Carmex, both of which contain *phenol.*

"Phenol can trigger drying and irritation," agrees Paula Begoun, author of *The Beauty Bible* (Beginning Press). "If the lip balm you are using contains irritants, your lips will *stay* dried up."

➤ **To heal rapidly, moisturize repeatedly.** Dr. Kunin suggests applying a moisture-rich product several times a day. "The more frequent the application, the better your results," she says.

Recommended: Lip Protectant SPF 30 from Vanicream and Soothing Skin and Lip Therapy from Murad.

➤ **Moisturize from the inside out.** "Chapped lips are often the first sign of not drinking enough water," says Victoria Nash, an esthetician in Phoenix, Arizona, and founder of the skin care company, Esenté Physioceuticals (*www.esente.com*). "In fact, I can tell if someone hasn't been drinking enough water simply by looking at their lips—they're *always* dry and cracked." She suggests quaffing a minimum of 8 eight-ounce glasses a day.

➤ **You can't lick this problem.** Your lips are dry—so you lick them. But saliva evaporates in a jiffy, leaving your lips even drier. Resist the impulse if you can, says Berg.

Trap: Avoid flavored lip balm, which can tempt you to lick your lips even more.

➤ **Lipstick can stick it to you.** "Some ingredients in lipsticks can dry lips," says Nash.

Avoid *phenyl salicylate* (salol), which can chap lips, says Dr. Kunin. Also look out for propyl gallate, which can cause a "contact allergy" that chaps lips.

Matte and gloss lipsticks can be particularly drying, adds Berg, who advocates cream lipstick.

Smart idea: Apply your lip balm over or under your lipstick, says Berg.

CHOLESTEROL PROBLEMS

High-Speed Remedies for High Cholesterol

Cholesterol clogs arteries, leading to heart attacks and strokes, which kill nearly 1 million Americans every year.

Fact: Reducing blood levels of cholesterol by only 10%—a small and potentially speedy decrease—can reduce the risk of heart attack by 30%.

But only 5% of Americans have achieved cholesterol levels that doctors deem protective—total cholesterol below 150 mg/dL (milligrams per deciliter), and "bad" cholesterol (which carries fat to arteries) below 100 mg/dL.

Yet cholesterol-lowering statin drugs—the most prescribed medications in the US—are not necessarily the best way to lower high cholesterol, says Joel Fuhrman, MD, a family physician in Flemington, New Jersey, and author of *Cholesterol Protection For Life: Lower Your Cholesterol Safely and Permanently* (Gift of Life Press).

"Cholesterol-lowering drugs can cause serious side effects, such as liver damage, muscle pain, severe fatigue and nerve damage. It's possible to avoid those side effects *and* reduce your risk of heart disease—by following an inexpensive, safe and effective program of nutritional excellence," says Fuhrman.

"You can lower cholesterol dramatically, without drugs, in just a few weeks, with a smart mix of foods scientifically proven to cut cholesterol," agrees Janet Bond Brill, PhD, RD, a nutritionist and wellness coach in Florida and author of *Cholesterol Down: 10 Simple Steps to Lower Your Cholesterol in 4 Weeks—Without Prescription Drugs* (Three Rivers Press).

Here are the best drug-free methods for quickly bringing high cholesterol under control…

➤ **Cut cholesterol fast—with Dr. Brill's All-Natural "Combination Therapy."** Dr. Brill targets "bad" LDL cholesterol—and she's in good company. The American Heart Association and the government's National Heart, Lung and Blood Institute both say that lowering LDL cholesterol is *the* most important goal for anyone with high cholesterol.

Start with a natural approach. "Americans turn far too quickly to drugs to solve their health problems," says Dr. Brill. "Yes, cholesterol-lowering statins are wonderful drugs. But they can have side effects, they're expensive and you have to take them every day for the rest of your life. Diet and exercise can work just as well, if not better, to control cholesterol—so it's smart to try them first, with your doctor's approval. If they don't work, *then* consider cholesterol-lowering drugs."

And the best way to lower cholesterol without drugs is with *combination therapy*—eating several cholesterol-lowering foods, every day. "Research shows that combining several, scientifically proven cholesterol-lowering foods with an exercise routine can be as effective as taking cholesterol-lowering drugs," says Dr. Brill.

Her top three recommendations…

1. Walk for 30 minutes every day. Walking burns up LDL. "It's one of the safest, simplest, most inexpensive and effective cholesterol-lowering strategies," she says.

Try this: If you haven't been exercising regularly, start with 20 minutes 2 to 3 days a week…after a few weeks, progress to 5 days a week…then 7 days a week…then increase walking time to 30 minutes…then pick up the pace.

⚠ *Caution:* Get the go-ahead from your doctor before starting a walking program.

2. Eat two meals a day rich in phytosterols. "Phytosterols are fats in plant foods—basically, the plant's version of cholesterol," says Dr. Brill. They work by blocking the absorption of dietary cholesterol and by reabsorbing cholesterol-building compounds in the intestinal tract. The government's National Cholesterol Education Program recommends eating 2 to 3 grams of phytosterols a day.

Problem: The typical American diet supplies about 80 milligrams (mg) a day of phy-

tosterols—so to meet that recommendation you'd have to eat about 30 times more food!

Solution: Eat foods enriched with phytosterols. *For example…*

• **Margarines,** such as Promise Activ Take Control Light (1 tablespoon supplies 1.7 grams) and Benecol Light (1 tablespoon supplies 0.85 grams).

• **Chocolate-containing products,** such as CocoaVia chocolate bars with almonds (1 serving supplies 1 to 1.5 grams), and RD Food's Right Direction chocolate chip cookies (1 cookie supplies 1.3 grams).

• **Orange juice,** such as Minute Maid Premium Heartwise Orange Juice (8 ounces supplies 1 gram).

"Most of the scientific studies that show phytosterols can lower LDL used margarine," says Dr. Brill.

She recommends adding 1 tablespoon of phytosterol-containing margarine to a meal, most days of the week. (Use it to butter toast, flavor hot cereal, on top of steamed vegetables or added to grain or pasta dishes.) Have another phytosterol-enriched food at a second meal.

Newest research: European scientists analyzed 84 studies on phytosterols and cholesterol and found an intake of 2 grams a day lowered LDL by an average of 9%. "This would reduce the risk of cardiovascular disease by about ten to twenty percent," say the researchers, in the *Journal of Nutrition*.

3. Eat oatmeal for breakfast. Oats are rich in beta-glucan, a fiber that acts like an intestinal sponge, soaking up cholesterol and driving it out of the body, says Dr. Brill.

Best: The type of oatmeal richest in beta-glucan is the least processed—steel cut oats. Dr. Brill's favorite brand is McCann's Quick-and-Easy Steel Cut Irish Oatmeal, which is widely available.

Speed Healing Success

Former Marine Battles High Cholesterol—And Wins!

Linda F.—a former marine and account executive in Seattle—had her cholesterol tested as part of a routine physical. When her numbers came back she was shocked. Her total cholesterol was 226 and her LDL was 131, way above the recommended 150 and 100. Her doctor recommended a statin. She said no.

"I'm in my mid-thirties, and didn't like the idea of going on a drug for the rest of my life." She began to research alternatives—and chose an all-natural "combination therapy," based on the program in *Cholesterol Down* (Three Rivers), by Janet Bond Brill, PhD.

Instead of taking a drug every day, she "took" a tablespoon of psyllium seed husks, two tablespoons of ground flax seeds and a bowl of oatmeal—each food scientifically proven to lower cholesterol, and to be even more effective when combined. She also exercised regularly.

After three months, her total cholesterol had dropped to 131 and her LDL to 91. Three years later, they're still normal.

Linda favors the Yerba Prima brand of psyllium seed husks (stirring it into an 8-ounce glass of juice)...Bob's Red Mill brand of flaxseeds (grinding up and refrigerating a large batch, for daily convenience)...and McCann's Steel Cut Oats.

"I've recommended combination therapy to many people with high cholesterol—and it's worked for everyone who's tried it and stuck with it," she says. "It's fast and simple. If you give it a chance, I think it will work for you."

Smart idea: She recommends adding several other foods proven to lower cholesterol to your oatmeal—soy, almonds and apples. "Mix the oatmeal with soy milk instead of water and zap it in the microwave. Then throw on a handful of almonds and some apple slices."

Rapid Resource: For more information about Dr. Brill's approach to lowering LDL cholesterol, visit her website at *www.drjanet.com*. E-mail specific questions to *Janet@DrJanet.com*.

➤ **Pistachios say "nuts" to high cholesterol.** Pistachios are rich in monounsaturated fat, phytosterols and fiber, all of which are known to lower cholesterol.

Recent scientific study: Researchers at Pennsylvania State University fed a group of 28 people three different diets over a period of several weeks—a cholesterol-lowering diet with 25% of calories from fat, a cholesterol-lowering diet with 10% of calories from pistachios (P1) and a cholesterol-lowering diet with 20% of calories from pistachios (P2).

LDL levels fell 9% on the P1 diet and 12% on the P2 diet, report the researchers, in the *American Journal of Clinical Nutrition*. (LDL levels stayed the same on the no-pistachio diet.)

"Pistachios, eaten with a heart-healthy diet, may decrease a person's risk of cardiovascular disease," says Penny Kris-Etherton, PhD, the lead researcher and a professor of nutrition.

What to do: The P1 diet included 1 ounce of pistachios, or about one handful, and the P2 diet included 2 ounces, or about two handfuls.

Red flag: When you add pistachios, subtract the same amount of calories from other dietary sources—otherwise, you'll gain weight. One ounce of pistachios is 160 calories.

➤ **Boost HDL—with niacin.** HDL is the "good" cholesterol that carries fat away from the arteries. You want to *increase* HDL, with healthy levels at 40 mg/dL or higher for men and 50 or higher for women.

Standout scientific evidence: Researchers at the University of Washington analyzed data from more than 83,000 heart patients and found that decreasing LDL by 40% *and* increasing HDL by 30% lowers the risk of heart attack or stroke by 70%—a much greater reduction than from lowering either total cholesterol or LDL.

What helps: One of the few reliable ways to increase HDL is with therapeutic doses of niacin, a B-vitamin—and niacin also lowers LDL and total cholesterol, says Allan Magaziner, DO, medical director of the Magaziner Center for Wellness and Anti-Aging Medicine in Cherry Hill, New Jersey, and author of *The All-Natural Cardio Cure* (Avery).

How to use: Start with 500 mg a day, says Dr. Magaziner. Every week, increase by 500 mg, until you reach 2,000 mg a day, in three divided doses, with meals.

Important: Use *nicotinic acid*, not *niacinamide*, a form of the B-vitamin that doesn't lower cholesterol.

⚠ *Caution:* If you take more than 2,000 mg a day, do so only with the approval and supervision of your doctor. In rare cases, niacin elevates levels of enzymes that can cause liver damage. Long-term, high-dose niacin therapy should include regular blood tests for those enzymes.

Rapid Resource: You can find out more about Dr. Magaziner's approach to health and healing at *www.drmagaziner.com*.

➤ **Cholesterol-busting supplements.** Recent studies show that two nutritional and herbal supplements are powerful aids in lowering cholesterol…

• **Red yeast rice and fish oil.** Researchers from the University of Pennsylvania studied 74 people, dividing them into two groups. One group took a statin. The other group took supplements of fish oil and red yeast rice (a yeast grown on rice that contains monacolin, a statinlike compound).

Eggs Are Okay!

"Study after study shows that eating six eggs a day for six weeks has no effect on cholesterol blood levels—yet the myth that eggs cause high cholesterol persists," says Jacob Teitelbaum, MD, a physician in private practice in Hawaii and author of *From Fatigued to Fantastic* (Avery).

After three months, LDL dropped by 40% in those taking a statin—and 42% in those taking fish oil and red yeast rice! And the regimen of two supplements decreased triglycerides (another blood fat that can hurt the heart) by 29%, compared to 9% for the statin. "These results show a potential benefit of a natural approach to the common medical condition of high cholesterol," says David Becker, MD, a study researcher.

Suggested intake: The daily amount of omega-3 fatty acids used in the study was 2.1 grams of EPA and 1.7 grams of DHA. The amount of red yeast rice was 2.4 to 3.6 grams, containing 5.3 mg of monacolin, with 2.5 in the form of monacolin K.

Product: Red yeast rice and fish oil supplements are widely available.

Rapid Resource: Res-Q 1250 was the omega-3 product used in the study. It's available at *www.myresqproducts.com*, or call 800-262-5483. Address: N3 Oceanic, Inc., 1862 A Tollgate Rd., Palm, PA 18070.

⚠ *Caution:* The independent testing company, *www.consumerlab.com*, found that four brands of red yeast rice were contaminated with a toxic substance—Walgreen's Finest Natural Red Yeast Rice, Natural Balance Red Yeast Rice Concentrated Extract, Solaray Red Yeast Rice and VegLife 100% Vegan Red Yeast Rice.

Also: Take 50 to 100 mg of CoQ10 with red yeast rice to help prevent side effects, such as muscle weakness.

• **Flavones.** In a study in the *Nutrition Journal*, an international team of researchers divided 45 people into two groups. For two months, one group took a supplement containing high levels of plant extracts rich in *flavones*, a compound shown to reduce cholesterol levels. The other group took a placebo. Among overweight people taking flavones, there was a 44% drop in LDL, a 10% drop in total cholesterol, an 11% increase in HDL and an 18% decrease in triglycerides.

Product: Flavoxine, by Next Pharmaceuticals. **Rapid Resource:** It is available from Kavalia in a product called VivaLean at *www.kavalia inc.com*, or by calling 888-795-3029.

➤ **Watch out for statin's side effects.** More than 15 million Americans take a *statin* (Altoprev, Crestor, Lescol, Mevacor, Pravachol, Zocor), a medication that inhibits the action of HMG-CoA reductase, an enzyme involved in producing cholesterol. Statins can lower total and LDL cholesterol, helping to prevent heart disease and stroke—and many doctors tout them as wonder drugs, with few (if any) side effects. *But statins aren't as safe as your doctor may think...*

Surprising: Six hundred fifty people who took a statin and reported a side effect were asked to complete a survey that included questions about how the doctor responded when told about the problem. About 50% of doctors dismissed the possibility that the statin caused the problem.

And what your doctor doesn't know about statins may hurt you...

Recent development: Beatrice Golomb, MD, PhD, and her colleagues at the University of California in San Diego, have gathered more than 5,000 reports from people who say they experienced one or more side effects after taking a statin. They also conducted a review of nearly 900 scientific studies on statin side effects, publishing their results in the *American Journal of Cardiovascular Drugs*. The most likely side effects from statins...

1. **Muscle problems.** This is the most common side effect, and includes pain, weakness, tenderness and exercise intolerance. In rare cases, the statin damages muscle tissue, a problem called *statin myopathy*. Myopathy can worsen, becoming *rhabdomyolysis*, a potentially fatal breakdown of muscle cells. (The statin Baycor was pulled from the market in 2001 after being linked to more than 400 cases of rhabdomyolysis, 31 of them fatal, as dead muscle cells overwhelmed kidney function.)

2. **Mental problems.** This is the second most common side effect, and includes memory loss, poor concentration and cloudy thinking. *Example:* Reporting in the *American Journal of Medicine*, researchers at the University of Pittsburgh found that people taking statins developed problems with attention span and reaction time.

3. **Nerve damage.** Peripheral neuropathy is the third most common side effect. The result of nerve damage, it is characterized by tingling, numbness or burning pain in the hands, arms, feet or legs.

Other side effects include high blood sugar, sleep problems, irritability, and sexual difficulties such as erectile dysfunction and low libido.

Preventing the "Niacin Flush"

The most common side effect of niacin is *flushing*—a warm, itchy, rashlike reddening of the face, neck and chest, lasting about 10 minutes. It is caused by *vasodilation*, the artery-widening power of niacin. Choose "flush-free" niacin, or *inositol hexanicotinate*, advises Dr. Magaziner. Combined with inositol, another B-vitamin, this form of niacin prevents the flush without reducing niacin's effectiveness.

What happens: Statins block the production of *Coenzyme Q10* (Q10), a compound crucial to the functioning of *mitochondria*, tiny energy factories inside every cell. Weakened mitochondria translate into weaker muscle, nerve and brain cells—and side effects. And the longer you take a statin, and the stronger the dose, the more likely you are to get those side effects, says Dr. Golomb.

Self-defense: If you develop a side effect, talk to your doctor immediately, says Dr. Golomb. Mitochondrial dysfunction can be reversed. But if cells have died because of prolonged mitochondrial dysfunction, it may be difficult or impossible to eliminate a statin-caused health problem. The sooner you and your doctor address the side effect, the more likely it can be eliminated.

Your doctor can stop the drug, to see if symptoms improve or resolve. If they do, consider taking a non-statin medication for preventing or treating heart disease.

Or your doctor can lower the dose. Research shows that people with one or more side effects from a statin are 45% less likely to experience the problem when put on a lower dose of the drug.

Also helpful: "If you take a statin, I strongly recommend that you take two hundred milligrams of Coenzyme Q10 daily as well," says Jacob Teitelbaum, MD, a physician in Hawaii and author of *From Fatigued to Fantastic* (McGraw-Hill). "If you stop your medication with your physician's approval, I would continue the Coenzyme Q10 for three months."

Product: Not all Coenzyme Q10 supplements are equally effective, says Dr. Teitelbaum. He favors the chewable brand from Enzymatic Therapy, which is widely available.

SPEED LIMIT Is a Statin Right for You?

Research shows that the ideal candidate for a statin is a middle-aged man with known heart disease (angina or heart attack) or one or more risk factors for heart disease, says Dr. Golomb.

Those risk factors include high LDL (over 190 mg/dL), low HDL (below 40 mg/dL), a family history of premature heart disease (a heart attack or sudden death in a father or brother under age 55, or a mother or sister under age 65), high blood pressure (140/90 mm Hg) or taking medications for high blood pressure and current smoking.

What most people don't realize: Research does *not* show that the benefit of taking a statin exceeds risk in women or in people over 70, says Dr. Golomb—even those at high risk for heart disease.

COLDS AND FLU

Triple Your Protection with Vitamin D

John Cannell, MD, the executive director of the Vitamin D Council, decided to conduct an experiment. On himself.

He stopped taking his daily dose of 5,000 IU (international units) of vitamin D. He stayed out of the sun. (The skin produces approximately 10,000 IU of vitamin D in response to 20 to 30 minutes of summer sun exposure.) And he waited for cold and flu season.

Sure enough, in October he got the first signs of a cold—the runny nose, the sneezing, the sore throat. Which he stopped *immediately* with high doses of vitamin D. (A cold or flu typically lasts about 10 days.)

"It was remarkable—the kind of response that makers of antibiotics dream of," says Dr. Cannell. "My symptoms completely cleared up and I never developed a full-blown infection."

But you can't wait until you've been sick for a couple of days to undo a cold or flu. "You need to take large doses of vitamin D *as soon* as you know you're getting the cold or flu," he says.

Dr. Cannell is not some nutritional rebel with a wild-eyed theory. His scientific paper proposing that low blood levels of vitamin D levels are the primary cause of the flu—*Epidemic Influenza and Vitamin D*—was published in Cambridge University's prestigious *Journal of Epidemiology and Health*, and was coauthored by some of the world's top vitamin D experts, from the Harvard School of Public Health, the University of California-San Diego and Georgetown University. He is one among many researchers who think vitamin D may be *the most important factor* for preventing colds and flu.

Here's how you can use his remarkable findings on vitamin D to help prevent colds and flu—and possibly stop an infection in its tracks.

➤ **The miracle of vitamin D.** Vitamin D is not technically a vitamin—a nutrient found in food. High levels of *cholecalciferol* (vitamin D-3) are produced in the skin when its exposed to sunlight. D-3 then turns into *calcitriol*, a hormone.

Scientists used to think calcitrol had one function—regulating blood levels of calcium. Now they know that it targets more than *2,000 genes* (10% of the human genome). Including genes that control the immune system.

"Vitamin D dramatically increases the production of the body's own *antimicrobial peptides*," says Dr. Cannell. "If you have sufficiently high levels of vitamin D, you'll have enough of those peptides to kill cold and flu viruses before they have a chance to penetrate the mucosal barrier."

New studies: A study in the *Archives of Internal Medicine* looked at health and nutrition

Say Good Night To Colds!

If you typically get less than seven hours of sleep a night, you're three times more likely to catch a cold, compared to people who sleep eight hours or more, say researchers from Carnegie Mellon University in Pittsburgh.

The study: The researchers studied 153 healthy people, asking them how many hours they slept on average. Then they quarantined them and administered nose drops containing the rhinovirus, which causes colds. The less a person had slept, the more likely he or she was to develop a cold.

data from almost 19,000 adults and adolescents. They found that those with the lowest blood levels of vitamin D were 40% more likely to have had a recent cold or flu than those with the highest levels. (Asthma patients with low levels of vitamin D were five times more likely to get a respiratory infection, and those with emphysema were twice as likely.)

"The findings of our study support an important role for vitamin D in the prevention of common respiratory infections, such as colds or flu," says Adit Ginde, MD, the study leader.

And in a study on bone loss, women took either 2,000 IU or 200 IU of vitamin D for three years. When the researchers who conducted the study read Dr. Cannel's paper on vitamin D and the flu, they reexamined their data. They found the women taking the higher dose of vitamin D had an average of nine episodes of colds and flu over the three years—while those taking the lower dose had an average of 30!

➤ **The best dosages of vitamin D for prevention and reversal.** For cold and flu prevention—and good health—Dr. Cannell recommends a dosage of 5,000 IU a day. "Anybody who takes this amount regularly should not get a cold or flu. And if they do get one, it should be mild."

For knocking out a cold or flu, he recommends a daily dose of 2,000 IU per kilogram (2.2 pounds) of body weight, for three or four days.

Example: A 180-pound man would take approximately 160,000 IU.

But isn't there a risk of vitamin D toxicity, as the nutrient builds up in the system? Not really, says Dr. Cannell.

"There is not a single case in the medical literature of vitamin D toxicity while taking regular doses of twenty-five thousand IU or less," says Dr. Cannell.

"People *need* five thousand IU a day to stay healthy." (To get that amount from milk you'd need to drink 50 glasses a day, he points out.) And short-term mega-doses to knock out a cold or flu pose no risk to health, he says. (Toxicity would only develop over many years of use.)

"Scientists use a term called the *therapeutic index* to calculate toxicity—the dose of a normal substance that would be toxic," says Dr. Cannell. "Water, for example, has a therapeutic index of ten—if you drink eight, eight-ounce glasses of water you're fine, but if you drink eighty, you die. Vitamin D has a therapeutic index of twenty—it's literally safer than water. Worrying about vitamin D toxicity is like worrying about drowning when you're dying of thirst."

Fact: Thirty-six percent of so-called healthy adults in the US are vitamin D deficient, as are 57% of people admitted to hospitals. Overall, say experts, the risk for vitamin D deficiency is about 50%—one out of every two people is likely to have blood levels below 20 nanograms per milliliter (ng/mL).

Helpful: However, if you decide to take 5,000 IU a day of vitamin D, Dr. Cannell suggests you take a *25-hydroxyvitamin D test* for blood levels of the nutrient, to ensure that

---

Unstuff Your Nose

All stuffed up? Here's a mucous-clearing suggestion from aromatherapist Cher Kore of Kameleon Healing Aromatherapy (*www.khealing.com*) in Massachusetts.

- *Boil a pot of water.* Add four drops of either eucalyptus or spearmint essentials oil or blend containing one or both of those oils. Put a towel over your head and breathe in the vapors for five to 15 minutes. Or use six to 10 drops in a hot bath.

Product: Sinus Scent, which contains both eucalyptus and spearmint essential oils. It is available at *www.khealing.com*, or call 617-254-5454.

---

your levels are adequately maintained and don't exceed the upper limits of the so-called "reference range" of safety.

"You want blood levels between fifty to eighty ng/mL, or one hundred and twenty-five to two hundred nm/L," he says. They generally shouldn't exceed 100 ng/mL.

Rapid Resource: You can find a link to an in-home vitamin D blood test from ZRT Laboratory at the website of the Vitamin D Council, *www.vitamindcouncil.com*.

The ZRT Lab contact information is *www.zrtlab.com*, ZRT Laboratory, 8605 SW Creekside Pl., Beaverton, OR 97008, call 866-600-1636 or e-mail *info@zrtlab.com*.

Bruce Hollis, PhD, professor of Biochemistry and Molecular Biology at the Medical University of South Carolina, and one of the world's leading authorities on vitamin D testing, has reviewed this test to make sure that it is accurate and reflects the "gold standard" of vitamin D testing.

Test yourself every six months, says Dr. Cannell.

Product: "I believe *cholecalciferol* (vitamin D-3) is the preferred oral form of vitamin D, as it is the compound your skin makes naturally when you go in the sun," says Dr. Cannell. "It is more potent and perhaps even safer than the synthetic analog, *ergocalciferol* (vitamin D-2), found in many supplements.

Rapid Resource: You can order supplements of vitamin D-3 (including 5,000 and 50,000 IU supplements) at the website of Biotech Pharmacal, *www.biotechpharmacal.com*, or call 479-443-9148 or 800-345-1199.

Dr. Cannell has also formulated a vitamin D-3 supplement that includes nutritional cofactors such as magnesium and vitamin K-2 that boost absorption. The product is Dr. Cannell's Advanced D and it is available at *www.purity products.com*, or call 800-256-6102.

Important: Seek a physician knowledgeable about vitamin D to guide you in your use of the nutrient, and in other approaches to preventing and treating colds and flu, such as the flu vaccine, says Dr. Cannell.

Super-Quick Fix

➤ **The seven secrets of effective hand-washing.** "The common cold virus can survive up to three days outside the nasal passages on objects and surfaces," says Allison Janse, author of *The Germ Freak's Guide to Outwitting Colds and Flu* (Health Communications). And 70% of people who have a cold have those infectious germs on *their* hands—passing them around.

The way to protect yourself? *Wash your hands!* But only 16% of people wash their hands well enough to kill germs, says Charles Gerba, PhD, Janse's coauthor, a microbiologist and a professor at the University of Arizona.

Here are Dr. Gerba's directions for doing it right…

1. **Hot water isn't necessary.** Warm water is best, because if the water is too hot or cold you're likely to stop washing before the germs are banished.

2. **Use old-fashioned hand soap.**

3. **Wet your hands and lather the soap all over,** rubbing between your fingers, the top and palm of your hands and under your nails. "It's this friction that gets the germs off, so rub for a full fifteen seconds," says Dr. Gerba.

4. **But *don't* rub while your hands are under the faucet,** because you'll wash the soap off too soon.

5. **Rinse your hands thoroughly.**

6. **The whole process should take at *least* twenty seconds,** says Dr. Gerba. To time yourself, sing "Happy Birthday to You."

7. **"Wash your hands frequently throughout the day,"** says Dr. Gerba. *Key times include…*
   - Before you eat.
   - After you use the bathroom.
   - After you come in from outside.
   - After you cough or sneeze (to protect others from your germs).

See Your Doctor If...

The American Academy of Family Physicians suggests you see a doctor if you have the cold or flu and the following symptoms…

- *A high, prolonged fever (above 102°) with aching and fatigue*
- *Symptoms that last for more than 10 days or get worse instead of better*
- *Trouble breathing or shortness of breath*
- *Pain or pressure in the chest*
- *Fainting or feeling as if you are about to faint*
- *Severe or persistent vomiting*
- *Severe sinus pain in your face or forehead*
- *Very swollen glands in your neck or jaw*

➤ **Press here to prevent a cold.** Acupressure is a massage technique that practitioners stay stimulates a fundamental life force called *chi*, which travels along channels or *meridians* in the body. "If you think you're about to get a cold or the flu, stimulating the *Heavenly Rejuvenation* acupoint may prevent the infection, says acupressure expert Michael Gach, PhD (*www.acupressure.com*), founder and former director of the Acupressure Institute in Berkeley, California, and author of numerous books and instructional DVDs and CDs on acupressure and other healing techniques, including *Acupressure's Potent Points* (Bantam).

Location: On the shoulders, midway between the base of the neck and the outside of the shoulders, one-half inch below the top of the shoulders.

What to do: There are two ways to stimulate this point.

1. **Curving your fingers,** hook your right hand on your right shoulder, and your left hand on your left shoulder. With your fingertips, firmly press the point and take three long, slow, deep breaths.

2. **If you don't have the flexibility to perform #1: Lie down on your back, on a firm mattress or carpeted floor, with knees bent and feet on the floor, as close to your buttocks as possible.** Bring your hands up above your head and rest the backs of your hands on the floor beside or above your head. Inhale, lift up your pelvis, pressing your feet against the floor to assist the lift. The higher your pelvis, the more weight will be transferred onto your shoulders, stimulating the point. Hold this posture for one minute, taking long, slow, deep breaths, with your eyes closed. Lower your pelvis and rest for three minutes.

CONSTIPATION

Get Regular Fast

Ask a gastroenterologist to define chronic constipation and you'll probably be told that…fewer than three bowel movements a week…stools that are hard and painful to pass…or a feeling of "incomplete evacuation"…qualifies you for the diagnosis.

Stella Metsovas, CN, a nutritionist in Laguna Beach, California, has a different opinion.

"I tell my clients that someone with healthy bowel function typically has two well-formed bowel movements a day—and that's the goal of nutritional therapy for a case of constipation."

And, says Metsovas, if you don't have at least *one* bowel movement a day (and tens of millions of Americans don't), you're likely to have other health problems along with constipation, such as headaches and fatigue—because stalled fecal matter clogs the colon, overloading the body with toxins, and health-giving nutrients are poorly absorbed.

But reversing constipation can be quick and easy as drinking a glass of water…

➤ **Re-hydrate for softer stools.** "Getting enough water is the number one action to counter constipation," says Metsovas. If you're dehydrated—and many people are—it's more likely your stool will be dry, hard and difficult to pass.

What to do: Drink an eight-ounce glass of water every hour or hour and a half, says Metsovas.

🕐 *Super-Quick Fix*

Also try: "The most important recommendation for regularity is to start every day with a glass of eight to twelve ounces of water, drinking it as fast as you can," says Elizabeth Yarnell, CNC, a certified nutritional consultant in Denver, Colorado (*www.effort lesseating.com*). "Once you get into the routine, you'll have no constipation problems."

> ➤ **Three constipation-curing breakfasts.** "The first dietary change I recommend for my clients with constipation is to eat a breakfast that supplies lots of the naturally occurring fiber necessary for well-formed stools. After about a week or so, nine out of ten of my clients have more bowel movements and are feeling better. At that point, they find they want to add more fiber-rich, constipation-curing fruits, vegetables, beans and whole grains to their diet."

• **Breakfast #1.** She recommends that her constipated clients eat a "Basic Smoothie" for breakfast four times a week.

It consists of a handful of organic fresh or frozen berries; ½ cup plain non-fat, Greek-style yogurt (a creamy, custard-type variety); 1 tablespoon of dried coconut; ½ banana; 1 serving of Hemp Protein Powder; and 1 serving of Detoxifiber (manufactured by Garden of Life).

Put all the ingredients in a blender and mix with water to the desired consistency.

"You can find all these ingredients at most Whole Foods stores, health food stores and online," says Metsovas.

She prefers hemp protein to soy- or whey-based protein powders because the protein in hemp is less processed and more easily absorbed. She recommends Detoxifiber because it supplies a moderate and balanced amount of natural fiber, from flaxseeds, pea hulls, alfalfa and barley leaf and chia seeds.

Red flag: She thinks psyllium seed husks and other fiber supplements commonly used for constipation tend to provide too much fiber too soon—leading to bloating, gas and discomfort— and are too abrasive for the lining of the intestine.

Rapid Resource: You can order Detoxifiber at *www.gardenoflife.com*, or call 866-465-0051.

• **Breakfast #2.** Once or twice a week, she recommends her clients eat a Yogurt Parfait.

It consists of 1 cup unsweetened yogurt with active cultures (lactobacillus acidophilus); a handful of fresh berries; 1 to 2 tablespoons of raw nuts; and 1 to 2 teaspoons of unfiltered, raw honey.

In a cup, layer one-inch of yogurt and top with half the berries and nuts, and then add a second one-inch layer and top with the honey.

Study: Researchers in Argentina studied 266 people with constipation and found that adding an acidophilus-containing yogurt to the diet increased the amount of weekly bowel movements by 17%.

• **Breakfast #3.** Once or twice a week, she recommends her clients have a breakfast of two pieces of toasted Sprouted Ezekiel Bread, with 1 tablespoon of raw almond butter, and a handful of berries or a teaspoon or two of raw honey on the two slices of bread.

She favors this brand of bread because it's high in fiber and the wheat berry hasn't been processed, robbing it of digestion-aiding enzymes.

Study: Doctors in Finland gave 59 people with constipation a regular breakfast of two pieces of fiber-rich bread and a cup of yogurt for three weeks—fiber to speed up and soften bowel movements and lactobacillus-rich yogurt to provide the "friendly" intestinal bacteria that would help decrease possible GI discomfort from an increase in dietary fiber. The addition of fiber increased the number of bowel movements per day and softened stools, and the yogurt reduced bloating, cramping and gas. The doctors recommend fiber-rich bread and lactobacillus-containing yogurt for the treatment of constipation, in the *European Journal of Clinical Nutrition.*

➤ **An apple a day keeps the laxatives away.** Apples contain pectin, a fiber that helps bulk the stool, says Metsovas. She asks her clients to eat two whole pieces of seasonal fruit a day—including one apple.

Other fruits can also help relieve constipation...

• **Mango and papaya.** "You can reverse chronic constipation by eating fresh mango or papaya every day, which function as natural laxatives" says Yarnell. Eat a few slices, or about 1 cup.

🕐 *Super-Quick Fix*

• **Plum juice.** Plum juice is effective in clearing up constipation, according to a study by researchers at the Johns Hopkins Bloomberg School of Public Health. They studied 36 people, dividing them into three groups. For six weeks, one group drank a daily, 8-ounce glass of plum juice (PlumSmart), one group took a psyllium fiber supplement, and one group took a placebo. Within 24 hours, 72% of the plum juice group said they felt "regularity benefits," compared to 50% of the psyllium group and 29% of the placebo group. And those on the plum juice had softer stools than the other two groups.

The daily use of plum juice may be an acceptable and effective treatment for stool softening and immediate relief of constipation symptoms, said the researchers.

• **Prune juice.** "One of the great remedies for constipation is good, old-fashioned prune juice," says Yarnell. "It's just what a lazy colon needs when it's stopped up."

• **Kiwifruit.** Doctors at the Queen Mary Hospital in Hong King gave 33 constipated patients a ripe kiwifruit in the morning after breakfast and in the evening after dinner, for four weeks. More than half of the patients improved, with average bowel movements per week doubled from two to four, and laxative used reduced by 50%.

"Kiwifruit is reported to have a laxative effect and is a good source of dietary fiber," says Annie On On Chan, MD, a gastroenterologist in Taiwan and the lead researcher for the study. "Based on this study, I recommend it to my patients with chronic constipation."

➤ **Take a footstool to the toilet.** "The modern flush toilet—as efficient and sanitary as it may be—forces you to assume a body position that cuts off the downward flow of feces in the colon," says Amil Minocha, MD, a Professor of Medicine at Louisiana State University and author of *Natural Stomach Care* (Avery).

"How did nature intend us to eliminate? By squatting, which relaxes the anal sphincter and allows an easy downward movement of the stool."

What to do: To simulate squatting while sitting on the toilet, Dr. Minocha says to place a foot-high footstool under your feet. "When you attempt to eliminate, bend forward as far as you can comfortably go. Placing a pillow on your thighs to rest your arms makes the forward bend easier and more relaxed. This position is especially useful in cases of chronic constipation."

See Your Doctor If...

Any sudden and unexplained change in bowel habits (*examples* include decreased frequency; a change in stool type, such as pencil-thin stools; new difficulty passing a bowel movement, with pain) could be a sign of a serious disease (such as colon cancer) and should prompt you to see a doctor, says Norton J. Greenberger, MD, Clinical Professor of Medicine at Harvard Medical School and author of *4 Weeks to Healthy Digestion* (McGraw-Hill).

➤ **Break up constipation with a castor oil pack.** "A castor oil pack applied to the lower abdomen can help break up a bad case of constipation," says Yarnell.

How to use: Use an old, unwanted flannel or cotton fabric. Saturate it in castor oil. Place it on the abdomen and cover it with plastic wrap and a heating pad. Keep it on the abdomen for 20 minutes.

Rapid Resource: You can find extensive resources for making and using castor oil packs at *www.baar.com*, under the category, "Castor Oil Therapy."

SPEED LIMIT Stay Away from Stimulant Laxatives

So-called stimulant laxatives that work directly on the intestine—castor oil (taken internally), *cascara sagrada*, senna (Ex-Lax) and *bisacodyl* (Carter's Little Pills)—can be harmful, says Dr. Minocha. That's because regular use can create a condition called "cathartic colon"—the colon wall becomes less responsive to the movements and stimulation of fecal matter, losing its ability to function properly. The result is laxative dependence.

"Except for occasional use in mild, short-term constipation, only use stimulant laxatives under a physician's supervision," says Dr. Minocha.

➤ **For more bowel movements—move your feet.** "Nothing helps constipation like exercise, which also gets the GI tract moving," according to the late Donna DiMarco, CN, a certified nutritionist in Florida and author of *Natural Relief from Constipation* (Keats).

Are you sedentary and don't know how to get started?

"Walk three minutes in one direction, then walk three minutes back," advised DiMarco. "Each day, add another minute, until you are walking twenty or thirty minutes each day. But be sure to get your physician's approval before starting any exercise program."

Study: Researchers in Holland studied 43 people with chronic constipation, dividing them into two groups. One group maintained their current sedentary lifestyle; the other group began to walk for 30 minutes a day. After three months, the walking group had more frequent bowel movements, fewer hard stools, less straining at stool and less incomplete evacuation. "In middle-aged inactive people with symptoms of chronic constipation, it is advisable to promote regular physical activity," say the researchers.

CHRONIC OBSTRUCTIVE PULMONARY DISEASE (COPD)

The Best Ways to Beat Breathlessness

Which diseases kill the most Americans? You can probably name the top three—heart disease, cancer and stroke. But few can name number four... *chronic obstructive pulmonary disease*, or COPD.

COPD kills 120,000 Americans every year—more than accidents, diabetes, Alzheimer's or the flu.

What happens: The airways of the lung are like an upside down tree—the trunk is the *windpipe*, the large branches are tubes called *bronchi* and the twigs are *bronchioles*. At the tip of the bronchioles are tiny air sacs called *alveoli*, where blood vessels shunt oxygen into the bloodstream and carbon dioxide out.

In COPD, airways and air sacs lose their elasticity, like old hoses and balloons…inflamed airway walls thicken, while their cells pump out scads of airway-clogging mucus (sputum) …and the walls of air sacs collapse. (Chronic bronchitis involves the bronchi while emphysema involves the bronchioles and alveoli. Most people with COPD have some degree of both.)

The earliest symptoms of COPD might be a chronic cough and sputum. Later, you may find yourself unexpectedly short of breath while carrying groceries, climbing stairs or going for a brisk walk. As the disease advances, respiratory difficulties can turn into disasters. You wheeze, can't take a deep breath and sometimes feel like you can't breathe at all. Walking across the room is a chore. Eventually, your best friend could be an oxygen tank.

Good news: COPD can't be cured, but it can be contained. "Timely tests, more effective drugs and smarter exercise routines can help you quickly control symptoms, lead an active, healthier life and slow the progress of the disease," says Robert G. Crystal, MD, Chief of the Division of Pulmonary and Critical Care Medicine at New York-Presbyterian Hospital/Weill Cornell Medical Center in New York City.

➤ **Get an early diagnosis.** Your doctor takes your blood pressure, orders a cholesterol test and schedules you for a colonoscopy. But what about spirometry?

Spirometry is a medical test using a spirometer, a breathing device that measures lung capacity (the amount of air lungs can hold) and strength (exhalation speed after taking a deep breath).

"Because the lungs have so much extra capacity and strength, or 'reserve,' the early stages of COPD are often symptom-free—but spirometry can detect the disease," says Dr. Crystal.

Problem: Half of the 24 million Americans with COPD don't know they have the disease. And that's because many primary care physicians don't use spirometry.

New finding: A study in the journal *Chest* of primary care physicians showed that only 22% chose to utilize the test—even in patients with symptoms of COPD. "Primary-care physicians under-diagnose COPD," say the study authors, and spirometry "is underused."

Solution: If you are a current or former smoker (the cause of 90% of all cases of COPD)… if you were exposed for years to secondhand smoke or occupational dust and fumes (other common causes of COPD)…if you have the early symptoms of COPD, such as a chronic cough or increased sputum production…tell your doctor that you want to know if there is any damage to your lungs, and ask for a spirometry and a chest x-ray, says Dr. Crystal.

➤ **The number-one recommendation —quit smoking.** Smoking is the cause of 9 out of 10 cases of COPD—with the remaining 10% probably caused by long-term exposure to secondhand smoke and occupational hazards such as fumes and dust. Quitting smoking is the most important step to slowing COPD and reducing severity.

What to do: Talk to your doctor about the approach that's right for you, says Dr. Crystal. Anti-smoking programs combined with drugs that help you quit have about a 15 to 20% success rate—you may have to try two to three times before quitting for good.

Anti-smoking drugs include the nicotine patch, gum, inhaler or spray, and *bupropion* (Wellbutrin).

➤ **Smokers, eat more broccoli.** The lungs of smokers with COPD fight disease-worsening inflammation with antioxidants that depend on a gene-activating "transcription factor" called

NRF2—and the lower the levels of NRF2 in the lungs, the worse the disease.

Broccoli might increase lung levels of NRF2.

New study: In the lab, researchers at Johns Hopkins Medical School in Boston exposed COPD lung tissue to sulforaphane, a compound in broccoli. It boosted NRF2 levels.

Also helpful: Wasabi—the green horseradish served with sushi—is also rich in sulforaphane.

➤ **Strengthen your breathing muscles.** Strengthening the muscles of breathing is important, particularly in the later stages of COPD, says Dr. Crystal.

New study: Researchers in the Veterans Administration Greater Los Angeles Health Care System studied 40 people with COPD, asking them to practice one of two techniques to improve breathing—either "pursed-lip breathing" or "expiratory muscle training." Those learning pursed-lip breathing had "sustained improvement" in breathlessness during exercise and in overall physical functioning. The researchers reported their findings in the *Journal of Cardiopulmonary Rehabilitation and Prevention*.

What to do: Here are instructions on pursed lip-breathing from the American College of Chest Physicians…

Step 1. Relax your neck and shoulder muscles. Inhale slowly through your nose, and count to two in your head.

Step 2. Pucker your lips as if you are whistling. Exhale slowly and gently through your lips while you count to four or more in your head. Always exhale for longer than you inhale. This allows your lungs to empty more effectively.

Practice this breathing technique until it works well for you, and use it often throughout the day.

➤ **Get more exercise.** Two medical organizations—the American College of Chest

---

Use Your Digestive Tract to Protect Your Lungs

Healthy diets with plenty of antioxidant-rich fruits and vegetables can build healthier, COPD-resistant lungs.

New findings: Researchers in the Department of Nutrition at Harvard Medical School analyzed diet and health data from more than 70,000 women. Those who ate what they called a "prudent pattern" (with plenty of fruit, vegetables, fish and whole-grain products) had a 25% lower risk of developing COPD, while those eating a "Western" pattern (with plenty of refined grains, cured and red meats, desserts and French fries) had a 31% higher risk.

They found similar results when analyzing diet and health data from more than 40,000 men. Those eating a prudent pattern had a 50% lower risk of being diagnosed with COPD, and those eating a Western pattern had a fourfold higher risk of developing COPD. The researchers reported their findings in the *American Journal of Clinical Nutrition*.

Physicians and the American Association of Cardiovascular and Pulmonary Rehabilitation—issued new exercise and lung rehabilitation guidelines for patients with COPD. They recommended a training program including *various* types of exercise, conducted under the supervision and guidance of a pulmonary therapist, to reduce and control breathing difficulties, improve quality of life and decrease the use of medical care and the length of hospital stays. *Among their recommendations…*

• **Lower body training.** Walking or riding a stationary bicycle. Both low- and high-intensity training produces benefits. But the higher the intensity, the greater the benefit.

Benefit: Strengthens leg muscles, to help you move about more easily, for longer periods of time.

- **Upper body training.** Strength-training exercises for the arm and shoulder muscles.

Benefit: Stronger muscles provide more support to the ribcage and improve breathing. Upper body training also decreases the amount of oxygen required for everyday activities, such as carrying groceries, cooking dinner, making the bed, vacuuming, taking a bath or shower, and combing hair.

- **Length of program.** Twelve weeks or more.

Benefit: Programs of six to 12 weeks produce benefits—but only for 12 to 18 months after the program ends. If you want sustained benefits, keep up the exercise.

Rapid Resource: To find an expert in pulmonary rehabilitation near you, contact the American Association of Cardiovascular and Pulmonary Rehabilitation at 312-321-5146, or your local chapter of the American Lung Association. (To find your local chapter, call 800-LUNGUSA, or type in your zip code under "In My Community" at the association's website, *www.lungusa.org.*)

SPEED LIMIT Are Drugs for COPD Safe?

Until recently, there hasn't been much research on the safety of medicine used to treat COPD, says Sonal Singh, MD, assistant professor of internal medicine at Wake Forest University School of Medicine, in Winston-Salem, North Carolina. But Dr. Singh and his colleagues analyzed data from 17 studies on several commonly used drugs, involving nearly 15,000 people—and the results were disturbing.

Daily, long-term use of the drugs *tiotropium* (Spiriva) and *ipratropium* (Atrovent, Combivent)—inhaled *anticholinergic drugs* that relax narrowed, mucus-clogged airways—was linked to a 50% higher risk for heart attacks, strokes and death from cardiovascular diseases.

Researchers at Northwestern University's Feinberg School of Medicine also looked at studies on ipratropium, and found that men using the drug were 34% more likely to die of a heart attack or arrhythmia (irregular heartbeat).

Meanwhile, another analysis of 18 studies, involving 17,000 people, linked the regular use of inhaled corticosteroids (found in combination with a bronchodilator, in drugs such as Advair and Symbicort) to a 60 to 70% increased risk for pneumonia.

"COPD patients who use the inhalers Spiriva, Atrovent and Combivent are at a high risk of heart attacks, strokes and death from heart disease," says Dr. Singh. "Patients and their doctors should decide whether these serious, long-term cardiovascular risks are an acceptable tradeoff in return for their symptomatic benefits. And doctors need to closely monitor patients with COPD who are taking these drugs, for the development of cardiovascular events."

Better: Dr. Singh suggests that you talk to your doctor about using a long-acting beta-agonist drug, such as *salmeterol* (Serevent) or *formoterol* (Foradil). These drugs, commonly prescribed for severe asthma, may work just as well for controlling the symptoms of COPD—and be a lot safer.

DEPRESSION

Every year, 13 to 14 million American adults suffer from a "major depressive disorder." *Maybe you are one of them...*

For several weeks or months, you feel depressed—sad or empty inside—most of the day, nearly every day. You lose pleasure in everyday activities...can't concentrate or think clearly...are indecisive...feel worthless and guilty...and may even imagine killing yourself. With other depressive symptoms, you're at one or the other end of the spectrum of sorrow—you have no appetite or you binge, losing or gaining a lot of weight...you can't sleep or sleep 10 hours a day...you're hyperactive or slow as a slug. You might not have all of those symptoms, but you have most of them.

Millions of other Americans suffer regularly from "minor" depression, with two or three of those symptoms.

Major or minor, depression takes a toll—and not just psychological. Scientists with the World Health Organization say depression is more damaging to health than angina, arthritis, diabetes or asthma.

Example: Scientists from Holland analyzed data from 28 studies and found that depression was linked to a 60% higher risk for heart attack. In fact, they found depression was *the most important risk factor* for developing heart disease.

Obviously, treatment is a must for so troubling a condition. And every year, doctors write more than 170 million prescriptions for antidepressant drugs. Unfortunately, those drugs often have side effects, including GI upset, headaches, nervousness, unwanted weight gain and sexual dysfunction. And they may not even work.

The actual benefit of antidepressant drugs is significantly less than is generally believed and only slightly greater than placebo, concluded a team of scientists in the *New England Journal of Medicine* in 2008, after reviewing 74 studies on the medications.

"Antidepressants should be used *rarely*, and generally for brief periods, in occasional life-threatening emergencies or when all other less potentially harmful approaches have been tried for a reasonable period and have been found wanting," says psychiatrist James Gordon, MD, the founder and director of the Center for Mind-Body Medicine in Washington, DC, and author of *Unstuck: Your Guide to the Seven-Stage Journey Out of Depression* (Penguin).

What *should* you do if you're depressed?

Seek out competent psychological guidance, says Dr. Gordon. And also consider using non-drug approaches, including nutrition and supplements, exercise and self-expression.

You might be surprised at how fast those approaches can work...

► **Use "behavioral activation" to overcome depression—step by step.** You stopped returning phone calls from friends. You stay in bed longer. You miss a lot of work. You're depressed. But rather than waiting to feel motivated to become more social...and get out of bed earlier...and go to work...commit yourself to carrying out specific actions, says Christopher Martell, PhD, a psychologist in private practice in Seattle (*www.christopher martell.com*), clinical associate professor at the University of Washington and coauthor of *Overcoming Depression One Step at a Time: The New Behavioral Activation Approach to Getting Your Life Back* (New Harbinger).

"Behavioral activation is committing to a depression-defeating action—even if you don't feel motivated to do it," says Dr. Martell. "You may not feel like going for a walk, but if you take

Speed Healing Success

Get It Done—Even When You're Depressed

Julie Fast has coauthored five books on bipolar disorder and depression that have sold tens of thousands of copies. But that doesn't mean she's not depressed.

"When you hear about my career accomplishments, you might think I no longer have depression—and that's why I can write and work successfully," she says. "Unfortunately, that's not the case. I'm still depressed more than I'm well. However, I've learned to *work through* my depression instead of letting my depression rob me of my ability to work or otherwise get things done. Depression may take over my mind, but it doesn't have to take over my actions."

Here are several strategies Fast has found effective for getting things done despite her mood...

- *Don't wait until you want to do something.* "Many people equate depression with the inability to work," she says. "In reality, the problem is often the inability to feel like working. After years of waiting for the elusive good feeling that comes with wanting to do something, I finally accepted the fact that I've never wanted to do certain things when I'm depressed and I never will. So I try to do them anyway."

- *Think like an athlete.* "How does a tennis player go to Wimbledon and play even when she's not at her best mentally? How does a baseball player play so many games in a season without taking a break? I think it's their ability to just do the physical and keep the mental thoughts on the physical game. They have to push aside doubt, pain and fear and just keep going. I try to do this when I'm faced with a physical task that I have to get done."

- *Feel the depression...and do it anyway.* "I wrote all my books while I was battling depression—sometimes I was even suicidal. What were my options? Twenty more years of not really getting anything done? Twenty more years of starting a project and quitting before I was even halfway through? I'd had enough of that. I still have days when nothing gets done—but I also know that these days make me feel terrible. So as much as possible I make myself work, even when it feels impossible."

a walk in spite of how you feel, you may improve your mood."

What helps: Break up actions into *small steps*, says Dr. Martell. "Say you've been getting out of bed at 10:00 A.M., so you decide to get up at 6:00 A.M. Well, that's not likely to occur. Instead, break the action down into small steps. Try to get up at 9:45 A.M. a couple of days during the week. Once you're doing that, get up at 9:30 A.M. In other words, take small, doable steps with a high likelihood of success.

"Set a limit on what you're going to accomplish, so that it's actually doable instead of having the continual experience of failing because you're trying to do too much—a common experience among those who are depressed."

One key to this process is to learn how to accomplish *short-term goals*, says Dr. Martell. *There are six manageable steps to reach short-term goals...*

One: Clearly define the goal. *Example:* Clean out the basement.

Two: Identify the steps necessary to achieve the goal. *Example:* Wash the floor and walls; clean windows; have a garage sale; buy a dehumidifier; open all the boxes, look through everything, sort into piles to throw away, keep, or sell; move piles to one side of basement.

Three: Arrange the steps in logical order. *Example:* 1. Open all the boxes, etc.; 2. Move piles, etc.; 3. Wash floors, etc.; 4. Have a garage sale; 5. Buy a dehumidifier.

Four: Make a commitment to each step. *Example:* Initial commitment to step 1: Spend one hour, from eight to nine each night for the next three nights, sorting things in the basement into piles.

Five: Take the step, no matter what your mood is like.

Six: Pat yourself on the back after each step is completed.

"You are not doomed to live life simply reacting to every mood you have," says Dr. Martell. "Making and pursuing goals, rather than allowing your moods to determine your behavior, is one of the effective ways to end your depression."

➤ **Nutrients to treat a happiness deficiency.** "There are many causes of depression, including stress, hormonal imbalances and genetic predisposition," says Alan C. Logan, ND, a naturopathic physician in New York and author of *The Brain Diet* (Cumberland). "But for many years, the *nutritional* cause has been overlooked—the fact that low blood levels of many individual nutrients can worsen depression, and that increasing your intake of those nutrients can help relieve the problem, and even boost the effectiveness of antidepressant medications."

How they work: The nutrients aid the function of *neurotransmitters*, brain chemicals that control mood.

If you're depressed, Dr. Logan recommends you consider increasing your intake of the following vitamins and minerals...

• **Folate—stopping relapse.** Studies show that adults with depression have blood levels

of the B-vitamin folate about 25% lower than those without depression. Blood levels of folate also predict whether antidepressant therapies will work—people on antidepressants with low blood folate levels had a 43% rate of relapse, compared to 3.2% for those with highest blood levels.

• **Vitamin B-12—helping depressed seniors.** Older adults with B-12 deficiency are 70% more likely to have severe depressive symptoms than those with normal levels, says Dr. Logan.

• **Zinc—boosting the power of antidepressants.** Low levels of zinc have been linked to low moods, he says. And research shows that adding 25 milligrams (mg) of zinc to an antidepressant regimen boosts the effectiveness of the drug.

• **Vitamin D—good for the winter blues.** A study showed that supplementing the diet with 400 to 800 IU of vitamin D improved mood during the winter months, says Dr. Logan. People taking the nutrient were more enthusiastic, motivated and alert.

• **Chromium—calming carbohydrate cravings.** Four studies show that supplementation with the trace mineral chromium improves the symptoms of depression, including carbohydrate craving and bingeing.

• **Selenium—beating depression *and* anxiety.** Studies have linked low blood levels of selenium to lowered mood states, and also show that supplementing with selenium improves the symptoms of depression (and anxiety).

Product: Dr. Logan recommends the supplement Multi+ Daily Joy, from Genuine Health (*www.genuinehealth.com*), which was formulated to supply therapeutic levels of all these nutrients.

➤ **A "brighter" brain—with omega-3 fatty acids.** The premier nutrient for preventing and treating depression isn't a vitamin or mineral. It's a fat—specifically, the omega-3 fatty acids found in fatty fish such as salmon, tuna and mackerel.

Standout scientific evidence: "The evidence for omega-3 in the treatment of depression is substantial," says Carol Locke, MD, a psychiatrist in Lincoln, Massachusetts.

• People living in countries where seafood is rarely eaten have a 65-fold greater risk of developing depression.

• Researchers in Taiwan analyzed 10 studies in which omega-3 was used to treat depression. They found "a significant antidepressant effect," with omega-3 supplements improving the condition by 69%.

• The same analysis found that omega-3 improved the symptoms of bipolar disorder (manic-depression) by 69%.

• Studies show that when pregnant women take omega-3 supplements during pregnancy, depression during and after pregnancy (postpartum) is reduced by 50%.

• A study showed that suicidal thinking was dramatically reduced among depressed people taking omega-3.

All of that evidence and more led the American Psychiatric Association to recommend *everyone* eat fish three times a week. They also concluded that an omega-3 supplement of 1 to 3 grams may be useful in treating depression and other "mood disorders" (such as anxiety).

Why it works: Without omega-3, the outer covering of brain cells (neurons) degenerates. With too little omega-3, neurons generate less *serotonin,* a neurotransmitter that helps control mood. The cellular receptors for *dopamine*— another neurotransmitter linked to mood— become malformed. *Dendrites,* the branching extensions that channel messages into and out of the cell, have fewer branches. And there are fewer *synapses,* the bridges between cells. In other words, an omega-3 deficiency is a sad story for your brain cells—and your mood.

Do You Have GOMS? (Grumpy Old Man Syndrome)

"Around middle-age, a man's testosterone levels start to go down—and so does his mood," says Dr. Locke. "But most of those men don't seek out treatment for depression. They assume, 'This is the way I am. I can't feel any better than this.' "

Your life might look something like this…

You feel grouchy. You can't concentrate as well. You're not as energetic. Your sleep is poor. You eat too much. Your libido drops. If you're retired, you might spend a lot of time watching TV. You'd rather stay at home than go out and you lose your social connections. You also lose your confidence—and your self-esteem.

Dr. Locke calls this condition GOMS—the Grumpy Old Man Syndrome. "It's important to reach these men and let them know, 'You can feel better—you can feel as positive and energetic as you used to feel.' " The two keys are omega-3 supplements and regular exercise.

These two lifestyle changes can dramatically improve mood and the symptoms of depression, she says. "They work together in the brain to generate the growth factors and proteins that help neurons work efficiently."

Product: There are two omega-3 fatty acids —EPA (eicosapentaenoic acid) and DHA (docosahexaenoic acid). Research indicates that an omega-3 combination with high doses of EPA is the most effective at alleviating the symptoms of depression. The omega-3 supplement OmegaBrite has been formulated to supply the quantity of EPA that can combat depression, says Dr. Locke.

Recommendation: For maintaining a positive mood even if you're not depressed, she recommends four capsules a day, with a total dose of 2,000 mg of omega-3s. "A lot of people who

Easing Your Depression with Paper and Pen

"I wouldn't have recovered from depression without my medical treatment, but I think creative writing was crucial in my healing as well," says Elizabeth Maynard Schaefer, PhD. So much so that she also started a writing class for depressed people, which meets at Stanford University (now in its 11th year) and wrote a book about writing and depression—*Writing Through the Darkness: Easing Your Depression with Paper and Pen* (Celestial Arts). Writing can help with depression in a number of ways, she says.

It can help you manage and organize your thoughts…create a plan for your treatment…help you become aware of and release difficult emotions…increase your acceptance of yourself and your life…lead to a sense of personal satisfaction, as you fill the page with words…give you a greater sense of purpose and meaning in life…and (studies show) even decrease the physical impact of stress and boost your immune system.

Here are Dr. Schaefer's tips for getting started…

- *Start out slow, writing for just a few minutes.* You could describe how you're feeling that day. *Important:* You might find yourself feeling a little bit sadder immediately after you write, as you consider your situation, but happier later.

- *Don't wait for the mood to strike you—just write.* After the first sentence or so, barriers tend to break down—and you may even find that you've written for 15 minutes or more.

- *Write several times a week.* But don't be hard on yourself. If you don't write one day, do it the next.

- *Write continuously.* Don't stop to think about the next word or sentence. Keep the pencil or pen going and write "as you go" rather than trying to construct a careful sequence, argument or narrative.

- *Branch out.* Instead of writing about how you feel today, consider writing about how you feel about your medicines. Or write about something other than your depression—your kitchen, your childhood, your thoughts and feelings about the color orange. *Important:* If a topic feels threatening, don't write about it—instead, discuss it with a therapist or friend.

"Creative outlets—whether it is writing, painting, dancing or making music—are an important component of healing from depression," says Dr. Schaefer.

Rapid Resource: You can find the author's blog on writing and depression at her website, *www.writingthroughthedarkness.com.*

don't think they are depressed feel better on four a day," she says. For depression, she recommends four to six a day. If you have been diagnosed with major depression or bipolar disorder, she recommends six to eight a day.

Smart idea: For best absorption, take the supplement with food.

Rapid Resource: To order Omega-Brite, visit *www.omegabrite.com* or call 800-383-2030. Address: Omega Natural Science, Inc., 8275 S. Eastern Ave., Suite 121, Las Vegas, NV 89123; e-mail: *updates@OmegaBrite.com.*

What most people don't know: "You may have heard that people on blood-thinning medications such as Coumadin or aspirin shouldn't take omega-3," says Dr. Locke. "And that the supplement shouldn't be taken before surgery, because of the risk of increased bleeding.

"But omega-3s *balance* the body and help regulate the clotting of blood," she says. "Yes, talk to your doctor before taking omega-3—but it's *not* contraindicated for people who take blood-thinning medications or for those about to have surgery. In fact, taking the supplement before surgery helps protect brain cells from anesthesia and decreases the risk of post-surgical infection."

➤ **St. John's Wort works.** "This well-known herbal antidepressant has received a lot of both positive and negative press over the last few years," says Dr. Logan. "Some studies support the botanical and some don't."

Recent development: In a review of 29 studies on St. John's Wort, involving 5,489 people, researchers found that the herb effectively treats the symptoms of major depression—in fact, just as effectively as medication, and with fewer side effects.

Product: "The brand of choice is Perika by Nature's Way, because it contains the St. John's Wort extract used in clinical studies," says Dr. Logan. The dose is typically 300 mg three times a day.

Red flag: St. John's Wort can speed up the elimination of medications from the body, says Dr. Logan. Used with an antidepressant, it can cause *serotonin syndrome,* an excess of serotonin that can trigger severe physical, mental and emotional symptoms. Use it only with the approval and supervision of your physician.

DIABETES

Dissolving the Sugar Disease

Blood sugar (glucose) is the primary fuel that powers cells. A normal fasting blood sugar level (measured in the morning after eight hours without eating) is below 100 milligrams per deciliter (mg/dL).

The problem: Nearly 24 million Americans (more than half of them over 60) have type 2 diabetes—the pancreas no longer manufactures sufficient insulin, the glucose-regulating hormone, and fasting blood sugar levels rise above 125 mg/dL. Another 57 million Americans have *prediabetes,* which is often related to insulin resistance—muscle, fat and liver cells no longer respond correctly to insulin, and fasting blood sugar levels to 100 to 125 mg/dL.

High blood sugar isn't sweet to your health.

Prediabetes and diabetes damage arteries, increasing your risk of heart disease and stroke two- to fourfold.

Developing diabetes before the age of 65 more than doubles your risk for Alzheimer's disease.

Diabetes is also the leading cause of blindness, from damaged blood vessels in the eyes... kidney failure, from diabetes-caused high blood pressure and damage to the kidneys...and non-traumatic amputation of lower limbs, as chronic foot ulcers, caused and complicated by poor circulation, progress to gangrene.

Writing in the *Journal of the American Medical Association,* experts from the government's Centers for Disease Control and Prevention estimate that a diagnosis of diabetes in a 40-year-old man shortens his normal life expectancy by 12 years, while a diagnosis in a 40-year-old woman shortens hers by 14 years.

What most people don't know: Everyone who develops diabetes is genetically predisposed to the disease, says Anne Peters, MD, professor of medicine at the University of Southern California, director of the USC Clinical Diabetes Programs and author of *Conquering Diabetes: A Complete Program for Prevention and Treatment* (Plume). But overweight and a sedentary lifestyle activate those genes. As the number of overweight people in America shot up in the past decade, so has the number of people with diabetes—by 90%. That's nearly twice as many people with the disease as 10 years ago.

Good news: You're not doomed to diabetes. *Research shows there are simple, speedy ways to prevent, control or even reverse the disease...*

⏱ *Super-Quick Fix*

➤ **Exercise four minutes a week.** "The risk of developing type 2 diabetes is substantially reduced through regular physical activity," says Professor James Timmons, at Heriot-Watt University in Edinburgh, Scotland. "Unfortunately, many people feel they simply don't have the time to follow current exercise guidelines of performing moderate to vigorous aerobic and resistance exercise for several *hours* every week. What we have found is that doing a few intense muscle exercises, each lasting only about thirty *seconds*, dramatically improves your insulin and glucose metabolism in just two weeks. You can do these exercises without even breaking a sweat."

The study: Professor Timmons and his colleagues asked 16 healthy but out-of-shape young men to exercise two days a week on a stationary bicycle, four times a day, in intense spurts of 30 seconds.

After two weeks, the men had a 23% improvement in how effectively insulin was clearing glucose out of their bloodstreams. In short, that seemingly tiny amount of exercise made them significantly less likely to become diabetic. Professor Timmons called the results, which appeared in the journal *BioMed Central Endocrine Disorders*, "remarkable."

Why it works: "This study looked at the way we break down glycogen—the glucose that's stored in the muscles," Professor Timmons told the BBC. "Think about diabetes this way—glucose is circulating in the blood rather than being stored in the muscles, where it belongs. If we take glycogen out of the muscles through exercise, then the muscles draw in that excess glucose from the blood. But if you go for a walk or a jog, you *don't* deplete the glycogen in your muscles. The only way to use up that stored glycogen is through intense contractions of the muscles—the type of exercise used in our study.

"If we can get people doing these exercises twice a week, it can have a very dramatic effect on the prevalence of diabetes."

And even though his research was on young men, he says this type of exercise will work for people of all ages, and for both men and women.

What to do: With your doctor's approval, ride on an exercise bike four times a day, each time performing a quick sprint at the highest possible intensity, for 30 seconds. Do this two times a week. Running in short sprints would also work, says Professor Timmons.

"This novel approach may make it easier for you to find time to exercise and lead a healthier life."

➤ **The fast-action food habits that make the biggest difference.** "If you commit to just a few good dietary habits that become part of your everyday lifestyle, you can control diabetes," says Johanna Burani, a registered dietician, certified diabetes educator and author of *Good Carbs, Bad Carbs* (Marlowe & Company). Take your pick...

• **Eat more fruits and vegetables.** Researchers in England studied more than 21,000 people for 12 years and found that those who had the highest blood levels of vitamin C from eating fruits and vegetables had a 62% lower risk of developing diabetes.

Also, scientists in England found that people eating diets emphasizing *low calorie density* foods (watery, high-fiber foods such as fruits and vegetables that fill you up while delivering few calories) had a 60% lower risk of developing diabetes, compared with people eating *high calorie density foods* such as meat, processed foods and soft drinks.

Similarly, researchers at the University of Pennsylvania found that emphasizing low calorie density foods is the best way to lose weight—a crucial factor in preventing and controlling diabetes.

- **Eat regular meals.** Swedish scientists studied more than 4,000 people aged 60 and older and found that those who regularly ate breakfast, lunch and dinner were 34% less likely to develop prediabetes compared to those with irregular eating habits.

- **Eat a handful of nuts.** Eating a handful of "tree nuts" (almonds, Brazils, cashews, hazelnuts, pecans, pine nuts, pistachios, macadamias and walnuts) five times a week may reduce the risk of diabetes by 27%, say Harvard researchers.

➤ **Diabetes-beating vitamins and minerals.** A range of vitamins and minerals are necessary to prevent and reduce the damage from diabetes, says Jacob Teitelbaum, MD, a naturally oriented physician in Hawaii (*www.endfatigue.com*) and author of *Pain Free 1-2-3* (McGraw-Hill). *Here are the most important...*

- **Magnesium.** In an analysis of studies involving nearly 300,000 people, researchers found that for every 100 milligram (mg) increase in the intake of magnesium, the risk of diabetes decreased by 17%.

Best food sources: Nuts, beans, whole grains, green leafy vegetables.

- **Vitamin D.** In a 22-year study from Finland of nearly 1,000 people, those with the highest blood levels of vitamin D were 72% less likely to develop diabetes than those with the lowest levels.

What to do: Taking a daily vitamin D supplement of at least 1,000 IU is the easiest and most reliable way to maintain healthy blood levels of vitamin D, says Michael Holick, MD, PhD, director of the Vitamin D, Skin and Bone Research Laboratory at Boston University.

- **Zinc.** Harvard researchers analyzed diet and health data in more than 82,000 women and

---

The Anti-Diabetes Diet That Works (But Not Like Magic)

There is no "magic" diet for diabetes, says Dr. Peters. Rather, you should follow the principles of healthy eating, she says.

- *Minimize refined carbs and starches,* such as sugar, white flour and potatoes.
- *Eat plenty of fruits, vegetables, legumes and whole grains.*
- *Eat balanced meals,* with half of calories from vegetables and salad, one-quarter from grains and other unrefined carbohydrates, and one-quarter from protein and fat. *Example:* A large green salad mixed with ½ cup of brown rice and two ounces of fish.

---

found that those with the highest dietary intake of this mineral were 28% less likely to develop diabetes.

What to do: "Snack on zinc-rich smoked oysters on whole wheat crackers," suggests Jennifer Adler, MS, CN, a Seattle-based certified nutritionist, natural foods chef and adjunct faculty member at Bastyr University. *Other good food sources:* Oysters have four times more zinc than any other food, but other good sources include shrimp, beef, turkey, pumpkin seeds, whole wheat and chickpeas.

- **Vitamin K.** Researchers at the Jean Mayer USDA Human Nutrition Research Center at Tufts University studied 355 people without diabetes aged 60 to 80, dividing them into two groups. One group received a daily vitamin K supplement; the other group received a placebo. Those receiving vitamin K had a significant improvement in insulin sensitivity—the ability of insulin to move blood sugar out of the bloodstream and into cells.

Suggested intake: 500 micrograms (mcg) per day in supplement form. Vitamin K supplements are widely available.

⏰ *Super-Quick Fix*

➤ **Stop after-meal grogginess—with Vitamins C and E.** For people with diabetes, it's not uncommon to experience "brain fog" for several hours after a high-fat meal, with memory loss and other cognitive problems.

"Consuming unhealthy meals for those with diabetes can temporarily worsen underlying memory problems," says Michael Herman Chui, in the Department of Nutrition Sciences at the University of Toronto.

But in a study conducted by Chui and his colleagues, people with diabetes took high doses of two antioxidant vitamins (1,000 mg of vitamin C and 800 IU of vitamin E) along with a high-fat meal. They had normal recall 90 minutes later—while another group with diabetes who ate the same high-fat meal but didn't get the nutrients performed poorly on memory tests.

How they work: High-fat foods such as those used in the study—pastry, whipped cream and cheddar cheese—trigger the production of free radicals, unstable molecules that damage brain tissue one to three hours after a meal. Antioxidants protect the brain.

➤ **The best sweetener for diabetes.** Date sugar, says Kalidas Shetty of the University of Massachusetts. Along with her colleagues from the University of San Paolo in Brazil, she tested the antioxidant content of dozens of sweeteners, from white sugar to maple syrup, publishing the results in the *Journal of Medicinal Food*.

"Depending on their origin and grade of refining, many sweeteners contain significant amounts of antioxidants, which have the

potential to control diabetes-linked high blood pressure and heart disease," says Shetty.

Example: Dark brown sugar contained 4,741 mcg per gram of phenolic compounds (the same plant chemicals that give red wine and tea their heart-healthy benefits), compared to 18 mcg for white sugar.

They also tested the sugars to see which inhibited an enzyme (alpha-glucosidase) that can raise blood sugar levels. The winner was date sugar, which inhibited the enzyme by 75%.

"These results indicate that a smart choice of dietary sweeteners—especially less refined sugars close to the original nature of the ingredients found in whole plants—may help you manage type 2 diabetes and its complications, such as high blood pressure and heart disease," says Shetty.

➤ **The best way to stick with a diabetes diet—don't follow any rules.** You've been diagnosed with diabetes. You've been told to follow a glucose-controlling diet and were handed a list of foods you should and shouldn't eat. Needless to say, you've very motivated to stay on the diet because you're worried about your health. And you do manage to "be good" for a few weeks. But like most people, your willpower has limits. And pretty soon you're eating the same foods you ate before you had diabetes. In fact, you felt so frustrated by all the dietary restrictions that now you're eating more "bad" foods. Is there a way out of this vicious, health-destroying cycle?

Yes, says Michelle May, MD, a family physician in Phoenix, Arizona, and author of *Eat What You Love, Love What You Eat: How to Break Your Eat-Repent-Repeat Cycle* (Greenleaf Book Group). The key to eating a healthful, diabetes-controlling diet is what she calls *mindful eating.* It's about freedom rather than rules...insight rather than willpower...self-nourishment rather than self-punishment.

Here are some of the strategies for mindful eating that Dr. May has used with thousands of people who have struggled to lose weight and control diabetes...

- **Before you eat, ask yourself this key question.** "People eat for reasons other than hunger," explains Dr. May. "Often the cues are emotional, such as loneliness, depression, anxiety, stress or boredom. These cues override our *internal* cues of hunger and fullness. You're likely to eat comforting, convenient, calorie-dense, highly palatable foods loaded with fat and refined carbohydrates—the foods that are the least helpful for a person with diabetes. And because you're not hungry when you *start* to eat, you don't know when to stop. You eat until the food is gone."

Being told to go on a "diabetic diet"—or any diet—ignores those underlying cues, she says. "Put aside any and all dietary rules about what to eat and what not to eat—they've never worked and they never will!" says Dr. May. *Instead, ask yourself this simple question before you eat...*

Why am I eating?

"Put a speed bump—a pause—between the desire to eat and the act of eating," says Dr. May. "Take a moment to realize what's *really* going on—whether you're physically hungry or responding to an emotional cue. If you discover you're not hungry, make a choice whether to use food to deal with something that isn't a physical need for food, or to redirect your attention to something else until you're actually hungry.

- **Learn to recognize the physical signs of hunger.** But how can you tell whether or not you're hungry? Dr. May says to "scan" your body—particularly your stomach—for physical signs.

"Get quiet for a moment. Scan your body from head to toe. Look for clues that your desire to eat *isn't* hunger—such as tension in your body, or pain, or worried thoughts. Also look for clues that your desire to eat is hunger—such as a hollow or empty feeling in your stomach, or rumbling and growling."

Best: Do this "scanning" whenever you feel like eating and also about every three hours, to see if you're truly hungry and need to eat.

- **Distract yourself.** If you're not hungry, one strategy is to distract yourself rather than eat, says Dr. May. Go for a walk. Pet your dog. Take a shower. Brush your teeth. Do your nails.

Or, if you've identified the underlying emotional need that you're using food to satisfy—meet the need instead, in a little way.

"Maybe you're overworked and stressed out and you need a vacation," says Dr. May. Take a few minutes to surf online and look at a travel site, or visualize being on vacation and resting in a hammock, or take a few deep breaths.

- **Learn to recognize when you feel full.** Being able to decide not to eat when you're not hungry is one feature of mindful eating. Deciding to stop eating when you're comfortably full is another.

"Mindful eating is not about *being good* but about *feeling good*," says Dr. May. "By identifying your signs of fullness—and stopping when you're comfortable—you'll have much better blood sugar control."

Smart idea: "Set an intention before you eat," says Dr. May. "Ask yourself, 'How do I want to feel when I'm done?' You probably want to feel good, energetic and satisfied—not bad, tired and stuffed."

- **Don't be a yo-yo—be a pendulum.** "Many of us are yo-yo dieters—we're wound up tight like a yo-yo, either up or down, on or off the diet, restricting ourselves or overeating" says Dr. May. "It's healthier to be like a pendulum—with a gentle arc in the middle."

Example: On a cruise ship, at the Midnight Chocolate Buffet, you enjoy a few bites of a few different things rather than gorging yourself.

Speedy Success

"I Knew My Life Depended On My Next Choice"

Sam Hoover, a 54-year-old from Oregon, was in trouble. He had been feeling bad for a long time—tired, peppered with aches and pains, his vision blurry, sick. Then things went from bad to worse—he was terribly thirsty all the time, urinated frequently and his eyesight dimmed. He went in for a blood test.

The dreadful result: His fasting blood sugar was over 400 (below 100 is normal) and his A1C (a measure of long-term blood sugar control) was 12.6% (more than double the normal level). In fact, his results were so bad that the hospital called him, told him he had advanced diabetes and to go straightaway to an urgent care center—where he was immediately put on twice-a-day injections of insulin.

"My dad had passed away from complications with diabetes, and I saw myself following in his footsteps," says Hoover. "But I refused to lay down and be a victim. I started to research diabetes to find out all I could. And I quickly discovered stories of not only *controlling* the disease but reversing it—with a low-fat, meatless vegan diet! I knew my life depended on my next choice. I purchased a book about the vegan diet—*Dr. Neal Barnard's Program for Reversing Diabetes* (Rodale)—and was prepared to suffer whatever I had to in order to save myself."

But, says Hoover, he didn't suffer at all. Instead, he discovered an "exciting new world" of eating right, feeling good and becoming healthier—and happier—than he had ever been.

The low-fat, meatless "vegan" diet Hoover went on had bested the standard American Diabetes Association in a 22-week head-to-head test, published in the journal *Diabetes Care*. Those on the vegan diet lost more weight, saw a bigger drop in A1C and had a greater reduction in the dosages of their glucose-controlling medications.

The vegan diet used in the study consists of no animal products (meat, poultry, fish, dairy, eggs)...a bare minimum of fat from high-fat vegetable foods such as avocados, olive oil, nuts and seeds...no carbohydrates high on the "glycemic index" (a measurement of how fast carbohydrates digest)...no foods with white sugar or white flour, no cold cereals (except for bran cereals)...no pineapples or watermelons, and no big baking potatoes. It emphasizes the "four new food groups"—vegetables, fruits, wholegrains and legumes. And it includes no caloriecounting—you can eat as much as you like of the foods allowed.

"The diet saved my life, plain and simple," says Hoover. "My A1C is now seven point two. My blood sugar levels have dropped to a normal range between meals. I am off insulin shots and on oral medication. My weight is steadily decreasing. And I have been telling everyone I meet about my life-changing experience."

"It's so much easier to manage blood glucose when you have a smaller arc of behavior," says Dr. May

"But mindful eating is not about being in control or out of control, she emphasizes. "It's about being *in charge*, so you get to make choices about what you want to do."

Rapid Resource: You can find out more about Dr. May's mindful eating program for diabetes and overweight at *www.amIhungry.com*. The site includes Dr. May's blog, books by her and others about mindful eating, as well as information about her workshops and seminars. Address: Am I Hungry?, P.O. Box 93686, Phoenix, AZ 85070, call 480-704-7811 or e-mail *MMay@AmIHungry.com*.

➤ **Herbs that help.** Three herbs can increase insulin sensitivity and are "very helpful" in the management of diabetes, says John Neustadt, ND, a naturopathic physician in private practice in Bozeman, Montana (*www.mon tanaim.com*).

• **Fenugreek.** This herb was used by healers in ancient Egypt, Rome, China and India—and is used today around the world. "Fenugreek helps control blood sugar by stimulating the release of insulin," says Dr. Neustadt.

Standout scientific evidence: More than 70 scientific studies on fenugreek and diabetes have shown that the herb can balance daily blood sugar levels…lower A1C, a measure of long-term blood sugar control…increase enzymes that help regulate blood sugar…activate insulin signaling in fat cells and liver cells…lower total cholesterol and increase HDL cholesterol, decreasing the risk of heart disease, which kills 70% of those with diabetes…and slow diabetic retinopathy, eye damage that can lead to blindness.

Product: "For people with diabetes, I recommend Fen-Gre from Standard Process," says Thomas Von Ohlen, MS, CN, former director of the Advanced Center for Nutrition in Fairfield, Connecticut. He suggests a 270 mg capsule, taken twice a day, with the approval and supervision of a physician. Fen-Gre is available online from *www.standardprocess.com*, or call 800-558-8740.

• **Gymnema.** This herb (*Gymnema sylvestre*) from India is also called *gur-mar* or "sugar destroyer," says Dr. Neustadt. It reduces blood glucose and stimulates insulin secretion.

Study: Indian doctors gave an extract of the herb to 22 people with type 2 diabetes—after 20 months, five of them were able to discontinue their diabetes medication. The herb may regenerate the insulin-generating cells of the pancreas, say the doctors, in the *Journal of Ethnopharmacology*.

Product: Gymnema is widely available. As with all herbs and nutritional supplements, use

Smart Ways to Manage Your Medication

The best way to control type 2 diabetes is with a healthy diet and regular exercise, says Dr. Peters.

Trap: People newly diagnosed with type 2 diabetes *intend* to control the disease with lifestyle changes, but studies show many are unsuccessful. Meanwhile, the disease may remain untreated and worsen.

Better: The American Diabetes Association now recommends that people newly diagnosed with diabetes use lifestyle modification *and* an oral diabetes medication (*metformin*) to control high blood sugar.

Medications for diabetes can help control the disease but they can also harm you—a fact demonstrated by research showing that Avandia (*rosiglitazone*), an oral medication commonly prescribed for diabetes, can increase the risk of heart attack by 42% and double the risk of heart failure.

Smart idea: Used appropriately, and in conjunction with a healthy lifestyle, most drugs are generally well tolerated, says Dr. Peters. Know the risks and benefits of every drug you take—and how to minimize the risks. (For more information, please see the section "Drug Side Effects," on page 111.) *Example:* If you are taking Avandia and notice that your ankles are swollen or that you are short of breath—signs of a possible heart problem—inform your doctor immediately. Your physician may switch you to another drug, or decrease the dose and add another diabetes drug to your regimen.

it only with the approval and supervision of a qualified health professional.

• **Banaba.** This southeast Asian plant increases the ability of the body to use the insulin it naturally produces, says Dr. Neustadt.

See Your Doctor If...

New research from the Centers for Disease Control and Prevention shows that 40% of people with diabetes are *undiagnosed*. And only 4% of the tens of millions of Americans with prediabetes know they have it!

"Most people who have prediabetes or diabetes have no symptoms," says Dr. Peters.

However, the more risk factors you have, the more likely you are to have prediabetes or diabetes. *Those risk factors are...*

- *Overweight,* with most of the weight around your middle

- *All or partially of African American, Latino, American Indian, Asian or Pacific Island origin*

- *Older than 45*

- *A family history of type 2 diabetes* (parent, grandparent or child)

- *High blood pressure*

- *Heart attack*

- *Triglyceride (a blood fat) above 150 mg/dL*

- *Low HDL* (less than 40 mg/dL in a male, less than 50 mg/dL in a female)

- *Previous gestational diabetes,* or a baby weighing more than 9 pounds

- *Impaired glucose tolerance or prediabetes*

- *Polycystic ovarian syndrome (PCOS)*

- *Rarely or never exercise*

"If you have any one of those risk factors, have a screening test for prediabetes and diabetes, particularly if you are over age forty-five or have a family history of the disease," says Dr. Peters.

Problem: You can have prediabetes or diabetes without any of these risk factors.

Solution: "The best way to find out if you have the problem is to ask your doctor for a fasting blood sugar test and then to follow your blood sugar level every year to be sure it remains normal," says Dr. Peters.

Red flags: If you have symptoms of advanced diabetes (such as frequent urination, excessive thirst, fatigue, frequent infections, unusual weight loss or blurry vision) see a physician immediately.

Recent studies: Japanese researchers in the Department of Diabetes and Clinical Nutrition at Kyoto University gave 31 people with diabetes and other blood sugar problems either corosolic acid (the active ingredient of banaba) or a placebo. Then they gave them a big dose of dietary sugar, in what's called a *glucose tolerance test.* An hour later...and 90 minutes later...and two hours later...those taking the banaba had much lower blood sugar levels. In a similar study conducted in the US, 10 people with diabetes were given banaba for two weeks—and their high blood sugar dropped by 30%.

Product: The US study used Glucosol, a soft-gel formulation found in many products, including Glucotrim from NSI, Gluco Trim from NOW Foods and Glucosol/Rx-Blood Sugar from Nature's Plus. Suggested intake: 32 to 48 mg a day of banaba extract standardized to 1% corosolic acid (CRA), the active ingredient.

▶ **Relief for diabetic neuropathy.** "A significant problem faced by people with diabetes is the development of nerve pain, called 'diabetic neuropathy,'" says Dr. Teitelbaum. "Usually tricyclic antidepressants such as nortriptyline have been a first-line treatment for this pain. Other medications such as Neurontin and Cymbalta can also be helpful."

But what has been ignored by most physicians is the power of nutritional support to eliminate and heal this pain, he says.

He recommends lipoic acid (300 mg, twice a day), acetyl-l-carnitine (500 mg, three times a day) and vitamins B-6, B-12 and inositol (in a high-dosage vitamin B supplement)—all of which work by nourishing and repairing nerves. "Give these nutrients three to six months to fully kick in, as they help the nerves to heal as opposed to simply masking the pain," says Dr. Teitelbaum.

To help the process occur more quickly, ask your doctor about B-12 shots, he says. "I like three thousand mcg per dose of methylcobalamin from a compounding pharmacy, given by intramuscular injections for fifteen doses, at whatever rate is convenient—daily to weekly—to quickly optimize blood levels. I then recommend the vitamin B-12 shots be given monthly, if needed, to help maintain pain relief."

New study: In a study reported in the *International Journal of Food Science and Nutrition*, doctors gave either vitamin B-12 shots or nortriptyline to 100 people with diabetic neuropathy. The B-12 shots were four times more effective in relieving the burning, freezing, tingling and stabbing sensations that are characteristic of this condition.

Also helpful: For immediate relief of diabetic nerve pain, try applying the Nerve Pain Cream or Gel from ITC Pharmacy (*www.itcpharmacy. com*, or call 866-374-0696), says Dr. Teitelbaum. "Your physician can call a prescription for the cream into the pharmacy and the pharmacist will be happy to discuss the treatment with your doctor. Apply one to three pea-size amounts of the cream or gel to painful areas, three times a day. You may have a significant degree of relief in two weeks. The pain cream contains a number of effective pain-relieving medications—but because they are being applied *directly* to the pain, they result in powerful relief without the side effects of taking the medications by mouth."

➤ **The vitamin that might stop kidney failure.** Ten to 20% of people with diabetes

suffer from kidney disease, or *diabetic nephropathy. Now there's a simple treatment that might stop it...*

New study: English researchers gave 40 people with diabetes and early-stage kidney disease either 300 mg of thiamine (vitamin B-1) a day or a placebo. Those taking the thiamine had a 41% decrease in the excretion of *albumin*—a protein that is a marker of early kidney disease in people with diabetes. In fact, 35% of those on the nutrient had a complete *normalization* of albumin levels.

"Thiamine supplements at high dose may provide improved therapy for early-stage diabetic nephropathy," say the researchers, in the journal *Diabetologia.*

Also helpful: People with diabetes who ate any kind of fish more than once a week were 14% less likely to develop early-stage kidney disease than people who didn't eat fish regularly, say English researchers in the *American Journal of Kidney Disease.*

DIZZINESS

Turn This Tough Problem Around

There are so many types and causes of dizziness that thinking about them can—make you dizzy!

But Jack J. Wazen, MD—a doctor at the Silverstein Institute in Florida (*www.earsinus. com*) and author of *Dizzy: What You Need to Know About Managing and Treating Balance Disorders* (Fireside)—is here to set the world of dizziness straight.

"Dizziness is a very general term—so the first step in understanding the condition is to accurately define it," he says.

Dr. Wazen divides *dizziness* into three types of symptoms…

- **Vertigo.** This is the sensation that either you or the world is turning. You could also feel as if you're falling or rocking back and forth. "It's almost a hallucination of movement," says Dr. Wazen.

- **Disequilibrium.** You're fine sitting or lying down or otherwise not moving. But when you get up to walk, you can't walk straight—you have to hold on to objects and you bump into things.

- **Dizziness.** Nothing is spinning…you can walk fine…but you feel light-headed and fuzzy.

Problem: There are many conditions and diseases that can cause one or more of these three types of dizziness.

You could have a problem with the inner ear, the main organ of balance (such as benign paroxysmal positional vertigo, Meniere's disease, recurrent vestibulopathy, motion sickness, labyrinthitis, vestibular neuronitis or an ear infection).

You could have a problem with your visual system, which helps you balance yourself (such as cataracts, glaucoma or macular degeneration).

You could have a problem with the brain, which makes sense out of physical sensations (such as a brain tumor, epilepsy, migraine, head trauma, multiple sclerosis or Parkinson's disease).

You could have a problem if the inner ear or brain isn't getting enough circulation (such as an arrhythmia, orthostatic hypotension, heart disease or a stroke).

You could have an imbalance in hormones or other metabolic systems that affect balance (such as allergies, anemia, chronic fatigue syndrome, diabetes, rheumatoid arthritis, lupus or a thyroid disorder).

A medication could be making you dizzy, such as an antidepressant. ("Read the *Physician's Desk Reference* and you'll find that nearly every drug has dizziness as a side effect," says Dr. Wazen.)

Or you might have a minor cause of dizziness (such as a cold or flu, fatigue, insomnia or sinusitis).

Solution: The first and most important step in dealing with dizziness is finding a doctor who can figure out *what* is causing the problem," says Dr. Wazen. "Getting the right diagnosis is paramount in shaping the correct treatment, which might include medications, surgery and physical therapy such as vestibular retraining." (These are exercises that help the brain compensate for the condition that is causing the dizziness, vertigo or disequilibrium.)

"There are literally no cases of dizziness—including Meniere's disease—where 'nothing can be done,' " he says. "No one should be disabled with dizziness."

➤ **Find the right doctor.** "The primary care doctor or internist should 'get the ball rolling,' " says Dr. Wazen. If they can't discover the cause of dizziness, then the next step is to see a specialist—a neurologist or otolaryngologist who has a *subspecialty* in dizziness and balance disorders (otology or neuro-otology).

Red flag: Most ear-nose-and-throat (ENT) doctors *don't* specialize in dizziness and balance disorders and are unlikely to provide the help you need.

Rapid Resource: To find a specialist near you, call either the American Academy of Neurology at 800-879-1960 or the American Academy of Otolaryngology-Head and Neck Surgery at 703-836-4444.

- American Academy of Neurology. Address: 201 Chicago Ave., Minneapolis, MN 55145.

- American Academy of Otolaryngology. Address: 1650 Diagonal Rd., Alexandria, VA 22314.

The Five-Minute Dizziness Cure

Benign paroxysmal positional vertigo (BPPV) is one of the most common causes of vertigo and dizziness, says Dr. Wazen. It's caused by the minute calcium carbonate rocks (otoliths) ending up in the ear's semicircular canal, where they don't belong.

Good news: BPPV responds "exceptionally well" to a five-minute treatment that your physician can perform in his office, which moves the ear rocks into a part of the ear where they don't cause vertigo, says Dr. Wazen.

The treatment...

1. **While you are sitting on a bed or examining table, the doctor will move you to a reclining position.** Your head will be placed over the end of the bed or table at a 45° angle.

2. **The doctor will turn your head to the opposite side.**

3. **You will be rolled over on to that side.** Your head will be angled slightly so that you will be looking at the floor.

4. **You will be returned to a sitting position.** Your chin will be tilted down.

After the maneuver, wait 10 minutes before leaving the office for the ear rocks to reposition themselves, says Dr. Wazen. "Do not drive home—arrange to have someone pick you up," he adds.

For the next five days, follow these precautions:

- *For the first two days,* sleep with the head at a 45-degree angle—in a recliner, or with a bed positioned at that angle. (Pillows don't work because you toss and turn and end up in a flat or near-flat position.) For days three to five after the procedure, sleep with two pillows under your head.

- *During the day, keep your head vertical.*

- *Don't go to the hairdresser or dentist*—their chairs recline and cause your head to lean back.

- *Don't do any exercises that cause you to move your head,* such as playing tennis, sit-ups or touching your toes.

- *If you use eye drops, do so without tilting your head.*

▶ **Make these simple dietary changes—right now.** "Simple dietary changes that you can make—beginning right now—may have a positive impact on your dizziness and balance problems," says Dr. Wazen. In fact, they can provide "most or all of the relief you need from dizziness," he says.

● **Reduce the amount of sodium in your diet.** "This is a healthy recommendation for anyone who experiences vertigo," says Dr. Wazen. "This advice is especially important for people who have Meniere's disease. In fact, a combination of a low-salt diet and short-term use of diuretics is the only treatment many people with Meniere's disease need to get better."

Dr. Wazen's recommendations...

To reduce salt look for foods labeled "salt-free" or "sodium-free"...don't put a salt shaker on the table...make liberal use of strong, nonsodium flavorings, such as lemon or lime juice, vinegar, freshly grated horseradish, minced fresh garlic and chopped onions...avoid processed foods as much as possible...when cooking, find low- or no-salt recipes...when drinking bottled waters, select sodium-free or low-sodium varieties...drink seltzer water instead of club soda, which is high in sodium...avoid adding salt to cooking water when you're making pasta, beans and grains...eat fresh or frozen vegetables instead of canned or jarred... avoid salty foods such as pickles, salty snacks, salted nuts, processed meats and fish and canned soups (except low-salt varieties)...watch out for salty condiments, such as ketchup, mustard, steak sauce and soy sauce...avoid MSG, which contains 12% sodium...if you use wine when cooking, use table or drinking wine (cooking wine and cooking sherry have added salt)...make your own air-popped, unsalted popcorn and season it with garlic or onion powder...eat unsalted, dry roasted nuts and sprinkle them with garlic or onion powder...when you eat out, insist that your food be made without added salt.

• **Cut the caffeine.** "Caffeine can impair the circulation to your inner ear, resulting in unsteadiness or light-headedness," says Dr. Wazen. But what about the severe symptoms—the headache, restlessness, depression, poor concentration and irritability—when you try to stop drinking coffee?

The best way to kick the caffeine habit is to do it gradually, says Dr. Wazen.

Reduce your intake of caffeine by about 20% per week over a four- to five-week period. "For example, if you drink five cups of coffee or five cans of cola daily, reduce your intake to four cups or cans the first week, three the second week, and so on."

Also helpful: Other dietary tips that have proven beneficial for many people with dizziness include...

• Reduce your sugar intake.

• Drink water regularly throughout the day.

• Check to see if you have food allergies. (For an excellent test to detect food allergies, please see the section "Irritable Bowel Syndrome" on page 216.)

• Avoid migraine-triggering foods. (For a list of such foods, please see the section "Headaches" on page 177.)

DRUG SIDE EFFECTS

PDQ Protection from Rx Risks

There are more than 3 *billion* prescriptions written every year in the US, with 50% of American adults taking at least one prescription medication...nearly 20% taking three or more...and over half of 65-year olds taking three prescription drugs or more daily.

Are we healthier for it? Well, some of us definitely aren't. *Just ask a coroner...*

Fact: Prescription drugs—taken correctly—cause more than 106,000 deaths each year. That makes "adverse drug reactions" (ADR)—the official term for side effects—the fourth leading cause of death in the US. Along with those deaths, there are more than 2 million other ADR every year.

"Almost every single prescription drug is in some way harmful," says Hyla Cass, MD (*www.cassmd.com*), author of *Supplement Your Prescription: What Your Doctor Doesn't Know about Nutrition* (Basic Health). "Just look at the warnings that come with each drug! So if you're going to use a medication, be sure it is the right one for the purpose, use it properly, and do what you can to minimize side effects."

You can do that PDQ...

➤ **Knowledge is safety.** "ADR aren't a rare and unusual phenomena—they're known and therefore largely preventable," says Larry Sasich, PharmD, the Chair of the Department of Pharmacy Practice at LECOM School of Pharmacy in Erie, Pennsylvania, and coauthor of *Worst Pills, Best Pills: A Consumer's Guide to Avoiding Drug-Induced Death or Illness* (Pocket Books).

But it's hard to get your hands on *reliable* information that tells you about the ADR for the drug you're taking—so you know exactly what symptoms to look out for. In fact, drug information leaflets typically passed out in drugstores are so second-rate that the government's Food and Drug Administration (FDA) called for an end to their distribution.

Good news: The FDA has created a consumer-friendly database on the Web that tells you the most important safety information about the riskiest drugs.

The website has been created by the FDA's Center for Drug Evaluation and Research, and is titled Postmarket Drug Safety Information for Patients and Providers. You can find it at *www.fda.gov/drugs/drugsafety*.

The section of the site that includes the riskier drugs is called "Medication Guides." You can find it on the Web page *www.fda.gov/drugs/drugsafety* under the heading "Drug Safety and Availability." It highlights more than 150 drugs, from *aripiprazole* (Abilify) to *olanzapine* (Zyprexa).

"These guides were written for consumers and approved by the FDA," says Dr. Sasich. "They contain detailed descriptions about a drug's ADR—what the person should look for, and what to do if the ADR occurs. The guides completely bypass any limitations in the information about the drug provided by the doctor or pharmacist."

Example: There is a Medication Guide for *ciprofloxacin* (Cipro), a fluoroquinolone antibiotic. It states that a common ADR for fluoroquinolones is tendon rupture—and that you should stop taking the drug at the first sign of tendon pain, swelling or inflammation and see your doctor. "This is an ADR most people wouldn't think about when taking an antibiotic," says Dr. Sasich.

Smart idea: Your doctor prescribes a drug. *Before you have the prescription filled,* check to see if it is among the "List of products with medication guides," says Dr. Sasich. If it is, *read the medication guide.*

You may read, for example, that the drug poses a risk of a life-threatening stomach ulcer—and you might decide that is too much risk for you.

New thinking: The patient should be a partner in a decision-making process as to whether or not to take a prescribed drug, says Dr. Sasich. "A well-informed individual can decide how much risk he or she is willing to take. Doctors should not be like parents, telling patients 'Do what I say and everything will be fine.' And patients should not be like obedient children. You're a *consumer.* Do some research before you buy and take the new prescription. If you don't want to take the drug, talk to your doctor about alternatives."

Also helpful: If the drug you've been prescribed isn't among the Medication Guides, you can find more information about it by reading its complete professional product label—by clicking the "DailyMed" link at the FDA drug safety site. DailyMed includes more than 5,000 product labels.

▶ **Don't take a drug that hasn't been on the market at least seven years.** "Not taking a drug until it has been on the market at least seven years is extremely good advice for consumers," says Dr. Sasich. He points out that since 1992, 20 new drugs have been withdrawn from the market for safety reasons—including the COX-2 painkillers *rofecoxib* (Vioxx) and *valdecoxib* (Bextra), which are estimated to have caused 55,000 deaths from heart attacks and strokes.

"The clinical trials used to approve new drugs are of relatively short duration and involve a limited number of patients," says Dr. Sasich. "Plus, there is no legal requirement for a new drug to be more safer—or more effective—than an older drug."

Useful: You can use the FDA safety database to find out the approval date of a drug you've been prescribed. Enter the link...*www.accessdata.fda.gov/scripts/cder/drugsatfda/index.cfm*...search for

Rules for Safer Drug Use

In the book *Bad Pills, Good Pills*, Dr. Sasich and his coauthors provide a number of "rules" for safer drug use. *They include...*

- *Make sure drug therapy is really needed for your medical condition.* Ask your doctor to explain all the alternatives.

- *If drug therapy is indicated, in most cases it is safer to start with a dose that is lower than the usual adult dose.*

- *When adding a new drug, see if it is possible to discontinue another drug that you are taking.* The fewer medications you take, the better.

- *Stopping a drug is as important as starting it.* Do not take a drug any longer than is necessary.

- *Assume that any new symptom you develop after starting a new drug may be caused by the drug.* If you have a new symptom, report it to your doctor.

- *Before leaving your doctor's office or pharmacy, make sure the instructions for taking your medicine are clear to you and a family member or friend.*

- *Ask your primary care doctor to coordinate your care and drug use.*

the drug by name...and click on the name. You will then be routed to a page that provides "Drug Details"—including the approval date.

▶ **Reduce the risk of side effects—with nutrition.**

"There is a little-known side effect of the most commonly used medicines—they can rob your body of the nutrients that are essential to your health," says Dr. Cass. They do that by decreasing appetite...reducing absorption... increasing the "burning" of nutrients...blocking the effect of nutrients at the cellular level...or draining the body of nutrients.

"Over months and years, that nutrient depletion can take a toll on your health and increase your risk of becoming ill—in some cases, with the very illness you're trying to prevent with the medication," she says. "Every person who takes prescription drugs needs to know about drug-induced nutrient depletion and how to effectively balance this side effect with nutritional supplements."

Here are Dr. Cass's recommendations for daily supplementation to prevent drug-induced nutritional deficiencies from some of the most commonly prescribed drugs. If you take one of the drugs listed—also take the suggested supplement or supplements. (Use these supplements with the approval and supervision of your prescribing doctor.)

- **Statins for high cholesterol:** *Atorvastatin* (Lipitor), *fluvastatin* (Lescol), *lovastatin* (Mevacor), *pravastatin* (Pravachol), *rosuvastatin* (Crestor) and s*imvastatin* (Zocor): CoQ10 daily (100 to 300 mg)

- **Calcium channel blocker for high blood pressure:** *Amlodipine* (Norvasc): Potassium (100 mg)

- **Bisphosphonate for osteoporosis:** *Alendronate* (Fosamax): Calcium (500 to 1,000 mg)

- **Proton pump inhibitors for heartburn and acid reflux:** *Omeprazole* (Prilosec) and *lansoprazole* (Prevacid): Calcium (1,000 to 1,200 mg) and vitamin B-12 (200 mcg)

- **NSAID (non-steroidal anti-inflammatory drug) for arthritis:** *Celecoxib* (Celebrex): Vitamin C (1,000 to 3,000 mg)

- **Diuretic for high blood pressure:** *Furosemide* (Lasix): Calcium (1,000 mg), magnesium (250 to 500 mg), potassium (100 mg), vitamin C (1,000 mg), vitamin B-1 (320 mg), vitamin B-6 (10 to 25 mg) and zinc (25 mg)

- **Beta blocker for high blood pressure and heart disease:** *Metoprolol* (Toprol-XL): CoQ10 (100 to 300 mg)

- **Anti-arrhythmia drug for heart irregularities:** *Digoxin* (Lanoxin): Calcium (1,000 to 1,200), magnesium (400 to 600 mg), phosphorous (700 mg), vitamin B-1 (25 mg)

- **Metformin for diabetes:** *Glucophage, Glumetza, Fortamet*: Vitamin B-12 (1.2 to 1.8 mcg)

DRY EYES

Healing on a Tear

What's the most common reason people visit eye doctors? Cataracts? Glaucoma? Nearsightedness?

No, no and no. It's dry eyes.

"Three out of ten American adults are afflicted with dry eye, a disorder of the tear film, the essential coating that protects the surface of the eyes, washes away debris and irritants and creates a crystal-clear window through which we see," says Robert Latkany MD (*www.dryeye doctor.com*), founder and director of the Dry Eye Clinic at the New York Eye & Ear Infirmary and author of *The Dry Eye Remedy: The Complete Guide to Restoring the Health and Beauty of Your Eyes* (Hatherleigh).

If you wear contacts…suffer from allergies…have rosacea…are peri- or postmenopausal…have an autoimmune disease such as Sjögren's Syndrome…have undergone laser eye surgery or cosmetic eye surgery…you might be especially prone to dry eye disorder, says Dr. Latkany.

But it's likely everyone will suffer from dry eyes sooner or later, he says. Maybe you already know one or more of the symptoms. Stinging, burning, grittiness and itching in the eyes.

Sensitivity to light. The feeling there's something in the eye. Soreness. Redness. Blurred vision.

You might have used eye drops for the problem. And gotten relief—for a few minutes. "Eye drops are soothing and temporarily relieve symptoms," says Dr. Latkany. "But they're not going to solve your problem."

Here's what does—and fast…

➤ **Adjust the computer.** "When you use the computer, you stare—which means you don't blink," says Dr. Latkany. Do that for two hours or so, and the symptoms of dry eye appear. But if you have to work in front of a computer all day, what are your options?

"Consider the angle at which you stare at the computer monitor," says Dr. Latkany. Most people work at eye level with the screen, he explains. That means your eyes are completely open most of the time, exposing a good portion of the ocular surface—the front of the eye. Some people even set their monitors on platforms so that they look up at the screen, stretching their eyelids open even further and exposing the widest possible expanse of the ocular surface to be "dried." "It's the worst way to look at a computer screen," he says.

Better: "The best way to look at a computer screen is down—at a small angle, at least," he says. "That allows the upper eyelid to close a bit, exposing less of the ocular surface and enabling the eye to coat the surface effectively."

What to do: Either raise your chair or lower the position of the monitor.

Also helpful: Take 10-second breaks, says Dr. Latkany. Turn away from the computer screen, close your eyes, move your eyeballs around underneath your closed lids to bathe and lubricate the eyes, count to 10, then open your eyes again. "Do this twice an hour—and you'll help prevent your dry eye symptoms from using a computer."

➤ **Lifestyle recommendations.** "There are many things you can do on a day-to-day basis that can alleviate the symptoms of dry eyes," says Dr. Latkany.

• **Sleep deep.** "I can't emphasize how important sleep is to reducing the discomfort of dry eye.

What it does: A deep sleep of at least eight hours bathes the eye, replenishes the tear film, and soothes the ocular surface.

• **Exercise regularly.** Exercise reduces inflammation, contributing to the health of the ocular surface, he says.

Recommended: At least 20 minutes of exercise, five times a week.

• **Take showers.** "A hot bath can be relaxing, but the steam tends to rise away from you and the temperature of the water goes down," says Dr. Latkany.

Better: Stand upright in a shower, with steam coming at you constantly and with the temperature remaining consistently hot. "Showering is as good a wash for your eyes as for your body," he says.

• **Drink water.** "Water is needed by all the body organs—and the eyes as well," says Dr. Latkany.

Recommended: Six to eight glasses of water a day.

• **Take a break.** "Perhaps the most important thing to avoid if you suffer from dry eye is a long stretch of consecutive visual tasking, whether it's working at a computer, watching TV or reading," he says. "It's the nonstop aspect of visual activity that you want to guard against, not the activity itself."

Red flag: "After an eight-hour stretch in front of the computer at the office, one of the worst things you can do for your eyes is to come

---

Use Restasis Right

"Restasis is the only FDA-approved eye drop that actually makes your eye make more tears," says Dr. Latkany. "There is nothing else like it available."

However: There is a lot of confusion about how to use Restasis correctly, he says.

For one thing, the product stings in about half the people who use it. For another, it takes six to eight weeks to start working, and doesn't reach its peak effect for four to six months. For these two reasons, many people stop using the drops.

Better: Refrigerate the drops, which will reduce the stinging, says Dr. Latkany. Use it regularly until you notice a benefit.

---

home and spend two hours in front of the TV, or working at the home computer, or doing heavy reading," says Dr. Latkany. "Instead, after a tiring day, call it quits on the staring and visual tasking. Spend the time visiting with your family, friends and neighbors…or take a walk…or consider listening to your favorite music in a dimly lit room."

• **Nourish your eyes.** "The omega-3 essential fatty acids promote tear secretion," says Dr. Latkany. "Their importance for relieving dry eye disorder is profound and unparalleled."

Study: Researchers at Harvard Medical School analyzed health data on more than 32,000 women and found that those who ate omega-3 rich tuna more than five times per week had 68% less chance of developing dry eye than those who did not. The study also found that those who ate more omega-6 fats—found in ice cream sundaes, pizza, cheeseburgers and Twinkies—raised their chance of getting dry eye.

Recommended: Barlean's Total Omega supplement, which has a balanced combination of omega-3, -6 and -9 fatty acids. It is widely available.

SPEED LIMIT | Drugs That Dehydrate Your Eyes

"There are at least seven categories of drugs that can be harmful for dry eye sufferers," says Dr. Latkany.

- Antihistamines/decongestants.
- Antidepressants, anti-psychotics and sleeping pills.
- Diuretics.
- Beta-blockers.
- Oral contraceptives and hormone treatments.
- Urinary bladder control medicines.
- Accutane and other systemic retinoids.
- Over-the-counter eye drops that claim they "get the red out" or relieve irritation.

"Consult with your internist, cardiologist or gynecologist," he says. "There may be an alternate dose or alternate medicine that can achieve the same endpoint without causing or contributing to your dry eye."

➤ **Your "Home Eye Spa"—a five-minute treatment for eye-drying blepharitis.** There are 50 *meibomian glands* along the edges of the top and bottom eyelids, explains Dr. Latkany. They pump oily, fatlike secretions on to the top of your tear film, coating the film and preventing it from evaporating. Until they get clogged up. Then the tear film evaporates faster—with resulting dryness, burning and irritation.

"This condition is called *blepharitis* and it's a common cause of dry eye," says Dr. Latkany. "And while there is no cure, it can be easily managed by my basic 'Home Eye Spa Treatment.'"

The treatment focuses on cleaning the eyelids using heat, massage and a gentle cleansing procedure, he explains. And it only takes five minutes.

Step 1. Heat up a moistened towel or the Eye Spa Pad, a heating/cooling pad that conforms to the shape of the eye. (It is available at *www.dryeyeshop.com* or call 877-693-7939.) Test the towel/pad with your fingers to make sure it's not too hot. Lie down on your bed or on a sofa, apply the moistened towel or pad to your eyes and relax for three minutes. "The heat is working to open the ducts of the meibomian glands and loosen the contents," says Dr. Latkany.

Step 2. "Next comes the massage," says Dr. Latkany. "Gently pull your eyelid slightly to the side. Then take a cotton swab dipped in hot water and, starting at the nose-end of your eye, gentle push at the lower eyelid margin just below the eyelash. Basically, you're pressing the eyelid ever so delicately against the eyeball, and this serves to push the contents of the meibomian glands up and out of the ducts. Do this very softly all along the bottom eyelid margin. Then, again starting at the nose, do the same thing on the top eyelid margin, pressing right above the eyelash line to express the contents of upper eyelid glands down and out. Repeat with the other eye. This is all very gentle and quick—it shouldn't take more than ten seconds or so."

Step 3. "Now cleanse the eyelid," he says. "Simply take the cotton swab and, with one stroke, gently wipe the eyelid below the eyelash line for the upper eyelid, above it for the lower eyelid. Repeat with the other eye. You're simply wiping away the gunk you've squeezed out of the eyelid margins."

⚠ **Caution:** Do not wipe inside your eyelid.

Step 4. "For the final cleanup, you'll need a bottle of refrigerated preservative-free artificial tears. I'm a big fan of preservative-free eye drops, and I suggest you refrigerate them. Chilled drops feel wonderful on an irritated eye, and you can tell with absolute certainty that the drop has hit the eye. Apply about five drops per eye—typically, that's one vial of the drops. You want to rinse out of your eye everything you may have stirred up with the heat and the massage."

Recommended: When you first begin treatment, do it on a daily basis, advises Dr. Latkany. "This kind of regular practice will help you get good at it and will begin to plant the habit. Once you have it down pat, keep it up at least three times a week."

⏱ *Super-Quick Fix*

"The heating pad or towel alone can make an enormous difference in just loosening the glands and opening the passageways of your eyelids. So doing just Step 1 of the Home Spa treatment is better than doing nothing for preventive and therapeutic purposes."

DRY MOUTH

Restore Your Teeth-Saving Saliva

Think of squeezing a lemon into your mouth or the smell of bacon cooking in the morning.

In a flash, your autonomic nervous system is activated to produce several types of saliva (some watery, some mucouslike) from three pairs of salivary glands in your mouth). At least that is what is supposed to happen.

But if you have dry mouth, or *xerostomia*—a condition that afflicts nearly 50% of people 65 and older—your salivary glands produce less than half the normal amount of saliva (three pints a day).

The result can be a desiccated life.

You might have…trouble speaking…trouble swallowing…bad breath…indigestion (from a

lack of *amylase*, an enzyme in saliva that triggers starch digestion)…and dry lips, with chronic cracks in the corners that are targets for nasty yeast infections. But perhaps the worst symptom of all is rampant decay, as teeth-destroying bacteria are no longer flushed out of the mouth by *lysozyme*, another saliva enzyme.

There are many possible causes of dry mouth, including menopause, diabetes, Parkinson's disease, depression, autoimmune diseases such as Sjögren's Syndrome and rheumatoid arthritis, and cancer treatments such as radiation and chemotherapy.

But maybe the most common cause should be dubbed Rxerostomia—because *medications* are responsible for 65% of all cases of dry mouth…

➤ **Double-check your drugs.** There are more than *400 medications* that can cause dry mouth, says Flora Parsa Stay, DDS, an associate clinical professor at the University of Southern California School of Dentistry and author of *Secret Gateway to Health* (Morgan James Publishing).

"Most physicians are more concerned with treating specific symptoms and diseases and less concerned with the side effects drugs have on the mouth," says Dr. Stay. "In fact, many physicians don't appear to consider this side effect at all."

What to do: "If you notice that your mouth seems drier than normal when you begin taking a medication, ask your physician if there is an alternative dose or alternative medication," says Dr. Stay. "If that isn't an option, then take other steps to deal with dry mouth."

Important: Make sure to tell your dentist about the medications you're taking, says Gigi Meinecke, DMD, RN, a dentist in private practice in Potomac, Maryland, and on the clinical faculty of the University of Maryland Dental School. "Oftentimes, people think there's nothing they can do about dry mouth. But a dentist can help

Medications That Can Cause Dry Mouth

The following classes of medications can cause dry mouth, says Dr. Stay.

- **Anti-acne,** such as *isotretinoin*
- **Anti-anxiety,** such as *alprazolam* (Xanax)
- **Anticholinergic/antispasmodic,** such as *oxybutynin*
- **Anticonvulsant,** such as *gabapentin* (Neurontin)
- **Antidepressant,** such as *citalopram* (Celexa)
- **Antihypertensive,** such as *captopril*
- **Anti-inflammatory/analgesic,** such as *naproxen* (Naprosyn) and *ibuprofen* (Advil)
- **Antinausea/Antiemetic,** such as *dyphenhydramine* (Dramamine)
- **Anti-Parkinsonian,** such as *carbidopa/levodopa* (Sinemet)
- **Antipsychotic,** such as *clozapine* (Clozaril)
- **Bronchodilator,** such as *ipratropium* (Atrovent)
- **Decongestant,** such as *pseudoephedrine* (Sudafed)
- **Diuretic,** such as *furosemide* (Lasix)
- **Muscle relaxant,** such as *cyclobenzaprine*
- **Narcotic analgesic,** such as *morphine* (MS Contin)
- **Sedative,** such as *flurazepam*

you deal with the problem and prevent xerostomia-triggered gum disease and decay."

▶ **Drink more water.** "If you have dry mouth, you should always have a bottle or glass of water with you—on your desk at work, in the cup holder in the car, on your bedside table," says Dr. Meinecke. "Sip constantly."

⏰ Super-Quick Fix

Helpful: Add a squeeze of lemon to the water, says Dr. Stay. "I get a lot of good feedback on this from my patients with dry mouth. They say it really helps, especially at bedtime."

▶ **Drink less alcohol and caffeine.** Alcohol and caffeine-containing drinks like coffee, tea and cola are drying, says Dr. Meinecke. "Steer clear of them."

Also helpful: Don't smoke—it also dries out oral tissue.

⏰ Super-Quick Fix

▶ **Chew sugarless gum after every meal.** Dry mouth sets you up for tooth decay. *But you can use your teeth to protect your teeth...*

Studies show that chewing on gum containing the sugar substitute xylitol for five minutes after meals can help reduce decay-causing bacteria by 40% to 60%.

"For someone with dry mouth, it's an easy and powerful way to prevent cavities and it also increases saliva," says Dr. Stay.

Recommended: There are many brands of xylitol-containing chewing gums on the market, such as Spry and Xylichew.

▶ **Create moister breath.** Breathing through your nose instead of your mouth will help keep your mouth from drying out, says Dr. Stay.

What to do: Keep your mouth closed and focus on breathing through your nose.

▶ **Avoid alcohol-containing mouthwashes.** "Most mouthwashes contain high levels of alcohol, which can dry out oral tissue," says Dr. Meinecke.

Better: Cleure Mouthwash, which is alcohol-free (*www.cleure.com*, 888-883-4276).

Also helpful: Cleure sells a toothpaste that does not contain sodium lauryl sulfate, a foaming agent found in nearly all brands of commercial toothpaste that is very drying.

➤ **Use a saliva substitute.** An over-the-counter saliva substitute—usually in spray form—can help control dry mouth, says Dr. Stay. Use it every 90 to 120 minutes, agrees Dr. Meinecke.

Recommended: Salivart spray, which is widely available. Biotène spray is also widely available. (Biotène also makes an alcohol-free mouthwash and toothpaste without sodium lauryl sulfate, *www.biotene.com*.)

DRY SKIN AND ITCHING

Take a Moment to Moisturize

Your skin feels stiff and tight and rough. It looks dull. Perhaps it's even flaky, cracked and itchy. In a word, *dry*.

In a word, *moisturize*.

"Realtors have a favorite line, 'Location, location, location,'" says dermatologist Audrey Kunin, MD, author of *The DERMAdoctor Skinstruction Manual* (Simon & Schuster) and founder and president of DERMAdoctor.com. "And dermatologists have a favorite line in fall and winter, when dry skin is at its worst—'Moisturize, moisturize, moisturize.'"

Here are the fastest, best ways to do just that...

➤ **Moisturize right after washing.** "After you take a bath or shower, the water evaporates from your skin, taking valuable moisture

---

The Best Cleansers for Dry Skin

There are hundreds of different facial and body cleansers on the market. Which ones are right for dry skin? "The key is to avoid any cleanser that is overly drying," says Brandith Irwin, PhD, a dermatologist in Seattle (*www.skintour.com*) and author of *The Surgery-Free Makeover: All You Need to Know for Great Skin and a Younger Face* (Da Capo). Her recommendations...

Sold in drugstores...

- Cetaphil Gentle Skin Cleanser
- Olay Foaming Face Wash
- Purpose Gentle Cleansing Wash

Sold in dermatologists' offices...

- MD Forte Facial Cleanser I
- SkinCeuticals Foaming Cleanser

---

with it and leaving your skin vulnerable to dryness," says Dr. Kunin.

What to do: "After you towel dry, increase the moisture content of your skin by applying a hydrating body cream like Korres Guava Body Butter or CeraVe Moisturizing Lotion," she says. "For particularly dry skin, use a moisturizer with an extra emollient base, such as CeraVe Moisturizing Cream or L'Occitane Shea Butter Ultra Rich Body Cream."

Rapid Resource: You can find these products at *www.dermadoctor.com*, or call 877-DERMADR. Address: DERMAdoctor, Inc., 1901 McGee St., Kansas City, MO 64108, email *service@DERMAdoctor.com*.

➤ **Moisturize more than once a day.** Most people only apply moisturizer in the morning. "Multiple applications of a moisturizer will help speed up hydration and skin healing for anyone whose dry skin has gotten out of control," says Dr. Kunin. "I often tell a patient with

Stop the Itch-Scratch Cycle

"Dry skin is often itchy skin," says Dr. Kunin. "And there is nothing harder to break than the itch-scratch cycle. The more you scratch, the more the inflamed skin will itch, and the harder it will be to heal the affected area."

Your best option is preventing dry skin, of course—with regular use of a moisturizer. But if the cycle has started, you need to treat the dry skin and the itch.

What to do: Oral antihistamines such as *cetirizine* (Zyrtec) and topical anesthetics such as PrameGel, L-M-X or Prax Lotion can keep you from scratching your skin raw, says Dr. Kunin. Prescription options such as oral *hydroxyzine* (Vistaril), *doxepin* or Zonalon cream may be helpful as well, she says.

parched, symptomatic skin that if she applies her moisturizer four or five times a day for a week she will see a significant and rapid improvement in her symptoms."

▶ **Keep moisturizer with you.** "I have somewhat dry skin, so I always have a moisturizer nearby," says Tanya Kormeili, MD, a dermatologist in private practice in Los Angeles (*www.kormeiliderm.com*). "I carry a moisturizer with me during the day and keep one in my car for when I'm driving home after work and keep one on my nightstand to use just before I go to bed. Whenever my skin feels dry, I moisturize."

▶ **For cracks and splits.** Use DERMAdoctor Handy Manum Medicated Skin Repair Serum with 1% Hydrocortisone, at least nightly, and ideally twice a day, advises Dr. Kunin. "It contains AHAs, salicylic acid and propylene glycol to quickly soften hard, dry skin, allowing fissures to heal.

"It also contains oat beta glucan and green tea extract to reduce itching and inflammation. And the base establishes a protective barrier on your skin to prevent further environmental insults."

You can find this product and other moisturizers at *www.dermadoctor.com*, or call 877-DERMADR. Address: DERMAdoctor, Inc. 1901 McGee St., Kansas City, MO 64108 or e-mail *service@DERMAdoctor.com*.

Also helpful: Apply Polysporin First Aid Antibiotic Ointment into the splits twice a day. *However:* "Do not use any topical antibiotic ointment that contains neomycin, which is a notorious skin sensitizer and cause of contact dermatitis," says Dr. Kunin.

▶ **During winter, use a "helper" ingredient.** These ingredients not only moisturize but also *exfoliate*, removing old, dead skin cells, explains Dr. Kunin. They include glycolic acid (AHA), lactic acid, urea and salicylic acid (BHA). "Their use can promote softer, supple skin that is less likely to crack during the depths of winter."

However: Don't apply them on a dried area with an open fissure.

Products: Dr. Kunin recommends you try AHA 20, AmLactin Moisturizing Cream or Carmol 20 Cream.

How to use: Twice daily, or once daily along with a regular moisturizing cream.

▶ **Add bath oil.** "If you like taking a bath, one way to help hydrate your skin is to add bath oil into your water," says Dr. Kunin. She suggests Robathol Bath Oil or L'Occitane Almond Shower Oil.

🕐 Super-Quick Fix

▶ **How to prevent dry hands.** "Most people wash their hands ten times or more a day," says Dr. Kunin. "This constant contact with water—not to mention harsh soaps—can cause dry cuticles and painful finger splits."

To prevent dry hands, carry hand cream with you and apply after every hand washing.

➤ **Mist your face.** Regular facial misting is an enjoyable and refreshing treatment that hydrates the skin, reducing dryness and fine lines, says Joni Loughran, author of *Natural Skin Care* (North Atlantic). *Her instructions…*

Use a bottle with a pump sprayer. Fill it with eight ounces of pure water mixed with 10 drops of an essential oil or blend of essential oils. (Use water alone if you're allergic to essential oils.) Shake vigorously before each use. Use as often as desired. "It is recommended at least three times a day—morning, noon and night, and is especially important in dry climates, air-conditioned rooms and airplanes, where there is little moisture in the air," she says.

⚠️ *Caution:* Take care not to get the misting liquid in the eyes, which could be irritating.

➤ **Moisturize from the inside out.** "Dehydrated skin is simple to treat with diet," says Susan Ciminelli, (*www.susanciminelli.com*) author of *The Ciminelli Solution: A 7-Day Plan for Radiant Skin* (Collins). "All you need to do is increase your water intake, eat more green leafy vegetables and adjust your diet to include foods that are rich in water such as melons and cucumbers. Do this on a daily basis and within one week you will see a difference. Even the fine lines—especially around the mouth and eye areas—will begin to diminish slightly."

ECZEMA

czema—the #1 reason people see dermatologists—afflicts 20 million American adults and 10 million children. Why so many sufferers?

New thinking: Eczema is a common genetic disorder. A set of 20 or so genes weakens the skin's "barrier"—the complex mixture of skin cells and lipids (fats) that creates a waterproof lining, sealing moisture in and keeping the environment out. In eczema, moisture escapes (leaving the skin dry and cracked) and microscopic irritants and particles enter (triggering an immune system response). The result?

You *itch*. So much so that sometimes you can't sleep, concentrate at work or pay much attention to your near and dear. And you *scratch*, causing or complicating a scaly, red, inflamed rash that is easily infected. In short, your skin is miserable and so are you. *But you don't have to be...*

"Because we now know the cause of eczema, we can provide accurate guidance for self-care that relieves these symptoms," says Adnan Nasir, MD, a professor of dermatology at Duke University and the University of North Carolina at Chapel Hill, and author of *Eczema-Free for Life* (Collins).

And relief is only a few minutes away...

➤ **Try a moisturizer with ceramide— and put it on *immediately* after bathing.** *Ceramides* are a key component of the lipids that link *corneocytes* (skin cells) to form the skin's waterproof barrier. They are now an ingredient in a new generation of moisturizers—which, when applied, "naturally mimic the barrier of the skin," says Dr. Nasir.

By using a ceramide-containing product every day, you can keep the barrier intact—

preventing the flares of dry, itchy, inflamed skin that plague so many eczema sufferers.

Recommended: CeraVe, which is widely available. A less expensive alternative favored by Dr. Nasir is Aquaphor Healing Ointment.

How to use: "The water layer in the skin is only about as thick as a sheet of paper," says Dr. Nasir. "You have to seal it in before it has a chance to evaporate. Many moisturizers don't work *unless* the skin is fully hydrated. So prune yourself up in the bath. And then, within three minutes of getting out, apply the moisturizer. Wait two to three minutes, and then apply a second thin layer on problem areas that are itchy, red and inflamed."

➤ **Bathe the right way.** "Proper bathing is one of the most important steps in managing

Cheap, Effective and OTC

The leading prescription moisturizer for mild to moderate eczema is MimyX Cream. Now, researchers have found that an inexpensive, over-the-counter moisturizer works just as well.

The study: Fifty-nine people with mild to moderate eczema used either MimyX Cream ($100 for a small tube) or Albolene Moisturizing Cleanser ($10 for a 12-ounce jar) for four weeks. Both products performed equally well, reducing redness, peeling, dryness, stinging and itching.

"It was very interesting to see that an over-the-counter moisturizing formulation that has been around for more than a hundred years was equally as effective as a more modern prescription moisturizing cream," says Zoe Diana Draelos, MD, a leading dermatologist for the study, published in the *Journal of Cosmetic Dermatology*. "If you have limited access to a dermatologist or prescription medications, this could be the moisturizer to treat mild to moderate eczema."

eczema—but many people don't know how it's done," says Dr. Nasir. His advice:

1. **Soak for at least 20 minutes—but no more than 30.** "Soak until your skin wrinkles or prunes—especially the tips of your fingers," he says. Smart idea: "If your skin is very dry, or you're experiencing frequent flares, take two baths a day, in lukewarm water."

2. **Don't use washcloths.**

3. **Don't rub or scratch.**

4. **Use the right soap—but not too much.** Most soaps are too alkaline, washing away protective acids, says Dr. Nasir. Best: "Dove Beauty Bar is neither acidic nor alkaline and is the best choice."

5. **If your skin is red and somewhat infected, add ¼ cup of chlorine (such as Clorox) to the tub.** "The chlorine will boost healing," says Dr. Nasir.

6. **Add bath oil if you like—but only at the end of the bath, when your skin is hydrated.**

7. **To relieve nighttime itching, bathe and shampoo just before bedtime.** "It gets rid of dust, dirt, pollen and other irritants that accumulate on your body and in your hair during the day," says Dr. Nasir.

Four Thousand Years of Relief

"Soothing, moisturizing and healing oatmeal baths have been used by those with eczema for over four thousand years," says Dr. Nasir. "An added benefit is that they clean, too, so you don't have to use soap." *His instructions…*

Put two cups of rolled oats in the blender, grind until fine and add it to your bathwater. You can also buy prepared oatmeal baths, such as Aveeno.

---

8. **After the bath, apply moisturizer.** This is crucial. "Bathing will dry your skin—if you allow the water your skin absorbed to evaporate. If you apply a moisturizer right after your bath, however, the cream will seal in the water."

🕐 Super-Quick Fix

▶ **Stop the itch in one minute—without drugs.** "In someone with eczema, the desire to scratch can be overwhelming," says Dr. Nasir. *Here is an easy way to ease the itch…*

"Apply firm deep pressure—about the equivalent to the weight of a bowling ball—to the site of the itching, for one minute," he recommends. "Now, apply the same deep pressure to the place that itches—but on the *opposite* side of the body. Why this works isn't known, but the anti-itching effect can last from minutes to hours."

▶ **The cold water cure.** Using a cool water compress for 10 to 15 minutes, up to four times a day, can relieve itching for hours, says Dr. Nasir. *His instructions…*

1. **Run cold tap water over a smooth cotton cloth.** Wring out the excess water.

2. **Gently lay the damp cloth on the itchy area.**

3. **Keep it there for 10 to 15 minutes,** or until it loses its cooling power. Re-cool as needed.

4. **When you're finished,** apply moisturizer to lock in the water.

Better: Although less convenient, cold milk works even better than cold water, he says. *His instructions for a milk compress…*

1. **Pour the milk into a bowl of ice cubes.** Let it sit for a few minutes.

2. **Dip a gauze pad into the milk,** then gently squeeze out the excess liquid.

3. **Put it on the itchy area for about 2 or 3 minutes or until it warms up.**

4. **Re-soak and reapply for a total of 10 minutes,** up to 4 times a day.

5. **Rinse your skin with clear water and immediately apply moisturizer.**

➤ **Soothing steroids.** An over-the-counter topical steroid cream containing 0.5% hydrocortisone can help control itching. "Use it once a day after your bath and after applying moisturizer to the skin," says Dr. Nasir. "Apply only to itchy areas."

Also try: Other medications that can ease itching include…

• oral antihistamines such as diphenhydramine (Benadryl)

• topical aspirin such as Gold Bond Medicated Powder ("Oral aspirin may worsen the itch," he warns.)

• topical doxepin cream (Zonalon), applied three to four times a day

• calamine lotion ("It's especially good for cracked, wet oozing skin," says Dr. Nasir.)

• lotions containing menthol and camphor, such as calamine lotion or Vicks VapoRub

• local anesthetic gels with 0.5 to 2% lidocaine ("They can soothe itching for about four hours," he says. "Use it two to four times a day.")

➤ **To prevent infections, try vitamin D.** The dry, cracked skin of people with eczema is vulnerable to infections. Now there's a quick way that might help prevent the problem—take a vitamin D supplement.

New study: People with eczema have low skin levels of *cathelicidin*, a component that protects against infection. Researchers at the University of San Diego School of Medicine asked 14 people with eczema to take 4,000 IU of vitamin D for three weeks, to see if the nutrient might boost cathelicidin levels. *It did…*

Don't Hold the Phone

Do you have an unusual red, itchy rash on your cheeks or ears? Call your doctor—but not on your mobile phone!

That type of facial rash might be caused by your mobile phone, says the British Association of Dermatologists. And it's the *nickel* in the phone that's probably causing the problem.

"Nickel allergy is the most common cause of a skin rash called *contact dermatitis*," says Audrey Kunin, MD, a dermatologist in Kansas City, Missouri, and author of *The DERMAdoctor Skinstruction Manual* (Simon&Schuster). "It's a reaction to minute amounts of nickel particles coming in direct contact with the skin."

Other sources of nickel that can cause contact dermatitis is jewelry ("*all* metallic jewelry—even gold and silver—contains some nickel," says Dr. Kunin), watches, zippers and eyeglasses.

If you have a rash from a mobile phone, use a headset rather than holding the phone to your face. "Avoidance is the best way to treat a contact allergy," says Dr. Kunin. "Stay away from what you're allergic to."

If you have contact dermatitis from a ring you wear every day (a common problem), Dr. Kunin says to…

• *Periodically coat the ring with nail polish* (favor a formaldehyde-free brand, which is easier on skin).

• *Use a moisturizing cream* to create a barrier between you and the metal. *Best brands for the purpose:* Triceram, Nouriva Repair or TheraSeal Hand Protection.

"Vitamin D dramatically induces cathelicidin production in the skin" of people with eczema, said the researchers in the *Journal of Allergy & Clinical Immunology*. Ask your dermatologist if a vitamin D supplement is right for you.

ENDOMETRIOSIS

After Years of Suffering, A Treatment That Works

Endometriosis is a disease in which tissue similar to the *endometrium* (the lining of the uterus) is found outside the uterus, usually in the pelvic cavity.

It is the most common cause of pelvic pain in women aged 15 to 40 (an estimated 95% of women with pelvic pain may have the disease) and can cause infertility.

For many women with the disease, life is a seemingly endless round of drugs with horrific side effects but little effectiveness…repeated surgeries…and continued suffering.

It doesn't have to be that way.

"The current treatment of endometriosis is wrong in so many ways and on so many levels—and does so much harm," says David Redwine, MD, a gynecological surgeon in Bend, Oregon, and author of *100 Questions & Answers About Endometriosis* (Jones and Bartlett). "It's been my mission in life to tell the *truth* about endometriosis—that it is a readily understandable condition, and potentially curable with surgery, *if* the surgery is complete and performed by a qualified surgeon with experience in dealing with endometriosis."

Dr. Redwine has used "complete surgery"—laparoscopic excision—to treat more than 3,000 women with endometriosis who had failed previous treatments.

And if you suffer with endometriosis, here's what he wants you to understand…

➤ **Understand why the current theory about the cause of endometriosis is incorrect.** The confusion about the *treatment* of endometriosis is due to confusion about the *cause* of the disease, says Dr. Redwine.

Doctors cling to a "theory or origin" first propounded by the gynecologist John S. Sampson in the 1920s. It says that endometriosis is the result of *reflux menstruation*, in which endometrial cells and tissue flow out of the fallopian tubes (which are connected to the inner cavity of the uterus) into the pelvic cavity. There, they attach to pelvic surfaces, invade and spread.

But if this "agricultural theory" of the disease were true, says Dr. Redwine, women would develop *more* disease with age, as the endometrial "seeds" blossomed and spread. But older women have *less* disease.

If this theory were true, doctors would have recorded photo-micrographic evidence of the process of attachment, proliferation and invasion. But no such evidence exists.

If the theory were true, all tissue samples of endometriosis would be identical to the uterine lining. But there are countless cellular differences between endometrial tissue and endometriosis. In fact, a cell-for-cell similarity between the two types of tissues almost never occurs.

If the theory of reflux menstruation were true, the disease would be incurable, because it could never be eradicated. It would always return. Well, it is incurable with the treatments used by modern medicine—because they are based on Sampson's theory.

➤ **Understand why current drug and surgical treatments—based on this incorrect theory—don't work and can't work.** The drugs commonly prescribed for endometriosis—such as *leuprolide* (Lupron) to mimic menopause or birth control pills to limit menstrual flow—are based on the Sampson theory. They don't work to cure the disease. And when the pain resumes, the doctor can tell the endometriosis patient that, yes, the medicine eradicated the disease—but it returned.

The two forms of surgery commonly used to treat the disease—laser vaporization and electrocoagulation, which "boil" and "burn" away the disease—only treat the superficial layers of endometriosis. When the pain resumes, the doctor can tell the patient the disease was eradicated—but it returned.

"Incorrect theories of the cause of the disease lead to incorrect treatments—and repeated rounds of treatments," says Dr. Redwine.

Why do doctors use these failed treatments?

There are several reasons, explains Dr. Redwine. "The drugs and surgical treatments are slickly marketed by their manufacturers. And the research justifying the use of the medications therapies has been paid for by drug manufacturers, who ignore negative results and manipulate statistics to emphasize positive results. The insurance reimbursement for effective surgical treatment is low, he points out. And neither the drug nor surgical treatments require a high degree of skill, and can be done by busy physicians.

"The stage is terribly set against women with endometriosis," says Dr. Redwine. "There are so many layers of ignorance, greed, confusion and deception—and the end result is that women experience endless rounds of unsuccessful treatments."

➤ **Understand the real cause of endometriosis—and the successful curative option that addresses the cause.** The probable cause of endometriosis is *embryologically patterned metaplasia,* or EPM.

Genetic and environmental factors cause embryological cells that should have ended up in the uterus, fallopian tubes and ovaries to end up in the pelvic cavity. When a woman starts producing estrogen at menstruation, these errant cells bloom into endometriosis.

The effective treatment is to *surgically excise* the endometriosis—to cut it out with a technique called laparoscopic excision.

"This treatment gives the doctor the opportunity to get around and underneath the disease

A New Voice for Women With Endometriosis

The Endometriosis Foundation of America (EFA) is a new organization that supports the use of laparoscopic excision as the best treatment for the condition.

"In contrast to the enigmatic picture often painted of endometriosis as an incurable condition, the EFA firmly believes that every stage of the disease is treatable and, with the correct surgical techniques, even curable," says their mission statement, at *www.endofound.org.*

The cofounder of the organization is Padma Lakshmi, cookbook author, actress, model and host of Bravo's *Top Chef* series. She was cured of endometriosis with laparoscopic excision.

"Endometriosis was a very trying ordeal," she says. "I had to be operated on. Now, I'm fine."

"Endometriosis is the most prevalent disease affecting reproductive health," says Lakshmi's surgeon and EFA cofounder, Tamer Seckin, MD, an expert in excision surgery for the disease. "It's also the most misunderstood, misdiagnosed, mismanaged and mistreated. And because of that, women end up being infertile and in chronic pain."

and completely remove it," says Dr. Redwine. "It is frequently curative and recurrence is uncommon.

"Patients come to me with complex histories of treatment," he adds. "They've used hormonal drugs, superficial surgery and painkillers, they've eaten less red meat, had acupuncture and tried heating pads. Whatever was working is no longer working. But excision surgery can work. It is the most effective treatment we currently have."

What to look for: A gynecological surgeon who performs laparoscopic excision of endometriosis, and has extensive experience treating the disease with this method.

Rapid Resource: You can access more information, including worksheets and pain profiles, at *www.endofound.org/resource-materials*. Address: Endometriosis Foundation of America, 205 East 42nd Street, 20th floor, New York, NY 10017; call 646-854-3337 or *http://www.endofound.org/contact*.

ERECTILE DYSFUNCTION

The Wise Way to Use Erection Medication

By age 50, half of all men complain about *erectile dysfunction* (ED)—often enough so that it bothers them, they can't achieve and maintain an erection sufficient for intercourse.

Those guys should just take some *sildenafil* (Viagra), right?

Well, here's the dirty little secret never mentioned in commercials for Viagra and other ED medications such as *vardenafil* (Levitra) and *tadalafil* (Cialis)…

What you may not know: "While many men have been helped by an erection medication, many have been disappointed," says Barry W. McCarthy, PhD, a clinical psychologist and marriage and sex therapist in Washington, DC, and coauthor of *Coping with Erectile Dysfunction: How to Regain Confidence & Enjoy Great Sex* (New Harbinger).

That's because erections medications work 65% to 85% of the time—not the 100% implied by the commercials.

And—contrary to popular belief—they don't turn back the clock on your sex life.

"If you're expecting an erectile medication to help you achieve an erection like you had in

your twenties, you're setting yourself up for frustration and failure," says Dr. McCarthy.

Good news: You can use erection medications in a wise way—by integrating the medication into the current sexual style of you and your partner, for more pleasure, eroticism and intimacy.

But first, there's a few things you have to understand about sex after 50…

➤ **You're not 20 anymore—and neither is your penis.** "There's a reason there are so few older athletes in competitive sports like basketball, baseball and football—a man's body no longer functions with the power and precision it did when he was in his teens and twenties," says Dr. McCarthy.

And that change in functioning includes the penis.

"When you are twenty, you have what sex therapists call *autonomous sexual functioning*—the ability to have an erection without any outside stimulation," says Dr. McCarthy. "But by the age of fifty, you require direct stimulation to have an erection. You require the sensual and erotic support of your partner—your sexual friend.

"But not getting a predictable, spontaneous erection a hundred percent of the time doesn't mean you can't have great sex—any more than you should stop playing basketball just because

Wax and Wane Exercise— How to Restore Confident Erections

"This exercise will show you how easy it is to get an erection, let it subside, and regain it when you stay relaxed and focus on arousal," says Dr. Mc-Carthy. "You are balancing the two physical conditions your body needs for erection—relaxation and stimulation. You'll want to practice this exercise several times, until you again feel confident with your erections."

His instructions…

1. **Soothing genital touch.** Rest on your back and ask your partner to gently and soothingly explore your testicles and penis with soft, slow touch for fifteen minutes. Concentrate on the quiet, calm sensations. Relax your pelvic muscle. (You can locate your pelvic muscle by imagining you are squeezing off urination or "twitching" your penis.) She can give you featherlike touching or fingering to pleasure your penis—but without producing an erection. Relax and concentrate on the calm sensations. Do this exercise at least twice.

2. **Finding your calm, easy erection.** Have your partner gently touch your genitals in a relaxing way. Then ask her to very gradually increase her fingering of your penis. Do not work to obtain an erection, but very slowly allow an erection by continuing your relaxation, keeping your pelvic muscle relaxed and focusing on the pleasure in your penis. The more relaxed and focused you are, the easier it will become erect. You are practicing getting an erection with *self-entrancement arousal*—maximum body relaxation, minimal touch and focus on your sensations.

- *Be patient.* Typically, it will take at least five to 10 minutes before an erection begins. Do not press it, or you will become distracted by spectatoring (watching and judging yourself, rather than sensuously participating) and undermine your physical relaxation. After several minutes of calm touch, she can increase the stimulation just a little. You are waiting to find the *minimum* touch you require to get an erection. Be sure you are not rushing it, because you would conclude that you need more stimulation than is really necessary. Keep your pelvic muscle relaxed and let her gradually increase penile touch. She may add stimulation by gently using both hands.

3. **Choosing to wax and wane.** After you've had an erection for three to five minutes, choose to let it subside about 50% by stopping or changing the penile touch. As you feel your erection subsiding, stay focused on your sensations. Then signal her to change the touch gradually to bring back a relaxed erection. Notice that when you're physically relaxed, it is easier to regain your erection. You can lose your erection and regain it easily when you are calm and focused.

you can't play like you did when you were in your twenties. You simply have to play with a different kind of style."

➤ **An older man's erection goes away and returns—and that's perfectly okay.** During a sexual occasion, an older man's erection is likely to go away and return…and go away and return again. That's only a problem if he thinks it is—if he considers sex a pass-fail test…that he's failing.

"*Knowing* that an erection that has gone away will return again is the best way to fight panic about losing your erection," says Dr. McCarthy. "It gives you some control over your

Exercise Is Sexercise

ED is often caused by poor circulation—there isn't enough blood flow to the penis to start and sustain an erection. Which is why you can prevent ED with heart-pumping, circulation-boosting exercise…

Study: Researchers at Harvard School of Public Health surveyed nearly 32,000 men aged 53 to 90—and found that those who exercised regularly had a 30% to 40% lower risk of developing ED compared to men who hardly exercised.

"Increasing exercise levels may be an effective, drug-free way to prevent and treat erectile dysfunction," says Elizabeth Selvin, PhD, an assistant professor in the Department of Epidemiology at Johns Hopkins.

What to do: Walking, pedaling on a stationary bicycle, jogging—any kind of regular, sustained exercise, for 30 to 60 minutes, most days of the week—can lower your risk.

experience. It lets you feel confident that if you relax and receive stimulation, your erection is likely to return."

➤ **Develop a flexible scenario.** And even if it doesn't return—or occur in the first place—that's not the end of the world.

Develop a *flexible* scenario for your sexual occasions, says Dr. McCarthy. "If intercourse doesn't happen, rather than apologizing or panicking, transition to erotic non-intercourse or sensual cuddling.

Result: Taking this approach means you'll probably have a lot more sex—into your 50s, 60s, 70s and 80s.

"When couples stop being sexual, it's almost always the man's call," says Dr. McCarthy. "The man has lost his confidence in erections and intercourse, and decides to stop having sex. And that's a terrible loss for the man, for the woman, for the couple.

"Sex isn't about passing or failing the intercourse test," emphasizes Dr. McCarthy. "It's about giving and receiving pleasure. That might include intercourse and orgasms—and it might not."

➤ **Let your partner decide on the moment of penetration.** Most men who take erection medication think that as soon as they get an erection—they should use it!

"That is absolutely the wrong technique or strategy," says Dr. McCarthy. "If you let your partner decide on the moment of penetration, it removes your performance anxiety—a major reason for ED. By letting your partner control the event, you can relax—and your confidence will be restored."

➤ **Cialis is better suited to most couples.** Cialis—the long-lasting erection-medication—is often a better choice for couples, says Dr. McCarthy. "It gives the couple the freedom to adapt to a 'good-enough' style of sexual play and sexual touching—enjoying both intercourse and non-intercourse—instead of the man feeling there's a window of opportunity when he *has* to perform."

Important: Although Cialis is advertised as working for up to 36 hours, it works best in the 24 to 30 hour range.

See Your Doctor If...

If you can obtain firm erections—erections at waking, masturbatory erections, erections with manual or oral sex—it's likely that your ED isn't the result of an underlying circulatory, hormonal or neurological problem.

But if you can't, you may have another health problem, such as diabetes, high blood pressure, heart disease or depression.

If you have ED, see your family doctor, who will review your health history and perhaps refer you to a urologist or sexual medicine specialist for other diagnostic tests.

Falls

Oops! The floor had a slippery spot, your foot slid forward, you toppled over backward—and in that instant your life changed. For the worse.

Forty percent of people over 65 suffer a fall every year, accounting for one out of every 10 visits to the ER and one out of every 15 hospitalizations among that age group. For 20 to 30%, those falls reduce mobility and independence. And lifespan.

Fact: Every 25 minutes, an older adult dies from a fall. And following a hip fracture—the most common injury after a fall—an estimated 50% of people over 65 die within one year, and most don't live more than two years.

But as bad as a fall can be, many doctors tell seniors they're a fact of life. Those doctors are wrong.

New finding: Researchers at Yale School of Medicine studied fall prevention programs in people 70 and older, publishing their results in the *New England Journal of Medicine.* They found the programs cut falls by 11% (and fall-related hip fractures and head injuries by 10%)—simply by educating people about what to do to prevent falls.

"Falling doesn't have to be an inevitable part of old age," says Mary E. Tinetti, MD, who led the study. "It is preventable."

And preventing a fall can be as fast as changing your shoes...

➤ **Wear shoes that grip.** Any rubber-soled, low-heeled shoe will help prevent falls, says Nanette Lavoie-Vaughan, MSN, APN, the director of Nurse Nan Consulting (*www.nanettelavoie-vaughan.com*) in North Carolina and author of *The Baby Boomers' Guide to Senior*

Care (American Media). If you favor house socks or slippers, wear a pair with nonskid treads, such as Sure-Grip terrycloth slippers, from Medline Industries, which are widely available.

🕐 Super-Quick Fix

➤ **In winter, beef up your boots.** Wear the Yaktrax Walker, a plastic netting that fits snugly over the bottom of a boot or shoe and provides extra traction.

New finding: In a study published in the *Journal of the American Geriatric Society,* researchers divided fall-prone older adults into two groups—one wore the Yaktrax Walker and one didn't. The group wearing the netting had a total of 19 outdoor falls; the group that didn't had 43. And only one fall in the Yaktrax group produced an injury, compared to 10 injurious falls in the non-Yaktrax group.

A pair of Yaktrax costs about $20, while the average cost for a fall-related hospitalization is $20,000, points out Fergus Eoin McKiernan, MD, of the Center for Bone Diseases at the Marshfield Clinic in Wisconsin.

Rapid Resource: You can order the Yaktrax Walker at *www.yaktrax.com*, or call 866-925-8729. Address: Yaktrax, LLC, 2001 T.W. Alexander Dr., Durham, NC 27709, fax 919-314-1960 or e-mail *help@4implus.com*.

➤ **Practice a balance exercise.** "I define balance as the ability of the body to keep its center of gravity in order to avoid a fall," says Betty Perkins-Carpenter, PhD, author of *How to Prevent Falls: Better Balance, Independence and Energy in 6 Simple Steps* (Senior Fitness Productions). And you can improve balance, she says—with balance exercises. *Here is an easy one...*

1. Stand with feet slightly apart. Place both hands on the back of a stationary chair in front of you.

Are You at Risk?

"There is a lack of awareness among older people and their doctors about who is at risk for falls," says David J. Thurman, MD, with the National Center for Chronic Disease Prevention and Health Promotion. "*Identifying* people at high risk for falls is a crucial step in preventing future falls." *Here are common risk factors for falls...*

- *Depression.* "People with depression are fifty percent more likely to fall than other older people," says Ngaire Kerse, PhD, at the University of Auckland in New Zealand, who studied 21,900 Australians over the age of 60.

- *Taking an antidepressant.* Those who are depressed and take an antidepressant are 66% more likely to fall. "In our study, three out of five women over eighty who were depressed and taking an antidepressant fell in the last year," says Dr. Kerse. Sleeping pills and antipsychotic medications can also increase risk.

- *Stroke.* "People who've had a stroke fall almost twice as often as people who haven't," says Dr. Kerse. In her study, 37% of stroke survivors fell in the six months after a stroke, and nearly 40% of those sustained an injury requiring medical treatment.

- *Parkinson's disease.* A recent study by the American Academy of Neurology found that people with Parkinson's disease are at a higher risk for falls.

The study also found an increased risk for those with...

- *Alzheimer's disease and dementia.*

- *Peripheral neuropathy.* Nerve damage in the feet that causes burning, tingling and numbness. Diabetes is the likely cause.

- *Vision loss,* from problems such as age-related macular degeneration or glaucoma.

- *Balance disorders,* such as Meniere's disease.

- *Prostate problems.* In men 65 and older, symptoms such as urinary urgency, straining at urination and frequent daytime and nighttime urination are linked to an increased risk of falling. Those with mild symptoms have a 21% higher risk; those with severe symptoms, 63%. "Ensure a clear path from the bedroom to the bathroom in your home," says Tomas L. Griebling, MD, a urologist and spokesperson for the American Urological Association.

- *Slower walking.* If your walking speed has decreased significantly, you're more likely to fall, says Manuel Montero-Odasso, MD, from the University of Western Ontario.

- *You've fallen in the past year.* This is a strong indicator you're likely to fall again.

2. Holding on to the chair, raise your right knee so your foot is a few inches off the floor (a little higher, once you've mastered the movements in this exercise). Allow your right leg, from knee to foot, to hang loose. Be careful not to tuck your foot under your thigh!

3. Hold this position for a slow count of three. Return your right leg to starting position and relax.

4. Perform the activity with your left leg. Now repeat once with right leg, then with left leg.

5. Now, "play the piano" by rippling your fingertips on the back of the chair. (You're practicing how it feels to balance without the complete support of the chair.)

6. While "playing piano," repeat lifting your right knee and then your left knee (Steps 1, 2 and 3 above) just high enough to sense how it might feel to let go of the chair completely.

7. Now, raise your right knee so that your foot is a few inches off the floor. Slowly, and relaxed, let go of the chair and gently raise your arms, little by little, until you find your balance point

Learn How to Fall Safely— Practice "The Slump"

You've probably never "practiced" falling, says Dr. Perkins-Carpenter. As a result, if and when you fall, your body will immediately become rigid—increasing your risk of a serious or even fatal injury.

New approach: But you can learn how to fall, she says—by practicing the Slump.

"The Slump exercise simulates a person with a loss of balance—but under conscious and thoughtful conditions. People who practice the Slump train what is known as their *proprioceptive sense*—the 'sixth sense' that subconsciously controls the correct positioning of your body. By continually practicing the 'art of falling,' your sixth sense allows you to instinctively relax and slump into a fall—preventing serious injury."

Her instructions…

The Slump: Into the Chair

1. **Stand tall in front of a stationary chair, with the seat brushing the backs of your legs.** Feet should be a comfortable distance apart and arms should be hanging loosely at your sides.

2. **Totally relax your body and SLOWLY let yourself relax and slump back into the chair.**

3. **Slump your shoulders and do you best "rag doll" impression.**

Repeat every time you sit down to read or watch TV.

The Slump: Into the Bed

1. **Stand in the center of the side of your bed, with your back toward the bed.** Stand tall, feet comfortably apart with the backs of your legs touching the bed and arms hanging loosely at your sides.

2. **Bending at the knees, SLOWLY and very loosely collapse into a sitting position on the bed.** Slump your shoulders and relax your entire body during this simulated "fall."

3. **Now collapse on either your left shoulder and side or right shoulder and side (whichever bedside you started on, with your head toward the headboard).** Still remaining as loose and limber as possible, bring your knees up slightly toward your chest.

Repeat every time you go to bed or lie down for a nap.

"Remember, a stiff body breaks, but a limp body bends," says Dr. Perkins-Carpenter. "You can avoid broken bones! Please practice every day!"

or center of gravity—the position in which, when you are balancing, your weight is evenly distributed and you feel comfortable and safe.

8. Hold this position for as long as you can. At first, it might be just a fraction of a second. But, gradually, you will be able to hold the position for longer intervals.

9. Return your hands to the chair and lower your right leg. Relax.

10. Repeat with your left leg.

11. Remember to "stand tall"—maintain a straight-backed posture.

12. Repeat the entire exercise four to five times a day.

Rapid Resource: How to Prevent Falls includes Dr. Perkins-Carpenter's entire Six-Step Balance System, with stretching-in-bed exercises, balance exercises, ball handling activities and other better-balance methods. You can order the book or an instructional DVD of the System, at *www.senior-fitness.com*, or call 800-306-3137 or e-mail *bpc@senior-fitness.com*. Address: Dr. Betty Perkins-Carpenter, Senior Fitness, 1780 Penfield Rd., Penfield, NY 14526.

⏱ *Super-Quick Fix*

➤ **Take vitamin D.** Australian researchers studied 302 women ages 70 to 90 with a history of falls. They divided them into two groups—one took 1,000 IU of vitamin D a day and the other took a placebo. Vitamin D reduced the risk of falling by 19%.

In another study, people in nursing homes (where approximately 50% of all residents fall every year) who took 800 IU of vitamin D decreased their risk of falling by 72%.

"Previous studies have shown that vitamin D could help prevent falls in seniors, perhaps by strengthening the muscles and bones," says Kerry Broe, at the Hebrew SeniorLife Institute for Aging Research at Harvard, who led the study. "But until now, we didn't know what dose would be effective."

She says to take 800 or more IU of vitamin D with the approval and supervision of your doctor.

➤ **Be careful in the bath.** Researchers at the University of Michigan Medical School asked 89 people ages 60 and older to show them how they typically climbed in and out of the shower or tub—and then videotaped them doing it. (Modesty prevailed—the volunteers were videotaped fully clothed.)

"We found that there are a lot of older adults who have trouble or are unsafe getting into and out of the tub or shower stall," says Susan L. Murphy, ScD, a research assistant professor in the Division of Geriatric Medicine at the medical school.

Problem #1. **Three-quarters of the people used the sliding glass doors of shower stalls for stability or balance.** "This is extremely unsafe, because shower doors were not designed to support a person's weight," says Dr. Murphy.

Solution: Don't use the door as support, she says. Or replace it with a shower curtain, which you definitely won't try to hold on to.

Problem #2. **Many of the participants used a towel bar for support.**

Solution: Install a "grab bar" in the tub, says Lavoie-Vaughan.

However, she says, make sure you choose the type that is attached directly to a stud in the bathroom wall, and not the type you purchase and install yourself, which is less likely to support your weight.

Rapid Resource: If you can't afford a grab bar, contact your local Agency on Aging, which will usually install them for free, says Lavoie-Vaughan. You can find the location of a nearby Agency on Aging at *www.n4a.org.* Click "Consumer" on the home page, or call 202-872-0888.

Lavoie-Vaughan's other tips for a safe bathroom include…

• Put a bathmat in the shower or tub.

• Use a shower bench or chair to sit in the tub.

• Use a handheld shower. "You can get them anywhere and they're easy to install," she says. "Just screw the shower head off and screw the attachment on. This brings the shower head down to you, so you don't have to stand as long."

➤ **Fall-proof your home.** There are many other ways to prevent falls at home, says Dr. Perkins-Carpenter.

You should be able to answer "Yes" to *all* of these questions, she says…

• **Lighting.** Can you turn on a light without having to walk into a dark room? Do you replace burned-out bulbs immediately? Do you have nightlights in your hallways, bedrooms, stairwells and living areas? Do you keep a flashlight by your bed? Are there lights and switches installed at both the top and bottom of stairways—and can you clearly see the outline of each step as you go up and down? Is the lighting bright but not creating glare?

- **Walkways.** Do you use nonskid wax or no wax at all, on polished floors? Are walkways kept clear of things that could trip you, such as cords, low furniture and toys? Do you immediately replace breaks in linoleum, broken floorboards or flooring that is buckling? Do you clean up spills on floors immediately?

- **Stairways.** Do all stairways have securely fixed handrails on both sides? Does your hand wrap easily and completely around the rail? Are all carpets and runners well fastened down? Are stairs kept free of clutter?

- **Furniture.** Do you arrange your furniture in each room so that a clear and wide walking lane is left open? Does your favorite chair have armrests that are long enough to help you get up and sit down? Are your chairs and tables stable enough to support your weight if you lean on them?

➤ **Get more sleep.** Women 70 and older who get less than five hours sleep a night are 1.4 times more likely to fall.

However: Sleeping pills aren't the answer. People who take *benzodiazepines* to help with sleep—either short-term or long-term—can *triple* their risk of falling. (Benzodiazepine sleeping pills are marketed under many names, including Valium, ProSom and Halcion.)

What to do: There are several ways for seniors with insomnia to improve their sleep, says B. T. Westerfield, MD, medical director of the Sleep Disorders Center of Lexington, Kentucky.

- Get treatment for sleep-disturbing medical problems, such as diabetes, arthritis or prostate problems.

- Talk to your doctor about your medications, which may be disturbing your sleep—particularly "psychoactive" medications for problems such as depression or anxiety.

- Don't drink alcohol within three hours of bedtime.

- Don't nap more than 30 minutes during the day.

- Exercise regularly. Walking is easy and convenient.

FATIGUE

Extra Energy—It's More Than Meets the Eye

Everybody wants more energy. And everybody has heard the standard recommendations for beating fatigue—get enough sleep…eat a "well-balanced" diet…exercise regularly…don't overwork…reduce stress.

So why are we all so worn out?

"Our high-tech society thrusts many of us into chronic physical, emotional and spiritual depletion," says Judith Orloff, MD, an assistant clinical professor of psychiatry at UCLA and the author of *Positive Energy: 10 Extraordinary Prescriptions For Transforming Fatigue, Stress & Fear Into Vibrance, Strength & Love* (Random House). "We're bombarded by information overload. We're confronted by hostile forces on a global scale. It's no surprise our energy suffers."

But what's most alarming, she adds, is that we've learned to tolerate tired, joyless states as *normal.*

Dr. Orloff practices what she calls "Energy Psychiatry." And she says that the traditional model of personal energy—a limited fuel replenished only by a healthy diet, sleep and exercise—is obsolete. "We need to teach people how

Shift Your Perspective On Your To-Do List

"Imagine you're on your deathbed looking back on your life," instructs Dr. Orloff. "Really get into it. Picture your face, your clothes, your surroundings. Pay witness to your life—notice the real highlights. Was it love? Family? Friends? That summer afternoon planting petunias with your son? How does your to-do list compare to those times? Do you even remember it? What about the all-nighters you pulled at work? Or the constant rushing? What was it all for? What was truly meaningful? Use these insights about how you expended your energy to restore a more enlightened perspective."

to sense and access the *full range* of their energy reserves. It's not your fault if you follow your doctor's orders and still feel drained. You just need a more complete prescription."

That "complete prescription" includes tapping into *subtle energy*—"the great, swirling, invisible energy fields that shape personal and planetary health." You can do that by protecting yourself from people who drain your energy... not letting the machinery of modern life grind you down...and harnessing the power of positive energy, through love and compassion. "All of us can soar with higher energy," says Dr. Orloff.

Prepare for takeoff...

► **Overcome technodespair.** "There's an energy affliction I call 'technodespair,' " says Dr. Orloff. Chronic energetic assault from a torrent of information—the Internet, email, voice mail, cell phones, texting, faxes—burns us out. "How do you know if you're a sufferer?" she asks. "You experience mild to intermediate nervousness, depression or fatigue after bouts with the complexities of technology."

What to do: Get in the habit of taking mini technology fasts, says Dr. Orloff. "Check your email less frequently. Watch a goofy movie instead of reading news updates on the Web. Go for a few hours without texting—take a walk instead."

Don't succumb to technology fiascos, such as the crash of a hard drive, she says. "Breathe deeply and take your pulse. This expels flipped-out vibes and awakens the positive. Also adjust your attitude. Don't catastrophize. Even if a technical snafu occurs, you'll probably be able to at least piece things together."

► **Swear off workaholism.** "Workaholism is the Puritan ethic gone haywire, an addiction to doing more, going nonstop until you drop," says Dr. Orloff. "If you keep pushing through fatigue when your intuition screams, 'Rest!' you're inadvertently punishing yourself. Fostering positive energy is about respecting your body's signals."

What to do: "Compassion, a subtle energy that comes from the heart, will help you stop pushing yourself," says Dr. Orloff. "Commit to at least one self-compassionate action a week— a short afternoon nap, for example, or hiring a babysitter to free up an evening. Planning regular downtime nurtures positive energy.

"Self-compassion also means realizing not everything has to be done today. Prioritize essentials—then stop there. From this perspective, much of our to-do list seems self-inflicted."

► **Protect yourself from energy vampires.** "Energy vampires roam the world sapping our exuberance," says Dr. Orloff. "But many of us mope around as unwitting casualties, enduring a preventable fatigue." Who are they?

"Intrusive parents who don't know what the word boundary means," she says. "Needy siblings who bleed their family dry. Coworkers with a penchant for exhausting drama. Friends whose nonstop whining on the phone leaves you

Speed Healing Success

"You Can't Believe What a New Thing Can Do for You"

A client of Dr. Kirshenbaum's (see page 137), Maura, shared her story of how newness saved her life…

"I'm a waitress at a steak house, plus I do catering jobs when I can. My husband owns a small auto body shop, and we have two sons, eight and ten. For most of our married life it's been about working hard and paying bills.

"We're like millions of people who've gotten ourselves into a place that's just good enough and just precarious enough where we pray nothing changes. Well, beware of getting what you pray for!

"But I got to the point where I just didn't want to get out of bed. I wasn't tired. It was more like, 'God, you look ahead and nothing is going to change. Because nothing *can* change.'

"Sometimes I get together with a few ladies and we talk about everything. And one day, one of the ladies out of nowhere says, 'You know, sometimes I could just scream.' And we looked at her, and there was a scary kind of haunted look on her face like you were looking into a secret you weren't supposed to know about. We talked about it, and it turns out that all of us were dying of boredom.

And I don't mean that we're very bored. I mean that boredom is really killing us.

"I asked myself what most made me want to scream. It was really just day-to-day routine. So I thought about what I could do that would be new. First I thought I could exercise. So I joined a gym in the next town. It had yoga. Imagine me doing yoga. Now that's new.

"I changed my look. I didn't want to look so small-town. I cut my hair short. I bought some black T-shirts.

"And my lady friends and I decided to take a trip to New York, see a show, go to a club, shop on Fifth Avenue—at least window-shop. Scare our husbands a little.

"You can't believe what a new thing can do for you. It's not about the thing itself. I mean, come on, who cares if you change your clothes? But it's like you're saying, 'Hey, I can rescue myself.'

"So while I was busy doing new things, I quit my job. I'd been waitressing because my catering wasn't taking off—because of the time I spent waitressing. Now I'm trying to get more catering jobs. I've taken out ads. Called places. It's scary. But I've gotten some jobs. It's exciting. It's *energizing*."

---

splayed. What's common to all vampires is that they take our energy and exhaust us."

Here are Dr. Orloff's descriptions of common types of energy vampires and ways to protect yourself…

● **The Sob Sister.** Whenever you talk to her, she's whining. She loves a captive audience and casts herself as victim, with the world always against her.

What to do: Limit the time you spend discussing a sob sister's gripes. (And remember—there are "sob brothers" too!) With a friend or family member, lovingly say, "I really value our

relationship, but when you keep rehashing the same points it wears me out. I can listen for ten minutes—that's my limit. However, when you want to talk solutions, I'm here for you." With a coworker, emphasize that you have work to do and can only listen a short time.

● **The Blamer.** The blamer has a sneaky way of making you feel guilty for not getting things just right. He berates, doles out endless servings of guilt or resorts to verbal abuse.

What to do: To deflect a blamer's vibes, you can use your own subtle energy as a shield. Imagine yourself enveloped in a cocoon of white light. Picture it as a shield forming a fail-safe barrier around every inch of you, a covering that stops you from being harmed. It's semi-permeable, allowing what's positive in, but keeping negativity out.

• **The Drama Queen.** She has a breathy flair for exaggerating small incidents into off-the-charts drama. Life is always extreme, either unbearably good or bad. She spends life flitting from crisis to crisis, energized by chaos.

What to do: The moment you sense a drama queen revving up, take a slow, deep breath to center yourself. Breathing is a wonderful way to reconnect quickly with your life force so her in-your-face intensity won't sear into your energy field and cause burnout. Keep concentrating on your breath. Tell yourself you know what's happening and you can handle it.

• **The Constant Talker or Joke Teller.** This chronically perky motor-mouth has no interest in what you're feeling and demands center stage. He's only concerned with himself, his stories, his opinions, his jokes.

What to do: Around these drainers, inhale deeply and slowly, feel your feet solidly planted in the ground and don't let exasperation override the calm you're striving for. Then, from a neutral place, set the parameters of your dialogue. With a stranger (on an airplane, for example), say nicely, "I hope you can appreciate this is my time to relax. I'd rather be quiet and read." With a neighbor or coworker, say, "I'm a very quiet person, so excuse me for not talking a long time." With friends and family, say, "I really feel left out when you dominate the conversation. I'd really appreciate a few minutes to talk too."

• **The Go-for-the-Jugular Fiend.** The most malevolent of bloodsuckers, she is vindictive and cuts you down with no consideration for your feelings. Driven by envy, competition or severe insecurity, she deflates your energy with just the right insult.

What to do: Move heaven and earth to eliminate her from your life. There's no gain to being exposed to such venom. If she must stay, never stoop to her level by countering meanness with meanness. If you must interact, break eye contact to stop the transfer of toxins. Use your breath to retrieve your life force. Let it function like a vacuum cleaner. With each inhalation, visualize yourself power-suctioning back every drop of energy she's snatched from you. Keep inhaling until the job is done. Do this in the presence of a vampire or later on.

Rapid Resource: You can find more energy-increasing, life-enhancing recommendations from Dr. Judith Orloff—and order her newest book, *Emotional Freedom: Liberate Yourself from Negative Emotions and Transform Your Life* (Harmony)—at *www.drjudithorloff.com.*

➤ **For more "emotional energy"—do something new.** "Emotional energy is the kind of energy you're really looking for," says psychotherapist Mira Kirshenbaum, cofounder and clinical director of the Chestnut Hill Institute in Massachusetts and author of *The Emotional Energy Factor: The Secrets High-Energy People Use to Beat Emotional Fatigue* (Delta). "It's a special energy that's all about feeling young and deeply connected to the fun and hope in life. It's an aliveness of mind, a happiness of the heart. How can you possibly feel energetic unless you have that kind of energy?"

And one way to get it is to *do something new.*

"We have a deep hunger for something new," says Kirshenbaum. "For most of us, that hunger is justified by the fact that there's very little new in our lives. This has a huge impact on our emotional energy. A life with little new in it is like a tire with a slow leak. It may not make a difference all at once, but the emotional energy will eventually leak out of it. You have to do something new to stop up the leak and fill up again with emotional energy."

Bottom line: "Tell yourself, 'If my energy's low, it's probably because I'm stuck in a routine, and so I need to do something new,' " says Kirshenbaum. "If you wouldn't ordinarily do it, it's new for you. Eat a new food. Eat an old food prepared in a new way. Drive home a new way. Wear socks that are a new color for you. Go to the bookstore and buy a new kind of book. Listen to a new kind of music. New things give big hits of emotional energy—and fast!

Rapid Resource: You can read Mira Kirshenbaum's blog—written with her husband and fellow psychotherapist, Charles Foster, PhD—at *www.chestnuthillinstitute.com*. The site also offers a way to initiate one-on-one counseling with Kirshenbaum or Dr. Foster. And you can order any one of Kirshenbaum and Dr. Foster's 14 books, which include *Feel Better Fast: Overcoming the Emotional Fallout of Your Illness or Injury* (M. Evans and Company) and *Everything Happens for a Reason: Finding the True Meaning of the Events in Our Lives* (Three Rivers Press).

FIBROMYALGIA AND CHRONIC FATIGUE

End Your Energy Crisis

Life demands energy. The energy to digest your food…to take a walk around the block…to think your way through a difficult tax return.

But what happens when your body can't make enough energy to meet life's demands?

What happens when you're under crushing stress, or always skimp on sleep, or eat a processed diet mostly devoid of vigor-giving nutrients—or find yourself faced with a toxic combination of these and other factors that block your body's ability to produce life-powering fuel?

Maybe you don't just feel tired or rundown. Maybe you have a full-blown, nonstop, body-dragging *energy* crisis.

A crisis called *fibromyalgia* (FM) or *chronic fatigue syndrome* (CFS).

"Fibromyalgia and chronic fatigue syndrome are two related conditions with the same cause—an energy crisis, in which the body spends more energy than it can make," says Jacob Teitelbaum, MD, medical director of the Fibromyalgia and Fatigue Centers and author of *From Fatigued to Fantastic!: A Clinically Proven Program to Regain Vibrant Health and Overcome Chronic Fatigue and Fibromyalgia* (Avery).

In CFS, the crisis is centered in the hypothalamus, the master gland in the brain that controls sleep, hormone levels, body temperature and blood flow. "You're exhausted but can't sleep," says Dr. Teitelbaum. "You might have low blood pressure and unusual sweating patterns."

In FM, the crisis targets the muscles, locking them in shortened positions. "Your muscles are tight and hurt, and you have widespread pain."

Among the estimated three to six million Americans with CFS and FM, the two conditions often overlap. For example, chronic insomnia is a common symptom of both disorders.

Good news: Dr. Teitelbaum (who once suffered from CFS himself) has discovered a medical and self-care protocol for restoring energy production. "Scientific research has shown that 9 out of 10 people with fibromyalgia or chronic fatigue who follow this protocol improve, and about half completely recover," he says.

The protocol is SHINE—Sleep, Hormonal Support, Infection Treatment, Nutrition and Exercise.

Study: Dr. Teitelbaum and a team of researchers studied 72 people with fibromyalgia and chronic fatigue syndrome, dividing them

Speed Healing Success

The Fastest Way to Find Out If You Have FM or CFS

"The predominant symptom of chronic fatigue syndrome (CFS) is fatigue that causes a persistent and substantial reduction in your activity level," says Dr. Teitelbaum. "The onset of fatigue might have been gradual, during a period of severe physical or emotional stress. Or it might have been sudden, starting with a 'drop dead flu' from which you never fully recovered. Other common symptoms include insomnia, achiness, difficulties with short-term memory and concentration, increased thirst, bowel problems, recurring infections, weight gain and low libido."

Fibromyalgia (FM) is characterized by muscle pain—consistent or transient—all over the body or in specific spots.

There is no specific lab test to confirm that you have CFS or FM, says Dr. Teitelbaum. "Diagnosis is often made by a practitioner and patient after medical evaluation and lab testing have eliminated all other possible causes, such as Lyme Disease, multiple sclerosis or depression."

Problem: It can often take months of evaluation before a person realizes they have CFS or FM, says Dr. Teitelbaum.

Solution: But you can discover if you have either or both of these conditions—today.

Dr. Teitelbaum has created a free, online computer program that will analyze your symptoms and lab results (if available)—using the same assessment criteria that he uses with each of his patients. The result is a possible confirmation of your condition—along with a list of the suspected underlying causes of your CFS/FM (such as disordered sleep, hormonal imbalances or unusual infections) and a detailed treatment plan tailored to your specific symptoms.

"Use this with your practitioner as a customized guideline for utilizing prescription remedies," says Dr. Teitelbaum. "You can begin the natural remedies on your own."

Rapid Resource: You can find the online program at *www.endfatigue.com*. Click on "Energy Analysis Program."

into two groups. One group received the SHINE protocol (sleep medications and natural sleep aids such as melatonin, various anti-infectious agents, hormone replacements and nutritional supplements) and the other a placebo treatment. After just six weeks, 28 out of 32 patients on the SHINE protocol said they felt either "much better" (16) or "better" (14)—they had more energy, deeper sleep, greater mental clarity, less pain and increased well-being. But among those in the placebo group, only 12 out of 33 people felt either "much better" (3) or "better" (9). The study was published in the *Journal of Chronic Fatigue Syndrome*.

If you SHINE, it's likely you'll feel better too...

▶ **S is for sleep restoration.** "If you have FM/CFS, the quickest way to recharge your batteries is to get more sleep," says Dr. Teitelbaum. "In fact, for FM/CFS patients to get well, it is critical that they take enough of the correct sleep medications to get eight to nine hours of sleep a night."

• **Prescription medications.** Talk to your doctor about taking 5 to 10 milligrams (mg) of *zolpidem* (Ambien) and 100 to 600 mg of *gabapentin* (Neurontin). The dangers of taking these medications is much lower than the ill effects of not sleeping, says Dr. Teitelbaum.

New approach: "I'm starting to believe that, to offer a margin for safety during periods of stress, it may be wise for a person with FM/CFS to stay on a half to one tablet of a sleep medication for the rest of their life," he says. "Your doctor may initially be uncomfortable with this. Nonetheless, our experience with over two thousand patients and two research studies shows this approach to be safe—and critical to people getting well. When one realizes that FM/CFS is a hypothalamic sleep disorder, this approach makes sense. Otherwise, it is as if your doctor would immediately try to stop blood pressure or diabetes medicines every time the patient was doing better!"

Dr. Teitelbaum also recommends natural sleep aids as an adjunct to sleep medications.

His favorite is a formula he developed— Revitalizing Sleep Formula, manufactured by Enzymatic Therapy. It includes *theanine* (a brain-balancing amino acid found in tea), and several relaxing and sleep-inducing herbs, such as Jamaican Dogwood, valerian, wild lettuce, passion flower and hops.

Rapid Resource: You can purchase this product (and the other supplements presented in this section) at Dr. Teitelbaum's website for people with FM/CFS, *www.endfatigue.com.* (One hundred percent of the royalty Dr. Teitelbaum receives from the sales of products he has developed is donated to charity.)

For better sleep, he also suggests…

• **Magnesium.** Take 250 to 500 mg of a sustained release form at bedtime.

• **Melatonin.** Take ½ mg of this sleep-regulating hormone at bedtime. "The standard dose is three milligrams, but studies show the lower dose is just as effective," he says. If you can't find a ½-mg pill, divide a larger pill.

➤ **H is for hormonal balancing.** "The hypothalamus is the main control center for most of the hormone-secreting endocrine glands in the body," says Dr. Teitelbaum. "Since the hypothalamus is weakened in FM/CFS, it's often necessary to treat the condition with thyroid, adrenal, ovarian and testicular hormones. In bio-identical form—chemically the same as the natural hormone found in the body—these treatments have been found to be reasonably safe when used in low doses."

But what if blood tests show you have "normal" levels of those hormones?

"Standard blood tests are horribly unreliable at diagnosing hormonal problems—they miss the vast majority of people who need hormonal support," says Dr. Teitelbaum.

Two hormonal treatments can take effect relatively quickly…

• **Thyroid hormone.** "A low level of thyroid hormones can cause fatigue, achiness, unexplained weight gain and cold intolerance," says Dr. Teitelbaum. "If you have two or three of these symptoms, talk to your doctor about a trial of Armor thyroid, a natural, or bioidentical, prescription hormone supplement. You may find yourself feeling dramatically better."

🕐 *Super-Quick Fix*

➤ **Adrenal support.** Signs of needing adrenal support—you find yourself irritable and fatigued when you are hungry, or you feel dizzy when you stand up, says Dr. Teitelbaum.

He recommends Adrenal Stress-End, from Enzymatic Therapy. It's a mix of adrenal glandulars (extracts from animal adrenal gland), the herb licorice, the amino acid tyrosine, and the nutrients pantothenic acid and vitamin C—all of which support the adrenal gland.

"People who take this product find that their energy smoothes out in a day or two and then builds over a period of weeks," he says. "It's a particularly good 'quick fix' for low energy."

Take one pill in the morning and one at lunch, he suggests.

▶ **I is for infection treatment.** "Many studies have shown immune system dysfunction in FM/CFS," says Dr. Teitelbaum. "It can result in many infections, such as viral infections, parasites and other bowel infections and infections with the fungus Candida.

"Although it's controversial, long-term treatment with an antifungal medication such as *fluconazole* (Diflucan) has been found to be very effective in FM/CFS."

The SHINE protocol also includes other anti-infectious prescription medications, depending on test results.

For all his patients, Dr. Teitelbaum suggests a no-sugar diet (because fungi feed on sugar) and taking a supplement of probiotics (friendly intestinal bacteria) to restore bacterial health in the digestive tract. *Product:* Acidophilus Pearls, from Enzymatic Therapy.

▶ **N is for nutritional supplementation.** Dr. Teitelbaum recommends two primary products to optimize nutrition in his patients with FM/CFS…

- **A multivitamin-mineral supplement.** "Which nutrients do you need more of if you have FM/CFS? All of them!" he says.

Product: To provide a complete supplement, he's formulated the Energy Revitalization System, a powdered product from Enzymatic Therapy. "You'd have to take thirty-five tablets of various supplements to get the fifty key nutrients in this mixture."

🕐 *Super-Quick Fix*

▶ **Ribose.** "A supplement of ribose is the ultimate 'quick fix' for FM/CFS," says Dr. Teitelbaum. "Ribose is a sugar that plays a role in the manufacture of RNA and DNA and is a key building block for the manufacturer of cellular energy. In fact, the main energy molecules in your body—ATP and FADH—are made of ribose plus B-vitamins and phosphate."

Study: Thirty-six people with FM/CFS—people who had been wearied by the disease for an average of seven years—took five grams of ribose, three times a day, for 25 days. Sixty-six percent—23 of the 36 people taking the supplement—had more energy, better sleep, more mental alertness, less pain and more well-being. On average, the increase in energy was 45%. "This is very dramatic for a single nutrient," says Dr. Teitelbaum.

You can find ribose at *www.endfatigue.com*.

▶ **E is for (moderate) exercise.** Exercise is good for just about everyone, says Dr. Teitelbaum. "But people with FM/CFS have an energy crisis—they usually can't exercise beyond a certain point. In fact, if they push too hard, the

---

Speed Healing Success

"I Feel a Huge Weight Is Being Lifted from My Chest"

"Several of the patients participating in the ribose study contacted me to tell me about the relief they found with this nutritional therapy," says Dr. Teitelbaum.

"They talked about the profound joy they felt when they were able to begin living normal, active lives, sometimes after years of fatigue, pain and suffering.

"One patient, an elementary teacher, wrote, 'I had so much fatigue and pain I thought I was going to have to quit teaching. When I take ribose, I feel like a huge weight is being lifted from my chest, and I'm ready to take on those kids again."

next day they might feel as if they'd been hit by a truck."

Recommended: Exercise at the level that *feels good for you*, whether it's 2 minutes a day or an hour a day. "If you feel wiped out after exercise, cut back," says Dr. Teitelbaum.

Working out in a warm-water swimming pool is particularly congenial for people with FM/CFS, he says. If you choose walking, he also recommends a pedometer—a clip-on device that records the number of steps you take per day. "Find out how many steps you typically take in a day without exercise. Then slowly increase that number, by adding one- and two-minute walks to your day."

FLATULENCE

What to Do When It's Not a Gas

Passing gas is normal—everyone does it about a dozen times a day, expelling a mostly odorless mix of nitrogen, carbon dioxide and oxygen.

But if your gas is excessive and perhaps excessively odorous…if you feel gassy and bloated a lot…then you want and need relief.

The Charcoal Cure

Charcoal absorbs toxins and gases, says Dr. Lipski. You can find activated charcoal capsules in most health-food stores and pharmacies. "It's inexpensive and very helpful," she says. "Take one to four tablets as needed, with a meal or immediately if you are having gas problems."

Warning: "Your stools will turn black—that's the charcoal leaving your body."

Here's how to find it like the wind…

➤ **Eat mindfully.** A common cause of excess gas is swallowed air, explains Joshua Levitt, ND, a naturopathic physician in private practice in Hamden, Connecticut (*www.whole healthct.com*).

"People swallow a lot of air when they eat too fast," he says. But you can slow down the speed of eating by eating *mindfully*—by paying more and better attention to your food.

"Turn your food-taking into a real meal rather than just a mechanism to alleviate hunger," says Dr. Levitt. Take a moment before you start eating to look at and appreciate your food. Smell it. Look at the color. Enjoy the shapes. Think about how it was grown or raised, and its journey to your plate.

And finally, really *chew* your food as you eat, masticating about a dozen times before you swallow. "When you swallow big chunks of food, you also swallow large volumes of air," he says.

Also helpful: Other ways to swallow less air when you eat include drinking through a straw…avoiding carbonated beverages…and not eating whipped foods such as egg whites and whipped cream.

Is Gum Giving You Gas?

"Sorbitol and xylitol are indigestible sugars found in most sugarless candy and gum," says Liz Lipski, PhD, CCN, a certified clinical nutritionist in private practice in Asheville, North Carolina, and author of *Digestive Wellness* (McGraw-Hill, third edition). "Large amounts of those sugars cause gas. But even small amounts can cause a problem for those who are sensitive."

What to do: If you chew sugarless gum and suffer from excess gas, forgo the habit for a few days and see if you feel better.

➤ **Feel better with a bitter.** A "bitter" is a pre-meal digestive aid that includes one or more herbs with a bitter flavor, such as gentian, wormwood, horehound or yarrow, says Dr. Levitt. "Stimulating the bitter taste receptors before a meal triggers the flow of digestive juices, improving digestion and helping to reduce gas."

What to do: Put one drop of gentian tincture on your tongue about 15 minutes before a meal, suggests Dr. Levitt. "For the first week or two you may feel the taste of the herb is too bitter," he says. "But once digestion improves, most people find they start to enjoy the taste—and even start enjoying other bitter foods, such as kale."

Product: A tincture of gentian from Herb Pharm. You can order the tincture at *http://herb-pharm.com* or call 800-348-4372. Address: Herb Pharm, P.O. Box 116, Williams, OR 97544, e-mail *info@herb-pharm.com*.

• **Take a digestive enzyme.** "As you age, your body manufactures fewer digestive enzymes and your ability to digest food decreases, possibly increasing flatulence," says Dr. Levitt. A supplement containing digestive enzymes can help remedy the problem.

Recommended: Dr. Levitt recommends the product Pancreatic Enzymes, from Vital Nutrients. You can order it at *www.professionalsupplementcenter.com* or call 888-245-5000. Take the supplement with meals, following the dosage recommendation on the label.

➤ **If fatty meals give you gas, try a supplement of bile acids.**

Bile is the fat-digesting fluid pumped out by the liver and stored in the gallbladder. If you have trouble digesting fat—if you've had your gallbladder removed, or you experience a lot of gas after every fatty meal—you may benefit from a bile acid supplement, says Dr. Levitt.

Product: Dr. Levitt recommends EnzyGest, from Priority 1. Follow the dosage recommendation on the label.

Rapid Resource: You can also find Enzy-Gest at *www.professionalsupplementcenter.com.*

🕐 Super-Quick Fix

➤ **Use ginger, fennel or anise.** "These spices are valuable tools for reducing gas," says Dr. Lipski. *Her suggestion…*

Put a few slices of fresh ginger or ½ teaspoon of dried ginger in a cup of boiling water and steep until cool enough to drink. "It will soon begin to dispel your gas from both ends."

Or simply chew on fennel or anise seeds to relieve gas.

● **De-gas your beans.** Beans are a superb food, high in fiber, good-for-you vegetable protein and cholesterol-lowering factors, says Dr. Lipski. "But they are notorious for producing gas."

What to do: There are several ways to reduce the "gassiness" of beans, she says.

1. **Soak the beans for four to 12 hours,** drain off the water, replace with new water and simmer for several hours until they are soft. "Some people find that putting a pinch or two of baking soda in the water also helps reduce the gas," she says.

2. **Use Beano, a product that contains the enzymes necessary for the digestion of beans.** "Place a drop or two on your food," says Dr. Lipski.

3. **Eat more beans.** "If you can't tolerate beans, you probably don't eat enough of them," says Dr. Levitt. Start out slowly, perhaps with ¼ cup a day. Wait two days, and eat ⅓ cup. Wait another two days, and eat ½ a cup. Increase by about 50% every two days, until you're able to eat a cup or more without gas.

   "You're teaching your intestinal tract to manufacture more bean-digesting enzymes," he says. "I eat twelve to sixteen ounces of beans a day and they never cause any gas."

FOOD ALLERGIES

One Supplement Can End Years of Misery

When you think of a food allergy, you probably think of this scenario…A child allergic to peanuts mistakenly eats a peanut-containing food and has an immediate and life-threatening allergic reaction, or *anaphylaxis*—hives burst out, the throat swells and Mom calls 911.

Well, that's one type of food allergy, in which an *allergen* such as a peanut activates the immune system's IgE *antibodies*, triggering a range of distressing and even life-threatening symptoms. Allergists estimate 1% to 2% of Americans suffer from this type of food allergy.

But there's another kind of food allergy, says Ellen Cutler, MD, a chiropractor in northern California, founder of the BioSET Healing System and author of *The Food Allergy Cure: A New Solution to Food Cravings, Obesity, Depression, Headaches, Arthritis, and Fatigue* (Harmony).

How to Detect a Food Sensitivity

"Imagine a large buffet offering every food imaginable," says Dr. Cutler. "Which food would you make a beeline for? The one you are most likely to crave and overindulge in—that's the one to which you most likely have a sensitivity."

Another way to tell if you're sensitive or intolerant to a food is your pulse.

"Take your pulse before and after you eat a suspected food," says Dr. Cutler. "If you're sensitive to a food you've just eaten, the pulse usually becomes faster and more forceful. But it can also become slower and weaker."

Speed Healing Success

Her Sugar Cravings Were Gone

"When I saw Claire for the first time, she was sixty-seven years old and about sixty pounds overweight," says Dr. Cutler. "The excess weight had already taken a toll on her knees and hips, which hurt constantly.

"Claire had tried several weight-loss regimens over the years, none of them successfully. As we talked, she mentioned that she experienced voracious sugar cravings, a common sign of carbohydrate sensitivity. She wondered about whether this sensitivity might be contributing to her weight problem.

"Sure enough, testing identified a number of food sensitivities, with carbohydrate being the most severe. I recommended a carbohydrate digestive enzyme, along with a carbohydrate-intolerance diet, which consists primarily of vegetables and proteins, with limited fruits and few or no grains.

"After ten days of enzyme therapy and the carbohydrate-intolerance diet, Claire's joint pain had improved noticeably. Just as important, her sugar cravings were all but gone, and she was pounds lighter."

Rather than an immediate allergic reaction, the food-weakened immune system triggers one or more *chronic health problems*, such as arthritic joint pain, fatigue, headaches, depression, overweight, irritable bowel syndrome or skin conditions such as eczema, hives and rashes.

Dr. Cutler estimates that 35 to 50 million Americans—one out of every four adults—suffers from this type of food allergy, which she calls a *food sensitivity* or *food intolerance*.

There are many reasons why a person develops food sensitivity, she says. It could be a genetic predisposition...or a digestive tract stressed by overeating...or intestines damaged by medications...or a nutritional deficiency.

If you have a chronic health problem that has resisted every attempt at a solution, it's time to suspect food sensitivity as a possible cause, says Dr. Cutler. *Here are her fast-action recommendations for controlling and clearing up the problem...*

🕐 Super-Quick Fix

➤ **Supplement every meal with digestive enzymes.** "Enzymes are complex proteins in the body that function as energy catalysts for the over 150,000 biochemical reactions in our bodies—particularly those involving digestion," says Dr. Cutler, whose book on the topic is *MicroMiracles: Discovering the Healing Power of Enzymes* (Rodale).

"Enzymes break down the various foods we consume—proteins, fat, carbohydrates and vitamins—into smaller compounds that the body can easily and healthfully absorb," she says. "Food sensitivities and deficiencies in digestive enzymes go hand in hand."

You can clear up 80% of food sensitivities by taking a digestive enzyme supplement with every meal, says Dr. Cutler.

Rapid Resource: Dr. Cutler has developed a digestive enzyme supplement with 18 different enzymes (such as protease for protein, amylase for carbohydrates and lipase for fats) that is intended to help people overcome food sensitivities. You can order online at *www.bioset.net* in the "Our Products" section or call 877-246-7381 or e-mail *info@bioset.net*. Follow the dosage recommendation on the label.

➤ **Identify the offending food—and minimize or avoid it.**

Seven foods cause 90% of food sensitivities, says Dr. Cutler. See the box on page 144 for helping you identify the food—and then see if eliminating it from your diet helps you clear up chronic symptoms. *The top seven offending foods are…*

- **Milk.** "It causes many chronic problems, including headaches, digestive problems and acne," she says.

- **Eggs.** "They are responsible for a lot of eczema, rashes and psoriasis."

- **Wheat.** "This sensitivity is a common cause of depression, irritability and fatigue."

- **Soy.** "The number one symptom from soy is bloating," says Dr. Cutler.

- **Tree nuts and peanuts.** "This is typically a classic allergy, with immediate onset of symptoms, but sensitivities can cause anything from headaches to herpes outbreaks."

- **Fish and shellfish.** "Again, this is typically a classic, immediate food allergy rather than a long-acting food sensitivity."

Super-Quick Fix

➤ **Chew more.** "Most people chew each mouthful only three or four times," says Dr. Cutler. That's not anywhere near the minimum number of 30 times necessary to permit the proper work of digestive enzymes—the natural cure for food sensitivities, says Dr. Cutler.

FOOD POISONING

The Antidote Is Prevention

Food poisoning—what experts call *foodborne illness*—sickens 76 million Americans a year. (That's 21,000 people a day.) Most suffer from a sudden and unexplained bout of the "stomach flu"—with symptoms such as stomach pain and cramps, nausea, vomiting, diarrhea and fever—as *salmonella, E. coli* or other germs blitz the digestive tract and the immune system fights back.

But every day, 25 of those 21,000—usually children under five with immature immune systems and adults over 65 with aging ones—*die* from food poisoning.

What can you do to protect yourself and stay healthy? Sometimes, not much.

"The recent spate of frightening and widespread food recalls—pot pies, peanut butter, pistachios—revealed fatal flaws in our systems of food production and safety oversight," says Marion Nestle, PhD, professor of Nutrition, Food Studies and Public Health at New York University and author of *Safe Food* (University of California Press). She points out that the food supply is now global, with untold ingredients and products migrating into our meals from all over the world, and that the understaffed and underfunded USDA (responsible for meat and poultry) and FDA (responsible for everything else) can't possibly meet the challenge of keeping our food safe.

"Given this situation, how can you protect yourself and your family from food contamination?" she asks.

Use caution in the kitchen.

"Food poisoning is not only caused by processed products and restaurant meals," says Elizabeth Scott, PhD, codirector of the Simmons Center for Hygiene and Health in Home and Community at Simmons College in Boston and coauthor of *How to Prevent Food Poisoning: A Practical Guide to Safe Cooking, Eating, and Food Handling* (Wiley). "Much of the meat and produce we buy in supermarkets is contaminated with pathogens that can cause food poisoning," says Dr. Nestle. But you can protect yourself by learning how to safely transport, store and prepare that food.

"Take to the Streets!"

"The United States does not have a food safety system that requires all foods—from farm to table—to be produced under standard, science-based food safety procedures and that holds food companies accountable for following these procedures in letter and spirit," says Dr. Nestle.

"What we do have falls far short of that. The present system divides foods between USDA and FDA—even though meat and vegetable safety are inextricably interlinked, with animal wastes contaminating plant crops in fields. The present system requires rigorous, science-based procedures for only a few foods. Most food producers are expected to use Good Manufacturing Practices, but these are rarely enforced.

"Food safety scandals make it clear that we need a much more effective system. The Government Accountability Office has been arguing for years that creating a more effective food safety agency should be an urgent congressional priority. What's stopping it?"

Politics, she says.

"And that's why food safety is about *democracy*," says Dr. Nestle. "The American public should be screaming bloody murder about unsafe food. People have a right to expect that the food they buy in grocery stores is not contaminated with dangerous pathogens. You can exercise your right as a citizen. Write letters! Join Food Democracy Now (*www.fooddemocracynow.org*), a grass roots organization that lobbies for safe and healthy food. Take to the streets!

"Let congressional representatives know that you want a unified, coordinated food safety system that requires all food producers to follow science-based safety procedures.

"Tell them that you expect your government to monitor and enforce those procedures. Democracy requires a safe food supply. Congress needs to take action. Now!"

Rapid Resource: You can read Dr. Nestle's blog on food safety and food politics at *www.foodpolitics.com*.

"Personal food safety requires four basic actions. *Clean* your hands and surfaces often. *Chill*, with prompt refrigeration. *Separate* foods to avoid cross-contamination. *Cook* to the proper temperature."

And none of them takes much time...

➤ **Clean.** "A golden rule of food safety is to keep high standards of kitchen hygiene," says Dr. Scott. *Her advice...*

• **Wash your hands.** "Before handling food, after handling raw foods and between handling different foods—wash your hands. Ditto for after using the toilet, changing diapers, touching or blowing your nose, handling garbage, gardening and handling pets."

Red flag: In a recent study, Dr. Scott and her colleagues videotaped people preparing foods in their homes and hand-washing before and after. The average time of a washing was *five*

seconds. "People completely underestimate the time it takes for a thorough hand-washing," she says. That would be *20 seconds*, about the time it takes to sing "Happy Birthday to You."

• **Wash counters and contact surfaces (handles, faucets, switches, knobs, etc.).** After any contact with raw food, use an antibacterial kitchen cleaner (when buying, check the label to make sure that it is registered by the Environmental Protection Agency, which assures its effectiveness for food surfaces), along with a disposable a paper towel.

• **Wash kitchen equipment and utensils.** After each use, wash in the dishwasher or wash with hot soapy water at the sink. Air dry, or dry with a clean towel or a paper towel.

• **Wash cutting boards.** After contact with raw food, wipe down with antibacterial

Doggie Bag 101

"The food in the doggie bag is probably nearing its germ-load limit of endurance by the time you take it out of the restaurant," says Dr. Scott. "It's already been prepared, served, pushed around your plate, contaminated from your fork and has sat unchilled while you finished your coffee and made your way home."

What to do: Get it in the fridge as soon as possible and eat it within 24 hours. To reheat, make sure it reaches a temperature of 160°F or higher or 185°F in the microwave.

Red flag: "If you leave the doggie bag in the car for a few hours or overnight, don't even think of trying to save it," says Dr. Scott.

cleanser, and then wash in the dishwasher or kitchen sink.

● **Wash sponges.** After contact with raw food, wash in the dishwasher or launder. Replace regularly.

Red flag: "Sponges and cloths are ideal breeding grounds for bacteria, and many studies have shown them to be the most contaminated items in the kitchen, even harboring salmonella," says Dr. Scott.

⏰ Super-Quick Fix

"Regularly put them in the laundry or through a dishwasher cycle."

➤ **Wash vegetables.** "That includes pre-packaged salads," says Dr. Scott. "The label may say something like, 'Triple-washed and Ready to Eat.' But they still need rinsing—because manufacturers reuse the water that supposedly cleans and decontaminates these foods."

Best: Before preparation, fill the sink with water and soak these and other vegetables for a few minutes.

➤ **Chill.** "The first step in preventing food poisoning at home is to store foods properly in order to ensure they remain in good condition when you're ready to eat them," says Dr. Scott. "As soon as you bring groceries home, get frozen and chilled foods back into a freezer or a refrigerator as quickly as possible. Once these foods begin to thaw and warm, any germs that are present can multiply rapidly."

Warning: Those germs will not be killed by any subsequent chilling or freezing.

➤ **Separate.** "Even the juices from raw meat and fish can carry food poisoning germs and contaminate other foods," says Dr. Scott. "This process of germs being carried from raw foods to other foods is called cross-contamination. It can happen when food poisoning germs get onto your hands or onto cutting boards, countertops, sponges, dishcloths, scrubbers and brushes."

What to do: "To minimize the risk of cross-contamination, keep the preparation of raw foods separate from that of other foods," says Dr. Scott. "If possible, complete the preparation of raw foods and then remove all items that have

Buy Local for Safety

What if you want your food raw? What if you want steak tartar, unpasteurized milk, a Caesar's salad made with raw eggs or a spinach salad? "You're taking a risk, and one of unknown magnitude," says Dr. Nestle.

Smart idea: You can minimize the risk by buying from local suppliers, she says. "Hamburger ground from one piece of meat is far less likely to be risky than industrial hamburger made from the parts of literally hundreds of animals. Lettuce grown locally might have harmful organisms on it, but the probability is smaller than for lettuce packed commercially and stored for days. Food safety is another good reason for supporting local farmers."

been in contact with raw foods, clean and sanitize the counters and wash your hands before starting on the preparation of other foods.

"Also keep a cutting board for raw meat and another for vegetables and fruits."

What many people don't know: "Recent scientific data doesn't support the common notion that the use of wooden cutting boards is more likely than plastics to produce cross-contamination of foods," says Dr. Scott.

⏰ *Super-Quick Fix*

"It was also found that wooden boards can be effectively sanitized by microwaving at high setting for four minutes—but plastic can't be effectively sanitized in the microwave," says Dr. Scott.

➤ **Cook.** "Fortunately, cooking takes care of a lot of food safety problems," says Dr. Nestle. "Bacteria usually don't survive heat. Cooking hamburger until it is well done or throwing a bunch of spinach into a pot of boiling water for just one minute will kill nasty bugs like *E. coli* and *salmonella*."

Important: Buy and use a cooking thermometer, says Dr. Scott. (Half of American households have one, but only 3% use them to test hamburgers and other high-risk foods.) And there is only one important temperature to remember—160°F. "This is the lowest temperature that reliably kills food poisoning germs and destroys heat-sensitive toxins," she says.

FOOT PROBLEMS

Kick Them Out

Life is a hike. By the time you're 50, you've walked about 75,000 miles—or three laps around the earth, says Paul Langer, DPM, clinical faculty member of the University of Minnesota, podiatrist at Minnesota Orthopedic Specialists in Minneapolis, and author of *Great Feet for Life: Footcare and Footwear for Healthy Aging* (Fairview Press). And all those miles take a toll on your tootsies—with four out of five 50-year-olds having at least one foot problem serious enough to see a podiatrist or MD.

Maybe it's a bulging, painful bunion...or a hard and hurting callous...or a fungus-infected nail...or a stabbing heel spur...or feet that throb and ache.

But feet are often the low man on the medical totem pole.

"I see patients with foot problems who have waited a year before seeking treatment," says Christine Dobrowolski, DPM, a podiatrist in Eureka, California, and author of *Those Aching Feet: Your Guide to Diagnosis and Treatment of Common Foot Problems* (SKI Publishing).

"The feet may be the most neglected part of the human body," agrees Dr. Langer. "Because painful conditions of the feet are so common, many people assume that foot pain is just a normal part of everyday life and there is nothing they can do about it."

But there's plenty you *can* do to solve everyday foot problems, says Dr. Langer. *And the journey to healthier, happier feet starts with a single step—into a well-chosen pair of comfortable shoes...*

➤ **Find the perfect fit.** "The most important action you can take to promote healthy feet is wearing shoes that fit and that also provide the right amount of cushioning and support," says Dr. Langer. But a study shows that two-thirds of people over 65—the age group with the most foot problems—wear shoes that don't fit.

And foot problems are often aggravated or even caused by those ill-fitting shoes, says Dr. Langer.

The Best Shoe

Feet hurt? "You can relieve a lot of foot pain by switching to proper footwear," says Dr. Langer. But with thousands of shoe types and styles, it's daunting to find the best shoe for you.

"I am constantly asked by my patients, 'What is the best shoe?' I wish there were a simple answer, but there are too many variables in individual needs—such as arch height, foot shape and previous injuries or surgeries—for everyone to be satisfied by one magical shoe."

But even if there's no ideal shoe, there are clues to help you identify top-quality shoes, says Dr. Langer. *They are...*

- *Soft leather or breathable mesh uppers.* "Poor-quality upper materials do not breathe as well and aren't as durable," he says.
- *Soft lining with no hard or poorly located seams.* This decreases the risk of blistering, provides more comfort and pulls moisture away from the skin.
- *Removable insoles.* "This is excellent for making modifications to the shoe—you can replace them with more supportive insoles, if necessary."
- *Slip-resistant outsole.* "This minimizes the risk of falls on wet or slippery surfaces," he says.
- *Flexibility at the forefoot.* "Shoes need to bend where the feet bend."

Here are his recommendations for making sure you buy a shoe that fits...

- **Stand up.** "You can only evaluate the fit of a shoe when you are standing with the shoe on," says Dr. Langer.

- **Check the heel-to-toe fit.** "The heel-to-toe fit is determined by where the longest toe falls within the tip of the shoe," he says. "And the longest toe isn't always the big toe—for one out of five people, the second toe is longer."

To locate that toe within the shoe, gently press the end of the toe box with your fingers or thumb. A properly fitting shoe will have about one-half inch of space between its tip and the end of the longest toe.

- **Check both feet.** "Most people have one foot that is slightly larger than the other," says Dr. Langer. "So make sure to check both feet for fit—the larger foot first. There's no problem having extra toe room in the shoe of the smaller foot."

Important: A good fit provides enough room for you to wiggle your toes without restriction—in both shoes.

- **Check the heel-to-ball fit.** Next, check the fit from your heel to the ball of your feet—the area where the toes join to the rest of the foot. To do this, ask the salesperson to watch you walk. In a good fit, the sole flexes directly under the ball of the foot as the heel is raised—with no pinching across the shoe upper.

- **Check the width.** "Place your thumb and forefinger across the widest part of the forefoot and squeeze," says Dr. Langer.

- The shoe is too narrow if the foot is stretching the upper tightly—especially if the upper is stretched wider than the sole.

- The shoe is too wide if the upper is loose and there is side-to-side movement in the forefoot.

"For shoes with removable insoles, check the width by removing the insole and standing on top of it, to make sure your foot is not wider than the footbed of the shoe," he says.

- **Check the heel.** "A good heel fit is important to limit slipping—and blistering as a result of slipping," says Dr. Langer.

The truest test of heel fit is walking, he says. "The heel doesn't need to be absolutely immobile—a quarter-of-an-inch play is acceptable. But if the heel is slipping noticeably on each step, look for another shoe."

- **Check the toe box.** This part of the shoe is often overlooked during fitting, he says. If your little toe feels crowded, choose a wider shoe or a shoe with a more rounded toe box.

- **Check the collar height.** This refers to how high the rim of the shoe opening sits on the ankle. "Women tend to have lower-set ankles than men, so they are more sensitive to pressure from the shoe's collar," says Dr. Langer.

Red flag: If you have ankles that are sensitive or have a tendency to swell, pay attention to how the collar fits around your ankle. Look for shoes with well-padded or low-cut collars.

- **Go for a walk.** "Lace up your prospective new shoes and take a stroll around the store," says Dr. Langer. "Don't hurry. Wear the shoes for as long as it takes to decide whether they're right for you."

- **Decide for yourself.** "Comfort is subjective," he says. "In the end, you have to decide whether the shoes look and feel right."

- **Prepare for an exchange.** Congratulations—you've bought a new pair of shoes. But you're not quite done. "After you've made your choice, write down the models and sizes of other shoes that were strong candidates, just in case an exchange is necessary later or you decide to purchase another pair."

- **Break your new shoes in—*inside* the house.** "Take the new shoes home and expect to spend a few days gradually breaking them in," says Dr Langer. "But avoid wearing the shoes outside until you are sure you want to keep them—most shoe stores will not make exchanges or refunds on shoes that have been worn outdoors."

- ➤ **Nail that fungus.** Fungal nails afflict up to 25% of adults, particularly those over 40, with weaker immune systems and thinner skin, says Dr. Dobrowolski, DPM. Her recommendations for foiling the fungus...

Athlete's Foot— Or Shoe Allergy?

"Much of what my patients call 'athlete's foot' is really *contact dermatitis*—an allergy to the material in shoes," says Robert J. Moore, III, DPM, a podiatrist at Moore Foot and Ankle Specialists in Houston (*www.mfasclinic.com*).

If the itching, burning and flaking is in a shoelike pattern—suspect your shoes. Usually the allergy-causer is a dye or a leatherlike material, he says. The only solution is to stop wearing the shoe that's causing the problem—probably a shoe you wear most days of the week.

As for *real* athlete's foot—don't play around with home remedies or natural treatments, he says. "Use Lamisil (*terbinafine*) or another antifungal spray or cream—every day, twice a day—to get rid of the problem."

Also helpful: To avoid getting re-infected with athlete's foot, take these precautions, says Dr. Dobrowolski...

- At the gym, wear shoes or sandals in the locker room.
- Bleach out your shower and tub weekly while you're using the medication.
- Put antifungal powder in your shoes every day.
- Change your socks once a day.

- **Bleach it.** "Roughen the surface of the nail with a nail file and apply a small amount of bleach to the nail with a toothbrush or Q-tip. Let it sit for five minutes. Do this twice a day, every day, for six months," she says.

⚠ *Caution:* Stop the treatment if you notice skin irritation—and don't soak your feet in the bleach.

- **Try Tea Tree Oil.** Studies show that this essential oil—from the leaves of a tree native

For Women Only— Instant Support

Four out of five visits to podiatrists are made by women—because too often shoes for women are, well, heels.

In a study of women's shoes and foot health led by Carol Frey, MD, associate professor of orthopedic surgery at the University of Southern California School of Medicine, she found...

- *80% of women* reported "significant" foot pain while wearing shoes.

- *59% wore uncomfortable shoes* on a daily basis.

- *88% wore shoes that were too small,* as measured by an orthopedic surgeon.

- *79% had not had their feet measured in the last five years when buying shoes.* (Better: Get them measured every time.)

But you can make even the most uncomfortable shoes a little more bearable—with a product called Instant Arches, says Dr. Stephen L. Rosenberg, a podiatrist from Santa Monica.

"Instant Arches are made of a unique and durable closed-cell foam material that creates maximum support, comfort and cushioning for sore feet, no matter what type of shoe you're wearing—dress, loafers, high heels, boots, athletics, casuals or sandals."

An adhesive backing allows for easy adjustments to any footwear, instantly helping to balance and stabilize the foot, he says.

Rapid Resource: You can order Instant Arches online at *www.instantarches.com* or call 310-828-3336.

to Australia—can dramatically reduce toenail fungus, says Dr. Dobrowolski. Apply it twice a day for six months.

- **Use an OTC to stop the spread.** Although they're only about 5% to 20% effective in curing the fungus, an OTC antifungal cream or spray can stop its spread. "I recommend using a topical once or twice a week or a few times a month to prevent the fungus from getting worse," she says.

- **Rx to the rescue.** Prescription topical treatments work about 20% to 30% of the time, says Dr. Dobrowolski. The best medication is Penlac (ciclopirox topical solution). "It's quite effective in decreasing the yellow discoloration and thickness," she says.

- **Think twice about oral antifungal medication.** Although the newer medications are safer, they can still take a toll on the liver. "I only recommend oral therapy to people who are having pain or who have chronic infections as a result of the fungal nails.

➤ **Soothe heel pain.** Heel pain—usually caused by *plantar fasciitis*—is one of the most common problems seen by podiatrists.

What happens: As the arch flattens with age, the long ligament on the bottom of the foot—the plantar fascia—tugs and pulls at the tissue in the heel, separating it from the bone. That area can become inflamed and fill with a mash of dead cells and calcified debris—a *heel spur.*

The main symptom is sharp pain at the heel, at the first step in the morning or after long periods of rest, says Dr. Dobrowolski. "The pain usually lessens after ten to fifteen minutes of walking, but gets worse by the end of the day." It can also worsen when you're exercising—for example, going for a walk, jog or run.

There are many quick ways to lessen the pain, say experts...

- **Self-massage.** "When you're sitting on the couch in the evening, take off your shoes and socks, grab your toes and pull them back toward you, stretching the bottom of the foot," says John Mulholland, DC, a chiropractor in Plattsburgh, New York, and a chiropractic consultant at the Lake Placid Olympic Training Center.

🕐 *Super-Quick Fix*

➤ **Stretch.** "A gentle stretching exercise called a heel lift can help you recover from plantar fasciitis and prevent future flare-ups," says Dr. Langer.

What to do: The heel lift is especially helpful for decreasing pain when getting out of bed in the morning, he says. Place the feet flat on the floor in a sitting position. Raise the heel while keeping the forefoot on the floor, 30 to 40 times for each foot.

● **Soak.** A warm footbath with ½ cup of Epsom salts reduces inflammation and pain, says Amy Rothenberg, ND, a naturopathic doctor and homeopath in Amherst, Massachusetts.

● **Ice.** Many podiatrists suggest an ice massage for the feet by rolling them on a cold juice can or a frozen water bottle.

Better: Cool-Soles, an ice pack in the shape of an insole. "I've treated a number of people with heel pain who have gotten freezer burns from icing their feet with a frozen soup can or a bag of peas," says Steven L. Rosenberg, DPM, a podiatrist in private practice in Santa Monica, California.

"Cool-Soles is an ideal alternative. "It has a woven nylon cover, so it's skin-friendly, and it stays cold for about twenty-five minutes. Take it out of the freezer, put it in a slipper or sandal, and put your feet up for a while."

Also helpful: "Sometimes women have chronically cold feet—they can put this in a microwave and warm their feet up."

Rapid Resource: You can order Cool-Soles at *www.instantarches.com*, or call 310-828-3336.

● **Homeopathic help.** The homeopathic remedy arnica gel effectively relieves heel pain, says Dr. Rosenberg.

Product: Traumeel, which is widely available.

➤ **The best way to treat a blister.** Blisters, a small pocket of fluid in the upper layers of the skin, are caused by friction—a shoe rubs on a sock that rubs on a foot. It happens when you walk hard and long in uncooperative shoes. If you hike, run, walk, jog, bike or climb, you can get a blister. New or rigid shoes can also cause the problem.

If you have a blister, here's the best treatment, says Dr. Dobrowolski...

Make a small hole with a sterile needle at the side of the blister, then drain all the fluid inside. *Do not* remove the top layer of skin. Make sure the area is dry, and then place adhesive tape on the blister and the surrounding areas.

Leave the tape on for three to five days. If after five days, the tape does not come off on its own, peel it off carefully—you don't want to remove the roof of the blister.

Once the blister is healed, take precautionary measures by placing the tape at that area before starting the activity or wearing the shoe that caused the blister.

➤ **Bunion relief.** A bunion is a deformity of the big toe joint, which angles toward the smaller toes, creating a large bump at the outside of the foot. Eventually, pain develops when you're wearing shoes or walking—a problem that is only correctable by surgery.

You can temporarily relieve bunion pain with this exercise, says Stephanie Tourles, author of *Natural Foot Care: Herbal Treatments, Massage, and Exercises for Healthy Feet* (Storey).

Sit in a chair with your feet flat on the floor. Place a nice, thick, moderately stiff rubberband around your big toes and pull your feet away from each other. Hold for five or 10 seconds and relax. Repeat 10 to 20 times.

⚠ *Caution:* If this hurts, or if you have arthritis or bunions in advanced stages, do only as many repetitions as you can and gradually increase as your toes gain strength.

➤ **Calm corns and calluses.** Corns and calluses are accumulations of dead skin in an area where there's pressure on a bone in the foot—a corn is on the top of the foot and a callus is on the bottom.

"Both can become extremely painful if they become large," says Dr. Dobrowolski. Pain relief is never corny…

"Donut hole pads that take pressure off the area are an effective way to treat a corn or callous," says Dr. Dobrowolski.

Or file down the corn or callous with an emery board or a fine piece of sandpaper, says Dr. Rosenberg. "They're more effective than a pumice stone and won't tear the skin up."

SPEED LIMIT

Skip the Medicated Pad

"There are corn and callous medicated pads at the drug store, but I don't recommend them," says Dr. Dobrowolski.

"They usually don't take away the corn— and may cause a chemical burn of the surrounding skin."

GALLSTONES

 Your gallbladder is a pear-sized holding tank that concentrates the daily quart of bile pumped out by your liver—and then releases it into the intestines after meals, where it disperses and dissolves fats.

But in 20% of Americans over 65, the gallbladder also ends up storing *gallstones.*

In many cases, those stones—usually made of cholesterol; small as sand or big as a golf ball; and numbering from one stone to hundreds of them—just sit there.

But for hundreds of thousands of people, they're the ammo for the symptoms known as a *gallbladder attack*—a post-meal (and sometimes nocturnal) onslaught that can include bloating, belching, nausea and pain (sudden or steady, moderate or intense) under the ribcage on the right side.

If you've had one attack, it's likely you'll have another. And another. And if you do, your doctor may suggest gallbladder surgery. Every year, 500,000 people with gallstones (three times more women than men) have their gallbladder taken out.

After the operation 25% will deal with six to 12 months of diarrhea, as the intestines adjust to bile delivered straight from the liver. Many of those will end up with irritable bowel syndrome.

Some experts think there are other options.

"Although prevention is a lot more effective than treatment, there is much that can be done nutritionally to help someone with gallstones control the condition and possibly prevent gallbladder surgery," says Jennifer Adler, MS, CN, a Seattle-based certified nutritionist, natural foods chef and adjunct faculty member at Bastyr University (*www.passionatenutrition.com*).

Here is what she and other nutrition experts recommend...

➤ **Beet back those stones.** Thick, sludgelike bile creates stones—and beets can help thin the bile, says Adler.

Problem: "Beets are not on most people's top ten list of favorite foods, she says. "In fact, many people say they hate them, because they've only eaten them boiled or canned."

Solution: "Roasting beets brings out the sweetness and intensifies the depth of flavor that's lost when they're boiled," she says. *Try this recipe for Simple Roasted Beets that she developed for her clients...*

Wash and quarter 1½ to 1¾ pounds of beets. (You don't need to peel—just trim skins of rough spots. Skins slip off easily after roasting.) Place them on a roasting pan, with 2 tablespoons melted butter and ¾ teaspoon salt. Preheat the oven to 425°F. Cook the beets until tender—usually about 40 minutes. Remove from the oven and splash with balsamic vinegar to taste.

"This recipe makes enough beets for the whole week," she says. "When you come home late from work, and you're hungry, you're not saying to yourself, 'What healthy vegetable should I make?' You're saying, 'Where's the take-out menu?' Well, these beets will be ready to take out—of the refrigerator."

➤ **Kale—for what's ailing your liver.** "Physicians familiar with natural therapies have favorable results treating gallstones without use of drugs or surgery by having their patients detoxify the liver and strengthen liver function," says Liz Lipski, PhD, CCN, CNS, the director of Nutrition and Integrative Health Programs at Maryland University of Integrative Health (*www.lizlipski.com*), and author of *Digestive Wellness* (McGraw-Hill, third edition) and *Digestive Wellness for Children.*

Stop Those Stones

Study after scientific study shows you can lower the risk of gallstones and gallbladder surgery. Here are the foods and lifestyle factors linked to lower (and higher) risk...

Eat more...

- *Fiber.* 17% lower risk. *Best:* Insoluble fiber, such as that found in whole grains.
- *Fruits and vegetables.* 21% lower risk.
- *Vegetable protein.* 21% lower risk. *Best:* Beans.
- *Nuts.* 30% lower risk. *Amount:* Five or more handfuls a week.
- *Monounsaturated fats.* 18% lower risk. *Foods:* Avocados and nuts.
- *Magnesium.* 32% lower risk. *Sources:* Whole grains, beans, dark leafy greens, broccoli, bananas.
- *Coffee.* 28% lower risk.

Eat less...

- *Saturated fat.* 41% higher risk. *Minimize:* Meat and full-fat dairy products.
- *Trans fats.* 23% higher risk. *Minimize:* Processed foods such as baked goods and margarine and deep-fried foods.
- *Iron.* In men, 21% higher risk. *Best:* Avoid multi vitamin-mineral supplements with iron and moderate intake of meat, fish and poultry.

Also Important...

- *Yo-yo dieting.* 42% higher risk with repeatedly losing and regaining weight
- *Regular exercise,* 57% lower risk.

"What is good for the liver is good for the gallbladder," agrees Adler. "And kale contains nutritional factors that support the detoxification of the liver."

Adler has developed an easy-to-make kale recipe that allows her clients to enjoy the vegetable all week—the *Massaged Kale & Currant Salad.* She likes it too. "I make this salad—which has a preparation time of only fifteen minutes—to ensure that I have dark leafy green ready on busy days. It tastes better as the days go by."

Cut one bunch of de-stemmed kale into bite-size pieces and put in a large mixing bowl. Add 1 teaspoon salt, massaging it into the kale for about 2 minutes. Gently stir in the remaining ingredients— ¼ cup olive oil, 2 tablespoons raw apple cider vinegar, ¼ cup diced red onion, ⅓ cup currants, ¾ cup diced apple (½ apple), ⅓ cup toasted sunflower seeds. Add additional salt and vinegar to taste. When the salad is at the desired flavor, add ⅓ cup crumbled gorgonzola cheese.

Also helpful: Foods high in sulfur can also help the liver, says Adler.

They include garlic, onion, eggs, broccoli, cauliflower, Swiss chard and radishes...

▶ **The dish on radishes.** Both Alder and Dr. Lipski recommend their clients with gallbladder problems eat more *Spanish black radish.* "Black radish has long been used as a folk remedy to stimulate bile production and aid in the digestion of fats," says Dr. Lipski. "In fact, radishes of all types seem to benefit the liver. Daikon radish, an Asian variety, is a mild tasting radish for people who aren't radish lovers."

How to use: "Shred a little bit of Spanish black radish or Daikon onto your salads," says Adler. You can find Spanish black and Daikon radishes at specialty or ethnic markets.

You can also take black radish in capsule or tablet form, says Dr. Lipski. Follow the dosage recommendation on the label.

▶ **Top two gallbladder supplements.** I. Harrison Moore, MD, of the Hills Medical Group in West Lake Hills, Texas (*www.center forhealthandhealing.org*), wishes he knew then what he knows now.

Twenty-five years ago, after the birth of their third child, his wife had several gallbladder attacks so severe that Dr. Moore felt there was no choice but gallbladder surgery. *However, if those* attacks happened today, he might prescribe his two favorite supplements for gallstones...

- **Gallbladder Nano-Detox.** This supplement contains Gold Coin Grass, a Chinese herb that thins the bile and softens gallstones, says Dr. Moore. It's combined with probiotics (beneficial intestinal bacteria) that aid its absorption.

"A typical dose for someone with gallstones is three to four tablespoons of the powder, in sixteen ounces of water, sipped for a few hours," he says. Used for four months, about 90% of gallstones are eliminated.

- **Gallbladder Complex.** He uses this supplement for patients with gallstones. "It contains herbal and nutritional factors that dilate the neck of the bile duct, perhaps reducing the pain of a gallbladder attack, which can be caused by stones or sludge distending the duct. (He recently had an onset of gallbladder pain himself, and took two to five pills, three times a day, with meals.)

Rapid Resource: These two supplements are available from the website of Premier Research Labs, *www.prlabs.com*, or call either 800-325-7734. Address: Premier Research Labs, 3500 Wadley Place, Bldg. B, Austin, TX 78728, e-mail *info@prlabs.com*.

Also helpful: Dr. Moore also suggests his patients with gallstones eat their fattiest meal for lunch, with low-fat meals in the morning and evening...take herbal supplements for liver support, such as Max-Stress-B, also available from Premier Research Labs...increase their intake of omega-3 fatty acids, from cod liver oil...avoid fried foods...increase their intake of raw fruits and vegetables...take a supplement of digestive enzymes with meals...and include generous amounts of mineral-rich sea salt (rather than standard table salt) in the diet.

GENITAL HERPES AND OTHER STDS

Just Because You're a Senior Doesn't Mean You're Safe

All the widowers, widows and divorcees who live in retirement communities are retired from sex too.

Of course they're not.

Study: Scientists at the University of Chicago surveyed the sexual habits of more than 3,000 adults 57 to 85 years of age, publishing the results in the *New England Journal of Medicine.* They found that 83% of men and 62% of women aged 57 to 64 had been sexually active within the past 12 months. And that the majority of sexually active adults in their 50s, 60s, 70s and 80s were having sex two or three times a month or more—the same rate as people in their 20s, 30s and 40s.

Some of those older adults ended up with genital herpes.

Fact: The virus that causes genital herpes (usually herpes simplex 2) infects 51 million Americans. With 500,000 new cases a year (transmitted skin to skin, and usually causing a painful 10- to 14-day outbreak of clusters of tiny blisters in the genital area), herpes accounts for about 70% of all newly acquired STDs.

And it's not an ageist virus.

"My patients tell me about outbreaks of STDs in their parents' retirement communities," says Jill Grimes MD, a physician in private practice at the West Lake Family Practice in Austin, Texas (*www.jillgrimesmd.com*), clinical instructor in the Department of Family Medicine at the University of Massachusetts Medical School and author of *Seductive Delusions: How Everyday People Catch STDs* (Johns Hopkins).

Anyone who is sexually active can end up with an STD, including genital herpes, genital warts (HPV), trichomoniasis, gonorrhea or the dreaded human immunodeficiency virus (HIV) that causes AIDS.

But seniors—particularly the newly widowed or divorced who are re-entering the sexual arena after decades of monogamy—are particularly vulnerable, often because of their attitudes and assumptions about safe sex, says Dr. Grimes.

"Seniors may think that only prostitutes, drug addicts and homosexual men get STDs," says Dr. Grimes. "Often, they don't think someone their age can get an STD—and certainly not from one of their peers. And because women aren't concerned about pregnancy—and men are concerned about erectile dysfunction—there is infrequent use of condoms."

If you're a senior having sex, you need to know how to keep yourself safe. And what to do if you're infected. (For herpes, relief is fast and easy.)

➤ **How to prevent herpes.** Unfortunately, it's not as simple as always wearing a condom.

What you may not know: Condoms are most effective for decreasing transmission of STDs carried through semen—HIV, chlamydia, gonorrhea and trichomoniasis (three bacterial STDs), says Lisa Marr, MD, author of *Sexually Transmitted Diseases: A Physician Tells You What You Need to Know* (Johns Hopkins). They don't offer the same protection for herpes, HPV (genital warts), syphilis and pubic lice, all of which are transmitted through direct, skin-to-skin contact.

But even though a condom might not provide 100% protection, to provide any protection it has to be used right, says Dr. Grimes.

"If you want a condom to be maximally effective, you have to use it consistently and correctly—not putting it on after pre-ejaculate has occurred, for example. And you have to use it for all types of genital contact, including oral sex and shared sex toys."

There's one more thing that's complex about preventing simplex…

After an outbreak, the herpes virus retreats into nerve endings, seemingly surfacing on the skin only during the next episode. But new research shows that people with herpes can "shed" and transmit the virus not only during an outbreak but *any* time. (However, a person with herpes is *most* contagious right before an outbreak—usually signaled by pre-blister tingling, itching and burning—as well as during and right after.)

What to do: "If you're thinking of having sex with a new partner, I advise both of you to be fully tested for all STDs," says Dr. Grimes. Even though they're not 100% effective against herpes, always use condoms. And if your partner has herpes, never have sex right before, during and right after an outbreak."

➤ **Fast relief for herpes.** The most effective treatment for herpes—preventing an outbreak or limiting the severity and duration of one that's just getting started—is to take one of a family of antiviral drugs that includes *acyclovir* (Zovirax), *famciclovir* (Famvir) and *valacyclovir* (Valtrex).

🕐 Super-Quick Fix

"As soon as you feel an outbreak coming on, you should take this medicine," says Dr. Grimes.

Zovirax is 200 milligrams (mg) and requires five daily doses, Valtrex is 500 mg and requires two daily doses and Famvir is 1,500 mg and requires one daily dose. "Ask your doctor for a recommendation," says Dr. Grimes.

If you get outbreaks more than once a month, consider taking "suppressive therapy" with Valtrex or Famvir to prevent them, she adds. Daily use of Valtrex or Famvir also reduces shedding and the risk of transmission.

Study: A study of more than 400 people with genital herpes who had six or more outbreaks a year found that over half of those people were outbreak-free after taking Valtrex

Herpes FAQ

Here are answers to the questions about genital herpes that Dr. Grimes says she's asked most frequently...

- *Can you catch herpes from a toilet seat? No.* The virus dies quickly outside the body, especially when it gets dry.
- *Can you catch herpes from oral sex? Yes.* This is a frequent source of transmission.
- *If you can't see or feel any sores, are you contagious? Yes.* If you have herpes, you are always potentially contagious.
- *If you develop herpes in a monogamous relationship, is your partner cheating? Not necessarily.* It can take weeks, months or years after exposure until you first notice an outbreak.

for six months. After a year, over one-third were outbreak-free.

"Although there are possible side effects, such as nausea and headaches, this is a very well-tolerated drug. I've never had anyone stop it because of side effects."

Also helpful: Dr. Grimes says some people find that taking daily supplements of the amino acid lysine (500 mg is often recommended) decreases the frequency and intensity of outbreaks, and that doubling the dose to 1,000 mg at the first sign of an outbreak (tingling, burning, itching) shortens it.

GLAUCOMA

Relieve the Pressure

Got glaucoma? Call your plumber. Well, no, not exactly...but close. In *open angle glaucoma* (the most common type, afflicting 70% to 80% of the millions of Americans with glaucoma), the canals that drain fluid from inside the eyeball clog up.

Fluid dribbles instead of flows out of the area, called the *aqueous humor*...pressure builds up...and damages the optic nerve, the bundle of nerve fibers that relay sight-giving electrical signals to the brain.

The possible result is you lose your peripheral vision...your visual field narrows more and more...and eventually you go blind. Glaucoma causes 10% of blindness in the US—and is the number-one cause of blindness among African-Americans, who have a higher genetic risk for the disease.

Doctors usually treat glaucoma with eye drops or oral medications intended to lessen intraocular pressure (IOP). If the drops or drugs don't work, surgery is often the next step. But those treatments aren't the only treatments.

"Nutritional support, supplementation and lifestyle changes can dramatically improve the condition of the eyes of a person with glaucoma," says Marc Grossman, OD, LAc, an optometrist in private practice in Rye and New Paltz, New York, and medical director of the website, *www.natu raleyecare.com*, an online eye-care guide that features eye exercises and free phone consultation.

Here are some of his recommendations for his patients with glaucoma. Discuss them with your primary care physician, optometrist or ophthalmologist.

➤ **Take your eyes for a walk.** As little as 20 minutes a day of exercise can decrease IOP, says Dr. Grossman.

Study: Glaucoma patients who took a brisk, 40-minute walk, five days a week for three months, reduced the pressure in their eyes by 2.5 millimeters—similar to the reduction achieved by beta-blockers, a medication commonly prescribed for glaucoma.

Dr. Grossman suggests 20 minutes of daily exercise or 40 minutes every other day—walking, swimming, cycling or rebounding on a mini trampoline. "The more sedentary you are, the more improvement you will see when you begin to exercise," he says.

➤ **Dr. Grossman's Glaucoma Juice.** "I consider daily juicing of mainly organic vegetables and fruits an essential part of any long-term healing program for glaucoma," says Dr. Grossman.

"Juicing provides a highly effective and efficient way to deliver essential nutrients into the blood and cells—in fact, it takes just a few minutes for the body to start utilizing nutrients from a glass of freshly prepared juice!" he explains.

Dr. Grossman has created the following juice combo for glaucoma, emphasizing eye-healing foods rich in beta-carotene, vitamin C and sulfur-bearing amino acids…

Does MSG Cause Glaucoma?

If you have glaucoma, you should avoid the food additive monosodium glutamate, popularly known as MSG, says Dr. Grossman. Why?

The amino acid glutamate in MSG targets receptor sites on nerve cells, creating *excitotoxicity*—overstimulation and destruction of the cells. Including the cells in the optic nerve. That fact led an international team of ophthalmologists to conclude, in the journal *Experimental Eye Research* that "a diet with excess [MSG] over a period of several years…may cause retinal cell destruction."

But MSG isn't always called MSG on food labels, say Marc Rose, MD, and Michael Rose, MD, ophthalmologists at the New Institute for Visual Wellness in Costa Mesa, California, and authors of *Save Your Sight!* (Warner). Watch out for foods with the following ingredient or ingredients listed on the label, which may indicate the presence of MSG: hydrolyzed vegetable protein, hydrolyzed protein, hydrolyzed plant protein, plant protein extract, textured protein, sodium caseinate, calcium caseinate, yeast extract, autolyzed yeast, hydrolyzed oat flour, malt extract, malt flavoring, bouillon, broth stock, flavoring, natural flavoring, natural beef or chicken flavoring, seasoning or spices.

Prepare 12 ounces of juice daily, using a combination of celery, carrots, cucumber, radish, turnip, parsley, beets and cabbage, adding a small amount of raspberries, plums or apple, to sweeten the mixture.

➤ **Drink more water.** To improve circulation inside your eyes, Dr. Grossman suggests you drink half your body weight in ounces every daily. *Example:* If you weigh 160, drink 80 ounces a day. Best: No more than four ounces at a time, so as not to overload your kidneys.

Red flag: Carbonated, caffeinated and alcoholic beverages can dehydrate the eyes, he says.

➤ **Supplements to protect your optic nerve.** Three supplements that Dr. Grossman recommends for his patients with glaucoma are the Optic Nerve Formula, the herb coleus from India and VitEyes Complete.

"Optic Nerve Formula contains alpha-lipoic acid, taurine, the herb ginkgo biloba and other nutrients and herbs that have been shown to help improve circulation to the optic nerve and protect it from damage," he says.

"Coleus is an herb in the mint family that is traditionally used in Ayurvedic medicine, the system of natural healing from India. Studies show that it can lower IOP by relaxing the smooth muscles of the eye."

"VitEyes Complete is the most comprehensive eye multivitamin available, and serves both as a multivitamin and an eye multivitamin."

Rapid Resource: You can order these three products (coleus is available in both pill and eyedrops) at *www.naturaleyecare.com* or call 845-255-8222. Address: Natural Eye Care, 3 Paradies Lane, New Paltz, NY 12561, e-mail *michael@naturaleyecare.com.*

➤ **An easy exercise for computerized eyes.** If you spend a lot of time at a computer, you may increase your risk of glaucoma—particularly if you're near-sighted or far-sighted.

Study: Researchers in Japan studied more than 9,000 Japanese workers and found that the heaviest computer users were 74% more likely to have limited peripheral vision—a change indicative of developing glaucoma.

What to do: "The increased use of computers—along with television viewing, and near work on the job—has created chronic, excessive stress on our visual system," says Dr. Grossman. "Eye exercises can strengthen eye muscles, help maintain flexible lenses and help maintain sharper vision. And certain eye exercises may help reduce eye pressure too—such as frequent eye

---

See Your Doctor If...

There are many different types of glaucoma. The type discussed in this chapter, *open angle glaucoma*, is the most common form.

It develops slowly, is painless and usually doesn't produce symptoms until it's advanced. See your ophthalmologist or optometrist for an eye exam every two years, to detect glaucoma before it can damage the optic nerve.

That's particularly important if you're at high risk for the disease—if you're an African-American over 40...if you're over 60 (with older Hispanics particularly prone)...if you have a family history of the disease...if you suffer from heart disease, high blood pressure, diabetes, overweight, or thyroid disease (hyperthyroidism)...or if you regularly take corticosteroid medications.

Another (rare) form of the disease is *narrow angle glaucoma*, in which pressure inside the eyeball rises quickly, with possible symptoms including severe eye pain, blurred vision, halos around lights, reddening of the eye, and nausea and vomiting (from the pain).

This is a medical emergency. If you have two or more of the above symptoms, seek medical care immediately, from an ophthalmologist or at the emergency room. Surgery can correct the problem.

---

movements in all directions, which can help the inner eye drain more efficiently in the long-term."

Here are Dr. Grossman's instructions for a pressure-reducing exercise he calls *scanning*...

🕐 *Super-Quick Fix*

You can do this exercise sitting, standing or moving around your environment. Take two deep breaths. As you look at objects—a clock, doors, lights—let your eyes glide easily over them, as if you were painting them with your

The Dirt on Glaucoma

Feeling pressured? So are your eyes.

"High levels of stress and pressure have been implicated as a major cause of glaucoma," says Dr. Grossman.

What happens: Stress causes us to breathe shallowly, which reduces the amount of oxygen in the bloodstream, affecting the eyes' ability to re-circulate fluids.

What to do: Dr. Grossman is an optometrist *and* an acupuncturist and expert in Traditional Chinese Medicine—which says that stress causes "liver energy" to rise, increasing pressure inside the eyes. One way to "bring the energy down," he says, is to literally get down to earth—put your feet in more contact with the earth by walking in nature, gardening or simply standing barefoot for a few minutes on your lawn.

eyes. Continue to breathe deeply and easily. As you shift your eyes from object to object, allow them to move easily without staring. They should move in a relaxed manner, without any tension. Continue to breathe and blink, releasing any tension in the mouth or jaw.

GOUT

Halt the Attacks Now

Five million Americans (80% of them men) suffer from *gout*—a type of arthritis caused by the buildup of uric acid, a waste product of urine production.

The excess uric acid congeals into miniscule crystals that are like tiny shards of glass—sharp-edged, pain-causing and joint-destroying. Those crystals often end up in the big toe, although you can get gout in other joints of the foot and in the joints of the fingers, wrists, elbows, knees and ankles.

How do you know the crystals are there?

Because you have a *gout attack*. The joint becomes hot, swollen and stiff…the skin around it turns shiny and red…you may have fever and chills. And the pain! It's so intense that even the slightest brush of a bedsheet on your toe can be excruciating.

The attacks—which can occur anywhere from once in a lifetime to once every couple of months—are bad enough. But over time, if the gout isn't treated properly, the crystals can form large, painful lumps called *tophi* that gradually deform and destroy joints and the tissue around them.

Problem: A recent study showed that only 22% of gout sufferers receive the proper medical care to stop attacks and control the disease.

"Errors in selecting the most appropriate medication and proper dose are common," says a report on gout, in the *American Journal of Medicine*.

Example: That was certainly the case with Victor Konshin, author of *Beating Gout: A Sufferer's Guide to Living Pain Free* (Ayerware Publishing).

First, his gout was misdiagnosed as osteomyelitis, a life-threatening bone infection. Then, he received second-rate treatments that didn't stop his gout attacks, which became more frequent and severe. Medications that were prescribed were given at the wrong dose, causing liver damage and life-threatening side effects. Finally, after a gout attack that lasted three weeks, Konshin teamed up with a gout expert and got his disease completely under control. Then, working with several gout experts, and reviewing over 300 scientific papers, he wrote a book to help other people with gout avoid his fate.

"The medical protocol described by Victor Konshin is the *best* way to treat and manage gout," says Ralph Argen, MD, a rheumatologist and gout specialist in Buffalo, New York.

Here is the doctor-approved approach that will help you stop a gout attack in a hurry—and never have another. However, these are *general* recommendations. Work with your primary care physician or a rheumatologist (arthritis specialist) to tailor your treatment to your condition.

Rapid Resource: You can order a copy of *Beating Gout* at *www.beatinggout.com*, or call 716-650-4040 or e-mail *info@ayerware.com*. Address: Ayerware Publishing, P.O. Box 1098, Williamsville, NY 14231.

▶ **Stop a gout attack.** The key to stopping a gout attack is to use anti-inflammatory medications to stop the inflammation as soon as possible, at the very first sign of attack. "Even if you wait a few hours, it might take days to get relief," says Konshin.

Most attacks start in the middle of the night. But attacks can start any time, so keep your medications with you at all times.

Medications to use: A non-steroidal anti-inflammatory drug, such as *naproxen* (Aleve), *indomethacin* (Indocin) or *sulindac*.

Recommended dosages: Naproxen—750 milligrams (mg) at first sign of symptoms and 250 mg every eight hours. (Do not take more than 750 mg a day after the first day and do not take for more than 10 days.) Indomethacin—100 mg at first sign of symptoms, 50 mg three times a day. (Do not take more than 200 mg per day or for more than two days.) Sulindac—200 mg at first sign of symptoms, 200 mg twice a day. (Do not take more than 400 mg a day or for more than seven days.) Stop the medication as soon as symptoms subside.

⚠ *Caution:* These medications can cause life-threatening stomach ulcers and other health

C Your Way to Prevention

Preventing gout is much better than treating it. Vitamin C might help.

New study: Researchers examined 20 years of health data from 47,000 men—and found a direct relationship between vitamin C intake and developing gout. Compared to those who got 250 mg or less of C a day, those who got...

- *1,500 mg supplemental C per day had a 45% lower risk*
- *1,000 to 1,499 mg had a 34% lower risk*
- *500 to 999 mg had a 17% lower risk*

Why it works: Vitamin C reduces the level of uric acid in the blood, says Hyon K. Choi, MD, DrPH, of Boston University School of Medicine. It also helps the kidneys reabsorb uric acid (so there's less in the blood) and it decreases inflammation.

"Given that vitamin C is generally safe—particularly in the ranges of intake in our study—the nutrient may provide a useful option in the prevention of gout," says Dr. Choi.

What to do: Increase your intake of vitamin C–rich fruits and vegetables, such as oranges, pink grapefruit, cantaloupe, kiwifruit, strawberries, pineapple, broccoli and peppers, and consider taking a daily vitamin C supplement.

problems, so you must use them carefully and only under a doctor's direct supervision.

▶ **Manage uric acid production—and prevent future attacks.** Once you've stopped your attack, it may be time to use medications to lower your uric acid levels and prevent future gout attacks. The goal is to get the level to less than 6 mg/dL (milligrams per deciliter).

Important: There is controversy as to when to start uric acid-lowering medications. Many experts advise waiting until after a second attack. But other experts say that if you have a history of

What's Diet Got To Do With It?

You may have read that if you have gout you need to follow a diet that is low in *purines*, a component of food that breaks down into uric acid.

"A low-purine diet is a waste of time," says Dr. Argen. "It was necessary in the days when effective medical treatments didn't exist."

So don't worry about eliminating meat, fish, seafood, beans, peas, spinach, asparagus, cauliflower or mushrooms.

However: Alcohol—particularly beer—has far more purines than the foods listed above and *is* a risk factor. If you have gout, you should limit yourself to no more than one drink a day, says Dr. Argen. Abstinence is best.

Also helpful: Losing weight can also help relieve gout, he says.

gout in your family, or very high uric acid levels (more than 12 mg/dL), you may want to start after the first attack.

Medication to use: Allopurinol (Zyloprim) stops the body from producing uric acid.

Recommended dosage: Start at 100 mg a day for one week. Then increase to 200 mg a day for the second week, and 300 mg a day after that. Your doctor will adjust your dose based on your uric acid levels, which should be checked periodically. The maximum safe dose is 800 mg a day.

⚠ *Caution:* You should wait two to three weeks *after* an attack before beginning this medication. But if an attack occurs, don't stop taking it.

Side effects occur in about 20% of people who take allopurinol, and in about 2% they are serious.

If you experience an adverse reaction, such as a rash or fever, see your doctor immediately.

Do not take allopurinol if you take *azathioprine* (Azasan), used to treat inflammatory bowel disease, autoimmune disease and organ transplants, or *mercaptopurine*, used to treat leukemia.

➤ **Practice prophylaxis.** Unfortunately, when you begin to lower blood levels of uric acid, the uric acid in body tissues begins to dissolve into the blood, triggering gout attacks.

Medication: So for the first few months of treatment, you have to take a low dose of a drug sometimes used to treat gout attacks—colchicine. Experts differ on the best length of treatment—some say three months while others say a year.

Recommended dosage: 0.5 to 1.8 mg a day.

⚠ *Caution:* If you take colchicine for prophylaxis, you should not take it for an acute attack, because of the risk of an overdose.

GUM DISEASE

Give It the Brush Off

In spite of all the ads for multi-ingredient toothpastes, bacteria-busting mouthwashes and high-tech toothbrushes, the gums of Americans aren't in very good shape.

Forty-eight percent of us have gingivitis—infected, swollen, bleeding gums. (The rate is 85% for Americans over 65.) Periodontal disease—advanced erosion of gum tissue and, eventually, the surrounding bone—afflicts 15% of the general population and 20% of those over 65.

Surprising new risk factor: If you have gum disease, you may be at increased risk for several other diseases, including killers such as heart disease, diabetes and cancer—and the more severe the gum disease, the greater the risk.

What happens: Bacteria in the mouth cause gum disease, explains Thomas Van Dyke, DDS, a professor in the Goldman School of Dental Medicine at Boston University. White blood cells flood the area to battle the bacteria, releasing chemicals in the process that create an *inflammatory response*—the telltale redness and swelling that signal your immune system is at work. But inflammation has a downside—it damages tissue. Scientists now understand that inflammation causes or complicates many diseases, including heart disease, arthritis and diabetes.

Inflammation from gum disease has been linked to these and other diseases in two ways...

1. **Bacteria from the mouth travels to other parts of the body,** causing inflammation.

2. **Local inflammation in the gums sparks systemic inflammation**—just as a local burn (on your hand, for example) raises inflammatory factors throughout the body.

Bottom line: Preventing and reversing gum disease can save your teeth *and* your life. *And it only takes a few minutes a day...*

➤ **Brush your teeth *and* gums.** "The initial stage of gum disease is nothing more than inflammation," says Flora Parsa Stay, DDS, associate clinical professor of dentistry at the University of Southern California, and author of *The Secret Gateway to Health* (Morgan James Publishing). "If you are very regular and thorough with brushing and flossing, you can easily reverse the condition."

Problem: Many people brush their teeth but neglect to brush their gums, says Dr. Stay.

Solution: "Put the toothbrush way up on your gums and brush the gums as well as the teeth," she instructs. "And brush every side of the tooth, not just the front. Take the time to do it right."

Are You at Risk for Gum Disease?

There are several risk factors for gum disease, says Dr. Van Dyke. Some are beyond your control, such as aging. Others you can do something about, such as good oral hygiene.

- ***Aging.*** Older people have more periodontal disease, probably because there's been more wear-and-tear on their gums.

- ***Smoking.*** The number-one risk factor for periodontal disease. If you're a smoker, you have yet another reason to quit.

- ***Overweight.*** Extra fat puts you at extra risk—probably because fat tissue generates inflammatory factors, worsening gum infections.

- ***Medications and dry mouth.*** Many medications cause dry mouth—and a lack of saliva contributes to gum disease. (For more information, please see the section "Dry Mouth" on page 117.)

- ***Genes.*** If there's a history of gum disease and tooth loss in your family, you may be at greater risk.

- ***Gender.*** Men have more gum disease than women, probably because their hygiene isn't as good.

- ***Oral hygiene.*** Gum disease is fueled by *biofilm*, or plaque—a multilayered, mineral-encrusted bacterial ecosystem. By disrupting plaque with brushing and flossing, you can prevent or control the disease.

Recommended: Dr. Stay recommends a toothbrush with bristles that are soft (so they don't damage the gums) and nylon (so they're easy to clean), with a large, comfortable handle for easy use, and tapered at the front so it's easy to reach the teeth in the back of the mouth. There is no

Speed Healing Success

"Whatever You're Doing, Keep It Up"

"Whenever I had my teeth cleaned, the dental hygienist would pull out gauze after blood-soaked gauze," says David Snape, of Kansas City. "But I never knew I had gum disease." Then Snape's dentist told him that he had *advanced* gum disease—and should have a procedure called root scaling and planing, which cleans below the gum line.

Rather than agreeing to the procedure, Snape decided to learn everything he could about gum disease...to see if he could reverse the problem himself.

After a thorough investigation, he decided to use an oral irrigator (the HydroFloss), an essential oil product to brush his teeth (OraMD), dental tape rather than dental floss ("It's thicker, wider and covers more surface area," he says), the Perio-Aid, a device to clean hard-to-reach areas, a pH balanced mouthwash (Perio-Therapy) and bacteria-reducing xylitol chewing gum.

"After five months of daily treatment, I returned to the dentist—and the dentist and the hygienist were visibly shocked at the excellent condition of my gums. They told me I no longer needed scaling and planing. 'Whatever you're doing, keep it up,' said my dentist."

His advice to those who want to prevent or reverse gum disease: "No matter what products you use, the main thing is that you have to break up the biofilm—the plaque—on a regular basis, every day, day in and day out."

Rapid Resource: David Snape wrote a book on the basis of his experience—*What You Should Know About Gum Disease: A Layman's Guide to Fighting Gum Disease* (Quantum Health Press). His website is *www.howtostopgumdisease.com*, where you can buy his book, order many of the products he uses in his regimen and download free reports about preventing and reversing gum disease.

research indicating a power toothbrush is more effective than a manual toothbrush, she adds.

Recommended: The Cleure Toothbrush, at *www.cleure.com*.

➤ **Choose the healthiest toothpaste.** Most commercial toothpastes contain the foaming agent sodium lauryl sulfate, which can dry the mouth, promoting gum disease, says Dr. Stay. They also contain salicylates for flavoring, an ingredient to which many people are sensitive. Salicylates can induce symptoms such as nasal congestion, itching and stomach pain. Toothpastes may also contain preservatives, artificial sweeteners and colors, and many other questionable ingredients, she adds.

Recommended: "Keep it simple. Toothpaste that contains baking soda is the best method for keeping a neutral pH in the oral environment—and that's what you want, because an acidic environment promotes gum disease.

Product: Cleure Toothpaste, which a scientific study at Indiana University demonstrated was uniquely effective in removing plaque.

➤ **Don't make this common flossing mistake.** Forty percent of Americans don't floss every day. They're gumming up their oral health.

Recent study: Researchers at New York University studied 51 sets of twins—asking one of the pair to brush their teeth every day and the other to brush *and* floss. After two weeks, the twin who didn't floss has significantly higher levels of the bacteria associated with gum disease.

"This study illustrates the tremendous importance flossing can have on oral health," says Kenneth Kornman, DDS, editor of the *Journal of Periodontology*.

"As a practicing periodontist, I am constantly telling my patients to clean between their teeth using dental floss or other interdental cleaners," says Susan Karabin, DDS, of the American Academy of Peridontology.

"Patients tend to think that flossing can't make that much of a difference. But this study demonstrates that the addition of flossing to your dental hygiene routine can significantly reduce the amount of bacteria that cause periodontal disease—even after just two weeks!"

However: People usually floss incorrectly, moving the floss straight up and down instead of curving it around the teeth and moving it gently under the gum, says Dr. Stay. *Her recommendations for effective flossing...*

1. **Use an arm's length (18 inches) of floss.** Wrap it around the middle finger of one hand. Leave approximately six inches and wrap that around the middle finger of the other hand, with about one inch of floss between the fingers of each hand.

2. **Hold the floss firmly,** but not so tightly that it cuts off circulation.

3. **Floss each tooth, forming a "C" shape with the floss.** Carefully clean each side of each tooth. Gently clean under the gums.

4. **Introduce a new area of floss into each area.**

5. **Don't forget to floss behind your last molar.**

   "By using this method you get at the bacteria in areas the toothbrush can't reach," says Dr. Stay.

🕐 Super-Quick Fix

➤ **Drink more green tea.** Teatime is teeth-time—if the tea is green.

New study: Japanese researchers studied nearly 1,000 men aged 49 to 59. They found that those who regularly drank green tea has less periodontal disease—for every additional cup of tea the men drank, there was a significant decrease in the depth of periodontal pockets (the grooves around the gum that deepen as gum disease advances)...a decrease in the loss of attachment of the gum to the tooth...and a decrease in bleeding. The study was published in the *Journal of Periodontology*.

Theory: Catechins, powerful antioxidants in green tea, decrease the inflammatory response to bacteria.

"Periodontists believe that maintaining healthy gums is absolutely critical to maintaining a healthy body," says David Cochran,

See Your Dentist If...

You have teeth and gums. "Regular, professional dental care—a cleaning at least every six months—is one of the best ways to prevent or help reverse gingivitis," says Dr. Stay.

However: If you have advanced gum disease, she recommends considering other options before gum surgery or tooth extraction. "Among many options, antibacterial gels can be placed under the gum to keep bacteria at bay, and splints can be made to hold teeth in place as the area heals.

"I'm not a big fan of gum surgery," she continues. "There is no 'one-time' cure for the disease, and a lot of times the problem returns. What is necessary is to make certain your home care is proper and that you get regular professional treatments—that you manage your disease to prevent further destruction."

DDS, PhD, past president of the American Academy of Peridontology.

"That is why it is so important to find simple ways to boost periodontal health—such as regularly drinking green tea, something already known to possess health-related benefits."

Also helpful: The same study found that people who regularly consumed dairy products such as milk, cheese and yogurt had less gum disease. "Millions of adults already suffer from periodontal disease," says Dr. Karabin. "By regularly consuming dairy products such as milk, the risk of developing gum disease may decrease."

➤ **Anti-gingivitis supplements.** If you have gum disease, there are several nutrients that can help reduce inflammation, boost the immune system (to beat back bacteria) and strengthen gum tissue, says Mark A. Breiner, DDS, a dentist in private practice at the Breiner Whole Body Health Center in Trumbull, Connecticut, and author of *Whole Body Dentistry* (Quantum Health Press). *They are…*

- **Vitamin C,** 500 to 1,000 milligrams (mg), morning and evening.

- **CoQ10,** 100 mg, twice a day.

- **Zinc,** 10 to 20 mg a day.

HAIR CARE PROBLEMS

Let's face it—bad hair days are a catastrophe, while good days are the best!" That's the enthusiastic opinion of Dimitri James, an internationally recognized beauty, hair and skin care expert, author of *Becoming Beauty* (SSpreSS) and founder and president of Skinn Cosmetics (*www.skinn.com*). *And he has lots of ideas to bring out your best—fast...*

➤ **Quick repairs for dry, damaged hair.** If you have dry hair—blame your parents. "Dry hair can be hereditary," says Dimitri. But, he says, it can also be the result of years of coloring... highlighting...perming...sun bleaching...and overwashing with harsh shampoos. *Here's what to do...*

• **Dye darker, not lighter.** "Coloring your hair *darker* rather than *lighter* is *healthier*," emphasizes Dimitri. "Lightening hair damages, dries and thins each strand. Coloring hair a shade or two darker hides damage and increases shine."

Hot oil treatment for overprocessed hair: "This do-it-yourself treatment for overprocessed hair is the same as you'd pay hundreds of dollars for in a salon," says Dimitri. *His instructions...*

You'll need two tablespoons of soy oil, two tablespoons of jojoba oil, two tablespoons olive oil, two tablespoons wheat germ oil, four cut-open capsules of vitamin E and two cut-open capsules of evening primrose oil.

Mix all the ingredients together and heat in the microwave until warm (not hot). Massage the mixture into your hair and scalp. Wrap your hair with plastic cling wrap and blow dry on hot for 10 minutes. Let cool for 10 minutes. Rinse with warm water and follow with a cold-water rinse.

➤ **Mask your split ends.** The best remedy for split ends is to have your stylist cut them off, otherwise they'll just keep splitting, says Dimitri. *In the meantime, try his Split Ends Mask...*

You'll need one ripe mashed banana, one cup yogurt and one tablespoon of honey. Mix all the ingredients together. Apply to your hair. Leave it on for 20 minutes. Rinse with warm water. Finish with a cold-water rinse.

➤ **Don't make this common hair care mistake.** It's over cleansing, says Dimitri. "Just like your favorite T-shirt, your hair gets frayed and worn out from daily washings," he says.

Is Your Hair Damaged?

There's an easy way to find out, says Dimitri.

Pluck a strand of hair and drop it in a glass of warm water. Dunk the strand once with your finger. If the strand sinks, your hair is damaged. If it floats, your hair is in good shape.

What to do: Don't let your heart sink along with your hair. Dimitri has several suggestions to undo the damage...

• *Cut down on shampooing. Try this:* Use a raw egg or two instead of shampoo for a couple weeks to repair the damage. Blend the raw egg with a little water and massage into dry hair. Leave on for 10 minutes and rinse out thoroughly with warm water. Finish with a cool water rinse.

• *Take a break from hairstyling.*

• *Stop backcombing.* Also known as *teasing* or *ratting*, this method of repeatedly combing hair toward the scalp is used to create "big hair" styles, such as beehives.

• *Purchase a protein reconstructor* (they are widely available) and use it twice a week, alternating with a hydrating treatment.

Red flag: Your hair could become brittle and break if you use a protein pack without alternating it with a hydrating system, he says.

The DERMAdoctor's Answer to Dandruff: Use Several Shampoos

"The flaking on your scalp is due to several genetically caused biological missteps," says dermatologist Audrey Kunin, MD, author of *THE DERMAdoctor Skinstruction Manual* (Simon & Schuster) and founder and president of *www.dermadoctor.com*.

"That's why dandruff doesn't respond well to a single therapy. If you want flake-free hair, you have to disrupt the dandruff pathway at several points, using several products that work together. *Here's what to do...*

- **Antifungal.** The natural yeast and bacteria that reside on the skin and scalp are an important trigger for dandruff, or what dermatologists call *seborrheic dermatitis*, says Dr. Kunin. That means you need a shampoo with an antifungal ingredient, such as *ketoconazole*. Shampoos with that ingredient include Carmol or Nizoral A-D.

- **Antibacterial.** Look for a shampoo with zinc pyrithione, which kills yeast *and* bacteria, such as DHS Zinc Shampoo.
- **Anti-flaking.** To get rid of scale—the fast-shedding skin flakes that are the sign of dandruff—look for a shampoo with salicylic (BHA) or glycolic (AHA) acids, such as Meted, Ionil Plus Conditioning Shampoo Salicylic Acid Formula or P&S Shampoo.

Bottom line: "Don't worry about being precise with your regimen—just use one shampoo for a few days and then switch to another." *Useful:* "Dandruff shampoos can be somewhat harsh on your hair," says Dr. Kunin. "I have found that Ionil Rinse is a very good choice for helping restore moisture."

Important: "If this round robin of shampoo therapy doesn't work, you'll need to talk to your doctor about incorporating prescription liquid drops, steroid-based shampoos, such as Capex, or prescription-level Nizoral or Loprox shampoo.

Smart idea: Try shampooing your hair only once a week.

"In between washings, simply rinse your hair with warm water while you rub your fingers back and forth, as though you were using shampoo. Then rinse with cold water, for extra shine."

Also try: "Rinse with apple cider vinegar, diluted fifty-fifty with distilled water," he says. "This really makes hair shine!"

➤ **Revive "lifeless" hair.** Does your hair have so little "body" it seems like a ghost of its former self? *Here's Dimitri's recipe for lively beauty...*

You'll need one ripe avocado, one tablespoon wheat germ oil and two tablespoons yogurt. Mix the ingredients together and massage into your hair. Leave on for 30 minutes. Rinse with warm water. Finish with a cold-water rinse.

➤ **Perk up a pooped-out perm—with stale beer!** This unusual but effective recipe requires "flat" beer and some aloe vera gel, says Dimitri. Mix equal parts of the two ingredients, rinse through your hair and leave on for 15 minutes. Rinse with cool water, leaving a small amount of the mixture in your hair.

➤ **Green hair repair.** Hair green from too much swimming in chlorine? Dimitri to the rescue. Mix 10 powdered baby aspirin and one cup of red wine. Rinse through your hair. Leave on for 10 minutes. Rinse well with cool water.

🕐 Super-Quick Fix

➤ **A trick to thicken fine hair.** Add a little powdered gelatin to your favorite shampoo, says Dimitri.

HAIR LOSS AND BALDNESS

Hair Today, Hair Tomorrow

Spencer David Kobren is the Ralph Nader of hair loss. As founder and president of the American Hair Loss Association, the author of *The Bald Truth: The First Complete Guide to Preventing and Treating Hair Loss* (Pocket Books) and *The Truth About Women's Hair Loss* (Contemporary Books), and the host of "The Bald Truth" radio show on XM radio, Kobren is widely recognized as America's foremost consumer/patient advocate on behalf of the 90 million Americans who are losing their hair—and trying not to. He's a tireless campaigner for effective treatments and against the (seemingly endless) barrage of hyped but useless hair loss products. "Spencer David Kobren is our voice of truth in the madness of hair loss and the hair loss industry," says Angela Christiano, PhD, associate professor of dermatology at Columbia University.

If you're dealing with hair loss—an often traumatic experience for men and women—here are Kobren's top suggestions for what *really* works to preserve, enhance or replace your vanishing mane…

▶ **Men—first, see a doctor—about** *finasteride* **(Propecia).** "Hair loss is a *medical issue*," emphasizes Kobren. "If you're beginning to lose your hair, you have to nip it in the bud—by using a medical treatment that hits hair loss at its hormonal base."

What happens: Half of all men experience the genetically inherited condition called *male pattern hair loss* by the time they're 50. It's caused by the testosterone by-product *dihydrotestosterone* (DHT), which shrinks hair follicles until they no longer produce visible hair. Solving the problem of hair loss at the "hormonal base" means blocking the production of DHT—and the drug *finasteride* (Propecia) does exactly that.

Study: In a five-year clinical trial of the drug, nine out of 10 men who took it had visible results—48% had regrowth of hair and 42% had no further hair loss.

"When you take Propecia, you're taking a drug that is going to keep hair on your head for the long haul," says Kobren. "I started losing my hair at the age of twenty-one and have been taking it for the last fifteen years. I would be bald if I wasn't using it."

Important: "You can't make an accurate assessment about the drug's effectiveness after three or even six months," he says. "Give it a year."

Red flag: About 2% of men who take the drug experience lowered libido and erectile difficulties. Those problems usually clear up when you stop taking the drug.

Update: Recent studies by the FDA show that in rare cases Propecia can cause long-term sexual dysfunction.

▶ **Women—think of Rogaine as a Band-Aid, not a treatment.** "Unlike Propecia, the topical treatment *minoxidil* (Rogaine) is a *vasodilator*," says Kobren. "It dilates the hair follicle, increasing circulation and the thickness of hair. But it doesn't stop hair loss or grow new hair. It's more like a Band-Aid than a cure."

However: Woman have few science-proven and safe options for hair loss, says Kobren. Rogaine is one of them.

▶ **Think twice about a hair transplant.** "I consider hair transplant surgery a last resort," says Kobren. "People see the infomercials for hair transplants, don't want to take a drug and think, 'I'll spend the money and get my hair back and I'll be fine.' But the surgery is far trickier—and frequently much less successful—than typically advertised. In fact, in some men, the surgery 'shocks' the remaining hair on the head, leading to *more* hair loss—and they look worse after the surgery than before.

Better: Take Propecia for a year, evaluate the results and *then* decide if you want to pursue a surgical option.

➤ **Think about a hairpiece—but don't buy it from a "hair club."** "I also recommend that you try a hairpiece before you try surgery," says Kobren. But don't join a "hair club," he says.

"That's one of the worst ideas in hair loss. You sign a maintenance contract for the hairpiece and end up spending fifteen hundred to three thousand dollars for a hairpiece you can get for one fifty to three hundred online."

Best: Buy a good "lace system" (the base of the hairpiece—lace is thin and provides a natural look) and have it cut and styled by a local stylist who has experience with hairpieces, says Kobren.

⚠ ***Caution:*** "In terms of the hair density of your piece, 'less is more' if you want a natural look," he says. "Unless you show some scalp in the hairline, the piece will look phony. But if the hairpiece is styled and maintained correctly, it can look undetectable."

Rapid Resource: Two online sources for hairpieces that have the American Hair Association Seal of approval are…

• *www.coolpiece.com.* Address: CoolPiece, 150 Hamakua Dr., PMB 506, Kailua, HI 96734, e-mail *help@CoolPiece.com*

• *www.toplace.com*, or call 888-986-7522. Address: TopLace, P.O. Box 577, Wayzata, MN 55391, e-mail *Info@TopLACE.us*

🕐 **Super-Quick Fix**

➤ **Consider "cover-up" makeup.** "I wear DermMatch, a cosmetic that makes me

---

Women and Hair Loss

"Forty percent of all hair loss in America is in women, says Kobren. "It's a problem people don't talk about—a silent epidemic of tremendous proportions. In contrast to male pattern baldness, it's usually more of an unpatterned, diffuse thinning of the hair. And it's not just postmenopausal women—it's becoming more prevalent at younger and younger ages."

What to do: See a dermatologist about the problem, suggests Kobren. Medications such as low-dose androgen (a male hormone) may help, as can 5% Rogaine, and hairpieces.

Rapid Resource: The Women's Hair Loss Project is a community of women experiencing hair loss who share their stories and practical ideas about the problem. Visit online at *www. womenshairlossproject.com*, or e-mail *women@ womenshairlossproject.com.*

---

look like a guy with a thinning crown rather than someone with no hair in that area," says Kobren. "There are plenty of people who are willing to jump into surgery and have their head cut open and pay thousands of dollars—but who won't put a little makeup on their head! This type of cosmetics is extremely empowering—it's one of the options that lets you get out of the house and into the world feeling one hundred percent comfortable."

Red flag: "Men with no hair use a scalp cosmetic and it doesn't look like hair—it looks like they painted their head," says Kobren. "These products are for men and women with thinning hair. They're not for bald areas."

Rapid Resource: *www.dermmatch.com*, or call 800-826-2824. Address: DermMatch, Inc., 900 Albee Rd., Nokomis, FL 34275.

➤ **Styling tips for hair loss.** "If you use hairspray, use it after the hair is *completely* dry," says Kobren.

"Avoid mousses and gels, which make hair look thinner.

"Don't be afraid of the blow dryer—it can't make hair fall out." Use it on medium setting to help avoid damaging your hair.

🕐 *Super-Quick Fix*

"Condition *before* you shampoo—if you condition afterward you weigh hair down, separating the hair more. Shampooing last gives hair a fuller, cleaner look," says Kobren.

➤ **Don't waste your time (or money) on hair loss supplements.** Many herbs and nutrients—such as saw palmetto and zinc—are advertised as helping to preserve or grow hair. Kobren doesn't support them.

"The products are not standardized and there is no established medical protocol for using them for hair loss," he says.

Red flag: Some people use DHT-blocking herbs such as saw palmetto along with Propecia and end up suffering sexual side effects that weren't there when they took the drug alone, says Kobren.

➤ **Above all else, don't panic.** "Hair loss is a medical condition that happens to a large percentage of the population and is nothing to be ashamed of," says Kobren. "Don't panic and rush out and buy questionable products."

Smart idea: Before you use a product, look for the seal of approval of the American Hair Loss Association (a round logo with the name of the association)—or contact the Association at *www. americanhairloss.org*, or e-mail at *info-ahla@ameri canhairloss.org* to ask about the product.

HAY FEVER

Unstuff in a Jiffy

Nearly half of Americans suffer from inhalant allergies—the stuffy, runny, itchy nose…the sneezing and coughing…the watery, itchy eyes…the fatigue…that is popularly dubbed hay fever and that doctors call *allergic rhinitis.*

What happens: Your body goes into "attack mode" against an *allergen*—a benign substance that it wrongly perceives as threatening, such as pollen, molds or animal dander, explains Dean Mitchell, MD, an allergist in private practice in New York (*www.allergydrops.net*) and author of *Dr. Dean Mitchell's Allergy and Asthma Solution* (Marlowe & Company). "When the body sounds this alarm, the immune system launches a vigorous and violent counterattack against the 'harmful' intruders."

That attack includes the release of *histamine* from *mast cells*—which produces the "collateral damage" you experience as allergy symptoms.

To control those symptoms, many people take an over-the-counter antihistamine such as *fexofenadine* (Allegra) or *loratidine* (Claritin), or an antihistamine combined with a decongestant, such as Allegra-D and Claritin-D. "Buyer beware," says Dr. Mitchell.

"While these combination drugs appear to be the solution to the problems of allergy sufferers, you should use them only on a limited basis because of their side effects, which can include high blood pressure, insomnia and worsened heartburn."

Fortunately, there are many non-drug alternatives that can effectively treat hay fever, says Nigma Talib, ND, a naturopathic doctor in private practice in West Vancouver, Canada (*www. healthydoc.com*).

They can work just as well—and, often, just as fast...

▶ **The hay fever cure—allergy drops (sublingual allergy immunotherapy).** Putting a liquid drop under your tongue (sublingual) of a minute amount of an allergen (immunotherapy) can dramatically reduce and even cure your hay fever, says Dr. Mitchell. "This breakthrough treatment—an alternative to immunotherapy with allergy shots—has been used successfully in Europe for decades and is now available here in the United States."

How they work: With immunotherapy, you are exposed to tiny doses of the very allergen you're allergic to, explains Dr. Mitchell. Gradually, higher and higher doses are used—until your body builds a tolerance to the allergen.

Using your immune system as a barrier to allergens is the optimal solution for long-lasting relief, he says. "In my practice, even the worst allergy cases see dramatic improvement that far exceeds their expectations."

Like allergy injections, the sublingual drops are directly absorbed into the bloodstream. Unlike injections, the majority of people who start the therapy continue it. "Ninety percent of patients on sublingual allergy immunotherapy are compliant—they don't miss treatments," says Dr. Mitchell. "With allergy injections, the compliance is around thirty to forty percent."

The process starts with a state-of-the-art blood test to detect allergies—a so-called "third generation" test, such as Pharmacia ImmunoCap, which is far more accurate than earlier versions. Once your allergens are determined—tree pollen, grass pollen, ragweed, animal dander, mold or any number of allergens—the drops are prepared and you are instructed in their daily use. After one month, you receive a stronger drop or a preparation with more allergens. And that process continues—until your allergies are under control.

To Breathe Easier, Turn Up Your Nose at These Foods

"People who have allergic rhinitis are often also allergic to certain foods," says Dr. Talib. When they eliminate those foods from the diet, their hay fever gets a lot better. In fact, says Dr. Talib, addressing food allergies *and* administering allergy drops cures 80% to 90% of her patients with allergic rhinitis.

The foods that typically worsen hay fever are tomatoes, peanuts, wheat, apples, carrots, celery, peaches, melon, eggs, pork and dairy foods.

What to do: Ask your doctor for a food allergy (ELISA) test from Genova Diagnostics, *www.genovadiagnostics.com*, which she considers the leading laboratory for this test. Avoid the foods you're allergic to.

"I consider allergy drops to be the single most important breakthrough in the treatment of allergy—a truly effective cure," says Dr. Mitchell.

Rapid Resource: To find an allergist near you who uses sublingual allergy shots, go to the website *www.allergychoices.com* and click on "Find a Provider."

▶ **Try these anti-allergy vitamins and herbs.** There are many supplements that can help relieve the symptoms of hay fever, says Dr. Talib. (Discuss their use with your primary care physician or allergist.)

● **Vitamin C.** This natural antihistamine stabilizes mast cells and is the most important supplement for an allergy sufferer, she says.

Suggested intake: During hay fever season, 2,000 milligrams (mg), three times a day. (High doses of vitamin C can cause diarrhea; if your stools are loose, cut the dose to 1,000 mg, three times a day.)

• **Quercetin.** This nutritional factor, found in foods such as apples, red grapes, berries and black tea, also stabilizes histamine-releasing mast cells, and is the second most important supplement for those with hay fever, says Dr. Talib. Take it with bromelain, an enzyme that enhances its absorption.

Product: Quercenase, from Thorne Research, which contains both quercetin and bromelain. It is widely available.

Suggested intake: Two capsules, three times a day.

• **Butterbur—as effective as Allegra.** This herb reduces the amount of histamine and also relaxes the respiratory tract, says Dr. Talib.

Study: Swiss researchers asked 330 patients with hay fever to take butterbur, *fexofenadine* (Allegra) or a placebo. Both butterbur and fexofenadine were equally effective in relieving symptoms—sneezing, nasal congestion, itchy eyes and nose, red eyes and skin irritation. Butterbur extract should be considered an alternative treatment for intermittent allergic rhinitis, say the researchers.

Suggested intake: 50 mg, twice a day.

Product: Petadolex, which is widely available.

• **Rosmarinic acid.** This extract of the herb rosemary is a superb anti-inflammatory and helps stabilize the immune system, says Dr. Talib.

Suggested intake: 200 mg, first thing in the morning.

Product: Dr. Talib prefers the Life Extension Brand, available at *www.lef.org*, or call 800-678-8989.

• **Goldenseal.** This herb can help clear up the chronic bacterial infection of the sinuses that often accompanies hay fever, says Dr. Talib.

Suggested intake: 200 mg, twice a day.

• **Stinging nettle.** This natural antihistamine is widely used in Europe for allergic rhinitis, she says. Use it for a short period of time when your symptoms are at their worst.

Suggested intake: 600 mg a day, for one week.

• **Omega-3 fatty acids.** This anti-inflammatory supplement can help *prevent* allergic rhinitis—a problem that is becoming more common with worsening air pollution (which damages the respiratory tract) and pollen-increasing global warming, says Dr. Talib.

Study: Japanese researchers found that people with the highest intake of the omega-3 fatty acids EPA (*eicosapentaenoic acid*) and DHA (*docosahexaenoic acid*) were 44% less likely to have allergic rhinitis. Similarly, German researchers found that those with a high intake of EPA had a 55% lower risk.

Recommended intake: 1 to 2 grams of omega-3 fatty acids.

Product: Dr. Talib prefers Eskimo 3, by Enzymatic Therapy, available at *www.enzymatic therapy.com*, or call 800-783-2286.

• **Probiotics.** "An allergy is the result of an imbalanced immune system," says Dr. Talib. "Well, the health of the gastrointestinal system plays a *huge* role in the health of the immune system. And probiotics—friendly intestinal bacteria—can keep your GI tract in good health."

Product: Dr. Talib prefers ProBio Sap-90, from NFS. You can order it at *www.bmsresources. ca*, or call 416-502-2665. Follow the dosage recommendation on the label.

➤ **Eat more broccoli.** Broccoli can douse inflammation in the airways, say researchers at UCLA.

New study: The researchers asked 65 people to eat either broccoli sprouts or alfalfa sprouts for three days. At the start and at the end of the three days, the researchers collected nasal rinses and measured levels of two powerful *antioxidant enzymes* (GSTP1 and NQO1)—compounds that decrease inflammation. After three days, those eating six ounces a day of broccoli sprouts had double the amount of GSTPI and triple the amount of NQO1; those eating the alfalfa sprouts had no change.

"This is one of the first studies showing that broccoli sprouts—a readily available food source—offers potent biologic effects in stimulating an antioxidant response in people," says Mark Riedl, MD, assistant professor of clinical immunology and allergy and the study leader. Dr. Riedl theorizes that it's the *sulforaphane* in the broccoli that does the trick.

What to do: If you have allergic rhinitis (or asthma or chronic obstructive pulmonary disease or want to battle the respiratory-damaging effects of air pollution), include broccoli sprouts, broccoli and other sulforaphane-containing cruciferous vegetables (such as kale, cauliflower, Brussels sprouts and bok choy) in your daily diet, says Dr. Riedl.

SPEED LIMIT | End Your Addiction To Nasal Spray

Over-the-counter decongestant nasal sprays such as Afrin and Neo-Synephrine—which can unclog your stuffed nose in seconds or minutes—are potentially *addictive*, says Dr. Mitchell.

What happens: The sprays work by constricting blood vessels inside the nose. But after a couple days of regular use, those vessels "rebound," becoming even more swollen—and blocking breathing again. To restore breathing, you use the nasal spray again. The vessels rebound again. You use the nasal spray again… and have to use more and more of it to breathe… and can't stop using it without a suffocating upsurge of congestion. You're hooked.

"Being hooked on nasal sprays is pretty common—about one out of every seven patients with nasal obstruction has abused nasal sprays," says Neil Bhattacharyya, MD, associate professor of otology and laryngology at Harvard Medical School.

What to do: Talk to your doctor about the problem and consider following this plan to get off the nasal decongestant, says Dr. Mitchell.

First, switch to an over-the-counter nasal cortisone spray—such as *fluticasone* (Flonase)—for a few weeks, which will keep your nose cleared while you're not using the spray.

Then switch to NasalCrom, a safe over-the-counter nasal spray with cromolyn sodium (neither a decongestant nor a steroid) as its active ingredient.

🕐 *Super-Quick Fix*

Try this: "NasalCrom is a good preventive for someone with seasonal allergies," says Dr. Mitchell. "Start using it a few weeks before allergy season begins. And if you're allergic to animal dander, you can use it right before visiting a friend who has a cat or dog."

- **Dodge the pollen.** "By taking care to avoid pollen, a person with allergic rhinitis can dramatically reduce their symptoms and the number of days they're out of commission," says Holly Lucille, ND, a naturopathic physician in private practice in Los Angeles (*www.drhollylucille.com*).
- **Use a nasal rinse.** "Flushing your nose with salt water helps flush out pollens," she says.

Product: SinusRinse, from NeilMed. It's available at most drugstores and many national retail chains.

- **Close your windows in the morning—and exercise in the afternoon.** Pollen counts are highest from 5 am to 10 am.

- **Encase mattresses and pillows in zippered, dustproof covers.** They help minimize the penetration of allergens.

- **Use a dehumidifier.** It helps reduce dust mites, the microscopic critters that live mainly in bedding. Ninety percent of people with allergic rhinitis are sensitized to dust mites, worsening allergic rhinitis.

- **Wash your bedding weekly in hot water.** This also helps kill dust mites.

⏰ *Super-Quick Fix*

➤ **Take off your shoes at the door.** "Most household dirt, dust and allergens come from the bottom of shoes," she says.

HEADACHES

Relief Can Be Surprisingly Simple

If you have chronic headaches—migraine, tension, sinus—everything you *think* you know about what causes them and how to relieve the pain...may be wrong.

That's the opinion of neurologist David Buchholz, MD, associate professor of Neurology at Johns Hopkins University in Baltimore and author of *Heal Your Headache: The 1·2·3 Program for Taking Charge of Your Pain* (Workman). And thousands of former headache sufferers treated by his approach would probably agree.

Here's what he wants you to know...

New thinking: "Nearly all headaches, of all types, arise from a *single* mechanism," says Dr. Buchholz. He calls it the *migraine mechanism*. When it's activated, it causes swelling and inflammation of blood vessels in and around your head—and the pain and other symptoms of headaches.

Fully activated, it causes the classic symptoms that conventional medicine labels a *migraine headache*—severe head pain, commonly accompanied by nausea, vomiting, sensitivity to bright light and loud noise and other symptoms.

Partially activated, it causes *tension headache* and *sinus headache* and their symptoms.

The migraine mechanism is activated in the *migraine control center*, probably located deep within the brain, in the hypothalamus. It is activated by *triggers*—certain foods and beverages, hormone levels, lack of sleep, cigarette smoke, low barometric pressure, stress and many other factors.

Your genes determine your personal triggers. They also play a role in determining your *threshold* for triggers—how many triggers it takes to set off the migraine mechanism.

Once triggered, the migraine mechanism can stay active for minutes, hours or days—or your threshold can be so low that you have constant headaches (a problem Dr. Buchholz says is far more common than generally acknowledged).

Self-defense: The key to preventing or healing migraines is to "keep your trigger level below your threshold," says Dr. Buchholz. Doing so is surprisingly simple...

➤ **Reverse the "rebound"—go cold turkey on headache drugs.** "When you have a headache, you just want to get rid of it," says Dr. Buchholz. "And if you're like most people, you rely on painkillers." But by taking headache medications too frequently, your headaches becomes *worse*—a phenomenon called *rebound headache*.

Trap: "Rebound is the greatest impediment to headache control," says Dr. Buchholz. Here's his explanation of how it works...

You take a fast-acting medication to relieve a headache. It works temporarily, by constricting the blood vessels around your head that become swollen because of migraine. Now, imagine what happens when the formerly swollen blood vessels escape from the temporary, artificial constriction brought on by the drug. They swell *with a vengeance*, in a process known as *rebound vasodilation*—and rebound headache.

In other words, *the drug* itself causes increased headache frequency and severity! And rebound also lowers your threshold, so that it takes fewer triggers to set off a headache.

If painkillers are used infrequently, rebound doesn't develop, says Dr. Buchholz. "But when you use the drugs several times per month, you soon start needing them once or twice per week, and then several times per week, and then more or less daily—and rebound headaches take you prisoner."

The drugs that can cause rebound headaches are...

• **Caffeine-containing analgesics**, such as Excedrin, BC Powder and others.

• **Butalbital compounds**, such as Fioricet and others.

• **Isometheptene compounds**.

• **Decongestants**, such as Sudafed, Tylenol Sinus, Dristan, Afrin, and many others, both OTC and prescription.

• **Ergotamines**, such as Migranal and DHE-45.

• **Triptans**, such as Imitrex, Amerge, Zomig, Maxalt, Axert, Frova, Relpax and Treximet.

• **Opioids and related drugs**, such as Tylenol with codeine, Percocet, OxyContin, Ultram and many others. (Opioid rebound works by changing the opiate receptors in the brain.)

What to do: If you have chronic headaches, the first thing you need to do is eliminate rebound, says Dr. Buchholz. And there's only one way to do so—stop taking the drugs that cause rebound headaches.

"To eliminate rebound, I recommend the 'cold turkey' approach," he says. Yes, about half of people will experience a temporary *increase* in their headaches for a few days or even a few weeks, from drug withdrawal. "Of my many patients who have toughed this out, I can't think of one who, after the fact, regretted it," he says.

What helps: "In place of the rebounding medications, you can take plain acetaminophen or aspirin without caffeine, or anti-inflammatories such as ibuprofen or naproxen. You may also use medication to control nausea and vomiting."

But why not just withdraw gradually and comfortably?

"Gradual withdrawal has a major flaw," says Dr. Buchholz. "It tends never to reach an end. Flush your headache medications down the toilet, where they belong. These drugs are not your best buddies—they're your worst enemies."

⚠ *Caution:* Withdrawing from high-dose narcotics or certain other drugs might be dangerous, says Dr. Buchholz. Check with the doctor prescribing the drugs to make sure that stopping abruptly is safe.

➤ **Delete these from your diet.** "The extent to which foods and beverages contribute to headaches escapes most headache sufferers," says Dr. Buchholz.

That's because the dietary triggers usually take a day or two to do their dirty work—making it difficult to link the specific food to the headache.

Also, the food may only trigger a headache sometimes, depending on your threshold level—for example, on a day when you're already on the verge of your threshold because you're under a lot of stress or didn't get much sleep.

Another factor is caffeine. "It's one of the most potent dietary triggers," says Dr. Buchholz. It's *helpful* for headaches in the short run—but *increases* them in the long run.

⏱ *Super-Quick Fix*

The Fastest Ways to Treat Infrequent Headaches

If you get mild-to-moderate headaches more than twice a week, or severe headaches more than twice a month, you should focus on *prevention*, says Dr. Buchholz. But if your headaches are infrequent, you can safely and effectively (and quickly) use over-the-counter drugs to treat the problem. *The best medication regimens...*

Mild to moderate headaches...

- *Acetaminophen (Tylenol)* (without caffeine), up to 1,000 milligrams (mg), every 4 hours.

- *Aspirin* (without caffeine), up to 1,000 mg, every 4 hours.

- *Ibuprofen (Advil, Motrin)*, 200 to 800 mg, every 4 to 6 hours.

- *Naproxen Sodium (Aleve, Naprosyn)*, 220 to 660 mg, every 6 to 8 hours.

⚠ *Caution:* These medications are generally safe, but not 100% so, says Dr. Buchholz. Acetaminophen can cause liver damage, especially with chronic, high-dose exposure. Aspirin, ibuprofen and naproxen can cause stomach irritation or bleeding, and raise blood pressure.

Severe headaches...

The class of drugs called *triptans* is the best treatment for infrequent severe headaches. "Approximately seventy-five percent of those who use a triptan obtain relief," says Dr. Buchholz.

- *Sumatriptan (Imitrex)*, 25, 50 or 100 mg tablet. "It's the original," says Dr. Buchholz.

- *Sumatriptan*, 5 or 20 mg nasal spray. "Faster than tablets."

- *Sumatriptan*, 6 mg self-injection. "Fastest."

- *Sumatriptan/naproxen (Treximet)*, 85/500 mg tablet. "Combination therapy."

- *Naratriptan (Amerge)*, 1 or 2.5 mg tablet. "Relatively well tolerated."

- *Rizatriptan (Maxalt)*, 5 or 10 mg tablet. "One of the best overall."

- *Zolmitriptan (Zomig)*, 2.5 or 5 mg tablet or 5 mg nasal spray. "Similar to sumatriptan."

- *Almotriptan (Axert)*, 6.25 or 12.5 mg tablet. "Challenger to rizatriptan."

- *Frovatriptan (Frova)*, 2.5 mg tablet. "Lasts long."

- *Eletriptan (Relpax)*, 20 or 40 mg tablet. "Latest generation."

Red flag: The line between limited, *appropriate* use of acute treatments for infrequent headaches, and the level of use that leads to rebound headaches, is a very fine one—which many headache sufferers cross at considerable peril, says Dr. Buchholz. "Do not use triptans more than twice a month."

Nausea and vomiting sometimes accompany a migraine. *Consider using...*

- *Prochlorperazine*, 5 to 10 mg up to 3 or 4 times daily orally, or 25 mg up to twice daily, as suppository.

- *Promethazine*, 12.5 to 25 mg up to every 4 hours, taken orally, rectally or by injection.

- *Metoclopramide (Reglan)*, 10 to 20 mg up to 4 times daily, orally or by injection.

Skipping meals is also a common trigger, so you might conclude you don't get headaches from food.

How do dietary items cause headaches? "The specific way they trigger migraine is unclear," says Dr. Buchholz. "I find it helpful to imagine that they directly feed into and stimulate the migraine control center in the brain, stacking with other, non-dietary triggers such as stress, hormones and barometric pressure changes, and pushing your total trigger level toward or above your threshold."

What to do: Everybody's dietary triggers are different, says Dr. Buchholz.

But here are the most common culprits...

- **Caffeine.** Coffee, tea, iced tea, chocolate drinks, cola and other caffeine-containing sodas and drinks. "Eliminate them completely and permanently," says Dr. Buchholz.

- **Chocolate.** It has migraine-triggering chemicals such as theobromine and phenylethylamine.

- **Monosodium glutamate.** It's commonly found in soups and bouillons...Accent and seasoned salt...flavored, salty snacks...croutons and breadcrumbs...gravies...ready-to-eat meals...cheap buffets...processed meats...veggie burgers...protein concentrates...and low-fat, low-calorie foods. (See page 160 in the "Glaucoma" section for a list of labeled ingredients that also indicate a food contains MSG.)

- **Processed meats and fish.** "Their nitrites and nitrates are powerful triggers of migraine," says Dr. Buchholz. They include aged, canned, cured, fermented, marinated, smoked, tenderized—or preserved with nitrites or nitrates. Hot dogs, sausage, salami, pepperoni, bologna (and other lunchmeats with nitrites). Liverwurst, beef jerky, certain hams, bacon, pates, smoked or pickled fish, caviar and anchovies. Also, fresh beef liver and chicken livers, and wild game.

- **Cheese and other dairy products.** "Tyramine, a protein byproduct, is the culprit here," he says. The more aged, the worse. Beware of cheese-containing foods, including pizza. Yogurt (including frozen yogurt), sour cream and buttermilk are also triggers. *Try this:* Permissible cheeses include cottage cheese, ricotta, cream cheese and good-quality American cheese.

- **Nuts.** They contain tyramine. Avoid all kinds, as well as nut butters. Seeds are okay.

- **Alcohol and vinegar.** Especially red wine, champagne and dark or heavy drinks. *Try:*

Vodka is best tolerated because it's low in congeners, a byproduct of fermentation. Clear (ideally, distilled) vinegar is allowable. Don't overdo condiments made with vinegar, such as ketchup, mustard and mayonnaise.

- **Certain fruits and juices.** Citrus fruits and their juices, pineapples, bananas, raisins (and other dried fruits preserved with sulfites), raspberries, red plums, papayas, passion fruit, figs, dates and avocados. *Try:* Apples, most berries, cherries, grapes, melons, peaches or pears.

- **Certain vegetables.** Onions especially. And sauerkraut, pea pods and certain beans (broad Italian, lima, fava, navy and lentils). *Allowed:* Leeks, scallions, shallots, spring onions, garlic and all other vegetables not listed above.

- **Fresh yeast-risen bread goods.** Less than one day old—homemade (or restaurant-baked) breads, especially sourdough, as well as bagels, doughnuts, pizza dough, soft pretzels and coffee cake.

- **Aspartame (NutraSweet).** Saccharin (Sweet'N Low) may also be a trigger for some. *Try:* Splenda.

- **Miscellaneous.** Soy products, especially if cultured, such as miso, or highly processed. Tomatoes and tomato-based sauces.

"You can begin to take control of your headaches by eliminating each of these potential triggers from your diet," says Dr. Buchholz. "The better you follow the diet, the more likely you are to achieve headache control. No one can follow the diet perfectly, but do your best."

Helpful: After four months of headache control, you can try reintroducing dietary items one by one and see what happens, says Dr. Buchholz. "Pick the item you miss the most and dedicate a week to it, consuming it daily. If, early in the week, headaches recur, terminate that trial. If you want, move on to another item."

Clarifying the Controversy

Why don't more headache specialists agree with the theory and treatments of Dr. Buchholz? "I would boil it down to two reasons," he says. "Preconceived notions and low expectations."

Preconceived notions: "There are deeply ingrained concepts of headache that pervade our thinking," says Dr. Buchholz.

One is that the so-called tension headache is characterized by muscular contraction in response to stress.

Fact: "Electrical studies measuring muscle contraction around the head and neck during this type of headache do *not* demonstrate excessive or abnormal activity," he says. "Tense muscles are *not* the source of your head and neck pain. This has long been known by headache specialists. But most headache sufferers—and most doctors—haven't gotten the word. And the misdiagnosis of tension headache persists."

Another preconception is that sinus headaches are caused by allergy, chronic infection or structural abnormalities.

"They usually are not," says Dr. Buchholz. "And this misdiagnosis—and the treatments for it—have created a confusing jumble. Over the years,

sinus headache sufferers are treated with innumerable courses of antihistamines, decongestants, steroid sprays, antibiotics, allergy shots, sinus irrigation and sinus surgery. Despite this accumulation of treatment failures, the stubborn myth and misdiagnosis of sinus headache lives on."

Low expectations: "Many headache sufferers have low expectations borne out by their experience of never getting better," says Dr. Buchholz. "After awhile, they give up and stop looking for an answer.

"And doctors who treat headache—often unsuccessfully, because the treatment is based on a wrong understanding—have low expectations too.

"All too often, they start to feel the headaches are the patients' *fault*—that the typical chronic headache patient is a whiner, griper, complainer or drug seeker. Or a neurotic who lives an unhappy, miserable life and doesn't *want* to get better. Or someone who has such a stressful life—from work, marriage and finances—that it's inevitable they suffer from headaches."

Bottom line: "The details of my model of migraine may not be completely accurate," says Dr. Buchholz. "But for headache sufferers, that's not so important. What's important is that it's effective in guiding you to control your headaches."

➤ **Are your other meds messing with your head?** Some non-headache medications directly stimulate the migraine control center, says Dr. Buchholz.

"In some cases, these medications are optional and therefore avoidable and in other cases they may be mandatory and therefore unavoidable. Talk to your prescribing doctor. However, from a headache perspective, the best approach is to eliminate a nonessential medication that may be contributing to headaches and decide later—after you've achieved control—whether to try adding it back."

Common medication triggers include...

➤ **Hormones,** such as hormonal contraception and hormone replacement therapy.

➤ **Adrenaline-like drugs, stimulants and diet pills,** such as bronchodilators for asthma (Advair), over-the-counter stimulants (No-Doz), methylphenidate (Ritalin, Concerta), dextroamphetamine (Adderall, Dexedrine), over-the-counter diet pills, and prescription diet pills.

➤ **Vasodilators,** such as nitrates for heart disease (Isordil, Nitro-Dur) and erection medications (Viagra, Levitra, Cialis).

➤ **Antidepressants,** such as selective serotonin reuptake inhibitors (Celexa, Paxil, Zoloft) and buproprion (Wellbutrin).

Important: Tricyclic antidepressants (nortriptyline and others) can help *prevent* headaches.

• **Proton pump inhibitors** (Prilosec, Nexium and others) for heartburn.

However: H2 blockers (famotidine, ranitidine) for heartburn do not trigger headaches.

➤ **Others,** including Isotretinoin for acne.

➤ **Stay on a schedule.** Regularity is key to avoiding headaches, says Dr. Buchholz. "Sleep, eat and exercise on a regular basis."

"Get enough sleep each night—eight hours or more—and don't oversleep sporadically on weekends.

"Don't skip meals—stay on schedule for three meals a day, no more than six to eight hours apart. Snack in between, if you wish.

"Exercise enhances endorphin product in the brain and is a natural way to help raise your migraine threshold. Aim for a half hour or more of aerobic exercise, three to four times a week."

HEARING LOSS

Hear This Now

Your spouse complains that you have the TV turned up way too loud—but it sounds perfectly normal to you. You're constantly asking people to repeat themselves. And when you're out to eat in a restaurant with a lot of background noise—well, forget about hearing the conversation clearly.

Those are all signs of *hearing loss,* a problem for nearly 40 million Americans, including one-third of all people age 65 and older, says Michael Seidman, MD, director of Otologic/Neurotologic Surgery and Otology Research at the Henry Ford Health System in Detroit, Michigan, and author of *Save Your Hearing Now: The Revolutionary Program That Can Prevent and May Even Reverse Hearing Loss* (Wellness Central).

Most hearing loss is what experts call *sensorineural*—damage to the hair cells within the cochlea, the part of the inner ear that translates sound vibrations into electrical impulses that are sent to the brain. *There are two main causes...*

Aging, a type of sensorineural hearing loss that is so common it has its own name—*presbyacusia.*

And noise—from a lifetime of hair dryers and garbage disposals, lawn mowers and chainsaws, rock concerts and loud work environments.

Hearing aids can help improve hearing loss, of course. But is there any way to *protect* and even *reverse* the damage to your ears—in the same way you protect your heart from arterial plaque by exercising and your cells from cancer by eating more fruits and vegetables?

Yes, says Dr. Seidman. "I have conducted research to identify natural means to prevent and reverse hearing loss, and I firmly believe it is now possible."

Here's what he suggests…

➤ **The top four nutrients to protect and repair hearing.** "These four compounds deliver state-of-the-art protection for the auditory system," says Dr. Seidman. "Typically, it is difficult—if not impossible—to obtain therapeutic amounts of these nutrients from food alone."

● **Alpha lipoic acid (ALA).** This powerful and versatile antioxidant is capable of counteracting the type of age-related damage that harms the auditory system, says Dr. Seidman. "Recent studies in our laboratory have demonstrated improvement in age-related hearing loss with ALA."

Recommended dosage: 100 to 750 milligrams (mg) per day.

● **Acetyl-L-carnitine (ALCAR).** This compound is important for the proper functioning of the mitochondria—the energy factories in every cell, says Dr. Seidman. It also supports a healthy nervous system and brain, where much of the auditory system is located. "Studies in our laboratory have shown that older people who took ALCAR had improved hearing, compared to older people who didn't."

Recommended dosage: 500 to 3,000 mg per day.

● **Glutathione.** This compound is a key element in combating the "free radical" damage that can harm hearing—the same cell-harming inflammatory and oxidative process implicated in the development of heart disease, diabetes and Alzheimer's, says Dr. Seidman. "Studies have demonstrated an age-associated eighty-eight percent reduction in glutathione levels in the auditory nerve—so it can be theorized that hearing loss may occur in part because of reduction of glutathione levels with age."

Recommended dosage: 30 to 300 mg a day.

● **Coenzyme Q10.** This vitally important nutrient protects the mitochondria—and

---

The Best Way to Clean Your Ears

"About once a month, I have to repair eardrums ruptured by cotton swabs, keys, hairpins or other objects that people were using to clean their ears," says Dr. Seidman.

Better: One option is to do nothing—because you don't have to. "The ears are self-cleaning," says Dr. Seidman. "Wax is slowly swept to the outer canal. From there, you can gently wipe it away with a washcloth and finger."

🕐 *Super-Quick Fix*

"If that doesn't feel clean enough, mix a little hot tap water with unheated hydrogen peroxide—about half and half. Test a few drops of the mixture on the inside of your wrist to make sure it's about body temperature. Use an eyedropper to fill one ear canal with the solution. Tip your head to the opposite side, in such a way that the solution stays inside the canal. Stay in that position for about one or two minutes. Then tip your head back to the other side, letting excess solution trickle out. Repeat the process in the other ear. Do this once a month if you feel it's necessary."

---

therefore hearing—and also plays a role in the production of cellular energy, says Dr. Seidman.

Recommended dosage: 60 to 320 mg per day.

"For best absorption, take these supplements with food and at least eight ounces of water. I recommend separating the daily dose you choose into two or three portions, so that your cells are nourished throughout the day."

Product: Dr. Seidman has formulated a supplement that contains all four of these nutrients—150 mg of ALA, 600 mg of ALCAR, 90 mg of Coenzyme Q10 and 60 mg of glutathione—the

Speed Healing Success

"My Family Doesn't Have to Shout at Me"

"The proof that ALA, ALCAR, CoQ10 and glutathione can protect hearing has been amply demonstrated by a number of glowing reports from my patients," says Dr. Seidman. "Ivan's story is a good example.

"After years of working as a baggage handler at a major airport, Ivan's hearing was deteriorating quickly, even though he always wore sufficient ear protection on the job. His family life was suffering because of the hearing loss. Frustrated by his inability to hear well—and the need to shout rather than talk in every conversation—Ivan's wife and children were threatening to stop speaking to him if he didn't get a hearing aid. But the price of a good hearing aid was an obstacle at that moment, so Ivan came to see me, wondering if there was something else he could do.

"I recommended Ivan start taking ALA, ALCAR, CoQ10 and glutathione. At first, he was reluctant. 'I already take vitamins and they aren't helping,' he said. I explained how these four ingredients are different and how my own research had proven that they could protect the ears. In spite of his doubts, Ivan decided to take the supplement.

"The next time I heard from him, things had improved considerably. He felt that his hearing was no longer getting steadily worse. He also found that conversations at home were improving. 'As long as the television isn't on, my family doesn't have to shout at me, so we turn it off at dinnertime and when we want to talk,' he said."

Anti-Age/Energy Formula. It is available from Body Language Vitamins, at *www.bodylanguagevitamin.com*, or call 877-548-3348. Address: 5310 Putnam Dr., West Bloomfield, MI 48323, e-mail *info@bodylanguagevitamin.com*.

➤ **A diet for your ears.** "If you want to protect your hearing, eating nutritious food is a must," says Dr. Seidman. "That's because like every other part of the body, your ears need a high level of nutrients—and a minimum of body-harming fats and refined sugars—to function at their best." His suggestions...

1. **Focus on whole foods with high antioxidant and fiber content.** Foods highest in antioxidants include prunes, raisins, blueberries, blackberries, strawberries, raspberries, plums, oranges, red grapes, kale, spinach, Brussels sprouts, beets, red bell peppers, onions and corn.

    Foods highest in fiber include beans (baked, kidney, black, pinto, lima, soy and navy, plus legumes such as peas and lentils), whole grains (brown rice, bran and all-bran cereals) and fruits and vegetables.

2. **Increase your intake of "good" omega-3 fats.** Eat more omega-3 rich fatty fish, such as salmon, cod, herring, sardines, tuna, anchovies and mackerel.

3. **Reduce your intake of refined and processed ingredients, especially sugar and high-fructose corn syrup.**

    Red flag: One unlikely place to find high sugar content is low-fat desserts, says Dr. Seidman.

    Smart idea: Satisfy your sweet craving with small amounts of dark chocolate.

➤ **Exercise in earnest.** "From the perspective of improved hearing, regular physical activity reduces the damage associated with aging," says Dr. Seidman. "Also, since circulation is increased, the flow of oxygen and nutrients into the ear and brain are enhanced."

What to do: "Find an activity you enjoy and that you'll do most days of the week," says Dr. Seidman. "Actually, find a few different pleasant activities—walking, bicycling, stretching, weight-training. That helps you avoid the injuries that can come with repetitive motions and provides a well-rounded workout."

Red flags: "If you like to exercise to music, keep the volume low," says Dr. Seidman. "And take earplugs to aerobics classes. The decibel levels of the music played during aerobics class can register well above the high nineties—equivalent to a power saw."

➤ **Shield your ears from noise damage.** "Minimizing the amount of noise in your life, and protecting your ears from noise that can't be escaped, are two crucial elements of saving your hearing," says Dr. Seidman.

"Many of my patients ask me when ear protection is appropriate. My answer—use it whenever you are exposed to loud noise of any kind. In terms of how the sounds affect your ears, there is very little difference between the roar of a lawn mower, the whine of a power saw, the bone-thumping bass of the latest popular music or a blow-dryer set on high."

What to do: Invest in earplugs, says Dr. Seidman. "They are tiny enough so that you can carry them everywhere, and they are easy to use."

Self-defense: Clean them between wearings, to eliminate bacteria that can cause ear infections.

Also helpful: Earmuffs—like those typically seen on individuals who work around airplanes—are one of the best solutions for protecting ears from noise, he says. New models feature noise

reduction with speech amplification so you can hear conversations, and others block loud noise but allow the wearer to hear AM or FM radio.

What most people don't realize: "Unlike earplugs or earmuffs, noise-canceling headphones are not rated for noise reduction and do not protect the ears from noise-induced damage," says Dr. Seidman. "Their purpose is to minimize background noise so that personal music players can be heard in noisy settings, such as in airplanes or subways, and to otherwise mask bothersome background sounds."

HEARTBURN

Douse the Fire Without the Drugs

Heartburn. Acid reflux. Gastroesophageal Reflux Disease, or GERD. Gastroesophageal Reflux, or GER. Acid indigestion. Gastric reflux.

That's a lot of different names for what is essentially the same problem...

What happens: When you swallow, food is propelled down the esophagus, the food tube between the mouth and the stomach. At the bottom of the tube is the *lower esophageal sphincter* (LES), a muscled valve that loosens its normally tight pressure to let the food through. But sometimes the valve loosens when it shouldn't—allowing stomach acid to "reflux" into the esophagus, producing the painful burning, belching, sour taste and other distressing symptoms that most of us call...heartburn.

No matter what you call it, chances are you've had it once or twice—or maybe three or four times, or three or four hundred.

Fact: An estimated 30% of Americans experience regular heartburn, says the American Gastroenterological Association (AGA). Twenty-five

See Your Doctor If...

If you think you may be suffering from hearing loss, have an evaluation by hearing professionals—an otolaryngologist/head and neck surgeon (also known as an ear, nose and throat doctor, or ENT) and an audiologist.

Is the Standard Dietary Advice for Heartburn Wrong?

You've been diagnosed with heartburn. *And your doctor has given you a "few" dietary recommendations...*

Don't eat chocolate. Or spicy foods. Or fried foods. Or fatty foods. As for beverages, skip the coffee. And the orange juice. And anything carbonated. Oh yeah, and the red wine. And whatever you do, don't have a mint after the meal!

You've done all that and now you're feeling fine, right? *Probably not...*

Surprising: There is *no* scientific evidence to support any of these standard dietary recommendations, says Lauren Gerson, MD, a gastroenterologist and director of the Esophageal and Small Bowel Disorder Center at Stanford University School of Medicine.

She and two colleagues surveyed more than 2,000 studies on heartburn that were published between 1975 and 2004, including 100 studies on lifestyle factors such as diet.

Only two lifestyle changes offered a clear benefit...

1. Losing even a few pounds reduced or eliminated heartburn.

2. Raising the head of the bed did the same for nighttime episodes of heartburn. ("Use a 4x4 or 4x6 piece of wood under the legs at the head of the bed," says Liz Lipski, CNN. "It's such a small change you won't even notice it, but it's enough gravity so that it works.")

Dr. Gerson decided to analyze those studies on lifestyle changes after seeing patient after unhappy patient with heartburn who restricted their diet—to no effect whatsoever. "The patients were on very bland diets and cutting out coffee and wine and everything that they enjoy—and basically their heartburn wasn't getting any better. In fact, it's very rare to see a patient who says, 'Oh, I just changed my diet and everything got better.' "

Dr. Gerson no longer counsels her heartburn patients to cut out foods.

However: "If a patient comes in and states, 'Red wine really gives me terrible heartburn,' then it may be reasonable to say, 'Well, you could avoid it, or you could take an antacid before you drink it.' "

percent have it once a month, 12% once a week and 5% every day.

It's no wonder that we spend tens of billions of dollars a year on acid-blocking drugs—the *proton pump inhibitors* (PPIs) such as Nexium, Prevacid and Prilosec...the *H2 receptor antagonists* such as Tagamet, Zantac and Pepcid AC... the *antacids* such as Maalox and Tums.

These drugs can do the trick, with the PPIs leading the pack in acid-suppressing effectiveness. But there's a catch.

Red flags: The PPIs were first approved in 2003. Now studies are showing their long-term side effects. For example, a recent study in the *Journal of the American Medical Association* showed that taking PPIs every day for four years can nearly *triple* the risk for hip fractures. "The general perception among physicians and the public is that PPIs are relatively harmless, but that may not be the case," says Yu-Xiao Yang, MD, the study leader. Studies also show the drugs double your risk of colds and flu and increase your risk of pneumonia by 63%—because there's too little stomach acid to kill viruses and bacteria and they migrate into your respiratory tract. And they increase your risk of *C. difficile*, a severe and possibly life-threatening infection.

And even their effectiveness is questionable. Forty percent of people who take prescription PPIs continue to suffer from heartburn and also take OTC antacids, says the AGA.

Speed Healing Success

Twenty Years of Heartburn— Gone in Two Days!

"I have been plagued by chronic heartburn for twenty years," says Norm Robillard, PhD. "Even though I was taking acid-reducing medicines, my condition continued to get worse. On a business trip to Seattle, after arriving at my hotel, I ate dinner, went back to my room, and went to bed. I woke up in the middle of the night choking for air. My lungs felt like they were filled with burning liquid. I had suffered severe acid reflux—stomach acid had traveled up my esophagus until I aspirated it into my lungs. I will never forget this moment."

Shortly after he suffered this horrendous attack of nighttime heartburn, Dr. Robillard decided to try a low-carbohydrate diet for another health problem—overweight.

"Within two days of starting the diet, the chronic heartburn completely vanished. I was amazed. I have continued to follow the low-carb diet—and have not taken one dose of heartburn medication since."

Theory: As a microbiologist who had studied carbohydrate digestion at Tufts University, Dr. Robillard returned to the scientific literature. And *he came to this conclusion about the true cause of GERD…*

Carbohydrates that aren't fully absorbed ferment in the small intestines…feeding the bacteria there…which multiply beyond their normal numbers…generating excess gas…that creates excess pressure in the small intestine and stomach… weakening the LES…and triggering heartburn.

"The consumption of excess carbohydrates is the root cause of GERD in susceptible individuals," he says.

He wrote about his theory and its practical applications in the book *Heartburn Cured: The Low Carb Miracle* (Self Health Publishing) and is currently working on his second book, *The Glycemic Choice Diet for Heartburn* (Self Health Publishing) which uses the glycemic index (a scale that measures how quickly carbs are digested) to guide heartburn sufferers to long-term relief.

Some of his key suggestions…

- **With your doctor's okay,** stop eating most carbohydrates for a few days, using a high-protein, low-carb diet such as the one featured in the book *Protein Power* (Bantam) by Michael Eades, MD.

- *Next, go on a diet that emphasizes foods low on the glycemic index,* such as *The New Glucose Revolution* (Da Capo).

- *Take your time eating and chew well.* Saliva contains *amylase*, a digestive enzyme for carbs.

Rapid Resource: You can find out more about Dr. Robillard's approach to heartburn and order his books at *www.digestivehealthinstitute.org*.

Another drawback is that the drugs reduce symptoms but don't solve the problem. "These medications are effective while you take them, but once you discontinue their use, your problem often recurs," says Liz Lipski, PhD, CCN, CNS, the director of Nutrition and Integrative Health Programs at Maryland University of Integrative Health (*www.lizlipski.com*) and author of *Digestive Wellness* (McGraw-Hill, third edition). Do you really want to take antacids for the rest of your life? *Maybe you don't have to…*

"There are many dietary and lifestyle actions you can take to allow stomach acid to continue doing its job without allowing it to travel outside the areas where it's supposed to be," says Martie Whittekin, CCN, a certified clinical nutritionist, host of the radio program *Healthy By Nature* (*www. hbnshow.com*) and author of *Natural Alternatives to*

Nexium, Maalox, Tagamet, Prilosec and Other Acid Blockers (Square One).

And many of those actions are fast…

⏱ Super-Quick Fix

➤ **Just add vinegar.** "Most people who are prescribed acid blockers are actually suffering from *low* stomach acid," says Whittekin. "Yet mainstream medicine balks at the idea that a fundamental cause of heartburn might be that meals are staying in the stomach too long because the acid is simply not concentrated enough to do the required digestion."

New approach: "A low-tech method of stimulating stomach acid is the use of vinegar," she says.

What to do: Mix one teaspoon of vinegar with a small amount of water. Drink this mixture at each meal. If it burns, you don't need this remedy—immediately neutralize the vinegar with a teaspoon of baking soda mixed with water.

On the other hand, if the vinegar is tolerated, gradually increase the amount by one teaspoon per day, until you are taking six teaspoons (two tablespoons) of vinegar (diluted in water) with each meal.

Product: Bragg organic apple cider vinegar is a good choice, says Whittekin.

⏱ Super-Quick Fix

➤ **Chew more, burn less.** "I've seen people with heartburn get off their medication simply by chewing more," says Ali Marie Shapiro, CHC, a certified health counselor in Philadelphia, Pennsylvania (*www.alishapiro.com*).

"You can reduce the workload of your gastric acid so that the amount you have will go further and work more effectively by chewing more thoroughly," agrees Whittekin.

What to do: Chew every bite 20 times, until the food is liquefied, she says. "Take a

small bite, be attentive to the food in your mouth and count how many times you chew. It may take a little while for this to become a habit, but it can make a huge difference."

➤ **Take digestive enzymes.** Enzymes are compounds that spark and speed chemical reactions in your body. *Digestive* enzymes—such as protease for protein, lipase for fat, and amylase for starches—spark and speed digestion.

"Many people find that taking a digestive enzyme supplement brings fast relief from heartburn because it goes to the heart of the problem—their food was not being properly digested," says Whittekin. "If you have heartburn, this is a very safe treatment to try."

Product: Whittekin recommends Enzyme Caps by Twinlab, which are widely available. Take with meals, following the dosage recommendation on the label.

➤ **Eat smaller meals.** "Smaller meals don't stay in the stomach as long as larger meals—they move more quickly to the intestines," says Elaine Magee, RD, a registered dietician in California (*www.recipedoctor.com*) and author of *Tell Me What to Eat If I Have Acid Reflux* (New Page). "And the shorter the time food is waiting around in the stomach, the shorter the time the stomach contents—including stomach acid—are splashing up into the esophagus."

Eat six times a day, says Magee—a small breakfast, a midmorning snack, a light lunch, an afternoon snack, a light dinner and maybe a nighttime snack.

One key to eating smaller meals is to eat when you are hungry and stop when you are comfortable, says Magee. (For more detailed information on following this strategy, please see page 104 in the "Diabetes" section.)

➤ **Drink lots of water.** "Some people find that increasing water consumption resolves acid reflux," says Dr. Lipski.

What helps: A gallon a day, or 128 ounces.

HEART DISEASE

Reverse It in Three Weeks

Every year, more than half a million Americans die of coronary artery disease (CAD). Three times that number suffer heart attacks. In total, half of American men and one-third of American women will have some form of heart disease during their lifetime.

But all of the standard treatments for heart disease—the cardiac drugs; the clot-dissolving medications; the surgical techniques that bypass clogged arteries or widen them with balloons, tiny rotating knives, lasers and stents—*do nothing to cure the underlying disease*, says Caldwell B. Esselstyn, Jr., MD, a surgeon, clinician and researcher at the Cleveland Clinic for more than 35 years and author of *Prevent and Reverse Heart Disease: The Revolutionary, Scientifically Proven, Nutrition-Based Cure* (Avery).

Good news: CAD is curable. The key is *plant-based nutrition*—eating fruits, vegetables, whole grains and legumes...not eating any meat, dairy, eggs, oils and nuts...and achieving a diet with 10% of calories from fat.

Study: Dr. Esselstyn studied the diet for 12 years, publishing his results in the *American Journal of Cardiology*. He followed 17 people with severe heart disease. Each had been told that modern medicine had nothing more to offer—not another open heart surgery, not more artery-widening angioplasty, not another and better drug. Those treatments were tried and they didn't work. For many of the 17, angina pain was so severe they couldn't walk across a room without excruciating chest pain. Every one of them was expected to die. And soon.

Today, 20 years later, every one of them is alive. The progression of their heart disease was *stopped*—and, in many cases, *reversed*. Their angina went away—for some, within three weeks. In fact, they became virtually "heart attack–proof," says Dr. Esselstyn. And there are hundreds of other patients with heart disease who have achieved the same remarkable results—by eating a plant-based diet.

Why it works: Heart disease develops in the endothelium, the cell-thick inner lining of the arteries. There, endothelial cells manufacture a compound called nitric oxide, which accomplishes four tasks crucial for healthy circulation.

1. **It keeps blood smooth and flowing,** rather than sticky and clotted.

2. **It allows arteries to widen when the heart needs more blood,** such as when you run up a flight of stairs.

3. **It stops muscle cells in arteries from growing into plaque**—the fatty gunk that blocks blood vessels.

4. **It decreases inflammation in the plaque** —the immune-sparked process that can trigger a rupture in the surface of plaque, starting

the clot-forming, artery-clogging cascade that causes a heart attack.

The type and amount of fat in the typical Western diet—from animal products, dairy foods and concentrated oils—assaults the endothelial cells, cutting their production of nitric oxide.

Low-fat vegetables, fruits, whole grains and beans are kind to the endothelium.

Study: A researcher at the University of Maryland School of Medicine fed a 900-calorie fast food breakfast containing 50 grams of fat (mostly from sausages and hash browns) to a group of students and then measured their endothelial function. For six hours, the students had severely constricted arteries and low levels of nitric oxide. Another group of students ate a 900-calorie, no-fat breakfast—and had no significant change in endothelial function.

"If a single meal can do that kind of damage, imagine the damage done by three fatty meals a day, seven days a week, three hundred and sixty-five days a year—for decades," says Dr. Esselstyn.

Well, you don't have to imagine…"All males over sixty-five years old, exposed to a traditional Western lifestyle, have cardiovascular disease and should be treated as such," concluded Lewis Kuller, MD, in his report on the 10-year findings of the Cardiovascular Health Study, from the National Heart, Lung and Blood Institute.

But male or female, you can prevent, stop or reverse heart disease with a plant-based diet…

The rules of the diet—which does not contain a single food known to cause or promote the development of CAD—are simple, says Dr. Esselstyn.

➤ **Don't eat anything with a face or a mother.** "This includes meat, poultry, fish and eggs," he says.

➤ **Don't eat dairy products.** "That means butter, cheese, cream, ice cream, yogurt and milk—even skim milk."

➤ **Don't consume oil of any kind—not a drop.** "That includes *all* oils, even virgin olive oil and canola," he says.

What you may not know: "Between fourteen to seventeen percent of olive oil is saturated fat—every bit as aggressive in promoting heart disease as the saturated fat in roast beef," says Dr. Esselstyn. "A diet that includes oils—including monounsaturated oils from olive oil and canola oil—may slow the progression of heart disease, but it will not *stop* or *reverse* the disease."

➤ **Generally, don't eat nuts or avocados.** If you are eating a plant-based diet to *prevent* heart disease, you can have a moderate amount of nuts and avocados as long as your total cholesterol remains below 150 mg/dL, says Dr. Esselstyn. If you have heart disease and want to stop or reverse it, you shouldn't eat these foods.

➤ **Eat a wonderful variety of delicious, nutrient-dense foods.** *That includes…*

• **All vegetables** except avocado. "Eat leafy green vegetables, root vegetables, veggies that are red, green, purple, orange and yellow and everything in between," says Dr. Esselstyn. Your list might include sweet potatoes, yams, potatoes (but never French fried or prepared in any other way that involves adding fats). Broccoli, kale and spinach. Asparagus, artichokes, eggplant, radishes, celery, onions, carrots. Brussels sprouts, corn, cabbages, lettuces, peppers. Bok choy, Swiss chard and beet greens. Turnips and parsnips. Summer squashes, winter squashes, tomatoes, cucumbers.

• **All legumes**—beans, peas, lentils of all varieties.

• **All whole grains and products,** such as bread and pasta, that are made from them—as

Why "Low-Fat" and Mediterranean Diets Don't Stop or Reverse Heart Disease

The most common objection physicians have to the plant-based diet is that their patients will not follow it, says Dr. Esselstyn. But many patients with heart disease who find out they have a *choice*—between invasive surgery that will do nothing to cure underlying disease, and nutritional changes that will stop and reverse the disease—willingly adopt the diet.

But why not eat a seemingly less demanding "heart-healthy" diet, such as the low-fat diet recommended by the American Heart Association (AHA) or the Mediterranean diet?

Surprising: Research shows that people who maintain the so-called "low-fat" AHA diet of 29% of calories from fat have the same rate of heart attacks and strokes as people who don't. That diet contains *three* times more fat than the plant-based diet that can stop and reverse heart disease, says Dr. Esselstyn.

And in the Lyon Diet Heart Study—widely regarded as proof of the heart-healing power of the Mediterranean diet—25% of people with heart disease who ate that diet experienced a new cardiovascular event.

"Plant-based nutrition is the *only* diet that can effectively prevent, stop and reverse heart disease, and make you immune to a heart attack," says Dr. Esselstyn.

"And the benefits of the diet go beyond beating heart disease," he adds. It also offers protection against stroke…high blood pressure…osteoporosis…adult-onset diabetes…senile mental impairment…erectile dysfunction …and cancers of the breast, prostate, colon, rectum, uterus and ovaries. And you will never again have to count calories or worry about your weight!

long as they do not contain added fats. The list includes whole wheat, whole rye, bulgur wheat, whole oats, barley, buckwheat (kasha or buckwheat groats), whole corn, cornmeal, wild rice, brown rice, popcorn.

There are also less well-known whole grains, such as couscous, kamut (a relative of durum wheat), quinoa, amaranth, millet, spelt, teff, triticale, grano and faro.

"You can also eat cereals that do not contain added sugar and oil," says Dr. Esselstyn. "That includes old-fashioned oats (not the quick-cooking variety), shredded wheat and brand names like Grape-Nuts."

Bread should be from whole grain and not contain added oil, he says. Whole-grain pastas are allowed.

⚠ *Caution:* "Be careful about restaurant pasta," says Dr. Esselstyn. "It is often egg-based and made from white flour, and there may well be oil lurking in the marinara sauce."

However: You should not eat refined grains, which have been stripped of much of their fiber and nutrients. Avoid white rice and "enriched" flour products, which are found in many pastas, breads, bagels and baked goods.

- **All fruits**—but limit your consumption to three pieces a day, and avoid drinking pure fruit juices.

What happens: Too much fruit rapidly raises blood sugar, triggering a surge of sugar-controlling insulin from the pancreas—which stimulates the liver to manufacture more cholesterol.

- **Beverages can include** water, seltzer water, oat milk, no-fat soy milk, coffee and tea. Alcohol is fine, in moderation. (No more than two glasses a day for men and one for women.)

Rapid Resource: Dr. Esselstyn's book *Prevent and Reverse Heart Disease* includes more than 150 delicious recipes using plant-based nutrition.

➤ **Take these supplements.** For maximum health, Dr. Esselstyn suggests the following four supplements—a multivitamin/mineral supplement; 1,000 mcg a day of B-12; 1,000 IU of vitamin D (if you're over 50); and one tablespoon of flaxseed meal per day, perhaps sprinkling it over cereal, for omega-3 fatty acids.

➤ **Expect a miracle.** "If you are a hundred percent compliant with this diet, within three to four weeks you will have strengthened the cap over the plaque so that it cannot rupture—you will be literally heart attack–proof," says Dr. Esselstyn.

"Long before the blockage of plaque begins to recede, the endothelial cells will have regenerated and started to produce healthy levels of nitric oxide. Blood vessels will begin to widen and chest pain will go away—in some patients, within ten days.

"And even that tiny increase in diameter of the vessels will create a huge increase in the flow of blood to the heart—possibly restoring total flow to blood vessels in three weeks.

"In my study, which was published in the *American Journal of Cardiology*, the treated patients had already experienced a total of for-ty-nine cardiovascular events, including four heart attacks, three strokes, fifteen cases of increased angina and seven cases of bypass surgery. During the next twelve years, among the seventeen patients compliant with plant-based nutrition, there were no cardiovascular events."

Important: People without heart disease who adopt this diet will never develop it, he says.

➤ **Consider a cholesterol-lowering statin drug—but don't depend on it.** Researchers from the Framingham Heart Study found that maintaining total cholesterol below 150 mg/dL is a virtual guarantee you will not have a heart attack, says Dr. Esselstyn.

However: If you eat the typical, high-fat Western diet and take a cholesterol-lowering statin drug, you will not protect yourself from heart disease—because the fat in the diet will damage the nitric oxide-producing cells of the endothelium, says Dr. Esselstyn.

Study: In a study in the *New England Journal of Medicine*, patients took huge doses of statin drugs to lower total cholesterol below 150 but didn't change their diets—and 25% experienced a new cardiovascular event within the next 30 months.

Recommended: "If you want to reverse heart disease, eat a plant-based diet and take a cholesterol-lowering statin," says Dr. Esselstyn. "This was the strategy used in my study—and it worked. The combination should lower your cholesterol to less than one fifty in fourteen days."

➤ **Be a good guest without going off your diet.** How do you eat a plant-based diet when you're an invited guest at someone's home? "The key in this situation is candor," says Dr. Esselstyn.

"Explain to your hosts at the time of the invitation that you follow an unusual nutrition plan and do not eat any meat, fish, fowl, dairy products or oils. Emphasize that you would very much enjoy the pleasure of their company, and

Won't I Crave Fat?

"That craving will disappear after three months of not eating any fat," says Dr. Esselstyn. "You'll develop a new taste for the natural flavors of foods. You'll discover new herbs, spices and sauces for seasoning."

Red flag: "Beware of the 'zero percent fat per serving' products such as salad dressing, butter substitutes, mayonnaise and pastries," says Dr. Esselstyn. "They may contain less than zero point five grams of fat per serving—the level necessary to qualify for the zero-percent claim on the label—but that little bit is enough to ensure that you will continue to crave fat."

Kitchen Tips for Plant-Based Nutrition

Dr. Esselstyn works with his wife Anne to orient new heart patients to plant-based nutrition. Here are her tips for making the diet work...

- *Use salt substitutes.* "Try vinegar, lemon, pepper, Mrs. Dash, Tabasco and other hot sauces," she says. "If you still miss salt, try adding a little Bragg Liquid Aminos, South River Sweet White Miso or low-sodium tamari."

- *Keep breakfast simple.* "Great basics for breakfast include cereals such as old-fashioned rolled oats, a brand of shredded wheat with no added sugar or a product such as Grainfield's raisin bran. You can top the cereal with Grape-Nuts for crunch. You might also add raisins, a banana or other fruit."

- *Start as many meals as possible with salads.* "They're healthy and filling," she says. "Add all the vegetables you can. Now that you are eating no oils, it is important to find a salad dressing you like. We have come to like salads dressed simply with a combination of balsamic vinegar and hummus that does not contain tahini, which is high in fat. *Product:* Fat-free hummus is available from Sahara Cuisine and Oasis Mediterranean Cuisine.

that you'd love to come, but don't want to cause any extra effort on your behalf."

But, says Dr. Esselstyn, the host will almost always insist that you come for food, and will ask what you can eat. "If that's the case, tell him or her that you'd be happy just to partake of plain salad and bread—or that simple steamed vegetables or a baked potato would be just fine."

▶ **Learn to navigate restaurants.** "Restaurants can be lethal if you don't think ahead," says Dr. Esselstyn. He suggests getting to know several in your area that already provide or are willing to fix a "safe" meal that you will enjoy.

"But if you must eat in an unfamiliar restaurant, try calling the chef or maître d' a few hours in advance—even sooner, if you have a chance," he says. "Explain that you need a meal that includes no food of animal origin and no oil."

The restaurant may surprise you, he says. "Often, restaurateurs are quite pleased to be challenged to accommodate you. And they will always be grateful you gave advance notice."

▶ **Travel smart.** "It's always easier to eat well on your home turf," says Rip Esselstyn. "That's why when you're not home, you need to pay special attention to following a plant-strong diet." *His suggestions...*

- **Plan ahead.** "Spend a few minutes packing a separate carry-on bag of foods that travel well," he says. They include healthy sandwiches, oranges, apples, plums, carrots, bell peppers, raisins, whole grain bagels, walnuts and almonds, and low-fat energy bars, such as Lärabars. "This will keep you away from airline snacks and convenience store junk," says Rip.

- **Pack your own breakfast.** "Whenever I travel, tucked securely in my suitcase is a Tupperware container filled with my Rip's Big Bowl Cereal," says Rip. *His recipe for a satisfying breakfast...*

  ¼ cup old-fashioned oats
  ¼ cup Grape-Nuts or Ezekiel brand equivalent
  ¼ cup bite-size shredded wheat
  ¼ cup Uncle Sam Cereal
  1 tablespoon ground flaxseed meal
  2 tablespoons raisins
  ½ handful of walnuts
  1 banana, sliced
  1 kiwi, sliced

Add slices from 1 grapefruit and ¾ milk substitute (rice, oat, almond) of choice. "Let your appetite be your guide as to the size of your bowl," says Rip.

Speed Healing Success

Put Out the Fire of Heart Disease with the Engine 2 Diet

The apple doesn't fall far from the tree, as they say—and neither, apparently, does the kale, the carrot, the kidney bean or the grain of brown rice...

Rip Esselstyn is the son of Caldwell B. Esselstyn, Jr., MD, the doctor whose work is featured in this section. Like his dad—who won a gold medal in rowing at the 1956 Olympics—Rip is a world-class athlete, competing professionally in triathlons, winning major competitions such as the Police and Fire World Games and the Escape from Alcatraz Triathlon. And like his dad, Rip's a lifetime adherent of a plant-based diet—or what he calls "plant-strong nutrition."

In 1997, at the age of 34, Rip became a fire fighter in Austin, Texas, working at the Engine 2 firehouse. In a spirit of camaraderie, firefighters compete about *everything*, says Rip—from Ping-Pong games to finding out who can climb the fire pole hand over hand without using his feet. One day, Rip and some of his colleagues at Engine 2 had a competition to find out who had the lowest cholesterol. The competition was lost by JR—who had a total cholesterol of 344.

Rip advised JR to try plant-based nutrition for three weeks—and JR's cholesterol dropped 146 points, to 196.

Rip then developed "The Engine 2 Diet"—a four-week, plant-strong regimen based on his father's groundbreaking work—and conducted two studies, testing the diet on 80 people, including many firefighters.

In the second four-week study, the total cholesterol dropped from an average of 197 to 135, the average LDL dropped from 124 to 74 and the average weight dropped from 203 to 189 pounds.

Based on those results, Rip Esselstyn offers two different four-week Engine 2 diets, for trying out plant-based nutrition.

He calls them the Fire Cadet option and the Firefighter Option...

Fire Cadet. This option is for those who don't like rushing into things, says Rip.

- **Week One.** No dairy of any kind—no milk, cheese, creams, yogurt, butter, ice cream or sour cream. No processed or refined foods—no white rice, white flour, white pasta, white bread and anything else that is processed—cakes, cookies, unhealthy chips, sodas, etc.

- **Week Two.** Stop eating meat, chicken, eggs and fish, while continuing to avoid dairy and refined foods.

- **Week Three.** Eliminate oil—olive, canola, coconut or any other. No baked goods, salad dressings or cooking with added oils.

- **Week Four.** The total Engine 2 diet—only plant-strong nutrition—fruits, vegetables, whole grains, legumes, nuts and seeds.

Firefighter. You start plant-strong nutrition on Day 1. What the Fire Cadet practices in weeks three and four, you practice for all four weeks.

Rip feels that envisioning a lifetime of plant-strong nutrition may be too daunting for many people—but that a 28-day trial run is a piece of (whole-wheat) cake. After four weeks, an Engine 2 dieter may find he or she feels so good—looking better, sleeping better, having more energy and eating as much food as desired without gaining weight—that the diet becomes a way of life.

"My mission," says Rip, "is a nationwide Engine 2 bucket brigade, in which 'buckets' of whole grains, legumes, fruits and vegetables douse the fires of heart disease and obesity that are running rampant in every city and town in America."

Rapid Resource: Rip Esselstyn's Engine 2 diet (along with 120 plant-strong recipes) is described in detail in his new book, *The Engine 2 Diet: The Texas Firefighter's 28-Day Save-Your-Life Plan that Lowers Cholesterol and Burns Away the Pounds* (Wellness Central). His website is *www.engine2.com*.

➤ **Eight high-speed heart healers.** The newest scientific research offers fast ways to protect your heart...

1. **Cut the risk of a second heart attack nearly in half—with Chinese red yeast rice.** Researchers in the US and China gave an extract of Chinese red yeast rice—Xuezhikang, or XZK—to 5,000 people who had suffered a heart attack within the previous year. *Compared to a placebo, those taking XZK had...*

   • 45% lower risk of another heart attack

   • 33% lower risk of dying from heart disease or another cause

   "It is very exciting, because this is a natural product and had very few adverse effects," says David M. Capuzzi, MD, PhD, director of the Cardiovascular Disease Prevention Program at Thomas Jefferson University. "We are pleased with the results."

   ⚠ *Caution:* "People in the United States should know that the commercially available over-the-counter supplement found in your average health food store is not what was studied," says Dr. Capuzzi. "Those over-the-counter supplements are not regulated, so exact amounts of active ingredient are unknown and their efficacy has not been studied yet."

   The patients in the study were given two, 300 milligram (mg) XZK capsules a day and then followed for a five-year period. Red yeast rice contains some ingredients similar to cholesterol-lowering statin drugs. "But we do not know exactly how Chinese red yeast rice works," says Dr. Capuzzi. "Still, the results were profound, with the supplement even outperforming statins."

   What to do: Talk to your cardiologist about whether XZK is right for you.

   Rapid Resource: The research on XZK was sponsored by Beijing Peking University, which has licensed the formulation to the manufacturers of the red yeast rice product HypoCol, marketed in retail stores in Asia (Singapore, Malaysia, China) and online at *www.hypocol. com.* Use HypoCol only with your cardiologist's approval and supervision.

2. **Lower cardiovascular risk factors, with Rooibos tea.** Rooibus tea is a popular beverage in South Africa, made from a local plant known as "red bush." In a study conducted at the Oxidative Stress Research Centre in South Africa, researchers asked 40 people with two or more heart disease risk factors (high cholesterol, overweight, high blood pressure or smoking) to drink six 7-ounce cups of Rooibus tea a day, for six weeks.

   The tea helped normalize cholesterol and blood pressure levels, and decreased a biomarker of *lipid peroxidation,* a process that helps turn LDL cholesterol into artery-clogging plaque.

   "With cardiovascular disease being the biggest killer of people in North America, this study's positive results may increase the relevance of rooibos as a beneficial beverage for consumers and healthcare providers seeking, safe, low-cost ways to reduce cardiovascular disease risk," says Mark Blumenthal, founder and director of the American Botanical Council.

   The tea is widely available.

   Also helpful: Researchers in Greece found that drinking green tea relaxed arteries by 4%. "This effect may be involved in the beneficial effect of green tea on cardiovascular risk," said the researchers, in the *European Journal of Cardiovascular Prevention and Rehabilitation.*

3. **Cut your risk of heart disease, with dark chocolate.** Italian researchers studied 2,000 people—some who ate dark chocolate

regularly and some who didn't—and found that regularly eating a small amount of dark chocolate was linked to a 33% lower risk of cardiovascular disease in women and 26% in men. The results were published in the *Journal of Nutrition*.

Theory: The antioxidants in chocolate decrease chronic, low-grade inflammation, the process that underlies heart disease.

⚠ **Caution:** You can eat too much of a good thing. The heart-healthy benefits of eating chocolate disappeared when people ate too much. The healthy amount is no more than 1.4 ounces per week.

4. **If you can't (or won't) exercise—take a hot bath.** "More than twenty-five scientific studies show that our bodies make physiological adjustments when we are immersed in water," explains Jonathan B. Smith, EdD, of Indiana University of Indiana, and author of *Hot Water & Healthy Living* (National Swimming Pool Foundation). "These changes are similar to those that occur when we exercise—increased circulation, more efficient breathing and improvements in mood."

"Soaking in a hot bath or hot tub may be the easiest and safest way for sedentary people to get their daily dose of heart and respiratory exercise," agrees Thomas Lachocki, PhD.

5. **Increase your intake of vitamin D.** Researchers from Austria studied over 3,000 people with heart problems, with an average age of 62, and found that those with the lowest blood levels of vitamin D had a 122% higher risk of dying from heart disease. The study appeared in the *Archives of Internal Medicine*.

What to do: Take at least 800 IU a day of supplemental vitamin D, an amount that several scientific studies have confirmed may help protect against deficiency.

6. **If you have heart failure and want to live longer—consider fish oil supplements.** Italian researcher studied nearly 7,000 patients with heart failure—a heart weakened in its pumping strength. They found that a daily 1 gram fish oil supplement rich in omega-3 fatty acids lowered the risk of hospital admission from heart disease by 8% and the risk of dying from heart disease by 9%.

"Although the improvements were modest, they were additive to other therapies that are the standard of care in heart failure, and the therapy was safe and very well tolerated," said Gregg Fonarow, MD, from the Ahmason-UCLA Cardiomyopathy Center in Los Angeles. "Supplementation with omega-3 fatty acids should join the list of life-prolonging therapies for people with heart failure."

7. **Believe your heart is healthy—and it will be.** Researchers at the University of Rochester Medical Center studied nearly 3,000 people over a period of 15 years. The men who believed that they were a low-risk for heart disease had a three times lower rate of death from heart attacks and strokes—whether they were actually at risk for heart disease or not!

"Clearly, holding a optimistic perception of the risk of heart disease has its advantages for men," says Robert Gramling, MD, who led the study, published in the *Annals of Family Medicine*.

8. **To stop calcium buildup, take vitamin K-2.** Dutch researchers analyzed the diets of 564 women, with an average age of 67, and found that those with the highest dietary intake of vitamin K-2—a form of vitamin K called *methaquinone*—had 20% less coronary calcification, or "hardening of the arteries."

"This study confirms once again that vitamin K-2 is clearly linked to the prevention of cardiovascular disease," says Leon Schurgers, of Maastricht University in the Netherlands.

The protective level of vitamin K-2 was 45 mg a day.

Rapid Resource: The supplement Osteo-K—which supplies 45 mg of K-2—is available at *www.nbihealth.com*.

⚠ *Caution:* If you are taking the anticoagulant *warfarin* (Coumadin), do not take Osteo-K or any other type of supplemental vitamin K, which can block the action of the drug.

HEMORRHOIDS

Put Them Behind You

Hemorrhoids bother the backsides of 50% of Americans over 50. The blood vessels around the anus swell and stretch, similar to a varicose vein in the leg. They can stay in the anus—an internal hemorrhoid. Or they can pop out—an external hemorrhoid. Typically, the hemorrhoid isn't dangerous—but it can bleed and hurt.

Pressure causes the problem—from...straining at stool during chronic constipation or diarrhea...heavy lifting...pregnancy and childbirth ...or constant sitting. (Genes and aging can also play a role.)

Relieving the pressure can solve the problem—fast...

🕐 *Super-Quick Fix*

➤ **Take psyllium seed husks.** They add bulk and water to stool, allowing for easier passage—and relief from hemorrhoids, says Liz Lipski, PhD, CCN, CNS, the director of Nutrition and Integrative Health Programs at Maryland University of Integrative Health (*www.lizlipski.com*) and author of *Digestive Wellness* (McGraw-Hill, Third Edition). In fact, she says, this treatment can help relieve both chronic constipation *and* diarrhea.

What to do: "To avoid gas and cramping from the sudden introduction of fiber, gradually build up to one teaspoon of psyllium with each meal." Start with one teaspoon at breakfast...three or four days later add a teaspoon at lunch...and then three or four days later add the teaspoon at dinner. Take it in an eight-ounce glass of water or juice.

➤ **Fiber heals.** "A high-fiber diet usually prevents hemorrhoids and allows them to heal," says Dr. Lipski. "Increase your intake of fruits, vegetables, whole grains and legumes, and drink plenty of fluids, including water, fruit juices and herbal teas.

As your dietary fiber increases, you will probably find you no longer need to take psyllium seeds, says Dr. Lipski.

➤ **Squat, don't sit.** "A squatting position on the toilet takes pressure off the rectum and can help during a flare-up of hemorrhoids," says Dr. Lipski.

Also helpful: Wipe gently with soft toilet paper and wash your anal area with warm water after each bowel movement, she says.

➤ **Use a salve.** "Salve can soothe inflamed tissue," says Dr. Lipski. "Spread it gently on the anus with your fingers."

See Your Doctor If...

Hemorrhoids can bleed—typically bright red blood with a bowel movement. But if you have rectal bleeding that lasts longer than a few days, see your doctor to rule out a more serious problem.

In some cases, an external hemorrhoid can become inflamed, swollen and painful, and develop a blood clot, requiring treatment and possible removal. If your hemorrhoid has become very painful and causes discomfort while sitting, see a doctor.

She recommends using one of the following—vitamin E oil, calendula ointment or goldenseal salve.

Also helpful: Witch hazel is also soothing to hemorrhoidal tissue, she says. "Put some on a cotton ball and press gently. Repeat the treatment several times a day."

▶ **Take a sitz bath.** This old-fashioned remedy for hemorrhoids is still in favor with the medical profession, says Dr. Lipski.

What to do: Place three to four inches of warm water in the bathtub and sit in it for 10 minutes, several times daily.

Better: "You can improve the results by adding a quarter cup Epsom salts or healing herbs," says Dr. Lipski. Useful herbs include chamomile, chickweed, comfrey, mullein, plantain, witch hazel or yarrow. Bring a large pot of water to a boil. Steep 1 to 2 cups of fresh herbs or 1½ cups of dried herbs until cool. Strain and add to the bathwater.

SPEED LIMIT – – – – – – – –
"H" Is for Hazardous

Preparation H is a leading over-the-counter remedy for hemorrhoids. *That "H" might stand for hazardous...*

"The over-the-counter drug Preparation H contains mercury and can be dangerous if used on a prolonged basis, because of the tremendous potential for the absorption of mercury from the anal canal," says gastroenterologist Trent W. Nichols, MD, coeditor of *Optimal Digestive Health* (Healing Arts).

▶ **Soothing supplements.** Several herbal and nutritional supplements can strengthen blood vessels and help prevent and heal hemorrhoids, says Dr. Lipski. Use with the approval and supervision of a qualified health professional.

● **Horse chestnut.** 500 milligrams (mg), three times daily.

● **Butcher's broom.** 100 mg of extract, three times daily.

● **Vitamin E.** 400 to 800 IU of d-alpha tocopherol and mixed tocopherols, daily.

● **Vitamin C and bioflavonoids.** 500 to 2,000 mg of vitamin C and 100 to 1,000 mg of bioflavnoids, daily.

HICCUPS

The World's Quickest Cures

You ate a lot. Or drank a lot. Or you ate and drank too fast. *And suddenly—hic... hic...hic...*

You have hiccups—involuntary contractions of the diaphragm (the sheet of muscle underneath the lungs and above the abdominal cavity) that snap shut your vocal cords. *Hic... hic...hic...*

Are hiccups serious? Almost never. (If you have frequent bouts or hiccups that won't stop, it's time to visit the doctor. Persistent hiccups can sometimes signal an underlying disease.)

Do you want to *stop* hiccupping? Of course, particularly if the bout lasts longer than a minute or two.

Well, here are the world's fastest hiccup "cures"—from health professionals and laypeople alike. Our hiccup experts may not always know *why* these cures work. *But they're confident they do work—if you give them a try...*

▶ **The Q-tip cure.** "There are several effective self-help methods for resolving hiccups," says Andrew Gaeddert, a herbalist in Oakland, California, (*www.healthconcerns.com*) and author of *Healing Digestive Disorders* (North Atlantic). "For one minute, massage the top of the back of your mouth with a cotton swab, moving it back and forth. Or swallow three tablespoons of vinegar."

For long-standing, recurrent hiccups: Supplement your diet with biotin, a B-vitamin, says Gaeddert. Follow the dosage recommendation on the label.

➤ **Calm the Rebellious Chi.** Traditional Chinese Medicine (TCM) says there is a fundamental life force called *Chi* that flows throughout the body along channels called *meridians*. "When your stomach and lungs are functioning properly, the Chi associated with those organs flows downward," says Jim Rohr, OMD, a doctor of Oriental Medicine in Bay Harbor, Florida (*www.jamesrohr.com*). "But when that Chi turns 'rebellious,' it flows upward and you have a problem such as hiccups—or a cough, acid reflux, nausea or vomiting."

Overeating is the main cause of rebellious Chi, says Rohr. Other Chi-imbalancing factors that can trigger hiccups include too much hot, spicy food or feeling angry and irritable.

What to do: Massaging the area called the Inner Gate—located on the inner wrist, about two inches from the wrist crease, in the middle of the forearm—is a good way to calm Rebellious Chi, says Rohr. "A gentle clockwise massage for thirty to sixty seconds on each wrist will help relieve hiccups."

You could also try massaging a point between your big and second toe, about an inch or two below the toe webbing. "This point is usually sore when firm pressure is applied," says Rohr. "Massaging the tender point on either foot will open up stuck energy, allowing the free flow of Chi to resume."

➤ **Chiropractic for chronic hiccups.** "I've found that Chiropractic Manipulative Therapy—using a physical adjustment to relieve pressure on nerves along the spinal line—can work to cure chronic hiccups," says Mark Levine, DC, a chiropractic physician in Torrington, Connecticut. "I've seen two cases of chronic hiccups in my nineteen years of practice—and both responded within days of the first treatment."

Why it works: A nerve arising out of the vertebrae in the neck—the Phrenic nerve—directly affects the functioning of the diaphragm.

➤ **"It works right away!"** Everybody swears by at least one hiccup cure. *Here are some of the most popular...*

● **Hold your breath.** "Put your chin down, hold your breath and swallow three times—give or take—until they go away," says Kama Linden, a singer in New York City. (Her latest, hiccup-free album is *Better Late Than Never*.)

"I hold my breath and swallow three times," says Denise Stephens, a public relations specialist. "Usually they're gone right away, but sometimes I have to do the routine again. It works for my ten-year-old son too."

"Plug your ears with your index fingers," says Ellen Hofstetter Jaffe, an educator. "Hold your nose with your thumbs. Do not breathe! Swallow hard and slowly a few times. Take your fingers away and breathe. No more hiccups!"

● **Bartender cures.** "In my many days as a bartender I've dealt with many people and their hiccups," says Casey Shreiber. "I've got a remedy that has never failed me. Take a slice of lemon, drop on some bitters and sprinkle on some sugar. Eat the lemon—and the hiccups are gone!"

"A bartender in Philly taught me this remedy," says Marisa Picker, an account executive in an advertising agency in New York. "You need two straws and one cup of water. Put one straw into the cup and one outside the cup. For about thirty seconds, suck through both straws—so you're drinking water and sucking in air at the same time. It works right away!"

"As a former bartender, I have a surefire cure for the hiccups," says Jeff Davis. "Take a small packet of sugar, open it, pour it on your tongue, press your tongue to the roof of your mouth—and hold it there until it dissolves. Works every time."

● **Sugar and honey.** Bartenders aren't the only people who use sugar to cure hiccups.

"A teaspoon of sugar has always been extremely reliable for me and my children and some of my patients," says Andrew Adesman, MD, associate professor of pediatrics at Albert Einstein College of Medicine in New York.

Sugar water works too. "An absolute hundred percent cure for hiccups—take two teaspoons of regular sugar with a six-ounce glass of water," says Nancy Fox, a business development specialist. "Works every time!"

And so does honey. "A spoonful of honey—that's it," says Owen Mead-Robins, vice president of a software company. "Our family has been doing it for generations. It works for me and everyone else. No idea why."

● **Peanut butter.** "My hubby gets hiccups all the time from drinking his beer—and he cures them by eating a tablespoon or two of peanut butter," says Deb Bailey.

● **Prove you have hiccups!** "I was a teacher for ten years," says Heidi Waterfield, an educational consultant in California. "Whenever a kid raised a hand and said, 'Can I go get a drink of water? I have the hiccups' I always said, 'Prove it and I'll give you a dollar.' For whatever reason, not a single kid was ever able to hiccup again."

"One thing that's never failed for me, is to ask someone with the hiccups if they have the hiccups," says Heather Cueva. "When they inevitably answer 'Yes,' I ask them, 'Prove it.' They are always amazed when their hiccups disappear from this simple exchange."

● **Drink a glass of water—straight up, upside down or with your fingers in your ears.**

"Fill a glass with water, tuck your chin into your neck and drink as much water as possible in this position—it will work!" says Dave K., from Little Falls, New Jersey.

"A nun in the eighth grade stopped a classmate's hiccups with this technique," says Sheilagh Weymouth, DC, a chiropractor in New York. "I've shared it with friends, family and patients for forty-two years—and it has never failed to stop a case of hiccups. Get on your knees, put your fingers in your ears and have a helper hold a glass of water to your lips while you drink four to six ounces. Keep your fingers in your ears and stay on your knees for another minute. I'm telling you—the hiccups are gone, kaput, history."

"I have a surefire cure that my aunt suggested to me years ago and it has *never* failed," says Stephanie Browne, a publicist in Santa Monica, California. "Fill a cup with water, bend over and drink from the far rim. Just a few swallows and you're good."

● **Think of a cow.** "Once I was riding with a carload of people and one of them started to hiccup," says Carol Penn-Romine. "Everyone was offering him remedies, none of which worked. Suddenly I blurted out, 'Barry! Think of a cow!' It went dead silent in the car as everyone tried to figure out what that was all about—and Barry realized his hiccups had gone away. I have used this several times since, and it works like a charm."

● **Why these cures work.** "The cause of hiccups is quite simple," says Bob Baker, a Hiccupologist (and former chemist and current technical writer) in Hillsborough, New Jersey. "They are caused by an excess of oxygen in the bloodstream. There is only one cure, which is to restore the proper balance between oxygen and the other gases dissolved in the blood, such as nitrogen and carbon dioxide. This requires reducing your oxygen intake for a few minutes. The easiest way is to simply hold your breath for as long as possible. This is why cures such as taking a long drink of water are actually effective. And as everyone knows, even scaring someone—which can cause a temporary interruption of breathing—can work."

Now if he could only explain how imaginary cows cure hiccups...

HIGH BLOOD PRESSURE

Lower It Fast—Without Drugs

It triples your risk of stroke and heart disease, increases your risk of heart failure sixfold and ups your risk of kidney disease. But you may not even know you have it—high blood pressure, or hypertension.

"High blood pressure is the silent killer," says Stephen Sinatra, MD, a cardiologist in private practice in Manchester, Connecticut, assistant clinical professor at the University of Connecticut Medical School and author of several books, including *The Sinatra Solution: New Hope for Preventing and Treating Heart Disease* (Basic Health) and *Lower Your Blood Pressure in Eight Weeks* (Ballantine).

What happens: In hypertension, there is a relentless, heartbeat-by-heartbeat, overly forceful push of blood against the walls of the arteries, wearing out the heart (which becomes enlarged and sluggish as it works extra hard to pump blood) and damaging the arteries (as blood races through the circulatory system and erodes and inflames arterial walls).

Hypertension is detected by a blood pressure test, which measures systolic pressure (the pressure

of blood against artery walls as the heart beats) and diastolic pressure (the pressure as the heart rests). A diagnosis of hypertension is made when systolic pressure is 140 or higher, or diastolic pressure is 80 or higher. And doctors make that diagnosis a lot.

Seventy-three million Americans have hypertension—including 50% of people over age 65. Another 69 million have *prehypertension*, a systolic blood pressure reading of 120 to 139, or a diastolic reading of 80 to 89.

Surprising: If you have high blood pressure, you can lower it fast. "You can create a lifestyle that lowers blood pressure—and see a drop to healthier levels in six to eight weeks," says Dr. Sinatra. *Here's what he suggests...*

SPEED LIMIT | The Trouble with Blood Pressure Drugs

"There are over sixty-five different drugs used to lower high blood pressure," says Dr. Sinatra. "Many people are on a cocktail of different medications that bring with them a host of unpleasant and often unbearable side effects.

"In my opinion too many people take potent drugs such as ACE inhibitors, diuretics and calcium channel blockers to control their hypertension—even when their blood pressure is only mildly elevated. All these drugs have potential side effects, including impotence, loss of libido, fatigue, drowsiness, dry cough, light-headedness and even depression.

"These adverse affects are particularly intolerable for people whose high blood pressure caused them no real physical symptoms—and that's most people! They're left frustrated, and often don't comply with medication schedules because the cure is so much worse than the disease. All too often, people start to skip pills or stop taking them entirely. They actually feel better without their prescribed drugs—even though the hypertension is silently continuing to weaken their heart and blood vessels."

What to do? "*Natural* blood pressure lowering is the preferred treatment," says Dr. Sinatra.

➤ **Cut 250 calories a day.** Even losing 10 pounds can help lower high blood pressure, says Dr. Sinatra.

Study: As many as 50% of overweight people with high blood pressure may have hypertension as a *result* of being overweight, says a team of Italian doctors, who reported their study findings at the American Heart Association's Annual Fall Conference of the Council for High Blood Pressure Research.

In the study, 50% of overweight, hypertensive adults, aged 29 to 65, achieved normal blood pressure after six months on a reduced-calorie diet. "The first step in blood pressure treatment should be to help the overweight person lose weight," says Robert Fogari, MD, study leader and professor of medicine at the University of Pavia in Italy. "Only after six months of trying to reduce the patient's weight can a decision be made about drug treatment."

⚠ *Caution:* This advice may not pertain to a person with very high blood pressure, such as 160/100 or higher.

What to do: "You can lose one pound a week by cutting two hundred fifty calories a day out of your food intake and walking one mile a day," says Dr. Sinatra. (More about walking in a moment.) "And cutting those two hundred and fifty calories is easy to do. It's the equivalent of cutting out the mayonnaise on a Big Mac, or cutting out one can of soda a day."

Also try: "Skip the bread and butter before dinner," says Jennifer Adler, MS, CN, a Seattle-based certified nutritionist and natural foods chef and adjunct faculty member at Bastyr University. *Her other suggestions...*

Try a Salt Substitute

You've taken the salt shaker off the table, just as Dr. Sinatra suggested. But now your food tastes bland. What to do? Talk to your doctor about using a salt substitute...

Study: Researchers in China found that when people with hypertension used a salt substitute for one year, their systolic blood pressure dropped by 7.4 points. Their arteries also became less stiff and more flexible. The study appeared in *Hypertension Journal*.

Replace afternoon cookies with fruit or yogurt. Trade your specialty latte for a small coffee with milk. Choose turkey over ham, roast beef, bologna and other fattier cold cuts—order lean roast beef instead of pastrami. Have a two-egg rather than a three-egg omelet. Have a scoop of chicken salad on a bed of lettuce instead of on a hard roll. Replace the fried onion rings with a small order of French fries. For a frozen pasta dinner, choose linguine with clam sauce rather than fettuccine Alfredo. For a frozen chicken dinner, choose baked rather than fried. For your tostado, use salsa rather than avocado, sour cream or grated cheddar cheese. Top your pasta with a half cup of tomato-basil sauce rather than a quarter cup of pesto sauce. Have a bowl of vegetarian chili rather than chili con carne. For pretzels, have hard minis rather than soft.

➤ **Put on a pedometer.** Dr. Sinatra puts all patients with high blood pressure on a daily walking program. *And for good reason...*

Study: Korean researchers studied 23 men with hypertension. The men walked briskly (three to four miles an hour, or a mile every 20 to 15 minutes) for either one 40-minute walk a day or four, 10-minute walks a day. After the 40-minute walk, systolic pressure dropped by an average of four points; after the 10-minute walks, it dropped by three points. The study was presented at the annual meeting of the American College of Sports Medicine.

What to do: Walk at least one mile a day, or about 20 minutes at a brisk pace, says Dr. Sinatra. "Walking is the easiest, safest exercise."

Smart idea: Buy a pedometer—a small device that is clipped to your waistband or belt and measures the amount of steps you take—and walk 10,000 steps a day, says Dr. Sinatra. A review of studies on pedometers, involving nearly 3,000 people, shows that using a pedometer with a daily step goal of 10,000 steps can increase the amount of walking by one mile per day (2,500 steps)—and lower systolic blood pressure by 3.8 points. The study was published in the *Journal of the American Medical Association.*

Dr. Sinatra's ideas to increase your steps per day...

"If you drive to your job, then park five, ten or even fifteen blocks away and walk to your office. If you commute by bus or train, then make time to get off a stop earlier and walk the rest of the way. If you have a furry four-legged friend, go out for a walk—it's good for your dog and good for you too!"

▶ **Pass on the processed foods.** "Some doctors believe that, except for a small group of salt-sensitive folks, sodium restriction isn't important for hypertension control," says Dr. Sinatra. "I disagree. It's been my experience that my patients do better when I limit their intake of this mineral."

What to do: "Taking the salt shaker off the table is the first step," says Dr. Sinatra.

However: "It's estimated that a whopping eighty percent of our sodium intake is ingested from hidden sources—mostly from packaged and prepared foods, such as frozen meals, soups, ice cream, bread, canned vegetables and pickles.

Smart idea: "In order to gauge their salt intake, I encourage my patients to keep a food diary for several days, and then go back and look up the sodium content of each item on their list. They're usually shocked to find that they've been consuming between five and ten grams of sodium every day—without sprinkling a single grain of salt on their food! To bring hypertension under control, I advise them to limit their sodium intake to two to three grams a day."

Red flags: Other packaged and processed foods typically high in sodium include salted nuts, potato chips and most crackers (unless labeled "unsalted" or "no added salt"), processed meats, olives, anchovies, soy sauce, bacon, most cheeses, most peanut butters, canned or bottled tomato juice, creamed cottage cheese, instant puddings and most instant hot cereals.

▶ **Eat five foods a day high in magnesium, potassium and calcium.** "These three nutrients are key for relaxing arteries and promoting healthy blood pressure," says Dr. Sinatra.

Smart idea: Eat at least five foods every day from the below lists of potassium-, magnesium- and calcium-rich foods. *The italicized foods are uniquely rich in the designated nutrient...*

Recommended foods high in potassium: *Adzuki beans*, anchovies, antelope, apricots, *avocado*, baked potato (with skin), bananas, beef, beet greens, black beans, blue fish, buffalo, cantaloupes, chicken (free range), chickpeas, clams, crabs (blue), dates, elk, *figs*, flounder, garlic, haddock, halibut, kidney beans, lentil, lima beans, lobster, mackerel, natto (soy product), nectarines, pinto beans, *prunes*, raisins, salmon, sea vegetables, snapper, sole, *soy nuts*, sweet potato, Swiss chard, trout, turtle beans, venison, *white beans*, wild goose, yogurt (nonfat and low-fat).

Recommended foods high in calcium: Asparagus, broccoli, cabbage, collards, *daikon*, dates, feta cheese, figs, *kale*, kelp, *milk* (1%), molasses, oatmeal, parsley, prunes, raisins, *ricotta cheese* (part skim), sesame seeds, *skim milk*, *tofu*, *yogurt* (nonfat and low-fat), white beans.

Recommended foods high in magnesium: Adzuki beans, All-bran, *apricots*, bananas, black beans, brown rice, *figs*, *kelp*, *pumpkin seeds*, seafood, sesame seeds, sunflower seeds, spinach, wakame.

➤ **Limit alcohol—especially beer.** "Anyone with high blood pressure must limit their alcohol intake to a drink or two a week," says Dr. Sinatra.

Red flag: If you're a beer drinker, switch to another form of alcohol, says Dr. Sinatra. "In my clinical experience, beer drinking along with munching on junk foods such as pretzels and potato chips is practically a guaranteed way to give yourself high blood pressure."

➤ **Just say no to cup after cup of Joe.** "Coffee should be regarded as a drug, not a food," says Dr. Sinatra. "It can stimulate the brain, relax small airways in the lungs and raise your stress hormone levels. And studies have shown that caffeine temporarily raises your blood pressure by a few points. I recommend you restrict your coffee to one cup daily."

Smart idea: Decide which time of day your body most craves its caffeine fix, and drink one cup of coffee at that time, says Dr. Sinatra. "Some of my patients find that splitting the single serving into a half cup at breakfast and another half cup in the afternoon satisfies their caffeine habit."

➤ **Eat oatmeal four times a week.** Several studies show that eating oatmeal regularly can help lower blood pressure, says Dr. Sinatra.

Study: A team of researchers studied 97 people with high blood pressure for three months, dividing them into two groups—one ate oatmeal and the other didn't. After the three months, those who were overweight and ate oatmeal had an average drop in high blood pressure of 8.3 systolic and 3.9 diastolic, compared to little change in

---

Speed Healing Success

Breathe Away High Blood Pressure

"I got high blood pressure several years ago—it came as a package deal with menopause," says Kathi Casey, a health coach, trainer and owner of the Healthy Boomer Body Center in Otis, Massachusetts. "My doctor put me on a beta-blocker, which I hated, so I began my search for alternatives. I found a couple that work—in fact, my blood pressure has been normal and I've been medication-free for about five years."

Casey's favorite pressure-lowering method is a yogic breathing exercise called Brahmari Breath. "It's easy to do and it works, because it releases endorphins—the brain's very own relaxation chemicals—and lowers stress hormones such as cortisol. One clinic in India uses it as their main treatment for high blood pressure."

Here are Casey's instructions...

- *Sit comfortably.* Relax your shoulders. Raise your hands and with your index fingers lightly push the flap on the outer edge of the ears closest to the face over the ear canals. Rest your tongue lightly against the roof of your mouth. Keep your lips closed throughout the exercise. Close your eyes and inhale deeply, to a slow count of four. Now exhale, while making a humming noise. Exhale as long as possible, perhaps to a slow count of eight. Repeat the inhalation and exhalation-humming three times.

"If you do this for three to five minutes a day, you can significantly lower your blood pressure," says Casey.

---

the non-oatmeal group. The study was published in the *European Journal of Clinical Nutrition*.

➤ **If diet and exercise don't work—add the "targeted nutraceuticals" omega-3**

and coenzyme Q10. After six weeks, if there's not a significant drop in blood pressure, it's time to continue the lifestyle modifications *and* add nutritional supplements, says Dr. Sinatra. Why supplements?

A key to reversing blood pressure is repairing and restoring the health of the *endothelium*, the innermost lining of the arterial wall, he says. "A healthy endothelium produces chemical substances that allow for the normal expansion and relaxation of blood vessels—and normal blood pressure. But the delicate endothelium can be damaged from a variety of factors, such as bad fats, a nutrient-poor diet, elevated insulin from too much sugar, excess stress and cigarette smoke—producing high blood pressure.

"Targeted nutritional therapy for high blood pressure is aimed at the *mitochondria* of the endothelial cells—the cellular power plants that generate ATP, the energy source for the primary biochemical reactions in the body. It's also aimed at decreasing *inflammation*, the secondary but significant damage created by the immune system as it tries to minimize and contain the effects of cellular breakdown in the arterial system."

Two nutrients that can do this are...

• **Omega-3.** The omega-3 fatty acids DHA and EPA reduce arterial wall inflammation and improve endothelial function.

• **Coenzyme Q10.** This nutritional supplement nourishes and supports the mitochondria. Research shows that 200 to 300 mg a day can lower blood pressure.

Recommended: Dr. Sinatra has formulated a product that supplies both these nutrients—Omega Q Plus. "I recommend two capsules, twice a day. If that doesn't work, I increase the dosage to four capsules, twice a day." Use this and any other nutritional supplement with the approval and supervision of a qualified health professional.

Millions Are Being Treated for Hypertension They Don't Have

"There is considerable evidence that at least twenty-five percent of those diagnosed with hypertension—millions of people—*do not have it* and *do not require treatment*," says Samuel Mann, MD, a cardiologist at the Hypertension Center of the New York Presbyterian Hospital-Cornell Medical Center in New York and author of *Healing Hypertension: A Revolutionary New Approach* (Wiley). The reason?

"The blood pressure is elevated only when it is being measured and is normal at all other times," he says.

What happens: This phenomenon is called "white coat hypertension"—you're nervous when your doctor checks your blood pressure, and pressure levels shoot up.

"For many people, a blood pressure check has become a stressful event," explains Dr. Mann. "Some are afraid that they are at risk of suffering a sudden stroke, particularly if a parent died of a complication of hypertension. Sometimes it's frightening simply because of what we read about hypertension. *Many* people have an extremely elevated blood pressure in the physician's office and yet a very normal blood pressure at home."

What to do: "I have almost every patient of mine do a home reading to confirm a diagnosis of hypertension," says Dr. Mann. "And most people can get a reasonable home reading."

He recommends using an automatic blood pressure monitor (which is placed around your wrist) rather than a manual arm cuff, and says the widely available Omron brand is accurate. "Sit for three to five minutes and take three readings a minute or two apart. Ignore the first reading, which is rarely accurate.

"If you find that your blood pressure is normal, talk to your doctor about your results. Your diagnosis may be wrong—and treatment for hypertension may be unnecessary."

Rapid Resource: You can order Omega Q Plus at *www.drsinatra.com*, or call 888-349-0481. Address: Healthy Directions, P.O. Box 531, Montoursville, PA 17754.

➤ **Then add magnesium and ribose.** "If the addition of those two supplements doesn't lower blood pressure, I add a broad spectrum magnesium supplement that includes a combination of magnesium citrate, glycinate, orotate and taurinate. It promotes the relaxation and widening of the blood vessels."

Product: Broad Spectrum Magnesium, available at *www.drsinatra.com*.

Suggested intake: 400 to 800 mg a day.

"I also add D-ribose—a sugar that is fundamental to the formation of the ATP molecule."

Product: The powdered supplement Ribo-Boost, available at *www.drsinatra.com*.

Suggested intake: Two scoops a day, at breakfast and lunch.

➤ **Then add garlic and hawthorne.** "If at this point the blood pressure is not coming down, I add the herbs garlic and hawthorne. They both contain compounds that are natural ACE-inhibitors, dilating arteries by blocking the production of angiotensin, a chemical that causes arteries to constrict."

Study: A team of Australian researchers analyzed 11 studies on garlic and high blood pressure and concluded that regular intake of garlic supplements reduced systolic blood pressure by an average of 8.4 points and diastolic blood pressure by an average of 7.3. "Supplementation with garlic preparations may provide an acceptable alternative or complementary treatment option for hypertension," say the researchers in *BMC Cardiovascular Disorders*.

Product: Daily BP Support, available at *www.drsinatra.com*.

Suggested intake: Follow the dosage recommendation on the label.

➤ **If blood pressure is still high, talk to your doctor about medication—but protect yourself from the side effects.** "If at this point blood pressure remains above 140/80, I will add a pharmaceutical drug to the regimen," says Dr. Sinatra.

"I usually begin with very low-dose of *indapamide*, a thiazide diuretic. At the same time, because this drug depletes magnesium and potassium, I put the individual on my Broad Spectrum Magnesium supplement and also encourage the person to increase magnesium and potassium in the diet, by eating a baked potato a couple times a week, an orange every other day, a banana every other day and an apple at least twice a week.

"I may also use a low-dose angiotensin receptor blocker, such as *losartan* (Cozaar/Hyzaar) or *valsartan* (Diovan), which are well-tolerated with minimal side effects.

"If the individual with high blood pressure is anxious and stressed, I may use a low-dose beta-blocker such as *propranolol* (Inderal). It works by blocking the beta limb of the autonomic nervous system, the part that's responsible for gearing up your body for action. Beta-blockers also blunt exaggerated physiological response to stress. If I give a beta-blocker, I also give Omega-Q Plus, since beta-blockers deplete the body of CoQ10."

HIVES

Bump Them Off

After the World Trade Center (WTC) attacks in 2001, the average number of visits to doctors for hives—those itchy, red bumps on the skin—increased by 28% among people living within 10 miles of the WTC.

Was the increase caused by stress...or allergens in the air...or medications people had started taking?

It's unlikely the experts will ever know—because the cause of 95% of hives are never discovered, says Audrey Kunin, MD, a dermatologist in Kansas City, Missouri, author of *The DERMAdoctor Skinstruction Manual* (Simon & Schuster) and founder and president of *www.dermadoctor.com*.

What happens: Hives—or what doctors call *urticaria*—are usually the result of an allergic reaction. An allergen triggers the mast cells of the immune system, which release histamine, which causes the hive (and the itching that goes along with them). What kinds of allergens?

Foods...food additives...medications...x-ray dyes—the list "seems just about endless," says Dr. Kunin.

The allergens can cause *acute hives*—one or more bouts of hives over a period of less than six weeks. You can also get *chronic hives*, bouts that last longer than six weeks. There are also *physical hives*—the mast cells are triggered not by allergens but by other factors such as stress, heat, cold, water, vibration...

But even if you can't figure out the cause, if you're one of the 50 million Americans a year who is targeted by one or more hives, you want some relief. *Here's how to get it...*

➤ **Block overheated hives.** One type of physical hives is called *cholinergic hives*, which is caused by the release of adrenaline from exercise, stress, heat or a hot shower.

"These hives pop up quickly and last for thirty to sixty minutes," says Dr. Kunin. "They look different from other types of hives, with multiple, tiny pink or red bumps that usually form in areas of higher blood flow and sweat, such as the face."

What to do: To prevent cholinergic hives, take the antihistamine *cetirizine* (Zyrtec) about

See Your Doctor If...

Hives can be one symptom of a generalized allergic reaction called *angioedema* that can include difficulty breathing, difficulty swallowing (because of a swollen tongue) and stomach cramping and that can proceed to life threatening anaphylactic shock. If you are having those symptoms, dial 911 or go immediately to a hospital emergency room.

Important: Anyone who has regular hives should carry an EpiPen, a device that injects epinephrine, a drug that can reverse angioedema.

Chronic hives can be a symptom of many different diseases and conditions, such as hepatitis B, tuberculosis, sinus infections, lupus, rheumatoid arthritis and colon cancer. If you're having chronic hives, see a doctor. Once underlying disease has been ruled out, consider seeing an allergist to help you detect the cause of the hives.

30 minutes before an event (such as exercise) that typically triggers them.

➤ **Block a cold-caused hive.** "Some people get hives when they walk into an air-conditioned building in the summer or go near the freezer case in the grocery store," says Dr. Kunin.

What to do: The antihistamine *cyproheptadine* is the therapy of choice, she says.

⚠ *Caution:* Cyproheptadine is not recommended for children.

➤ **The best anti-hive medications.** "Treatment for hives is focused on controlling itching and stopping new hives from forming," says Dr. Kunin. And the best way to do this is to block the histamine-releasing trigger points on the surface of mast cells—the H and H2 receptors. *You can do that with...*

• **Antihistamines.** They block the H1 receptor. "My prescription antihistamine of choice is *hydroxyzine*," says Dr. Kunin. "It comes in a ten-milligram tablet, taken every four to six hours. The dose can be increased as needed—and tolerated—to control hives."

Red flag: "I find that nonsedating antihistamines are relatively worthless for controlling itching related to hives," she says.

● **Heartburn medications.** "When I see patients with hives, they're usually miserable," says Dr. Kunin. "So I don't settle for blocking just the H1 receptors. I also routinely prescribe a drug that blocks the H2 receptors—they're a small percentage of the overall number of receptors, but blocking them really makes a difference in whether or not the patient improves."

Surprising: The class of medicines that block H2 sites are heartburn medications such as *ranitidine* (Zantac) and *cimetidine* (Tagamet). "I usually prescribe a twice-daily dose of Zantac, which tends to be better tolerated than Tagamet," she says.

● **Antidepressant.** "If a patient's hives don't improve with H1 and H2 blockers, I sometimes prescribe *doxepin*, an antidepressant that has incredible H1 and H2 blocking ability."

➤ **Topical treatments.** Effective hive therapy will also include use of topical treatments that speed relief, says Dr. Kunin. "It's always better to apply something to reduce itch-ing than to scratch." *Your topical emergency kit may include any of the following...*

● Topical steroid creams (over-the-counter or prescription Cortaid). *Caution:* Chronic use can thin skin—read the label, and use only as directed (for no more than seven days).

● Topical anesthetics (PrameGel, Prax Lotion, Caladryl Clear, Aveeno Anti-Itch cream or lotion)

● Topical Zonalon (prescription topical antihistamine)

● Aveeno Oatmeal or baking soda baths

➤ **Discover your food triggers.** According to Dr. Kunin, the foods that most commonly cause chronic hives are peanuts, nut-containing products, strawberries, citrus fruits, tomatoes, seafood, shellfish, eggs, dairy products and yeast (including yeast-containing foods like fresh-baked breads, beer, blue cheese and yogurt). That's a lot of foods. What to do?

"First try a reasonable approach," says Dr. Kunin. Eliminate the top food suspects and also all vitamin pills and other supplements for six weeks, she advises. Then add them back one at a time, allowing at least four days (and preferably a week) after each addition. "If you get hives when you add back the food or supplement, it's possible you've isolated the culprit."

INFERTILITY

Researchers at Cornell University looked at the level of psychological distress caused by cancer and found only one other condition could match it for producing depression, anxiety, anger and upset.

Infertility.

But infertility isn't a life-threatening disease. What's so stressful about it?

"These days, couples plan their lives around when they are going to build a family," explains Alice Domar, PhD, author of *Conquering Infertility* (Penguin), executive director of the Domar Center for Mind/Body Health at Boston IVF (*www.domar center.com*) and assistant professor of Obstetrics, Gynecology, and Reproductive Biology at Harvard Medical School. "They figure out when to marry, how long to wait before trying to have a baby—and then they throw away the birth control in September and expect to have a baby by June. It's a huge shock when pregnancy doesn't happen like it's supposed to." *And that shock quickly turns into stress in every area of a couple's life...*

- **Relational stress**—with the man typically taken aback by the intensity of his wife's upset, and the woman seeing her husband as somewhat stoic and uncaring.

- **Sexual stress**—with the woman only wanting sex when she is ovulating, and the man feeling like the only reason she wants sex is to extract his sperm.

- **Social stress**—when the couple doesn't want to be around other fertile couples, with their bellies, babies and birthday parties.

- **Work stress**—with intensive fertility treatments demanding extra and often unpredictable days off.

- **Financial stress**—to pay for those treatments, which can cost $12,000 a try and are often not covered by insurance.

- **Spiritual stress**—as a couple prays to God for a baby but God doesn't answer their prayers.

"And to top it all off," says Dr. Domar, "the couple is *blamed* for the problem, with well-meaning but misinformed family and friends telling them if they'd 'just relax' they could get pregnant."

All that unrelenting stress doesn't help with the process of conception and pregnancy. "Both my clinical experience and scientific research indicate that couples who are highly stressed and depressed are less likely to become pregnant, either naturally or via assisted-reproductive techniques," says Dr. Domar.

Good news: Research conducted by Dr. Domar and others shows that relieving stress can double the chances of getting pregnant and conceiving.

And there are quick and easy ways to shed stress, she says...

Super-Quick Fix

➤ **Enjoy mini-relaxation.** "Mini-relaxations—or 'minis' for short—are among the most useful tools for coping with stress," says Dr. Domar. When you're under stress—say, when a friend calls to announce she's pregnant—you start to take shallow breaths from your chest, rather than deep breaths from your abdomen. An alarm sounds in your brain and body...the "fight-or-flight" response kicks in...triggering stress hormones...that lock you into anxiety and shallow breathing—and more stress.

"You can stop that chain of events immediately with a mini," says Dr. Domar. "In just a few seconds, a mini can shift you from shallow chest

Dr. Domar's Fast-Fertility Lifestyle Changes

"These are the lifestyle changes I recommend for my patients," says Dr. Domar. "I believe they contribute to the success my patients have in getting pregnant."

- *Stop exercising.* "I believe that exercising vigorously enough to bring your heart rate over a hundred and ten beats per minute can have a dampening effect on fertility. I advise my infertility patients to take a three-month exercise vacation. I have seen so many pregnancies occur in infertile women who simply stopped exercising that I feel compelled to make this recommendation."

- *Lose or gain a little weight.* "If you suspect or have been told that you are underweight, you may well increase your chances of getting pregnant if you gain a few pounds," says Dr. Domar. "Being very overweight can also impair your ability to conceive—and losing even a moderate amount of weight, such as ten to fifteen pounds, can return your chance of pregnancy to normal."

- *Can the caffeine.* "Several studies have linked caffeine consumption to reduced fertility as well as to an increased rate of miscarriage. I advise my patients to eliminate caffeine completely."

- *Abstain from alcohol.* "Two studies have found that alcohol consumption can interfere with conception in fertile women. That's enough evidence to recommended abstinence for infertile women."

- *Don't smoke.* "Many studies support the claim that smoking can cut your chances of getting pregnant and carrying."

- *Check your herbs with your doctor.* "In a study at Loma Linda University, the herbs St. John's wort, Echinacea purpurea, and ginkgo biloba made eggs harder to fertilize and reduced the viability of sperm. Let your infertility doctor know if you're taking herbs. Your doctor will likely suggest that you stop all herbal remedies until you've completed your family."

- *Men, tell your sperm to cool it.* "Warm temperatures—from saunas, hot tubs, heated car seats, exercising while wearing a cup—can harm sperm. So can undue pressure—I treated one couple where the man stopped bicycling and they got pregnant. Another risk factor is laptops. If you want to keep your sperm happy, take your laptop off your lap."

breathing to deep abdominal breathing, speeding oxygen to your cells and giving you a chance to step back, gather your emotional resources and cope with whatever challenge is facing you. Minis *instantly* break the cycle of stress and tension. Most of my infertile patients love minis." *She suggests infertile women use them...*

- Before and during blood tests.
- Before and during injections (in-vitro fertilization, or IVF, involves numerous self-administered injections of fertility drugs).
- During any stressful phase of preparation for medical tests or procedures.
- Before and during ultrasounds.
- Before calling the doctor's office for test results.
- When you're waiting for your doctor to call you back.
- When you're put on hold by the doctor's office.
- When you see a pregnant woman in the grocery store.
- When an invitation to a baby shower arrives in the mail.
- When your neighbor says, "When are you going to have a baby? You're not getting any younger, you know!"

- If you've suffered miscarriages and are pregnant again—any time you go to the bathroom.

- When you walk past a baby-clothes shop in the mall.

Here are two versions of mini-relaxations taught by Dr. Domar...

- **Count down.** Count down from 10 to zero while taking one complete breath—one inhalation and exhalation with each number. (If you start to feel light-headed or dizzy, slow down your counting.) When you get to zero, you should feel better. If not, try doing it again.

- **Slowly.** As you inhale, count very slowly from one to four. As you exhale, count slowly back down, from four to one. Do this for several breaths.

➤ **Savor self-nurture.** "Infertile women often feel as if their bodies belong to their doctors," says Dr. Domar. "They poke you and prod you and take your blood and harvest your eggs and tell you when you can and can't be intimate with your husband. By nurturing yourself, you reclaim your power to make yourself happy and to be in control of your body." *Some of her suggestions...*

See Your Doctor If...

"The official definition of infertility is failing to produce a pregnancy that results in a live birth after one year of unprotected regular intercourse if you're under thirty-five, and after six months if you're over thirty-five," says Dr. Domar. If you fit that description, talk to your family practitioner or gynecologist about assisted-fertility treatments and whether they're right for you.

- Have a manicure or pedicure.

- Sit on a chaise lounge in the backyard with a cool drink and the latest issue of your favorite magazine.

- Take an afternoon nap.

- Plant an herb garden.

- Make some popcorn and watch a mushy movie.

- Borrow a friend's puppy and romp with it in the grass.

- Visit an art museum.

- Eat an ice cream cone—without punishing yourself with warnings about fat and calories.

"What you choose to do doesn't matter, as long as you're indulging in a pleasure you would normally deny yourself," she says. "Pick something that emphasizes enjoyment, play and a sense of fun—self-nurturance should never feel like just another chore on the daily to-do list."

Rapid Resource: Dr. Domar's book, *Self-Nurture: Learning to Care For Yourself as Effectively as You Care for Everyone Else* (Penguin).

➤ **Keep your chin up.** Infertility is a *temporary* crisis, says Dr. Domar. "Most infertile couples try to have a baby for only a few years—and more than fifty percent get pregnant. And even if you don't get pregnant, you can adopt, or use donor eggs or donor sperm. If you really want to be a parent, you are going to be a parent."

Dr. Domar says that when she talks to her patients months or years later, they're fine. "Many of them tell me they are stronger, their marriages are more robust and their lives are more satisfying than they were before infertility—whether or not they've had a biological child. That's doesn't mean they're glad they were infertile. But they did survive it, and most of the time they emerge stronger."

INFLAMMATORY BOWEL DISEASE

Cool the Inner Fire

More than 1 million Americans have *inflammatory bowel disease* (IBD)—inflammation of the lining of the digestive tract. If the inflammation is in a single, continuous area in the rectum and colon, it's called *ulcerative colitis*. If the inflammation occurs in patches anywhere in the digestive tract and burrows deep into the tissues, it's called *Crohn's disease.*

In either case, IBD is a *serious disease* (with its cause or causes still hotly debated by experts). During periodic flare-ups, symptoms can include frequent, bloody stools, abdominal pain and cramping. Long-term developments can include arthritis and colon cancer.

Important: Inflammatory bowel disease requires medical supervision and a treatment plan that may include multiple drugs and possibly surgery.

But there are several nondrug options that may help control the problem, says Liz Lipski, PhD, CCN, a certified clinical nutritionist at Maryland University of Integrative Health (*www.lizlipski.com*), and author of *Digestive Wellness* (McGraw-Hill, Third Edition).

Discuss these ideas with your gastroenterologist...

➤ **Take a probiotic.** "Numerous studies have shown that the use of a *probiotic*—a nutritional supplement containing friendly digestive bacteria—is beneficial for people with IBD," says Dr. Lipski. Probiotic bacteria like *L. acidophilus* and bifidobacteria provide competition for other symptom-triggering "unfriendly" microbes, pushing them out of the gut and creating a healthier bacterial environment, she explains.

A probiotic supplement can help stop active disease...help keep people with IBD in remission, limiting repeated flare-ups...help treat "pouchitis" a complication of colon surgery for the disease...and improve the symptoms of arthritis, a common complication of IBD.

Product: In many studies on ulcerative colitis and probiotics, doctors have used VSL#3, a supplement with eight different strains of friendly bacteria. (Four strains of *lactobacillus*, three strains of *bifidobacterium* and one strain of *streptococcus*.) Use it only with your doctor's approval and supervision.

Rapid Resource: It is available at *www.vsl3.com*, or call 866-438-8753.

➤ **Take glutamine.** "Glutamine is the first nutrient I recommend for bowel and intestinal health," says Dr. Lipski.

Glutamine is an amino acid, a component of protein. The digestive tract uses it as the primary nutrient for intestinal cells, and it is effective for IBD, explains Dr. Lipski.

Suggested intake: 10 to 30 grams a day of the powdered supplement, in water or juice. (*Not* in a hot drink, because heat breaks down the nutrient.)

⚠ *Caution:* Glutamine can cause constipation. If the problem develops, discontinue use of the supplement.

➤ **Increase the intake of omega-3 fatty acids.** The omega-3 fatty acids DHA (*docosahexaenoic acid*) and EPA (*eicosapentaenoic acid*)—found in cold-water fish such as salmon, mackerel, herring, tuna, sardines and halibut—can reduce the inflammation of IBD, says Dr. Lipski. "Eating these fish several times a week can supply your body with these essential fats.

"You can also take capsules of EPA/DHA oils daily."

Study: In 11 people with IBD, the use of fish oil supplements decreased disease activity by 58% over a period of eight months. None of the 11 worsened, and eight were able to reduce or discontinue medications.

Product: Max EPA, from Twin Labs.

Dosage: 15 capsules a day, supplying 2.7 grams of EPA and 1.8 grams of DHA.

INSOMNIA

Take the Express to Dreamland

Many of us are sleeping less—a lot less. The number of people reporting sleep problems has jumped 13% since 2001, with the number of Americans sleeping less than six hours *rising* from 13% to 20% and those sleeping more than eight hours *dropping* from 38% to 28%, according to the National Sleep Foundation.

For those 60 and older, sound sleep is even harder to come by...

Fact: Fifty-eight percent of adults age 59 and over report having difficulty sleeping at least a few nights a week. Eighty-five percent never receive treatment. The other 15% typically get a prescription for sleeping pills—which, in people over 60, can cause daytime confusion, drowsiness, falls and fractures and side effects from interactions with other medications.

Are you among the tossing and turning millions?

The official definition of insomnia is having trouble falling asleep or staying asleep, or waking up too early, at least three times a week, for more than a month.

If that describes you, there's plenty you can do about it—starting tonight...

➤ **Don't let *acute* insomnia turn into *chronic* insomnia.** Most insomnia starts with *stress*—a loved one dies, you lose your job, your

Is Deep Sleep Cherry-Flavored?

Tart cherries are rich in melatonin, a compound that controls sleep-wake cycles. Could drinking a glass of super-charged cherry juice—developed at the food science labs of Cornell University, and containing the extracts of 50 tart cherries—help people sleep?

To find out, researchers at the University of Rochester Medical Center studied older adults with insomnia, dividing them into two groups. Twice a day, one group drank an eight-ounce bottle of CherryPharm, the high-cherry juice. The other group drank a look-alike, taste-alike beverage without cherries.

Result: Those drinking CherryPharm fell asleep faster and spent less time awake after falling asleep.

"This clinical trial suggests that CherryPharm, a natural juice, improves sleep in individuals with insomnia," says Wilfred Pigeon, MD, the study's lead researcher.

Rapid Resource: You can order a tart cherry juice similar to CherryPharm (now called Cheribundi) at *www.cheribundi.com*. The product is also widely available in supermarkets.

retirement account is dwindling. You feel worried, anxious and upset. You can't stop thinking about the problem. And you can't sleep...

Fact: One-third of Americans are losing sleep over the state of the US economy and personal financial concerns, says the National Sleep Foundation.

Good news: That kind of acute insomnia usually lasts a couple of weeks and then you start sleeping soundly again, says Lisa Shives, MD, the medical director of Northshore Sleep Medicine, in Evanston, Illinois (*www.nssleep.com*).

But *acute* insomnia can become *chronic* insomnia—and that's what has happened to an estimated 10% of Americans under the age of 60, and 30 to 50% over the age of 60.

Here are fast and effective ways to stop acute insomnia from developing into a long-term problem...

> **Don't spend extra time in bed.** You're not sleeping well. You're tired during the day. You have trouble focusing at work and you're grumpy at home. So it makes sense to hit the hay earlier, right? After all, you *need* the sleep. Wrong.

If you go to bed early and sleeplessly toss and turn—because you're worried, anxious and upset about whatever factor is causing the acute insomnia—you'll quickly develop a *negative association* with the bedroom. It will become the place where you can't sleep—where you feel tormented, emotionally, mentally and physically. And that new connection between your bedroom and sleeplessness is the seed of chronic insomnia, says Dr. Shives.

Best: Even if you're tired, go to bed and get up on a *regular schedule*—say, 11:00 P.M. to 7:00 A.M.—no matter how much you do or don't sleep while you're in bed. "This is crucial for not developing chronic insomnia," says Dr. Shives.

> **Don't wheel the TV into the bedroom or use your laptop in bed.** You're not sleeping. You're bored. So you start watching TV in the bedroom or you bring your laptop to bed or you text a friend on the cell phone. UR making a big mistake!!!

All that electronic activity creates a scenario where the bedroom becomes the place where you hang out late at night—but not the place where you sleep, says Dr. Shives. And that's a wide open doorway to chronic insomnia.

Better: If you feel you need to do something in bed, read—as long as it's not reading for work. Enjoyable (or boring) reading can help put you to sleep, says Dr. Shives. So can listening to relaxing music.

Sleeping Pills Can Make You Dead Tired— Literally

Every year, doctors in America write 24 million prescriptions for sleeping pills, such as *zaleplon* (Sonata), *eszopiclone* (Lunesta) and *zolpidem* (Ambien). They're for the *temporary* relief of insomnia, and not recommended for long-term use.

However: A survey of nearly 1,500 adults, conducted by *Consumer Reports*, found that 5% used sleeping pills every night of the month, 14% took them at least eight times a month—and 38% of those taking sleeping pills said they'd been using the medication for at least two years. *It could be suicide by Rx...*

New study: Researchers at the University of California in San Diego analyzed data from more than one million people and found that those who took more than 30 sleeping pills a month were at three times the risk of dying, while those who took between 1 and 29 pills had a 50 to 80% higher death risk. (The researchers don't know why sleeping pills are linked to increased mortality rates.)

What to do: "Try lifestyle changes—such as a standard sleep-wake schedule, a conducive bedroom environment and regular exercise—before you start taking sleeping pills," says Dr. Shives.

> **Don't let Fido in bed.** Allowing a pet to start hanging out with you in bed during a bout of acute insomnia—because you're distraught or bored—trains you to be a chronic insomniac, says Dr. Shives. "For most people, a pet in the bedroom disturbs sleep. So while your pet might be a consoling presence, sleeping in the same room with your animal companion is a bad habit to start."

> **Don't nap.** Daytime naps of longer than 10 or 15 minutes can interfere with nighttime sleeping, says Dr. Shives. "They're another

way to turn yourself into a chronic insomniac." (This is also good advice for people who have developed chronic insomnia, says Dr. Shives.)

➤ **Don't worry about not sleeping.** Becoming intensely and constantly concerned about getting enough sleep is the hallmark of chronic insomnia, says Dr. Shives.

Acute insomnia is a normal part of stressful, modern life—it has a beginning and end, usually in about two to three weeks.

The best advice: Don't worry about it.

➤ **For chronic insomnia—evaluate how bad the situation really is.** "People with chronic insomnia have developed dysfunctional beliefs about sleep," says Dr. Shives. "During acute insomnia, they worried about whatever life stressor triggered the problem. Now, they're mostly worried about *not sleeping.* They tell themselves, 'Oh my God, if this goes on I'm going to lose my job or wreck my car or ruin my marriage.' "

Well, says Dr. Shives, a poor night's sleep does impair alertness and performance, and chronic sleeplessness can increase the risk of chronic diseases, such as diabetes, heart disease and depression.

But if you have chronic insomnia, you need to take a very realistic view of the day-to-day impact of sleeplessness on your life. In fact, *don't* think about your sleep, advises Dr. Shives. Think about *daytime function.*

"Most chronic insomniacs will quickly realize that their daytime function is *not* all that impaired," she says. "They are not drowsy all day. They are not falling asleep at the wheel and wrecking the car. In fact, it's okay if they *don't* get eight hours of sleep every night or even most nights."

This mental shift will help relieve a lot of your anxiety about sleeping—anxiety that is keeping you awake at night!

Try this: Make a list of all the beliefs you have about sleep, such as, "I think my insomnia is going to wreck my health" or "I'm going to get fired from my job." Then look at all the evidence that supports your beliefs. Is there any? Maybe your doctor gave you a clean bill of health at your last physical checkup. Maybe you've had stellar performance evaluations at work for three years in a row.

"When you find yourself worrying about sleep—remember the evidence that shows your insomnia is *not* a problem," says Dr. Shives.

🕐 *Super-Quick Fix*

➤ **Think a happier thought.** "When you start playing your usual 'mental tape' about a lack of sleep harming your life, immediately start daydreaming about something positive and pleasurable," says Dr. Shives. "Whatever makes you happy is a good daydream, whether it's moving to Paris and opening a hotel—my own personal favorite—or marrying a movie star."

➤ **Wake up at the same time every morning.** A chronic insomniac feels like sleep is something he or she can't control, says Dr. Shives. By setting an alarm for the same time every morning, you bring sleep under your control—and also begin to regularize your sleep-wake schedule, which research shows is key to overcoming chronic insomnia.

"Don't worry about how you'll feel the next day—even if you haven't slept," says Dr. Shives.

➤ **Understand the difference between being *tired* and being *sleepy*—and don't go to bed until you're sleepy.** "Tiredness and fatigue come from physical and mental effort," explains Dr. Shives. "Sleepiness, on the other hand, is a phenomenon in which you feel the pressure to sleep—in your brain, in your eyes and in your mind—and you start to doze off. Do not get into bed until you feel truly sleepy."

➤ **Don't drink caffeine.** Many chronic insomniacs have a biochemical imbalance that keeps them on edge all the time—and caffeine can worsen the situation. Avoid coffee, black, green and white tea, cola and chocolate, says Dr. Shives.

➤ **Turn on the lights in the morning, dim them at night.** Light levels are crucially important to a normal sleep-wake cycle, says Dr. Shives.

"When you wake up in the morning, immediately expose yourself to bright light. Turn on all the lights in the bedroom or, if the sun's out, go outside for a short walk.

In the two or three hours before bedtime, avoid staring at bright electronic media—the TV or the computer, she advises. For entertainment, read, using a small reading light that attaches directly to the book rather than an overhead light or lamp in the bedroom.

Best: The best books to help you fall asleep aren't plot-driven, says Dr. Shives. Those include religious works and books of poetry. Or read a novel you've already read.

➤ **Exercise in the evening.** The outdated advice: Don't exercise three to four hours before bedtime.

New thinking: Exercising three hours before bedtime can help you sleep, says Dr. Shives. That's because your body begins to *cool down* naturally after exercise—and a cooler body temperature is conducive to falling asleep.

Best: Three hours before bedtime, exercise and then also take a hot shower or bath.

IRRITABLE BOWEL SYNDROME

Easygoing Relief

An estimated 10% to 20% of Americans suffer from IBS, two-thirds of them women. The symptoms include abdominal pain, cramping and bloating...constipation, diarrhea or an intestinal seesaw of both...

Speed Healing Success

She Wrote the Book on IBS

"My grandfather had IBS, my mother has IBS, my sister has IBS—and I have IBS," says Elaine Magee, MPH, RD (*www.recipedoctor.com*). So she decided to do something about it. She wrote a book—*Tell Me What to Eat If I Have Irritable Bowel Syndrome* (New Page), which has sold more than 100,000 copies.

Here are some of Magee's recommendations for fast relief from the symptoms of IBS...

• **Fast relief from diarrhea.** The best foods include banana, white rice, rice crackers, rice milk and chicken (white meat).

For rehydration, try Pedialyte. *Red flag:* Not Gatorade, says Magee—"It's high in fructose, which causes bloating."

Use the probiotic *Saccharomyces boulardii*. *Product:* Florastor. *Suggested intake:* One tablet a day.

• **Fast relief from constipation.** Try five servings a day of high-fiber foods such as oatmeal, berries, pear, peach, plum, papaya, mango, kiwi, raisins, prunes or prune juice, chickpeas, carrots, celery, snap peas and snow peas.

Drink five glasses of water a day and herbal tea—more if you can.

Avoid the foods and supplements that improve diarrhea.

Smart ideas: "If you have constipation-predominant IBS, you probably know how important fiber-rich foods are to your comfort, says Magee. To help you reach the daily target of 25 to 30 grams, set by the American Dietetic Association, she suggests foods such as 1 cup of Raisin Bran (8 grams)...½ cup of Ortega Fat Free Refried Beans (9 grams)...1 to 2 slices of whole grain bread (4 grams)...9 Reduced Fat Triscuits (4 grams)...1 apple (3 grams)...1 cup cooked carrot slices (5 grams)...or 1 sweet potato (4 grams).

• **Bloating no-no's.** The following foods are notorious for causing bloating, says Magee... cheese...all carbonated beverages, including beer and seltzer...all artificial sweeteners... Zone Bars and Power Bars...any food with fructose corn syrup...onions and garlic...and any food with MSG.

lumpy or loose stools...straining to defecate or having to make an emergency dash to the bathroom. Those symptoms can range from the mild and inconvenient to the severe and incapacitating.

Most experts say IBS is a *functional disorder*—you have a definite set of dysfunctional digestive symptoms, but no blood test, x-ray or probe ever finds a definite, physical source of the problem.

Most people with IBS feel it's a *frustrating disorder,* says William Salt, MD, a gastroenterologist in Columbus, Ohio, clinical associate professor in medicine at Ohio State University and author of *Irritable Bowel Syndrome and the MindBodySpirit Connection* (Parkview Publishing).

"Many doctors don't have helpful advice for sufferers," he says. "Many people with IBS lead restricted lives."

But don't despair. "If you suffer from IBS, the most important thing for you to know is that there *is* hope," says Dr. Salt. "Healing is possible." *And in some cases, it can be quite fast...*

Super-Quick Fix

➤ **Try peppermint oil.** "Peppermint oil is a muscle relaxant that is widely used in England for IBS," says Liz Lipski, PhD, CCN, a certified clinical nutritionist at Maryland University of Integrative Health (*www.lizlipski.com*) and author of *Digestive Wellness* (McGraw-Hill).

See Your Doctor If...

Medical treatment is a must for IBS, says Stephen Wangen, ND, founder of the IBS Treatment Center in Seattle, Washington, (*www.ibstreatment center.com*) and author of *The Irritable Bowel Syndrome Solution* (Innate Health Group). "There are several common causes for the symptoms of IBS, and they vary from individual to individual," he explains. You might have a food allergy to the gluten in wheat, rye and barley or to dairy foods or to other foods...or *dysbiosis*, an imbalance of the bacteria in the intestinal tract...or an intestinal overgrowth of a yeast such as candida...or intestinal parasites...or a combination of those factors.

To discover the cause, says Dr. Wangen, you need two digestion-focused medical tests—a food allergy test (which is a blood test) and a test for bacteria, yeast and parasites (which is a stool test). "These tests are available, reasonably straightforward and affordable."

He suggests you talk to your doctor about ordering the following two tests...

- *A complete food allergy panel* (measuring IgE, IgE and IgA antibodies) from US BioTek Laboratories, *www.usbiotek.com*. Address: 16020 Linden Ave. N., Shoreline, WA 98133, call 877-318-8728.

- *A test for stool microbes,* from Genova Diagnostics, *www.gdx.net*. Address: Genova Diagnostics, 63 Zillicoa Street, Asheville, North Carolina, 28801, call 800-522-4762 or use the email form at the website.

The results of the food allergy tests will indicate which foods and ingredients you should avoid to control IBS symptoms, says Dr. Wangen. The results of the stool test will point toward treatments to eradicate the problem, whether it is bacterial, fungal, parasitic or a combination.

You can find out more information about Dr. Wangen's protocols for treating IBS at *www.ibstreat mentcenter.com*, or call 888-546-6283. Address: 11301 Pinehurst Way NE, Seattle, WA 98125.

New study: Researchers in England analyzed studies on three IBS treatments, involving more than 2,500 people. They found peppermint oil was the *most effective treatment* for relieving the symptoms of IBS—twice as effective as anti-spasmodic medications, and four times as effective as a high-fiber diet.

Peppermint oil has been overlooked because of the introduction of newer, more expensive drugs for IBS, say the researchers, who suggest that treatment guidelines for IBS be revised to include peppermint oil.

What to do: "To get the oil into the intestines intact, use an enteric-coated peppermint oil, which will prevent it from dissolving in the stomach," says Dr. Lipski.

Product: Pepogest Enteric-Coated Peppermint Oil, from Nature's Way.

Suggested intake: One to two capsules daily, between meals, says Dr. Lipski.

🕐 Super-Quick Fix

➤ **Try a probiotic.** "In numerous studies, probiotic supplements—a capsule containing 'friendly' intestinal bacteria—have been shown to help regulate IBS," says Dr. Lipski.

New study: Researchers at Northwestern University reviewed 16 studies and found the most effective probiotic for the control of IBS symptoms is a strain called *Bifodobacterium infantis 35624*. The study appeared in the *American Journal of Gastroenterology*.

"Probiotics are gaining in popularity for the treatment of multiple gastrointestinal disorders, including IBS," says Darren M. Brenner, MD, in the Division of Gastroenterology at

Northwestern. "After assessment of these studies, B. infantis 35624 was the only probiotic that showed repeated effectiveness."

New thinking: We think that imbalance in gut microflora leads to a chronic, low-level inflammation in the intestines that may produce the symptoms of IBS, says Liam O'Mahony, MD, a researcher who conducted a study on B. infantis. The probiotic may help other inflammatory conditions, such inflammatory bowel disease and even arthritis, he adds.

Product: Align, a B. infantis-containing probiotic, from Procter & Gamble. Follow the dosage recommendation on the label.

Rapid Resource: To order the product, and for more information, visit the website *www. aligngi.com*, or call 800-208-0112.

➤ **For constipation, get going—out the door.** If your primary IBS symptom is constipation—start exercising.

New study: Researchers at the University of Birmingham in England studied 56 people with constipation-predominant IBS, dividing them into two groups. One group attended two exercise consultations to provide exercise skills, knowledge, confidence and motivation, with the goal of beginning and sustaining a regular exercise routine—30 minutes, five days a week. The other group was give standard care for the condition.

After three months, the group that received the exercise consultations was exercising a lot more—and defecating a lot more. They had "significantly improved symptoms of constipation," say the researchers, in the *International Journal of Sports Medicine.*

Best: For people with IBS, "a gradual exercise program utilizing low-impact aerobic activities such as walking, biking, swimming or water aerobics is most likely to be successful," says Dr. Salt. "In the beginning, some forms of exercise may upset your stomach a bit, and that

discomfort can be discouraging. But with time, exercise will reduce your IBS symptoms."

Start with five minutes at a time, he suggests. "Do this at least three times a day, if you can," says Dr. Salt. "Your goal is to gradually increase to thirty minutes, on most days of the week."

➤ **Prepare ahead of time for an embarrassing situation.** One of the potential *emotional* difficulties of IBS is experiencing digestive upset in public—a loudly rumbling gut, passing gas or even incontinence, says Barbara Bradley Bolen, PhD, a clinical psychologist in Farmingdale, New York (*www.drbarbarabolen.com*), and author of *Breaking the Bonds of Irritable Bowel Syndrome: A Psychological Approach to Regaining Control of Your Life* (New Harbinger) and *IBS Chat: Real Life Stories and Solutions* (iUniverse).

And one key to handling such a situation is knowing the difference between *embarrassment* and *shame*, she says. "We feel shame based on a sense of *personal failure*—for which we are either judging ourselves too harshly or imagining that others are doing so," says Dr. Bolen.

Better: Remind yourself that what is happening is *not* shameful. It's only *embarrassing*—and it's not the end of the world. Also remind yourself that other people are probably not going to judge you—because everyone experiences digestive symptoms, not just people with IBS.

You can also use *calming self-talk* in an embarrassing situation, says Dr. Bolen. "Calming self-talk is a strategy for reducing anxiety by talking to yourself in a calm, rational manner regarding the things that usually set off your anxiety."

What to do: Write down and memorize calming phrases that you'll use later—at work, at a party, in a restaurant, when you're traveling. *Examples:* "If my stomach rumbles or I pass gas, it isn't such a big deal. It happens to everyone at one time or another. Other people will most likely be supportive and understanding, not judgmental and critical."

KIDNEY STONES

 If you've had one kidney stone, you definitely don't want another. "I've had women tell me they would rather give birth again than pass another kidney stone—that's how excruciating the pain can be," says Bryan Kansas, MD, a urologist in Austin, Texas (*www.urologyteam.com*). What's behind all that agony?

Four out of five kidney stones are made of *calcium* (a mineral) and *oxalate* (what chemists call an *acid salt*). Normally, these microscopic crystals stay dissolved in the urine. But triggered by one or more factors—such as drinking too little fluid, a diet too high in protein and salt, overweight, high blood pressure, a genetic predisposition—the calcium and oxalate pile up and *crystallize*. You form a stone. And your life is deformed with pain, especially if the stone moves out of the kidney and into the *ureter*, the tube connecting the kidney and the bladder.

If you form and pass one stone, you have a 50% risk of passing another within five years. And another one after that. But you don't have to be between a stone and a hard place.

You can *reduce* your risk of forming more stones, says Dr. Kansas. *Start by turning on the faucet…*

➤ **Drink a gallon of water a day.** But isn't 128 ounces—16, eight-ounce glasses of water a day, an average of one glass every waking hour—a lot of water? Who would drink that much, day after day?

"Well, it depends on how badly you don't want to have another stone," says Dr. Kansas.

Reason: Three to four quarts of intake equals two quarts of output, he says. And two quarts of urine is the amount needed to keep calcium and oxalate dissolved and prevent stone formation.

Speed Healing Success

"His Stones Are Under Control"

"I experienced my first kidney stone a couple months ago," says Karen Timsley-Kim, of Orlando, Florida. "My father has also suffered with them for years—but his stones are under control with his current regimen. So I decided to follow it too.

"For daily prevention, we stay hydrated. We also take a calcium-magnesium supplement, with one thousand milligrams of calcium and four hundred milligrams of magnesium. We take two thousand IU of vitamin D, which aids calcium absorption. And we drink one cup of corn silk tea a day, which is a traditional kidney tonic."

Helpful: Stop drinking water two hours before bedtime, so you don't have to get up and urinate throughout the night, says Dr. Kansas.

Dr. Kansas asks his stone-formers to drink 64 of their daily 128 ounces of water mixed with four ounces of lemon juice. "Lemons have a lot of citrate, which inhibits the formation of stones," he says.

⚠ *Caution:* People with heart failure need to limit their fluids and shouldn't follow this protocol.

Recent study: Researchers from the Comprehensive Kidney Stone Center at Duke University studied 11 patients with kidney stones who had been on long-term "lemonade therapy." Stone formation decreased from an average of one per year to 0.13 per year—a reduction of 87%. And none of the stone-formers needed any medical intervention during their three and a half years on lemonade therapy—no drugs, no surgery, no other treatments of any kind.

Important: To prevent a first stone, Dr. Kansas suggests drinking at least 60 to 80 ounces of fluid a day, in any form—water, juice, coffee, tea. "People think they're drowning themselves in fluid—but most people aren't even drinking forty ounces a day," he says.

🕐 *Super-Quick Fix*

➤ **Take a stone-preventing supplement.** Another factor that controls stone formation—the pH (a measurement of alkalinity and acidity) of urine. "Urine that is slightly more alkaline is less likely to form stones because the crystals are more likely to stay in solution," says Dr. Kansas.

He asks his stone-forming patients to take a supplement that contains magnesium oxide, magnesium citrate and potassium citrate—three nutrients that help keep urine alkaline.

Better: Potassium citrate is often prescribed for kidney stones but can cause nausea and diarrhea. Combining it with magnesium increases "gastrointestinal tolerability," say researchers from Washington State University.

The supplement also contains vitamin B-6. Researchers at Harvard Medical School found those with a high dietary intake of B-6 had a 36% lower rate of kidney stone formation.

Study: Researchers at Stony Brook Medical School in New York gave kidney stone formers a supplement with magnesium oxide, magnesium citrate, potassium oxide and vitamin B-6. It decreased urinary oxalate levels by 29%. It also decreased by 27% the calcium oxalate "saturation" that leads to crystallization.

Product: TheralithXR, available at *www. theralogix.com*, or call 800-449-4447.

➤ **Change your diet—but don't overdo it.** If you passed a kidney stone a decade ago, chances are you would have been given a list of 100 or more oxalate-containing foods that you were never supposed to eat again. You also may have been told to forgo calcium-rich milk and

Should You Cut Calcium?

If most kidney stones are made of calcium, wouldn't eating less calcium-rich foods lower your risk for more stones?

No, says Laurie Beebe, RD (*www.mycoach laurie.com*), a registered dietician in Illinois who helped conduct research to answer this question.

"If a stone-former has relatively low dietary calcium intake, oxalate is absorbed and ends up in the kidney, prompting crystallization of stones. If a person *increases* their calcium intake—which a well-intended but misinformed physician might tell them to reduce—the calcium and the oxalate are attracted to each other, form a compound in the gut, and are excreted, never reaching the kidney. In short—you reduce the oxalate content of urine by increasing your calcium intake."

cheese—because calcium was thought to make calcium stones.

"Those aren't recommendations we make today," says Dr. Kansas. "It's now understood that avoiding all oxalates is far too restrictive and that low-calcium diets can cause stones."

What's the current recommendation? Dr. Kansas asks his stone-forming patients to reduce by 50% the types of foods that can cause stones. They include red meat...salt and salty foods, such as chips...and coffee, tea, chocolate, nuts, spinach, kale, collard greens and rhubarb—all of which are very high in oxalates.

➤ **An herbal formula to relieve the pain and pass the stone.** A herbal formula developed by world-renowned herbalist and acupuncturist Michael Tierra, LAc, O.M.D, works in several ways to relieve the pain of a kidney stone and allow it to pass easily, says Tom Dadant, a fellow herbalist. *The formula includes the herbs...*

• **Gravel root.** Dissolves calcified deposits in the body, such as kidney stones.

- **Turmeric root.** Reduces the inflammation in the ducts, allowing them to relax and expand so you can pass the stone.

- **Dandelion root.** Works as a diuretic, increasing urinary output, which aids in passing a stone.

- **Parsley root.** Also a diuretic and anti-inflammatory.

- **Marshmallow root.** Lubricates the inner linings of the body—much the same as the herb slippery elm is used to coat and soothe a sore throat. "It allows the stone to pass with less irritation," says Dadant.

- **Lemon balm.** A so-called "anti-spasmodic" herb, lemon balm gently calms and soothes body and mind. "It allows the body to open up, so the stone can be passed without undue tightening and contracting of the ducts."

- **Licorice and ginger roots.** Also lubricate and reduce inflammation.

Dadant tells the following story about someone with a kidney stone who used the formula...

"A man who lived in Chicago had excruciating pain when urinating and went to a urologist, who conducted an ultrasound test and told him he had a very large kidney stone that would require surgical removal. Not wanting to undergo an operation, the man went home and searched the Internet under 'kidney stones' and saw that gravel root was a frequently mentioned herbal treatment. He went to the health food store looking for the herb, and was directed to this formula. He bought a bottle and took a five-tablet daily dose that night and another five tablets when he woke up. Later that day, he passed the stone—with some pain, but not nearly as much as he had been experiencing. When passing it, he urinated into a strainer, trapping the stone. He took it to a urologist, who examined it and told him he could not possibly have passed a stone that big. However, when the urologist conducted an ultrasound test, there was no sign of the original stone."

Helpful: The formula also works to prevent and dissolve gallstones, says Dadant.

Product: Stone Free, from Planetary Herbals. You can find an online retailer of Planetary Herbals at *www.planetaryherbals.com/retailers.* The product is also available through health food stores and other retail outlets where herbs are sold.

If you are a stone-former, use Stone Free only with the approval and supervision of a qualified health professional.

See Your Doctor If...

The pain of a kidney stone—beginning in your side or back, just below your ribs, and zinging to your lower abdomen and groin—should send you to a doctor. Although most stones pass without inflicting any permanent damage, you may need pain medication. Or possibly a medical procedure to dissolve or remove the stone.

If you've had one or more stones, see a urologist for a complete medical workup, says Dr. Kansas. In some cases, there are underlying causes of kidney stones, including parathyroid disease.

LACTOSE INTOLERANCE

On this troubled planet, where conflict is rife, there is one point that 75% of the global population can agree on.

They have a hard time digesting dairy products.

The problem is their bodies don't manufacture lactase, the enzyme that digests lactose, the sugar in milk.

And in the melting pot of America, milk often isn't part of the mix. Twenty-five percent of Americans—including many African-Americans, Asian Americans, Caucasian Americans of Mediterranean and Jewish descent, Hispanics and Native Americans—are lactose intolerant. If they consume dairy, they pay the gastrointestinal price of bloating and gas.

Surprising: Being lactose intolerant doesn't mean calcium-rich, protein-rich dairy products have to be banished from your diet. Here's what experts suggest...

➤ **First, figure out if you *are* lactose intolerant.** Take dairy out of your diet for two weeks and then have dairy three times in a day—maybe a glass of milk, a chunk of cheese and a bowl of ice cream, says Jennifer Adler, MS, CN, a certified nutritionist and natural foods chef (*www.passionatenutrition.com*) and adjunct faculty member at Bastyr University in Seattle, Washington. "If you notice that digestive symptoms such as gas, bloating and diarrhea go away during those two weeks and then *return* when you add dairy—you're probably lactose intolerant," she says.

Helpful: "In eliminating dairy to test yourself for lactose intolerance, double-check your

Lactose Intolerance or Dairy Allergy?

"There is a huge difference between lactose intolerance and an allergy to dairy products," says Steve Wangen, ND, a naturopathic doctor and founder of the IBS Treatment Center in Seattle, Washington.

"With lactose intolerance, you get *digestive symptoms*, such as gas, bloating, abdominal cramping and loose stools—and that's it. With a dairy allergy, you can have a wide range of digestive *and* non-digestive symptoms, such as headaches, acne and eczema, fatigue, joint and muscle pain and brain fog.

What happens: "In a dairy allergy, the immune system attacks dairy products, producing one or more of hundreds of possible symptoms—digestive, skin, emotional, mental, musculoskeletal, respiratory, and on and on," explains Dr. Wangen. "Eating dairy products—even if they are lactose free, or even if you take a pill with lactose enzymes, such as Lactaid—will continue to cause health problems. That's because an immune reaction against dairy is far more comprehensive than lactose intolerance. And all indications are that it is a genetic reaction—there is no reintroducing dairy into the diet or outgrowing a dairy allergy."

Bottom line: "If eating dairy produces symptoms other than digestive upset—you have a dairy allergy and not lactose intolerance," says Dr. Wangen. "It's that simple."

diet for less obvious sources," says Liz Lipski, PhD, CCN, CNS, the director of Nutrition and Integrative Health Programs at Maryland University of Integrative Health (*www.lizlipski.com*), and author of *Digestive Wellness* (McGraw-Hill, Third Edition).

Those sources include bakery items, cookies, hot dogs, lunchmeats, milk chocolate, most non-dairy creamers, pancakes, protein powder drinks,

The Non-Dairy Queen

Alisa Marie Fleming has taken the cow by the horns.

She's the author of *Go Dairy Free: The Guide and Cookbook for Milk Allergies, Lactose Intolerance, and Casein-Free Living* (Fleming Ink) and runs a website of the same name, *www.godairyfree.org*, which offers a wealth of information—recipes, dining tips, product reviews and the like—for dairy-free living. Her mission is to help people with lactose intolerance or dairy allergy find tasty alternatives to milk and dairy products. *Some of her ideas for dairy-free substitutions...*

- **Half and half.** Combine ½ cup of regular (not light) coconut milk (shaken) with seven tablespoons of plain or unsweetened milk alternative (such as oat, almond or rice) to get a half-and-half consistency.

- **Butter.** Blend up apple pulp or a handful of prunes to create an excellent, healthy butter substitute for baking sweets and quick breads. In fact, pureed bananas, pineapple and pears also give an excellent "fat" consistency to recipes with an added jolt of health and flavor. *A few recommendations to maximize results...*

- Because the fruit will add more sweetness than butter, reduce the sugar in your recipes a touch.

- Think of the flavor of your recipe to judge which fruit flavor will work best. For example, prune puree works particularly well in chocolate desserts, such as brownies, and pineapple can add a tropical flair to most quick breads.

- Use a half cup of pureed fruit in place of one cup of butter. You may need to add a tablespoon or two of vegetable shortening or oil back into the recipe to achieve the best results.

- **Cottage cheese.** This style of cheese is one of the easiest to mimic. For a simple option, blend up some firm silken tofu with a dash of lemon juice. Silken tofu will do wonders as a replacement for cottage cheese or ricotta in dips, sauces, smoothies, pies and pasta dishes.

---

ranch dressings and anything that contains casein, caseinate, lactose, sodium caseinate or whey.

Problem: If you are sensitive to other foods in addition to dairy—such as the gluten found in wheat, rye and barley—the self-test might not be conclusive, says Dr. Lipski.

Solution: "Your doctor can order a simple, noninvasive hydrogen breath test to pinpoint if lactose intolerance is causing your problem," she says. "This challenge test is ideal for people who find it difficult to complete a self-test or are confused about their findings.

"After you breathe into a bag to collect a baseline sample, you drink a small amount of lactose solution and breathe into a different bag. Lab technicians measure the levels of methane and hydrogen gas you exhaled in both samples.

"Normal methane levels are zero to seven parts per million.

If levels increase at least 12 parts per million between the two samples, it indicates lactose intolerance—even if your hydrogen levels are normal.

"Normal hydrogen levels are ten parts per million. Levels of twenty parts per million or more are commonly found in people with lactose intolerance."

When both methane and hydrogen are tested, false tests results are far less likely, says Dr. Lipski.

➤ **Double-check the cow.** One key to dealing with lactose intolerance is the *quality* of the dairy, says Adler. "I am not a fan of dairy products from cows raised in feedlots," she says. "Dairy products should come from grass-fed cows. For example, they have more conjugated

Speed Healing Success

The Health Coach Who Trained Herself to Enjoy Dairy

Meredith Sobel is a health coach in New York and the owner of Luscious Organics Catering and Personal Chef Services. And she's lactose intolerant. And she enjoys dairy products. Just about every day. Here's how she does it…

"The best thing to do is have any highly cultured dairy product, such as yogurt or kefir with live cultures.

"Also hard cheese that has been aged more than two years is fine, though I avoid soft cheeses such as mozzarella and cottage cheese.

"I use lactase enzyme pills and also drink Lactaid milk.

"Raw milk is great—I drank it all last summer with no problem.

"I also find goat's milk quite tolerable. I wouldn't have a cup of it, but I'll have a drop in coffee or tea with no problems.

"There are also loads of non-dairy alternatives that are quite yummy, such as ice cream made from coconut milk. I avoid soy milk because I don't like the taste, but I find almond milk quite nice and mild."

linoleic acid [CLA], which has been shown to be protective against cancer.

"Even raw dairy from grass-fed cows is often tolerable to someone with lactose intolerance," she says. "A lot of times when people with lactose intolerance drink raw dairy, they say, 'Wow, I can drink this milk and it's no problem at all.' Raw milk has the bacteria and enzymes that naturally come along with milk and help the digestive process."

Rapid Resource: To find grass-fed fairy products, see the website *www.eatwild.com*, which provides a state-by-state directory of more than 1,100 pasture-fed farms and a state-by-state list of local farmers markets, stores, restaurants or buying clubs that feature grass-fed dairy products.

➤ **Take a lactase enzyme replacement.** "Taking a supplement containing lactase, such as Lactaid, before drinking milk or eating dairy-containing foods can help control lactose intolerance," says gastroenterologist Trent Nichols, MD, coeditor of *Optimal Digestive Health* (Healing Arts).

➤ **Try low-fat and hard cheeses.** "Low-fat cheeses such as Swiss, sharp Cheddar, Edam and Jarlsberg are lactose-free and used in moderation are a good source of protein," says Dr. Nichols.

People with lactose intolerance can often handle hard, aged cheeses, such as aged Gouda, Parmigiano Reggiano and Pecorino Romano, says Adler.

➤ **Try fermented milks.** Fermented milk products such as yogurt and kefir (which is cultured with different bacteria than yogurt) are often tolerable to the lactose intolerant—because the fermentation process break down the lactose, says Adler.

➤ **The best non-dairy sources of calcium.** If a person can't tolerate dairy, there are other ways to get calcium, says Adler. One of her favorite sources is stinging nettle. (The "sting" goes away when the nettle is dried, she says.)

What to do: Put one ounce of dried nettles in 32 ounces of water. Let it steep for four to 10 hours. Drink.

"One cup of stinging nettle tea delivers two thousand milligrams of calcium, compared to three hundred milligrams for a cup of milk," says Adler. "It blows milk away."

Also helpful: Adler says other good sources of calcium include dark leafy green vegetables such as kale…salmon in the can…and bone broth (roast a chicken, put the bones in a pot with water, vegetables and vinegar, cook for 12 hours, strain liquid and use to make soup, rice or beans).

LEG DISCOMFORTS

Step Away from the Pain

From an excruciating charley horse in your calf...to "restless legs" that won't let you sleep...to aching varicose veins...to leg cramps from peripheral arterial disease...there are many times when your health needs a leg up. *Here's how to get the help you need...*

➤ **The stretch that cures nighttime calf cramps.** "I see patients who are absolutely desperate because they have a 'charley horse'— a painful cramp in the calf that wakes them every night in the middle of the night," says Robert Moore, DPM, a podiatrist at Moore Foot and Ankle Specialists (*www.mfasclinic.com*) in Houston, Texas.

What happens: Poor circulation starves the muscle of oxygen, causing the cramp, says Dr. Moore.

What to do: The best way to treat a charley horse is *stretching*, which relaxes the muscle, says Dr. Moore. But you have to do the right kind of stretch—which can stop the cramp on the spot *and* prevent new cramps. *His instructions...*

1. **Standing next to a table and supporting yourself,** stand on your tiptoes.

2. **Contract the calf muscles in your left leg** for three to four seconds.

3. **Relax,** letting your heels drop to the floor.

4. **Wait 10 seconds.**

5. **Flex your left foot up toward your knee,** for three to four seconds.

6. **Relax for 10 seconds.**

7. **Repeat the exercise,** three times with each calf.

Do this stretch when you have a cramp, to relieve it, and also morning and night. "The nighttime leg cramps will go away in two or three days or two or three weeks, depending on the person," says Dr. Moore. "It's the best relief on the planet."

➤ **More quick ways to treat nighttime leg cramps.** There are several quick and easy ways to counter nighttime leg cramps, says Jacob Teitelbaum, MD, a doctor in Hawaii and author of *Pain Free 1-2-3!* (McGraw-Hill).

• **Take 200 milligrams (mg) of magnesium 30 minutes to one hour before bedtime,** which will help relax muscles.

• **Eat a banana every other day and drink a glass of tomato juice every day.** Both supply high levels of potassium, another mineral that helps relax muscles.

The Best-Looking Compression Stockings

Compression stockings can help prevent varicose veins in pregnancy, says Audrey Kunin, MD, a dermatologist in Kansas City, Missouri, and founder and director of *www.dermadoctor.com*. They're also the best way to prevent venous ulcers from forming," says Dr. Moore.

Problem: Most women don't want to wear them because they're too ugly.

Solution: "The manufacturer JOBST makes a variety of high-fashion knee highs, athletic socks and fashion hosiery that help provide high style *and* reduce your venous worries," says Dr. Kunin.

Rapid Resource: You can find a store near you that sells Jobst products by visiting the website *www.jobst.com* and clicking "Where to Buy" on the home page. Also consider lightweight compression stockings from *www.solutions.com*.

- **Stretch your calf muscles before you go to sleep.** Pull your toes toward you when you're sitting up in bed.

- **Wear socks to bed.** Cold feet can sometimes be a trigger, he says.

- **Leave a bar of soap under your bed sheets.** "It works, according to some," says Dr. Teitelbaum. "It seems odd, but it's cheap, safe and easy to try."

➤ **For varicose veins, try horse chestnut.** Aging, overweight, genes and standing all day as part of your job description are the main factors that can produce varicose veins—the blue, thick, twisty cords lashed to the legs of 20% of Americans (and an estimated 50% of those over 50).

What happens: Veins carry blood to the heart, and with each muscle-powered pump up from the legs, tiny valves shut to stop blood from flowing backward. If those valves weaken and fail, blood pools in your veins—and you have a *varicosity.*

You might not have any symptoms, or your heavy-feeling legs might ache, throb, burn, swell or cramp.

And varicosities can turn into a crisis—an ulcer that forms on the skin over the stranded blood.

Short of injections that shut down the veins, or surgery to "strip" them out of the body, medical care doesn't offer much in the way of help, except for compression hosiery, which most people won't wear because it's uncomfortable and ugly.

Good news: A supplement of horse chestnut seed extract works just as well as hosiery.

New study: Researchers in England analyzed the six most rigorous studies on the use of horse chestnut seed extract (HCSE) for varicose veins. They found the supplement helped relieve leg pain, reduced swelling and improved the appearance of veins—just as effectively as compression stockings. HCSE is a safe and

Speed Healing Success

"I Just Walk, Walk, Walk"

Charles Meadows—a 64-year-old Chicago resident and retired telephone company manager—measured his life in footsteps. How far was it to walk to the milk in the grocery store—and could he make it to the dairy case before cramps knifed through his left leg, immobilizing him and leaving him breathless in the aisle?

Meadows has peripheral artery disease, with blocked arteries in his legs that prevented oxygen from reaching the muscle, triggering sharp pain after just a few steps. And it had robbed him of life's pleasures, such as going to a Cubs baseball game or his family's summer picnics.

But then Meadows participated in a study from Northwestern University's Feinberg School of Medicine that tested whether regular exercise could improve the symptoms of people with PAD. The answer was yes.

The study showed that 40 minutes of treadmill walking, three times a week, for six months, allowed people to walk 70 feet further during a six-minute walk than they could at the start of the study. People who didn't work out on the treadmill walked an average of 49 less feet after the six months.

"This is the first study to show that exercise improves walking endurance for people with PAD who have the classic symptoms of calf pain," says Mary M. McDermott, MD, the study's lead researcher.

Meadows now strides—mostly pain-free—along the shore of Lake Michigan in Chicago for 30 minutes at a stretch. "I just walk, walk, walk," he says. "It has given me my vigor back."

effective treatment for varicose veins, say the researchers.

How it works: The active ingredient in HCSE is *aescin*—it strengthens veins, blocks

High-Speed Surgery for Varicose Veins

"This is a real breakthrough in treating varicose veins," says Cynthia Shortell, MD, in the Division of Vascular Surgery at the University of Rochester Medical Center.

She's talking about VNUS Closure surgery—an alternative to the surgical "stripping" of varicose veins that has been a standard medical treatment for the past 40 years—with 1- to 3-inch incisions, the risk of bruising, swelling, scarring and nerve damage, and six weeks of recovery.

How it works: The surgeon makes a tiny puncture, a catheter is inserted into the varicose vein, and a surge of radiofrequency heats the vein, collapsing and sealing it. "There are fewer complications, a faster recovery time of just a few days, and it's appropriate for nearly everyone with symptoms from varicose veins," says Dr. Shortell.

Rapid Resource: To find out more about the procedure, visit the website *www.veindirectory. org,* where you can also find a physician near you who performs VNUS closure surgeries.

enzymes (metabolic triggers) that play a role in forming varicose veins and calms vein-weakening inflammation.

Suggested intake: Look for a "standardized supplement" (it contains the therapeutic amount of aescin—50 to 75 mg per dose), and take 300 mg, twice a day.

HCSE supplements are widely available.

➤ **Prevent peripheral arterial disease—with vitamin D.** You couldn't find a parking spot close to the mall entrance and had to walk a hundred yards or so—but halfway there your calves were seized by a pain as vicious and debilitating as the bite of a pit bull. You have *peripheral artery* disease, or PAD. Eight to 12 million Americans are in the same listing boat.

In PAD, the arteries of the legs are clogged and narrowed with plaque. Whenever you ask your legs to do a little extra work—walk up stairs, stroll to the mailbox—your leg muscles can't get enough oxygen, and your calves, thighs or hips start to cramp, a symptom doctors call *intermittent claudication.*

Treatments include exercise (a start-and-stop walking regimen that takes your pain into account), lowering cholesterol with diet and medications or even surgery to clear clogged arteries. But people with cardiovascular disease can help prevent it from advancing to PAD—with vitamin D.

New study: Researchers at Albert Einstein College of Medicine analyzed diet and health data from nearly 5,000 people. Those with the lowest blood levels of vitamin D (less than 17.8 nanograms per milliliter, or ng/mL) were 64% more likely to have PAD than those with the highest levels (more than 29.2 ng/mL). In fact, for every 10 ng/mL drop in vitamin D from the highest level, the risk of ending up with PAD increased by 29%.

Why it works: "A growing body of evidence suggests that low levels of vitamin D may adversely affect the cardiovascular system," says Thomas J. Wang, MD, of Harvard Medical School. "Cellular receptors for vitamin D are found in many different types of tissue, including muscle cells of the circulatory system and the endothelium, the inner lining of the body's blood vessels."

What to do: Taking a vitamin D supplement of 1,000 IU a day is the easiest and most reliable way to maintain healthy blood levels of vitamin D, says Michael F. Holick, PhD, MD, director of the Vitamin D, Skin and Bone Research Laboratory at Boston University Medical Center.

Important: Please see page 253 in the chapter "Osteoporosis" for more information on the healthiest blood levels of vitamin D (50 to 80 ng/ml) and bi-yearly testing to ensure your levels are in that range.

➤ **Rest your restless legs—with valerian.** When you sit, lie down or sleep, you have unpleasant sensations in your legs—creeping, crawling, jittery, tingling, burning, aching, pulling or tightening sensations. And the only way you can get rid of those sensations is by jiggling your legs or pacing or otherwise moving around.

You have restless legs syndrome (RLS)—along with an estimated 5% to 10% of other Americans. And because of it, you have trouble falling asleep or staying asleep—and you're tired during the day. Doctors don't know the cause of the problem. Drugs used to treat it can have harsh, strange side effects (such as altering brain chemistry in a way that turns you into a compulsive gambler!) *But experts may have found an effective, drug-free alternative to the problem...*

New study: Researchers at the University of Pennsylvania studied 37 people with RLS, dividing them into two groups. One group took 800 mg a day of valerian, a relaxing herb. The other took a placebo. The people taking the herb had significant decreases in RLS symptoms and in daytime sleepiness.

"Valerian may be an alternative treatment for the symptom management of RLS, with positive health outcomes and improved quality of life," say the researchers, in the journal *Alternative Therapies in Health and Medicine.*

LIVER DISEASE

Immediate Support

Pity your poor liver. It has to clean up after everything that enters your body—medicines, the fatty fallout from a rich meal, funky food additives, vagrant viruses, alcohol. And although your liver is very lively (unlike other organs, it can rebuild itself), sometimes it's overwhelmed by years of fatty foods, aggressive germs or mega-grams of alcohol. And you develop liver disease.

"Liver disease can range from mild inflammation or minimal scar tissue to cirrhosis and liver failure," says Trent Nichols, MD, CNS, a gastroenterologist and certified nutrition specialist, and coeditor of *Optimal Digestive Health* (Healing Arts Press). The symptoms are also wide-ranging, from fatigue and loss of appetite to vomiting and the yellowed skin of jaundice.

If you've been diagnosed with liver disease, you should be under the regular care of a gastroenterologist or hepatologist, says Dr. Nichols.

Talk to your doctor about whether you might benefit from one or more of the liver-supporting options offered in this chapter...

Nonalcoholic fatty liver disease (NAFLD)—in which at least 20% of liver cells are filled with fat globules—afflicts an estimated *one-third* of all Americans, says Stephen Harrison, MD, a gastroenterologist in the Department of Medicine at the University of Texas Health Science Center in San Antonio.

As the incidence of obesity soared to nearly 70% of Americans...as rates of type 2 diabetes doubled in the past decade...more and more people are diagnosed with NAFLD.

New thinking: NAFLD is the liver-related manifestation of the *metabolic syndrome*—poor blood sugar control, overweight, high blood pressure, high triglycerides (a blood fat) and low "good" HDL cholesterol. Like the metabolic syndrome, it is caused by overeating and a sedentary lifestyle.

There are two types of NAFLD, one more serious than the other.

• **Steatosis** is also called simple *fatty liver*—fat accumulates in liver cells but the tissue isn't damaged.

• **Nonalcoholic steatohepatitis (NASH)** —liver cells are fatty and liver tissue is inflamed and possibly scarred.

Diagnosing Fatty Liver Disease

The mild form of NAFLD—steatosis—usually doesn't have any symptoms, although 10% of people suffer from tenderness or pain in the right side of the upper abdomen, where the liver is located, says Dr. Harrison. The condition is detected by ultrasound examination of that area. If the ultrasound shows 20% to 30% of the liver cells are fatty, you have steatosis.

If ultrasound detects steatosis, your doctor may refer you to a gastroenterologist for a liver biopsy—the only way to find out if you have NASH, the more serious form of the disease.

Important: If you have steatosis, several risk factors make it more likely you'll develop NASH…

- *Age 50 or older*
- *Being a woman*
- *A BMI (body mass index) above 28.* (Examples of BMI of 29 include 5'4" and 169 pounds, 5'8" and 190 pounds, 6' and 213 pounds.)
- *Type 2 diabetes*

After 10 years, 8% to 10% of those with NASH develop cirrhosis. Some go on to develop liver failure, requiring a transplant. Others develop liver cancer.

➤ **Nutrition for NASH.** Studies show that people with NASH tend to eat 400 to 500 more calories a day than those who don't have NASH, says Dr. Harrison.

They also eat more saturated fat (found primarily in red meat and dairy products) and less monounsaturated fat (found primarily in olive oil, nuts and avocados.

Research also shows that losing only 9% to 10% of body weight improves NASH.

Based on those findings, Dr. Harrison offers the following advice to help control or reverse NASH…

- **Bag the bagels.** Emphasize low-calorie carbohydrate foods such as vegetables, whole grains and beans.

De-emphasize high-calorie carbohydrate foods made with processed grains, such as bagels, muffins, crackers, pretzels, breakfast cereals such as Frosted Flakes, white bread, white rice, cookies and cake.

Recent finding: A study in the *American Journal of Clinical Nutrition* showed that people eating a diet low in processed carbohydrates lost weight twice as fast as those on a low-fat diet.

- **Reduce red meat.** Cut down on beef, lamb and pork. Limit yourself to a four-ounce serving (about the size of a pack of cards) three times a week.

Eliminate whole-fat cheese, milk and yogurt; eat low-fat or non-fat versions.

Use butter substitutes with cholesterol-lowering plant sterols such as Benecol, Take Control or Promise.

- **Go fishing in the refrigerator.** A study by Italian researchers found that people with NASH who took a daily one-gram supplement of omega-3 polyunsaturated acids from fish oil had an improvement compared to those not taking the supplement.

Eat fatty fish such as salmon or mackerel two to three times a week, or take a one-gram omega-3 supplement daily.

- **Eat a handful of walnuts.** They're a good source of monounsaturated fats. Also eat ½ an avocado two to three times a week, and use ½ teaspoon of olive oil and lemon as a salad dressing.

- **Can the soda.** Table sugar (sucrose) and high-fructose corn syrup wreck havoc with blood sugar and turn into fat in your body.

Eliminate all sources of sucrose and fructose, including soda and fruit juices.

• **Lace up your sneakers.** NASH is improved by three to four weekly sessions of exercise that burn at least 400 calories per session, such as 45 minutes of brisk walking.

Cirrhosis kills 26,000 Americans every year—the twelfth leading cause of death.

"Scar tissue replaces normal tissue, and blocks the flow of blood and nutrients," explains Liz Lipski, PhD, CCN, CNS, the director of Nutrition and Integrative Health Programs at Maryland University of Integrative Health and author of *Digestive Wellness* (McGraw-Hill, third edition).

The most common causes are alcoholism and advanced hepatitis (a viral infection of the liver, discussed below).

Dr. Lipski's suggestions for those with cirrhosis…

➤ **Try alpha lipoic acid.** "Studies show that this powerful antioxidant protects the liver against chemical poisoning," says Dr. Lipski. *Suggested intake:* 200 to 300 milligrams (mg), twice daily.

➤ **Try SAMe (S-adenosylmethionine).** In a study, this nutrient reduced itching and fatigue in patients with liver disease. *Suggested intake:* 1,600 mg. daily. *Caution:* Do not use SAMe with antidepressants, which can cause too-high levels of serotonin.

➤ **Try milk thistle (silymarin).** "Milk thistle is a traditional remedy for liver disease," says Dr. Lipski. "There is little or no risk and the possibility of great benefit." *Suggested intake:* 420 mg daily. "Look for a product that has been standardized for silymarin content," she says.

➤ **Try sho-saiko-to.** "Also called TJ-9 [or HO-9], this Chinese remedy contains bupleurum and six other herbs," says Dr. Lipski. "It is being used extensively in Japan for people with cirrhosis and hepatitis and to prevent the development of liver cancer." *Suggested intake:* 2.5 grams, three times daily. *Caution:* "It shouldn't be used in combination with interferon therapy," says Dr. Lipski. It is widely available on the Internet and in some retail outlets.

Hepatitis is an inflammation of the liver, most commonly caused by a viral infection. There are many types. The most common is hepatitis C, which has infected four million Americans and kills 11,000 yearly. It accounts for 50% of all cases of cirrhosis, end-stage liver disease and liver cancer.

"Hepatitis is a serious illness," says Dr. Lipski. "For best results, use several healing agents in combination." (The remedies for cirrhosis may help hepatitis, too, she points out.)

➤ **Try zinc.** "People with hepatitis are commonly zinc deficient," she says. *Suggested intake:* 50 to 75 mg daily.

➤ **Try N-acetyl-cysteine (NAC).** This antioxidant can reduce the "viral load" on the liver, says Dr. Lipski. *Suggested intake:* 1,000 to 2,000 micrograms (mcg) daily.

➤ **Try vitamin C.** "Vitamin C is well known for its antiviral effects," says Dr. Lipski. *Suggested intake:* A minimum of 2,000 mg daily.

➤ **Drink green tea.** It contains catechins, a compound that may help reduce liver damage. "Drink green tea as often as you like," says Dr. Lipski.

MACULAR DEGENERATION

An estimated 20% of Americans ages 65 to 74, and 35% over age 75, have age-related macular degeneration (AMD)—the number-one cause of vision loss and blindness.

What happens: At the back of the eyeball is the retina, which converts light into electrical impulses that are sent to the brain. In the center of the retina is the macula, a tiny collection of cells that delivers your sharpest vision. In AMD, the cells of the macula begin to break down—along with your eyesight…

It starts with bent or wavy lines in the center of your vision. The lines widen to a blotch that is blurry, blank or dark. The blotch slowly spreads like a fog, enveloping everything in a hazy, sight-erasing monochrome—the pages of a book, the faces of family and friends, the TV screen, the stairs, a road sign, the road.

Good news: If you don't have AMD, you can do a lot to prevent it. If you do have AMD, you can do a lot to slow its progress. *And you can start preventing or slowing the disease in the blink of an eye…*

➤ **Take lutein and zeaxanthin.** These two pigments (part of the *carotenoid* family of nutrients, famous for coloring carrots orange) function like internal sunglasses, shielding the macula from damage. They're found in dark green and yellow vegetables, including broccoli, Brussels sprouts, carrots, corn, green beans, green peas, kale, mustard greens, parsley, pumpkin, spinach, squash and yams.

New study: Scientists from the Age-Related Eye Disease Study analyzed six years of health data from 4,500 people ages 60 to 80. They found that those with the highest dietary intake of lutein and zeaxanthin were the least likely to develop sight-robbing AMD.

What to do: Maximize your intake of foods rich in these nutrients. But for the most reliable protection against AMD, consider taking a supplement containing the nutrients, says Larry Jebrock, OD, a behavioral optometrist in Novato, California (*www.natural-vision-correction.com*).

Recommended: Dr. Jebrock favors the product Pure Focus, a highly absorbable liquid supplement that includes 1.5 milligrams (mg) of lutein and 0.03 mg of zeaxanthin, and also vinpocetine, an herbal extract that improves circulation to the macula.

Rapid Resource: You can purchase Pure Focus on the Internet at *www.nutritionalfocus. com* or call 800-530-5010. Address: Nutritional Focus, 2382 Camino Vida Roble, Ste E., Carlsbad, CA 92011.

Are You at Risk for AMD?

Scientists theorize that chronic, low-grade inflammation—a process that damages cells—plays a key role in the development of heart disease, type 2 diabetes, Alzheimer's and age-related macular degeneration. Decreasing chronic inflammation with a diet rich in fruits, vegetables, whole grains, legumes and fish can help prevent AMD. *And eating that kind of diet is particularly important if you have one or more of the following risk factors for damage to the macula…*

- *Aging (over 65)*
- *Blue, green or hazel eyes* (brown eyes have more macula-protecting pigment)
- *Frequent exposure to sunlight without sunglasses*
- *Smoking*

Wake Up Your Macula— With Color

"The macula has photoreceptors that respond to light and color," says Dr. Jebrock. "Although AMD is mainly caused by cellular inflammation, it also seems as if the cells of the macula are 'sleepy'— and could be 'woken up' if properly stimulated. And the way to do that is with light and color."

He recommends purchasing a set of color gels—small sheets of semi-transparent plastic in several colors. (Please see "Rapid Resource" below for purchasing information.)

Place the blue and green gels on top of each other, creating a blue-green combination. On a table, prop the gels up at a 40-degree angle, about an arms-length away from your eyes, using an inverted clear glass or other transparent support. In an area fairly close to and behind the gels, place a lamp with a 40-watt incandescent bulb. Look at the backlit blue-green gel twice a day, for 10 minutes each time. After two weeks, switch to an orange-green combination.

Smart idea: "You can use a piece of graph paper with a dot in the middle—which optometrists call an Ansler Grid—to see if this therapy is improving your condition," says Dr. Jebrock.

"Put a dot directly in the middle of a sheet of graph paper. Hold the sheet of paper about sixteen inches away from your eyes and cover one eye. Look directly at the cross in the box that encloses the dot and notice if there are any distortions in the boxes around the cross. For example, the boxes may be misshapen, looking more like barrels, or they may be missing. These visual distortions correspond to the areas of the macula that are damaged.

"Do this test every two weeks or so to see if there is any improvement. For example, perhaps the boxes to the left of the dot used to be gone but now you can see them. If color therapy is improving your vision, continue it, alternating two weeks of blue-green with two weeks of orange-green."

Rapid Resource: You can purchase an inexpensive set of six color gels at Amazon.com. (*www.amazon.com/Colored-Film-Gels-Colors-Sheets/dp/B004A9PMGE*) or at *onlinesciencemall.com* (call 205-683-9765) Address: Online Science Mall, 6433 Clay Palmerdale Rd., Pinson, AL 35126.

➤ **Eat more fish or take a fish oil supplement.** Omega-3 fatty acids—found in fatty fish such as albacore tuna, herring, lake trout, mackerel, salmon and sardines—help protect the macula, says Dr. Jebrock. They boost circulation to the area, reduce the cell-harming effects of sunlight, cut inflammation and improve the communication between cells (cell signaling) that keeps them young and healthy.

New study: Researchers at Harvard Medical School analyzed the diets of 681 older men, including 222 with AMD. The men who had eaten two or more servings a week of fatty fish were at a 22% lower risk of AMD. In a similar study, scientists at the Centre of Vision Research at the University of Sydney found a 40% reduction in AMD risk for those eating fatty fish once a week.

What to do: Consider a salmon steak for lunch or dinner, once or twice a week. Or take a daily fish oil supplement, which are widely available.

➤ **Minimize refined carbohydrates.** Call it a nutritional whiteout—sugar, white flour and other refined carbohydrates can make it very hard to see anything...

New study: Researchers at the Laboratory for Vision Research at Tufts University in Boston analyzed dietary and health data from more than 4,000 people. They found those eating a diet including a lot of foods high in refined carbohydrates such as sugar, white bread and white rice

See Your Doctor If...

If you suspect you have AMD—if normally straight objects appear bent or wavy...if a spot appears in the center of your vision...if you cover up one eye, and what you're looking at changes size or color—see an optometrist or ophthalmologist.

If their examination indicates you have the disease, they should take another test (often given by a retinal specialist) called a *fluorescein angiography*, which indicates whether you have the "dry" or "wet" type of the disease.

Ninety percent of people have the slow-progressing dry type.

However, 10% have the quick-advancing "wet" type, with leaky blood vessels in the macula. It may require surgery.

were more likely to develop advanced, vision-robbing AMD. In fact, the more refined carbs they ate, the higher the risk.

"Many cases of AMD could be prevented if individuals ate a diet rich in unrefined carbohydrates," such as whole wheat, oats and brown rice, says Allen Taylor, PhD, director of the Laboratory.

➤ **Exercise your focus.** "The macula is responsible for sharp, focused vision," says Dr. Jebrock. "Since it is not functioning properly, you want to do something that stimulates and improves the focusing mechanism of the eye."

To do that, look at a near object for a few moments—such as your fingertips—and then switch your attention to a far object—such as trees in the distance. Do this several times a day, every day.

➤ **Wear UV-blocking sunglasses.** "Ultraviolet rays from sunlight can damage the macula," says Dr. Jebrock. When buying sunglasses, look for a pair with a UV400 rating, which means it blocks out most of the damaging rays.

🕐 Super-Quick Fix

➤ **How to read with advanced AMD.** If your AMD is advanced, Dr. Jebrock suggests getting reading glasses with a +5 to +10 magnification and holding the print about three to four inches away from your eyes.

"It's not normal vision, but it's better than not being able to see anything at all," he says.

MEMORY LOSS

Retain Your Brain

It is no longer necessary to accept 'senior moments,' waning memory or poor memory as an inevitable part of growing older," says 84-year-old Harry Lorayne, memory-training specialist and author of *Ageless Memory: Simple Secrets for Keeping Your Brain Young* (Black Dog and Leventhal). "You can acquire a memory you never imagined you could have—and you can have it for the rest of your life! In fact, you can *quickly and simply* learn to regain the memory you had when you were younger—and surpass it."

"People who commit to a four-pronged approach of improving memory and keeping the brain young—memory exercises, a healthy brain diet, physical conditioning and stress reduction—report almost *immediate* results," agrees Gary Small, MD, director of the UCLA Center on Aging and the Semel Institute Memory Research Center and coauthor of *The Memory Prescription* (Hyperion).

Here are the best high-speed recommendations for boosting memory from these and other experts...

➤ **Five rules for remembering names.** "The universal complaint about memory is not being able to remember names," says Lorayne.

Doodle Your Way to Better Recall

When you doodle in a meeting or while you're on the phone, you're inattentive and less likely to remember what went on.

No, say scientists—to doodle is good for the old noodle.

New study: Researchers at the University of Plymouth in England asked 40 people to listen to a two-and-half minute tape of names of people and the places they were traveling to, such as a party. Twenty participants were asked to shade in spaces on a piece of paper while they listened, without paying any attention to neatness—in other words, to doodle.

After listening to the tape, both the doodlers and non-doodlers were asked to recall the names of people who were going to a party and the names of places.

The doodlers recalled an average of 7.5 names and places; the non-doodlers, 5.8.

Why it works: "If you're doing a boring task, such as listening to a dull telephone conversation, you may start to daydream," says Jackie Andrade, PhD, a study researcher. "A simple task such as doodling may stop the daydreaming without affecting listening. This study suggests that doodling may be something you can do to help keep you on track with a boring task—and not an unnecessary distraction that you should resist."

"But that's a lie! Most of us don't forget a name—because we never remembered it in the first place. The name goes in one ear and—zip—right out the other." *So, says Lorayne, the first rule of remembering a name is…*

Rule #1. Be sure you hear the name. "Don't think it's embarrassing to say, 'I'm sorry, but I didn't hear your name—could you tell it to me again.' No, you're flattering the person by paying attention to their most prized possession—their name."

Rule #2. Try to spell the name. "I don't care if the name is 'Jones' or 'Smith'—it's not silly to ask. Say, 'Do you spell that 'S-m-i-t-h.' By applying this second rule, you enforce the first—because you have to hear the name to spell the name."

Rule #3. Make a remark about the name. "Any remark will do—because it's reinforcing the impression," says Lorayne. "Perhaps the person's name is 'Bentavena.' Well, you could say, 'Gee, I went to school with a guy named Carl Bentavena. Could that be a relative?' "

Rule #4. Use the name in your conversation with the person. "For example, after the individual makes a comment, you could say, 'Gee, Mr. Bentavena, that's an interesting thought.' "

Rule #5. Use the name when you say good-bye. "Say, 'Mr. Bentavena, it was a pleasure meeting you.' "

"I've been doing memory training for over six decades and have taught millions of people—and this fast and simple method works!" says Lorayne.

▶ **Your mitochondria and your memory.** "Brain cells need fuel to run memory—and that fuel is supplied by mitochondria, tiny energy factories inside each cell," says John Neustadt, ND, a naturopathic doctor, and medical director of Montana Integrative Medicine. "Studies in laboratory animals show that when mitochondria are *damaged*, memory *decreases*—but when mitochondria are *repaired*, memory *increases*."

Mitochondria are damaged by oxidation, a kind of internal rust. Oxidation is caused by aging…by a diet with too many refined carbohydrates and too much saturated fat…by pollution and other environmental insults…and by many other causes. *The two most important nutrients to prevent and repair the oxidation of mitochondria are…*

Do You Think Memory Worsens with Age? Then Yours Probably Will!

Are you convinced that memory decays with age? Then yours will probably decay!

That was the unusual result of a study on memory from researchers at North Carolina State University. "We found that people aged sixty and older perform more poorly on a memory test—if they were told beforehand that older people do poorly on that type of memory test," says Tom Hess, PhD, a study researcher. "But when more positive views of aging were reinforced prior to the memory test, older people had significantly higher levels of memory performance."

Bottom line: "Please stop thinking that your mental capacity and your memory capabilities must inevitably decline as you move through middle age and beyond," says Lorraine. "Robert Frost, Georgia O'Keeffe, Pablo Casals, Helen Hayes, Albert Einstein, George Burns and Carl Sandburg are just a few people who would tell you that it isn't so. They had highly functional memories and agile minds through their 'golden years'—and there is no reason for you to accept a steep decline in your ability to remember as an inevitable part of growing older."

● **Acetyl-L-Carnitine (ALCAR).** This nutrient crosses the blood-brain barrier and improves mitochondrial functioning in the brain, says Dr. Neustadt. "It also decreases age-related damage to the hippocampus, the brain structure responsible for forming memories."

● **Alpha lipoic acid (ALA).** Research shows that combining ALCAR with ALA boosts memory, says Dr. Neustadt.

Product: The supplement MitoForte delivers ALCAR, ALA and several other mitochondria-protecting nutrients and herbs, such as N-Acetyl-Cysteine (NAC), the B-vitamin biotin and the herb turmeric, says Dr. Neustadt.

Suggested intake: 2 to 4 capsules daily.

Rapid Resource: You can order MitoForte at *www.nbihealth.com*, call 800-624-1416 or e-mail *info@nbihealth.com*. Address: Nutritional Biochemistry Inc., 1184 North 15th Ave., Suite 1, Bozeman, MT 59715.

Also helpful: Another memory-enhancing nutritional supplement is the antioxidant Pycnogenol, derived from the bark of the French maritime pine tree. *New study:* Australian researchers studied 101 people aged 60 to 85, dividing them into two groups. For three months, one group took 150 milligrams (mg) of Pycnogenol daily and the other group took a placebo. After three months, those taking the Pycnogenol had lowered levels of oxidative damage to nerve cells. They also had a significant improvement in memory tests. The group taking a placebo didn't have a decrease in oxidative damage or an increase in memory. The research was presented at the World Congress on Oxidants and Antioxidants in Biology.

➤ **Feed your memory.** "Food is like a pharmaceutical compound that affects the brain," says Fernando Gomez-Pinilla, PhD, a professor of neurosurgery and physiological science at UCLA who analyzed the results of 160 studies on food and aging, and published the results in the journal *Nature Reviews Neuroscience. Some of the best foods for memory...*

● **Salmon, walnuts and flax seeds** are uniquely rich in the omega-3 fatty acids that can improve memory. Omega-3 fatty acids keep the synapses that link brain cells more flexible, says Dr. Gomez-Pinilla. (Based on his findings, he now eats salmon three times a week.) Other good sources of these fats include halibut, shrimp, cod, tuna, kale, collard greens and Brussels sprouts.

● **Spinach and orange juice** are rich in folic acid, a B-vitamin that can help prevent

Speed Healing Success

The Nutritional Secrets of a Memory Champion

Chester Santos can memorize 99 faces and names, two decks of shuffled playing cards or a sequence of 1,000 random numbers—in a matter of minutes. He recently won the National Memory Championship, a yearly competition. What's the secret of his success?

Spending at least two to three hours a day practicing memory-enhancing exercises. And taking nutritional supplements.

"I strongly believe that taking the right vitamins and supplements, coupled with the proper mental training, can help to dramatically improve memory," says Santos. "That's what I've done for years to help me achieve greatness in the field of competitive memory. Every day, I take a fish oil supplement for the omega-3 fatty acids, which helps to improve brain function, a B complex vitamin for concentration and a daily multivitamin to help maintain my overall health."

memory loss in aging, he says. Folic acid supplements have also been shown to reduce age-related memory decline. Other good sources of folic acid include folic acid-enriched foods (such as breakfast cereals, bread and pasta), dark green leafy vegetables (such as collard greens, mustard greens, turnip greens and broccoli), legumes (such as dried beans and peas) and peanuts, asparagus, avocado and strawberries.

Red flag: Researchers in England found a link between high consumption of the soy product tofu and poor memory in people over 65.

➤ **Reduce calories, increase memory.** German researchers found that when people cut their calorie intake by 30% they performed better on memory tests.

New study: The researchers studied 50 people aged 60 or over, dividing them into three groups. One group cut calories by 30%. One group cut saturated fat by 20%. A third group didn't make any dietary changes. After three months, the calorie-cutting group had a 20% improvement in scores on a memory test. There were no significant changes in the other two groups.

"These results provide the first experimental evidence that caloric restriction improves memory in the elderly," say the researchers, in the *Proceedings of the National Academy of Sciences.*

What to do: The best way to cut calories is to emphasize low-calorie, filling foods such as fruits, vegetables, whole-grains and legumes, and to minimize high-calorie, low-fiber foods such as meats, dairy products and processed snacks and baked goods, says Jeffrey Novick, MS, RD, director of nutrition at the Pritikin Longevity Center in Aventura, Florida.

Example: "The most useful way to think about calories is to think of foods in terms of *calories per pound,* says Novick. Of course, you wouldn't eat a pound or broccoli or a pound of butter. *But a pound-for-pound comparison between the two foods shows just how many calories each packs* and the differences between them…

- 100 to 200 calories per pound—vegetables

- 200 to 300 calories per pound—fresh fruits

- 500 calories per pound—whole grains and legumes

- 600 to 650 calories per pound—lean proteins, such as seafood and the white meat of chicken

- 1,000 calories per pound—fatty proteins, such as a steak served at a restaurant specializing in "premium" steaks

- 1,200 to 1,500 calories per pound—refined, processed carbohydrates, such as breads, bagels and crackers

• 2,000 calories per pound—junk food, such as sugary cookies made with white flour

• 2,800 calories per pound—nuts and seeds

• 4,000 calories per pound—oils and fats

➤ **Relax to remember.** "Chronic mental stress triggers the release of stress hormones that cause wear and tear on the brain—and on memory," says Dr. Small. He suggests practicing a relaxation technique daily to reduce stress and protect memory.

Here are Dr. Small's instructions for an easy, effective stress-relieving relaxation technique…

• **Tighten and release muscle unwinder.** Lie down or sit in a comfortable chair. While the rest of your body remains comfortable and relaxed, slowly clench your right fist as tightly as you can. Focus on the tension in your fist, hand and forearm. After five seconds, relax your hand and let your fingers and wrist go limp. Notice the contrast between the sensation of tension and relaxation in those muscles, and hold that tension for five seconds. Then let your arm straighten and drop gently to your side. Feel the sensation of your muscles relaxing. Repeat the exercise for your left side. Continue this sequence of tensing and releasing different muscles groups throughout your body, including shoulders, abdomen, buttocks, thighs and legs.

Also helpful: "The other way to decrease stress is to become more realistic about what you can and can't take on," he says. "Many people commit to too much. Delegate some responsibilities."

➤ **Ask your doctor about *donepezil* (Aricept).** Aricept is typically used to slow memory loss and mental decline in people with Alzheimer's. But Dr. Small and other researchers at UCLA decided to test the drug on people with mild, age-related memory loss. They divided them into two groups. One group took the drug, one group took a placebo and both groups had PET scans at the beginning and at the end of the 18-month study.

Results: The brains of those taking Aricept had an increased rate of metabolism (and sign of health) and looked more normal than those taking the placebo, says Dr. Small.

Treatment of early symptoms of memory loss may protect the brain and help people with mild, age-related memory impairment, says Dr. Small. Talk to your doctor about whether Aricept is right for you.

SPEED LIMIT Are Common Drugs Sapping Your Memory?

Anticholinergic medications relax the "smooth muscles" that line various systems in the body, such as the circulatory system, the respiratory tract, the digestive tract and the genitourinary tract. They are prescribed for high blood pressure, heartburn, urinary disorders, COPD (chronic obstructive pulmonary disease), asthma, Parkinson's disease and many other health problems. They work by blocking the action of the neurotransmitter *acetylcholine*, which relays messages between brain cells (neurons).

Examples: *Ipratropium* (Atrovent) for chronic obstructive pulmonary disease (COPD), *ranitidine* (Zantac) for heartburn, *nifedipine* (Procardia) for high blood pressure and *tolterodine* (Detrol) for incontinence.

These drugs may also block memory.

New study: For one year, doctors in the Yale University Department of Medicine studied more than 500 healthy men age 65 and older with high blood pressure who were taking one or more anti-cholinergic medications. They found that regular use of the medications had detrimental affects on memory and the ability to perform the tasks of daily living, such as managing finances...that there were significant declines in memory over the year of the study... and that the more anti-cholinergic medicines a man was taking, the worse the decline.

Physicians should take the possibility of memory loss into account when prescribing anti-cholinergic medication, says Jack Tsao, MD, associate professor of neurology at Uniformed Services University in Bethesda, Maryland, a doctor who has conducted research on anti-cholinergics and memory. Talk to your doctor about whether you're at risk.

▶ **Walk away from poor memory.** "A convincing body of scientific evidence indicates that regular aerobic conditioning not only improves your memory performance in the short run, but also may delay the rate at which your brain ages," says Dr. Small.

Standout scientific evidence: Australian researchers studied 138 people aged 50 or over with mild memory problems, dividing them into two groups. One group was asked to exercise 50 minutes, three times a week, for six months. (Most of the participants walked.) The other group didn't exercise. From the start of the study and over the next 18 months, the researchers gave the participants standard memory tests. After 18 months, the exercisers scored far higher on the tests than the non-exercisers.

This is the first study to show that exercise improves memory in older adults with mild memory impairment, say the researchers. They note that the power of exercise to strengthen memory continued even after the exercise "intervention" had stopped. They also note that regular exercise has other benefits, such as helping lift depression, preventing falls and strengthening the heart. The study appeared in the *Journal of the American Medical Association.*

In another study, researchers at the University of Illinois at Urbana-Champaign found that older people (aged 59 to 81) who are more physically fit also have bigger *hippocampi*—the part of the brain that plays a key role in forming memories. They also have better *spatial memory*—your ability to remember where you are, where you've been, and how to get from place to place.

"This is a really significant finding because it supports the notion that your lifestyle choices and behavior may influence brain shrinkage in old age," says Kirk Erickson, PhD, a study researcher. "Basically, if you stay fit, you retain key regions of your brain involved in memory and learning."

"Impairment of spatial memory is one of a number of reasons why older people end up losing their independence," adds Art Kramer, PhD, another study researcher. "Here is yet more evidence that becoming fit has a direct effect on how well you're going to live your life."

What to do: Walk briskly a minimum of 45 minutes a day, three days a week.

In a study published in the *British Journal of Sports Medicine*, Drs. Erickson and Kramer found that people who walked that amount improved their ability to perform so-called "executive function" tasks—everyday or "working" memory, planning, scheduling and multitasking. Regular, moderate aerobic exercise can "reliably reverse age-related mental decline," they write.

➤ **Computerize your brain.** A common computer term is RAM, or *random access memory*. But if you use your computer to *improve* your memory, there might not be anything random about it, say scientists.

New study: Researchers from the USC Davis School of Gerontology and the Mayo Clinic studied 487 people over the age of 65, dividing them into two groups. One group used the "Brain Fitness" memory-training computer program for 40 hours over two months. The other group watched educational DVDs, followed by quizzes.

After two months, those using the Brain Fitness program had an increase in "information processing" ability of 131%—and processed information twice as fast as the group that didn't use the program. On average, the memory and attentiveness of the Brain Fitness group was the same as people 10 years younger. Many of the participants reported improvement in remembering names or understanding conversations in noisy restaurants, say the researchers.

"The changes we saw in the Brain Fitness group were remarkable," says Elizabeth Zelinski, PhD, a study leader. "What the results mean is that cognitive decline is no longer an inevitable part of aging."

"This study has profound personal implications for aging baby boomers and their parents," says Joe Coughlin, PhD, director of the AgeLab at the Massachusetts Institute of Technology. "They now have tools for maintaining an independent future—all the great and little things we call life."

The study was reported in the *Journal of the American Geriatrics Society.*

How it works: The program features six computer-based exercises that the company says

are "designed to be very easy to use, even for computer novices."

The exercises improve "working memory," explains Dr. Zelinski—the type of memory that retains information (new names, a shopping list, directions from the airport to your niece's wedding) long enough to either act on it or transfer it to long-term memory.

It also improves "narrative memory"—the details of the stories told to you every day by a spouse, coworkers, friends and teacher. Better narrative memory allows you to engage confidently in new and enjoyable activities, such as taking a class or traveling.

And the exercises are designed to increase the levels of *neuromodulators*—neurotransmitters and hormones that keep the mind sharp but typically decline with age.

Rapid Resource: A version of "Brain Fitness" is now sold as brainHQ by Posit Science at *www. brainHQ.com* or call 800-291-2826. Address: Posit Science Corporation, 160 Pine St., Suite 200, San Francisco, CA 94111. Other apps and software programs to help boost brain power include Lumosity (*www.lumosity.com*), VigorousMind (*www. vigorousmind.com*), and CogniFit (*www.cognifit.com*).

➤ **Quilt yourself a better memory.** Participating in crafts can prevent or delay memory loss, say scientists.

New study: Researchers at the Mayo Clinic studied 1,300 people aged 70 to 89, some with diagnosed memory loss. They asked the participants about their mental habits from when they were 50 to 65 years old. And they found that those who participated in activities such as crafting (quilting and pottery), reading books, playing games and using the computer had a 40% lower risk of memory loss.

Red flag: People who watched TV for more than seven hours a day were 50% more likely to experience memory loss.

"This study is exciting because it demonstrates that aging does not need to be a passive process," says Yonas Geda, MD, a study researcher. "By simply engaging in mental 'exercise,' you can protect your brain against future memory loss."

MENOPAUSE PROBLEMS

Change for the Better

Forty-three million American women are postmenopausal—and they'll be joined by 17 million of their sisters by 2020. In fact, by 2015, nearly 50% of women in the US will be menopausal.

Perimenopause (the time immediately before menopause) usually starts in a woman's 40s, when the length of the menstrual cycle starts to change and then there are missed menses. You're "officially" menopausal 12 months after your final period—on average, that's around the age of 51.

But whenever you enter menopause—you're not dealing with a disease that requires a cure, says Tori Hudson, ND, medical director of A Woman's Time clinic in Portland, Oregon, and author of *Women's Encyclopedia of Natural Medicine: Alternative Therapies and Integrative Medicine for Total Health and Wellness* (McGraw-Hill).

"Except when triggered by surgery, medications or radiation, menopause is a normal, natural event of aging," she says. "It is not a disease process. It is not a sign of impending disability or frailty. It can be—and often is—the beginning of a new phase of life, with new options, new learning opportunities and new adventures."

However: "Even though it is a normal process of aging, the natural transition from the reproductive years to the postmenopausal years is not necessarily a smooth one," says Dr. Hudson.

As the hormones estrogen and progesterone fluctuate and drop with perimenopause, you can start to have hot flashes, insomnia, mood swings, poor concentration and other symptoms. The intensity of those symptoms can range from the mild (one hot flash per month, for example) to the severe (one hot flash per hour).

For 75% to 90% of women, symptoms last four to seven years and then disappear. For 10 to 25%, they persist. *For 100%, relief is within reach...*

➤ **Cool off your hot flashes.** About 85% of perimenopausal and menopausal women in the US report hot flashes—a wavelike sensation of heat over the body, particularly the upper torso, face and head. (When they happen at night, drenching you in perspiration, they're called *night sweats*.)

Experts still don't know what causes hot flashes. But they do know safe, self-care methods that can reduce their intensity and severity or even stop them completely.

● **Black cohosh.** This is the best-researched herb for hot flashes and night sweats, with the most positive therapeutic results, says Dr. Hudson.

Recent study: Chinese doctors studied 244 menopausal women for three months, giving them a black cohosh extract or tibolone, a synthetic steroid with estrogen-like effects. (Tibolone is used in 70 countries to treat the symptoms of menopause, but has not been approved by the FDA for use in the US.)

After three months, the women taking the black cohosh extract had an average 68% drop in their "Kupperman Score," a standard measurement of menopause symptoms.

That means after taking black cohosh extract, they had fewer and less intense hot flashes...fewer and less intense night sweats... were less nervous and irritable...were less depressed...and their concentration improved. Tibolone produced similar benefits. But it also

But Didn't That Big Study Show Black Cohosh Doesn't Work?

Wrong *form* of black cohosh. Wrong *dose* of black cohosh.

Unfortunately, that's what was used in a major study sponsored by the National Institutes of Health to find out if the herb black cohosh (*Cimicifuga recemosa*) really works to reduce hot flashes and night sweats in menopausal women, says Francis Brinker, ND, a naturopathic doctor, clinical assistant professor at the Program for Integrative Medicine at the University of Arizona College of Medicine and author of *Complex Herbs—Complete Medicines* (Eclectic Medical Publications).

The one-year study, involving 351 women who were perimenopausal or menopausal concluded "Black cohosh…shows little potential as an important therapy for relief" of hot flashes and night sweats.

But says Dr. Brinker, rather than using Remifemin—the extract of black cohosh proven effective in dozens of other studies—the researchers used an entirely different type of extract (much higher in ethanol), at a 20 to 40 times higher dosage.

"When you increase ethanol in an herbal extract, you increase the amount of resinous components from the herb and decrease the amount of water-soluble components," says Dr. Brinker. "Well, the active components of black cohosh are not known. So by changing the composition of the extract, you could easily change the herb's activity in the body—and its effectiveness.

"As for dosage—you would think that a dosage that was twenty to forty times higher would be *more* effective, but that's not how pharmacology works. Sometimes a small dose works, but a larger dose has the *opposite* effect.

"The form of an herb matters and the dose of an herb matters—and sometimes you can give the wrong form and the wrong dose and make the herb ineffective."

produced vaginal bleeding, breast pain and abdominal pain.

"The efficacy of black cohosh is as good as tibolone for the treatment of menopausal complaints, even for moderate to severe symptoms," say the researchers. "Black cohosh is an excellent option for treatment of menopausal conditions."

Product: This study used the form of black cohosh that has been tested successfully in more than 90 scientific studies—Remifemin, from Enzymatic Therapy. It's available at *www.enzymatictherapy.com*, or call 800-783-2286.

Suggested intake: Follow the dosage recommendation on the label, says Holly Lucille, ND, a naturopathic physician in Los Angeles—one tablet in the morning and one in the evening, with water.

Why it works: For many years, doctors theorized that black cohosh extract reduced hot flashes because it contained *phytoestrogens*—estrogen-like plant compounds. But black cohosh does not appear to be estrogenic whatsoever, say researchers at the University of Illinois in Chicago, who analyzed the estrogenic properties of the herb. Now, that same team of researchers, led by Z. Jim Wang, PhD, has discovered the way that black cohosh might work.

Your brain has opiate receptors—chemical sensors that respond to opiates such as morphine and endorphins, Dr. Wang explains. When the opiates attach to their receptors, they trigger key brain functions, such as the regulation of pain, appetite and body temperature.

"We found that elements in black cohosh extract bind to the 'mu' opiate receptor," says Dr. Wang. "This particular opiate receptor system affects several aspects of female reproductive neuroendocrinology, such as the levels of sex hormones and neurotransmitters that are important for temperature regulation."

In other words, black cohosh might work in your brain to correct the drop in neurotransmitters that disrupts your personal thermostat.

⚠ *Caution:* In rare cases, black cohosh may affect the liver. If you have a known liver disease such as chronic hepatitis C, or you consume three or more alcoholic drinks a day, you probably shouldn't use black cohosh, says Dr. Hudson—or, if you do, a doctor should regularly test your liver enzymes to check that the herb is not starting to cause damage.

● **Siberian Rhubarb Extract.** This herbal extract has been used as a menopause-soothing folk remedy in Russia and as an over-the-counter remedy in Europe.

Standout studies: In a study published in the medical journal *Menopause*, 109 perimenopausal women took either the extract or a placebo for three months. Those taking the extract had fewer hot flashes and night sweats, better sleep, less depression, anxiety and irritability, less fatigue, more sexual satisfaction, less vaginal dryness, and less bleeding and spotting.

Over the next eight months, many of the women on the extract continued to take it—and many of the women on the placebo switched to the extract. Those already taking the extract experienced a "further decrease" in their symptoms—and, after four months on the extract, those who previously had been taking the placebo had the same degree of relief.

The extract, concluded the German researchers, is "effective and safe in the long-term

Are Bioidentical Hormones Safer?

Suzanne Somers takes them—and says they turn menopause into the "sexy years." A doctor's book claims they're a "miracle" for menopause. Another physician says they will turn you into a "Natural Superwoman." What's behind all the ballyhoo?

Bioidentical hormones. One hormone that is *not* "bioidentical" is the estrogen in the estrogen replacement (Premarin) that's been marketed for more than 50 years—it's derived from the urine of pregnant mares.

But when the Women's Health Initiative study showed that hormone replacement therapy (HRT) with "conjugated equine estrogens" and synthetic progesterone increased the risk of heart disease, stroke and breast cancer—many women started looking for alternatives to reduce the symptoms of menopause. One of them was bioidentical hormone replacement therapy (BHRT).

BHRT uses synthetically created versions of human estrogens—a combination of *estriol* (a hormone that is elevated during pregnancy), along with *estradiol* or *estrone*. Bioidentical forms of progesterone, testosterone and dehydroepiandrosterone (DHEA) are sometimes included.

And many women consider them safe. In one survey, 71% said that BHRT has fewer risks than HRT—or no risks at all. And 62% said they were just as or more effective than HRT for managing menopausal symptoms.

Studies show BHRT *can* work just like HRT to reduce hot flashes, improve mood and ease vaginal dryness. *But they may not be any safer...*

Red flag: "There is no scientific evidence that bioidentical estradiol has a better safety profile than non-bioidentical estrogens," says Dr. Hudson. "For example, research shows that bioidentical estradiol is no safer in breast tissue than any other kind of estrogen.

"I think health practitioners need to be cautious, careful and judicious with *all* hormone replacement therapy—HRT and BHRT. We need to always use the lowest doses to accomplish whatever therapeutic objective we're trying to accomplish."

treatment of menopausal symptoms in perimeno-pausal women."

In another study from Germany, published in *Alternative Therapies in Health and Medicine*, 252 perimenopausal and menopausal women took the extract—and after six months, the severity of their symptoms was cut by 56%.

Product: The extract used in the studies—ERr 731—is marketed in the U.S. as Estrovera, from Metagenics (*www.metagenics.com*).

Suggested intake: "Estrovera is a safe and effective product for managing menopausal symptoms," says the Cleveland Clinic, adding, "...the only intervention to achieve similar response rates has been treatment with estrogen itself." They advise taking one tablet daily.

Why it works: Compounds in the extract (glycosylated hydroxystilbenes) activate estrogen receptors on cells, according to a study by German investigators in the journal *Phytomedicine*.

⚠ **Caution:** For maximum safety, women with a history of breast or endometrial cancer shouldn't use Estrovera, says the Cleveland Clinic.

• **Pycnogenol.** Doctors in Taiwan studied 155 menopausal women, dividing them into two groups. One group took Pycnogenol—a potent antioxidant derived from pine bark. The other group took a placebo.

After six months, there was no change in the placebo group. But the women taking pycnogenol had an average decrease in the severity and frequency of hot flashes—and also an overall reduction in other symptoms of menopause, such as insomnia, fatigue, headache, vaginal dryness, memory and concentration problems, and low libido. (There was also a drop in blood pressure and "bad" LDL cholesterol—important benefits for menopausal women, who have an increased risk for heart disease.)

The Jury Is Still Out on Soy

The best diet to help ease menopause symptoms is rich in whole, natural and unprocessed foods, with an emphasis on fruits, vegetables, whole grains, beans, seeds, nuts and healthy fats, and low in saturated fats, fried foods, white flour, alcohol, sugar and salt, says Dr. Hudson.

But should it also include generous amounts of soy, which are high in plant compounds called phytoestrogens (specifically *isoflavones*) that might ease menopausal symptoms?

"There are hundreds of studies on soy and dozens on hot flashes, some showing effects and others not—making it difficult to make a conclusion," says Dr. Hudson.

She cites three major reviews of isoflavones and menopause symptoms—one looking at 10 studies, one looking at 25 studies and one report from the North American Menopause Society. None of them found convincing evidence that soy worked for menopause symptoms. "I'm sure the three reviews are disappointing news for advocates of soy," she says.

However, she adds, for some women, soy protein and soy isoflavones can be helpful in reducing the frequency and severity of hot flashes.

Best: If you choose to increase soy foods or take soy beverages, powders or supplements, a reasonable approach would be to ingest a daily level of isoflavones that does not exceed the amount consumed in ethnic diets that contain high amounts of isoflavones, says Dr. Hudson.

Suggested intake: 50 to 150 mg of isoflavones per day for adults.

Example: ¼ cup roasted soy nuts (60 mg), ½ cup tofu (35 mg), 1 cup soy milk (30 mg).

Why it works: Pycnogenol increases circulation and decreases inflammation, both of which could help ease menopause symptoms, say the researchers.

Suggested intake: The women in the study used 100 milligrams (mg), twice daily.

➤ **Sleep through the night.** If you're tossing and turning at night, you should turn toward help. "It's crucial to stop insomnia as soon as it starts in perimenopause or menopause, because poor sleep leads to fatigue and depression, which quickly worsens a woman's quality of life," says Dr. Hudson. *There are several types of insomnia that can bother a menopausal woman...*

• **Waking up with night sweats.** If that's the case, try black cohosh, says Dr. Hudson.

Also helpful: Another possible product to use is Women's Phase II, from Vitanica. It contains ingredients a study shows can reduce hot flashes and night sweats *and* improve sleep— dong quai root, licorice root, burdock root, motherwort leaf and wild yam root. It's available at *www.vitanica.com*, or call 800-572-4712.

• **Difficulty falling asleep.** This is the easiest kind of insomnia to clear up, says Dr. Hudson.

She recommends that about 30 minutes before bedtime you try either valerian (1 to 2 capsules, or 1 to 2 teaspoons of a liquid extract)... melatonin (start at 2 mg and increase up to 10 mg)...L-tryptophan (1,000 mg)...or 5-HTP (100 to 300 mg, 45 minutes before bedtime).

"It's a trial-and-error process," she says. "Usually one of them will do the trick."

• **For insomnia and depression.** 5-HTP and L-tryptophan boost mood-elevating serotonin levels, so either supplement is a good choice if you have insomnia and depression, says Dr. Hudson.

• **For insomnia and anxiety.** Valerian is calming and is a good choice if you have insomnia and anxiety.

• **Difficulty staying asleep or waking early and not being able to go back to sleep.** If you wake up and can't fall back to sleep, you might try an over-the-counter medication such as Tylenol PM or Benadryl.

See Your Doctor If...

The start of perimenopause is an important time for a comprehensive health and lifestyle evaluation, says Dr. Hudson. "A thorough medical history, complete physical exam and selected tests, depending on your age, your symptoms and other medical problems, should be done by a licensed healthcare practitioner."

What about self-care and medical care for menopause symptoms?

"Most women who are perimenopausal can feel comfortable starting on their own with herbs and nutritional supplements for the relief of menopause symptoms," says Dr. Hudson. (A healthy diet and regular exercise are also crucial.) "If you don't find adequate relief, see a licensed primary care provider—such as a naturopathic doctor, medical doctor, osteopathic doctors, nurse-practitioners or physician's assistant—who is educated in the range of options for menopause, and not just in conventional HRT."

If you're chronically anxious or depressed, you might take an herbal preparation during the day, such as kava, which a study shows can help alleviate these emotions in perimenopausal women. Dr. Hudson recommends 100 to 210 mg of an extract standardized to 70% kavapyrones.

However: These two types of insomnia are difficult to treat with self-care and require medical attention, says Dr. Hudson.

She sometimes uses hormonal replacement therapy...sometimes tests neurotransmitters and then treats with specific amino acids that balance neurotransmitters...and sometimes tests levels of the stress hormone cortisol, and, if it's high at night, uses intensive natural treatments to lower it.

"These aren't self-care methods, but they can really work," she says.

▶ **The best treatment for vaginal dryness.** "Vaginal dryness, vaginal thinning—with irritation, itching and pain with vaginal sex—are very common problems for menopausal women, but they usually don't become troublesome until several years after menopause," says Dr. Hudson.

What happens: When estrogen levels decline, the vulva loses its collagen, fat and water-retaining ability and becomes flattened, thin and dry, and loses tone. The vagina also shortens and narrows, and the vaginal walls become thinner and less elastic.

Best: "The remedy that works the quickest and the best is prescription vaginal estrogen—it's a miraculous medicine," says Dr. Hudson. It comes in creams, gels, suppositories and vaginal rings. Dr. Hudson favors bioidentical estriol, which she says has more affinity to vaginal tissue than other estrogens. "A common prescription is one milligram of estriol per one gram of cream. One gram of cream is inserted in the vagina daily as a loading dose, then twice a week as a maintenance program." Talk to your doctor about this treatment.

A possible alternative—particularly for breast cancer survivors concerned about exposure to estrogen—is the over-the-counter product Replens, a vaginal moisturizer. "It has less of an effect than vaginal estrogen, but still significantly improves the elasticity and integrity of vaginal tissue," says Dr. Hudson. Replens is widely available.

Another possible choice is an all-natural vaginal moisturizer—the Personal Moisturizer, from Emerita, available at *www.emerita.com*, or call 800-888-6041.

▶ **Lift depression, ease anxiety.** "Depression and anxiety are very common during perimenopause, especially in women with a history of depression," says Dr. Hudson. Irritability and mood swings are also common.

What happens: Fluctuating hormones impact brain chemistry, causing more intense emotional ups and downs.

An herbal formula that includes both the antidepressant herb St. John's Wort and black cohosh is a "perfect combo" for a woman with hot flashes and mild depression, says Dr. Hudson.

Product: Woman's Passage, from Vitanica, which includes hops extract (shown to reduce hot flashes and help with sleep), St. John's wort extract (for depression) and black cohosh extract (for hot flashes).

Another possible treatment, says Dr. Hudson, is SAMe (*S-adenosyl-methionine*), a natural compound that helps produce neurotransmitters (brain chemicals that regulate mood) and phospholipids (crucial factors in strong, well-functioning brain cells).

Suggested intake: 1,600 mg a day, in 800 mg or 400 mg doses.

⚠ *Caution:* Don't take St. John's wort or SAMe if you are taking a prescription antidepressant. The combination may cause too-high levels of serotonin, triggering a range of physical, mental and emotional symptoms

For anxiety, Dr. Hudson suggests black cohosh and one or more of several anti-anxiety compounds, including...

- **GABA** (gamma-aminobutyric acid), a calming biochemical, which works in a few days to a week or two, at a dose of 750 mg, twice a day.

- **Kava**, a calming herb, which works in a day, with a maximum daily intake of 210 mg.

- **Magnesium**, a mineral that balances the nervous system, at 300 mg a day.

- **B-complex vitamins**, which also balance the nervous system, using a B-50 or B-100 supplement.

- **Fish oil**, which has been shown to be effective for many emotional difficulties, including depression, anxiety and hostility—1 to 2 grams a day.

NAIL PROBLEMS

What do Jennifer Lopez, Kim Cattrall, Britney Spears, Gwen Stefani and Angelina Jolie have in common, besides gracing the pages of *People* magazine?

They all had their nails beautified by Roxanne Valinoti, a New York–based nail stylist and nail educator. Here's her best (and speediest) advice for preventing and reversing your nail problems. *Your fan base will appreciate the results...*

➤ **How to heal brittle, split, chipped or torn nails.** If your nails are thin—a genetically determined trait—they tend to tear more easily, like a sheet of paper, explains Valinoti. If your nails are thick (ditto on the genes), they tend to chip, split and break.

Problem: In either case, you might decide to buy a nail hardener to strengthen your nails. Which it does—by drying out the nail. And that's not a plus, because healthy nails require strength and flexibility, says Valinoti.

🕐 *Super-Quick Fix*

Solution: Oil the nail daily, which creates strong and supple nails.

Product: SolarOil, from Creative Nail Design. "It contains naturally light oils that penetrate the nail plate and provide more flexibility," says Valinoti.

What to do: "Apply the SolarOil every night," says Janet McCormick, MS, MNT, a manicurist and consultant in the nail industry (*www.medinail.com*) and author of *Spa Manicuring for the Salon and Spa* (Milady). "Use the pad of your thumb to dab the oil onto the area where the nail comes out of the cuticle. Then, moving your thumb pad across

the nail, rub the oil into the nail and around the sides.

"For brittle, split or torn nails, don't use a hardener. Oil, oil, oil."

Rapid Resource: You can find a salon or store that sells SolarOil and other Creative Nail Design products at the website *www.cnd.com*. On the Home Page, click "Products."

➤ **Stop nail polish from peeling, cracking, chipping and fading.** The most common complaint about nails? Polish doesn't last long enough, says Valinoti.

What happens: Did you or the manicurist soak your hands in soapy water before the polish? The water causes the nail to curve and swell, explains Valinoti. When the nail flattens into its normal shape after a day or two, the polish starts to loosen, peel, crack and chip—like wallpaper in a moist bathroom.

Better: Rather than soaking your hands in water, soak them in warm oil.

🕐 *Super-Quick Fix*

Also helpful: Before the application, use ScrubFresh from Creative Nail Design, which cleans and temporarily dehydrates the nail plate.

A Better Way to Remove Nail Polish

"Acetone is the fastest and safest solvent to remove nail polish remover," says Valinoti.

However: Using it more than once a week can dry out the nail plate, weakening nails.

Better: Dilute the acetone with one part water to 10 parts acetone, to prevent excessive drying. Add a drop of SolarOil to the mix.

Feed Your Nails

"Your nails reflect what's going on inside your body," says Jennifer Adler, MS, CN, a certified nutritionist and natural chef (*www.passionate nutrition.com*) in Seattle, Washington, and an adjunct faculty member at Bastyr University. "If you have a nutritional deficiency, it can show up on your nails. *Watch to watch out for...*

- *Flat, sharply angled or spooned nails.* This can indicate an iron deficiency, says Adler. *What to do:* Ask your doctor for a CBC (complete blood test) to see if you have an iron deficiency and need an iron supplement. If so, eat more red meat.

- *Soft or slow-growing nails.* This can indicate a generally low intake of minerals, says Adler. *What to do:* Eat more dark leafy green vegetables, such as kale.

- *Hangnails, inflamed cuticles, white spots.* These problems can signal low levels of zinc, a common deficiency, says Adler. *What to do:* For more zinc, eat more red meat, or snack on smoked oysters in olive oil on whole-wheat crackers.

- *Ridges.* Vertical ridges could be a sign of vitamin B deficiency—either from low intake, or from too much stress, which drains the body of Bs. *What to do:* Eat more whole grains and chicken. Take time to relax.

➤ **Help for hangnails.** "Nightly treatment with SolarOil can also help fix a hangnail," says McCormick.

Red flags: "Never clip into skin, which can trigger an immediate infection," she says. "Only clip dead skin. And never pull a hangnail—even ones around the cuticle and on the side of the nail that seem to scream out, 'Pull me, pull me!'

➤ **How to rid yourself of ridges.** "As we age, *keratin*—a protein in our skin, hair and nails—becomes drier," explains Valinoti. The nails literally shrink, which creates ridges. *There are several ways to solve the problem, she says...*

- **Use oil.** Daily application of SolarOil will help keep nails moist.

- **Use a ridge-filling base coat on the nail.** This will temporarily fill in the gaps.

Products: Get Even Ridge Filling Basecoat, from Zoya; Ridge Filling Basecoat, from Essie.

- **Buff.** Buffing can restore a smooth surface. But don't overbuff the natural nail plate, which could lead to thin, easily torn nails.

Best: Buff no more than once a month.

Try this: The new Glossing Buffer, from Creative Nail Designs, which gives an instant shine without thinning the nail.

➤ **How to stop biting your nails.** "I specialize in helping people break the habit of nail-biting," says McCormick. *She explains her method...*

Is Your Nail Salon Safe?

"There are several things you need to look for when you enter a nail salon, to make sure it's safe," says McCormick.

- No reuse of emery boards.
- All implements and tools are clean.
- No implements are removed from a drawer —they should be sterilized in an autoclave.
- The manicurist asks you to wash your hands prior to the service.
- No dust and clutter, in the waiting room or elsewhere.
- No manicures for under $18, which indicates cost-cutting and less-than-safe service.

Rapid Resource: For a state-by-state listing of salons approved by the Medical Nail Technicians association, visit the website *www. westerilize.com.*

1. **Find a nail technician who does acrylic or gel artificial nails,** which will help your nails grow out healthfully during this process. Have the technician put on the nails.

2. **Return every week for a manicure.** If you have a broken or rough area that is bothering you, you *will* put it in your mouth.

3. **Buy a squeeze-ball and always have it with you—**whenever you are tempted to bite your nails, squeeze the ball instead. Wear gloves while you drive—right-handed people bite the nails on their left hand, and visa versa.

4. **When you bite your nails, they grow faster because of the constant stimulation.** Once the growth has slowed down—which should take two weeks to one month—you can have the acrylic or gel nails removed. Continue to have regular manicures every other week.

5. **Start using a hardener.**

6. **Have a nail file at home with a 240 grit—**you can buy this at Sally's or another beauty supply store—and take care of every rough edge on your nails.

7. **Oil the nail nightly.**

"This is not a psychological problem," says McCormick. "It is simply a habit, probably formed from watching a parent bite his or her nails. You can break it by following the above protocol. It might not be easy. But it works."

OSTEOPOROSIS

You're a woman in her 40s or older—and you're bombarded with warnings about your *bones*.

Are they weakening? Disappearing? Are you among the tens of millions of Americans with osteoporosis, the bone-thinning disease that can snap hips and crush spines? Or the tens of millions who have *osteopenia*, the prelude to osteoporosis? Should you take more calcium? Or a drug to prevent or reverse the problem?

"The challenge for many women who want to prevent bone loss is finding helpful, accurate information," says Susan E. Brown, PhD, director of the Osteoporosis Project and author of *Better Bones, Better Body: A Comprehensive Self-Help Program for Preventing, Halting and Overcoming Osteoporosis* (McGraw-Hill, Second Edition). "Most experts communicate about osteoporosis from a fragmented, partial view—frequently determined by an agenda that is related to economic interests, such as those of the drug or dairy industry."

If you've been confused about osteoporosis, don't be discouraged, says Dr. Brown. The latest scientific information points to simple, natural methods as the best ways to improve your current bone health, prevent future bone loss and reduce your risk of osteoporosis.

➤ **The first step—clear up the confusion.** "The first step in preventing, halting and reversing osteoporosis naturally is finding out the *facts* about the disease," says Dr. Brown. *She debunks what she calls "The Top 10 Myths" about osteoporosis…*

Myth 1. Osteoporosis is the result of normal aging. Yes, most people lose bone mass as they age, says Dr. Brown. "But the remaining bone should be healthy and capable of constant self-repair. In osteoporosis, however, bone loss goes *beyond* that of normal aging—the bone becomes excessively fragile because of a loss of the mineral and protein matrix in the bone." These problems arise, she says, because of poor nutrition, lack of sunlight exposure, low vitamin D levels, high caffeine intake, lack of exercise, an acid-forming diet, the use of various medications and other bone-destroying factors. "Osteoporosis is *not* the result of normal aging," she emphasizes.

Myth 2. Osteoporosis is a disorder of the elderly. Even the young are not free from the specter of osteoporosis, says Dr. Brown. Among the groups most affected are those with anorexia, ballet dancers, athletes in training who undereat trying to stay slim, and people with celiac disease and other digestive disorders.

Myth 3. Women are predisposed to osteoporosis. An estimated 25% of men over 50 will have an osteoporosis-related fracture during their lifetimes.

Myth 4. Osteoporosis is caused by low estrogen. "Women all over the world experience a lowering of estrogen at menopause—but not all women develop osteoporosis," says Dr. Brown. "In fact, in various cultures postmenopausal women have lower estrogen levels than women in the US—yet they have less osteoporosis and fewer osteoporotic fractures."

Myth 5. Osteoporosis is caused by low calcium intake. "Because bone is largely composed of calcium, it might appear logical to link calcium intake to bone heath," says Dr. Brown. "But cross-cultural data show that most areas of the world have a *lower* calcium intake than we do—and lower rates of osteoporosis. In fact, the countries with the highest calcium intake have the highest hip fracture incidence!" Yes, *adequate* calcium is essential for the development and maintenance of bone, she says. But what is "adequate" depends on many other factors. They include the intake of other bone building nutrients...the intake of potentially calcium-depleting substances such as excess protein, salt, fat and sugar...the use of certain medications and of alcohol and tobacco...the level of physical activity, exposure to sunlight, environmental toxins and stress...and many other factors.

Myth 6. Osteoporosis is common all over the world. Osteoporosis occurs in some places much more than in others, just as the incidence of cancer, heart disease and diabetes varies from one culture to another, says Dr. Brown.

Myth 7. Osteoporosis is caused by faulty bone metabolism. "Osteoporosis is our body's intelligent response to long-term imbalances and stressors," says Dr. Brown. "The bone is a nutrient reservoir. When the blood is low in minerals, nutrients are drawn out of the bone to compensate. And when areas of the body's alkali reserves run low, compounds are drawn from the bone to buffer body acids and maintain our all-important pH balance. The immediate effect of drawing minerals and buffering compounds out of the bone is positive—blood mineral levels are returned to normal and pH balance is maintained. But if the mineral compounds are not redeposited into bone, osteoporosis ensues."

Myth 8. Osteoporosis fractures are caused by low bone density. "For decades, it was assumed that thin bone was the only cause of osteoporosis—that once bone reached a certain level of thinness, it fractured more easily," says Dr. Brown. "But now it's clear this isn't the full story. Low bone density by itself *does not* cause bone fractures—because many people with thin, osteoporotic bones don't have fractures, and more than half of fractures occur in people who aren't osteoporotic." So why do bones fracture?

"Because they have an inability to repair themselves properly from the micro-fractures that regularly occur due to normal stress and strain," says Dr. Brown. "And this self-repair is inhibited by many factors—including lack of nutrients and exercise, an acid-forming diet, various medications and an overload of chemicals and pollutants."

Myth 9. Once bone loss occurs, it's impossible to rebuild bone. "Bone is a dynamic, living tissue that constantly repairs itself," says Dr. Brown. "We have the capacity to rebuild lost bone mass."

Myth 10. Osteoporosis is a stand-alone medical condition that can happen to an otherwise healthy person. "Osteoporosis is not an isolated disease process," says Dr. Brown. "Lifelong patterns of poor eating, little exercise, smoking, surgeries and medication use and excessive stress take their toll on the whole body—including the bones."

Bottom line: "Bone loss is not a 'mistake' made by your body," she continues. "It's the long-term end result of a protective mechanism developed to maintain balance in the short-term. Bones only become fragile if they haven't been given the nutrients and support they need. If you eat an imbalanced diet and live an imbalanced lifestyle, you'll get imbalance in your body—and osteoporosis will develop as your body looks to your bones to supply the minerals and other nutrients it needs to sustain life.

"The opposite is true as well—the more balanced your diet and lifestyle, the more balanced your body will be, resulting in a decreased need to sacrifice bone for the maintenance of biochemical homeostasis."

Rapid Resource: For more information about osteoporosis, please visit the website *www.betterbones.com*. It includes Dr. Brown's blog (Osteo Blast), with the latest updates on the natural approach to retaining and building bone...a questionnaire to assess your fracture risk... studies that underlie Dr. Brown's approach to natural bone health...and many other features. Dr. Brown is also available for private consultations about your bone health, at 888-206-7119, or e-mail *info@betterbones.com*. Address: The Center for Better Bones and the Better Bones Foundation, Dr. Susan E. Brown, PhD, 605 Franklin Park Dr., East Syracuse, NY 13057.

SPEED LIMIT The Problem With Fosamax

"The common misconception that bone loss is 'forever' has led many people to turn to biphosphonate drugs such as *alendronate* (Fosamax), which is one of the osteoporosis medications known as 'anti-resorptive' drugs," says Dr. Brown.

"These medications dramatically reduce bone loss by bringing premature death to *osteoclasts,* the cells that break down and recycle old, worn-out segments of bone," she explains. However, bone breakdown and bone buildup are tightly coupled. So as Fosamax dramatically reduces bone breakdown, it also dramatically *decreases* new bone formation. In fact, studies show that the bone-forming surface of bone is suppressed by 60% to 90% by Fosamax.

Yes, Fosamax often *appears* to increase bone density. But, as Susan Ott, MD, explains: "This is because the bone is no longer remodeling and there is not much new bone. The older bone is denser than the newer bone—there is less water and more mineral in the bone, and radiographic techniques thus measure the higher density." So while this *looks* like added bone tissue—it is not. "Many people believe that these drugs are *bone builders.* But the evidence show they are actually bone *hardeners,*" says Dr. Ott.

Surprising: Anti-resorptive drugs such as Fosamax and *risedronate* (Actonel) simply halt bone breakdown—they do not actually build new bone.

Here are Dr. Brown's recommendations to balance your life and save your bones...

➤ **Vitamin D—the most important nutrient for your bones.** "It's common knowledge that calcium is essential for bone health," says Dr. Brown.

What it does: Bone is made of a mineral compound embedded in a living protein matrix," explains Dr. Brown. "This mineral compound is a crystalline structure, called *hydroxyapatite,* formed of calcium and phosphorus. Calcium—and the hydroxapatite crystal it forms with phosphorus—is essential to bone development and maintenance."

However: "The effect of calcium on reducing fracture risk is marginal," she says. She points out that the cultures with the *lowest* calcium intake also have the lowest rate of fracture—because they don't drain the calcium in bones through an acidic diet, alcohol, medications and stress.

"The whole calcium story will be revisited and we'll realize that we're recommending way too much calcium for people—and nowhere near enough vitamin D."

The importance of vitamin D: "Scientists now know that people low in vitamin D absorb sixty-five percent less calcium than those with adequate levels of this vitamin," says Dr. Brown.

"Needless osteoporotic fractures are much more common in folks with low levels of vitamin D, and the incidence of fractures can be dramatically reduced with vitamin D supplementation," she continues. For example, a recent study from England found that 95% of those suffering a hip fracture were deficient in vitamin D, while other research in England and the US shows that daily supplementation with 800 IU of vitamin D, with some calcium, can reduce hip fracture incidence by 33 to 50%.

Suggested intake: Take 2,000 IU of supplemental vitamin D a day—and get your vitamin D blood levels tested regularly to make sure they are within safe parameters," suggests Dr. Brown.

However, if you have been diagnosed with osteoporosis, she says to talk to your doctor about taking 7,000 IU a day for eight weeks to rebuild your blood levels of the nutrient—since half of all people treated for osteoporosis have low blood levels of vitamin D.

"Calcium is *not* the most important nutrient for bones—vitamin D is," says Dr. Brown. "We could achieve a fifty percent worldwide reduction in fractures by bringing everyone up to normal blood levels of vitamin D." What's normal?

"You want blood levels of vitamin D between 50 to 80 ng/mL [nanograms per milliliter]," says John Cannell, MD, executive director of the Vitamin D Council. They generally shouldn't exceed 100 ng/mL.

Rapid Resource: You can find a link to an in-home vitamin D blood level test from ZRT Laboratory at the website of the Vitamin D Council, *www.vitamindcouncil.org.*

The ZRT Lab contact information is *www.zrtlab.com*, or call 866-600-1636. Address: ZRT Laboratory, 8605 SW Creekside Pl., Beaverton, OR 97008, e-mail *info@zrtlab.com.*

Test yourself every six months, says Dr. Cannell.

➤ **The newest nutrient for your bones is vitamin K.** "This little-known nutrient is extremely important for bone health," says Dr. Brown.

Vitamin K (phylloquinone) is a fat-soluble nutrient (like vitamins A and D) found abundantly in leafy green vegetables, asparagus, green beans and vegetable oils. Vitamin K-2 (menaquinone) is formed in the body from K-1.

Vitamin K-1 helps the liver manufacture proteins that control blood clotting. Vitamin K-2 has many functions, including building collagen in bone—and preventing fractures.

Standout scientific evidence: Doctors from England analyzed the data from 13 studies on osteoporosis and vitamin K, given in a dose of 45

milligrams (mg) and a form called MK4. They found vitamin K decreased hip fractures by 73%, spinal fractures by 60% and all non-spinal fractures by 81%. Their results were published in the *Archives of Internal Medicine.*

Important: Medications called *corticosteroids* (cortisone, prednisone, hydrocortisone) are a synthetic version of cortisol, an adrenal hormone. They are often prescribed to help control the symptoms of chronic diseases with an inflammatory component, such as rheumatoid arthritis, inflammatory bowel disease, lupus and severe asthma. Taken regularly for six months or more, they can cause osteoporosis. Taking vitamin K with corticosteroids can help prevent or slow that bone loss.

Recommended: There is only one vitamin K supplement on the market in the US that contains the same amount and type of the nutrient used in clinical trials to decrease fracture risk—Osteo-K—which also contains calcium, vitamin D, magnesium and boron, says John Neustadt, MD, a naturopathic physician in Bozeman, Montana. It is available at *www.nbihealth.com.*

⚠ **Caution:** If you are taking the anticoagulant *warfarin* (Coumadin) do not take Osteo-K or any other type of supplemental vitamin K, which can block the action of the drug.

Also helpful: Dr. Brown has created a nutritional supplement program that provides all 18 of the nutrients (including vitamin K) research shows are key to maintaining and building bone. You can find out more about the supplement program by calling the Better Bones Foundation at 888-206-7119.

➤ **Don't let internal acids dissolve your bones.** The human body operates best in an *alkaline* state and the internal environment of a healthy body is slightly alkaline, maintaining a pH just above 7.0, explains Dr. Brown. "Because the pH level is so critical, the body has many

The Strange, Bone-Saving Power of Prunes

Dried plums—known to scientists as *Prunus domestica*, and to the rest of us as *prunes*—are loaded with powerful natural compounds that fight cell-damaging oxidation and inflammation. Could they protect bones?

In a study conducted in 2002, postmenopausal women who ate nine to 10 prunes a day for three months had big boosts in two biomarkers that indicate bone growth. A group that ate dried apples didn't have an increase.

In 2005, female rats that had eaten a bone-eroding diet were given diets rich in prunes, and bone mass returned. The animals had incurred a type of bone damage that scientists up to then thought was irreversible—but prunes reversed it, says Bahram H. Arjmandi, PhD, RD, a professor at Florida State University and the lead researcher on all the prune studies.

In 2006, Dr. Arjmandi and his colleagues showed that prunes prevent bone loss in male rats.

In 2007, a study showed that prunes strengthen the structure of bone in male and female laboratory animals.

In 2011, 236 women who had been postmenopausal from 1 to 10 years ate either 5 or 6 prunes or the equivalent amount of dried apple for one year. At the end of the year, the bone mineral density in the hip and forearm of the bone group was "significantly increased" compared to the apple group. The prune group also had lower levels of two biomarkers of "bone turnover"—in other words, they had less biochemical activity leading bone loss. "The findings," wrote Dr. Arjmandi, "confirmed the ability of prunes in improving bone mineral density in postmenopausal women."

Want to include more prunes in your diet?

Try this: The California Dried Plum Board (which calls prunes dried plums) offers the following ideas…

- Sprinkle prunes on oatmeal or ready-to-eat cereal, or into pancake batter as a complement to sliced bananas.

- Add chopped and pitted prunes to apple butter, orange marmalade, peanut butter or low-fat cream cheese.

- Add halved and pitted prunes to turkey or chicken salad.

Rapid Resource: You can find dozens of prune recipes at *www.californiadriedplums.org*.

---

checks and balances to maintain its pH within a narrow range. One of the major mechanisms for bringing pH back into line when it has become too acid is to draw calcium and other alkalinizing minerals from the bones to buffer this acidity and alkalinize the body." In other words, excessive and prolonged acidity can drain bone of calcium reserves and lead to bone thinning.

Problem: An imbalanced, acid-forming diet high in animal protein, sugar, caffeine and processed foods can disrupt pH balance.

Solution: "Ideally, our diet should be composed of sixty-five percent alkaline-forming foods and thirty-five percent acid-forming foods," says Dr. Brown.

What to do: For every 10 foods you eat, six should be vegetables (especially leafy greens), two should be fruits, one should be protein and one should be high in starch, such as potatoes.

Also helpful: "*The following simple changes are especially helpful for quickly alkalinizing the body,*" says Dr. Brown…

- **Drink the juice of one-half lime, lemon or apple cider vinegar in water a few times during the day.** "Although these citrus fruits contain organic acids, when metabolized by the body, they leave an alkaline residue," says Dr. Brown. "The same holds true for apple cider vinegar made from whole apples, which are high in alkalinizing minerals."

● **Add yams and sweet potatoes to your diet** on a regular basis, as well as lentils. "All these foods help to alkalinize the body quickly," says Dr. Brown.

● **Eat one cup of alkalinizing greens daily.** They include kale, mustard and turnips greens, collards or endive. "Use lettuce as well, but in *addition* to these other greens," says Dr. Brown. Grated daikon radish is a wonderful alkalinizing condiment, she says.

● **Use miso and seaweed in soups and other dishes daily,** even if only a small amount. "Miso soup with daikon radish, ginger and seaweed is both a great digestant and an alkalinizer," says Dr. Brown.

● **Favor the alkalinizing grains,** which include oats, quinoa and wild rice.

● **Enjoy liberal amounts of fruits.** "In season, eat plenty of watermelon and its juice along with the other melons and fruits and berries," says Dr. Brown.

Also helpful: If you suffer from gas, bloating or weak digestion, favor cooked fruit and small amounts of fresh juices.

Rapid Resource: You can find the *Acid Alkaline Food Guide* by Dr. Brown at her website, *www. betterbones.com.* You can also purchase *Better Bones ph Paper*, which allows you to monitor the pH of your urine on a daily basis.

➤ **Eliminate or minimize these bone-robbers.** Several lifestyle factors can steal the strength from your bones, says Dr. Brown. *Watch out for…*

● **Smoking.** Women who smoke one pack a day during adulthood have 5 to 10% less bone mass at the age of menopause than nonsmokers.

● **Alcohol.** Alcoholics have an estimated five times more fractures than non-alcoholics—and even a few drinks a day could be detrimental to bone.

Is Bone Mineral Density the Best Measurement?

If you're concerned about osteoporosis, you may have had a DEXA (dual energy x-ray absorptiometry) test to measure the bone mineral density (BMD) in your hip, spine and wrist. If your score was -1 to -2.5 below the normal bone mass for healthy women or men in their twenties, you have osteopenia; a score under -2.5 signals osteoporosis.

Surprising: BMD does not accurately reflect fracture risk. In one study, 82% of women who reported fractures of the wrist, forearm, hip, rib or spine in the year after a BMD test *didn't* have a score of -2.5 or lower.

Overall, BMD predicts only 44% of fractures in women and 23% of fractures in men.

Better: FRAX, a fracture-risk assessment tool, is a diagnostic device that uses a computer program to calculate the 10-year fracture risk for a person 50 or older. It is based on 12 risk factors such as bone mineral density (BMD), history of fractures, sex, weight and height, smoking, and level of alcohol intake.

You can take the FRAX test online at *www. shef.ac.uk/FRAX/index.htm.* Discuss the results with your physician.

Helpful: For the test, you enter your weight in kilograms (not pounds) and your height in centimeters (not feet and inches). You can find online tools that automatically calculate those conversions at *www.unit-conversion.info.*

● **Dieting.** "Lifelong low nutrient intake guarantees low bone mass," says Dr. Brown.

● **Medications.** Corticosteroids, thyroid hormones, aluminum-containing antacids, diuretics and antibiotics—all encourage bone loss.

● **Stress.** "Believe it or not, stress also contributes to osteoporosis," says Dr. Brown. She recommends regular meditation.

➤ **Exercise regularly.** "I believe that our sedentary lifestyle ranks right beside inadequate nutrition as a major cause of our current osteoporosis epidemic," says Dr. Brown. "It is well known that exercise—especially lifelong exercise—is one of the most important factors in building and maintaining healthy bones."

What to do: "The exercises you choose should be activities you enjoy or that you can learn to enjoy," says Dr. Brown. She recommends an exercise based on a proven program that showed a 6.1% increase in bone density among postmenopausal women after two years. "Postmenopausal women actually gained bone density at a time when they otherwise would have rapidly lost bone!" she says.

Those exercises include a combination of weight-bearing, strength-training exercises (walking, jogging, stair-climbing, weight lifting) with nonweight-bearing aerobic exercises (cycling, rowing), 50 to 60 minutes a session, at least three times a week. Talk to your doctor before beginning an exercise program.

Warning: "Exercise in which you bend over frontward are not recommended for those with osteoporosis because they put undesired pressure on the spinal vertebrae," says Dr. Brown.

OVERWEIGHT AND OBESITY

Shed Pounds Fast

Normal-weight people are going out of style. *Fact:* Eighty-six percent of adults in the US will be either overweight or obese by 2030, say researchers from the Johns Hopkins School of Public Health, in the journal *Obesity.* (Please see page 257 for definitions of overweight, obesity and severe obesity.)

They also estimate that one out of every six dollars spent on health care will go toward problems caused by extra pounds. What kind of problems? It's a long list.

- Bladder problems
- Cancer (breast, colon, esophagus, kidney, prostate)
- Depression
- Gallbladder disease
- Gout
- Heart disease
- High blood pressure
- High cholesterol
- Infertility
- Liver disease
- Menstrual irregularities
- Metabolic syndrome
- Osteoarthritis
- Pregnancy complications
- Sleep apnea
- Stroke
- Type 2 diabetes

Another way to look at the health risk of extra pounds—if you're overweight at 18 you have *double* the risk of dying prematurely, and if you're obese you have triple the risk (about the same as somebody who smokes 10 cigarettes a day).

There are many reasons why extra pounds are extra trouble. For example, excess fat clogs cells and mucks up their normal functioning. Hormones generated by fat cells trigger chronic, low-grade inflammation, causing and complicating many conditions, from heart disease to Alzheimer's. And extra pounds damage bones and joints.

Good news: You don't have to achieve normal-weight to prevent, control or reverse weight-caused or weight-complicated health problems.

"Losing about five to ten percent of your body weight can dramatically lower your risk from many obesity-caused health problems," says

Michael Zemel, PhD, Director of the Nutrition Institute at the University of Tennessee.

"The message out there is that if you don't lose an extraordinary amount of weight on a diet, something is wrong," adds M.R.C. Greenwood, PhD, a professor emerita in the Department of Nutrition at UC-Davis. "This perpetuates an unrealistic approach to weight loss that sets you up for failure. Losing *any* amount of weight is a *success*."

So get ready to successfully (and healthfully) shed some pounds—and shed them fast…

▶ **Lose an extra pound per week—with calcium and vitamin D supplements.** Have your diets failed again and again? The problem might be too little *calcium*.

New study: Researchers at Université Laval in Canada found that women with a low dietary intake of calcium (less than 800 milligrams a day) lose nearly one pound more a week when

---

The Definition of "Overweight"

Overweight, obesity and severe obesity are scientific definitions, based on "body mass index," or BMI, a number calculated from a formula that divides weight by height.

A person is considered *overweight* with a BMI of 25 to 29.9; *obese*, with a BMI of 30 to 39.9; and *severely obese* with a BMI of 40 or above.

Example: A five-foot-five-inch woman is overweight at 150 pounds, obese at 180 pounds and severely obese at 240 pounds. A five-foot-ten-inch man is overweight at 174 pounds, obese at 209 pounds and severely obese at 278 pounds.

Rapid Resource: You can find an online device to instantly calculate your BMI at *www. nhlbi.nih.gov* (search BMI), the website of the Obesity Education Initiative of the National Heart, Lung and Blood Institute.

---

they take a calcium and vitamin D supplement while dieting.

In their 15-week weight-loss study, low-calcium women who received the supplement lost an average of 13.2 pounds—while low-calcium women not receiving the supplement lost 2.2 pounds.

Theory: "Our hypothesis is that the brain can detect the lack of calcium and seeks to compensate by spurring food intake, which obviously works against the goals of any weight-loss program, says Angelo Tremblay, PhD, the study leader. "Sufficient calcium intake seems to stifle the desire to eat more and is important to ensure the success of any weight-loss program."

Red flag: More than half of all overweight women *don't* get 800 milligrams (mg) of calcium a day.

Recommendation: The dieters took a nutritional supplement containing 1,200 mg of calcium and 400 IU of vitamin D (which aids the absorption of calcium).

⚠ *Caution:* Chronic use of high-dose calcium supplements may increase a women's risk of cardiovascular disease. If you decide to take 1,200 mg of calcium, do so with the approval and supervision of your physician.

▶ **Eat eggs at breakfast—and lose 65% more weight.** Why did the chicken cross the road? *To help the dieter on the other side…*

New study: Researchers at Louisiana State University studied people eating a reduced-calorie diet, dividing them into two groups. One group ate two eggs for breakfast; the other group ate a bagel breakfast with the same amount of calories.

After two months, the egg-eaters had lost 65% more weight, had a 34% smaller waistline and consistently reported feeling more energetic. And their cholesterol levels stayed the same.

"People have a hard time adhering to diets, and our research shows that choosing eggs for breakfast can dramatically improve the success

The Scent Diet

You probably associate delicious food aromas with wanting to eat more of whatever you're smelling, whether it's the scent of fresh-baked cookies or bacon sizzling in the skillet.

But a recent study suggests that powerful food smells actually may help you eat *less*... and lose weight in the process.

René de Wijk, PhD, a Dutch sensory scientist, wanted to explore whether the smell of food influences how big a bite we take. Previous studies have shown that when we take smaller bites, we feel full on fewer calories than when we take bigger bites.

Dr. de Wijk hooked 10 volunteers to machines that pumped a custard dessert directly into their mouths. At the same time, the subjects were randomly exposed to either a slightly detectable aroma of natural cream...or a moderately detectable aroma of natural cream...or no aroma at all. During the experiment, the participants could press a button whenever they wanted to stop the flow of custard, which determined their "bite" size. The key result? People pressed the button more quickly—in essence, took smaller bites—when the aroma was stronger.

Dr. de Wijk theorized why the smell may have worked. "A cream aroma is associated with calories, and we regulate calories via bite size," he said. Or, it could also be that we have an innate tendency to try to moderate intense sensations of any kind, so we take smaller bites as a protective measure.

Creamy aromas aren't the only ones that might help you eat less. For example, aromas that are strongly spicy, meaty, buttery, fishy, vinegary, lemony, garlicky or oniony—anything other than bland—might also do the trick. And whatever the aroma, eating your food warm or hot might help you eat less than eating it cold, since warmth brings out aromas more strongly. Heat up those leftovers!

of a weight-loss plan," says Nikhil V. Dhurandhar, PhD, the study's lead researcher.

"Eggs are a good source of all-natural, high-quality protein, so they can help keep you satisfied longer, making it easier to resist tempting snacks," says Jackie Newgent, RD, a nutritional consultant and chef in New York City (*www. jackienewgent.com*).

Smart idea: "You can prepare an egg breakfast in less than sixty seconds," says Newgent. Beat one egg in a microwave-safe mug and then cook it in the microwave oven on high for 60 seconds. Slide the egg onto a whole grain English muffin. Add flavor with a sprinkling of fresh herbs, salsa or cheese. Serve fruit slices—such as peaches in the summer—on the side, for a balanced meal.

➤ **Burn 278 more calories when you exercise—take a red chili supplement.** Red chili peppers are so hot they burn up calories.

A lot of calories...

New finding: A study by researchers in the Department of Health and Exercise Science at the University of Oklahoma shows that people who take a red chili pepper supplement before exercising burn hundreds of more calories than people taking a placebo.

The researchers asked the participants to take the supplement or a placebo one hour before walking on a treadmill. Those who took the supplement burned...three times more calories before the exercise...3% more during the exercise...and 12 times more for an hour after the exercise. The cumulative total was 278 more calories.

The supplement works by heating the body and boosting metabolism.

Product: X12, from GNC, containing Capsimax. Follow the dosage recommendation on the label.

🕐 *Super-Quick Fix*

➤ **Sit farther away from the all-you-can-eat buffet.** (And don't face it, either.) *What* you eat in a restaurant is important for weight control. But *where* you eat and *how* you eat is important too.

Study: Researchers at Cornell University's Food and Brand lab studied 23 diners at 11 all-you-can-eat Chinese restaurant buffets. They found normal-weight and overweight diners approached the experience very differently.

- 42% of the overweight diners faced the buffet, compared to 27% of the normal-weight diners.
- Overweight diners sat an average of 16 feet closer to the buffet.
- 71% of normal-weight diners browsed the buffet before servings themselves, while 67% of the overweight diners served themselves immediately.
- 24% of normal-weight diners used chopsticks rather than forks. Among the overweight, the number was 9%.

"The overweight people were generally unaware of what they were doing," says Brian Wansink, PhD, lead author of the study, and author of *Mindless Eating: Why We Eat More Than We Think* (Bantam). "They're unaware of sitting closer, facing the food, chewing less and so on."

Bottom line: "When food is more convenient, people tend to eat more," says study coauthor Collin R. Payne, PhD, of New Mexico State University.

So make it a little less convenient. Sit far away from the buffet...don't face it...and browse before making your selections.

➤ **Feel less hungry after you eat— take a fish oil supplement.** One of the biggest problems with calorie-restricted dieting is that

The Best Snack for Dieters

Snacking is bad for weight loss, right? Well, it depends on the snack.

Researchers at the Yale University's Prevention Research Center found that dieters who ate two KIND Fruit & Nut Delight bars per day were more successful at losing weight than dieters who didn't.

"Snacking can add calories to the diet and cause weight gain," says David L. Katz, MD, the study's lead researcher. "But snacking on wholesome foods can help control appetite and weight, while providing excellent nutrition—and displacing less filling foods that contribute empty calories. KIND bars are just that kind of food, made principally of nuts and fruits."

KIND Fruit & Nuts bars are widely available in health food stores.

you always feel hungry. Taking omega-3 fish oil supplements might help.

New study: An international team of researchers asked 232 overweight and obese people to supplement an eight-week calorie-restricted diet with either 260 or 1,300 mg of daily omega-3 fish oil supplements. During the last two weeks of the study, they measured the dieters' level of hunger and satisfaction after meals (satiety).

Those taking the higher dose of omega-3s had fewer hunger sensations and felt fuller.

Omega-3 supplements are widely available.

Also helpful: Researchers from the University of Barcelona found that omega-3 fatty acids may protect you against two of the complications of overweight: high insulin levels and nonalcoholic fatty liver disease.

"Doctors are always looking for simple and easy ways to counter the harmful effects of

Any Diet Will Do

Low-fat? Mediterranean? Atkins? Which is the best diet for helping you lose weight? All of the above.

Researchers in Israel and the US studied 322 overweight people, average age of 52, assigning them to three different calorie-reduced diets (1,200 calories a day)—a low-carbohydrate, high-protein diet similar to the Atkins Diet; a low-fat diet, similar to the American Heart Association diet; and a Mediterranean diet, rich in monounsaturated fats and low in animal protein.

After two years, *all* the groups had lost about the same amount of weight—9 pounds, with a 2-inch reduction in waist size. And they *all* got healthier, with fewer risk factors for heart disease and diabetes.

Because Mediterranean diets and low-carbohydrate diets are effective alternatives to low-fat diets, you can take *your* preferences into account when choosing a diet, says Meir Stampfer, MD, of Harvard Medical School, the study's lead researcher.

obesity—and the great thing about this finding is that the information can be used right away," says Gerald Weissmann, MD, of the NYU School of Medicine.

➤ **Save 18,000 calories a year—replace beef with Portabello.** Want to cut calories without feeling deprived? Switch from roast beef to roasted mushrooms.

New study: For four days, researchers at the Johns Hopkins Weight Management Center fed a group of men lunch entrees made with either beef or mushrooms—lasagna, napoleon, sloppy Joe and chili. The following week, those who ate the beef entrees switched to mushroom, and visa versa.

When the participants ate the beef entrees, they ate 420 more calories a day—and 30 more grams of fat. But when they ate the mushroom entrees, they didn't ask, "Where's the beef?" They said the mushroom entrees were just as tasty, hunger-satisfying and filling as the beef entrees.

"The most intriguing finding of this study was that the participants seemed to accept mushrooms as a palatable and suitable culinary substitute for meat," says Lawrence Cheskin, MD, director of the center. "They didn't compensate for the lower calorie mushroom meal by eating more food later in the day."

Dr. Cheskin estimates that if men substituted a 4-ounce portabello mushroom for a 4-ounce grilled hamburger every time they ate a grilled hamburger, in a year they'd save more than 18,000 calories, or 5.3 pounds.

➤ **Prevent weight-gain—walk!** Want to stop yourself from gaining weight as you age? Walk thirty minutes a day.

New study: Researchers at the University of North Carolina at Chapel Hill analyzed 15 years of health data from nearly 5,000 people. Those who walked more gained less weight.

The researchers found, for example, that heavy women who walked at least 30 minutes a day gained fifteen fewer pounds than heavy women who didn't.

This is the first study to show that walking stops long-term weight gain, says Miriam Nelson, PhD, of the John Hancock Center for Physical Activity and Nutrition at Tufts University.

"If we can increase walking participation by Americans, the evidence is strong that we will improve weight control," adds Penny Gordon-Larsen, PhD, a study researcher.

PARKINSON'S DISEASE

Deep within your brain is a structure called the *substantia nigra*. There, brain cells (neurons) produce *dopamine*, a *neurotransmitter* that relays messages between neurons, helping regulate movement, thinking, perception, behavior, motivation and many other physical, mental and emotional functions.

In the more than one million Americans with Parkinson's disease (PD), those dopamine-producing neurons begin to malfunction and die. (By the time a diagnosis is made, 60% to 70% are dead.)

The result is the typical physical symptoms of PD. Tremors. Rigid muscles. Slow movements.

In many cases, PD also produces a range of mental and behavioral symptoms, such as fatigue, apathy, depression, anxiety, sleep disorders, dementia and hallucinations.

However: Many doctors, people with PD and their caregivers often don't associate these symptoms with the disease, says Joseph Friedman, MD, director of the Parkinson's Disease and Movement Disorders Center of NeuroHealth, clinical professor of Clinical Neurosciences at the Warren Alpert School of Medicine at Brown University, and author of *Making the Connection Between Brain and Behavior: Coping With Parkinson's Disease* (Demos Health).

Parkinson's is typically treated with medications that either replace dopamine, such as *carbidopa* and *levodopa* (Sinemet), or dopamine agonists (such as *pramipexole* and *ropinirole*).

But if you have PD, there is a more important treatment than medications, says Dr. Friedman. *A treatment that requires little more than a pair of sneakers…*

➤ **Walk 30 minutes a day.** "The most important recommendation for anyone with Parkinson's—more important than taking medications—is to walk thirty minutes a day, every day," says Dr. Freidman.

Reason: "Gait dysfunction is one of the most disabling features of Parkinson's," he says. "I believe the more you walk, the more likely it is that you will forestall walking dysfunction.

"Regular exercise is the best way people can protect themselves against the long-term symptoms of Parkinson's," he continues. "I tell my patients, 'Regular exercise may not make you feel better today or tomorrow, but it is the most effective treatment for being in the best possible shape five to ten years from now.'"

New study: Researchers at the Sackler School of Medicine at Tel Aviv University in Israel asked people with PD (average age 70) to participate in a program of treadmill walking—30 minutes of walking, 4 days a week, for six weeks. After the six weeks, their walking speed increased by 12% and the normalcy of their gait (a measurement called "swing time variability") improved by 23%. In addition, their quality of life had improved by 31% and their Parkinson's symptoms had decreased by 24%. The results were reported in the *Archives of Physical Medicine and Rehabilitation*.

➤ **Stretch out.** "I also recommend stretching exercises for everyone with Parkinson's," says Dr. Freidman. "The disease tends to flex everyone into stooped postures, with bent knees, elbows and wrists—as if they were going back into the fetal position. Stretching can help counter that."

What to do: "When movements get smaller with Parkinson's, it helps to move big—to make big movements with the body, the arms and the legs," says David Zid, a professional fitness instructor and author of *Delay the Disease: Exercise and Parkinson's Disease* (Columbus

261

Health Works). And there are three such exercises he thinks are particularly effective.

"If you perform one exercise each day—or become motivated to do two or three each day—I guarantee you will become stronger, more flexible and have better balance," says Zid. "These activities will help your brain cells become healthier and delay the progression of the symptoms of Parkinson's Disease."

Perform all the exercises either standing or seated in a chair, says Zid. He also says to "train to tolerance"—that is, if you begin to experience muscular or any other type of pain, stop.

1. **Big Rope Pull.** Reach up high with both hands, above your head, and grab an imaginary rope either on the right or left side. Pull it toward the floor on the opposite side of your body. Repeat five times per side.

2. **Hamstring Stretch.** Sit with one leg straight in front of you, the other knee flexed with your foot flat on floor. Place both hands just above the knee on the straight leg. Move your belly button toward your toe, pulling your toes up and flexing your foot. You should feel a nice stretch up the back of your leg. Hold for a 10 count. Repeat the stretch three to five times with each leg.

3. **Arm Circles.** Stand or sit with your arms straight out and shoulder blades pinched—make a giant T. Hold the pinch throughout the following three moves. With your palms facing down, perform two small circles, two medium circles, and two large circles, forward and backward. Do the same movement with your palms facing forward (thumbs up). Do the movement a third time with your palms facing back (thumbs down). Perform to tolerance—and remember to keep your shoulder blades pinched back.

Rapid Resource: Several routines of easy calisthenics, stretches, walking and balance drills, strength training, facial and vocal exercises—all specifically designed for people with Parkinson's—have been developed by Zid, Jackie Russell, RN, and Thomas Mallory, MD. The routines are available in the book *Delay the Disease* and also the DVD of the same name. You can order them at *www.delaythedisease.com* or e-mail *delaythedisease@ohiohealth.com*.

➤ **Preventing Parkinson's Disease.** Risk factors for Parkinson's are debated among experts. But there is general agreement that if you are…older…male…with a parent, brother or sister with Parkinson's…you're at higher risk for the disease. Women who have had a hysterectomy are also at increased risk. Are there any ways to *lower* risk?

New research points to several possibilities…

● **Eat a Mediterranean diet.** Italian researchers analyzed 12 studies involving more than 1.5 million people and found that those who followed a strict Mediterranean diet were 13% less likely to develop Parkinson's. The diet emphasizes vegetables, fruits, whole grains, legumes, fish, olive oil and red wine, and minimizes saturated fat from red meat and dairy products.

● **Take vitamin D.** Researchers from Emory University in Atlanta tested the blood vitamin D levels of 297 people—100 with Parkinson's, 97 with Alzheimer's and 99 healthy people. They found that 55% of people with Parkinson's had insufficient blood levels of vitamin D, compared to 41% with Alzheimer's and 36% of healthy people. Low vitamin D levels may play a role in causing the disease, say the researchers, in the *Archives of Neurology*.

Theory: The dopamine-generating cells in the *substantia nigra* have high levels of vitamin D receptors, and the nutrient may play a role in their normal functioning.

What to Do: Take a daily supplement that provides 1,000 IU of vitamin D. "It's the quickest and most reliable way to maintain healthy blood levels of vitamin D," says Michael F. Holick, MD, PhD, director of the Vitamin D, Skin and Bone Research Laboratory at Boston University Medical Center.

Important: Please see page 253 in the chapter "Osteoporosis" for more information on the healthiest blood levels of vitamin D (50 to 80 ng/ml) and bi-yearly testing to ensure your levels are in that range.

- **Drink green tea.** Antioxidants in green tea protected dopamine neurons in laboratory animals, say researchers in China.

- **Take DHA, an omega-3 fatty acid.** The omega-3 fatty acids DHA and EPA are found in fatty fish such as salmon, tuna and mackerel. In a recent study, DHA protected the dopamine-producing neurons of mice given a toxic compound that causes the same type of damage as Parkinson's. "Our results suggest that DHA deficiency is a risk factor for developing Parkinson's disease," say researchers from the Université Laval in Canada.

- **Exercise.** Researchers at the Harvard School of Public Health analyzed 10 years of health data from more than 143,000 people with an average age of 63 and found that those who engaged in regular moderate to vigorous physical activity were 40% less likely to develop Parkinson's.

What to do: "Make sure you get some moderate or vigorous exercise several times a week," says Evan L. Thacker, the study leader.

- **Stay away from pesticides.** People who reported exposure to pesticides—particularly herbicides and insecticides—are 70% more likely to develop Parkinson's, say Harvard researchers. The risk was the same for farmers and non-farmers.

POSTSURGICAL PROBLEMS

Prepare—and Heal Faster

Coronary artery bypass graft. Hysterectomy. Lumbar spinal fusion. Mastectomy. Cholecystectomy. Arthroscopy of the knee. Just the *names* of surgical procedures are frightening.

But the reality of "going under the knife" is a lot scarier. The blank of anesthesia. The slice of the scalpel. The struggle to wake up in the recovery room. The drugged days of post-op pain. The looming threat of "complications."

And yet a trip to the operating room seems almost inevitable. There are 60 million surgical procedures in the US a year—one for every five Americans. Is there any way to approach surgery *positively*—with less anxiety, less pain afterward and a shorter recovery time?

Yes, yes and yes, says Peggy Huddleston, a psychotherapist in Cambridge, Massachusetts, and author of *Prepare for Surgery, Heal Faster: A Guide of Mind-Body Techniques* (Angel River Press). Whether your surgery is minor or major, she says you can feel calmer before surgery… have less pain after surgery…use less pain medication…recover faster…and save money on medical bills. How? By using her "Five Healing Steps" for surgical preparation. Doctors at Tufts University Medical School would agree.

Standout scientific evidence: Doctors at the Lahey Clinic, a teaching hospital at Tufts University Medical School, studied 56 patients undergoing colorectal surgery. Half the patients used the five-step program developed by Huddleston and half didn't. Those who went through the program left the hospital 1.6 days sooner (saving $3,200 per patient). By the second day at home, they were using 60% less pain medication.

In similar research at another Tufts teaching hospital, New England Baptist, doctors studied patients undergoing total knee-joint replacement. Again, they divided them into two groups—one used Huddleston's five-step program and the other didn't. The Huddleston group went home an average of 1.3 days sooner.

"The five steps to prepare for surgery give you specific ways to feel more in control at a time you often feel helpless and vulnerable," says Huddleston. "They are easy to use, cost you and the hospital nothing and have no negative side effects."

Here are the five steps...

Step 1. Relax to feel peaceful. "Remember the last time you were deeply relaxed?" asks Huddleston. "Your body felt loose and comfortable, your mind peaceful. Maybe you were lying in the summer sun or listening to music or watching clouds drift across the sky. The situation—the warmth of the sun, the sweep of the music, the drifting clouds—caused you to let go of the tension.

"Now, in preparing for surgery, you need to learn how to trigger this deep relaxation within yourself. Knowing how to relax—anywhere and anytime—is one of the best ways to cope with surgery. Within a week or two of practice, you'll be so relaxed that you will feel peaceful in a noisy hospital hallway, waiting for your operation. And if you have a stressful medical test, you will be able to relax in the waiting room and during the test, making the process much easier."

What to do: "Find a quiet place where you will not be disturbed," says Huddleston. "If you are at home, turn on your answering machine. Turn off the bell on your phone or put a pillow over it. If others are at home, tell them not to disturb you. At first, minimizing distracting noises is helpful. Once you have learned to relax, you'll be able to do so with noise around you.

"Choose a comfortable position, sitting or lying down. Stretch out on a bed or sit in a chair.

If you sit in a chair, be sure the back of your head is supported, so you can completely let go. Loosen your clothing, such as a belt or necktie, so you can take easy, deep breaths. Do whatever you need to get very comfortable.

"Take a deep breath, and while exhaling, feel a deep letting go. Focus your awareness on your neck. Release and relax, and let go of any tension in this part of your body. Next, relax your shoulders, arms and hands. As you relax your hands, imagine tension draining out through your fingertips. Then relax your chest, stomach, abdomen and back—the muscles and ligaments that go from the base of your neck all the way down to the small of your back. Next, relax your pelvis, hips and legs. Imagine a door in the bottom of each foot. Picture opening the door and letting tension drain away. When the tension is gone, close the door.

"Now, imagine yourself in your ideal place of relaxation—for example, lying in the spring sun, enclosed in a secret place in a garden, smelling the sweet honeysuckle and hearing the birds singing around you. It can be a real place or one you create in your imagination. Be sure the place you choose is completely serene and makes your whole body relax—and imagine yourself in your ideal place rather than looking at a picture of yourself there.

"Next, think of a person or pet who is easy to love, or a guardian angel or a spiritual figure who embodies qualities of divine love. Let your mind go back to a time you felt a great deal of love for and from the other. Feel these emotions now. Recalling the love, you may experience a warm glow in your heart—let it fill your heart and surround you. Love is profoundly healing, emotionally and physically.

"Next, remember a time you felt a sense of oneness—a time you felt connected to something larger than yourself. Maybe you experienced it in nature, feeling the vibrancy of being one with everything—the earth, trees and sky. You may also have had a sense of oneness playing golf, jogging, listening to music or being with someone you love.

"Now that you are in a deep state of relaxation, you are ready to picture your healing," says Huddleston.

Step 2. Visualize your healing. "You can help your recovery by visualizing your ideal surgical outcome," says Huddleston. "Create a beautiful image of the healed outcome that makes you feel peaceful whenever you call up the image. Use your senses to make it come alive, the way you imagined your ideal place of relaxation.

"At first, it's all right if a part of you doesn't quite believe your positive visualization. With daily practice, you'll discover that soon you *will* believe it. At that point, you'll experience an ease with which you *see* and *feel* the healed outcome.

"And when worries about your operation pop into your mind, switch the worries to pictures of your healed outcome, much like changing the channel on television.

"In the days or weeks before surgery, visualizing your healed end-result will calm you. Some have found it also improved their physical condition.

"Also, before and after the operation, ask the part of your body that is healing, 'What comforting feeling do you want me to give you?' 'How many times a day and for how long do you want this feeling?' "

Example: "A man scheduled for back surgery asked his lower back, 'What emotion would comfort you?' It answered, 'Emotional support.' Recalling a time he felt believed in and supported, he bathed his back in this sensation before and after surgery."

Step 3. Organize a support group. "The emotional support you receive from your family and friends strengthens your immune

---

🕐 ***Super-Quick Fix***

After Colon Surgery, Chew Gum

A common complication after surgery to remove all or part of the colon is *postoperative ileus*—the intestines don't work.

It is seen as an inevitable response to the trauma of abdominal surgery, and it's a major factor in postoperative pain and discomfort from bloating, nausea, vomiting and abdominal cramping, says Dr. Sanjay Purkayastha, at St. Mary's Hospital in London. But he and his colleagues have figured out a new way to solve the problem. Chew gum.

New study: The doctors studied 158 people undergoing colon surgery, dividing them into two groups. After the surgery, one group chewed sugarless gum three times a day for five to 45 minutes each time. The other group didn't.

On average, the gum-chewers starting passing gas (a good thing, in this case) 0.66 days sooner. They had their first bowel movement 1.1 days sooner. And they left the hospital a day earlier.

How it works: The doctors theorize that gum chewing stimulates nerves in the digestive system, triggering the release of digestive hormones and increasing the production of saliva and pancreatic secretions.

If you're scheduled for colon surgery, talk to your surgeon about writing you a prescription…for Wrigley.

---

system, boosting your recovery from surgery," says Huddleston.

"When friends say, 'How can I help?' ask them to send you peace, tranquility or love for the half hour before your operation. Decide which emotion will comfort you the most—for some it's love, for others it's peace or tranquility. When you tell your friends the emotion you want to feel, express it in a colorful picture. Saying, 'Wrap me in a pink blanket of love' conjures up a more vivid image than merely saying 'Send me love.'

"An anxious spouse and friends will discover that sending you love will also comfort them at a time they are worried about you.

"In addition to having your friends send you love before surgery, also arrange for your spouse or closest friend to be with you until you go into the operating room.

"Also make a list of the specific ways you want to be helped before and after your operation. You may need a friend to feed your cat, water your plants and collect your mail. Several friends can take turns bringing you home-cooked meals."

Step 4. **Use healing statements.** "Research from around the world shows that—contrary to what has been commonly believed—when you are anesthetized and unconscious, you hear what is said during surgery," says Huddleston. "Furthermore, you are powerfully influenced by what you hear, much like a person under hypnosis."

Standout scientific evidence: Studies at Beth Israel Medical Center in New York, Emory University School of Medicine in Atlanta, St. Thomas' Hospital in London and the Royal Infirmary in Glasgow all show that patients who had positive statements spoken to them during general anesthesia recovered more quickly and with less pain and complications than patients who didn't hear statements.

The implications of this research are remarkable, says Huddleston. "Having your surgeon and anesthesiologist say specific healing statements to you during your operation can directly affect your health, your comfort, your time spent recovering and the cost of your hospitalization."

What to do: "If your surgeon does not use therapeutic statements, explain that you have read about and believe in the benefits of positive

statements during surgery," says Huddleston. "Then tell your doctor, 'There are four statements that I would like you or the anesthesiologist to say to me during my operation.' Give your doctor a page of the 'Healing Statements.' The surgeon should repeat each statement five times." *They are...*

- **At the beginning of surgery...**

1. Following this operation, you will feel comfortable and you will heal very well.

- **Toward the end of surgery...**

2. Your operation has gone very well. I am very pleased with your _____. (Fill in the blank: hip, shoulder, etc.)

3. Following this operation, you will wake up hungry for _____. You will be thirsty and you will be able to urinate easily. (Fill in the blank with the name of your favorite light food, such as ice cream, sherbet or broth.)

4. Following this operation, _____. (Fill in the blank with your surgeon's specific, positive recommendations suggestions for a speedy recovery.)

Step 5. **Meet your anesthesiologist.** For years, anesthesiologists have combined drugs to calm patients before surgery, says Huddleston. "It turns out that one of the most active ingredients for calming you is not a drug, but rather an informative and supportive doctor-patient relationship with your anesthesiologist. It puts your mind at ease to have your questions answered and meet the doctor to whom you'll entrust yourself."

Standout scientific evidence: Researchers at Harvard Medical school studied 218 patients awaiting surgery—half were given a sedative and half had a brief, reassuring meeting with an anesthesiologist. The patients who received the drug felt drowsy but nervous. The patients who met the anesthesiologist reported feeling calm before surgery. In a similar study, patients who spent more time with an anesthesiologist after

Double-Check Your Surgeon's Checklist

Major complications occur in up to 16% of inpatient surgeries. But those complications could be cut by more than one-third. With a checklist.

New study: In a study involving more than 7,000 surgical patients in eight hospitals around the world, researchers at Harvard Medical School and the World Health Organization found that when surgeons used a "Surgical Patient Safety Checklist," major complications fell from 11 to 7%. And deaths fell from 1.5 to 0.8%. The study appeared in the *New England Journal of Medicine.*

How it works: The checklist is simple. At three critical points during surgery (prior to anesthesia, immediately prior to incision and prior to the patient exiting the operating room), a member of the surgical team verbally confirms the completion of each step for preventing infections...anesthesia safety...and other essential steps, such as confirming the surgery site is marked...and counting the number of sponges and instruments used at the end of surgery to ensure nothing was left inside the patient.

Rapid Resource: Let your surgical team know they can find out more about the checklist (including a three-minute video titled, "How to Use the Checklist") at the website of the World Health Organization, *www.who.int/patientsafe ty/safesurgery/en/index.html.* The scientific citation for the study is: *N Engl J Med.* 2009 Jan 29;360(5):491–9.

surgery used 50% less pain medication and went home 2.7 days earlier.

Huddleston's recommendations...

● **Arrange the meeting as early as possible.** "The sooner you meet your anesthesiologist and understand the procedures, the less preoperative anxiety you will have," she says. "Also, if you do not feel comfortable with this person, you will have time to request to meet another. It is your choice, especially since you are paying for their professional services."

● **Make a list of questions about the anesthesia and how it will be administered.** "Your anesthesiologist will be guided by your questions and will be glad to provide the information you want," she says.

● **Will you need preoperative medication? If so, make sure it matches your coping style.** "The wrong preoperative medication can actually create stress," says Huddleston. "For example, if you are vigilant and like being in control and knowing lots of medical facts before surgery—you may want *diazepam* (Valium) or morphine, which relaxes the body like a rag doll while allowing the mind to go on thinking. If your style is avoiding and denying—which is perfectly appropriate—you may want *scopolamine*, a drug that makes it hard to hang on to thoughts."

● **If you will be awake during surgery, ask your doctor to explain the procedure for the local or regional anesthesia.** "You'll feel better prepared knowing what to expect," she says. "If you plan to listen to a relaxation tape during surgery, tell your doctor."

● **If you will be unconscious during surgery, discuss what the anesthesiologist will say to you as you go under the anesthesia.** "As you are given the anesthesia, some anesthesiologists like to use imagery, such as 'Imagine yourself on a beautiful beach.' Choose a scene that is right for you and tell your anesthesiologist the scene so that he or she can evoke this image."

● **Explain how you would like to be treated as you are given anesthesia.** "You may want your anesthesiologist to hold your hand or stroke your forehead," says Huddleston.

● **If you have any fears about the anesthesia, talk these over with your doctor.** "Usually your fears can be allayed with straightforward information about what will happen," she says.

● **Discuss your medications and allergies.** "Carefully review this information with your doctor, asking if there are any medications you should stop taking before surgery."

● **Know when you should stop eating or drinking the night before surgery.** "The cutoff times for food and liquids are crucial," says Huddleston. "Follow the doctor's rules."

● **Know what medications will be available to reduce postoperative discomfort or pain.** "The more you know, the more in control you will be after your operation."

● **Discuss instructions about how to move and care for your body after surgery.** "Your surgeon will usually give you written instructions about how to move your body during recovery," says Huddleston.

"As you can see, an informative and supportive meeting goes a long way toward reducing your stress and preparing you for an optimal outcome."

Rapid Resource: The program that Huddleston developed to use in hospitals consists of the book she wrote and also a relaxation CD for you to learn how to relax and to listen to in the hospital.

"At home, you can use any type of listening device you like," she says. "But at the hospital, you'll need a listening device with headphones. Remember to take along several extra batteries as well as the electric cord to the device. Using the CD at the hospital will let you create your own private, healing atmosphere. Wherever you are, the headphones will block out distracting noises and give you privacy."

You can order the book and the CD (either together or separately) at *www.healfaster.com*, or call 800-726-4173 or e-mail *peggy@healfaster. com*. The website includes excerpts from her book, interviews with Huddleston and detailed information about scientific studies on her programs. Huddleston also offers one-on-one phone consultations to help you prepare for surgery.

PREGNANCY PROBLEMS

Nine Months of Minute-by-Minute Relief

Here's the good news for moms-to-be—almost all of the aches and pains of pregnancy are *not* a pressing medical problem.

"They are usually annoyances and inconveniences," says Laura Riley, MD, author of *Pregnancy: The Ultimate Week-by-Week Pregnancy Guide* (Wiley), medical director of labor and delivery at Massachusetts General Hospital in Boston and assistant professor of obstetrics, gynecology and reproductive biology at Harvard Medical School.

"The discomforts are usually not an illness, nor are they going to harm your baby. And they are usually fleeting, getting better in a week or two," she says.

But that doesn't mean you don't want relief. *And there are plenty of ways to get it—fast…*

🕐 *Super-Quick Fix*

➤ **For morning sickness—suck on a popsicle.** Nausea and vomiting—otherwise known as morning sickness—is the most common complaint in pregnancy, particularly during the first trimester. "They're often caused by dehydration," says Dr. Riley. She suggests drinking 80 ounces of water a day.

Problem: Many pregnant women in their first trimester don't like drinking plain water.

Solution: Get your liquids in other ways.

- Eat popsicles or Italian ices. (Yes, you're right to be concerned about sugary, empty calories, says Dr. Riley. But when you're nauseous in the beginning of your pregnancy, you should eat whatever makes you feel better.)
- Suck on ice chips.
- Favor watery fruits and vegetables, such as watermelons and cucumbers.
- Drink lemonade.

➤ **Press nausea away.** Pressing an acupuncture point on your wrist can help relieve nausea, says Dr. Riley.

What to do: "Press three fingertips gently but firmly on the base of your palm, just above where you'd take your pulse on your wrist. Breathe deeply and press that area with your fingertips for a minute or more, gradually increasing pressure until you feel slight discomfort."

Rapid Resource: Try BioBands, a wristband that applies steady pressure to the nausea-relieving acupuncture points. You can order from the company website, at *www.biobands. com*, or call 800-246-2263. Address: BioBands, P.O. Box 393, Roslyn, NY 11576.

➤ **Eat something.** "You may not feel like eating, but an empty stomach will only make the problem worse—because morning sickness is worsened by low blood sugar."

What to do: "If you crave a food and can keep it down, eat it—no matter what it is," she says.

"It might also help to eat food that is cold or at room temperature, because that will cut down on potentially nauseating odors."

The Nausea Kit

"In case you're seized by a bout of nausea while you're out and about, keep an emergency kit handy," says Dr. Riley. It should include…

- *Plastic bags*
- *Wet wipes*
- *Napkins*
- *Water for rinsing your mouth*
- *Toothbrush and toothpaste*
- *Breath mints*

Two other good ideas…

- **Before you get out of bed,** nibble on crackers.

- **Before you go to bed,** eat a small carbohydrate snack, such as a whole grain muffin, so that you stomach will feel less queasy.

➤ **For back pain, mimic an angry cat.** "About half of women complain of back pain as their pregnancies progress," says Dr. Riley.

What to do: "To help relieve the problem, lay on your side and push your back out like an angry cat," says Dr. Riley. "That helps release all the contracted muscles. This stretch is especially helpful in the eighth and ninth months of pregnancy, when your back is killing you after a long day."

➤ **Help for heartburn.** About half of pregnant women experience heartburn during their second and third trimesters, typically after meals or at bedtime, says Dr. Riley. That's because pregnancy hormones slow down emptying time from the stomach and cause the muscle between the stomach and the esophagus to relax.

Some easy ways to douse the burn…

- Combine acidic foods such as oranges and tomatoes with less acidic foods. *Examples:* Eat tomatoes on your sandwich instead of in your salad. Don't drink orange juice until after you've had a bowl of cereal.

- Eat six small meals rather than three large meals.

- Try an over-the-counter antacid like Tums or Mylanta. They can safely reduce the acidity of your stomach contents during pregnancy without harming your baby, says Dr. Riley.

▶ **For varicose veins, relief that rocks.** Your legs feel heavy, tired and achy. Like 50% of pregnant women, you have varicose veins—"evidence that your circulatory system is struggling to move forty percent more blood through veins and arteries," says Dr. Riley. Some of that extra blood has stretched out veins, causing their valves to malfunction and blood to pool rather than flow—further stretching and even twisting the vein.

"Varicose veins can be permanent and tend to worsen with each pregnancy, so it's worth trying to prevent them or to ease the discomfort they cause," says Dr. Riley.

Her recommendations...

- Sit in a rocking chair several times a day, using your legs to gently rock back and forth.

- When you rest, keep your legs elevated higher than your heart.

- Don't cross your legs when you sit down.

- Avoid standing or sitting for long periods of time.

- Walk 30 minutes every day.

- Wear sheer maternity pantyhose.

▶ **The best treatment for leg cramps.** "Leg cramps usually occur in the lower leg, often at night," says Dr. Riley. "They can be quite painful and interrupt your sleep."

What to do: "Stand barefoot on a cold tile floor and lift your toes up," she says. "This stretches the calf and often brings relief."

▶ **For foot pain, rotate your ankles.** "Higher hormone levels cause you to retain water, making your feet swell," says Dr. Riley.

See Your Doctor If...

"The number one reason to see the doctor right away is vaginal bleeding," says Dr. Riley. "If you're bleeding during the first trimester, it may be a miscarriage. If it's the second trimester, it's not normal. Same for the third trimester.

"Yes, there may be a little spotting when you're about to deliver. But otherwise, see the doctor.

"You should also see your doctor if there is any ache or pain that is not going away and is escalating in intensity."

What to do: "Sit with one leg raised, rotating your ankle a dozen times in each direction. Then switch legs and do the same thing with the other leg."

▶ **Soothe carpal tunnel with a pillow.** Twenty-five percent of pregnant women get carpal tunnel syndrome—pressure on a nerve- and tendon-filled area in the wrist, which causes numbness, tingling and burning in the hands and arms. "It can be particularly aggravating at night, when fluid has pooled in your extremities," says Dr. Riley.

What to do: "Sleep with your hands propped up on a pillow to encourage fluid to drain to other regions of your body," she advises.

▶ **Quick TLC for your post-delivery bottom.** The vagina can tear during delivery, leaving you with a sore bottom, says Dr. Riley.

Her recommendations...

- Apply ice to ease soreness and swelling in the first 24 hours.

- Keep the area clean to speed healing and prevent infection.

- Use a squirt bottle with warm water to gently cleanse the area several times a day and after you urinate. (Pat rather than rub dry.)

• Take a warm (not hot) sitz bath a few times a day. Fill a small plastic tub with water, position it over your toilet and sit in it. (The same recommendation works for hemorrhoids during pregnancy.)

PREMENSTRUAL SYNDROME (PMS)

Breaking the Cycle of Upset and Pain

Maybe your thinking isn't as clear, your concentration isn't as focused and your memory isn't as sharp. Maybe you're more irritable, depressed and tense. Maybe you've developed back pain, a headache or pelvic cramps. Maybe your body has become bloated and your breasts tender. Maybe you've started to crave sweets and salty food. What's happening to you?

Premenstrual syndrome, or PMS.

"PMS is an array of symptoms—emotional, cognitive, physical, behavioral—that occur cyclically during the premenstrual phase of the cycle and are followed by relief during the menses," says Lori Futterman, RN, PhD, director of the San Diego Premenstrual Syndrome Clinic, an assistant professor at University of California, San Diego, and author of *PMS, Perimenopause, and You* (Lowell House).

An estimated 70% to 90% of women experience PMS, with 10% to 40% saying the symptoms interfere with daily life—one or more of the 150 distressful symptoms linked to the syndrome. Why so many?

"The reason that PMS can have such far-reaching effects is that people have receptors for estrogen and progesterone—two of the hormones that are involved in PMS—throughout their entire bodies," explains Diana Taylor, RN,

PhD, professor emerita at the School of Nursing at the University of California, San Francisco (UCSF), and coauthor of *Taking Back the Month: A Personalized Solution for Managing PMS and Enhancing Your Health* (Perigee).

"That's why PMS can affect how a woman feels from literally head to toe."

But she can also feel better from head to toe.

"I have seen women with PMS overcome their symptoms with vitamins, minerals, herbs and lifestyle and nutritional changes," says Linda Woolven, a herbalist and acupuncturist in Toronto Canada, and author of *Smart Women's Guide to PMS and Pain-Free Periods* (Wiley).

Here's what she and other experts say can help clear up your month-to-month symptoms in three months or less...

➤ **Take a multivitamin-mineral and PMS supplement.** "In my research with the UCSF PMS Symptom Management Program, vitamin and mineral supplements were the most frequently used strategy for PMS, and for most women helped relieve PMS severity within three months—particularly fluid retention, constipation, concentration problems and mood swings," says Dr. Taylor.

Recommended: "I recommend a general multivitamin-mineral supplement that is taken for half the month, from the first day of the period to mid-cycle," she says. "Then stop taking the multivitamin-mineral supplement and start taking a PMS formula supplement, and take it every day from mid-cycle until the start of the period.

"If you continue to have PMS symptoms a few days into your period, it's fine to continue taking the PMS formula for a few more days," says Dr. Taylor. "Just be sure to switch back to the regular multivitamin-mineral formula, and stop taking the PMS formula by the end of your period."

Suggested intake: Dr. Taylor suggests a multivitamin-mineral formula with approximately these levels of nutrients: Vitamin A,

The PMS Diet

What can you eat to prevent and treat PMS? "It's actually quite simple," says Woolven.

Her recommendations...

- *Increase your consumption of fiber.* It helps lower estrogen, which helps reduce PMS.

- *Reduce your consumption of saturated fats.* "If you decrease the amount of saturated fat in your diet—from animal and dairy products—you'll also dramatically reduce estrogen," she says.

- *Increase your consumption of essential fatty acids.* These fats—found in fatty fish such as salmon, tuna and mackerel, and in flax seed and flax seed oil—improve PMS symptoms and overall health.

- *Reduce your intake of simple sugars and carbohydrates.* "Simple sugars are simply bad for PMS," says Woolven. "The more sugar you eat, the more severe your PMS symptoms will be."

- *Reduce or eliminate caffeine.* "If you suffer from breast tenderness, mood disorders, irritability, insomnia and depression during the days on which you have PMS—caffeine must be strictly avoided," says Woolven. "Even one cup a day significantly aggravates symptoms."

- *Reduce salt.* "Salt can cause water retention, one of the leading problems experienced by women with PMS," she says.

- *Eat more soy foods.* Soy foods contain phytoestrogens, which bind to estrogen receptor sites in your body and balance your estrogen levels.

- *Eat foods rich in sulfur.* "It's one of the key nutrients for eliminating excess estrogen from the body," says Woolven. *Good food sources:* Garlic, onions and beans.

15,000 IU; vitamin D, 400 IU; vitamin E, 600 IU; vitamin C, 1,000 milligrams (mg); folic acid, 50 mg; thiamine (vitamin B-1), 50 mg; riboflavin (vitamin B-2), 50 mg; niacin, 50 mg; vitamin B-6, 200 micrograms (mcg); vitamin B-12, 50 mcg; biotin, 30 mcg; pantothenic acid, 50 mg; calcium, 150 mg; magnesium, 300 mg; iodine, 150 mcg; iron, 15 mg; zinc, 25 mg; manganese, 10 mg; potassium, 100 mg; selenium, 25 mcg; chromium, 100 mcg.

Product: "The PMS supplement I recommend most often is the Schiff PMS 1 Nutritional Supplement," she says. "It's well tolerated by most women and requires taking no more than eight small gelatin capsules a day."

▶ **Chasteberry for PMS.** "Chasteberry—*vitex agnus castus*—is the most important herb for normalizing and regulating the menstrual cycle," says Woolven. "In Europe, it is a standard treatment to relieve PMS symptoms, including depression, cramps, mood swings, water retention and weight gain."

Study: Researchers in Germany asked more than 1,600 woman with PMS to take a chasteberry supplement. After three cycles, 93% of the women reported a decrease or complete cessation of PMS symptoms. Less depression. Less anxiety. Less food cravings. Less bloating. Less breast tenderness. The study was reported in the *Journal of Women's Health and Gender-Based Medicine.*

Suggested intake: 175 to 225 mg daily of a tablet standardized for 0.5% agnuside, the active ingredient. Or 30 drops of a tincture, three times a day.

Also helpful: Woolven suggests you consider the following treatments for PMS symptoms if dietary changes and chasteberry haven't worked after three months...

- **Water retention.** Take 50 mg of B-6 three times a day with food. It acts as a diuretic.

- **Depression.** Add 50 to 100 mg of 5-HTP, three times a day. It boosts serotonin, a brain chemical that regulates mood.

- **Anxiety.** Add a tincture of passionflower—40 drops, three or four times a day.

- **Insomnia.** Add valerian, 150 to 300 mg, standardized for 0.8 percent valeric acid, 30 minutes before bed.

- **Acne.** Add zinc, 25 to 50 mg, once a day.

Important: Use these herbs and nutritional supplements with the approval and supervision of a qualified health practitioner, says Woolven.

➤ **Foot reflexology for menstrual cramps.** Reflexology is a healing modality that says the feet (and the hands and the outer ears) are "maps" of the rest of the body, with specific points that correspond to organs and areas,

explains Bill Flocco, director of the American Academy of Reflexology in Burbank, California. By *applying therapeutic pressure to those points, you can help your body heal from a wide range of health problems. Including menstrual cramps…*

The study: Women with PMS were divided into three groups. One group received reflexology for several months, one group received "placebo" reflexology (pressure on points that weren't linked to PMS) and one group didn't receive any treatment. The group receiving reflexology had a 47% reduction in symptoms, including menstrual cramps. The study appeared in the journal *Obstetrics and Gynecology.*

What to do: The primary point for menstrual cramps is the "uterine reflex" on the back lower corner of the inside of the foot, says Flocco. To work the area, place your left foot on your right knee. With the thumb of your right hand, apply pressure to the area below the protruding anklebone, between the ankle and the back of the heel bone. "Start off lightly, gradually increasing the pressure," says Flocco.

Use a technique Flocco calls the "thumb roll"—place the tip of your thumb directly on the skin and then roll it forward, applying pressure. Then move the tip of the thumb slightly forward, and perform the maneuver again. (It is like the movement of an inchworm.) Repeat until the entire area is covered.

After working on your right foot, switch to your left.

Work the left and right foot for a total of 10 to 15 minutes a day, four to five days before your period starts, says Flocco. "Usually within a month or two, women report a dramatic reduction in or elimination of their menstrual cramps," he says.

⚠ ***Caution:*** Since this technique stimulates the uterus, do not perform it if you are in the first trimester of pregnancy.

See Your Doctor If...

Do you need to see a doctor for your PMS? "Ask yourself if there is interference in your quality of life from PMS symptoms," says Dr. Futterman. "How would you rank yourself on a scale of one to ten, with ten being the most disabling? If you score five or above, you need assistance. If you score seven or above, you definitely need assistance."

The best treatment approach to PMS is a *team* approach, she adds. "Talk to a gynecologist who specializes in menstrual cycle-related difficulties. You could also consult with a nutritionist, a personal trainer and a psychologist. There are clinics throughout the country that offer this type of multi-discipline approach."

Rapid Resource: Gynecologists who specialize in menopause are often competent to treat PMS, she says. You can find a list of certified practitioners at the website of the North American Menopause Society, *www.menopause.org.*

Rapid Resource: The website *www.ameri canacademyofreflexology.com* offers reflexology charts, books about reflexology, dates of reflexology classes and other information about the modality. Address: American Academy of Reflexology, Bill Flocco, Director, 725 E. Santa Anita Ave., #B, Burbank, CA 91501, call 818-841-7741 or e-mail *aareflex@aol.com*.

PROSTATE PROBLEMS

Restore the Flow

I'm a sixty-one-year-old man—so I'm speaking from experience when I talk about this health problem," jokes Angelo Druda, a certified practitioner of Traditional Chinese Medicine in northern California (*www. traditionalbotanicalmedicine.com*) and author of *The Tao of Rejuvenation: Fundamental Principles of Health, Longevity and Essential Well-Being* (North Atlantic).

The experience is urinary problems. The cause is a swollen prostate, or what doctors call *benign prostatic hypertrophy* (BPH).

What happens: The prostate is a walnut-size, semen-producing gland that circles the urethra, the tube that transports ejaculate and drains urine from the bladder. Around the age of 40—probably because of age-related changes in the levels and action of testosterone—prostate cells begin to expand. The swollen organ squeezes and narrows the urethra.

Four out of five men over 40 have BPH, with about 50% of men 60 or older experiencing urinary symptoms. They can include urgency…more frequent urination, including waking up several times a night to urinate…difficulty starting the stream…a weaker stream…straining…difficulty stopping the stream…dribbling at the end…and incomplete emptying.

There are many medical treatments for BPH, depending on the severity of the symptoms, which range from mild to emergency (completely blocked urine flow). You can take an *alpha-blocker* such as *tamsulosin* (Flomax), which relaxes the muscular junction where the bladder and urethra meet. You can take a *5 alpha reductase inhibitor* such as *finasteride* (Proscar), which blocks an enzyme that converts testosterone to *dihydrotestosterone* (DHT), a hormone that pumps up prostate cells. A doctor can insert various devices through your urethra to shrink the prostate with microwave radiation or radio waves or a laser. Or a surgeon can slice away some of the swollen gland.

Red flags: But these treatments can have undesirable side effects. For example, many men who take Flomax develop ejaculatory difficulties (pleasureless or painful orgasms, or an inability to have an orgasm), says James Occhiogrosso, CNC, a certified nutritional counselor and herbalist in Florida and author of *Your Prostate, Your Libido, Your Life* (Glenbridge).

Good news: If your symptoms have started recently, you can reverse them quickly with natural therapies, says Druda. "If you address the problem when symptoms begin, you can have a swollen prostate on Monday, and by Friday the problem is handled."

Here is what Druda and other naturally oriented practitioners suggest for fast, effective ways to reverse BPH without the risk of drug- or surgery-caused side effects. *Discuss these options with a qualified health practitioner…*

➤ **Try saw palmetto and pygeum—together.** What's the first treatment for BPH typically prescribed in Europe, Asia, Africa and India? Flomax? Proscar? Neither. It's Permixon—an *herbal medication* that is a formulation of

Speed Healing Success

"I Rarely Wake Up More Than Once During the Night to Urinate"

James Occhiogrosso was 18 years old when his father died…of a swollen prostate. "All the men in my family have a significant history of prostate symptoms," says Occhiogrosso. "My father had severe BPH and was hospitalized for prostate surgery when he was 54. He entered the hospital on Sunday afternoon and my family was making funeral arrangements on Monday evening."

Occhiogrosso began developing BPH symptoms in his 40s. "I would wake up more and more frequently during the night—first once, then twice, then three times a night and then every hour on the hour. By my late 50s, the condition was intolerable." But it didn't stay that way.

"Today, at the age of seventy, I rarely wake more than once during the night to urinate. I don't have to stake out the location of every rest room before I take a trip. In short, my prostate— and my overall health—is better now than it was more than two decades ago." What did Occhiogrosso do?

He began to eat a diet rich in plant foods, with no red meat or dairy products. "A diet that emphasizes plant foods can help to balance hormoane levels," he says.

He started taking saw palmetto and pygeum. He also took a flower pollen extract, which European studies show can help reduce the symptoms of BPH.

He used several other supplements, exercised regularly and practiced stress reduction.

"My condition has been stable for about the past ten years," he says. "I am very satisfied with my approach to prostate health." He suggests that anyone diagnosed with BPH "try the natural approach for at least a year" before turning to medications.

Rapid Resource: You can find out more about Occhiogrosso's approach to prostate health and the supplements he takes for his condition at *www.prostatehealthnaturally.com.*

---

saw palmetto, an extract from the berries of the serona repens bush. It works by reducing DHT.

Glenn S. Gerber, MD, an associate professor of surgery and urology in the Division of Urology at the University of Chicago Medical School analyzed more than 30 studies on Permixon— including studies showing it worked as well as Proscar and Flomax, but without the side effects. "Permixon significantly reduces the symptoms of BPH, increases urinary flow, improves the quality of life and is well tolerated," he says, in the *British Journal of Urology.*

In a similar analysis, researchers at the Minneapolis Veterans Center looked at 18 studies on another herb often used to treat BPH—*pygeum arficanum.* Compared to a placebo, men taking the herb had a 23% increase in urine flow and 20% fewer episodes of nighttime urination. Pygeum africanum may be a useful treatment option for men with lower urinary tract symptoms from BPH, say the researchers, in the *American Journal of Medicine.* Pygeum works by strengthening the bladder and reducing inflammation.

"I find a formula with both these herbs does the trick in reversing BPH," says Druda.

Important: "You want to start treating prostate issues as soon as you get the symptoms," he says. "Otherwise, if you ignore the problem for five or ten years, the gland gets engorged and hard as a rock—to treat the problem, you have to do something like zap the prostate with a laser or shave it with surgery."

Product: Serageum, a combination of saw palmetto and pygeum, developed by Subhuti

Dharmananda, PhD, director of the Institute for Tradition Medicine, in Portland, Oregon. It also includes several Chinese herbs traditionally used for BPH.

Suggested intake: 1 capsule, three times a day.

Rapid Resource: Serageum is available on the web from Shakti Enterprises at *www.chinese herbs.net*, call 828-505-2300 and from *www. maxnature.com*, call 626-415-7375.

➤ **Take beta sitosterol.** This common plant component reduces DHT, says Druda. He uses it along with the saw palmetto and pygeum herbal formula. "It's tremendously effective," he says. Beta sitosterol supplements are widely available.

➤ **Zinc for the prostate.** "The prostate gland contains ten times more zinc than any other organ in the body," says Nigma Talib, ND, a naturopathic doctor in private practice in West Vancouver, Canada (*www.healthydoc.com*). And a dietary deficiency of zinc—common in North America, where soils have become depleted of minerals because of modern farming practices—contributes to the enlargement of the gland.

Suggested intake: 45 mg a day.

Also helpful: "Every man should eat zinc-rich pumpkin seeds," says Dr. Talib. She suggests ¼ to ½ cup a day. "You can add them to a protein smoothie or sprinkle them on your cereal."

➤ **Cut out coffee, alcohol and hot, spicy foods.** "Over the past thirty years I've successfully treated more than ten thousand patients with uri-

---

See Your Doctor If...

If you develop any of the urinary symptoms described in this section, see your doctor to rule out other possible causes, such as prostate cancer, prostatitis (an infection of the prostate), bladder infection and kidney disease—and to discuss a treatment plan if you do have BPH.

---

nary difficulties of all kinds—including BPH and the inflammation of chronic prostatitis—with a simple dietary approach," says Milton Krisiloff, MD, a urologist in Santa Monica, California and author of *The Krisiloff Anti-Inflammatory Diet Revolution* (One World Press).

His diet eliminates caffeine, alcohol and hot, spicy foods.

Research: "To quantify my observations, I examined almost twenty-four hundred charts of patients from my medical practice," he says. "For patients on the Krisiloff Diet, eighty-seven percent of men and eighty-nine of women were cured of their urinary problems."

Why it works: He theorizes that caffeine, alcohol and hot, spicy foods cause an "allergy-like reaction" leading to inflammation—an inflammation that he thinks underlies not only BPH and chronic prostatitis, but many other conditions, including arthritis, heartburn, chronic sinusitis, skin rashes and chronic headaches.

His advice about eliminating these foods...

● **Caffeine.** "Many people think caffeine is synonymous only with coffee," he says. "But caffeine is also found in tea, decaffeinated coffee, decaffeinated tea, cola drinks, some non-cola drinks, such as energy drinks, and in chocolate. Caffeine-free herbal tea or grain beverages are acceptable drinks."

● **Alcohol.** "Eliminating alcohol means all alcohol, including beer and wine," he says.

● **Spicy foods.** "Forbidden hot spicy foods include salsa, red pepper, hot mustard, horseradish, chiles, Tabasco sauce, pepperoni, curry and wasabi. Mild spices such as salt, black pepper and onion are not irritants and are acceptable."

Bottom line: "People ask if they have to stay on the diet permanently," says Dr. Krisiloff. "If they want to never have symptoms again, the answer is yes."

Rapid Resource: You can order the book at *www.krisiloffdiet.wordpress.com.*

PSORIASIS

Diet Can Make the Difference

Only 120,000 Americans have what dermatologists consider extensive psoriasis—large skin areas of red, flaky, scaly lesions that can itch, crack, bleed and hurt.

For them and every other psoriasis sufferer, a glitch in the immune system (with an unknown cause) forces skin cells to recycle too quickly—every three to four days rather than the typical month, leading to an unsightly pileup on the skin surface.

Well, 120,000 is a small number, as diseases go. But what's happening to the other estimated five to seven million Americans with a "mild" or "moderate" version of the disease? Their psoriasis is confined to a smaller area—usually the elbows, knees, scalp, nails, palms or soles. And it comes and goes in flare-ups. Is it nothing more than a now-and-then annoyance? Definitely not.

A study conducted by the National Psoriasis Foundation (NPF) found that nearly 2 million Americans with psoriasis say their skin condition is a daily problem for them—and more than 1 million are dissatisfied with their current treatment.

"All too often, we hear from psoriasis patients who have given up on their treatment, and who have given up hope," says Gail M. Zimmerman, former president of the NPF. "Psoriasis can have such a significant negative impact on lives—physically, socially and emotionally. This study is a powerful reminder that even those patients whose psoriasis is not considered 'severe' by traditional measurements nevertheless deserve and need additional treatment options that will work for them."

Deirdre Earls, RD—a registered dietician in Austin, Texas, and author of *Your Healing Diet: A Quick Guide to Reversing Psoriasis and Chronic Diseases with Healing Foods* (BookSurge)—offers people with psoriasis one of those options. An option that she says healed her of a 25-year case of psoriasis on her hands and elsewhere—psoriasis so bad, she couldn't turn a steering wheel or unscrew a jar without opening cracks in her hands.

▶ **The diet that defeated psoriasis.** "I had tried various drugs and topical treatments for my psoriasis—including spending days in the hospital covered with coal tar," says Earls. "My doctor was recommending methotrexate, an oral drug that can cause liver damage with long-term use, and I didn't want to go that route—it was too expensive, and I envisioned myself getting sicker than I already was.

"Well, I began researching on the Internet—where I found many sources suggesting diet as a possible approach. I had spent two decades in professional dietetics, and even though no one had ever suggested that diet had anything to do with psoriasis, I figured I had nothing to lose by giving it a shot—and committed myself to natural healing with food.

"Within six months, my hands had cleared eighty-five to ninety-five percent—without any medications. Now I am completely clear—and it's been seven years since I've had any flare-ups. I also no longer have allergies and lost twenty pounds of unwanted weight. I've never turned back."

Why did the diet work? "It's simple," says Earls. "Psoriasis is a systemic, inflammatory disease. A plant-based, whole-foods diet is an anti-inflammatory diet."

Earls describes the principles of that diet…

1. Increase consumption of complex carbohydrates, especially whole grains, legumes

See Your Doctor If...

There are many medical treatments for psoriasis (and for psoriatric arthritis, which accompanies the disease in 20% to 30% of cases), with various levels of effectiveness, side effects and expense, says Abby S. Van Voorhees, MD, director of the Psoriasis and Phototherapy Treatment Center and associate professor of dermatology at the University of Pennsylvania Medical School. They help to slow the rapid growth of skin cells, and to soften and lift the psoriasis scales, reducing redness, and controlling itching and inflammation. If you have psoriasis that is causing you discomfort (physical or emotional), see a dermatologist. Treatments include…

- **Topical treatments,** such as coal tar; moisturizers; bath solutions; corticosteroids; anti-itch creams; *calcipotriene* (Dovonex), a vitamin D derivative; *calcipotriene* and *betamethasone dipropionate* (Taclonex); and *tazarotene* (Tazorac), a vitamin A derivative.

- **Light therapy (phototherapy),** exposing the skin to controlled ultraviolet (UV) light, either UVA or UVB.

- **Psoralen and UVA (PUVA),** a combination of a medication and phototherapy.

- **Lasers,** which have various effects, such as destroying the tiny blood vessels that contribute to psoriasis lesions.

- **Retinoids,** oral drugs related to vitamin A.

- **Cyclosporine,** an immunosuppressive drug.

- **Methotrexate,** an immunosuppressive drug.

- **Biologics,** a new class of drugs given by injection or IV infusion, which work by blocking the action of immune cells.

and fresh vegetables and fruits. "When in doubt, eat a plant," she says.

2. **Reduce consumption of refined sugars—** white sugar, cane juices, high fructose corn syrups, etc.

3. **Reduce consumption of animal foods,** such as meats, poultry, eggs and dairy. "If you crave meat, try to limit yourself to four ounces of red meat per week, eight ounces of white chicken or fowl, two eggs per week, eight ounces of low- or nonfat yogurt, and two ounces of low-fat or nonfat cheese," she says.

4. **Reduce total fat consumption,** especially of saturated fats, which are found in animal products.

5. **Eat from a wide variety of fresh foods,** to ensure a balance of vitamins and minerals.

6. **Eat more fresh and organic foods,** and less chemically processed foods. "Fresh is always best and frozen is the next best option," says Earls.

7. **Avoid all alcohol.**

Important: Earls counsels those who want to try the diet to approach it with the right mind-set for maximum success. "You need to be convinced of the diet's efficacy and committed to it before you try it," she says. "Otherwise, you'll *force* yourself to do it—and fail, because there will be an inevitable backlash.

"You also have to realize that mistakes will happen—you'll go off the diet. Well, no one is perfect—and perfection is not required. Approach the diet with the attitude that you can eat *whatever* you want to eat—and that you have decided to make certain food choices more often than others. If you're rigid, you're sure to fail."

Smart idea: "Don't let yourself get hungry," says Earls. "When you're really hungry and you don't have any quality food at your fingertips, you invariably get frustrated and eat whatever is available. Pack healthy snacks in your refrigerator, car, purse and office. Almond butter, raisins,

Odwalla bars, LäraBars, fiber-rich juices such as Odwalla Superfood, Naked Juices or Amazake and brown rice cakes are great snacks that can travel almost anywhere."

She also counsels all her clients to check with a physician before beginning any dietary change.

➤ **Tazorac—a uniquely effective treatment.** "I have been amazed by the effectiveness of Tazorac [tazarotene], a form of topical vitamin A," says Audrey Kunin, MD, a dermatologist in Kansas City, Missouri, and founder and president of *www.dermadoctor.com*. "In fact, I haven't had a single psoriasis patient treated with Tazorac fail to improve. I consider it one of the best therapies for moderate plaque psoriasis, the most common kind."

Better: "However, I ask my patients to alter their treatment from the normal, daily recommended use," says Dr. Kunin. "I ask them to use it the way experience has taught me is the best for skin to tolerate a topical vitamin A cream—every other night, very sparingly, on dry skin.

"Plus, I add a second element to the treatment regimen. Every morning, I have the patient apply the steroid clobetasol to her psoriasis—except for thinner areas of skin, such as the face, groin, flexures such as the elbow crease, and the neck, because steroids can thin the skin.

"So, every other night they use Tazorac. I start with stronger 0.1% Tazorac Gel, unless the affected areas are in the same thin regions, in which case I choose the lower-potency 0.05% in a cream base. Within four to six weeks, clearing is seen. For stubborn areas, I increase the Tazorac to every night, if the patient's skin can tolerate it. Children have more delicate skin, and I prescribe Tazorac 0.05% cream only on a case-by-case basis.

"The biggest problem with Tazorac has been irritation or initial enlargement of the involved sites—this routine is great at preventing that problem.

"Again, I have to say that Tazorac has been one of the most impressive therapies for psoriasis that I have ever prescribed."

⚠ *Caution:* "Of course, there may be situations where it is not appropriate—for pregnant women, for a person with generalized psoriasis or for pustular psoriasis," says Dr. Kunin. "Ask your dermatologist if it is right for you."

REPETITIVE STRAIN INJURY (RSI)

You work (or play) on a computer for hours at a time, clicking your mouse. Or you pound away for hours at pavements with a jackhammer. Or you snip, snip, snip with a scissors, cutting hair. Or you hit a golf or tennis ball hundreds of times. Or you check out customers in a supermarket, scanning hundreds of products over a barcode detector. You *repeat* the same motion over and over. And because of that, you might develop *repetitive strain injury*, or RSI.

RSI is the most common cause of occupational injury, with a $20 billion a year price tag for workers' compensation. Eight million Americans suffer from carpal tunnel syndrome, an RSI in which inflamed tendons, bone spurs, or other structures squeeze on the median nerve as it passes through the wrist.

Theory: No one knows exactly what causes RSI. But a common explanation is that inflamed muscles and strain-thickened connective tissue (tendons and ligaments) pinch nerves and blood vessels, causing pain, tingling, numbness or weakness.

There are two easy ways to lessen the discomfort of (and maybe even reverse) RSI, says Jonathan Mulholland, DC, a chiropractic physician in Plattsburgh, NY, and a chiropractic consultant at the Lake Placid Olympic Training Center. One is to increase blood flow to the area of the injury. The other is to break up *adhesions*, scar tissue that presses on and binds nerves.

And there's a five-minute self-massage that can do both…

➤ **Use the "active release technique."** This uniquely effective self-massage technique was invented by James Cyriax, MD, a British orthopedic surgeon, says Dr. Mulholland, who suggests you do it five minutes once a day for pain from *any* RSI.

Find the spot that is the sorest and the tightest. Apply enough pressure so that it "hurts good"—uncomfortable but not excruciating, providing relief without too much accompanying pain. With your index finger in place on the sore spot, simply roll back and forth across the spot (there will be enough give in the skin and muscle to do this easily) in an area about an inch wide. Do not pick up the finger and move it around.

"Do this massage for five minutes while you're watching TV at night," says Dr. Mulholland.

Also helpful: Another effective massage is to apply and maintain direct pressure with the index finger—without moving it—straight into the sorest spot. "A sharp radiating pain will gradually dull," says Dr. Mulholland.

➤ **When you're in acute pain, use ice.** "When pain is intense, ice is the best treatment," says Dr. Mulholland.

What you may not know: Heat at the wrong time can increase inflammation. "Don't use it until your pain is under control," he says.

What to do: Apply ice at 20-minute intervals—20 minutes on, 20 minutes off, as many times a day as possible. "Ice is never going to hurt your condition, as long as you don't keep it on too long," he says.

Use ice packs or a sandwich bag filled with ice. You can also freeze water in a paper cup, hold the cup, and massage the painful area with ice for 10 or 15 minutes.

➤ **RSI-easing postures for sitting, working at a computer, driving and sleeping.** Proper posture can ease carpal tunnel syndrome, says Scott Fried, DO, of the Upper Extremity Institute in Blue Bell, Pennsylvania, (*www.nervepain.com*) and author of *The Carpal Tunnel Helpbook* (Perseus).

His suggestions…

- **Sitting.** Keep your head and neck upright, with your ears directly over your shoulders.

- **At the computer.** The computer display should be directly in front of you, at eye height, and adjustable for comfort. "As you type or use a mouse, your wrists should be straight, resting in a neutral position using arm rests and wrist rests," he says. Place the mouse in a position that requires minimal stretching of your arm—consider keeping it at the same height as the keyboard. "The key is to avoid straining your neck or arms and to remain comfortable while working."

Smart idea: "Some "ergonomic" keyboards work well for some people, but common sense and overall ergonomics—proper posture and positioning—are more important, says Dr. Fried. "My recommendation for any ergonomic keyboard is to try it out for at least a half an hour before you buy it. If it feels good, it may be helpful, but nothing works for everyone."

Your chair should have a firm but not hard seat, says Dr. Fried. Your feet should be firmly on the floor, with your knees at a 90° angle, sticking out at few inches from the front of the seat. The backrest should support your back—if the seat doesn't have an adjustable backrest, use a small pillow or rolled-up towel. Armrests are best—"they help support the shoulders, allowing you to relax the muscles around the neck," he says.

- **Driving.** Hold the steering wheel low, rather than at the middle or the top. "Hold it securely, but try to relax the arms and hands," he says.

Smart idea: For long trips, rest your forearm on a pillow for support.

- **Sleeping.** "Certain sleeping positions can worsen the symptoms of RSI," says Dr. Fried.

Red flags: Sleeping on your arm. Using more than one supporting pillow under your neck.

The Best Mouse for RSI

"For my patients with RSI, I recommend the Zero Tension Mouse," says Dr. Mulholland. "It uses a lateral device—a kind of thick joystick—and prevents the hours of micro-movement with a mouse that can cause RSI."

Rapid Resource: You can order the Zero Tension Mouse at *www.ergoexpress.com*.

Sleeping on your stomach with your head turned to one side. Lying on the side where you experience symptoms. Placing your arm over your head.

Best: Sleep on your back. "Or lie on the unaffected side with one pillow under your head and another pillow in front of you, in line with your trunk, using the second pillow to prop up the affected arm."

➤ **A super-stretch for RSI.** Doing the following shoulder roll two or three times a day can dramatically reduce the tension in your shoulders, arms, wrists and hands, preventing or reducing the pain of RSI, says Sharon Butler, a certified practitioner of Hellerwork (a structural bodywork and movement therapy) in Paoli, Pennsylvania (*www.selfcare4rsi.com*), and author of *Conquering Carpal Tunnel Syndrome* (New Harbinger).

Her instructions…

Raise your shoulders toward your ears and let your arms hang loosely by your sides. Very slowly, rotate your shoulders toward the front of your body. Continue rotating them to the lowest point, reverse direction and rotate them toward the back, then return to the starting position.

Take at least 30 seconds to do this exercise, making the widest circle possible, then do another complete revolution in the opposite direction.

➤ **How to prevent and ease tennis elbow.** "There are some common problems that cause most cases of tennis elbow," says Dr. Mulholland.

A Surgeon's No-Surgery Recommendations for RSI

Of people who have surgery for carpal tunnel syndrome, one-third say they have long-term scar discomfort and only poor to fair recovery of hand strength and 57% have a recurrence of their pain. But there are other ways to reduce the pain and restore function, says Robert E. Markison, MD, a hand surgeon in San Francisco. *His suggestions…*

- *Try ginkgo.* This herb can improve circulation to your arms and hands, reducing RSI symptoms, he says. *Suggested intake:* 60 milligrams (mg) in the morning. Use with the approval and supervision of a physician.

- *Try glucosamine and chondroitin.* These nutrients can also reduce the pain of RSI, he says. *Suggested intake:* 500 mg of glucosamine and 400 mg of chondroitin.

- *Drink water.* Staying well-hydrated improves circulation, delivering pain-relieving oxygen and nutrients into areas hit by RSI. *Minimum:* 64 ounces a day.

- *Drink vegetable juice.* An eight-ounce glass of carrot-celery-beet-parsley juice delivers a big dose of anti-inflammatory phytochemicals. Drink every morning, adjusting the ingredients to taste.

- *Don't drink coffee.* "If you have RSI, you should eliminate caffeine from your diet," says Dr. Markison. *Reason:* Caffeine is a diuretic and drains water out of your body. Smart idea: If you must have a morning cup of coffee, drink twice as much water at the same time.

- *Stop smoking.* A single puff of a cigarette can cut blood to the hands by as much as 60%. "There is no hope for smokers with RSI," he says.

- *Lose weight.* Twenty to 30 extra pounds quadruples your risk of RSI. "I've seen many cases of carpal tunnel that have been controlled by weight loss alone," he says.

Don't bend your arm and lead your backhand swing with your elbow, he suggests. Do keep your racquet and forearm lined up.

Experiment with a slightly larger grip size. "The narrower the grip, the tighter you hold the racquet, and the more strain you put on your muscles," he says.

Loosen the string tension a bit. Higher tension stresses muscles.

Choose a lighter racquet, which puts less load on the forearm and elbow.

Stretch your forearm. "Hold your arm out and gently pull your wrist down and back," says Dr. Mulholland. Hold this for a few seconds.

➤ **To ease golf elbow—stretch with a golf club.** "The main cause of golfer's elbow is a lack of flexibility in the back and shoulders that limits rotation in the hips, requiring more 'muscle' at the elbow and wrist to make up for lack of club speed," says Dr. Mulholland. That's why the following three stretches are good ways to help prevent or ease the problem.

His instructions…

Stretch #1. **Keep one hand on the grip and the other hand close to the club head.** Stand with the club in front of you. Raise the club up over your head and stretch for a few seconds.

Stretch #2. **Using the same hand placement,** hold the club behind your buttocks and bring your arms up toward your head.

Stretch #3. **Holding the golf club over your head,** slowly lean to the left and then to the right.

"These are good stretches for before the round, while you're waiting for tee-time," says Dr. Mulholland.

➤ **An effective stretch for a frozen shoulder.** "Frozen shoulder has many causes, including tendon inflammation," says Jacob Teitelbaum, MD, a doctor in Hawaii and author of *Pain-Free 1-2-3* (McGraw-Hill). "The shoulder gradually loses mobility and scar tissue can form

See Your Doctor If...

If you feel any numbness or tingling in your arms or hands or have constant pain that interferes with your activities for more than a week, you should see a health professional who specializes in RSI, says Dr. Fried.

around the shoulder joint, causing it to become frozen."

He suggests these stretches for the frozen shoulder. Use the hand opposite to the frozen shoulder to lift the other to the top of a door, so that your hand holds on to the top of the door. Then gently squat down to stretch the shoulder. Hold for 10 or 15 seconds—to the point of mild pain, but not pushing through pain, which can injure a joint. Next, put your arm behind your back and use your other hand to pull gently on it and stretch it. This stretch can also be done with your arm over your head.

Best: "It is good to be sure that you maintain your range of motion any time you have shoulder pain, to prevent a frozen shoulder," he says.

ROSACEA

Erase the Red

It can lower your self-confidence and self-esteem. It can cause you to say "No" to an RSVP, cancel a dinner date, even avoid going out shopping or to the movies. It can make you call in sick or derail your career. It's *rosacea*, a skin condition that affects 14 million Americans—three times more women than men, most between the ages of 25 to 55.

"Rosacea is a constellation of skin symptoms," says Audrey Kunin, MD, a dermatolo-gist in Kansas City, Missouri and author of *The DERMAdoctor's Skinstruction Manual: The Smart Guide to Healthy, Beautiful Skin And Looking Good At Any Age* (Simon & Schuster). "While not everyone has every symptom, it's typical to have a few."

These can include redness of the face... flushing...skin sensitivity or dryness...enlarged oil glands and oiliness...the presence of small "broken" blood vessels (also called spider veins)... acne in all its forms (blackheads, papules, pustules and cysts)...occasional surface irregularities of the nose (rhinophyma)...and eye symptoms (including redness, irritation and sometimes clear discharge).

There's no known cause or cure for rosacea.

But there's a quick and easy way to look (and therefore feel) a whole lot better...

➤ **Correct all the symptoms—with one skin cream.** "Clearing the skin of acne is a fundamental therapeutic goal of rosacea treatment," says Dr. Kunin. "Yet, I can't tell you how many times I've talked to women with rosacea who were concerned not only about their blemishes, but also about having to deal with acne *and* wrinkles," she says. "And they were often struggling with a host of *other* rosacea symptoms not addressed by their acne therapy. Sensitive skin. Dry skin. Oil spots, because the skin can go both ways in rosacea. Redness.

"Ideally, effective treatment for rosacea would address the *entire* spectrum of concerns, including blemishes," says Dr. Kunin. "That's why I decided to develop the rosacea cream Calm, Cool and Corrected—to be an effective, *multi-functional* treatment. Using a sophisticated complex of scientifically proven ingredients, it controls oil production, reduces inflammation, fights blemishes, lessens cellular buildup, minimizes bacterial production on the skin—and helps diminish signs of aging."

Those ingredients include...

• **Nordihydroguaiaretic acid (NDGA) and oleanolic acid.** Together, these two ingredients improve the appearance of blemishes and redness, says Dr. Kunin.

Medical journals report that NDGA possesses the ability to reduce 5-alpha-reductase activity—the enzyme necessary for converting testosterone to its active metabolite, DHT, or dihydrotestosterone. "DHT is responsible for all those undesirable masculine skin traits such as acne, facial hair growth and female hair loss," says Dr. Kunin. "If you can lower the DHT, the blemishes should improve."

Oleanolic acid reduces sebum (oil) levels in the skin, creating an environment that is hostile to the normal skin bacteria that contribute to rosacea and reducing rosacea-related inflammation and redness, say Dr. Kunin.

• **Sebum sequestering micro-particles,** a form of polymer technology, helps absorb excess surface skin oils without causing skin dryness, she says.

• **Hyaluronic acid, aloe vera, chamomile extract, squalane and shea butter** protect and moisten the delicate, sensitive skin often associated with rosacea, but without worsening acne.

• **White tea** is the most potent antioxidant form of tea extract, further reducing inflammation.

• **Superoxide dismutase and vitamin E** are other potent antioxidants that can help rejuvenate the skin.

"In many cases, Calm, Cool and Corrected may replace the need for additional rosacea therapy," says Dr. Kunin. "However, it was designed to *complement* all prescription rosacea regimens, working synergistically against rosacea symptoms and delivering the ideal rejuvenation factors for rosacea-riddled skin."

Rapid Resource: Calm, Cool and Corrected is available at *www.dermadoctor.com*, or call 877-DERMADR.

SPEED LIMIT | Antibiotics and Breast Cancer

Daily, low-dose antibiotics are often prescribed for rosacea. They may be riskier than most doctors realize.

The study: Researchers at the University of Washington, Seattle analyzed health data from more than 10,000 women. They found that daily use of antibiotics—including antibiotics for rosacea—was linked to a significantly increased risk of breast cancer.

"The results of this study support the continued need for prudent long-term use of antibiotics," say the researchers, in the *Journal of the American Medical Association*. Talk to your dermatologist about whether or not antibiotics are right for you.

➤ **Watch out for redness triggers.** A variety of environmental factors can worsen the redness of rosacea, says Dr. Kunin. The National Rosacea Foundation (NRF) has surveyed people with rosacea, quantifying the worst triggers and offering ideas to minimize their impact.

See Your Doctor If...

If you have any of the following warning signs of rosacea, see a dermatologist for diagnosis and treatment, says the National Rosacea Foundation...

• Redness on the cheeks, nose, chin or forehead.
• Small visible blood vessels on the face.
• Bumps or pimples on the face.
• Watery or irritated eyes.

- **Exposure to sun.** A trigger for 81% of those with rosacea, informs the NRF.

Smart idea: "Sunscreen is essential for anyone with rosacea," says Dr. Kunin. "Make sure you wear it daily. This will go a long way in helping minimize your redness."

- **Emotional stress.** A trigger for 79%. (Please see the section "Stress and Tension" on page 300 for ideas and suggestions to control stress.)

- **Hot weather.** A trigger for 75%.

Smart idea: Stay in a cool, air-conditioned environment as much as possible, advises the NRF.

⏰ *Super-Quick Fix*

Chew on ice chips or spray your face with cold water.

- **Heavy exercise.** A trigger for 56%.

Smart idea: Use low-intensity exercise regimens, such as walking, yoga and tai chi, advises the NRF. Exercise for shorter intervals.

- **Alcohol.** A trigger for 52%.

Smart idea: If it's a trigger, reduce your intake or avoid entirely, says Dr. Kunin.

- **Spicy foods and beverages.** A trigger for 45%. Common triggering spices are white and black pepper, paprika and red pepper and cayenne.

Smart idea: Substitute two teaspoons cumin and one teaspoon oregano for chili powder.

- **Certain skin care products.** A trigger for 41%.

Smart idea: "Washing with M.D. Forte Replenish Hydrating Cleanser, Free & Clear Liquid Cleanser, or Vanicream Cleansing Bar gently removes makeup, oils and other debris without further irritating skin," says Dr. Kunin.

Cutanix Dramatic Relief moisturizing formulations contain quadrinone, an ingredient that helps reduce inflammation, she says. "Other moisturizers appropriate for those with rosacea include M.D. Forte Replenish Hydrating Cream, Wibi Dry Skin Lotion and Nutraderm Therapeutic Lotion (Original Formula)."

Rapid Resource: For more information on rosacea, visit the website of the National Rosacea Society, at *www.rosacea.org,* or call 888-NO-BLUSH. Address: 196 James St., Barrington, IL 60010, e-mail *rosaceas@aol.com.*

Scars

 If you suffer a *shallow* wound—a skinned knee, paper cut or minor burn—your new skin grows back, filling the injured area with fresh tissue that is virtually identical to the original.

But if you suffer a *full thickness wound*, with a depth of ½ inch or more—a wound that pierces the skin's outermost layer (the epidermis) and the dermis beneath it—the repair won't be quite so perfect.

What happens: To heal the deeper wound, your body relies on *collagen*, an elongated protein that provides structural support, like girders in a building. And the result is a scar—an area containing a lot more collagen and a lot less of other skin components, such as elastin (the protein that allows skin to stretch and resume its shape) and sweat glands.

But you can do something about scars. And fast.

"It's quick and easy to prevent many scars—or at least achieve the smallest, least noticeable scar possible," says James Spencer, MD, a dermatologist in private practice at the Spencer Dermatology & Skin Surgery Center in St. Petersburg, Florida, and a clinical professor of medicine in the Department of Dermatology at Mount Sinai School of Medicine. And dermatologists and plastic surgeons offer some expeditious treatments to minimize or disguise scars that are already there.

However: If an accident, surgery or disease inflicts a full-thickness wound—*you will scar.* The goal is to produce the smallest and least unsightly scar possible. And there are no treatments to remove scars *completely.*

➤ **The best way to prevent a scar.** "Proper self-care after a wound is the fastest way to prevent a scar," says Dr. Spencer.

What you may not know: Many people believe that a dry, uncovered wound heals best, he says. But scientific studies show that keeping a wound wet is ideal for scar-minimizing healing.

A quick and simple approach works best…

● **Moisten the wound.** Use an over-the-counter antibiotic ointment (preventing infections is also a must for effective healing).

● **Cover the wound.** Hundreds of products are available. Choose one you find comfortable and easy to use.

● **Keep the wound covered 24/7 until it's completely healed.** Change the ointment and covering every day or two.

Important: A scab is dry—delaying wound healing and possibly creating a scar. The three steps above should prevent a scab. But if a scab forms, don't tear it off.

● **Don't pick at your wound.** Don't squeeze acne bumps, scratch mosquito bites or dig at ingrown hair—you may deepen the wound, leading to a scar.

SPEED LIMIT Popular Scar Remedies That Don't Work

● **Mederma.** This over-the-counter topical gel, made from onion extract, is often recommended as a way to minimize new or established scars, says Dr. Spencer.

Recent study: Dermatological surgeons at Harvard Medical School studied 24 surgical patients, treating half their scars with onion extract and the other half with petroleum-based gel. There was no difference between the two areas in appearance, redness or size of scar.

• **Vitamin E.** In a study conducted at the University of Miami and reported in *Dermatological Surgery*, dermatologists found no difference in scarring in wounds treated with or without vitamin E.

Why these remedies seem to work: Most new scars get better with time—less red and smaller—whether you treat them or not, says Dr. Spencer.

➤ **Fast ways to minimize a scar.** "Talk to a dermatologist or a plastic surgeon about your scar, explaining what you see as the problem," says Dr. Spencer. Its appearance may bother you. It may itch. Or because scar tissue is less stretchable, it may limit movement—for example, a scar on your hand can restrict your fingers. The doctor should recommend one or more solutions, and help choose the best for you.

The speediest options...

• **Fillers.** Made from a material such as collagen, a filler is injected with a fine needle two to three times over three months into one or more indented areas, temporarily lifting the area. It typically takes more than one treatment to see results, which last six to eight months. Popular fillers include Dermalogen, Restylane, Hylaform, Cosmoderm, Cymetra and Artecoll.

Best for: Indented scars, typically from acne or chicken pox.

• **Cortisone injections.** Injecting cortisone—a synthetic version of a hormone produced by the adrenal gland—can shrink and flatten a scar. (The mechanism is unknown.) Typically, three or four injections are needed, every two to four weeks.

Best for: Keloids (scar tissue that is raised and pours outside the boundaries of the wound over surrounding skin) and hypertrophic scars (red, thick scars that stay within the boundary of the wound but extend above the skin's surface).

• **Interferon.** The immune system produces this protein when battling viruses, bacteria and other infectious agents. Injected, it can flatten a scar and reduce redness. (The mechanism is unknown.) The number and timing of injections is the same as for cortisone.

Best for: Keloids and hypertrophic scars.

• **Botox.** The muscle-paralyzing toxin, used cosmetically to relax forehead wrinkles, can also minimize scars from forehead wounds.

Recent study: Injections of Botox around a (closed) forehead wound from injury or surgery improved the appearance of the wound six months later by 20%, compared to non-injected wounds.

Best for: Wounds on the forehead.

• **Aldara.** A keloid can be surgically removed. But it's a risky procedure—chances are 50-50 it will grow back, perhaps larger. Aldara cream is an *immune response modulator* that stimulates the production of interferon. Applied after surgery, it may help keep a keloid from returning.

Best for: Surgically removed keloids.

• **Silicone sheeting and gels.** Although scientists don't know why it works, applying a bandagelike sheet of silicone gel can help stop a new scar from becoming hypertrophic or keloidal, or help reduce an old scar. For new scars, the sheeting should be applied about one week after the injury or removal of sutures.

Best for: Keloids and hypertrophic scars.

• **Massage.** After healing is complete, cover a scar with petroleum jelly and massage it gently but firmly with the tips of your fingers, for 10 minutes or so a day, for one to two months. This will soften the scar.

• **Makeup.** Heavier makeups such as Dermablend Coverage Cosmetics (*www.derma blend.com*) can hide scars.

SHINGLES

Prevent the Outbreak, Prevent Years of Pain

The virus that caused your chicken pox—*varicella-zoster virus*, or VZV—didn't go away. Instead, it went into a kind of hibernation, in sensory nerves along the spinal cord or near the brain. Years passed. You aged. The cellular guardians of your immune system became weaker. And VZV woke up, crawled out of the root and along a nerve fiber and onto your skin—where it caused the infection known as *shingles*, or *herpes zoster.*

Shingles afflicts one in 100 people over the age of 50—and one in two of all those who live to 85. It shows up as a painful rash—a semicircle of blisters that wraps itself around your trunk, from your mid-back to one side of your chest. Or it can hit you in the face, around the eye (where it can cause glaucoma and blindness). It can also strike the scalp, the neck, an arm, a leg.

The rash heals in 30 days or less. But that doesn't mean VZV is done with you. Because in 14% of those with shingles (and 50% of those 70 or older), the reactivated virus damages nerves—triggering a condition called *postherpetic neuralgia* (PHN). Or maybe PHN stands for *postherpetic nightmare.*

The pain of PHN can last for weeks…or months…or years. It can dominate your day and steal your sleep. In some cases, the skin at the site of the now-vanished rash becomes so sensitive that even the slightest stimulus—the touch of a shirt you're wearing, a breeze brushing your face—causes excruciating pain. In fact, PHN can *ruin* your life…as you take pain medications…that leave you unable to drive… so that you become isolated and depressed…and move into a nursing home.

"That devastating consequence—the loss of independence—happens to a significant number of older people because of PHN," says Michael N. Oxman, MD, a professor of medicine and pathology at the University of California, San Diego, and a staff physician in the Infectious Diseases Section at the Veterans Administration Medical Center in San Diego.

But it doesn't have to, he adds. Because now there's a vaccine that can reduce your chance of getting shingles—and dramatically lower your risk of PHN if shingles occurs.

➤ **Get the shingles vaccine.** If you had the opportunity to be inoculated against a horrific disease that could drive you into a nursing home—would you do it? If your answer was yes, talk to your doctor about inoculation with Zostavax, the shingles vaccine.

Landmark study: Led by Dr. Oxman, researchers in 22 sites around the US enrolled nearly 40,000 people aged 60 and over in a trial of the shingles vaccine—half got the vaccine and half got a placebo. The remarkable results were reported in the *Journal of Infectious Diseases.*

• **Less shingles.** The vaccine reduced the incidence of shingles by 51%.

• **Less severe shingles.** Among those who did get shingles, the vaccine reduced the severity of the disease by 35%—less pain, shorter duration, less interference in the activities of daily life.

• **Less PHN.** And the result Dr. Oxman considers the most important—among those who did get shingles, the vaccine reduced the incidence of subsequent PHN by 66%. "That means if you are 60 or older, the shingles vaccine reduces your risk of getting PHN by two-thirds," he says.

• **Safety.** The vaccine is very safe, says Dr. Oxman.

A possible risk of being injected with any vaccine—a weak form of the same virus that causes the disease—is that it will trigger the

Turbocharge the Vaccine— With Tai Chi

Tai chi—a meditative, relaxing, slow-moving martial art from China—may help an older immune system defend itself against shingles.

New study: Led by Michael R. Irwin, MD, researchers at the University of California in Los Angeles and UC-San Diego studied 112 people (ages 59 to 86; average age, 70), dividing them into two groups. One group took 40-minute tai chi classes, three times a week. The other group spent those 40 minutes attending educational classes about health. After four months, both groups received an injection of the chickenpox vaccine. (The shingles vaccine was not available when this study was conducted.)

A sign of the effectiveness of the vaccine is "cell-mediated immunity" (CMI)—a measurement of the immune system's specific activation against the virus: in this case against the *varicella zoster virus* (VZV) that causes both shingles and chickenpox. At the start of the study, the two groups' CMI to VZV were the same. But within 10 weeks of receiving the vaccine, the Tai Chi group had developed twice the CMI to VZV as the education group—and the same level typically seen in 30- to 40-year-olds who receive the vaccine!

Perhaps even more remarkable, the Tai Chi group had a level of CMI to VZV about 40% higher than typically produced by the vaccine alone. (They also had more vitality, more mental clarity, better physical functioning and fewer aches and pains than the education group.)

"Dr. Irwin's research team has demonstrated that a centuries-old behavioral intervention, Tai Chi, resulted in a level of immune response similar to that of a modern biological intervention, the varicella vaccine, and that Tai Chi boosted the positive effects of the vaccine," says Andrew Monjan, PhD, of the government's National Institute of Aging, which funded the study.

Why it works: "There are several ways Tai Chi may affect immunity and health, including relaxation and exercise, both of which have been shown to strengthen the immune system" says Dr. Irwin.

Good news: "These are also exciting findings because the positive results of the study have implications for other infectious diseases," says Dr. Irwin. "Since older adults often show blunted protective responses to vaccines, this study suggests that Tai Chi is an approach that might complement and augment the efficacy of other vaccines, such as influenza vaccines."

Recommendation: Dr. Irwin recommends receiving personal instruction in Tai Chi rather than learning from a DVD. "In our study, the Tai Chi instructor spent a lot of time observing and correcting technique. I think hands-on instruction is critical in gaining the full benefit."

Look in the yellow pages under "Tai Chi" to find a course near you. Tai Chi courses are often taught at the local YMCA.

You can also find lists of Tai Chi schools and instructors at the website *www.thetaichisite.com*.

illness it is intended to prevent. In the study, the shingles vaccine did not cause shingles.

During the study, there was no difference between the vaccine group and the placebo group in the percentage of those who experienced one or more "severe adverse events"—1.4% of the vaccine group, compared to 1.4% of the placebo group. In other words, there were no serious health problems that could be attributed to the vaccine.

Bottom line: "I recommend that anyone who is sixty or over and has no contraindications, get the vaccine," says Dr. Oxman. (The FDA has approved the vaccine for anyone 50 and over, but insurance only pays for the vaccine in those 60 and over.) That's the same recommendation made by the Centers for Disease Control and Prevention, which lists these contraindications:

- People who have had a life-threatening allergic reaction to gelatin or the antibiotic neomycin. (The shingles vaccine may contain trace amounts of these.)

- People who have a severe allergy to any component of the vaccine.

- People with a weakened immune system as a result of leukemia, lymphoma or any other blood or bone cancer.

- People with HIV/AIDS who have T-cell counts below 200.

- People being treated with drugs that affect the immune system, including high-dose steroids.

- Women who are or might be pregnant.

▶ **If you start to have an outbreak of shingles, see a doctor—immediately.** Shingles is a *medical emergency*, says Anne Oaklander, MD, PhD, an associate professor of neurology at Harvard Medical School and Director of the Center for Shingles and Postherpetic Neuralgia at Massachusetts General Hospital.

"If you start to develop symptoms that might be shingles, you should be seen by a medical professional that day. In most cases, you can call your primary care provider and be seen that day. But if the primary care provider is not available, you should go to the ER—do not wait for the doctor, or make an appointment for the following week, even if that is what the receptionist suggests. Push for same-day care."

Reason: "Almost everyone who has a case of shingles should immediately start taking an antiviral medication—not only because it will lessen the severity of the rash and the pain that goes with it, but because it will cut the risk of PHN by about fifty percent," says Dr. Oaklander.

Main treatment: The drugs used to treat an outbreak of shingles are *acyclovir* (Zovirax), *famciclovir* (Famvir) and *valacyclovir* (Valtrex).

"They are very safe medications," says Dr. Oaklander.

What to look for: Shingles announces itself with odd sensory symptoms in the area where the rash will develop, says Dr. Oaklander. You might have tingling, itching or pain, and the area might feel particularly tender or sensitive.

However: "I urge everyone to do whatever they can to get vaccinated for shingles," says Dr. Oaklander. "Prevention is the best cure."

SINUSITIS

Breathe Easier

In 1980, at the age of 33, Robert Ivker, DO, made a commitment to himself to *cure* his own chronic sinusitis—an ongoing infection in the air-filled cavities located behind and around the nose and the eyes.

Dr. Ivker had been told by an ear, nose and throat specialist that there was *no* cure for the chronic, low-grade infection—that he'd have to "learn to live with" the constant runny nose and postnasal drip, and with the repeated flare-ups of acute sinusitis, with its head congestion, headache, facial pain, fatigue and gobs of yellow-green mucus.

"I was miserable," says Dr. Ivker. "There was no way I was going to live with that." But he wasn't aware of any conventional doctors who had cured the problem. So he set out on a journey beyond the boundaries of conventional medicine—beyond antibiotics, corticosteroids and sinus surgeries—to *holistic medicine*.

"Holistic medicine is the art and science of healing that addresses the care of the *whole* person—body, mind and spirit," says Dr. Ivker. "It pays attention to *causes* rather than just treating *symptoms*, which is what conventional medicine does."

With chronic sinusitis, the holistic process has three objectives, says Dr. Ivker. First, to heal the mucus membranes of the sinuses by reducing chronic inflammation. Next, to reduce levels of the yeast (fungus) candida—"because all people with moderate to severe sinusitis have some degree of fungal sinusitis," he says. Third, to strengthen the immune system.

The program of diet, supplements, exercise, emotional and mental uplift and management of the personal environment that he used to cure his sinusitis eventually developed into the total approach presented in the book *Sinus Survival: The Holistic Medical Treatments for Allergies, Colds, and Sinusitis* (Tarcher/Putnam, Fourth Edition) and the e-book *Love Your Nose Naturally!*

After curing his own sinusitis, he turned his attention to other people with the problem, founding the Ivker Center for Respiratory Healing. "I've been largely focused on treating sinusitis for the past thirty years," he says. And there are many people to treat.

About 40 million Americans suffer from chronic sinus problems. And suffer and suffer and suffer. "The majority of chronic sinus sufferers have learned to accept their condition and have adjusted to a compromised quality of life," he says. But they don't have to. *Here are Dr. Ivker's key recommendations for quick-to-implement ways to prevent and clear up acute and chronic sinusitis…*

➤ **Release your repressed anger.** The scientific field of psychoneuroimmunology shows that your thoughts, emotions and attitudes can directly influence your immune system, says Dr. Ivker. In practical terms, this means that you can either *weaken* or *strengthen* your immune system, depending on what you think and feel.

And there is *one* emotional pattern in particular that sets you up for chronic sinus infections…

"Repressed anger is probably the primary emotional trigger that causes most sinus infections," says Dr. Ivker. "If you suffer from this problem, you are typically a high-achiever who sets very high standards for yourself. You give yourself a hard time for making a mistake, you're very unforgiving of yourself—and much of your anger is directed at yourself."

That suppressed anger weakens the immune system and triggers sinus infections. But, he says, the safe *expression* and *release* of anger can help reverse the problem.

How it works: Traditional Chinese Medicine (TCM) believes that the energy of anger is stored in the liver, says Dr. Ivker. They also believe that there is a particular sound that corresponds to every organ of the body. The sound that corresponds to the liver is the *SH* sound. (The same sound begins an English-language, four-letter expletive commonly used to express and release anger, Dr. Ivker points out.)

Dr. Ivker has wed these traditional insights from TCM with the modern psychological insight that the most effective way of releasing anger is through a combination of sound and body movement. "Think of the martial artist who grunts as he punches and kicks, or the tennis player who yells as she hits the ball, or the child who kicks and screams while throwing a tantrum."

🕐 *Super-Quick Fix*

What to do: Kneel down in front of a sofa or bed with a pillow on it. Bring to mind a person or situation that makes you angry just by thinking of him/her or it. Say to yourself, "My intention for this exercise is to simply release my anger and not to inflict pain on anyone." After that, clench your fists, bring your fists up alongside your ears, so that your elbows are bent, inhale, and as you exhale, bring your forearms down on the pillow and say the SH sound as you strike the pillow. Repeat that movement and sound continually—about 10 or 15 times—keeping the person or situation in mind.

Do this every day, once a day. You can also do it if there is a situation during the day that triggers your anger.

"It takes one to two minutes and it's a fantastic, safe way to release anger," says Dr. Ivker. "This is the most effective technique for defusing the primary trigger for sinus infections."

 ## Antibiotics Don't Work For Sinusitis

Every year, millions of Americans get *acute sinusitis*—a mucus-packed viral, fungal or bacterial inflammation of the sinus cavities that is the caboose on the train of one out of every 50 colds. Twenty million people a year go to doctors with the problem. Ninety percent are prescribed antibiotics. In fact, 15% to 20% of *all* outpatient antibiotic prescriptions are for acute sinusitis.

But antibiotics don't work for sinusitis, says Dr. Ivker. And they contribute to the increasingly common problem of *antibiotic resistance*—untreatable bacterial infections. (The more antibiotics prescribed—individually and collectively—the more bacteria mutate to resist them.)

New findings: Two hundred forty people with acute sinus infection were given one of four treatments for the problem—an antibiotic, a nasal corticosteroid, both or neither. None of the treatments was any better than the other treatments. "Among patients with the typical features of acute bacterial sinusitis, neither an antibiotic nor a topical steroid alone or in combination are effective in altering the symptom severity or the duration of the condition, say the researchers in the *Journal of the American Medical Association.*

In other recent research, doctors in Switzerland analyzed nine studies on acute sinusitis and

antibiotics, involving more than 2,500 people. "Antibiotics offer little benefit for patients with acute sinusitis," they conclude in the *Lancet.* "Given the cost, adverse events and bacterial resistance associated with antibiotic use, they are not justified, even if a patient reports symptoms for longer than ten days."

More new anti-antibiotic evidence: Finnish researchers reviewed 57 studies involving more than 15,000 people with acute sinusitis. The studies showed that people typically recover after two weeks—whether they take antibiotics or not. "Clinicians need to weigh the small benefits of antibiotic treatment against the potential for adverse effects for both individuals and the general population," say the researchers.

Bottom line: "Antibiotics do not help in resolving a sinus infection," emphasizes Dr. Ivker.

In fact, he points out, repeated use of antibiotics can *worsen* a chronic fungal infection—one of the main causes of chronic sinusitis. In other words, this useless treatment for acute sinusitis can *cause* chronic sinusitis!

➤ **The best supplements for sinusitis.** Supplements can help prevent, treat and reverse sinusitis in several ways, says Dr. Ivker.

Taken at the first sign of a cold, they can stop that infection in its tracks. "*The* most important action to prevent sinusitis is effectively preventing and treating colds," says Dr. Ivker. "It stops the whole cascade of inflammation that results in an acute sinus infection—which in turn causes greater inflammation to the mucous membranes, resulting in *chronic* sinusitis."

You can also use supplements to counter acute sinusitis and chronic sinusitis, he says.

● **Allimed/Allimax.** "This is the most powerful supplement for the treatment of chronic sinusitis," says Dr. Ivker. It is antibacterial, antifungal and antiviral. It works so well because it is 100% pure allicin—the active ingredient in garlic. "None of the supplements you can buy in health food stores are anywhere near one hundred percent," he says.

Allimed is the capsule form and Allimax is the nasal spray. This supplement (as well as the other supplements discussed in this section) is available at *www.sinussurvival.com*, or call 800-869-9159. Address: Sinus Survival, 5415 W. Cedar Lane, Bethesda, MD 20814.

Suggested intake: Take at the first sign of a cold, for acute sinusitis, and to reverse chronic sinusitis. Follow the dosage instructions on the label.

● **Sinupret.** The herbal remedy Sinupret has been the number-one over-the-counter remedy for sinusitis for the past 75 years. Why haven't you ever heard of it? Because it is number one… in Germany, where science-proven herbal remedies get the respect they deserve.

"There have been many 'gold standard' clinical studies—randomized and double-blind—that show this herbal formulation is effective," says Narinder Duggal, MD, PhD, an internist and pharmacologist in Seattle, Washington.

The herbal extracts in Sinupret (from gentian, primula, verbena, sorrel and elderberry) reduce inflammation, kill viruses and bacteria, liquefy and thin mucous, strengthen the immune system, and help regenerate the *cilia*, tiny hairs on the mucus lining of the nose that wave in pulses, sweeping out germs and other invaders.

"Sinupret is the logical, science-proven first-line choice for the treatment of acute or chronic sinusitis," says Dr. Duggal. "It is far better than any drug on the market for sinusitis, none of which have been proven effective in clinical trials.

"For acute sinusitis, Sinupret works in one day, and you continue the treatment for seven to ten days. For chronic sinusitis, you can take the herbal formulation every day. Four out of five of my patients have excellent results with Sinupret."

Suggested intake: Take three tablets a day the first sign of a sinus flare-up, says Dr. Duggal. Take it regularly to heal chronic sinusitis. Also take it at the first sign of a cold, says Dr. Ivker.

Sinupret is widely available, including at the website of the manufacturer, *www.bionoricausa. com*, or call 800-641-7555

● **Echinacea.** "This is at the top of the list of immunity-enhancing herbs," says Dr. Ivker. It stimulates the immune system, reduces inflammation and kills bacteria and viruses.

Suggested intake: For a cold or acute sinusitis—as a liquid (tincture), 20 to 30 drops, four to five times a day; in capsules, 200 milligrams (mg), three times a day.

Don't take it for longer than three weeks—after that point, your immune system builds a tolerance to the drug, says Dr. Ivker.

Echinacea products are widely available.

● **Grape seed extract.** Sinusitis is a type of inflammation—and inflammation generates cell-damaging *oxidants*, or *free radicals*. Proanthocyanidin—found in grape seed extract—is 20 times more powerful an antioxidant than vitamin C and 50 times more powerful than vitamin E, says Dr. Ivker.

Product: OPC GrapeGold, formulated by French professor Jacque Masquelier at the University of Bordeaux in France. It is available widely and at *www.sinussurvival.com*.

Suggested intake: One, 100 mg capsule daily, for a cold, for acute sinusitis and for chronic sinusitis.

Also helpful: "European physicians consider it to be their first choice for hay fever and it is also widely used for asthma," says Dr. Ivker.

● **Vitamin C.** "In my experience, vitamin C has been extremely effective in the treatment and prevention of colds and sinus infections," says Dr. Ivker.

Speed Healing Success

"Within Ten Days I Felt a Noticeable Difference"

"I had suffered from chronic sinusitis for twenty years," says Wendy C., of Indian Hills, Colorado. "I was resistant to nearly every antibiotic I tried. I had endured surgery twice, with no results. I was depressed and frustrated because I was always sick. And I didn't think I had any options left."

Then Wendy began Dr. Ivker's program of anger release and other emotion-balancing mind-body techniques, a healthy diet, supplements, nasal hygiene, regular, moderate exercise and avoiding allergens and pollutants as much as possible.

"Within the first ten days, I felt a noticeable difference," she says. "Over the next six weeks, my sinus problems vanished.

"I continue to follow the program, which I feel saved my life. I have not been on antibiotics for more than two years. What doesn't make sense to me is why other doctors and ear-nose-and-throat specialists don't find solutions for their patients other than drugs or surgery."

Rapid Resource: Dr. Ivker's holistic program for chronic sinusitis is available through web-based video, tutorials and guides, at *www.sinussurvival.com*. He is also available for personal consultations and programs, by calling 303-978-1474.

Suggested dosage: 3,000 mg a day for prevention.

At the first sign of a cold or acute sinusitis, 15,000 mg a day, three times a day, with meals; or 2,000 to 3,000 every two to three hours. Maintain the high dosage for several days, or until your symptoms begin to improve. "Taper off very gradually over the next two weeks to get back down to the usual daily dose of three thousand milligrams," says Dr. Ivker.

Product: He suggests ascorbate or the product Ester C. "These are much more easily absorbed and more potent than ascorbic acid."

⚠ *Caution:* "Possible side effects of dosages above three thousand are diarrhea, gas and cramps," says Dr. Ivker. "But these symptoms are more likely to occur with the pure ascorbic acid form of vitamin C. If you experience these symptoms, cut back your next dose by a thousand milligrams."

● **Ionic silver.** A nasal spray containing ionic silver can kill cold viruses and immediately knock out a cold, says Dr. Ivker. You need to use the spray every 20 to 30 minutes at the first sign of a cold.

Product: Cold Rescue, from Peaceful Mountain. It is available at *www.peacefulmountain.com*, or call 888-303-3388.

➤ **Use a nasal irrigator.** "Using a nasal irrigator is extremely helpful for treating acute sinusitis and healing chronic sinusitis," says Dr. Ivker.

Best: "The most effective strategy is pulsatile irrigation, which involves rapidly but gently rinsing your nose with a stream of saltwater (saline solution) that pulses at a rate matching the normal pulse rate of healthy cilia," says Murray Grossan, MD, an otolaryngologist and head and neck surgeon with the Tower Ear, Nose and Throat Clinic at Cedars-Sinai Medical Center in Los Angeles and author of *Free Yourself from Sinus and Allergy Problems Permanently* (Hydro Med).

"Clinical trials involving thousands of patients have shown that pulsatile irrigation increases blood flow to the nasal passages and helps restore function to damaged cilia."

Product: Several pulsatile irrigation devices are available from websites specializing in allergy or medical products, such as National Allergy at

Hummm Your Sinus Problems Away

Humming or singing the letter "M" can help heal sinusitis, says Dr. Grossan.

Why it works: Researchers from around the world have found that humming increases the level of the compound *nitric oxide* in the sinuses by 15 to 20 times—and nitric oxide is antifungal, antibacterial and antiviral.

Newest research: A patient with chronic sinusitis eliminated his symptoms in four days by humming 18 times per minute for one hour at bedtime and humming 60 to 120 times, four times a day, for the next four days.

"The morning after the first humming session the patient awoke with a clear nose and found himself breathing easily through his nose for the first time in over one month," says the researcher, in the journal *Medical Hypothesis*. "Symptoms were eliminated in four days."

What to do: Sing "oooommmmm" in a low tone, says Dr. Grossan. "Make this sound often throughout the day. As an alternative, buy a toy kazoo and hum into it for ten minutes daily."

www.natlallergy.com (800-522-1448) or Health Solutions Medical Products at *www.pharmacysolutions.com* (800-305-4095).

"For best results, I recommend using this form of irrigation twice daily," says Dr. Grossan.

➤ **Exercise—but don't overdo it.** Aerobic exercise such as brisk walking can strengthen the immune system.

What most people don't realize: If you already have a weakened immune system, too much exercise can weaken it even more—"and it doesn't take much to be too much," says Dr. Ivker.

What to do: If you have chronic sinusitis, exercise gently, at no more than 60% of your maximum heart rate.

To figure out that number, use this formula—220, minus your age, multiplied by 60%.

Example: If you're 60 years old, that would be 220 minus 60 (160), multiplied by 60% (96 beats per minute).

For the first week of aerobic exercise—such as walking, swimming, rebounding (jumping on a mini trampoline) or cycling—maintain that pulse rate while exercising for five minutes. For the second week, 10 minutes. For the third week, 15 minutes.

Increase the time you exercise week by week by five minutes, until you're exercising for a minimum of 30 minutes, five or more times a week.

After you are exercising regularly for 30 minutes at 60% of your maximum heart rate, gradually begin to increase the intensity of your exercise, from the mild to the moderate level, or a pulse rate that is no more than 70% of your maximum heart rate.

Useful: "I make sure that all my patients know how to take their pulse," says Dr. Ivker. *His instructions...*

Use your index and middle finger to feel the pulse on the thumb side of your wrist or at your neck, just below the jaw. Using a watch with a second hand, count the number of beats in 60 seconds, which will give you your heart rate in beats per minute. Or count by 15 seconds and multiply by four.

SLEEP APNEA

Stop the Snoring— In Five Minutes

Twenty to 30 million Americans have *obstructive sleep apnea*, with overweight men over 65 the most common victims. They're all very tired.

What happens: During sleep, the muscles at the back of the throat relax. In snoring, the sagging soft tissue that lines the throat vibrates. If it vibrates a little, you snore softly. If it vibrates a lot, you snore loudly. But in sleep apnea, the tissue doesn't just sag. It *plugs* the airway, which narrows and shuts—and breathing *stops*.

You snort. You grunt. You gasp. You cough. You start breathing again. And then you fall back asleep, never remembering you woke up.

That mini-suffocation of 10 seconds or so occurs over and over, all night long—at least five times an hour, and maybe as many as 60.

And even though you don't know you're waking up, your spouse probably does. Because when people with sleep apnea snore, they snore *loudly*—loud as a vacuum cleaner, sucking up someone else's good night's sleep.

If you have a bad case of sleep apnea, you wake up headachy and tired—maybe even feeling less refreshed than when you went to sleep. And you spend the day tired—so tired, you can nod off while idling at a stoplight. You're probably depressed or cranky. You don't think clearly.

And because a good night's sleep is crucial to well-being, you're at a higher risk for a wide range of diseases, including heart disease, stroke, type 2 diabetes, depression and erectile dysfunction. In fact, you have nearly a five times higher risk of dying from *any* cause.

"There's probably not a single health condition that's not worsened by sleep apnea," says Craig Schwimmer, MD, an otolaryngologist, clinical assistant professor at the University of Texas Southwest Medical School and medical director of the Snoring Center, in Dallas and Fort Worth, Texas.

Dr. Schwimmer treats thousands of cases a year of sleep apnea—but not with the same-old, same-old. He doesn't send most of his patients off to a sleep laboratory for an all-night diagnostic procedure to confirm they have sleep apnea. And he offers options if you don't want to spend the rest of your lifetime's nighttimes doing a Darth Vader imitation while tethered to a CPAP—a *continuous positive airway pressure* machine that generates a constant flow of pressurized air into a flexible tube connected to your strapped-on breathing mask. (Only about 45% of people with sleep apnea who start using CPAP stick with it, and then often for only a couple of hours a night, a couple of nights a week—because they can't cope with the skin irritation, the claustrophobia, the dry mouth, the noise, the smell and the other downsides of the intrusive equipment.)

Instead, Dr. Schwimmer is the world leader in offering his patients procedures that in about 80% of cases can dramatically improve and even cure sleep apnea. And each procedure takes only a few minutes.

Here are Dr. Schwimmer's breakthrough remedies for sleep apnea—breakthroughs that thousands of people have found faster, easier and a lot more effective than more standard types of medical care...

➤ **Spare yourself a night in the sleep lab.** "In America, we spend 3.5 billion dollars a year sending people to sleep laboratories to confirm a diagnosis of sleep apnea," says Dr. Schwimmer. "But if you snore, and your spouse says you stop breathing at night, and if you're tired during the day—you have sleep apnea. You don't need to spend a night in the sleep lab to confirm what's obvious." Plus, research shows that apnea-confirming sleep studies *don't* change treatments or improve outcomes for people with the condition.

New approach: If you want a test for sleep apnea, consider a home test, says Dr. Schwimmer. A recent study shows they are just as accurate as lab-based sleep studies. And Medicare and Medicaid now cover the cost of the test, which uses a simple and comfortable device. Ask your doctor about this option.

Speed Healing Success

"I Experienced Immediate Relief"

"I've had sleep apnea for fifteen to twenty years, but I never knew it," says Tim Costa, a professional bass fisherman from Texas. "I literally always felt like I was dying. I underwent the Pillar Procedure (see right). The procedure itself was virtually painless, and I experienced immediate relief. My snoring has completely stopped. Even my complexion is better. Before this, I couldn't tell you when I last had a good night's sleep. Now, I can fish all day and I don't even need to nap."

"Before Tim had the Pillar Procedure, I never had a good night's sleep, because of his snoring and because I had to listen for him to stop breathing," says Carol Johnson, Tim's wife. "It was rough on the kids too, because he was cranky twenty-four/seven. And he was so tired all the time. After he had the procedure, we saw an immediate improvement. His breathing was better, as was the snoring. It's improved our relationship too. He's quite pleasant these days."

➤ **Consider three minimally invasive, office-based treatments for sleep apnea.** "There are two types of sleep apnea patients—those who can tolerate CPAP and those who can't," says Dr. Schwimmer.

For those who can't, one of the main medical options has been an invasive surgery called *uvulopalatopharyngoplasty* (UPPP), in which a large chunk of tissue is cut out from the rear of your mouth and the top of your throat, along with your tonsils. You're under general anesthetic, you're in a lot of pain afterward, recovery requires takes two weeks at home—and the surgery has a 50% to 60% success rate.

Instead of UPPP, Dr. Schwimmer offers these three procedures…

● **The Pillar Procedure.** This outpatient procedure takes about five minutes. The doctor places about five tiny, woven inserts into the tissues of the soft palate. The inserts reduce the vibration that causes snoring and support the palate, helping stop its tissues from sagging during sleep.

Since the palate is the most common site of obstruction in obstructive sleep apnea, this procedure is sometimes all that's needed. But in 40% of people with sleep apnea, other procedures are required.

● **Turbinate Coblation.** Some cases of sleep apnea have more than one obstruction—for example, the soft palate *and* a nasal obstruction. In those cases, Dr. Schwimmer may also perform a 20-minute procedure called a *turbinate coblation*—a reduction of small structures in the nose using radio frequency, which is similar to microwave energy.

● **Laser Tonsillectomy.** In some cases, Dr. Schwimmer will also perform this alternative to tonsillectomy. In the 20-minute procedure, the laser vaporizes the outer surface of the tonsils, significantly reducing their size.

Rapid Resource: To find out more about these procedures—which Dr. Schwimmer also uses to treat "socially disruptive snoring"—you can visit the website *www.snoringcenter.com.*

The Snoring Center, which treats patients from all over the world, has 11 offices. Call 877-655-5826.

➤ **Talk to your dentist about an oral appliance.** Another fast solution for sleep apnea is a mouthguard–like oral "appliance," worn during sleep. It works by pulling the lower jaw forward, opening up more space at the back of the throat.

However: Many people find them uncomfortable, and they can cause aching jaws in the morning and long-term shifting of teeth.

"I have about a dozen dentists with sleep apnea as patients—they stopped using their oral appliances and have undergone some of the procedures I offer," says Dr. Schwimmer.

Red flag: Don't buy an over-the-counter or television-advertised oral appliance for sleep apnea, says Dr. Schwimmer. "If you're going to sleep with something in your mouth, you want it of the highest-grade material and you want it custom-fitted and adjustable. That way, there's the maximum likelihood that you'll tolerate the device and it will help decrease the apnea.

300 "Cures" for Snoring—And None of Them Work

Spray your throat. Clip your nose. Position your head with a special pillow. Waste your money.

There are about 300 over-the-counter antisnoring devices on the market, says Dr. Schwimmer. And none of them work. "The scientific literature shows overwhelmingly that these devices are ineffective at significantly reducing snoring," he says. "Don't spend your time, energy or cash on them."

➤ **The four best self-help actions for sleep apnea.** "There is a lot you can do on your own to help snoring and sleep apnea," says Dr. Schwimmer.

● **Lose weight.** "Shedding pounds has been shown to dramatically improve the condition," he says.

However, sleep apnea patients have a hard time losing weight—they're typically too tired to

exercise…and tend to snack on sugary food to combat daytime sleepiness.

● **Don't drink in the evening.** Sleeping relaxes the throat muscles. Sleeping and alcohol relaxes them even more.

● **Don't eat late at night.** "There is a close connection between heartburn and sleep apnea," says Dr. Schwimmer.

● **Don't sleep on your stomach.** You're more likely to snore. However, this is easier said than done. "Most people sleep in whatever position they're comfortable, and that's that," says Dr. Schwimmer.

STOMACHACHE

Solve Your Tummy Troubles Fast

Your stomach hurts. And you've had plenty of tests to figure out the cause. Well, it's *not* heartburn…*not* an ulcer… *not* stomach cancer…*not* an injury from taking a stomach-irritating non-steroidal inflammatory drug (NSAID) such as aspirin. The diagnosis? *Functional dyspepsia,* a fancy way of saying you have a set of abdominal symptoms with an unknown cause—some combination of gnawing or burning pain in the upper abdomen, above the navel…feeling uncomfortably full after eating only a little food…bloating and belching… and nausea or vomiting.

Chances are you've tried OTC and prescription remedies for the problem—there are dozens, from Alka-Seltzer to Zantac.

Problem: Three out of five people with functional dyspepsia still have symptoms after a year of taking stomach medications.

Solution: An herbal remedy from Europe that may be more effective than any drug…

🕐 *Super-Quick Fix*

▶ **Try Iberogast.** This digestive remedy from Germany consists of nine digestion-regulating herbs—an extract of clown's mustard plant (*Iberis amara*, an herb bound in Spain and Western Europe), lemon balm leaf, chamomile flower, caraway fruit, peppermint leaf, licorice root, angelica root, milk thistle fruit and greater celandine. Nine may be your stomach's lucky number.

Standout scientific evidence: German doctors asked 315 patients with dyspepsia to take either Iberogast or a placebo for eight weeks. Compared to the placebo group, those taking Iberogast had a much greater reduction in symptoms such as abdominal pain, nausea and fullness.

In another German study, published in the journal *Digestion*, 43% of people with dyspepsia taking Iberogast had "complete relief" after eight weeks—compared to 3% of people taking the placebo.

Swiss doctors from University Hospital Zurich and German researchers from the University of Heidelberg analyzed the results of several studies on Iberogast, involving 273 people. The herbal preparation was effective in reducing stomach pain, abdominal cramps and nausea. "From the point of view of efficacy and safety, Iberogast is a valid therapeutic option" for the treatment of dyspepsia, says Jorg Melzer, MD, one of the doctors who conducted the study.

"Iberogast is the best-studied and safest preparation available for indigestion, and should be the first choice for treating this problem," says Olaf Kelber, MD, a German doctor who has studied the remedy.

Why it works: Researchers at the Royal Adelaide Hospital in Australia gave either Iberogast or a placebo to 29 healthy men and then repeatedly measured their stomach function for two hours after a meal. The herbal formula relaxed the muscles of the stomach, increasing its size by 41% compared to the placebo group. (More stomach room means less uncomfortable feelings of fullness.) It also improved *antral motility*—the strength of muscular "pressure waves" in the part of the stomach that connects to the small intestine. (Faster digestion means less chance indigestion can take hold.) These two effects might underlie the effectiveness of Iberogast in dyspepsia, say the researchers, in the *American Journal of Gastroenterology*.

New thinking: Writing in the journal *Phytomedicine*, an international team of doctors from Germany, Poland and Australia say dyspepsia is caused by many different mechanisms. But, they continue, drugs for dyspepsia typically target only *one* of those mechanisms—increased acid secretion—and are "unlikely to be effective in all patients." Iberogast, on the other hand, with its nine plant extracts, addresses the range of mechanisms that can trigger dyspepsia. The herbal treatment—not drugs—is the treatment more likely to be "advantageous" in treating dyspepsia, say the doctors.

Suggested intake: Twenty drops a day, three times a day, says Dr. Kelber. You can take the drops directly, or mix them with one to two ounces of warm water and drink before, with or after a meal.

Product: Iberogast is available from Tribute Pharmaceuticals at *www.iberogast. ca* or call 888-333-4401.

▶ **Massage your belly.** "When you were young and had a tummy ache, your mom may have rubbed it lovingly to make it all better— and it worked!" says Alyce Sorokie, founder of the Partners in Wellness holistic health clinic in Chicago, Illinois (*www.gutwisdom.com*), and author of *Gut Wisdom: Understanding and Improving Your Digestive Health* (New Page). "Now it's your turn to rub your belly." *Her instructions...*

1. Lie on your back with a pillow under your knees.

2. Take three deep breaths.

3. Starting at the lower right side of your belly, directly above the hipbone, move your fingertips in a circular motion, slowly moving up the right side until your fingers are just below your ribcage. Stop often to take a few deep breaths.

4. Using the same circulation motion, massage across your upper belly, just above your navel, to your left side, directly above your left hipbone.

5. If you notice any tender or tight areas, apply light pressure with your fingers on that area and imagine your breath is entering into that space. Notice how that can relieve the discomfort.

6. Complete the massage by placing both palms on the center of your abdomen and allow a deep breath to fill your abdomen.

7. Place a hot water bottle or heating pad on your abdomen—and notice how relieved your gut feels!

➤ **Don't eat too fast.** "The *way* you eat can cause dyspepsia," says Norton Greenberger, MD, clinical professor of medicine at Harvard Medical School and author of *4 Weeks to Healthy Digestion* (McGraw-Hill). In particular, eating too *fast*. "I recommend that you spend fifteen to twenty minutes eating a meal," he says.

His suggestion...

Put your fork down between bites. "Savor each bite of food, take the time to chew it properly and don't rush to stuff the next bite in your mouth," he says. "Take a moment to breathe, inhale the aromas and enjoy the flavor of what you are eating."

Also helpful: Have a conversation. "In Europe it is considered polite during a meal to put one's utensils down and ask accompanying family or friends about their day or to engage them in a lively discussion," says Dr. Greenberger. "Even if you are eating alone, pause between bites to reflect on positive developments in your day and in your life."

➤ **Don't drink when you eat.** "You can avoid overfilling your stomach—which can cause dyspepsia—by eating and drinking separately," says Dr. Greenberger. "A few sips of water at a meal are fine, but try not to fill your stomach with liquid in addition to a full meal."

STRESS AND TENSION

Instant Relaxation for Lifelong Health

Stress is sickening. Literally. "It is estimated that seventy-five percent of all medical complaints are stress-related," says Edward Charlesworth, PhD, a clinical psychologist, president of Stress Management Research

Associates in Houston, Texas, and author of *Stress Management: A Comprehensive Guide to Wellness* (Ballantine). "The list of these disorders is long and still growing—migraine and tension headaches, high blood pressure, rapid and irregular heartbeats, immune dysfunction, insomnia, back pain, muscle aches, skin disorders and many psychiatric disorders."

Why is stress so bad for us?

Because the *stress response*—programmed into our bodies from our days as cave dwellers, when an instant "fight-or-flight" reaction to danger was a must for survival—is now triggered dozens (if not hundreds) of times a day.

By bored baristas and bullying bosses...by ringing alarm clocks and jingling cell phones...by traffic jams and jammed printers...by an endless epidemic of e-mails and a tsunami of Twitter's tweets...by mounting debts and dwindling bank accounts...and by a 24/7 "news cycle" that spins your emotional wheels with the lowdown that the planet is too hot, the economy is too cold and the peanut butter cookie you're about to eat may be supplying you with your RDA for salmonella. (And that's not even mentioning your stressful encounters with your spouse, your kids, your coworkers and Snarl, the neighbor's Rottweiler.)

That nonstop stress derails your digestion, tightens your muscles, weakens your immunity, thickens your blood, harries your heart and cooks your cells in a stew of stress hormones.

But it doesn't have to. You can defuse the fight and cancel the flight. You can *relax*. And it doesn't require taking a yoga class, meditating or signing up for an apprenticeship with St. Teresa.

New thinking: There are two types of stress, says Fred Luskin, PhD, a senior consultant in health promotion at Stanford University and coauthor of *Stress Free for Good: 10 Scientifically Proven Life Skills for Health and Happiness* (HarperOne).

"Type 1 stress is *short-term stress*—it occurs when the source of the stress is immediate

Stress in the USA

What are America's biggest stressors? A recent "Stress in America" report from the American Psychological Association, *www.apa.org*, found that more than half of Americans said their stress had increased in the past year—with 81% of Americans stressed by money, 67% by work, 67% by health problems affecting the family and 60% by family responsibilities. The most common stress-caused symptoms were irritability and anger (60%), fatigue (53%), insomnia (52%), feeling nervous or anxious (49%), feeling depressed or sad (48%), headache (47%) and upset stomach (35%).

and identifiable and you can resolve the stress in a short period of time," he says. *Examples:* Avoiding a traffic accident. Regaining your footing while climbing a mountain.

"This kind of stress can be pleasurable," says Dr. Luskin. "Think of the excitement you feel when you navigate a downhill run on a ski slope or hit a perfect golf stroke."

"Type 2 stress is *long-term stress*—it occurs when the source of the stress isn't an immediate crisis," he says. *Examples:* Conflict with your boss or co-worker. Worry over your finances. An ongoing health problem. Marital difficulties.

"When you experience Type 2 stress for too long or too often, you can feel tired or anxious or irritable, or make more mistakes at work, or get sick more often," says Dr. Luskin. "Eventually, Type 2 stress can cause or aggravate a wide array of diseases."

Bottom line: The key to reducing or managing stress is to "Break up the destructive, cumulative negative effects of Type 2 stress into more manageable, short-term and even pleasurable Type 1 experiences," says Dr. Luskin. "Doing this is simpler than you think."

In fact, he offers several easy methods to defang Type 2 stress, all of which have been proven effective in research at Stanford University. And none of which take more than a couple minutes.

Important: "Everyone should practice the first two methods—'Breathe from your belly' and 'So much to appreciate,'" says Dr. Luskin. "These are core life skills. Then evaluate the others and see which feel like a need for you. For example, if you feel frazzled, try 'Slow down.' If you want to feel more happiness and connection, try 'Smile because you care.'"

Super-Quick Fix

➤ **Breathe from your belly.** This is the simplest and most effective form of stress management, says Dr. Luskin.

Why it works: The *sympathetic nervous system* gears us up to respond to danger and deal aggressively with life's challenges, he explains. The *parasympathetic nervous system* relaxes us. Slow, regular, abdominal deep breathing activates the parasympathetic nervous system. "By *voluntarily* activating the parasympathetic in stressful situations—facing such 'dangers' as an angry boss or an overloaded schedule—you calm down your body. And since your mind and body are in constant communication, a calm body will give your mind a break."

What to do: Dr. Luskin's instructions...

1. As you inhale, imagine that your belly is a big balloon that you're slowly filling with air.

2. Place your hands on your belly while you slowly inhale.

3. Watch your hands as you slowly breathe out, letting the air out of the balloon.

4. As you exhale, make sure your belly stays relaxed.

5. Take at least two or three more slow and deep breaths, making sure to keep your attention on the rise and fall of your belly.

When to use: When you get angry. Before getting on an airplane, if you're nervous. When you need to pause and think before speaking, to avoid saying something you might later regret. When you need help falling asleep. Whenever you notice that your breathing is shallow, rapid, tight or tense.

What helps: Do this every single day—sometimes for five to 10 minutes at a time. And do it even when you're not under stress—while you're sitting in your car, watching TV or sitting at the computer.

➤ **So much to appreciate.** "Appreciation is the simple act of noticing good in your life," says Dr. Luskin. "An unrelenting stress response ensures that your body won't let you appreciate a sunset or the smile of a baby. The practice of appreciation reverses this trend. It teaches you to treasure the good and spend time thinking about your blessings. Looking for things to appreciate reduces stress and actually retrains your nervous system to make it easier to relax."

What to do: Dr. Luskin's instructions...

1. Before you begin you day's activities, review the things you need to do during the day, and include on your list two specific things to be thankful for.

2. During a stressful time, take two slow, deep belly-breaths. When inhaling for your third breath, think deeply on one of the following—someone you love, a beautiful place, an act of kindness done for you.

3. During the day, do each of these exercises for 15 to 30 seconds—focus your full attention on someone you love, appreciate a place you find beautiful and think fondly about a kindness someone did for you.

When to use: When stress and difficulties pile up. When there's too much to do. When you have to make a decision. Before making a difficult phone call. When you feel underappreciated. When talking with a family member, lover or friend—to remember how much that person means to you. When you feel lonely or isolated.

What helps: When you think about someone you love, think of someone with whom you're still in a good relationship. When you think of a place, think about a place that evokes good memories or is particularly beautiful. When you think about a kind act, think clearly about what someone did that was loving. Appreciating positive things is enhanced when combined with belly-breathing.

➤ **Tense to relax.** "Tight muscles and clenched fists are indications that stress has a hold on your emotional and physical well-being," says Dr. Luskin. But you can instruct your body to have the opposite, relaxed response, he says. "One of the interesting things about muscles in the human body is that they relax to their utmost right after they've been tensed. Tensing and relaxing is a skill so simple that you can practice by gripping and releasing the steering wheel of your car at a stoplight or in a traffic jam. Whenever you practice, you will notice how quickly the shift from muscle tension to muscle relaxation happens."

What to do: Dr. Luskin's instructions...

1. Take two slow, deep belly-breaths.

2. On the third inhalation, tighten your right arm from your shoulder to your hand.

3. Hold tightly for two or three seconds.

4. As you exhale, relax fully and let your arm drop.

5. Repeat the first four steps with the other arm, each leg and then your entire body.

6. As you practice, repeat a relaxing affirmation, such as, "I have all the time in the world" or "I am relaxed and at peace."

When to use: Before going to bed. To feel alert when you awaken in the morning. Before physical exercise. When your neck or shoulders are tight. When you're sitting at your desk. When you're stuck in traffic. When you're sitting in an airplane.

What helps: When you tense your muscles, really tense them. When you relax, really relax. Sometimes practice with only your arms and legs, and sometimes with your entire body. Pay attention to what it feels like to be relaxed. Remind yourself how calm and relaxed you are and remember that you're capable of this kind of relaxation at any time. Think often during the day, "I'm relaxed and at peace."

➤ **Slow down.** "People everywhere complain of having too much to do and not enough time to do it—and being in a hurry is a normal state for most of us," says Dr. Luskin. "The problem is that this constant hurrying creates more stress than it eliminates—and it doesn't even necessarily mean we get more done."

The solution is to learn...to...do...things...more...slowly, says Dr. Luskin.

"It's important to work productively, of course, since we all have many tasks we need to accomplish. However, it's only by slowing down that we get a glimpse of life's deepest gifts. It's not necessary to slow down all day long. What is necessary is to have an 'Off' switch that allows you to slow down when you chose to. Slowing down means doing whatever you're doing with attention and care...doing one thing at a time... and paying attention to what you're doing, while thinking as little as possible about whatever else you have to do."

What to do: Dr. Luskin's instructions...

1. Do a common activity slowly, carefully and with focused attention. Start by taking a couple slow, deep belly-breaths. Then pay close attention to how good something smells (a rose or some food)...notice how beautiful something looks (nature, a loved one, or a piece of art)...look carefully at every aspect of something (the marvel of your hands, for example). Drink in wonderful tastes, colors, shapes and textures.

2. When you're in a hurry, tell yourself, "I have all the time that I need."

When to use: When waiting in line in a grocery store or airline security area. When rushing to an appointment. When you notice that you are driving too fast. When you feel impatient. When you feel bored. When making dinner for family, friends or yourself.

What helps: Remind yourself that you can't go any faster than the maximum you're capable of. Practice doing something the usual way and then slow down and practice again. Sometimes speed up what you're doing so you can notice how uncomfortable that feels.

➤ **Smile because you care.** "Almost everyone who is stressed misses the power that comes from recognizing how much of what they do is done because they love their family, friends and community, or because they have a desire to make the world a better place," says Dr. Luskin. "These strong feelings of love and care, if brought to the surface and remembered, can provide the necessary energy to work hard, be creative, endure difficulty and persevere. When we recognize and acknowledge the love is our true motivations, it connects us with our deepest purpose and soothes our stress. *In short:* Learn to recognize the good that you do *because you care.*

"And we know that adding a smile to appreciation creates happiness and well-being—a positive state of mind that is literally right under your nose! A smile is the expression of contentment and joy. When you feel happy, you smile. Try a smile right now—think of the love you offer and smile, holding that smile for about ten seconds. Every person asked to do this reports feeling better. In other words, not only do you smile when you feel happy, but you feel happy when you smile."

What to do: Dr. Luskin's instructions...

1. Reflect back on your day.
2. Start by taking a couple slow deep breaths.
3. Ask yourself why you did these things.
4. When you remember that you did them because you care, smile.
5. Think about how much you care about the people you do things for—and smile.
6. Feel your experience of love and care and let it warm the area around your heart—and smile again.

When to use: When you're feeling discouraged or down in the dumps. When you're feeling overworked. When you're doing routine things such as laundry or cooking or mowing the lawn.

What helps: Remember that often we do things because we want to be of help. Reflect on how much you care for all the people around you. Remember how much help you are to them. Think about how what you do would be missed if you stopped. Smile whenever you can for a mood lift. Smile at people and they'll more than likely smile at you.

➤ **Just say no.** "A huge proportion of people under stress are trapped in simple situations that they want to get out of but can't, because they don't know how to say no," says Dr. Luskin. "When we say yes but really mean no—when you inhibit your true thoughts, feelings or actions—it creates a split between mind and body that causes stress."

It's not that becoming assertive will be easy, he says. "The skill of just saying no requires practice. If saying yes to things you don't want to do is a habit, then that habit will have to be changed. The only way to change a bad habit is by making a clear intention, rehearsing what you want to do differently, and then regularly practicing that new behavior."

What to do: Dr. Luskin's instructions…

When someone asks you to do something you know you don't want to do…

1. Take two or three slow, deep belly-breaths.

2. Then say, "I need a few moments to think about this. Can I get back to you in a little while?"

3. When you offer your response, choose one of the following: "I've thought about this, and unfortunately I'm not going to be able to help you out this time. I realize this may be disappointing to you, but it's what I've decided." Or, "I'm not going to be able to help you out in the way you asked—maybe together we can come up with a solution that works for both of us."

When to use: When you're asked to take on extra work. When you're asked to help over and over in your family. When you need to resist the bad habit of peers. When salespeople are pushing you to buy something you do not need. When a friend wants you to come over and you're exhausted.

What helps: At first, practice saying no with people you trust, knowing that they will respond well. Remember that you can choose to say no. Give the answer you *want* to give. You don't have to do something just because

---

Just-in-Time Stress Relief

The methods of stress relief described by Dr. Luskin are offered online and live to individuals, companies and organizations and health service providers through the company Just In Time Stress Relief, on the Web at *www.jitsr.com.*

---

someone asks you to. If you're not sure what answer you want to give, always ask for time to think over your request. You don't have to say no more than you have to say yes—the choice is always yours.

STROKE

Speed Can Save Your Life

Nearly 800,000 times a year—every 40 seconds—the brain of an American comes under attack. From a stroke.

What happens: A clot blocks the flow of blood to the brain—an *ischemic stroke*, accounting for 83% of strokes. Or a blood vessel in the brain ruptures—a *hemorrhagic stroke*, accounting for 17%. Those "brain attacks" are often deadly or disabling.

Stroke is the third leading cause of death (after heart disease and cancer), killing 143,000 yearly. It's the leading cause of disability—the paralysis, spasticity, pain, speech problems, memory loss and other harrowing symptoms that make stroke one of the most dreaded of diseases.

Good news: Researchers are discovering new and more effective ways to prevent and treat stroke—with the death rate from stroke falling 30% in a recent 10-year span.

Here are the breakthroughs that will help you survive…

➤ **Rush to the ER.** Stroke experts have a saying, *Time is brain,* says Ralph L. Sacco, MD, chairman of the Department of Neurology at the Miller School of Medicine at the University of Miami.

What happens: If you're having a stroke, the *faster* you call 911 and get to the emergency room…and, if your stroke turns out to be of the ischemic variety, the *sooner* you are treated with tissue plasminogen activator (tPA), the blood-thinning, clot-dissolving intravenous drug that restores blood flow to the brain…the less amount of brain tissue is likely to die…and the *better* the likely outcome, in terms of preventing death and disability. But many people who are having a stroke don't go the ER right away—because they don't realize they're having a stroke!

Study: Less than half of 400 patients who were diagnosed at the Mayo Clinic's emergency department with either a stroke or a transient ischemic attack (TIA, or mini-stroke) thought they were having a stroke. Most said they thought the symptoms would simply go away, say the Mayo Clinic researchers, in the journal *Emergency Medicine.* The average time of arrival at the ER was *after* the three-hour period from the onset of stroke during which tPA is effective.

"Time is crucial in treating a stroke," says Latha Stead, MD, an emergency medicine specialist and the study's lead researcher. "The sooner a patient experiencing a stroke reaches emergency care, the more likely the stroke can be limited and the condition managed to prevent further damage and improve recovery."

In another study, researchers in the Division for Heart Disease and Stroke Prevention at the Centers for Disease Control in Atlanta surveyed more than 86,000 adults for knowledge of the five warning signs of stroke. They reported their results at the American Stroke Association's International Stroke Conference.

Trap: They found that people at the highest risk of having a stroke—the elderly and those who had a previous stroke—were the least likely to know the five warning signs of stroke. Overall, only 37% of those surveyed knew all five signs.

"We were really surprised to see people who have had a stroke were *less* aware of symptoms than those who had not had a stroke," said Jing Fang, MD, the study's lead researcher.

The five signs of a stroke are…

• Sudden weakness in the face, arm or leg, particularly if the weakness occurs on only one side of the body;

• Sudden, severe headache with no known cause;

• Sudden visual disturbance in one or both eyes;

• Sudden confusion or difficulty speaking; or

• Sudden dizziness, loss of balance, loss of coordination or difficulty walking.

Watch Out for the Aspirin/Ibuprofen Combo

Are you taking aspirin to prevent a second stroke? Then you might not want to take ibuprofen (Advil, Motrin) regularly for arthritis or other pain problems such as headaches.

Study: German researchers found that 28 stroke patients who were taking aspirin and ibuprofen had no blood-thinning effect from the aspirin. In fact, 13 of them had a second stroke. When 18 of the patients stopped taking ibuprofen, aspirin's ability to thin blood returned.

"This interaction between aspirin and ibuprofen or prescription NSAIDs is one of the best-known but well-kept secrets in stroke medicine," says Francis M. Gengo, PharmD, a study researcher.

And he notes that the ibuprofen has the same effect on the prescription medication Aggrenox—a combination of aspirin and extended-release dipyridamole (an anti-clotting medication).

What to do: Dr. Gengo has this to say to doctors: "When you counsel a patient to take aspirin/extended release dipyridamole to lower stroke risk, tell your patients they may have some transient headaches, but to avoid ibuprofen. You may have prevented that patient from having another stroke."

Red flag: Three out of five stroke deaths occur in women. However, women are 30% less likely than men to receive tPA in the ER, report researchers from Michigan State. The possible reason is women who are having a stroke may not have any of the five classic stroke symptoms. Instead, they may suffer a loss of consciousness or sudden pain other than a headache.

Rapid Resource: The American Heart Association/American Stroke Association have created Stroke Hero, a campaign offering simple tutorials and quizzes that instruct how to tell if someone is having a stroke. For more information, visit *www.strokeassociation.org.*

Other crucial steps in getting to the ER...

• **Don't call the doctor's office.** Calling a primary care doctor at the first sign of stroke can delay patients from reaching the ER, say researchers at West Virginia University-Morgantown. In their study, the researchers called primary care physicians' offices seeking advice for hypothetical stroke or heart attack symptoms. Nearly one-third of receptionists recommended scheduling an appointment for later in the day if symptoms continued. "Calling 911 is the only correct answer," says Stephen Davis, adjunct assistant professor of emergency medicine and a study researcher.

• **Ignore the advice of the hospital helpline** if you're having strokelike symptoms and the operator tells you to call your doctor. A study in the journal *Stroke* showed that nearly a quarter of hospital helpline operators mistakenly routed a caller describing classic stroke symptoms to primary care doctors rather than to 911.

"So many of our patients arrive at our stroke center more than three hours after their symptom onset—sometimes even days after their symptoms started," says Brett Jarrell, MD, an emergency department doctor and study researcher. "I would ask them why they waited, and many replied that they called their local

Preventing Depression After Stroke

Depression occurs in *more than half* of the 700,000 people who have a stroke every year. It's a dark cloud over recovery.

"The success of stroke rehabilitation depends on patients playing an active role in their own treatment," says Peter Sawicki, MD, who studied the problem. "If people become depressed, it is very difficult for them to have the necessary motivation." Worse, people who become depressed after a stroke are four times more likely to die than those who don't, says Robert G. Robinson, MD, in the Department of Psychiatry at the University of Iowa.

Self-defense: Researchers at Iowa State University studied 176 stroke patients for a year after their stroke. Some of the patients took the antidepressant medication *escitalopram* (Lexapro); others took a placebo. Those taking the placebo were 4.5 times as likely to be become depressed than those taking the drug. "Patients who are given escitalopram...following acute stroke may be spared depression and perhaps its adverse consequences," writes Dr. Robinson, in the *Journal of the American Medical Association.*

hospitals, only to be told that they should contact their primary care doctor instead of calling 911."

➤ **Start treatment immediately after a TIA.** What the chest pain of angina is to a heart attack, the *transient ischemic attack* (TIA, or mini-stroke) is to stroke—a sign that there has been a temporary lack of blood flow to an area of the brain, usually due to a blood clot, and a warning that you are at a high risk for stroke, says Dr. Sacco. In fact, studies show that you have a 12% risk of a stroke within 90 days of a TIA—and *half* that risk is within the first 48 hours. *But you can decrease your risk of a stroke after TIA—with fast medical treatment...*

New study: A study in the journal *Lancet Neurology* shows that *rapidly* starting drug therapies after a TIA—with a blood-thinning agent such as aspirin, blood pressure medications and cholesterol-lowering statins—can decrease the risk of stroke by about 80%.

"Urgent assessment and early initiation of a combination of existing preventive treatments can reduce risk of early recurrent stroke after a TIA," says Peter Rothwell, MD.

What to do: If you've had a TIA, see your doctor *immediately* to discuss a treatment plan. That is likely to include blood-thinning medications such as aspirin…medications to lower high blood pressure…and cholesterol-lowering statin medications.

➤ **To prevent a first stroke, consider cholesterol-lowering statin medication.** A study in *Lancet Neurology* analyzed the results of dozens of studies on statins, involving 165,792 people. They found that for every decrease of LDL by 39 mg/dL, there was a 21.1% decrease in the risk of stroke.

"Stain therapy is the most important advance in stroke prevention since the introduction of aspirin and antihypertensive treatments," say the researchers.

➤ **Prevent a second stroke.** Of the 795,000 people who have a stroke every year, 185,000 are having a *second stroke*. Those strokes are preventable with the type of medication strategy that can prevent a stroke after a TIA.

New study: A study reported at the American Academy of Neurology's Annual Meeting showed that stroke victims who achieve "optimal levels" of four risk factors—high LDL cholesterol, low HDL cholesterol, high triglycerides and high blood pressure—were 65% less likely to have another stroke, compared to people who did not reach optimal levels on any risk factor. Those who reached optimal levels on three risk factors were 38% less

likely to have another stroke…on two risk factors, 22% less…and on one risk factor, 2% less.

New thinking: There is a *cumulative* effect of treating all risk factors that is greater than treating the individual factors, says Pierre Amarenco, MD, a study researcher. "People need to work with their doctors to reach the optimal level on all these risk factors."

Best: The optimal levels are an LDL "bad" cholesterol of lower than 70…an HDL "good" cholesterol of higher than 50 in men and 60 in women…triglycerides less than 150…and blood pressure less than 120/80.

➤ **Eat more fish.** A study in the journal *Neurology* showed that people who ate broiled or baked tuna and other fish high in omega-3 fatty acids (salmon, mackerel, herring, sardines, anchovies) three times or more per week had a nearly 26% lower risk of stroke, compared with people who didn't eat fish regularly.

The Low-Stroke Lifestyle

Researchers at Harvard who analyzed health data from nearly 115,000 men and women discovered five lifestyle factors that cut the risk of stroke by 80%…

- *You don't smoke.*
- *You're not overweight.*
- *You exercise*—moderately or vigorously—for at least 30 minutes every day.
- *You eat a diet that emphasizes vegetables, fruits, chicken, fish, nuts, beans and fiber*—and minimizes saturated fats and trans fats.
- *You drink moderately*—one drink a day for women and two a day for men.

"More than half of ischemic strokes may have been prevented through adherence to a healthy lifestyle," says Stephanie E. Chiuve, ScD of the Harvard School of Public Health.

Trap: "While eating tuna and other types of fish seems to help protect against stroke, these results were not found among people who regularly ate fried fish," says Jyrki Virtanen, PhD, RD, at the University of Kuopio in Finland.

Best: To help prevent stroke, the American Stroke Association recommends the Mediterranean diet—emphasizing fruits, vegetables, whole-grains, beans, fish and the monounsaturated fats found in avocados, olive oil and nuts, and minimizing the saturated fats found in red meat and full-fat dairy products and the trans fats found in many processed foods.

➤ **Avoid fast foods.** People who live in neighborhoods with the highest number of fast-food restaurants had a 13% higher risk of ischemic strokes compared to those living in areas with the lowest number of the restaurants, reported researchers from the University of Michigan.

However: This study doesn't prove that fast food causes stroke, says Dr. Sacco. But it is one more piece of evidence pointing to a stroke-preventing power of a healthy diet and the stroke-causing potential of an unhealthy one.

➤ **Drink tea.** Researchers at UCLA analyzed studies involving nearly 195,000 people and found that, compared to people who didn't drink tea, those who drank six cups of green or black tea a day had a 42% reduction in stroke, while those who drank three cups had a 21% reduction.

"These findings are so exciting," says Lenore Arab, a professor of medicine at the David Geffen School of Medicine at UCLA and a study researcher. "If we can find a way to prevent stroke that is simple and non-toxic, that would be a great advance."

Also helpful: Women who drink two to three cups of caffeinated coffee a day had a 19% lower risk for stroke than women who drank less than one cup per month, say Dutch researchers, in the journal *Circulation*.

SUNBURN

Get Out of the Red

Solar radiation does us a lot of good, from triggering the photosynthesis at the foundation of the world's food supply to powering homes with solar panels.

But you can get too much of a good thing. A hefty dose of ultraviolet B radiation (UVB), a component of sunlight, can cause *sunburn*.

If the sun has put your well-being temporarily in the red, here's what to do for fast relief of the pain, burning and itching...

🕐 *Super-Quick Fix*

➤ **Apply a cold compress.** Soak a washcloth in cold water and put in on the sunburned areas, says Paul S. Auerbach, MD, a Clinical Professor of Surgery in the Division of Emergency Medicine at Stanford University and author of *Medicine for the Outdoors: The Essential Guide to Emergency Medical Procedures and First Aid* (Mosby). A cold shower is soothing too, he says.

Is Your Spouse a Risk Factor for Stroke?

Yes, if your spouse is a smoker.

New study: If you're a non-smoker married to a smoker, you have a 42% increased risk of stroke, compared with being married to a non-smoker, says a study in the *American Journal of Preventive Medicine*. If you're a former smoker married to a current smoker, you have a 72% increased risk.

Good news: The risk is eliminated if your spouse stops smoking.

How Often Should You Apply Sunscreen?

"The best way to treat a sunburn is not to get one," says Dr. Kunin.

However: Only 28% of adults use sunscreen when outside for an hour or more on a sunny day.

She recommends using a sunscreen with a minimum SPF (sun protection factor) of 15—and preferably 30. And she suggests using it *often*.

"It needs to be reapplied every two hours while you're outdoors, as well as after swimming," she says. "Waterproof sunscreens also need to be reapplied after water exposure."

She also suggests wearing sun-protective clothing, hats (with a four-inch brim) and sunglasses with UVA and UVB protection.

Rapid Resource: The Environmental Working Group claims that—because of a lack of FDA regulation—four out of five sunscreens contain chemicals that may pose health hazards or don't adequately protect skin from the sun's damaging rays. They provide consumers with a free list of the 169 sunscreens they say provide "very good sun protection." You can find it online at *www.cosmeticsdatabase.com.*

Also try: You can also brew up a batch of green tea, chill it and make compresses, says Audrey Kunin, MD, founder of *www.derma doctor.com* and author of The *DERMAdotor's Skinstruction Manual: The Smart Guide to Healthy, Beautiful Skin and Looking Good at Any Age* (Simon& Schuster). The EGCG found in green tea works as a natural anti-inflammatory ingredient, she says.

▶ **Moisturize.** Use a non-sensitizing skin moisturizer, such as Vaseline Intensive Care, says Dr. Auerbach.

▶ **Take an anti-inflammatory drug.** Over-the-counter ibuprofen (Advil) or naproxen (Aleve) will help relieve some of the discomfort and diminish the inflammation, says Dr. Kunin.

Also helpful: For a bad, total-body sunburn —with symptoms such as low-grade fever, loss of appetite, nausea and weakness—a five-day course of prednisone "can do wonders," says Dr. Auerbach. His suggested intake is 80 mg on the first day, 60 mg on the second, 40 mg on the third, 20 mg on the fourth and 10 mg on the fifth.

▶ **Try distilled white vinegar.** "My mother always rubbed distilled white vinegar on our sunburns, and it really did take the sting out of the burn, once the initial sting from the vinegar wore off," says Dr. Kunin. The reason it's effective is the acetic acid in the vinegar works as a sort of topical non-steroidal anti-inflammatory drug (NSAID).

See Your Doctor If...

If you have symptoms of heatstroke, such as nausea, vomiting or fainting, or if your sunburn blisters, see the doctor, says Dr. Kunin.

THYROID PROBLEMS

Do these symptoms sound familiar... You're tired a lot of the time—in fact, you *wake up* tired. (But you also have trouble falling asleep.) You hurt all over, with muscle aches and joint pains that don't seem to have any cause. You're anxious, even panicky. Other times, you're depressed. Mentally, you're sluggish, unfocused and forgetful. Your sex drive is stalled. You're overweight—and have a lot of trouble shedding pounds, even when you don't eat much. Your menopause has been a nightmare, from severe hot flashes to migraine headaches. You have poor digestion. You're bothered by allergies. Your skin and hair are dry. Even your feet are affected—you often feel chilly, and always wear socks to bed.

If that list reads like a résumé of your misery—or even if you only have a couple of those symptoms—you may very well have thyroid disease.

"When the thyroid gland is hampered by illness, causing reduced production of thyroid hormone, every bodily function is diminished," says Richard Shames, MD, a doctor in Sebastopol, California (*www.feelingfff.com*), and coauthor of *Thyroid Power: 10 Steps to Total Health* (Collins).

The hormone Dr. Shames is talking about is thyroxine (T-4, the storage form of thyroid hormone), which turns into thyronine (T-3, the active form). Thyroid hormone is like the body's gas pedal. It regulates the rate of metabolism of every cell, affecting cell function, cell temperature and cell growth. In short, the thyroid gland controls every chemical reaction in every organ in the body.

And, he says, an estimated 50 million Americans may be struggling with low levels of thyroid hormone—an epidemic of underactive thyroids. Why is that happening?

Theory: The tens of thousands of artificial chemicals in our environment—many of them chemically similar to the body's hormones—have confused and imbalanced the immune system, so that it mistakenly attacks the thyroid, a condition known as an *autoimmune disease*.

Is a low level of thyroid hormone causing or complicating your health problems? There's a fast way to find out.

▶ **Take a test for thyroid hormone levels.** Low thyroid is easy and inexpensive to treat once it is diagnosed—but it is frequently *misdiagnosed*, says Dr. Shames. Instead, doctors treat the anxiety...or the digestive problems...or the depression...and never test for low thyroid levels. And even if they *do* test you for thyroid levels—they often misinterpret the results.

"Most physicians are not up to date with the research that shows that TSH (thyroid-stimulating hormone)—the main test used to check your thyroid—is very unreliable, missing most of the people who have low thyroid function and need treatment," says Jacob Teitelbaum, MD, a doctor in Hawaii and author of *From Fatigued to Fantastic* (Avery). "And even if you take the so-called 'more reliable' free T4 test, you are considered to have non-normal, low thyroid function only if you are in the lowest two percent of the population for T4 levels." Which means there are *many* people *with* low thyroid hormone levels who are being told they have a *normal* thyroid.

Standout scientific evidence: "In two studies conducted by Dr. G. R. Skinner and his associates in the United Kingdom, patients who were thought to have hypothyroidism (an underactive thyroid) because of their symptoms had their blood levels of thyroid hormone checked," says Dr. Teitelbaum. "The vast majority of them had technically normal thyroid blood tests. This data was published in the *British Medical Journal.* Dr. Skinner then did another study, in which the patients with normal blood tests who had symptoms of an underactive thyroid—those who your doctor would likely say had a normal thyroid and would not need treatment—were treated with thyroid hormone. A remarkable thing happened when this was done. The large majority of patients, despite being considered to have a normal thyroid, had their symptoms improve upon taking thyroid hormone [Synthroid], at an average dosage of a hundred to a hundred and twenty micrograms a day."

Bottom line: "Current thyroid testing will miss most patients with an underactive thyroid," says Dr. Teitelbaum.

What to do: You can have your own thyroid testing done by the Canary Club, at *www. canaryclub.org,* says Dr. Shames. (Their vision statement reads: "The Canary Club is dedicated to helping people receive the best health testing at the best possible price. Our mission is to educate, support and empower people, whose hormone health has been compromised.") Their "Thyroid Profile Kit" tests for free thyroxine (fT4), free triiodothryronine (fT3), thyroid stimulating hormone (TSH) and thyroid peroxidase antibody (TPO). Once you have the results, you can read the "Interpreting Results" article on the website, and then discuss the results with your physician.

If you want to find a doctor near you who knows how to effectively treat low thyroid levels, visit the website *www.endfatigue.com*, go to the "Community" tab and click on "Find a CFS/ FM Practitioner" for a list of Fibromyalgia and Fatigue Centers—which specialize in treating fatigue-related problems such as underactive thyroid, fibromyalgia and chronic fatigue syndrome. You'll also find a list of practitioners trained by Dr. Teitelbaum in effective protocols for treating low thyroid levels (among other problems).

Bottom line: A one-month trial of a low dose of thyroid medication will indicate whether or not your problem is low thyroid, says Dr. Shames. "If you show any improvement, that clinches the diagnosis." At that point, you can work with your doctor to establish a safe and effective daily dose of thyroid hormone to correct your problem.

➤ **Over-the-counter alternatives to thyroid hormone.** "If you can't find a doctor who will write a prescription for thyroid hormone, there are alternatives," says Dr. Teitelbaum. For many people, natural thyroid glandular supplements can be very helpful, he says.

Product: Dr. Teitelbaum suggests using BMR Complex, from Integrative Therapeutics, which includes iodine, the amino acid L-tyrosine (these two nutrients create thyroid hormone in the body), zinc, copper and the blue flag root (an herbal thyroid stimulant).

Suggested intake: Take one or two capsules three times daily between meals, says Dr. Teitelbaum. "But after one month, try lowering it to two to three capsules each morning."

Rapid Resource: BMR Complex is available at *www.endfatigue.com*, or call 800-333-5287 or e-mail…*customerservice@endfatigue.com.*

Another effective over-the-counter product for underactive thyroid is MedCaps T3, from Xymogen, says Dr. Shames. It is available online at *www.xymogen.com*, or call Xymogen at 800-647-6100.

⚠ *Caution:* If you develop rapid heartbeat or restlessness, it's likely you are taking too high a dose. Discontinue use and see your doctor.

TINNITUS

Turn the Noise Down

Buzzing like a bee. Ringing like a phone. Humming like an annoying coworker. Hissing like a snake. Clicking like a keyboard. Roaring like the ocean. Whistling like a referee. Whooshing like traffic.

Those are just *some* of the sounds you might hear if you're one of the estimated 35 million Americans with *tinnitus*. And you're not hearing them because you're a John Cage fan, the composer who made music out of everyday sounds. No, the source of the noise is *inside* your head. And the noise can be anything from a minor distraction to a maddening dilemma—about half of those with tinnitus say the noise is bothersome.

Tinnitus can have many causes, including a lifetime of exposure to loud noise (tinnitus often accompanies hearing loss)...prescription and OTC drugs...Ménière's disease (an inner ear disorder)... TMD (a misalignment of the jaw)...earwax...and even cancer. (If you've developed tinnitus, see a doctor to help you determine the cause.)

Unfortunately, if no underlying cause is found, treatments for tinnitus are rarely satisfactory. "People with tinnitus have tried almost everything in an attempt to stop the problem— drugs, surgery, diet, therapy, tinnitus-maskers, you name it," says Neil Bauman, PhD, a hearing loss coping skills specialist in Stewartstown, Pennsylvania (*www.hearinglosshelp.com*), and author of *When Your Ears Ring!: Cope With Your Tinnitus* (GuidePost Publications). "All of these have had only limited success, if any."

But that doesn't mean you should give up.

"If you've heard the statement, 'There's nothing that can be done about your tinnitus,' you're listening to the wrong person," says Marc Fagelson, PhD, director of Audiology at East Tennessee State University.

Here are some of the best recommendations for turning down the noise...

➤ **Try gingko biloba.** "Several studies show that this herb can improve tinnitus symptoms by rebuilding blood vessels," says Michael Seidman, MD, director of Otologic/Neurotologic Surgery and Otology Research at the Henry Ford Health System in Detroit, Michigan, and author of *Save Your Hearing Now: The Revolutionary Program That Can Prevent and May Even Reverse Hearing Loss* (Warner).

"If you are living with tinnitus, ginkgo biloba is certainly worth discussing with your doctor and trying."

Suggested intake: 120 to 240 milligrams (mg) twice a day, in the morning and evening. Look for an extract standardized to 24% ginkgo-flavoglycosides.

⚠️ **Caution:** Do not take ginkgo if you are taking blood-thinning medications such as aspirin or *warfarin* (Coumadin).

🕐 *Super-Quick Fix*

➤ **Try zinc and niacin.** "A combination of zinc and the B-vitamin niacin can sometimes completely resolve the tinnitus, particularly if the onset of symptoms is recent," says Dr. Seidman. "If it's longstanding, frequently the tinnitus can be diminished."

Why it works: The highest concentrations of zinc are found in the inner ear and low levels may affect hearing. Niacin may work by improving circulation to the inner ear.

Suggested intake: 25 mg of zinc once a day and 50 mg of niacin twice a day. (Niacin supplements may cause harmless, temporary but intense facial "flushing," or redness.)

➤ **Try a garlic supplement.** "A garlic supplement can ease tinnitus symptoms," says Dr. Seidman. "It assists in blood pressure management, stress control and minimizing cholesterol deposits that can block the small artery leading to the inner ear."

Suggested intake: 300 mg daily. Deodorized garlic supplements are useful for people who don't want to live with the constant smell of garlic on their breath, he says.

Speed Healing Success

The Journey from Hell to Peace

Psychotherapist Kevin Hogan, PsyD, calls his recovery from tinnitus a "journey from hell to peace."

"I heard sounds at an unbelievable volume day and night for two and a half years," he says. "Today, I occasionally experience some head noise—perhaps once each week or month, and it's faint when it pays a visit."

In the process of overcoming his own problem, the outgoing Hogan—an expert on sales and motivation—became a helper to thousands of other people with tinnitus. Eventually, he wrote *Tinnitus, Turning the Volume Down: Proven Strategies for Quieting the Noise in Your Head* (Network 3000). *Here is his advice for you…*

Tinnitus is part of an "attention" disorder, says Dr. Hogan. In other words, if you don't pay attention to the sound, you don't hear it. *Therefore, the starting point of improvement is to…*

1. **Become immersed and engrossed in activities** that take up a lot of time and attention.

   Example: Take a long walk and really take in the scenery, almost as if you were analyzing each thing you see. This creates less "space" in your awareness for tinnitus.

2. **Talk to your doctor about an anti-anxiety medication** such as *alprazolam* (Xanax) to reduce the "fear factor" about having tinnitus.

After the "volume" of fear is lowered, the noise will likely follow.

3. **SSRI antidepressants such as *escitalopram* (Lexapro) and *sertraline* (Zoloft)** can reduce severe depression, which can reduce tinnitus. When you are severely depressed, you focus inward—and notice the noise. When you feel better, you focus externally—and don't notice the noise as much.

4. **Go to the beach.** Tinnitus is "masked" for almost everyone by the sound of falling water. The beach, a noisy stream or a waterfall can provide a great deal of relief.

⏰ Super-Quick Fix

5. **Wear an MP3 player** (such as an iPOD) if your tinnitus is severe. Keep the volume of the music lower than the volume of the tinnitus. You don't want to try to drown out the tinnitus because that isn't going to work. You want to desensitize yourself to the noise.

---

6. **If you grind your teeth because of temporomandibular joint disorder (TMD),** have your dentist make you a splint (mouth guard) that you can wear during the day or night. TMD is a common cause of tinnitus.

7. **Get an MRI** to make sure that there is not a tumor pressing against the eighth auditory nerve.

Rapid Resource: To learn more about tinnitus, visit the website *www.kevinhogan.com/FAQ.htm*.

➤ **Learn to ignore tinnitus.** You can teach your brain to unlearn its conditioned reflex of anxiety, worry and distress about tinnitus and relearn another conditioned reflex—ignoring the tinnitus, says Dr. Bauman. *He explains…*

"If you become anxiously focused on the sound of tinnitus, your brain's limbic system—the subconscious part of your brain that responds to emotions—says, 'Whoa, this sound must be important because my owner is concerned about it—I'll turn it up.' The tinnitus isn't actually louder. But your *perception* of the sound is that it is louder and more intrusive.

"To reverse tinnitus, you must enlist your limbic system in turning the volume down. But the limbic system doesn't respond to what you *say*, it responds to what you *do* and *feel*. If you *ignore* the tinnitus by focusing on something else, then your limbic system says, 'My owner isn't worrying about this anymore. Why have I got it flagged with a triple red flag? I'll reduce it to a double red flag.'

"Every time you focus on something other than the tinnitus—your limbic system will turn the volume down. Eventually, tinnitus will fade into the background."

Example: "You can *learn* to ignore tinnitus just like you learn to ignore the sound of traffic after you move to a city," says Dr. Bauman. "When you first move to the city, the constant, loud sound of the traffic may drive you batty. After a year, you hardly even hear it. You've learned that traffic noise is normal and—even though you can attend to it and listen to it any time you want—you usually filter it out.

"You can do the same with tinnitus—by not worrying about it and by consciously and constantly turning your attention to something else."

➤ **Watch out for drug-caused tinnitus.** "There are more than four hundred fifty over-the-counter and prescription drugs known to cause tinnitus," says Dr. Bauman. "These drugs—called *ototoxic drugs*—can either trigger tinnitus in the first place, make your existing tinnitus louder or trigger a new tinnitus sound."

Drug-caused tinnitus usually appears first as a continuous high-pitched sound, he explains. "The reason for this is that ototoxic drugs generally damage the hair cells at the base of the cochlea first—which is where the high-frequency sounds are detected and passed on to the brain."

He points out that tinnitus can precede or accompany hearing loss from ototoxic drugs. "In fact, tinnitus is the number-one indicator that you may be doing damage to your ears. It may be the *only* warning you'll ever get. Pay attention to it! If your ears begin to ring after you begin taking any drug, you should immediately report this to your doctor.

"You and your doctor should then decide what to do—whether to reduce the dosage, change the medication or stop taking the medication altogether," Dr. Bauman says.

Good news: Tinnitus resulting from taking ototoxic drugs is often temporary and goes away soon after you stop taking the drug.

TMD

Quick Relief for Your Stressed Jaw

Maybe you complained to your doctor about a mysterious set of symptoms including poor concentration, headaches, dizziness, sinus problems, ringing in your ear, and neck and shoulder pain. And maybe after extensive testing—and finding nothing—the doctor told you the symptoms were "all in your head."

Well, the doctor was right, in a way. It's possible the symptoms *were* all in your head—specifically, in your *jaw*.

"TMD, or temporomandibular joint disorder, is a very real, diagnosable disorder of the jaw—that is frequently misdiagnosed," says Flora Parsa Stay, DDS, clinical associate professor of Dentistry at the University of Southern California and author of *The Secret Gateway to Health* (Morgan James Publishing).

What happens: The jaw's temporomandibular joint (TMJ) makes two kind of movements, explains Dr. Stay. When you open the mouth slightly, there's a hingelike movement. When you open wide, the jaw slides forward and down. "In TMD, the jaw joints are not functioning properly and smoothly, and you hear noises as the joint changes from a hinge position to the sliding movement." The crunching or grinding noises are called crepitus. You might also have *tinnitus*, or ringing in the ears.

But because a misaligned jaw can affect so many other structures—among them, the ears, eyes, sinuses, neck, shoulders and back—there can be *many* distinct symptoms associated with TMD, says Dr. Stay. *They can include...*

- Clicking, popping, ringing noises in the inner ear
- Headaches
- Pain and pressure behind the eyes
- Jaw pain
- Pain in the neck area
- Problems with jaw movement during eating or yawning
- Lockjaw and limitations in opening and closing the jaw properly
- Sinus problems
- Pain on chewing, especially hard foods
- Problems with the bite

TMD has many possible causes, from genes to head trauma from a car accident, with an estimated 5% to 15% of Americans suffering from the problem. Are you one of them?

Self-test: "By placing your fingers directly in front of the ears and slowly opening and closing your mouth, you will feel the movement of the jaw and the jaw joints," says Dr. Stay. "If you hear any noises when you do this, or feel any pain, you may have TMJ."

Also, if you have normal range of motion when you open and close your mouth, you should be able to place three fingers vertically in your mouth between your upper and lower teeth while your mouth is open, and feel no pain, says Dr. Stay. "If you can fit only one or two fingers in your mouth, then you have limited range

of motion and should consult your dentist for treatment."

Good news: By correcting the positioning of the jaw with a mouthguard...or using self-hypnosis to overcome nighttime tooth clenching and grinding, one of the most common causes of TMD...you can help correct the problem and find relief within a week.

➤ **See your dentist for a mouthguard.** The easiest and fastest way to correct TMD is with a mouthguard or orthotic splint, which you wear in your mouth over your teeth, says Dr. Stay. "It moves the jaw into normal position and the pressure is relieved. Patients usually feel some relief and less pain within a week."

You may have to wear the mouthguard during the day and night, or only at night, depending on the cause and severity of your problem.

Red flag: Although mouthguards are available over-the-counter, Dr. Stay does not recommend them. "For best results, the mouthguard should be custom-made and custom-fitted by a dentist," she says. (The dentist will take an impression of either the top or bottom jaw or both, and then fashion the splint from clear acrylic.) "It is very important that the bite is adjusted correctly, or you'll likely to encounter *more* problems."

➤ **Practice self-hypnosis to overcome nighttime tooth-grinding.** Nighttime tooth-grinding is a common cause of TMD. In fact, says Scott Sulak—a certified clinical hypnotherapist with offices in Los Angeles and Seattle—they're virtually synonymous.

"Calling it TMD is a misnomer," he says. "Bruxism—nighttime tooth-grinding—is the condition, and it affects the temporomandibular joint."

Sulak explains that the source of bruxism is *subconscious*—generated by a part of the mind in which we're not typically aware. The bruxism could be the result of an "unresolved internal conflict" from a previous trauma, he says, such as an alcoholic parent typically returning home at two in the morning. It could be part of an unconscious habit formed during childhood as a way to cope with stress, such as chewing the inside of the mouth. Bruxism is so much a part of the subconscious that most people don't even know they're doing it, he points out.

"People who grind their teeth at night generally don't believe they actually do it until they're told by a spouse or dentist that it's the case," says Sulak. And because the problem is subconscious, he says, "it is highly responsive to *suggestions*—thoughts, ideas and intentions that can be implanted into the subconscious by a self-hypnosis CD that you listen to while you're in a relaxed state as you fall asleep."

Examples: "Your jaw is parted slightly… your lips barely touching…your teeth apart…as you lie there in a very natural, peaceful, relaxed state….Your jaw is like the screen door of the cottage, barely swinging, hanging in the wind…. Your jaw feels loose, slack, like a handful of loose rubber bands."

"I have fifteen self-hypnosis titles for various health problems, and the CD for TMD is by far my biggest seller—because nighttime tooth-grinding is rooted in subconscious thought," says Sulak. "Listening to the CD before going asleep, when you're highly suggestive, is often enough to solve the problem without any other treatments."

Rapid Resource: You can buy a copy of the self-hypnosis CD, *Eliminate TMJ* at *www. changeforgood.com.* The website also includes self-hypnosis programs develop by Sulak for weight control, insomnia, stopping smoking and pain relief.

➤ **Easy ways to soothe the TMD discomfort.** There are a number of easy ways to reduce TMD symptoms, says Dr. Stay.

● **At bedtime, take a hot shower or bath.** "This helps tense muscles to relax, helping you sleep better, and perhaps will help with clenching or grinding if that is a nighttime habit," says Dr. Stay.

● **Apply moist heat or ice.** "Heat increases circulation, decreases joint stiffness, pain and muscle spasms, and is mostly helpful in a chronic situation," says Dr. Stay. Her suggestion…

Soak a washcloth in hot water, cool it to a comfortable temperature, apply it to the area for a few minutes and repeat.

"Cold application is usually helpful for acute pain, to help relieve muscle spasms or acute inflammation," she says. Use either an ice bag or a cold pack.

● **Correct your posture.** For a mouthguard to work in managing symptoms, you need to address other factors, such as proper posture, says Dr. Stay.

Smart idea: "A key to correct sitting posture is to lift your breastbone as you sit," says Pamela Adams, DC, a chiropractic physician and yoga instructor in Larkspur, California. "Pretend that a string is attached to the middle of your chest and is nudging your breastbone upward. You want to lengthen the space between your belly and your breastbone. Do this exercise whenever you notice you are leaning back or slumping over."

● **Don't overuse your jaw.** "When you have jaw pain for an extended period of time, you have to treat the jaw as if you had a sprained ankle and are told not to walk on the ankle," says Dr. Stay. *Here are a few ways she suggests to keep from overusing the jaw…*

Don't yawn too widely. Eat soft foods if your jaw is painful—avoid hard foods such as crunchy French bread, pizza or carrots. Don't talk with the telephone held between your neck and your shoulder. Don't carry heavy purses or other such items. Don't wear high heels. If you use a computer, take regular breaks and stretch.

● **Don't put anything in your mouth.** That includes biting your fingernails, chewing gum or holding pencils or other items in your mouth, says Dr. Sulak. "All of these habits accentuate and aggravate bruxism," he says.

● **Keep your teeth apart during the day.** "Keep your lips parted so that they are barely touching and your teeth *aren't* touching," says Sulak. "If you position your mouth that way during the day, you condition your subconscious mind as to how you want your jaw positioned during sleeping."

● **Minimize the use of caffeine.** Caffeine-containing foods and drinks—coffee, tea, energy drinks, chocolate—tighten the muscles and worsen the tendency to clench and grind the teeth, says Dr. Sulak.

TOOTH PROBLEMS

Solutions with Bite

From dimmed enamel to decay to loose dentures—a problem with your teeth is a problem with your *life*.

"Our teeth are basic to our self-esteem and the way others view us," says Mark A. Breiner, DDS, a dentist in private practice at the Breiner Whole-Body Health Center in Trumbull, Connecticut (*www.wholebodymed.com*), and author of *Whole-Body Dentistry* (Quantum Health Press). "That's why people will go to extreme lengths and spend thousands of dollars to protect and save their teeth."

But extreme lengths aren't always necessary. Although tooth problems such as a toothache, tooth sensitivity and tooth decay require a visit to the dentist, there is a lot *you* can do in a very short time to help prevent and repair everyday tooth problems…

➤ **The best sugar-free gum.** Studies show that chewing sugar-free gum with xylitol for five minutes after a meal can help prevent tooth decay and cavities—and even re-mineralize the enamel that protects teeth. But what's the *best* sugar-free gum?

New study: Dental researchers at the University of Melbourne in Australia tested three sugar-free gums with xylitol and found that Trident White and Trident Xtra Care re-mineralized teeth at about twice the level of the other gums. *Reason:* They contain milk-derived calcium "nanocomplexes"—tiny packets of re-mineralizing calcium that are absorbed directly into the tooth.

➤ **Protect your enamel.** One in 15 Americans has erosive tooth wear—acids have eaten away at the tooth's hard enamel coating and trickled into the bonelike material underneath, causing the tooth to soften and weaken—and possibly decay. The main culprit is acidic beverages. *Here's what to watch out for…*

● **Soft drinks.** Soft drinks contain citric acid and phosphoric acid, both of which can corrode teeth. (In fact, some sodas contain more than twice as much acid as battery acid!)

Best: Root beer doesn't contain the acids that harm teeth, says a study in the journal *General Dentistry*.

● **Sports drinks.** "Citric acid in sports drink has been linked to erosive tooth wear," says Mark Wolff, DDS, professor and chairman of the Department of Cariology and Comprehensive Care at New York University of Dentistry. "Consume sports drinks in moderation," he says. If you consume them frequently, talk to your dentist about using acid-neutralizing, re-mineralizing toothpaste. *Example:* Arm & Hammer Enamel Care Toothpaste.

Speed Healing Success

He Cured His Tooth Decay With Beef and Butter

Ramiel Nagel, a writer in Los Gatos, California, had a mouthful of misery. His teeth felt loose, and when he touched his molars near the gum line he felt sharp pain. Concerned, he went to the dentist for a checkup—and was told he had four cavities. And he wasn't the only one in his family with dental problems. His young daughter had several cavities and one tooth beyond repair.

"Now, nearly three years after my original decay, my cavities are gone and my loose teeth are firmly embedded and strong," says Nagel. "The sensitive spots have hardened dramatically and are pain-free. And although my daughter's teeth continued to decay a tiny amount, she has no pain, no sign of infection and no problem eating hard foods."

But neither one of them was fixed by a dentist.

"I didn't want to subject my daughter to traumatic anesthesia and surgery or have her teeth pulled," says Nagel. Nor did Nagel want synthetic fillings or other dental work for his problem.

After extensive research, Nagel encountered the work of Weston Price, DDS, a dentist who theorized that poor nutrition—specifically, eating a Western diet loaded with processed foods—deprives the teeth of the crucial nutrients.

Those nutrients include high levels of the fat-soluble vitamins A and D, the minerals phosphorus and calcium, and a mysterious "Activator X" that some theorize might be vitamin K. The way to ensure adequate intake of those nutrients—and prevent or heal tooth decay—is to eat a so-called "primitive" diet that eliminates processed foods and emphasizes raw meats, dairy products, eggs and vegetables, said Dr. Price.

And that's what Nagel and his family did.

Their diet emphasizes grass-fed, organic meat (including organ meats), often prepared in slow-cooked soups and stews or seared…raw organic milk, cream and butter…raw eggs…one-half teaspoon a day of cod liver oil…uncooked shellfish and wild fish (such as sashimi)…vegetables, including two to four cups of raw vegetable juice a day…and fermented foods such as sauerkraut and yogurt. They completely avoid "processed, modernized and denatured food," says Nagel, such as boxed breakfast cereals or potato chips.

For older people with cavities (Nagel points out that 62% of Americans ages 60 and older have tooth decay), he advises to try a highly absorbable nutrition-rich tonic for helping prevent and reverse decay—The Raw Egg Tooth-Strengthening Formula. *To prepare the daily tonic, blend…*

- *1 cup raw milk or yogurt*
- *2 to 4 ounces of raw cream*
- *2 raw eggs*
- *Small amount of raw honey or stevia for sweetness.* You can also use vanilla extract, carob powder or nutmeg for flavoring.

⚠ *Caution:* Talk to a qualified health professional before adding this high-fat tonic to your diet.

Nagel says that nutrient-rich raw eggs are very purifying—literally expelling old toxins from the body—and that for a day or two you may feel a little worse as your body cleanses. But then, says Nagel, it's likely you'll feel a whole lot better—and so will your teeth.

Rapid Resources: Nagel wrote a book about his dental discoveries, *Cure Tooth Decay: Heal & Prevent Cavities with Nutrition* (Golden Child Press).

For more on Weston Price's approach to healthy nutrition, he suggests the book *Nourishing Traditions* (New Trends), by Sally Fallon.

For the best online sources of raw meat, dairy and eggs, he suggests *www.realmilk.com, www.eatwild.com* and *www.uswellnessmeats.com*. He also favors the New Zealand product, Anchor Butter. To find a local supplier, call 888-869-MILK or go to *www.anchorbutter.com* and click on "Store locator."

• **Energy drinks.** A study in the journal *General Dentistry* found that energy drinks can erode enamel.

Helpful: To prevent acidic beverages such as sodas, sports drinks and energy drinks from damaging your teeth, follow these guidelines from Raymond Martin, DDS, a spokesperson for the Academy of General Dentistry...

1. **Use a straw positioned at the back of the mouth** so that the liquid avoids the teeth.

2. **Drink quickly rather than slowly,** to limit contact with your teeth.

3. **To neutralize the acids after drinking the beverage,** rinse your mouth with water, eat cheese or use a fluoride rinse.

4. **Chew sugar-free gum** after drinking the beverage.

5. **Don't drink an acidic beverage right before bedtime**—the production of acid-neutralizing saliva decreases during sleep.

Red flag: Brushing your teeth right after you drink a sports drink—or any tooth-eroding drink—*worsens* the problem, because the softened enamel is particularly sensitive to the abrasives in toothpaste. "Wait at least thirty minutes before brushing your teeth to allow softened enamel to re-harden," says Dr. Wolff.

➤ **Temporary relief for a toothache.** "With tooth pain, the first thing you should do is seek professional treatment," says Flora Parsa Stay, DDS, a clinical associate professor of dentistry at the University of Southern California, author of *The Secret Gateway to Health* (Morgan James), a book about gum disease, and founder of Cleure all-natural health, beauty and dental products (*www.cleure.com*). But until you can see the dentist, here are some speedy ways she suggests to reduce the pain.

• **Use an over-the-counter ointment containing lidocaine or benzocaine.** These numbing products include Campho-Phenique, Orajel or Anbesol. Put the ointment directly on the tooth.

Also helpful: "Soak a cotton ball with clove or wintergreen oil, and place it directly on the sore tooth," says Dr. Stay.

• **Take an over-the-counter pain reliever.** Use whatever works for you, whether it's aspirin, acetaminophen (Tylenol) or ibuprofen (Motrin, Advil), she says.

Red flag: "Aspirin and other pain relievers should never be applied topically to the area surrounding a sore tooth," says Dr. Stay. "These products contain strong acids that can burn the gum tissues."

• **Rinse with saltwater.** "Warm saltwater rinses or a solution of warm saltwater mixed with a tablespoon of aloe vera gel may reduce gum irritation and tooth pain," says Dr. Stay.

• **Use ice.** "For a toothache from an impacted tooth, a small piece of ice placed over the swollen gums may bring temporary relief," says Dr. Stay.

However: This is an exception, she points out. Otherwise, never apply ice directly to a sore tooth or any other area within the mouth.

➤ **Don't ignore denture problems.** "A lot of times, people with dentures will have gum irritation and think, 'Oh, that's nothing' and ignore the problem," says Dr. Stay.

Problem: "You should never ignore dental irritation," says Dr. Stay. "It can turn into a severe problem, such as oral cancer."

Solution: You should have your dentures adjusted or repaired at least once every five years. "Over time, the jaw loses bones and the dentures don't fit—and ill-fitting dentures are the cause of most denture problems," she says.

Also helpful: To clean your dentures effectively, first brush them with water and toothpaste and then soak them overnight in a solution of 1 cup water, ¼ cup vinegar, 1 teaspoon of baking soda and 1 capful or teaspoon or hydrogen peroxide.

If you can't find a brush soft enough to clean your gums, use a soft washcloth, says Dr. Stay.

To soothe inflamed and tender gum tissue, rub aloe vera gel on your gums or rinse with a mouthwash that contains peppermint oil, says Dr. Breiner.

Red flag: "Don't place a chipped or broken denture in your mouth, especially if it has sharp edges," says Dr. Stay. "Leave it out of your mouth until you can see your dentist."

SPEED LIMIT Go Easy on the Denture Cream

Researchers in the Department of Neurology at the University of Texas Southwestern Medical Center in Dallas reported that four denture-wearing patients developed neurological problems such as weakness in the arms and legs, balance problems and cognitive problems.

They found each of them were using six to 20 times the recommended amount of denture cream (Fixodent and Poli-Grip)—and that they had absorbed high levels of the zinc from the cream, driving down blood copper levels, triggering the neurological problems.

"Denture cream contains zinc, and chronic, excessive use may result in serious neurological disease," they conclude, in the *Archives of Neurology.*

Better: If you're using large amounts of denture cream because of ill-fitting dentures— see your dentist to fix the problem, say the researchers.

➤ **How to deal with dental anxiety.** Nearly 50% of Americans avoid preventive dental care—because of fear and anxiety. "If you're among them, you need some healthy coping strategies to overcome your fears," says Dr. Stay. *Here's what she suggests…*

• **On the day of your visit, avoid caffeine for six hours before the visit.** "If you are keyed up to begin with, caffeine will only heighten your anxiety," she says.

Better: "Opt for a high-protein snack or meal before you head to the dental office. This will actually calm you."

• **Practice slow, deep breathing.** "People who are anxious tend to hold their breath," she says. "The more oxygen you have available, the less panic you will feel."

• **Daydream in the dental chair.** "Dream about beautiful places where you would rather be or make plans about the weekend or the holidays," says Dr. Stay. "Let your mind wander far and wide, but keep your thoughts pleasant."

White Wine Stains Too

You probably know that red wine can stain teeth. But white wine? *Well, dentists have some bad news for you Chardonnay lovers out there…*

New study: Researchers at the New York University of Dentistry tested the capacity of white wine to increase staining—and found that it did. "The acids in wine—including white wine—create rough spots and grooves in the tooth," says Dr. Wolff. "This enables chemicals in other beverages that cause staining—such as coffee and tea—to penetrate deeper into the tooth."

What to do: "The best way to prevent staining caused by wine, as well as other beverages, is to use a toothpaste containing a whitening agent," he says. *Example:* Colgate Total Plus Whitening Toothpaste.

• **Ask questions before the dentist gets started.** "Make sure you're comfortable with what the dentist plans to do."

Also helpful: "Work out a hand signal to let the dentist know if you want a break or if you feel pain," says Dr. Stay.

➤ **Try homeopathic cell salts for tooth sensitivity.** "I like to use homeopathic cell salts to help with tooth sensitivity," says Dr. Breiner. The salts help replenish the calcium and magnesium that are important to healthy teeth, he says.

Product: Calcarea Phosphorica 3X and Magnesia Phosphorica 3X cell salts. They are widely available in health food stores and on the web.

Suggested intake: Three of each, morning and evening.

TRAVELER'S ILLS

Stay Healthy Away From Home

What threat kills the most Americans traveling to developing countries? Malaria? Dengue fever? Terminal tourista?

None of the above. The correct answer is…*cars.*

Twenty-five percent of Americans who die in developing countries do so in a car accident, usually as a passenger or pedestrian, says Christopher Sanford, MD, co-director of the Travel Clinic at the University of Washington in Seattle and author of *The Adventurous Traveler's Guide to Health* (University of Washington Press). Only 1% die of infectious diseases.

"The biggest fallacy of travel to developing countries is that the number-one threat is infectious diseases," he says. "If you're traveling by car in a developing country, always use a seat belt, if one is available. If you're driving, *never* assume you have the right of way, even on a divided road. And if you're walking, be cautious and vigilant.

"And if the taxi is driving too fast or erratically, say, 'Slow down or let me out,' " adds Herbert DuPont, MD, founding president of the International Society of Travel Medicine, director of the Center for Infectious Disease at the University of Texas and chief of internal medicine at St. Luke's Episcopal Hospital in Houston.

That's smart advice for not having your final destination be more final than you'd planned. *Here are other top recommendations from these two world-class experts in trotting the globe without tripping up your health…*

➤ **Put a travel clinic on your itinerary.** Are you headed to the developing world—to Asia (except for Japan or Singapore), Africa or Latin America? Then go to a travel clinic beforehand to make sure you receive the appropriate vaccinations (for example, for hepatitis A, tetanus and influenza) and preventive medications (for example, anti-malarial drugs). "There is a real reduction in risk by taking these precautions," says Dr. Sanford.

Study: Researchers at Tuft University found that only 34% of international travelers sought travel health advice in advance…only 46% of travelers to high-risk regions for malaria were carrying anti-malarial medications…and only about 10% of international travelers to risky areas had received the appropriate vaccinations.

Rapid Resource: You can find a state-by-state directory of travel clinics by visiting *www.istm. org*, the website of the International Society of Travel Medicine. On the home page, click on "Global Travel Clinic Directory."

There is another state-by-state directory of specialists in travel medicine at *www.astmh.org,* the website of the American Society of Tropical Medicine and Hygiene. On the home page, click on "Education & Resources," then click on "Clinical Consultants Directory."

Or look in the Yellow Pages under "Travel Medicine."

➤ **Buy evacuation insurance.** "Say you're in a car crash in Asia, Africa or Latin America and break a thigh bone—not an unlikely scenario," says Dr. Sanford. "Well, the medical quality in much of the developing world is sub-standard, with the risk of hepatitis and HIV from the blood supply. It's not where you want to stay for medical care. You want to get your situation stabilized and leave the region, for Europe or the US.

"But normal health insurance and Medicare don't cover that kind of contingency—and hiring a medical jet to fly you out will set you back seventy-five thousand dollars," explains Dr. Sanford.

Better: Buy evacuation insurance from a company such as Medex.

"By paying a little money upfront, you can guarantee that you'll be able to leave an area of sub-standard care," he advises.

Rapid Resource: You can find out more about travel evacuation insurance (and other types of travel assistance and insurance) at *www.medex assist.com,* or call 800-732-5309. Address: 8501 LaSalle Rd., Suite 200, Baltimore, MD 21286, e-mail *medex_info@uhcglobal.com.*

➤ **For traveler's diarrhea—pack an antibiotic.** Before traveling to the developing world, get a prescription filled for an antibiotic that you can take immediately if you develop traveler's diarrhea, says Dr. Sanford. It should shorten the length and severity of the episode.

For Africa and Latin America, the antibiotic of choice is the fluoroquinolone antibiotic Cipro (*ciprofloxacin*).

Your Mobile Personal Pharmacy

"If you're planning an international trip, you need to create a personal medical kit," says Dr. DuPont.

It should include…

1. **A duplicate set of your prescription drugs.** "While traveling, always divide your medications, keeping one supply with you, so that you have your medications if your luggage is lost, stolen or delayed," he says. Ask your prescribing physician for a duplicate set of prescription drugs, so you can carry both sets in their original, labeled containers.

2. **Over-the-counter or prescription medications** for heartburn, colds, insomnia, sunburn, skin rashes (an anti-itch cream containing steroids) and cuts and scratches. It should also include Band-Aids and scissors, disinfectant for scratches and cuts, ear plugs and eye shades, and a thermometer.

3. **If you're flying longer than six hours:** Compression stockings to wear on the airplane, to prevent deep vein thrombosis, a blood clot in your leg.

4. **If you're traveling to tropical or semitropical countries:** Medications for prevention and treatment of traveler's diarrhea.

5. **If you're traveling to areas with malaria:** Insect repellant and preventive drugs for malaria.

⚠ *Caution:* Cipro should not be taken by anyone under 18.

For Southeast Asia and India—where bacteria have mutated to resist Cipro—the antibiotic of choice is *azithromycin* (Zithromax).

Take the antibiotic if you develop liquid diarrhea, he says. For milder diarrhea (loose stools), you can use the over-the-counter drug Imodium A-D. (You can also use Imodium A-D *with* the antibiotic, to ease all-out traveler's diarrhea.)

Red flag: Buy your antibiotic *before* you leave the US, rather than abroad. "One in three antibiotics purchased in developing countries are old, adulterated or bogus," says Dr. Sanford.

Also helpful: A subset of traveler's should take a *preventive* antibiotic for traveler's diarrhea, says Dr. DuPont. That includes anyone whose schedule can't tolerate an illness of at least 12 hours (such as a politician, a couple on a honeymoon, a traveler on important business or a flight attendant). It also includes people who have an underlying medical problem where a bout of traveler's diarrhea could be catastrophic (such as someone with insulin-dependent diabetes, congestive heart failure, inflammatory bowel disease, cancer, AIDS).

Talk to your doctor about an antibiotic that will work for you.

➤ **Apply DEET to your skin and *permethrin* to your clothes.** If you're traveling to the tropics, using insect repellants on exposed skin and on clothes is a must, says Dr. Sanford.

Malaria is not the only hazard, he points out. Mosquito-borne dengue fever (with severe headache, muscle and joint pain, rash, vomiting and diarrhea) is now at epidemic levels in 100 countries and becoming more common every year.

What to do: "Spray twenty-five to thirty percent DEET on any skin that is exposed to the air, including your face, neck and hands," he says.

DEET is safe. "You practically have to drink it to get sick," he says. "You can use it two or three times a day." (Very rarely, a person develops a rash. It that happens, discontinue use.)

Spray permethrin on your clothes once every two weeks. "This insecticide is non-toxic, inexpensive, has no smell and stays on your clothes through multiple launderings," says Dr. Stanford.

"Study after study shows that these precautions make an enormous difference in getting or not getting insect-borne diseases," he says.

Head Spinning From Crossing Time Zones? Try Twirling...

"Twirling—spinning the body in a clockwise or counterclockwise direction—is an excellent remedy for jet lag," says Dan Bouwmeester, MD, director of the Radiant Life Health Clinic in California, who learned the technique from his spiritual teacher, Adi Da. "It works by realigning the body's physical and subtle energies with the 'twirling' rotation of the earth, he explains.

"If you've flown east, twirl west—left over right. If you've flown west, twirl east—right over left. Do it several times. Afterward, rest in the yoga pose known as the 'Corpse Pose'—lying on your back with your legs extended and spread comfortably apart and with the arms extended to either side of your body at a comfortable distance."

Here are the detailed instructions…

1. Stand erect, facing straight ahead with arms extended straight out to the sides (parallel to the floor and the front of the body) at shoulder level, with the right palm facing the floor and the left palm facing up.

2. Spin or twirl the body in a clockwise (left to right) or counterclockwise (right to left) direction.

3. Keep the eyes and relaxed, looking straight ahead as you twirl.

4. Hold the head, arms and upper body erect, in the original position, throughout the exercise. Breathe deeply, feeling the breath descending into the belly around the navel.

5. As you rotate, the feet should remain in the same general area of the floor.

6. End slowly.

⚠ **Caution:** Do not twirl if you have chronic dizziness or balance problems or if you do not exercise regularly.

Products: Dr. Sanford recommends 3M Ultrathon for DEET. It has a 34% concentration and is in a time-release formula that stays on the skin longer.

He also suggests Sawyer Permethrin.

Both products are widely available, including at REI and other retail outlets that cater to outdoor recreation and travel.

➤ **For jet lag, take a sleeping pill.** You travel east across several time zones. And as your body clock slowly resets to local time, you live in the chronobiological chaos known as *jet lag*—unable to fall asleep...waking up in the middle of the night...exhausted during the day. Can you prevent it? Cure it quickly? *Not really...*

Neither Dr. Sanford nor Dr. DuPont—top travel docs who do a lot of international traveling—think there are good solutions for the problem of jet lag, which is more bothersome when you're flying west-to-east and losing time.

"I no longer worry about jet lag," says Dr. DuPont, who was flying from Houston to Budapest on the day he was interviewed. "I don't acclimate to the new time zone and am chronically tired, but I know I won't be jet lagged when I return home."

"I feel spacey for about a week," concurs Dr. Sanford.

But they do offer a few, hopeful suggestions...

Take a prescription sleeping pill such as *zolpidem* (Ambien) for the first few nights at your new destination, to help get yourself on a regular schedule, says Dr. DuPont.

Many travelers swear by melatonin, the over-the-counter sleeping supplement, says Dr. Sanford.

Other possibly helpful recommendations are...

• *Plan* on being jet lagged for a couple days—one day for each time-zone crossed.

Take This Supplement At 30,000 Feet

Natto is a cheeselike Japanese food made from fermented soybeans that contains the enzyme *nattokinase*, which can break down *fibrin*, the protein in blood that forms blood clots, explains John Neustadt, ND, a naturopathic doctor and medical director of Montana Integrative Medicine.

To reduce the risk of DVT from airplane travel, Dr. Neustadt suggests taking a supplement with nattokinase and pine bark extract, an antioxidant—a combination shown in a clinical study to reduce the risk of blood clot formation by 24%.

Product: NattoPine, available at *www.pure formulas.com.*

Suggested intake: Two capsules daily, for three days before the flight and on the day of flying. Take only with the approval and supervision of a qualified health professional.

• While flying, drink non-alcoholic and non-caffeinated beverages every chance you get.

• Get on the local schedule—and get into the daylight—as quickly as possible.

Super-Quick Fix

➤ **If you're flying with a clogged nose, use nasal spray.** Usually, the air pressure inside and outside of your ear is the same, thanks to the Eustachian tube, which connects the middle ear and the back of your nose—when you swallow, the tube opens up and equalizes pressure. But if your nose is clogged from a head cold, allergy or sinus infection—interfering with the tube's mechanism—the air inside your ears will expand as pressure changes during the ascent and descent of a flight. The air then presses on your eardrums—possibly causing intense pain.

What to do: Before ascent and descent, use a decongestant nasal spray such as Afrin, suggests Dr. Sanford. "Using it for more than three days can be habit-forming, but short-term use may be helpful in this situation." Chewing gum may also help.

➤ **Prevent deep vein thrombosis.** The metal bar at the edge of the seat is pressing into the back of your thighs. You're in the same cramped position for hours. You're dehydrated. And if your flight has been six hours or longer, by the time you land, and for the next three days, you have a two to four times higher risk of developing *deep vein thrombosis* (DVT)—a blood clot in your leg.

Your calf could become painful, swollen and hot. Or the clot could travel to your lungs, causing a pulmonary embolism, which is fatal in 3% of cases.

You're at higher risk for DVT if you are over age 60, overweight, have heart disease, smoke, take estrogen, are pregnant, have cancer, had leg surgery (such as a knee replacement) or have had a previous DVT.

What to do: To prevent DVT, drink non-alcoholic and non-caffeinated beverages every chance you get, says Dr. DuPont.

Never stay in your seat for more than two hours at a stretch—get up and walk around.

And—particularly if you're at higher risk—wear compression stockings, which improve circulation in your legs. Studies show they reduce the risk of DVT by around 90%.

➤ **Patch up motion sickness.** You're on a bobbing boat. Or sitting in the backseat of a car on a winding mountain road. Or watching the scenery from a speeding train. Or gripping the armrests of a bucking 747. And all of a sudden, your balance system is no longer in sync with the

Speed Healing Success

Preventing Altitude Sickness

Altitude sickness—or *acute mountain sickness* (AMS), as travel doctors call it—occurs in about 50% of cases when your body doesn't have time to gradually acclimate to low-oxygen living above 7,000 feet, says Dr. Sanford. (Think Aspen, Colorado; Bogota, Columbia; Machu Picchu in Peru; Mexico City, Mexico; and Flagstaff, Arizona.) You can develop nausea and a headache (much like a hangover) for a day or two. Less than 1% of those with AMS develop life-threatening complications in the brain or respiratory tract.

"I recently traveled to Peru and flew from Lima, at five thousand feet, to the mountains at eleven thousand feet," he says. "When I arrived in Lima, I started taking the prescription medication *acetazolamide* [Diamox]—one pill, twice a day, for three days. The drug markedly reduces the risk for AMS—and I didn't get it. It's okay to stop the drug once you're at altitude. You can also take the drug if you begin to develop AMS—it should help relieve symptoms. The main side effect is increased urination. In rare cases, a person may develop stomach upset or rash—if that occurs, stop taking the drug."

⚠ **Caution:** Don't take Diamox if you have an allergy to drugs that contain sulfa.

outside world—and you develop motion sickness. You're nauseous, dizzy and sweaty, and feel like you might throw up.

What to do: To prevent motion sickness, take a preventive medication before you travel, says Dr. Sanford. "I think the best is *scopolamine* (Transderm Scop), a patch you place behind your ear six to eight hours before travel. It yields the most results for the lowest risk, which include dry mouth, blurry vision and drowsiness. Talk to your doctor about whether this medication is right for you."

If you don't want to use scopolamine, consider the over-the-counter medication *meclizine* (Antivert), says Dr. Sanford.

He doesn't endorse bracelets that press on anti-nausea acupuncture points on the wrist or ginger, two oft-recommended remedies for motion sickness. "They are unproven," he says. *Other practical suggestions include...*

- **Car.** Sit in the front seat. Turn the air vents toward your face.

- **Airplane.** Sit toward the front or by the wing.

- **Boat.** Ask for a cabin on the upper deck or toward the front of the ship. Keep your eyes on the horizon.

- **Train.** Don't sit in a seat facing backward.

- **Any conveyance.** Don't read. Keep your head still. Don't smoke.

ULCERS

Stomach acid is, well, acid— if it sloshed on to your skin, it would burn you. The stomach lining is protected from the acid by a thick layer of mucous and by acid-buffering bicarbonate. Sometimes, however, acid seeps down to the lining and burns a hole in it. And you have a *peptic ulcer.*

An estimated 10 to 20% of Americans will suffer a peptic ulcer in their lifetime. There are two types—a *gastric ulcer* in the stomach and a *duodenal ulcer* in the section of the small intestine right next to the stomach.

In 80% of cases, the ulcer is caused by an infection with *Helicobacter pylori* (*H. pylori*), bacteria that burrow into and weaken the mucous layer. In 10%, the ulcer is caused by the regular use of a stomach-irritating NSAID (non-steroidal inflammatory drug) such as aspirin, ibuprofen (Advil, Motrin) or naproxen (Aleve, Naprosyn). In 10% the cause isn't discovered.

Good news: There are fast and easy ways to help your doctor with medical therapy for *H. pylori...*

➤ **Support "triple therapy" with natural remedies.** "When *H. pylori* is eradicated, ulcers heal and don't recur," says Liz Lipski, PhD, CCN, CNS, the director of Nutrition and Integrative Health Programs at Maryland University of Integrative Health and author of *Digestive Wellness* (McGraw-Hill). And your doctor should eradicate *H. pylori*, she adds. "Long-term infection not only increases the risk of peptic ulcers but also chronic indigestion and stomach cancer."

The bacteria is typically eradicated with a combination of three medications called *triple therapy*—an antibiotic to kill the bacteria...an H2 blocker or proton-pump inhibitor (the same type of acid-suppressing drugs used for heartburn) to stop the production of acid while the ulcer heals...and bismuth to protect the stomach lining. The success rate is high. Natural therapies can improve it.

● **Lactoferrin and probiotics—boosting success rates.** *Lactoferrin* is a peptide (protein sub-fraction) of milk. Studies show that it strengthens immunity and kills harmful bacteria, including *H. pylori*. Probiotics are "friendly" bacteria that help protect and restore the health of the digestive tract. Together, they can boost the power of triple therapy.

New study: Italian researchers from the University of Pisa gave 206 ulcer patients either standard triple therapy (Group A) or triple therapy with lactoferrin and probiotics. (Group B). The therapy was a success in 72% of the patients in Group A—and 89% of the patients in Group B.

"The addition of lactoferrin and probiotics could improve the standard eradication therapy for *H. pylori* infection—lactoferrin serving to increase the eradication rate and probiotics to reduce the side effects of antibiotic therapy," say the researchers, in the *American Journal of Gastroenterology.*

What to do: Lactoferrin and probiotic supplements are widely available. Talk to your doctor about adding them to the triple-therapy treatment regimen.

● **Saccharomyces boulardii—decreasing side effects.** Triple therapy is effective—but potentially unpleasant. The combo of medicines can cause nausea, dizziness, headaches or diarrhea. Some patients decide the treatment isn't worth it and stop taking the drugs. Supplementing triple therapy with *Saccharomyces boulardii*—a strain of yeast that normalizes the functioning of the digestive tract—might help.

New study: Turkish doctors in the Department of Gastroenterology at Gazi University in Ankara studied 124 patients with *H. pylori* infection who were receiving two weeks

Twenty percent of people under age 40 and 50% of people over age 60 are infected with *H. pylori*. Why do only some of them get ulcers? A diet high in salt might be one reason.

New study: Epidemiological research—data on health and disease in thousands of individuals—has linked a high intake of salt with a higher risk of *H. pylori* infection causing an ulcer.

To see if that data has a biological basis, scientists in the department of Microbiology and Immunology at the Uniformed Services University of the Health Sciences in Bethesda, Maryland, studied the effect of salt on *H. pylori* bacteria. They found that high concentrations of salt warped *H. pylori* cells—they stopped dividing normally and became elongated. They also found that extra salt activated a gene that makes it more likely *H. pylori* bacteria will turn nasty and trigger an ulcer.

"These changes may help explain why a high-salt diet is associated with increased risk of ulcers in people infected with *H. pylori*," says D. Scott Merrill, PhD, one of the researchers who conducted the study.

For ways to lower the salt in your diet, please see page 203 of the section "High Blood Pressure."

of triple therapy, dividing them into two groups. One group took daily supplements of *S. boulardii*; the other group took a placebo.

During the therapy, twice as many people in the placebo group experienced diarrhea. Three times as many had stomach pain. After the therapy, the placebo group had 38% more gastrointestinal discomfort.

Product: Talk to your doctor about using Florastor, a widely available *S. boulardii* supplement proven effective in more than a dozen clinical studies. Follow the dosage recommendation on the label.

➤ **Rapid pain relief.** While you're waiting for a doctor to diagnose and treat what might be an ulcer, you still have to deal with the pain. But many pain relievers *irritate* the stomach. *Here are some nondrug remedies that can help...*

● **Water.** One very simple remedy for ulcers is to drink large amounts of water, says Dr. Lipski. "Drink four to six glasses during the pain and it may disappear."

New study: Researchers in Greece found that healthy people who drank one, eight-ounce glass of water had lower stomach acidity after just one minute—twice as fast as an antacid, and hundreds of times faster than acid-suppressing drugs. The study was reported in the journal *Digestive Diseases and Sciences.*

● **Aloe vera gel.** "It is soothing and healing to mucus membranes," says Dr. Lipski.

Suggested intake: "I recommend two ounces, two to three times a day," says Julie Wilson, DC, CCN, a chiropractor and nutritionist in Chicago, Illinois (*www.drjuliewilson.com*).

● **DGL licorice.** *Deglycyrrhizinated licorice* (DGL) is a type of licorice that doesn't cause high blood pressure, says Dr. Lipski. "It helps heal the stomach's mucus lining," she says.

Suggested intake: 400 to 500 milligrams (mg) with each meal, says Dr. Wilson.

● **Gamma oryzanol.** This compound found in rice bran oil normalizes the production of gastric juices.

Study: Researchers in Japan found that gamma oryzanol reduced ulcer symptoms by 80 to 90%.

Suggested intake: 100 mg, three times daily, for three to six weeks.

➤ **Protect yourself from an aspirin-induced ulcer—with a proton-pump inhibitor.** One hundred and seven thousand people are hospitalized each year with complications from aspirin and other NSAIDs and 16,000 die—usually from bleeding ulcers.

New finding: Doctors in Japan found that people taking low-dose aspirin were more than twice as likely to develop gastric ulcers if they weren't taking either a proton-pump inhibitor such as *omeprazole* (Prilosec) or *esomeprazole* (Nexium).

What to do: "Talk to your doctor about using acid-blocking proton pump inhibitors such as Prilosec or Nexium with NSAIDS," says Jason Theodosakis, MD, author of *The Arthritis Cure* (St. Martin's Griffin) and assistant clinical professor at the University of Arizona College of Medicine in Tucson. "They can reduce the risk of stomach ulcers from twenty to five percent or less."

If you take a proton pump inhibitor, take a multivitamin-mineral supplement too—these drugs can causes deficiencies in B12, magnesium and other key nutrients.

URINARY INCONTINENCE

Stay Dry Every Day

Ninety percent of cases of urinary incontinence are *stress urinary incontinence* (SUI)—incontinence when you are coughing or sneezing or laughing or lifting something heavy. Thirty to 50% of women experience it now and then.

Unfortunately, the problem can become increasingly common with age, with a loss of tone in the bladder and the urethra—one in six women between the ages of 40 to 65 has SUI.

The typical recommendations are to take a drug, have surgery or wear diapers.

But those therapies should be *last* resorts, not first-line care, says Kathryn Burgio, PhD, director of the continence program at the University of Alabama at Birmingham.

The first resort is *Kegel exercises* to strengthen the *pubococcygeous* (PC) muscle, which you already tighten automatically when you squeeze your urethra and stop the flow of urine.

New study: Researchers in Australia recently analyzed 24 studies on using Kegel exercises—or what they call "pelvic floor muscle training (PFMT)"—for urinary incontinence. They found the exercises *cured* women of SUI in 73% of cases, and vastly improved the situation in 97% of cases.

Problem: Most doctors and their patients think Kegels *don't* work to cure SUI.

Solution: "That's because Kegels usually aren't taught properly," says Dr. Burgio.

Here's her advice on how to do them right...

➤ **Do Kegel exercises right.** "First, you need to know where the muscles are," she says. "You can locate them by stopping or slowing the stream of urine the next time you go to the bathroom. The muscles you use to do that are the pelvic floor muscles. Another way to identify them is to tighten the same muscles that you use to stop yourself from passing gas in public. You can also find them by tightening the vaginal muscles.

"Several times a day, squeeze the muscles and hold the contraction for ten seconds," she says. "At first, you may not be able to hold for very long, but don't worry. Start by holding for a count of three—one Mississippi, two Mississippi, three Mississippi—then let go. Over time, build up to a count of ten.

"You may have a tendency to contract your abdominal muscles by mistake," she continues. "Breathing normally and regularly while doing the Kegels will help you keep those muscles relaxed. You can also put one hand over your abdomen to double-check that you're not tightening the muscles there.

"When you're doing Kegels correctly, you'll feel a lifting sensation in the area of your vagina or a pulling sensation in your rectum," she says.

What's the right amount of Kegels to cure incontinence?

"Do forty-five Kegels a day," she says. "It's best to do them fifteen times in a row, three times a day."

Red flag: "The most common error is that people simply forget to do them," says Dr. Burgio.

Smart idea: "The best way to remember to do your Kegels is to pick a few activities that you do every day—such as taking a shower or brushing your teeth—and do the exercise during those activities."

Also helpful: "Exercising your pelvic floor muscles can reduce incontinence, but to get the most out of Kegels, you need to use those muscles," says Dr. Burgio. "Remember to squeeze the muscles right before and during those activities that cause leakage, such as coughing and sneezing. This helps to close the opening to the bladder and prevent urine loss."

Good news: "Don't be discouraged," she says. "At first you'll have to concentrate quite a bit. But after they become a habit, you'll start doing Kegels automatically."

Rapid Resource: If you'd like to find a nearby practitioner with expertise in incontinence—urogynecologist, nurse practitioner or physical therapist—visit the website of the American Urogynecologic Society, *www.augs.org*, and click "Find a Provider" on the home page. Address: 2025 M Street NW, Ste. 800, Washington, DC 20036, call 301-273-0570 or e-mail *info@augs.org*.

➤ **Watch out for the caffeine.** Caffeine is a *diuretic*—it causes the bladder to fill more quickly, which means you'll have to urinate more urgently and frequently, says Diane Kaschak Newman, RN, co-director of the Penn Center for Continence and Pelvic Health at the University of Pennsylvania Medical Center in Philadelphia and author of *Overactive Bladder: Your Complete Self-Care Guide* (New Harbinger).

What to do: Limit your caffeine intake to 200 milligrams (mg) daily. An eight-ounce cup of brewed coffee contains 100 to 165 mg. Black or green ten contains about 40 mg. Other common sources include iced tea (70)...cola (46)...chocolate (1 to 15 per ounce for milk and 20 per ounce for dark)...and some over-the-counter medications, such as Excedrin (65 mg per tablet).

➤ **But don't decrease fluids.** "If you're like millions of women with bladder-control problems, you probably think reducing the amount of fluids you drink will lead to less urine and less urination," says Newman.

Surprising: "Adequate fluid intake is necessary to eliminate bladder irritants and help prevent incontinence," she says. In fact, she explains, concentrated urine (dark yellow, strong smelling) may actually irritate the bladder and cause you to go to the bathroom more frequently.

What to do: Drink 60 to 64 ounces of fluids a day. "Spread your intake throughout the

See Your Doctor If...

"Incontinence is usually evaluated by a doctor with a special interest in the problem—generally a gynecologist, urologist or urogynecologist," says Amy E. Rosenman, MD, assistant clinical professor of Obstetrics and Gynecology and Urogynecology at the David Geffen School of Medicine at UCLA and coauthor of *The Incontinence Solution: Answers for Women of All Ages* (Fireside).

The doctor will determine what type of incontinence you have. *There are five types, says Dr. Rosenman...*

- *Stress incontinence.* Urine loss with some type of physical stress to the body, such as a cough, sneeze, physical activity or laughing.

- *Urge incontinence.* Urine loss preceded by a sense of needing to urinate before reaching the bathroom.

- *Mixed incontinence.* Urine loss with features of both stress and urge.

- *Overflow incontinence.* Urine loss occurring when the bladder is full but the bladder does not contract properly to push the urine out. The urine then trickles out of the overfull bladder.

- *Total incontinence.* The constant loss of urine.

"Expect to be asked a lot of questions," she says. "Put aside any sense of discomfort and embarrassment and answer as completely as you can."

Smart idea: "It is a good idea to think carefully about these questions even *before* you see the doctor—and to take the answers with you to the doctor's appointment." *Questions you are likely to be asked include...*

What activities cause you to leak? Is the amount of urine lost small, or do you flood? Do you wear panty liners, pads or adult diapers to protect your clothes from wetting? Do you have an urge to urinate before you lose any urine? Do you lose urine before you get to the bathroom? Do these urges occur only with a full bladder? How often do you urinate during the day and during the night? Does your bladder feel empty after you urinate? Is there pain or burning when you urinate? Do you get more than one or two bladder infections a year? Do you have any difficulty starting a stream of urine? Do you have any trouble stopping the flow of urine once it stops? Do you feel any bulging in the vagina? Do you feel a pulling or pressure in the pelvis, especially when you are on your feet for any length of time? Do you leak constantly? Do you have any neurological problems, especially of the lower back or legs? Do you have diabetes? Have you previously had bladder surgery?

day, avoiding high volumes at any one time," says Newman. To help prevent nighttime incontinence, drink the majority of fluids *before* 6:00 pm, and don't have any alcohol or caffeine with your evening meal.

➤ **Watch out for little-known bladder irritants.** Some surprising foods can irritate the bladder, worsening incontinence, says Newman. *They include...*

- **Highly acidic foods,** such as tomato-based products, spicy foods and Mexican foods.

- **Milk-containing foods** can reduce bladder control.

- **Artificial sweeteners** can also reduce bladder control.

- **Alcohol** acts as a diuretic and can irritate the bladder.

- **Citrus-based juices** may cause bladder overactivity.

- **Carbonated beverages** can contribute to the problem.

URINARY TRACT INFECTIONS

Beat Back the Bacteria

Ten million times a year, American women visit doctors because of a urinary tract infection, with symptoms such as urgent, frequent and burning urination, cloudy (and maybe bloody) urine, and back and groin pain. An estimated 30 million other women have the infection but never see a doctor.

One out of three women will experience a UTI sometime in her life, says Elizabeth Kavaler, MD, a urologist in private practice in New York (*www.nyurological.com*), and the author of *A Seat on the Aisle, Please!: The Essential Guide to Urinary Tract Problems in Women* (Copernicus Books). Twenty percent of those women will have a second UTI—and two-thirds of those will suffer *several* a year. Men, on the other hand, rarely have UTIs. What's up with this sexist infection?

Reason: Women have a two-inch *urethra*, the tube between the genital opening and the bladder. In men, the urethra is eight inches long. Which means that, in women, the *E. coli* bacteria that harmlessly hang around the rectum and vagina have an easy scoot upstream to the bladder, where they morph from harmless passengers into infection-causing pests.

What causes UTI? Genes, which predispose some women. Sex, which pushes bacteria toward the bladder. (However, you can't "catch" a UTI from a partner—the infecting bacteria are *your* bacteria.)

What most people don't know: "The infection is *not* caused by poor genital hygiene—by being 'dirty' instead of 'clean,'" says Dr. Kavaler. "Nobody's vagina is dirtier than anybody else's vagina." That means women should *not* douche to prevent UTIs—a practice that can disturb the natural bacterial balance of the vagina and trigger recurrent infections. "Showering and cleaning the vagina with warm water once a day is enough to maintain excellent hygiene," she says.

If you think you have a UTI, visit your doctor, who will determine if you have the infection. If you do, you'll probably receive a prescription for bacteria-killing antibiotics. In four out of five cases, that's that—infection defeated, once and for all.

But for those with *recurrent* UTIs, there's an effective but little-used strategy—a faster, safer strategy—that can quickly clear up UTIs *and* minimize your risk of antibiotic-caused side effects…

➤ **Self-medicate for success.** Most of the time, doctors overmedicate recurrent UTIs with too large a dose of antibiotics, says Dr. Kavaler. This eliminates healthy bacteria in the vagina, often leading to vaginal yeast (fungal) infections. Other common side effects include diarrhea and digestive upset. "The goal should be to treat recurrent UTIs with the *least* amount of antibiotics," she says.

To accomplish that goal, she recommends you ask your doctor for a *preventive* prescription of antibiotics—either TMP-SMX (Bactrim, Septra), *nitrofurantoin* (Macrobid) or *fluoroquinolone* (Cipro, Levaquin).

"I tell my patients to fill the prescription and keep the antibiotics available. When a woman thinks she's getting a UTI—at the first sign of burning and itching—she takes a pill twice a day. Usually, the symptoms begin to subside one day into the treatment, which is when ninety percent of the bacteria are destroyed. If she's still not feeling well on the second day, she can continue taking the antibiotics."

One to three days of treatment is all a woman usually needs, says Dr. Kavaler. "Taking a 'full course' of antibiotics for seven days is *not* necessary. Low doses are more than enough to knock out a UTI.

Commonsense Precautions

These following fast-action practices may help you avoid recurrent UTIs, says Dr. Kavaler...

- *Clean the genitalia from front to back,* to avoid spreading bacteria from the rectum toward the vagina.
- *Wear cotton-crotch underwear*—it doesn't lock in the moisture that can promote the growth of bad bacteria.
- *Don't delay urination;* urinating helps wash away bad bacteria.
- *Urinate immediately after sex.*

"Even if this strategy doesn't reduce the *frequency* of UTIs, it will reduce the *amount* of antibiotics you take—and that's a big health benefit."

⚠ *Caution:* This strategy is appropriate for a healthy woman with no other medical problems and no fever with the infection.

⏰ Super-Quick Fix

➤ **OTC is TLC for the weekend UTI.** It's the weekend. You think you're getting a UTI. You don't have antibiotics on hand. You can't get to the doctor. What should you do?

Drive to the drugstore and pick up some *Pyridium* (Phenazopyridine), an over-the-counter urinary tract anesthetic that can help relieve the burning, urgency, frequency and irritation of a UTI. "It's like aspirin for the bladder," says Dr. Kavaler.

While you're at it, buy some Cystex, an OTC drug that stops UTI bacteria from multiplying as rapidly. "It can either keep the UTI in check or clear it up," says Dr. Kavaler.

And don't worry about the day or two wait to see a doctor.

"There are three things that can happen—the UTI can get better by itself, it can stay the same or it can get worse," says Dr. Kavaler. "But whatever happens, it's not an emergency—you're not going to die of a kidney infection over the weekend."

➤ **Cranberry—take away the bacterial toehold.** Cranberry juice is a classic remedy to prevent recurrent UTIs. Scientists used to think cranberry worked by acidifying the urine, creating an inhospitable environment for the *E. coli* bacteria. But cranberry is more like a Natural Enforcer, kneecapping the bacterial bad guys.

New finding: Scientists at the Worcester Polytechnic Institute in Massachusetts found that cranberry juice cripples *fimbriae*—the sticky, hairlike projections that *E. coli* use to attach themselves to bladder walls.

"In the presence of cranberry juice, the *fimbriae* fold in and form a coil, so the bacteria no longer have an attachment with which to grab on to the bladder," says Terri Camesano, PhD, associate professor of chemical engineering.

The juice also helps form an "energy barrier" between the bacteria and bladder—a barrier 20 times stronger than in a no-juice environment.

But the bacteria-busting isn't permanent—which is why cranberry juice only works if you use it regularly, says Dr. Camesano. "You need to drink one or two, eight-ounce glasses of cranberry juice a day if you want to maintain the preventive effect."

Her study used the type of juice you can buy at any supermarket, with 27% of juice from cranberry.

Also try: Other experts think a cranberry supplement is the way to go. "I recommend that my patients with recurrent UTIs take Cran-Max, a one-a-day chewable supplement from Enzymatic Therapy," says Holly Lucille, ND, a naturopathic physician in private practice in Los Angeles (*www.drhollylucille.com*).

New study: Researchers at the University of Dundee in Scotland studied 137 older women who had two or more UTIs in the past year, dividing them into two groups. For six months, one group took 500 milligrams (mg) of Cran-Max, while the other took 100 mg of the antibiotic *trimethoprim* (Primsol), which is used to prevent recurrent UTIs.

Both treatments performed about the same, in terms of preventing UTIs, but Cran-Max caused fewer side effects, says Marion E. T. McMurdo, MD, the study leader. "Older women with recurrent UTIs can consider with their doctors whether they want to use a cheap, natural product like cranberry extract or a drug that poses the risk of antibiotic resistance, fungal infections and super-infection with *Clostridium difficile* bacteria (a possible side effect of antibiotic treatment)."

UTERINE FIBROIDS

Lower the Estrogen, Shrink the Fibroid

Seventy percent of American women, many of them in their 30s and 40s, have *fibroids*—growths on the wall of the uterus, or womb. There's usually more than one and size often varies, from as small as a seed to larger than a grapefruit.

But even though these growths are technically tumors, they're benign tumors—in more than 99% of cases they're not cancerous nor do they turn into cancer, says Michael Broder, MD, assistant clinical professor of obstetrics and gynecology at the David Geffen School of Medicine at UCLA and author of *What Your Doctor May Not Tell You About Fibroids* (Warner).

"Benign" also means they don't usually require treatment—unless they're causing troublesome symptoms, such as lengthy, heavy periods and bleeding between periods…pain (often back pain or leg pain)…urinary problems… constipation…and abdominal pressure.

"Only you can decide what makes symptoms troublesome enough to need treatment," says Dr. Broder. And an estimated 20% to 50% of women with fibroids do have symptoms they consider bothersome, many of them deciding to have surgery or undergo another conventional medical treatment. (Those options are listed in the *See Your Doctor If…*box on page 336 of this section.)

But Holly Lucille, ND, a naturopathic physician in private practice in Los Angeles (*www. drhollylucille.com*), says there are many non-surgical, non-drug options a woman with fibroids can consider. Options that don't work overnight but are quick to implement.

"The cause of most uterine fibroids is a metabolism in which the hormone *estrogen*

See Your Doctor If...

Many women are diagnosed with fibroids during a pelvic exam or an ultrasound. In most cases, the fibroids aren't causing any problems.

But sometimes fibroids can cause symptoms such as constant pelvic pain...heavy, painful periods...bleeding between periods...pain during intercourse...urinary incontinence...or constipation—any or all of which should prompt a visit to the physician.

In many cases, doctors will recommend a hysterectomy, or surgical removal of the uterus—the second most common operation performed on American women (after cesarean section), with 300,000 operations per year, or more than one per minute, says Dr. Broder.

Red flag: Research conducted by Dr. Broder and his colleagues showed that in 76% of operations, doctors failed to meet professional treatment criteria set by the American College of Obstetricians and Gynecologists when recommending hysterectomies.

"Too often, important diagnostic tests, as well as less invasive and more conservative treatments, were skipped, as doctor after doctor rushed their female patients on to the fast track for a hysterectomy," he says. "While hysterectomy does get rid of fibroids along with the uterus, and improves the quality of life for most women who choose it, there are many other treatment options."

They include watchful waiting (no treatment)...medications to suppress the fibroid-triggering hormones...surgery where the fibroids are removed but not the uterus (myomectomy)...a non-surgical procedure where the blood supply to the fibroids is cut off (uterine artery embolization)...and a new, non-invasive procedure that destroys the fibroids using sound waves (focused ultrasound surgery).

"The range of treatment possibilities is enormous," says Dr. Broder. "Find a doctor who is a partner in your treatment—someone willing to have a conversation with you about all your options."

---

rather than *progesterone* is dominant, stimulating the abnormal growth of uterine tissue," says Dr. Lucille. Estrogen dominance is caused by several factors, she says. One is the widespread presence of *xenoestrogens* in the environment—from insecticides, food additives and industrial chemicals—that function like estrogen in the body. Another is poor estrogen metabolism, often caused by a toxified liver. A third is the depletion of progesterone by chronic stress. "By addressing estrogen dominance, you can reduce and even eliminate fibroids," she says.

Here are her suggestions for you to discuss with a qualified health professional...

➤ **Take DIM (*diindolylmethane*).** This is a nutritional supplement of a compound found in cruciferous vegetables such as broccoli, Brussels sprouts, cabbage and kale. It promotes normal estrogen metabolism, says Dr. Lucille.

Suggested intake: 200 milligrams (mg) daily.

Product: EstroBalance, from Enzymatic Therapy, available at *www.enzymatictherapy.com*, or call 800-783-2286.

➤ **Eat more cruciferous vegetables.** Dr. Lucille suggests three to four servings a day. A serving is 1 cup of raw vegetables or ½ cup of cooked vegetables.

➤ **Take calcium-D-glucarate.** This compound breaks down in the body into D-glucaric acid, which blocks the action of an enzyme (beta-glucuronidase) that boosts estrogen production.

Suggested intake: 200 micrograms (mcg) daily.

Product: Dr. Lucille uses the Thorne brand of calcium-D-glucarate, which is widely available on the web. (This supplement can cause hot flashes, so use it only with the approval and supervision of your doctor.)

▶ **Try flax seeds.** Flax seeds supply lignans, a type of plant compound called a *phytoestrogen*, which can block estrogen from reaching receptor sites on cells. "Fresh ground flax seeds are best because they supply the most lignan," says Dr. Lucille.

Suggested intake: Grind two tablespoons a day in a coffee grinder and sprinkle on your breakfast cereal or salad, or stir into yogurt or juice.

▶ **Take choline and inositol.** These two vitamin-like compounds help support liver function, decreasing estrogen levels, says Dr. Lucille.

Product: Tyler's Lipotropic Complex, available on many sites on the web.

Suggested intake: 1 to 4 tablets a day.

▶ **Take pancreatic enzymes.** These digestive enzymes can literally digest the proteins that promote the cellular growth of the fibroid, says Dr. Lucille.

Product: Mega-Zyme, from Enzymatic Therapy.

Suggested intake: Two, three times a day, between meals.

▶ **Take Chaste Tree Berry.** This herb stimulates the production of progesterone, says Dr. Lucille.

Suggested intake: 200 mg a day.

Product: Chaste Tree Berry from Vitanica, at *www.vitanica.com*, or call 800-572-4712.

▶ **Drink a herbal tea of dandelion root and burdock root.** Both of these herbs help cleanse the liver, increasing the metabolism of estrogen, says Dr. Lucille.

How to use: Take ½ cup of each of the herbs and put in 32 ounces of water. Bring to boil and then turn to low, allowing to simmer for 30 minutes. Strain. Add sweetener to taste. Drink throughout the day.

▶ **Eat a whole-foods diet.** "Eating a high-fiber, low-fat diet that emphasizes fruits, vegetables, whole grains and legumes and limits or cuts out saturated fats, sugar and alcohol is very helpful in shrinking uterine fibroids," says Dr. Lucille.

VAGINAL INFECTIONS

If you're confused about vaginal infections, join the club. "Many women are confused," says Amanda Levitt, ND, a naturopathic physician in private practice in Hamden, Connecticut (*www. wholehealthct.com*).

Many, because vaginal infections are common, accounting for 10% of all visits by women to health care practitioners.

Confused, because it's often hard to know what type of infection you have. "Women often say, 'I have a yeast infection,' when that's not the cause of the problem," says Dr. Levitt.

To add to the confusion, *bacterial vaginosis* (BV) is not an infection at all, but an overgrowth of normal bacteria.

And *irritant vaginitis* isn't caused by *any* kind of organism. The red, inflamed tissues of the vulva (the exterior part of the vagina) might be reacting to a product (or product ingredient) that has contacted the vaginal area, such as a soap, detergent or douche. Or the cause might be tight jeans or a tampon.

But 90% of all cases of "vaginitis" *are* from bacteria, fungus and other germs. And the first step in healing is figuring out what type of infection you have. "Accurate diagnosis is the most important key to efficient and appropriate treatment," says Tori Hudson, ND, a professor of gynecology at National College of Naturopathic Medicine, medical director of A Woman's Time clinic in Portland, Oregon, and author of *Women's Encyclopedia of Natural Medicine* (McGraw-Hill).

Good news: After identifying the problem, healing can be fast. "Vaginitis is often easily treated," she says.

➤ **Identify your infection.** "Vaginal infections are frequently misdiagnosed by women," says Dr. Levitt. *Here's what you can do to get it right—and when you need the doctor's help...*

• **Bacterial vaginosis (BV).** Accounting for 90% of all vaginal infections, this is the most common type—though it's actually the result of an *overgrowth* of normal bacteria, which irritate the vagina.

Symptoms: It's usually accompanied by a thin, white-gray discharge, itching and a fishy odor (though in more than half of cases there are no symptoms at all).

Common causes: Taking an antibiotic can disturb the balance of bacteria in the vagina. Unprotected intercourse is a frequent cause. Douching can disturb the bacteria. Aging can trigger the problem, as lower levels of estrogen cause vaginal cells to produce less glucose, the fuel for healthy lactobacillus bacteria.

Self-diagnosis and treatment: If you've had BV before—and have no doubt that your current infection is an encore—you can self-treat the problem, as long as your symptoms don't persist, says Dr. Levitt. If symptoms persist, it's important you receive the correct diagnosis and appropriate treatment.

Medical diagnosis: The doctor might take a sample of vaginal discharge and examine the cells under a microscope, looking for the type and mix of bacteria that indicates BV. The doctor might also check the pH of the vagina—an alkaline pH means you probably have BV. The doctor may also conduct an "amine test"—adding a drop of potassium hydroxide to the discharge. If there's a fishy odor, you probably have BV.

• **Yeast infection (vulvovaginal candidiasis, or VVC).** This infection is usually caused by the fungus *candida albicans*. An estimated three out of four women will have at least one bout of VVC in their life. About 45%

Soothing Atrophic Vaginitis

"As you get older and estrogen levels drop, you develop drier, thinner, more easily irritated vaginal tissue," says Marie Savard, MD, an ABC News medical contributor and author of *Ask Dr. Marie: Straight Talk and Reassuring Answers to Your Most Private Questions* (GPP Life).

Some suggestions for pampering your private parts…

"For cleaning, don't use toilet paper," she says. "Use two-ply, unscented, Natural Aloe Pampers Baby Wipes." (She says they are great for irritant vaginitis at any age.) "They are so much more cleansing and less irritating than soap and water, and minimize the drying out of tissue.

"Use a water-based lubricant during sex," she advises. Don't use petroleum-based products such as Vaseline, which can further irritate delicate vaginal tissue. You may also want to consider using estrogen cream, once or twice a week, says Dr. Savard. "It has minimum bad effects and maximum good effects—it can help your vaginal tissue feel healthier and younger."

of those women will have another infection, and 5 to 8% will have recurrent infections—four to five a year.

Symptoms: The most common symptom is itching. Other possible symptoms include a thick, white, cottage cheeselike discharge…burning…painful urination…painful sex…and a swollen vulva (the external part of the vagina) that has pinpoint red lesions, like a baby with a diaper rash.

Common causes: Antibiotics, using birth control pills or an IUD, diabetes, pregnancy, HIV.

Self-diagnosis: Vagisil Screening Kit is available over-the-counter and measures the *alkalinity* of your vagina. If it's more alkaline, it's more likely that you have BV—"and you don't

have to spend money on an over-the-counter remedy for yeast infection," says Dr. Levitt. You'll also need more testing to confirm whether or not you have BV.

If the pH is acidic (less than 4.5), you probably don't have BV and you *may* have a yeast infection—and can try the self-care remedies in this section.

Medical diagnosis: The doctor may take a culture and look at it under a microscope, to spot the yeast, or send the culture to a lab.

- **Trichomoniasis.** This a sexually transmitted disease, with five million new cases a year.

Symptoms: In 20% to 50% of cases, there are no symptoms. When they're present, they include large amounts of a frothy, green-yellow discharge…pain with urination…itching…and bleeding after intercourse.

Cause: Unprotected sexual intercourse with an infected partner.

Medical diagnosis: The doctor looks at the discharge under a microscope for the presence of the trichomonad protozoa that cause the problem. If they're not seen, a culture is sent to the laboratory.

Medical care: This disease is treated with an anti-protozoal drug *metronidazole* (Flagyl). It's important your sexual partner is also treated.

➤ **Speedy self-care for BV.** If it's definitely a repeat case of BV, consider the following self-care suggestions, says Dr. Levitt.

- **Eat a whole-foods diet, low in sugar and alcohol.** "I ask a BV patient to clean up her diet," says Dr. Levitt. She suggests plenty of fruits and vegetables, whole-grains and legumes, "good quality protein" from grass-fed beef, free-range poultry and wildfish, and limiting the amount of refined carbohydrates and alcohol. "Such a diet gives you everything you need for a healthy immune system and balanced vaginal flora."

- **Take a probiotic.** To help balance that flora, she also recommends taking a probiotic supplement—which supplies friendly bacteria—twice a day. She suggests PharMax, a professional brand that is widely available on the web.

- **Use a probiotic suppository.** You can also use the PharMax probiotic as a suppository, inserting one capsule vaginally, at bedtime, says Dr. Levitt. Use for five nights.

- **Consider Yeast Arrest suppository.** Another option is a suppository containing boric acid, berberine and other herbs. "In spite of its name—Yeast Arrest—this product works wonderfully in clearing up BV quickly," says Dr. Levitt. She suggests using it twice a day, morning and night, for seven days.

Rapid Resource: You can order Yeast Arrest from the manufacturer Vitanica, at *www.vitanica.com*, or call 800-572-4712.

- **Ask your partner to wear a condom.** Not being exposed to alkaline semen will help restore the acidity of the vagina.

➤ **Speedy self-care for a yeast infection.** "Most yeast infections go away on their own," says Dr. Savard. *Here's what to do to speed up that exit...*

- **Cut out sugar, alcohol and refined carbohydrates.** Yeast feed on excess sugar.

- **Take a probiotic.** A supplement of friendly bacteria helps normalize the environment of the vagina, says Dr. Levitt. Use the same product recommended for BV.

- **Put plain, unsweetened yogurt on the labia.** If you have a mild infection, this can help soothe the tissue, says Dr. Levitt.

See Your Doctor If...

If you have the symptoms of a vaginal infection or vaginal irritation, you should see the doctor if...

- *It's your first episode*—you have new or painful symptoms.
- *You're not sure* what kind of infection you have.
- *The symptoms are persistent*—you have recurrences.
- *You're pregnant.*
- *You have an underlying chronic health condition,* such as diabetes, cancer or AIDS.
- *Your sexual partner* is also experiencing symptoms.

- **Use a boric acid suppository.** "The most successful natural treatment for VVC that I've encountered is boric acid suppositories—even in cases of resistance to antifungal prescription drugs," says Dr. Hudson. She cites a study in which 100 women with chronic resistant yeast infections who had failed extensive and prolonged conventional therapy were treated with 600 milligrams boric acid vaginal suppositories twice a day for two or four weeks. "The regimen was effective in curing ninety-eight percent of the women," she says. Product: You can use Yeast Arrest or another boric acid suppository; they are widely available.

- **Use an over-the-counter antifungal.** "If your yeast infection is uncomfortable and you can't bear to wait until your body is back in balance, use an over-the-counter anti-fungal preparation such as Monistat [miconazole]," says Dr. Savard.

WARTS

Dermatologists call it the *verruca vulgaris* —the common wart. But each wart is really a colony of viruses that is replicating on the skin—*human papilloma viruses*, with more than 100 types.

Most warts grow on the hands and fingers, often near your fingernails. Plantar warts grow (often painfully) on the bottom of the feet. And all of them tend to be persistent.

But sometimes, a wart meets its match…

➤ **Duct tape to the rescue.** "The duct tape treatment for warts was proven effective in a scientific study," says Lauren McCabe, DC, a chiropractic physician in Portland, Oregon. "In fact, I met a dermatologist a few years ago who said he had completely changed his approach to wart treatment after this study. My fiancé has had success using this treatment on a few small warts."

Study: Researchers at the Children's Hospital Medical Center in Cincinnati studied 51 people with warts, dividing them into two groups. One group received cryotherapy—liquid nitrogen was applied to the warts for 10 seconds, every two to three weeks. The other group received *duct tape occlusion*—the warts were covered with duct tape for two months.

Eighty-five percent of the duct tape group had "complete resolution" of the wart, compared to 60% of the cryotherapy group, say the researchers. Their conclusion is that "the simple application of duct tape was more effective than cryotherapy in the treatment of the common wart."

They note that duct tape is more practical, especially when compared with the multiple clinic visits required for freezing of a wart. Duct tape causes fewer side effects—no pain, no

blisters, no discoloration, no infection. And duct tape therapy is a lot cheaper, they say.

Important: Although their study lasted two months, duct tape typically worked after three weeks.

What to do: In the study, people with warts were instructed to cut a piece of duct tape as close to the size of the wart as possible, apply it to the wart, and leave it on for six days. If the tape fell off, the patients were instructed to apply a new tape. At the end of the six days, the patient removed the tape, soaked the area in water, and gently reduced the wart with an emery board or

See Your Doctor If…

Most warts don't require treatment, but if the wart is painful (as is often the case with plantar warts), or threatening to cause permanent destruction of the nail, see a dermatologist to have the wart removed, says Tanya Kormeili, MD, a dermatologist in private practice in Los Angeles (*www.kormeiliderm.com*) and a clinical professor of dermatology at UCLA.

You should also see a doctor for genital warts, which are not amenable to the anti-wart recommendations discussed in this section. For more information on genital warts, please see the section "Genital Herpes and Other STDs" on page 157.

Treatment options can include…

- *Freezing,* or cryotherapy, using liquid nitrogen.
- *Imiquimod (Aldara),* a medication that revs up the immune system to destroy the wart.
- *Retinoids (Tazorac),* a vitamin A derivative that disrupts the growth of the wart.
- *Surgery,* cutting out the wart or destroying it with an electric needle (electrodessication) or laser.
- *Cantharidin,* an extract that makes the area blister, after which the doctor removes the dead wart.

pumice stone. The tape was left off overnight and reapplied the following morning, for another six days. This cycle of treatment was continued for two months, or until the resolution of the wart—which was usually after about three weeks.

➤ **Oil them off.** "I've found that using pure oregano oil on a wart causes it to heal rapidly," says Leslie Irish Evans, an aromatherapist and massage therapist in Bellevue, Washington. "Get a dropper and carefully put the oil only on the affected area two times a day." (Pure oregano oil is caustic and can irritate healthy skin, she warns.) "It makes you smell like pizza—but it works!"

"I use lemon essential oils to get rid of warts," says Lesley Hobbs, an aromatherapist in Washington. "Put one to two drops directly on the warts, nightly, for two to three weeks. One of the things I most appreciate about this treatment is that I don't have to be concerned about this oil touching the surrounding skin."

➤ **Try celandine.** "I've used lots of different remedies for my patients over the past thirteen years, and this herbal treatment is one of the most reliable," says Sheilagh Weymouth, DC, a chiropractic physician in Manhattan (*www.wholelifehealthcare.com*).

What to do: Bend the stem of a greater celandine plant (a poppy that is native to North America and that you can grow in a pot) until it breaks open and the inner juice oozes out. "Apply it topically to the wart, protecting the skin around the wart with tape," she says. It works by inhibiting cell replication, says Dr. Weymouth.

⚠ *Caution:* The orange-colored, acrid juice is an irritant and should not contact normal skin.

Also try: An herbal tincture of the plant can also work. "Great celandine tincture has worked quickly—for myself and some of my clients," says Colorado-based herbalist Susan Mead.

Speed Healing Success

"After a Few Weeks the Wart Was Gone—And It Never Came Back!"

You don't have to be a health professional to know how to get rid of warts…

- *Neem oil.* "Neem oil is an effective, all-natural wart remover," says Ann H. "It smells a little strong, but it's quick—usually less than a week, in my experience. It helps to put a Band-Aid over the wart after applying the oil."

- *Duct tape.* "I had a wart on the middle finger of my left hand," says Cathy Fowler of Washington. "It got to be pretty huge, so I went to the dermatologist to have it frozen off. After about a month, it started to grow back—and got to be about the same size it had been before it was removed. A friend then told me to try duct tape. I wrapped a piece of the tape and left it on for a week. After a week, it was significantly smaller, and after I removed the tape it continued to shrink. After a few more weeks, it was totally gone—and never came back. I recommend this to anyone with a stubborn wart."

- *Nail polish.* "Sally Hansen Hard As Nails clear formula—put in a wart and it falls off," says Terri Jay. "I don't know why."

- *Garlic supplement.* "I had warts for several years," says Lynn Christianson. "I tried lots of things and had given up. Then I used a supplement of aged garlic extract—Kyolic 103—to boost my immune system during flu system. It also includes immune boosters such as mushroom complex, vitamin C, astragalus, oregano and olive leaf. Suddenly, I noticed my warts had disappeared. No warts since!"

Rapid Resource: Greater celandine tincture is available from Eclectic Institute, at *www.eclectic herb.com*, or call 800-332-4372. Address: Eclectic Institute Inc., 12960 Ten Eyck Rd., Sandy, OR 97055, e-mail *customerservice@eclecticherb.com*.

➤ **Give your wart the slip.** People slip on banana peels. Apparently, so do human papilloma viruses.

"A colleague swore to me that if someone has a plantar wart, the very best nontoxic treatment was to cut a section of banana peel larger than the wart, tape it on the wart, with the inside of the peel on the skin," says Jill Grimes, MD, a family practice physician in Austin, Texas. "You wear it all day and replace it the next day. I have had patients try this—it works!"

"The inside of banana peels work quite well in curing warts," concurs Dr. Weymouth.

WRINKLES

Look Younger Tomorrow

Wrinkles are the scars of time…With time, your skin becomes drier. You lose collagen and elastin, the protein fibers that provide strength and support. Solar rays damage the skin. The binding "cement" around skin cells erodes. The fat layer thins. A lifetime of using your facial muscles freezes expressions in place. And the surface layer of dead cells thickens, robbing skin of its youthful luster.

The result, of course, is crows' feet… frown lines…upper-lip lines…lines around the mouth…lines from the nose to the mouth… loose skin around the jaw line—*wrinkles*, fine, deep and in between.

The result can also be a confusing, frustrating search for effective ways to prevent, slow, stop or even reverse your wrinkles. What ingredients, products and procedures *really* work?

"When it comes to skin rejuvenation, separating fact from fiction is practically a full-time job," says Audrey Kunin, MD, a dermatologist in Kansas City, author of *The DERMAdoctor Skinstruction Manual* (Simon & Schuster) and founder and president of *www.dermadoctor.com*.

Well, time may not be on your side—but that doesn't mean you have to surrender to the clock. "I don't believe in aging gracefully—I believe in aging vigorously, with intention and vitality" says Brandith Irwin, MD, a dermatologist in Seattle, Washington (*www.skintour.com*), and author of *The Surgery-Free Makeover* (De Capo).

And that means taking a few simple steps to change the things you'd most like to change about your face, she says…

➤ **The best ingredients to beat wrinkles.** "Currently, there are only a few primary active ingredients that have been proven to be helpful in skin rejuvenation and that you should look for in skin care products," says Dr. Kunin.

• **Vitamin A.** "Vitamin A creams—which increase cell turnover—are the gold standard for repair of sun-damaged and aging skin," says Dr. Irwin. "They can help prevent future wrinkles and give the skin more of a glow."

Vitamin-A creams go by many names, including Renova, Retin-A, Tazorac, Tretinoin (generic Renova and Retin-A) and Retin-A Micro, all of which are available by prescription only. Retinol is a weaker form, available without a prescription. "But there are several Retinol products that are almost as strong as the prescription form," says Dr. Irwin.

Recommended: SkinMedica Retinol Complex. The product is available at *www.skintour.com*.

⚠ *Caution:* You may have some redness, irritation or flaking with a vitamin A cream, says Dr. Irwin. If you do, she suggests the following:

"First, wash with a gentle cleanser. Second, use a light moisturizer. Third, let your face dry for ten to fifteen minutes. Last, use a pea-size amount of vitamin A cream on your entire face. Also, always apply a retinol at night, because light inactivates them. And always use a sunscreen when you are using vitamin A creams."

● **Glycolic acid.** Alpha hydroxy acid (AHA) is a family of acids, including lactic, citric, malic, tartaric—and glycolic, the most effective for skin rejuvenation, says Dr. Kunin.

"It works through exfoliation, smoothing out fine wrinkle lines. It also moisturizes, helps bleach unwanted skin discoloration and helps draw other skin treatments more deeply into the skin," she says.

"AHAs are safe when used with caution and according to directions, but don't forget this is an acid—using too much can result in a chemical burn."

Smart idea: Alternate nighttime applications of glycolic acid with a Retinol. The glycolic acid will cut down on flaking from the Retinol, hydrate the skin and provide a second active rejuvenating ingredient to your skin care regimen, says Dr. Kunin.

Products: DERMAdoctor Wrinkle Revenge Antioxidant Enhanced Glycolic Acid Facial Cleanser 1, containing 12% buffered glycolic acid—best for those with sensitive skin or just starting a glycolic acid routine.

DERMAdoctor Wrinkle Revenge Antioxidant Enhanced Glycolic Acid Facial Cleanser 2, containing 15% buffered glycolic acid—best when a higher strength is desired.

DERMAdoctor Wrinkle Revenge Antioxidant Enhanced Glycolic Acid Facial Cleanser 3, containing 20% buffered glycolic acid—for when skin is already accustomed to Facial Cleanser 2.

Rapid Resource: These products are available at *www.dermadoctor.com* or call 877-DERMADR.

● **Vitamin C (L-Ascorbic Acid).** Technically, vitamin C is an citric acid, a type of AHA. It's also an *antioxidant*, helping to stop the rust-like process of *oxidation* that can age skin. It's required for the creation of collagen and it also stimulates the activity of fibroblasts.

Products: Cellex-C Advanced C Serum and other Cellex-C products; SkinCeuticals Serum 10 AOX+ and other SkinCeutical vitamin C products.

Best: Use a vitamin C product once daily.

Smart idea: If your skin is dry, it might be sensitive to vitamin C, says Dr. Kunin. Apply hydrating products at the same time, such as Cellex-C Hydra 5 B-Complex.

● **Peptides.** Age destroys collagen, the firmness-giving fibers within the skin—1% a year, starting at age 40. Peptide-D58 can help stop the damage. Peptides are amino acids, a component of protein—and Peptide-D58 helps repair broken collagen by sparking the activity of *fibroblasts*, collagen-producing cells.

Products: DERMAdoctor Wrinkle Revenge Rescue & Protect Facial Cream and DERMAdoctor Wrinkle Revenge Rescue & Protect Eye Balm.

Another wrinkle-beating ingredient containing peptides is GHK copper peptides. GHK is a protein in the skin; copper allows it to arrive at skin cells in an active, usable state. GHK copper peptides can stimulate collagen and elastin formation, reducing fine lines, firming the skin and cutting down on sagging…they boost the production of the extra-cellular "cement" that binds skin cell to skin cell…they help oxygenate skin…and they work as an antioxidant.

A study shows that the application of GHK copper peptides boosts the formation of an early stage of collagen 70% more than Tretinoin, a proven ingredient.

Products: Neova Copper Peptide Therapy and Neutrogena Visibly Firm.

Speed Healing Success

Yoga for Your Face

"As a yoga teacher, I felt very in control of my body, training and sculpting it—and I began to realize I hadn't put the same attention on my face," says Annelise Hagen, a yoga instructor in New York and author of *The Yoga Face: Eliminate Wrinkles with the Ultimate Natural Facelift* (Avery).

So Hagen began to study the muscular anatomy of her face—where it was sagging or drooping, and where she wanted to bring it to life. She developed facial exercises to counter the changes—and practiced them with the same diligence she did her yoga.

"After doing the exercises for a while, people began asking me if I'd gotten a facelift," she says. "My nasal labial folds are less dramatic—I'm plumper in that area—and my crow's feet have lessened." Hagen then developed a complete routine for every area of the face, and began teaching it in classes.

"Pick one or two that address your problem areas," she says. "Try to do them once a day. The best time is after you've cleaned your face and applied a moisturizer—make the exercises part of your daily cleaning ritual. They just take a couple of minutes."

Whatever your results, Hagen emphasizes that true youthfulness radiates from the inside out. "The soul is eternal," she says. "Let go of the fear of aging, connect to your ageless spirit and tap into the joy that radiates eternally."

Here are three exercises from her complete routine…

● *Cheeks and lips: Satchmo.* "This exercise is called 'Satchmo,' after the inimitable Louis Armstrong," says Hagen.

"If you observe photographs of his cheeks—or any other trumpet player's cheeks—you will see that they are firm and strong, long into old age."

Her instructions…

Puff up both cheeks with air, and then transfer air from cheek to cheek. Alternate back and forth until you are out of breath. Repeat three or four times.

● *Forehead and eyes: Crow, Crow, Go Away!* "This exercise works to prevent or reverse drooping and sagging in the lower lids of the eyes, and also to uncrease crow's feet," says Hagen.

Start by smiling. Next, place your index finger on the crease between the eyelid and the cheek. Now pulse your lower eyelid muscles against the resistance of the index finger's pressure. This is an isolation movement, so do not move any other facial muscles. After you become adept, try 40.

● *Jaw, neck and shoulders: Baby Bird.* "This exercise will assist in firming the chin, neck and cheeks," says Hagen. "It helps prevent jowls from forming and is a good antidote for existing ones." *Her instructions…*

"Tilt your head back and look at the ceiling. You must be relaxed when doing this—it is a bit challenging at first. Swallow while pressing the tip of the tongue to the roof of your mouth. Then tilt your head slightly to the left and swallow. Tilt your head slightly to the right and swallow. Do three to four times in each direction."

Best: If you use Neova as your only rejuvenation product, use it twice daily.

● **N-6 furfuryladenine (N6, Kinetin).** This ingredient—a growth hormone in plants—is a boon for people with tender, delicate skin who can't tolerate exfoliating or acid rejuvenation products, says Dr. Kunin. "It helps retain moisture and reduces the signs of aging."

Products: Almay Kinetin, from Revlon. Kinerase, previously a prescription product, now available over the counter.

See Your Doctor If...

Botox. Fillers. The Fractal laser. Thermage. Sculptra. A facelift.

Yes, you've decided to see a dermatologist to help you eliminate wrinkles and smooth your skin—with Botox or fillers or the Fractal laser or Thermage or Sculptra, or maybe even a facelift. But how do you find the best dermatologist—and work with that doctor to choose the treatment or treatments that are right for *your* face (and your budget)?

"There are many safe and effective options—non-surgical and surgical—to reduce the wrinkles you have and minimize the formation of new ones," says Tanya Kormeili, MD, a dermatologist in private practice in Los Angeles (*www.kormeili derm.com*) and a clinical professor of dermatology at UCLA. But, says Dr. Kormeili, you also want to make sure your *doctor* is safe and effective.

"There are now so many 'medical spas' and physicians and nurses and technicians offering lasers and other antiaging treatments—and many of these doctors and their assistants are *not* qualified to effectively and safely deliver those therapies," she says.

Best: Choose a dermatologist board-certified by the American Academy of Dermatology. A board-certified dermatologist will know if your skin needs a cosmetic or medical treatment, such as for pre-cancerous skin changes, says Dr. Kormeili. Working with a dermatologist who is interested in both your *health* and your *beauty* will also enable you to build a long-term relationship of trust—so you know that you're not being oversold procedures, or paying too much for them. A board-certified dermatologist can also treat complications, if they are any. And they can also refer you to a plastic surgeon, if you choose to have a eyelift or other procedure.

Best: To avoid possible irritation, apply at a separate time of day from other skin rejuvenation products.

➤ **Don't forget about the moisturizer.** Skin becomes drier as you age, particularly after menopause, as oil glands dry up. "That's why one of the most overlooked—and quickest—solutions for aging skin is a moisturizer," says Dr. Irwin.

Best: Don't use the same moisturizer as you did in your 40s, she says. "You need something thick and creamy that will make an immediate difference. People tend to under-moisturize as they age, so use it twice or even three times a day."

Products: Cetaphil Cream (rather than lotion). Aquaphor Healing Ointment. Vanicream Free and Clear. Vivite Skin Replenishing Cream.

➤ **Supplements (and snacks) for younger skin.** Why would one middle-aged twin have more wrinkles than his or her sister twin—why would one twin "look older for his/her age," compared to the other?

Because of heart disease. Or kidney disease. Or stress. Or smoking. In other words, because of *poor health*.

"A wrinkle is *not* just a wrinkle," says Alan C. Logan, ND, a naturopathic physician and author of *Your Skin, Younger: New Science Secrets to Reverse the Effects of Age* (Cumberland House). "The visible signs of aging are often the result of poor health—and you can prevent or lessen them by a nutritional approach that improves the health of the entire body and also specifically targets the skin."

Recent finding: Researchers looked at nutrient intake and skin aging in more than 4,000 women aged 40 to 74. They found that women with the highest intake of vitamin C were less likely to have a wrinkled appearance... women with the highest intake of linoleic acid (found in vegetable oils) were less likely to have dry skin...and women with the highest intakes of fat were more likely to have wrinkles. "Healthy dietary behaviors may have additional benefit for skin appearance, in addition to other health outcomes," say the researchers, in the *American Journal of Clinical Nutrition*.

Dr. Logan recommends the following science-proven nutrients for healthier, more youthful skin...

• **Lycopene.** This phytochemical colors plants such as tomatoes and watermelons. Ingested in sufficient quantity, lycopene provides a "sun protection factor" of two to three on skin. In fact, a study shows that people who consume more lycopene have a 30% lower risk of non-melanoma skin cancer.

Foods rich in lycopene include tomatoes, guava, apricots, watermelon, papaya and pink grapefruit. Lycopene supplements are widely available.

• **Fish oil.** Japanese researchers found that taking EPA (eicosapentaenoic acid)—an omega-3 fatty acid found in fatty fish such as salmon and mackerel, and in flax seeds—help stopped sun-caused damage of fibroblasts, the cells that help manufacture collagen.

In another study on omega-3, researchers in Germany asked 24 women aged 40 to 60 to take fish oil supplements—after three months, skin elasticity (an indication of firmness) had increased by 10%.

Look for an omega-3 supplement with at least 1,000 mg of EPA, says Dr. Logan.

• **Cocoa flavonoids.** Dark chocolate is like a pair of dark glasses from your skin—it protects it against photoaging from sun exposure, the number-one cause of aging skin.

New study: German researchers studied 24 women, aged 18 to 65, dividing them into two groups. Every day for 12 weeks, both groups drank a 3.4 ounce (100 milliliters) mixture of cocoa powder and water. But one group used a dark chocolate powder high in *flavanols*, an antioxidant; the other group used a low-flavanol powder.

At the beginning of the study, after six weeks, and after 12 weeks, the researchers exposed a tiny patch of the participants' skin to "solar-stimulated radiation" (the same type of sunburn-and-wrinkle-producing rays beamed at you by the sun) and then measured reddening, a sign of skin damage.

After six weeks of drinking the cocoa, the high-flavanol group (HF) had 15% less reddening than at the beginning of the study; after 12 weeks, the reddening was 25% less. Meanwhile, the low-flavanol group (LF) didn't have any change in the degree of reddening—or in any other measurement of skin health and youthfulness. But after 12 weeks, the HF group also had...11% thicker and 13% denser (firmer) skin...11% moister skin...28% less skin dehydration...30% less roughness...43% less flaking...and 100% better blood circulation in the skin.

"The regular consumption of...cocoa flavanols can confer substantial photo-protection as well as help maintain skin health by improving skin structure and function," says Ulrike Heinrich, MD, in the *Journal of Nutrition*.

What to do: Try HealthySkin Chocolate Soft Chews, says Dr. Logan. Three chews supply 329 mg of cocoa polyphenols, as well as other skin-supporting ingredients, such as lycopene. Each chew is 70 calories.

• **Evening primrose oil.** In a three-month study, researchers in Switzerland found that people who took supplements of evening primrose oil—rich in gamma-linolenic acid—had skin that was 13% moister, 5% more elastic, 17% firmer and 22% less rough.

Product: The scientists used the supplement Efamol, which is widely available.

Index

About the Author

Bill Gottlieb, CHC, is a health coach certified by the American Association of Drugless Practitioners. He is the author of 16 health books that have sold more than 3 million copies and have been translated into 10 languages. He is also a health journalist whose articles have appeared in many publications, including *Bottom Line Personal*, *Bottom Line Health*, *Prevention*, *Reader's Digest* and *Men's Health*. From 1976 to 1995, Bill worked at Rodale Inc., where, as editor-in-chief of Rodale Books and Prevention Magazine Health Books, he creatively conceived and edited health books that sold more than 50 million copies, including *The Doctors Book of Home Remedies* and *New Choices in Natural Healing*. He lives in northern California. BillGottliebhealth.com